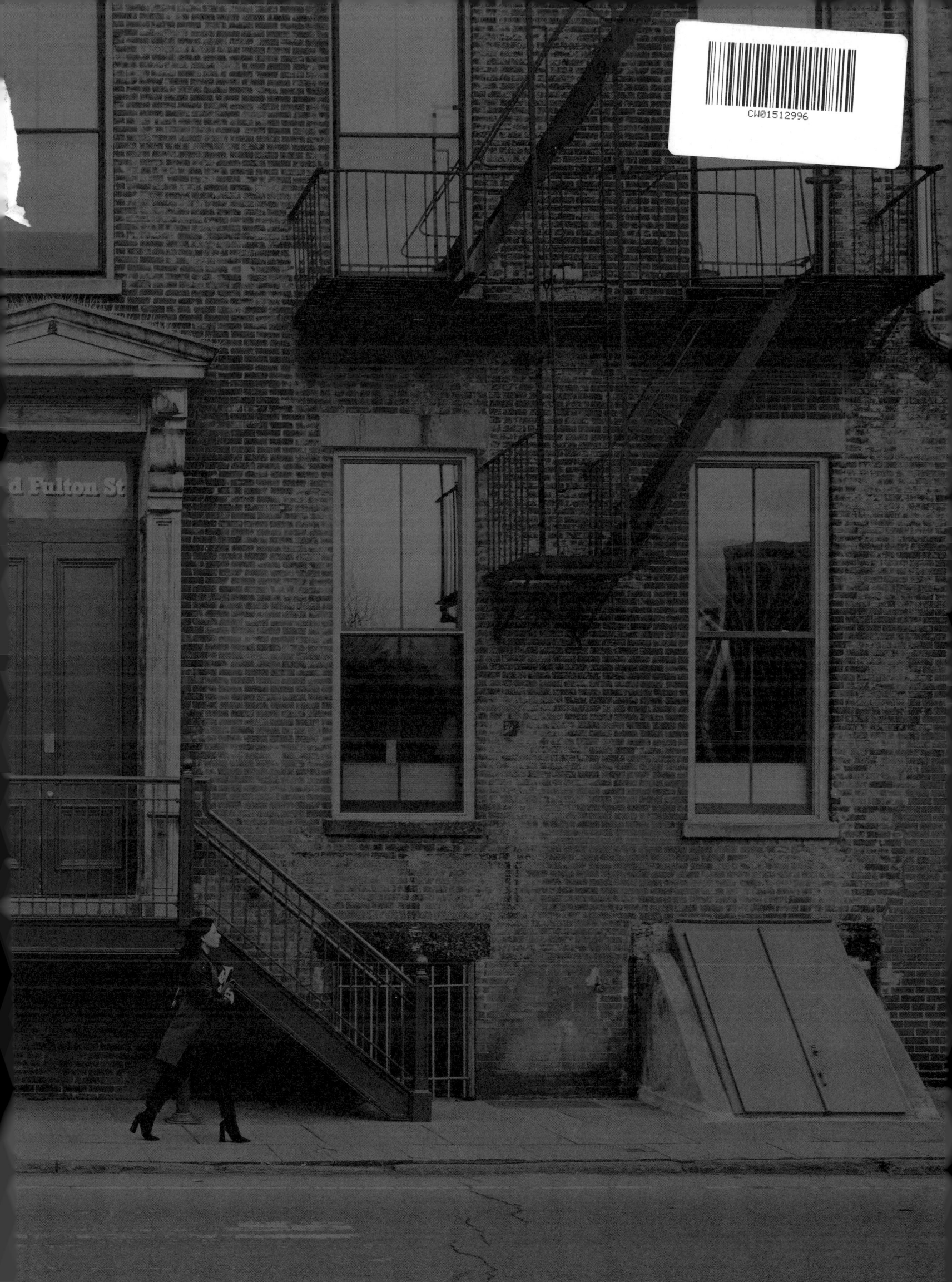

NEW YORK INTERIORS

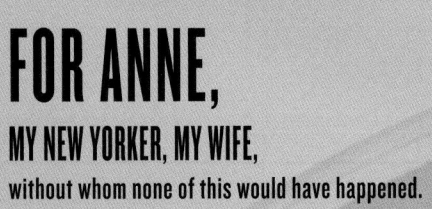

FOR ANNE,
MY NEW YORKER, MY WIFE,
without whom none of this would have happened.

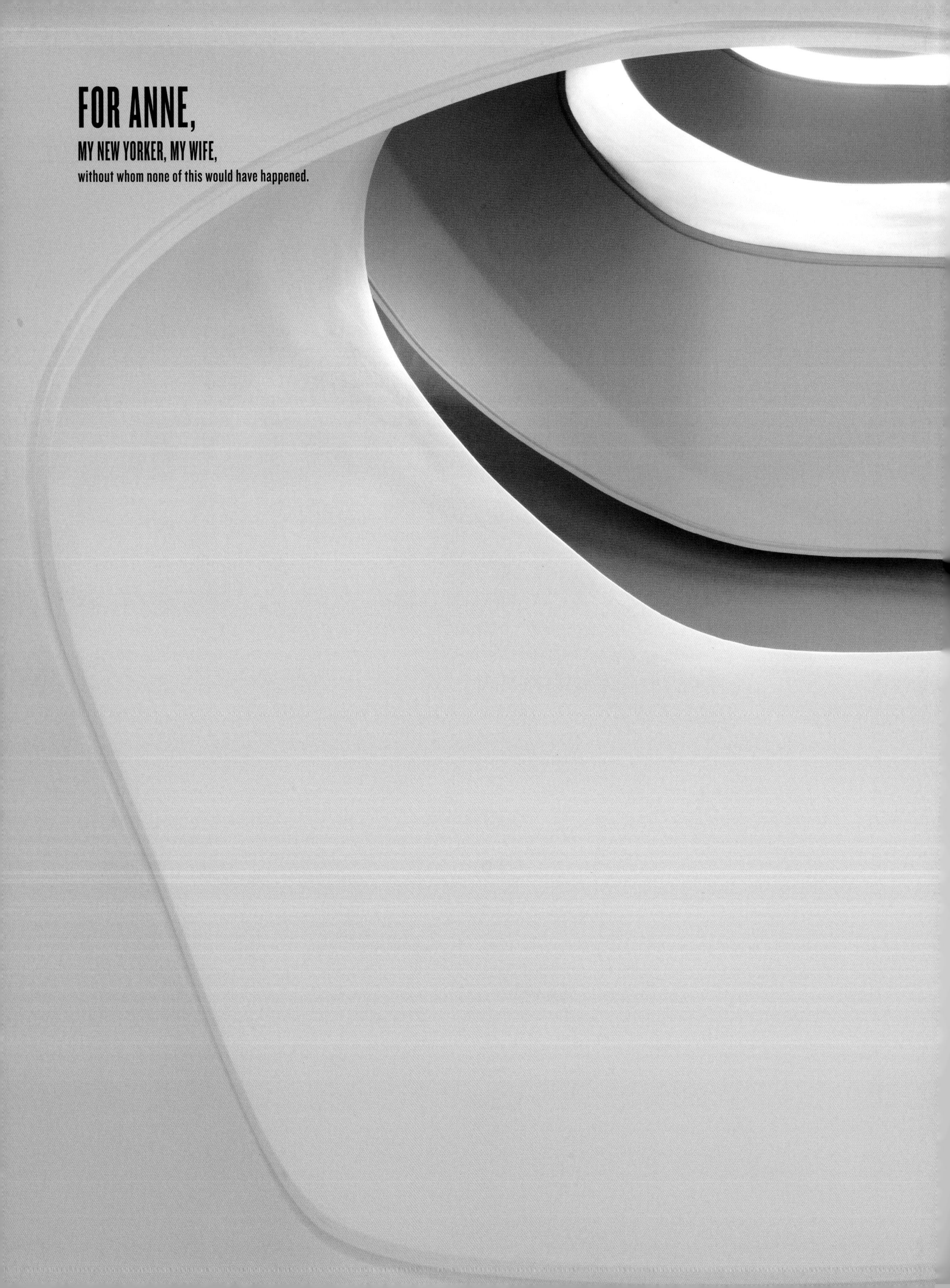

NEW YORK INTERIORS

SIMON UPTON

VENDOME

NEW YORK · LONDON

CONTENTS

GETAWAY 246

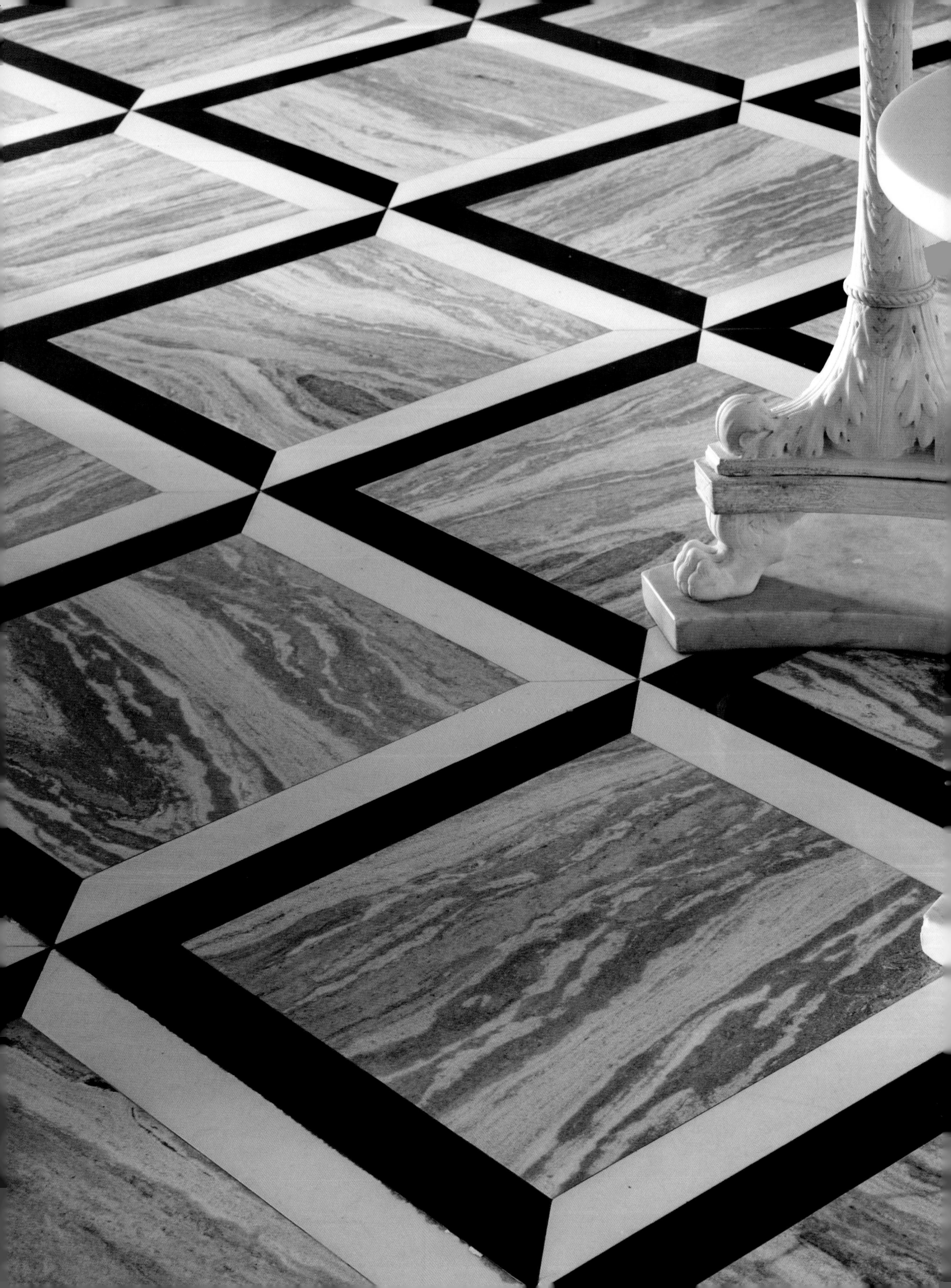

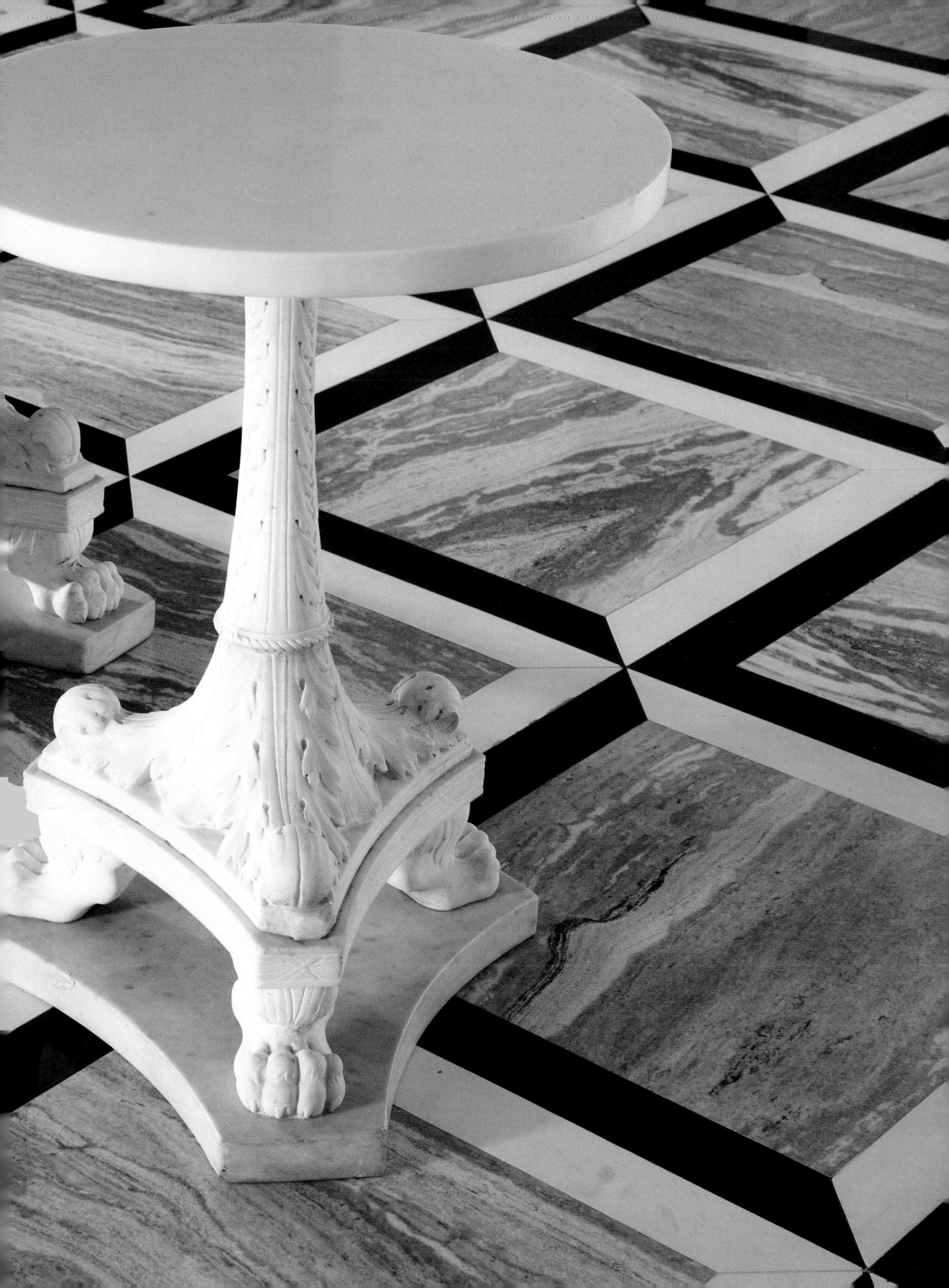

PREFACE

MY LOVE AFFAIR WITH...

SIMON UPTON

New York would never have kept me so faithful for so long were it not for the wonderful people I have met along the way.

In a reflection of the city itself, the inhabitants of New York represent a melting pot of some of the most creative, interesting, resilient, hard-working, and fun-loving characters that it has been my pleasure to get to know. Whether New Yorkers born and bred, Americans from elsewhere who have gravitated to the city and made it their home, or "foreigners and Europeans"—like me—attracted to a city that recognizes and rewards talent, motivation, and success, each has their own enduring relationship with this extraordinary place.

When I first thought about doing a book on New York, it became clear that this would be a way in which I might thank some of those people with whom I have not only worked but also become friends; people who supported me at the start of my photographic career and who are still here for me 25 years later.

The selection of interior designers and architects, stylists, artists, writers, and "free spirits" revealed in this book—each of whom offers a personal glimpse into their own relationship with the place they call "home"—reflects the remarkable diversity of private spaces to be found both in New York City and the countryside beyond. From art-filled lofts and penthouse apartments to intimate and cozy pieds-à-terre, and from cool coastal dwellings to idyllic country plots, some of the locations featured have never been seen before, while others have been revisited especially for this book. It has been my privilege to photograph them all.

Thank you, New York!

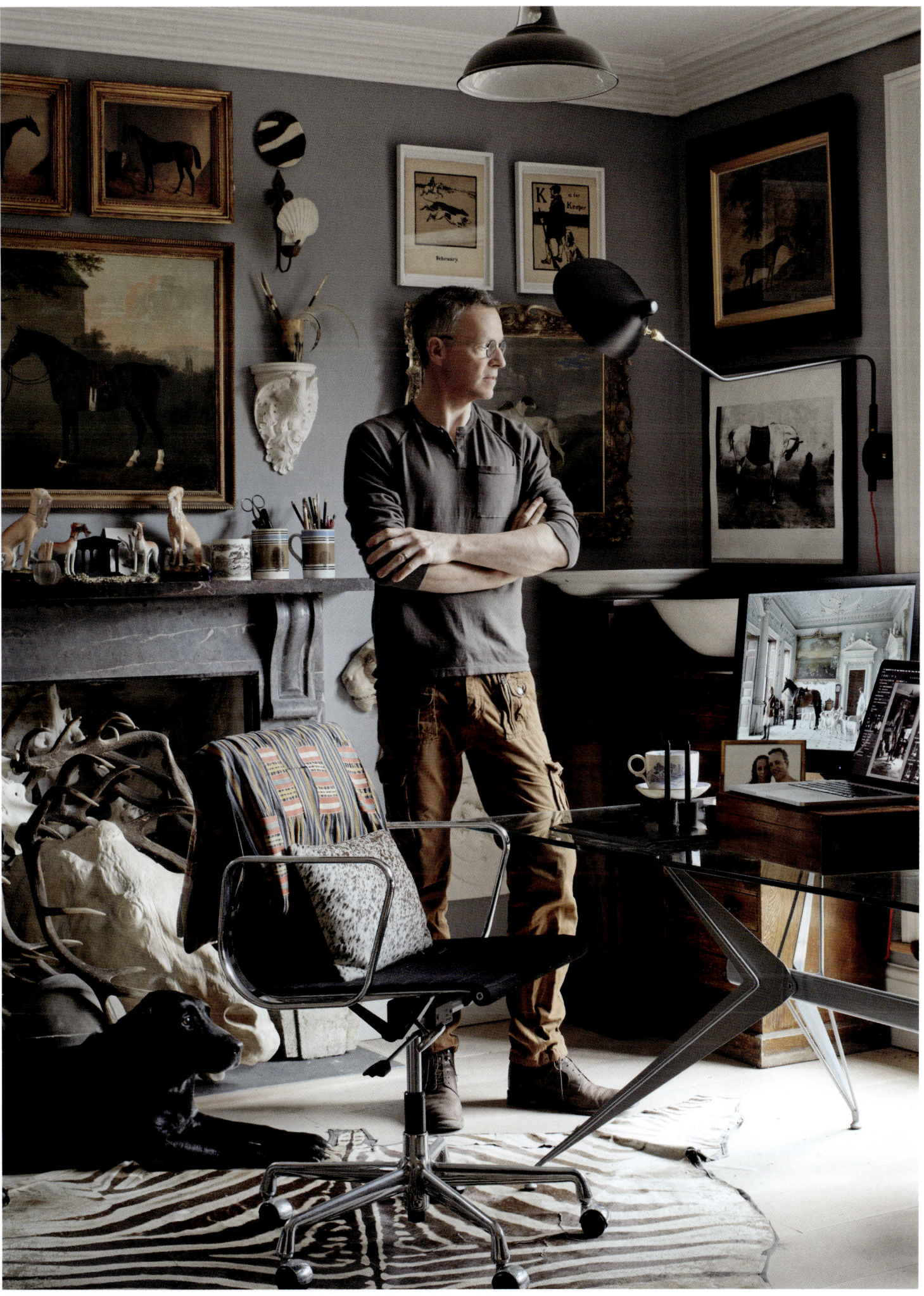

FOREWORD
RUPERT THOMAS
EDITOR,
THE WORLD OF INTERIORS

Think about New York and the word "serene" doesn't naturally spring to mind. Energetic, exciting, stimulating to the point of frenzy: yes. Tranquil, calm, and almost meditatively harmonious? Surely some mistake there. But Simon Upton has an unrivaled ability to bring elegance to the rooms he photographs without losing any of their intensity or dynamism.

Accordingly, here are some of Manhattan's most gloriously personal spaces captured in their myriad finery, yet distilled with quiet, understated beauty. It's as if he's caught the city that never sleeps as it emerges from a restorative moment of shut-eye: calm, poised, and ready for its close-up. Pictures of rooms don't get more refined than this.

It's perhaps ironic that a photographer devoted to the country should choose to focus his lens on what he describes as "the ultimate city." But, over three decades, Manhattan has burned its way into Simon's heart and seen him work with—and befriend a huge variety of its creative talents. The objectivity of the insider/outsider enabled him to see how vital it is to carve out a domestic sanctuary for oneself there—a place beyond the ceaseless bustle. So, this is his homage to rooms that keep the outside world at bay, but into which we are now lucky enough to be invited.

Simon makes capturing the souls of his four-walled subjects look effortless. But the best interior photographs are hard-won: the endless waiting for the right fall of light; divining from exactly which angle a room is shown to most impactful effect (which, he says, inevitably means wedging himself unglamorously into a corner); to say nothing of the painstaking tweaks to ensure chairs, tables, cushions, and curtains are at their natural best. All this and much more go toward making a truthful representation of a space and, as an inevitable consequence, an intimate depiction of those behind it.

So here is a book that no other photographer could have put together. A lasting portrait of that most fleeting but heartfelt of creations: the very private places people call home. Drawn from uptown and downtown, the heart of the city and rural upstate, the rooms themselves are wide-ranging: from rigorously empty to pleasingly jam-packed, rainbow bright to chicly monochromatic, put together on a (relative) shoestring or lavishly decorated with money no object. But all are lucky to have been shot by Simon. None could have been photographed with more clear-eyed sophistication.

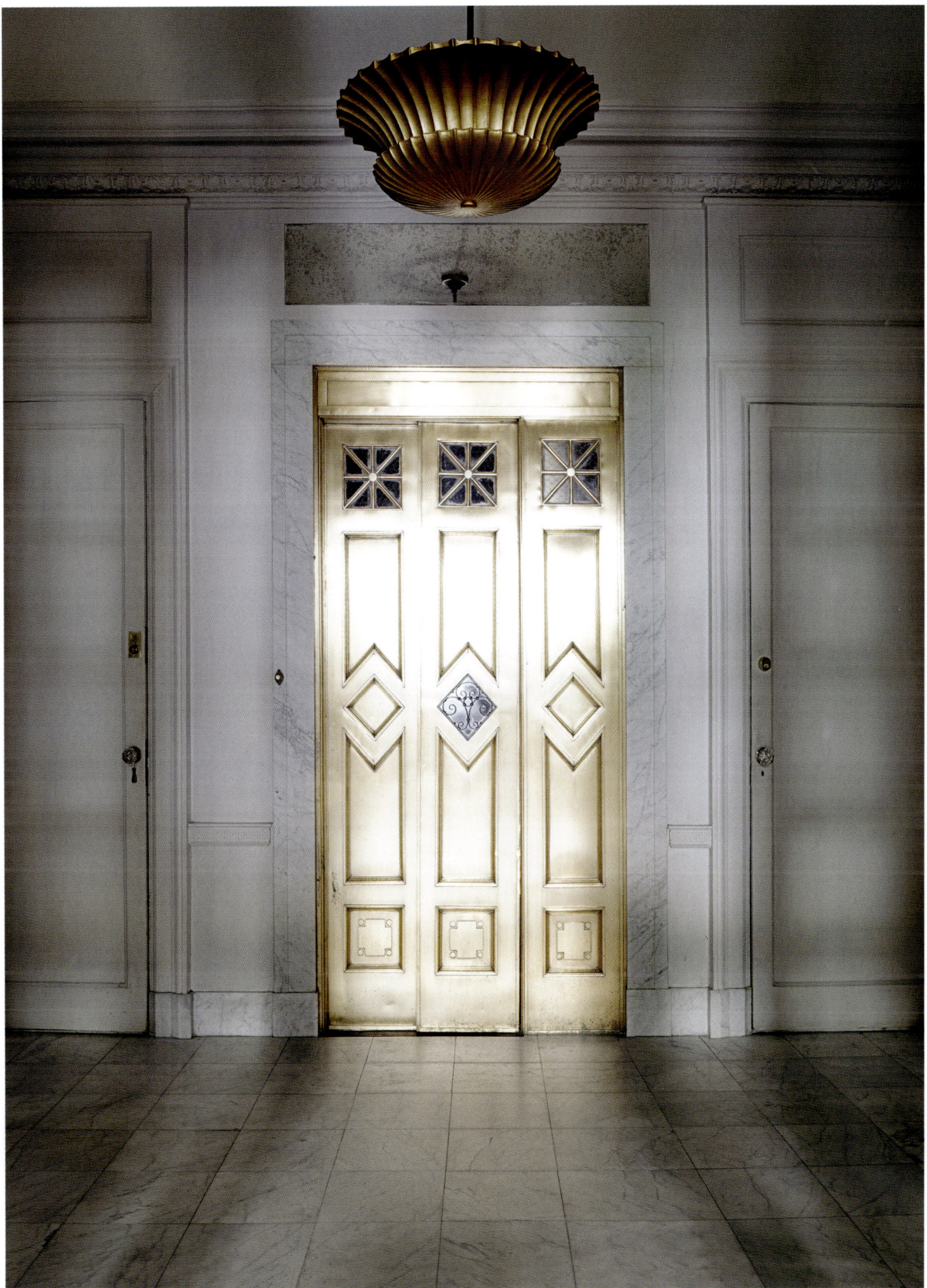

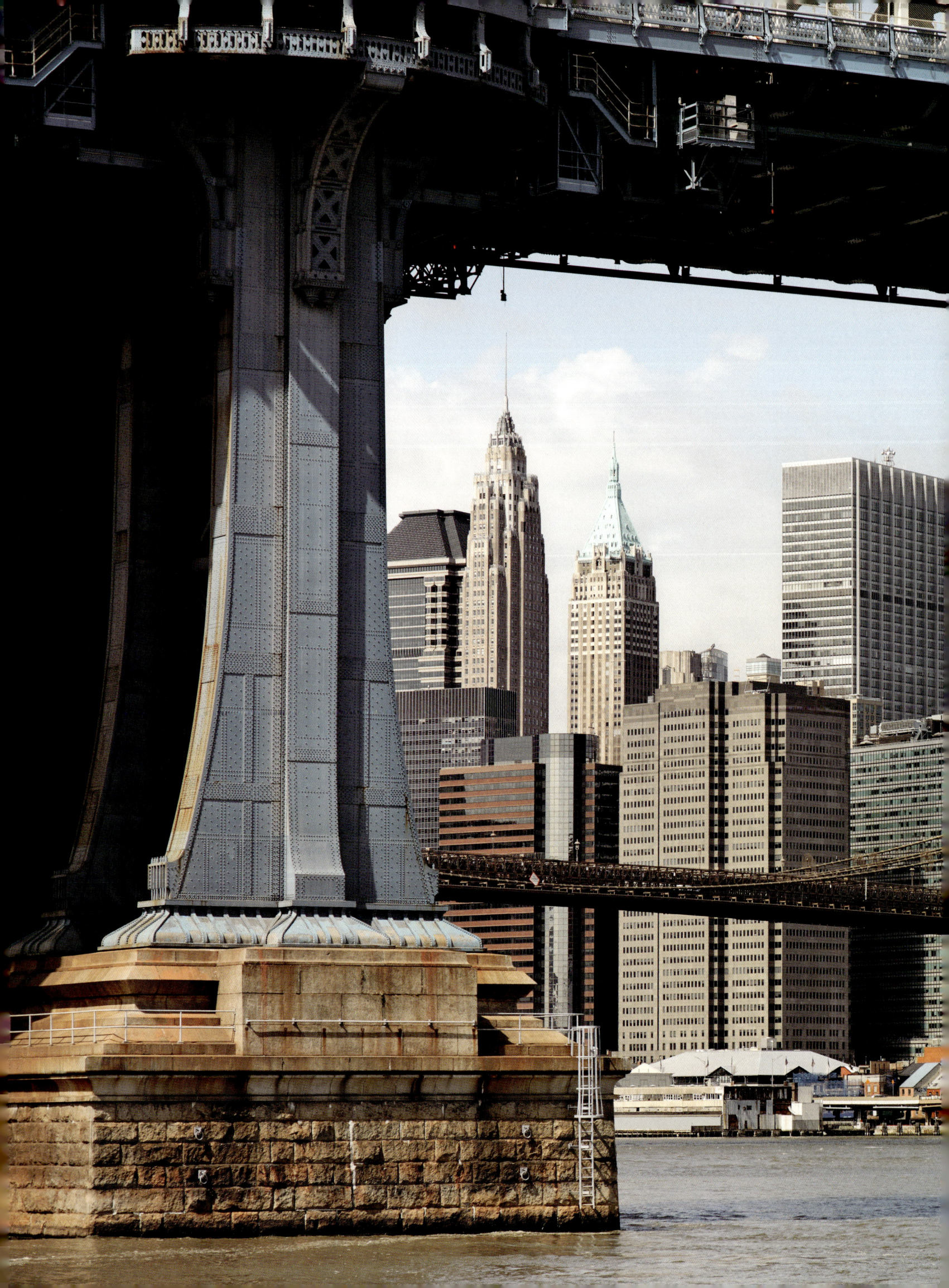

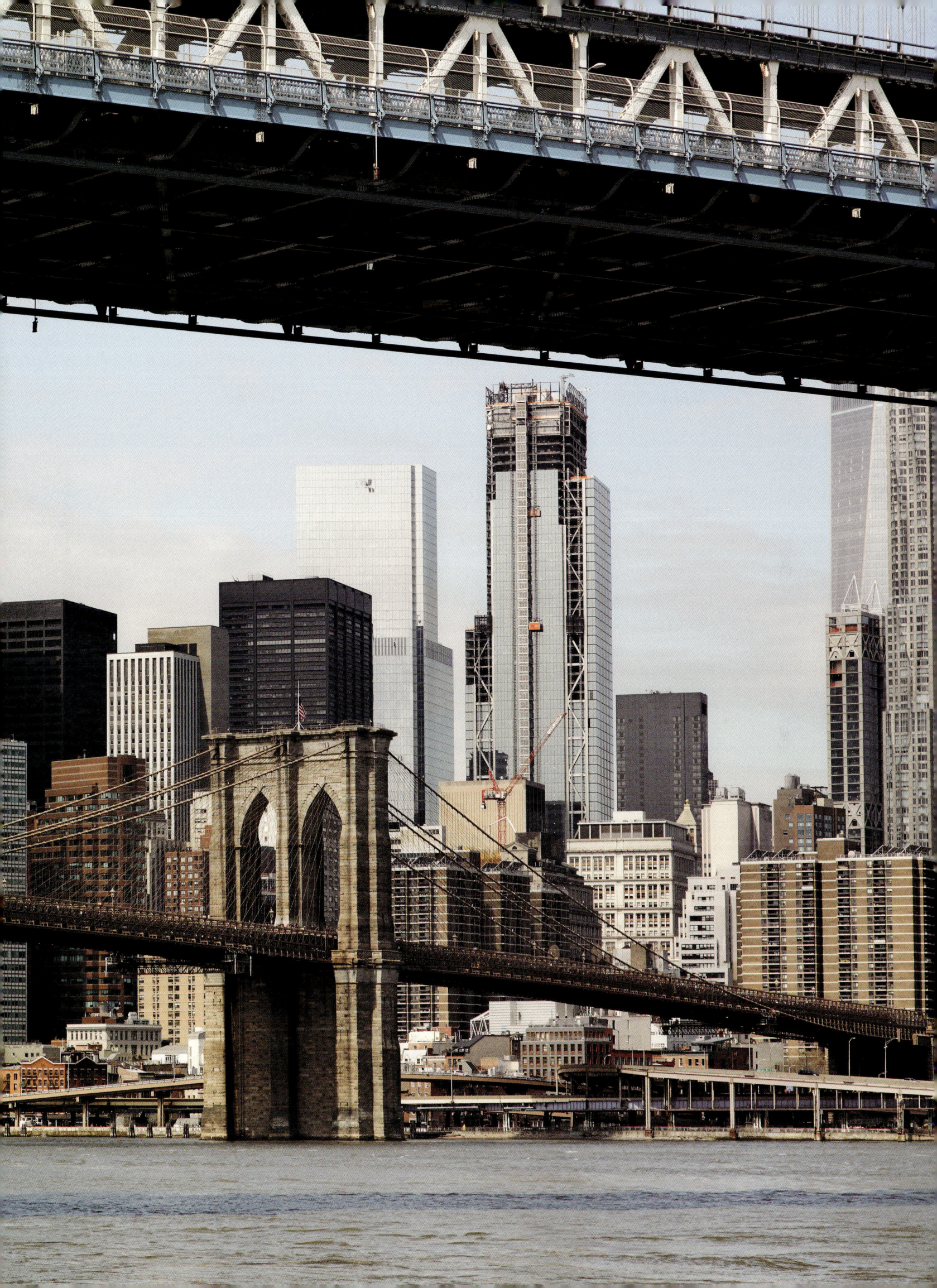

CITY

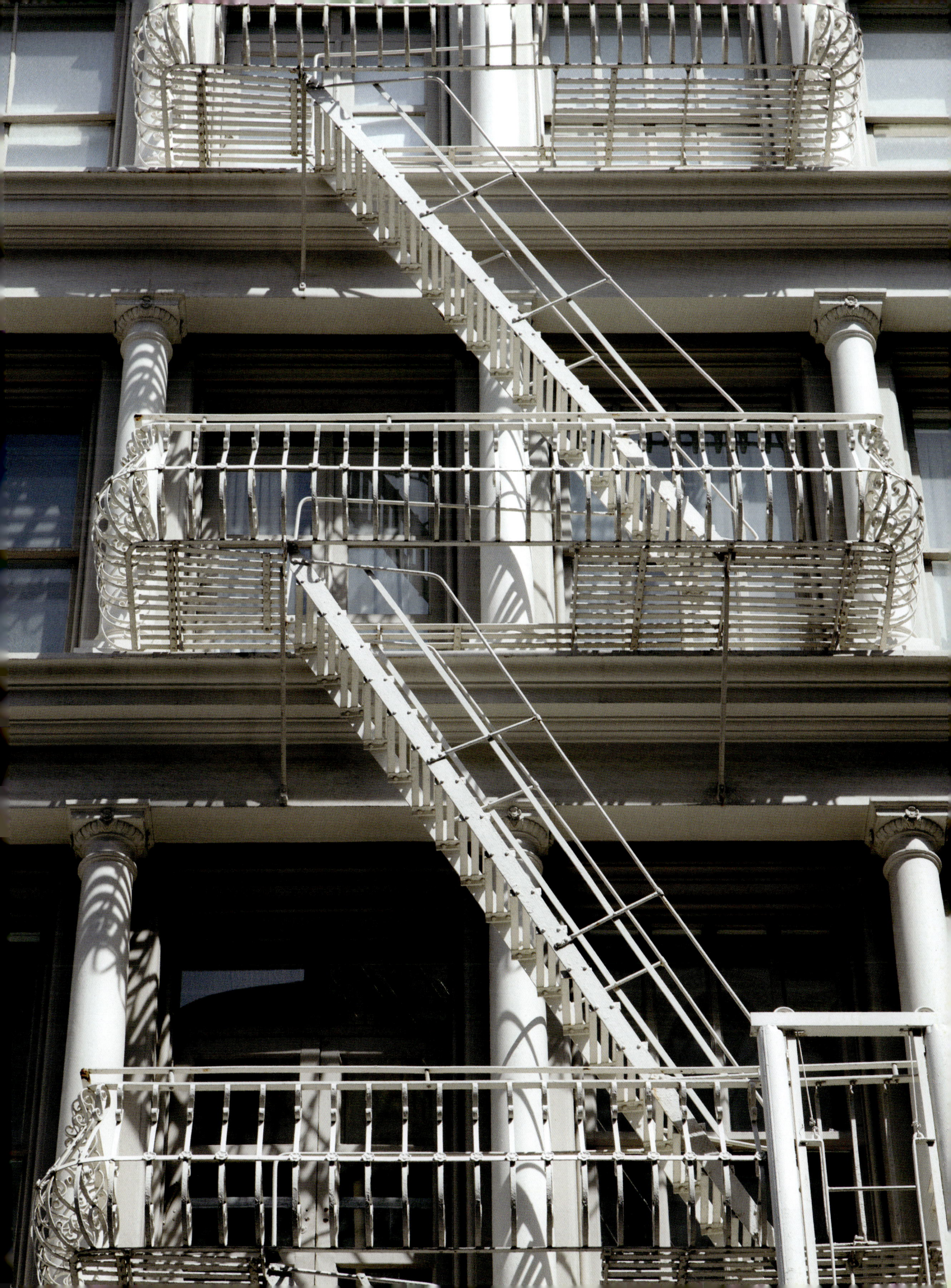

ENGLISHMAN IN NEW YORK

HAMISH BOWLES

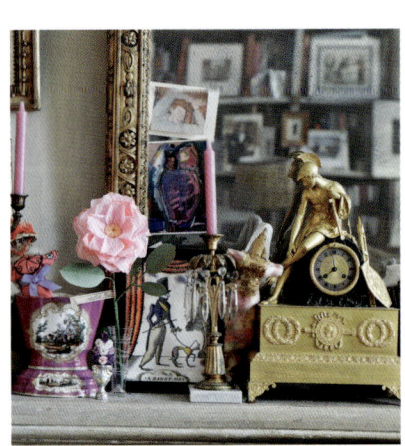

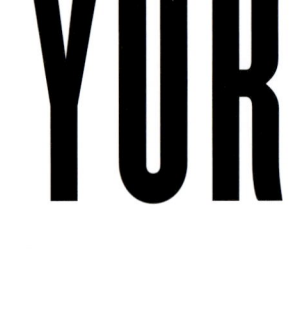

I find my building aesthetically very pleasing, one of three sister structures separated by two gardens. Dating from 1925 and situated just north of Washington Square, between the East and West Villages, each has an attractive lobby in New York baronial style, with double-height apartments (oh, how I always coveted one!) and Juliet balconies.

When I first arrived in New York I lived in the West Village, and after a brief and somewhat lonely sojourn in Sutton Place, I returned to this area about 12 years ago. It's lively, with the New York University campus around the square, giving it that dynamic energy that young people bring. The former owner of my apartment was a distinguished literary agent who had lived here since the 1950s. Apart from being rather shabby, all the apartment's architectural detailing and original structure were intact. The joy of discovering a place still *dans son jus* was thrilling and, despite its parlous state and forlorn quality, I was smitten and began to plan a radical renovation.

Roberto Peregalli and Laura Sartori Rimini of Studio Peregalli are good friends and creative visionaries and, while I would never have presumed to ask them for advice, happily they were in New York at the time I acquired the apartment, so I asked if they would take a look, keen to get their perspective Roberto did a perfect sketch of the living room on the back of an envelope. Structural alterations accomplished, they culled my collection of furniture and we then set about decorating and furnishing. My most serious investment was the drawing-room carpet, which completed the look and gave a background to the objects and furniture, amplifying their effect, but perhaps my favorite space is my bedroom, which acts like an enveloping bower and proudly displays my portrait of Truman Capote by Renée Boucher, bought with my first American paycheck.

A lot of my furniture has resonance, but the marmalade sofa is my pride and joy. It has been a reassuring presence in all my apartments and was originally upholstered in an ivory trellised jacquard. Perfect 1930s. Perfect Syrie Maugham! I would never have thought of the color, wickedly introduced by Studio Peregalli in hand-dyed and ruinously costly silk velvet, yet it complements beautifully my beloved lilacs and purples.

Before the pandemic, I led a strangely peripatetic life and my New York apartment was a wonderfully comforting place to return to. During the pandemic, it has been a salvation. If I am honest, I have always found being English an asset here: New York is an anglophile city. There is a different pace and energy here and it has been a marvelous place for me to call home.

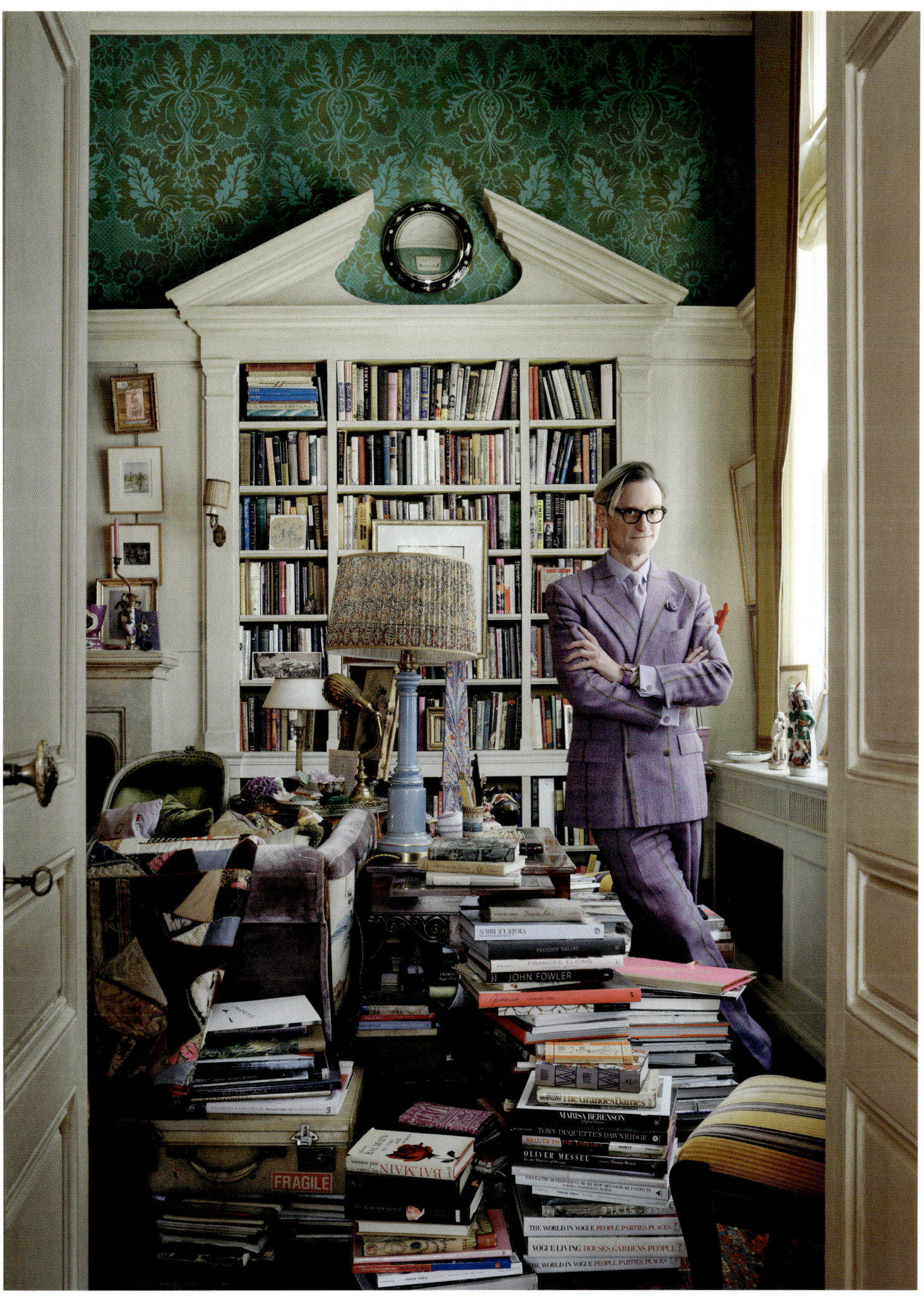

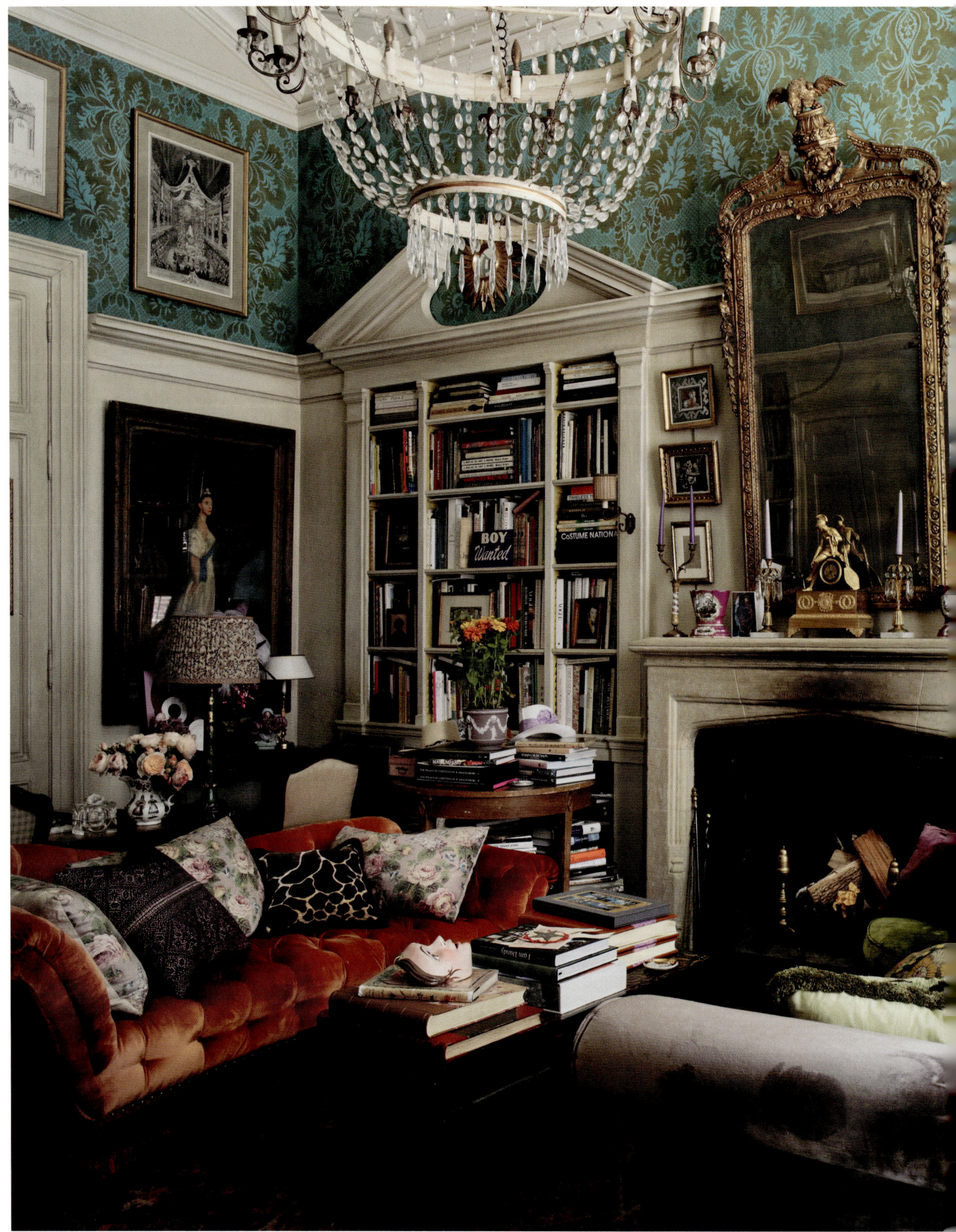

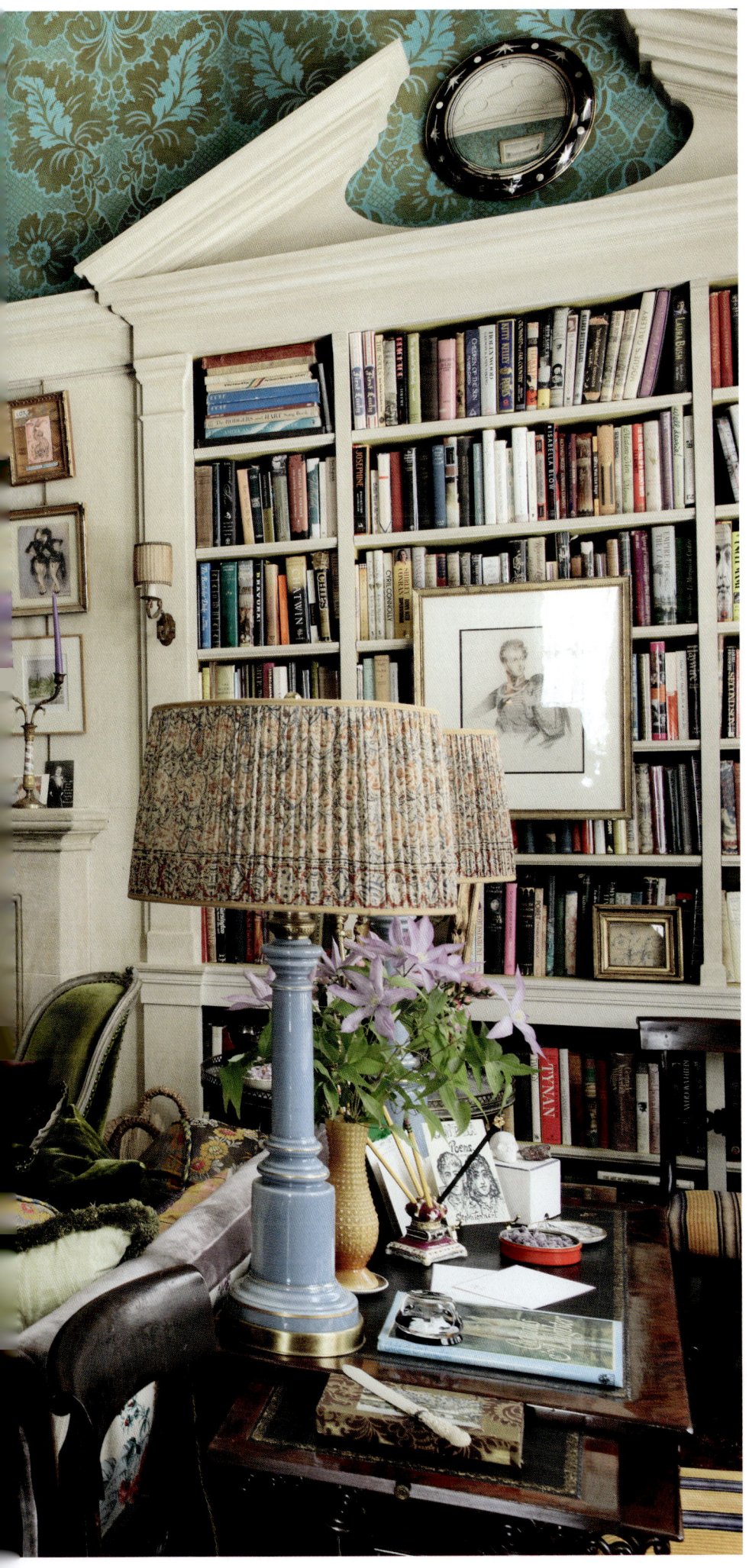

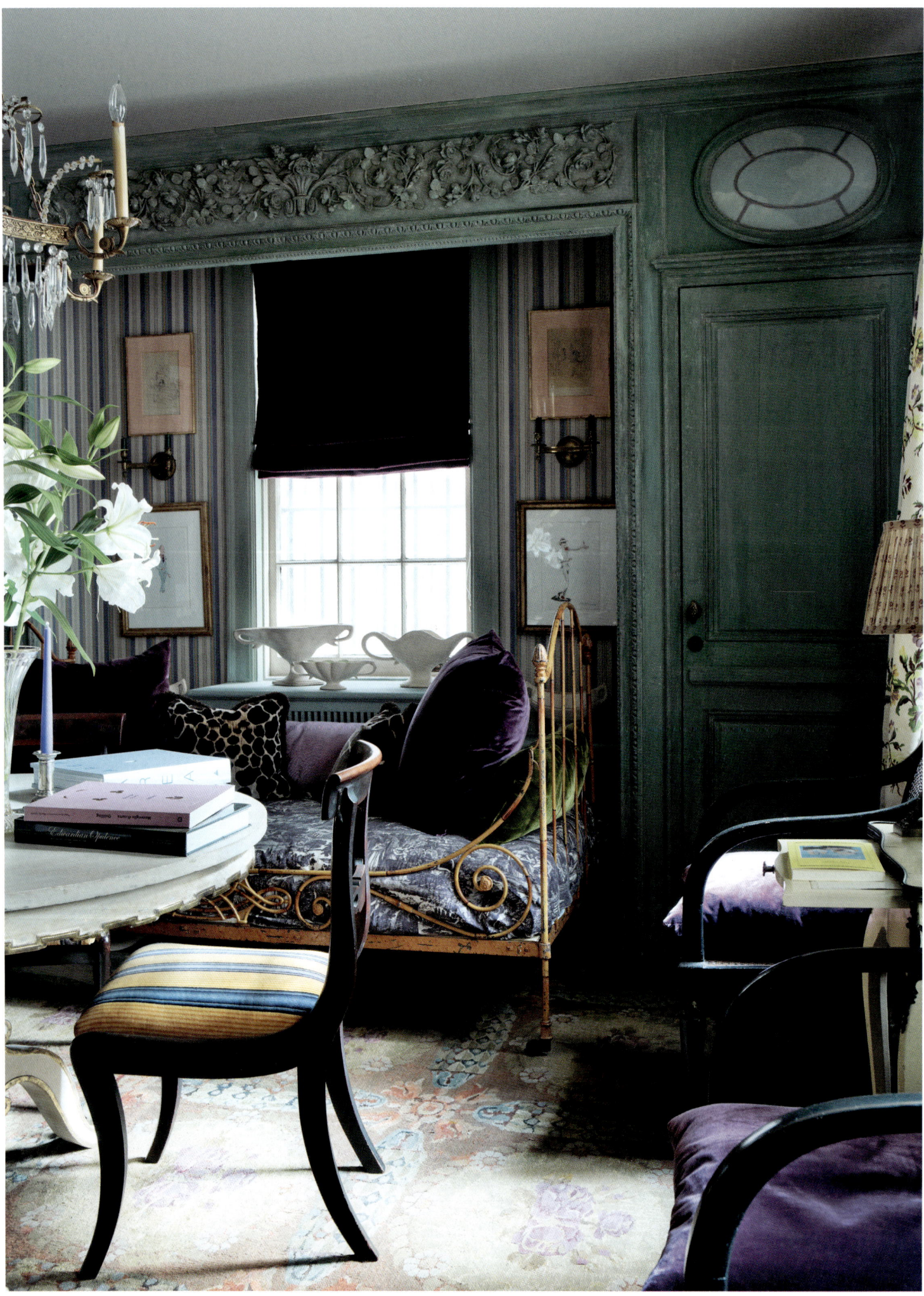

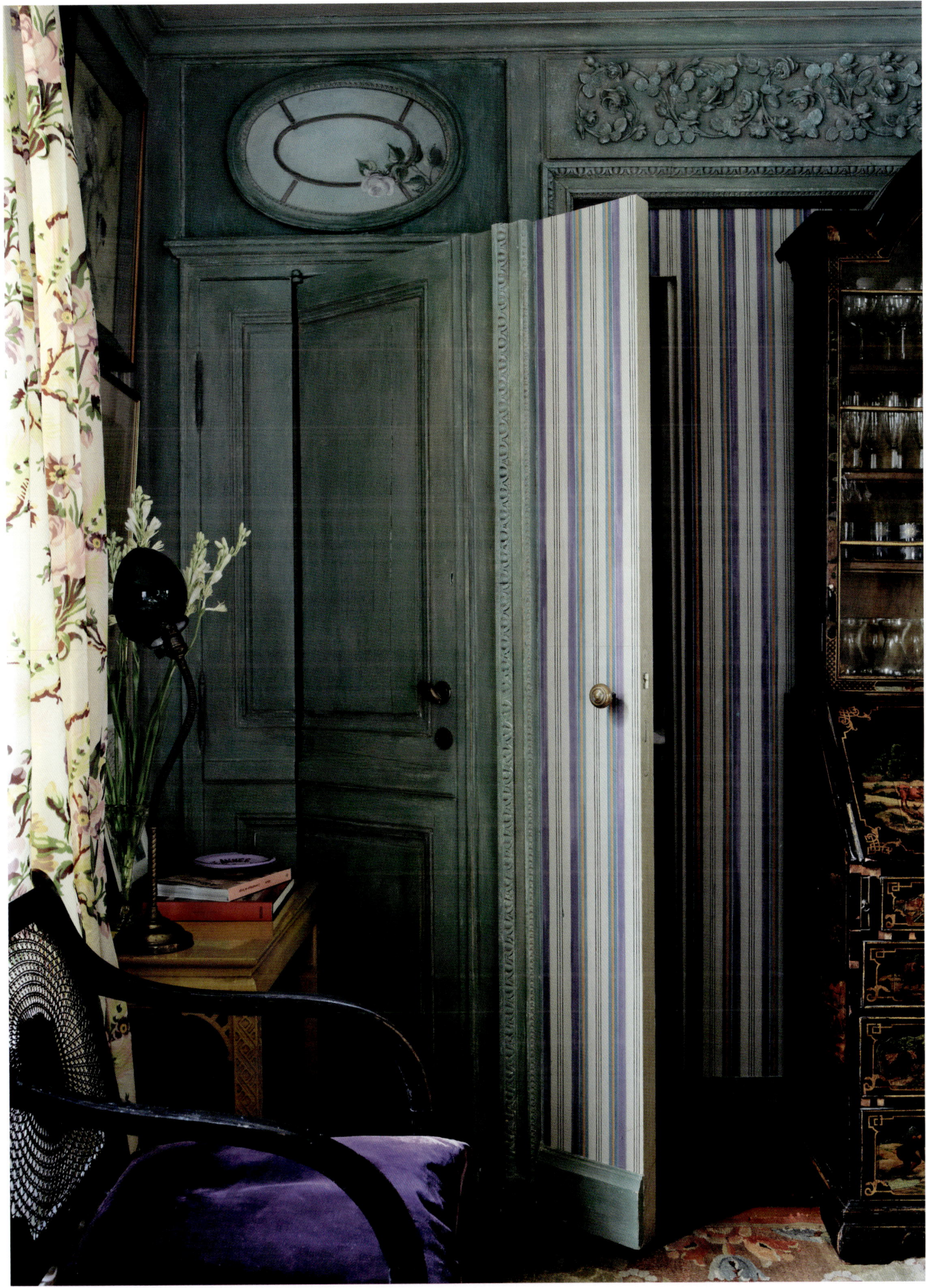

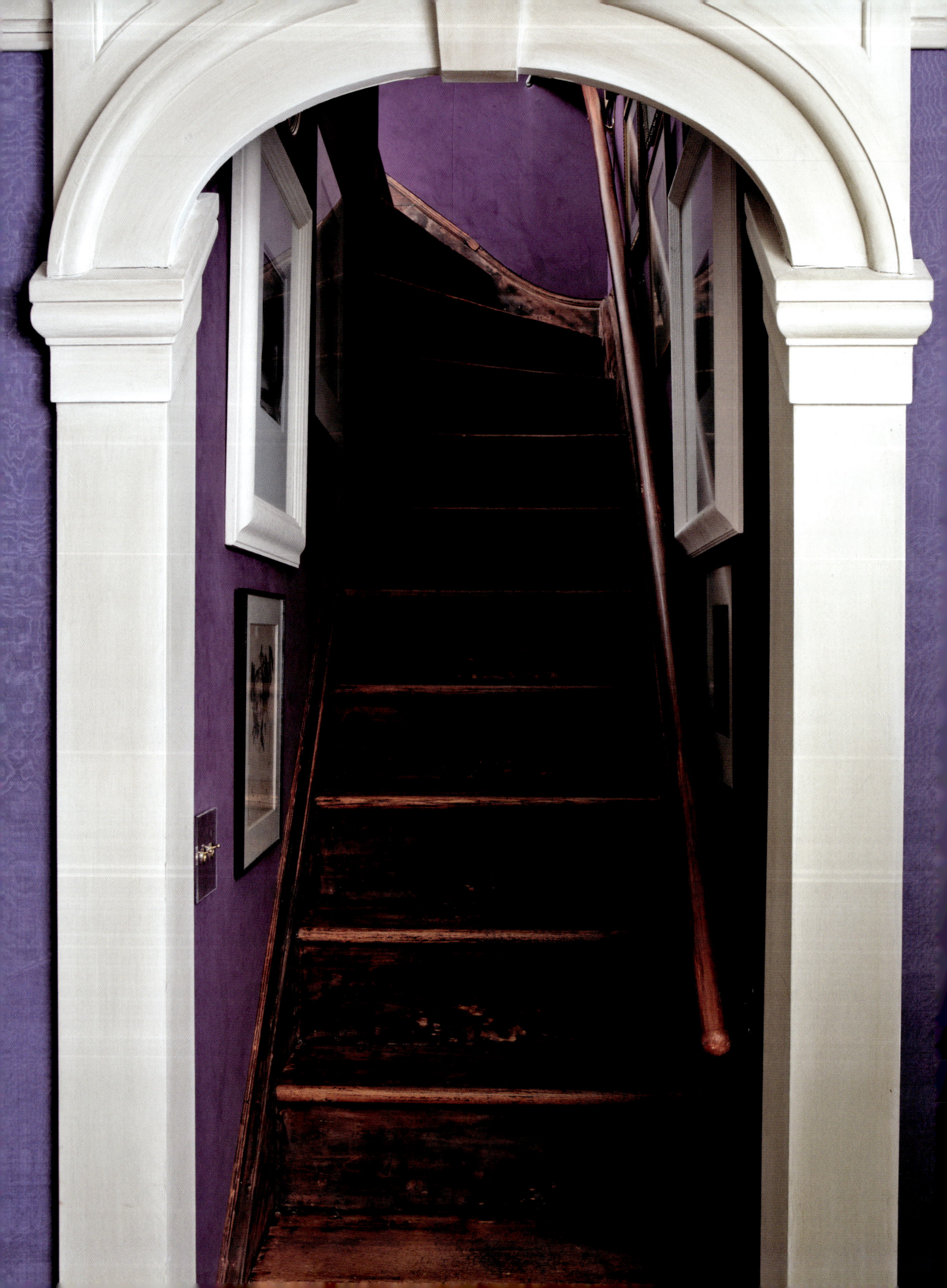

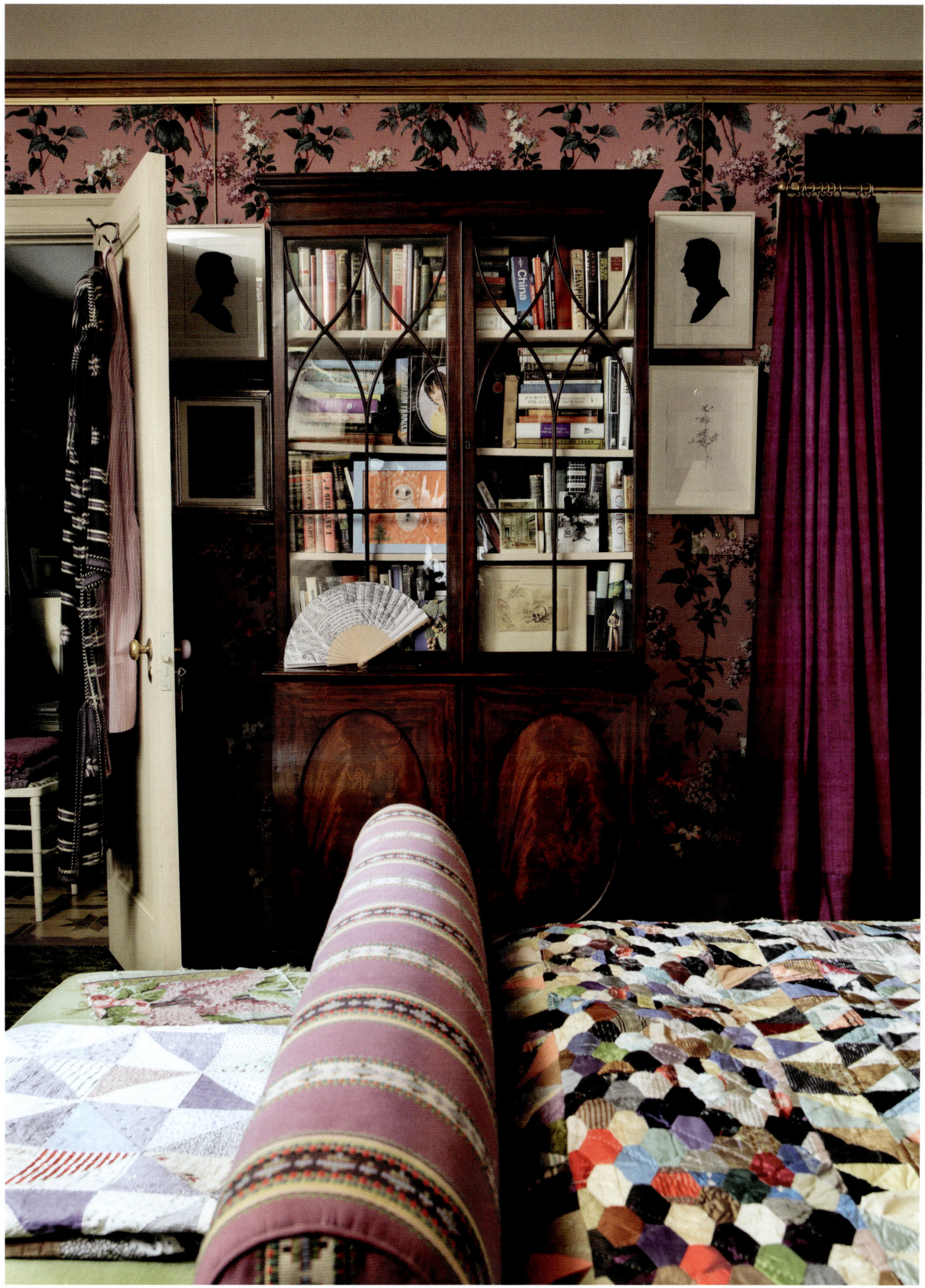

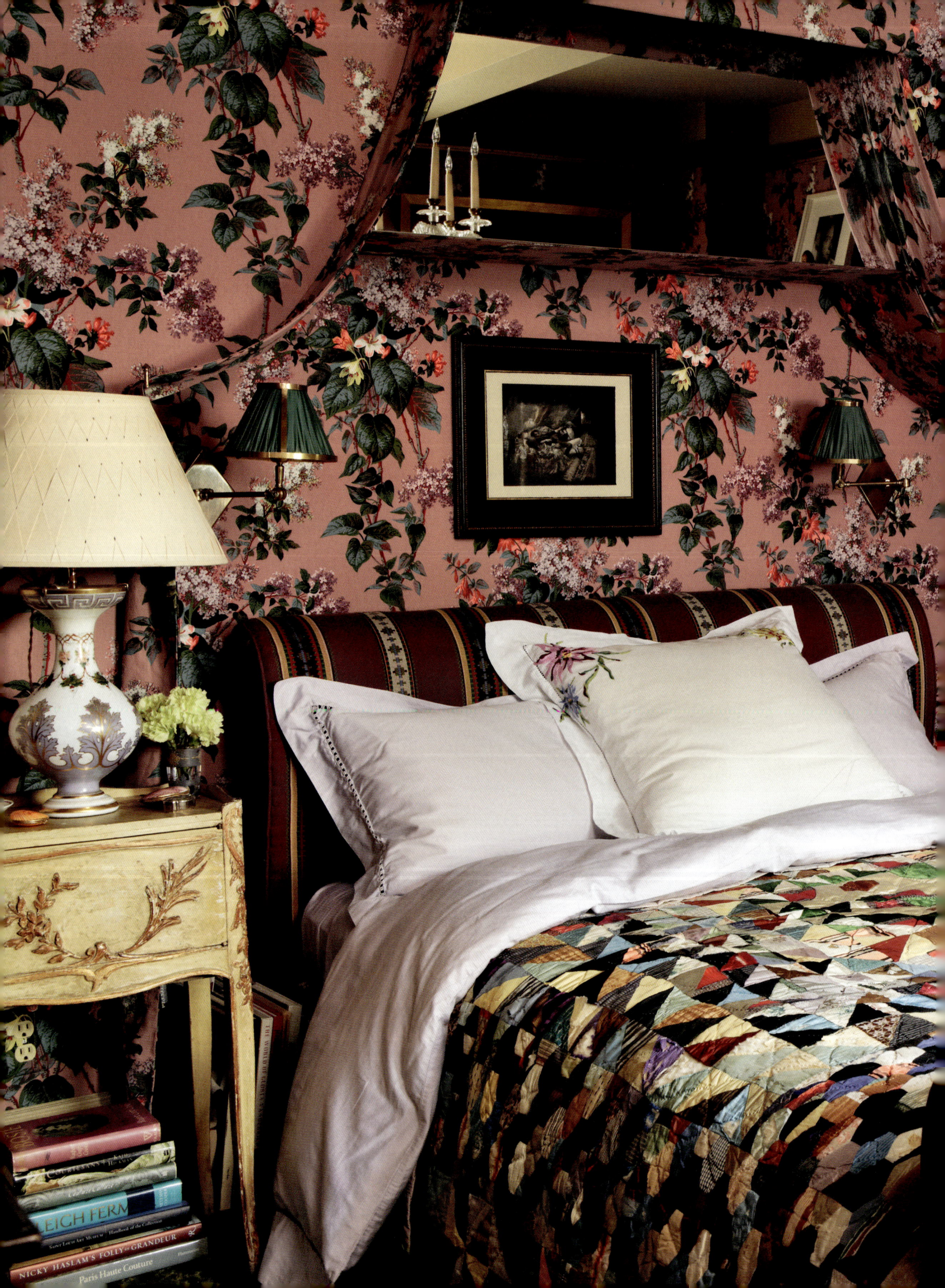

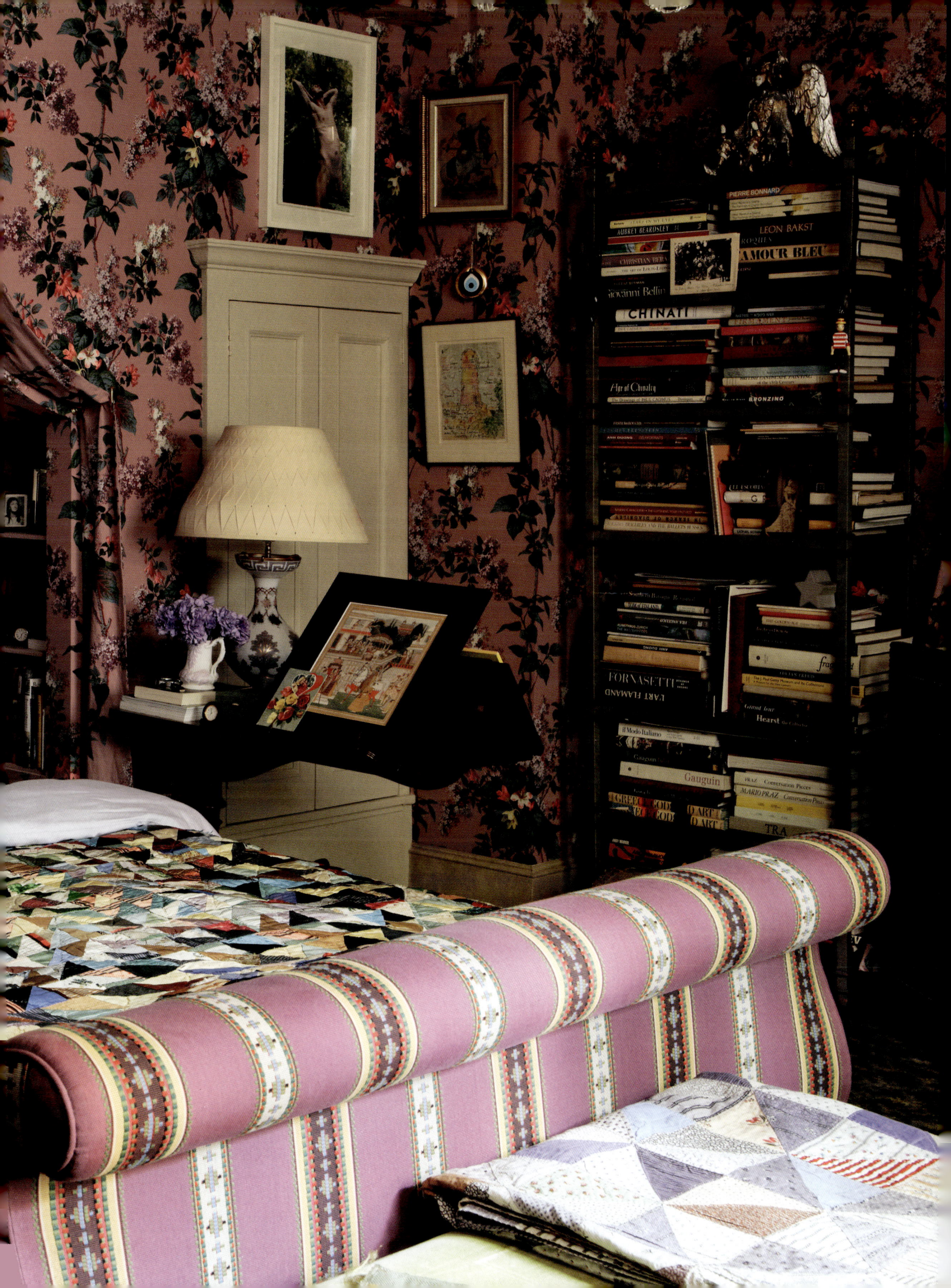

INFORMED REVERENCE

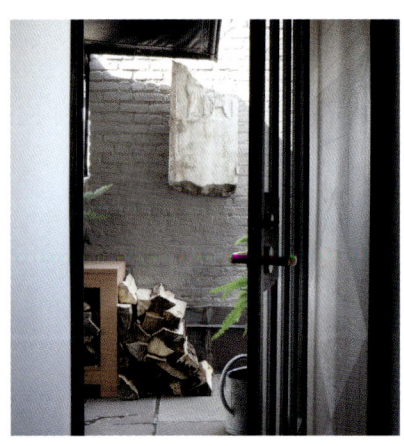

STEPHEN SILLS

Back in the 1980s I was living in a one-room apartment on 83rd Street, in a neighborhood I loved, right across from The Metropolitan Museum and close to Central Park. A friend who was already living in the apartment block where I live now told me that a penthouse on 86th was coming up for sale and that I should take a look. It was a tiny, ramshackle place, and quite horrible! In those days, I had absolutely no money, so my Dad offered to buy it for me. He couldn't believe the price he had to pay "for a shack on top of a building," as he put it. I shall always be grateful to him for providing me with a place to live. I have been here ever since and over the years have completely rebuilt and redecorated it four times. Each time it has been redone, it's been published in some magazine or other. I guess you might consider it my "calling card."

I was born in Oklahoma, literally in the middle of nowhere, but it gave me a perspective on the rest of the world. I love New York! The city is phenomenal—the people, restaurants, and different cultures and personalities are just fascinating. It's one of those places to which people tend to gravitate—people who don't seem to fit into the rest of America, or the rest of the world, for that matter. Anyone who is creative, musical, cultured, resilient, and inventive ends up here.

The only thing I love doing is interiors; mine is not so much a profession as a passion. Managing client expectations all day long, it's wonderful to come home to the tranquility of my apartment, which is flooded with natural light on three sides. I chose a neutral background in which to live, with just a splash of richness from the curtains in the living room and bedroom, which are made of purple taffeta lining material. My favorite room is the living room, which features a working fireplace and is home to my treasured Jean-Michel Frank daybed in shagreen. A piece by Oklahoma artist Harold Stevenson reminds me of my roots and hangs above the desk in my dressing room. I have him to thank for introducing me to so many people in Europe.

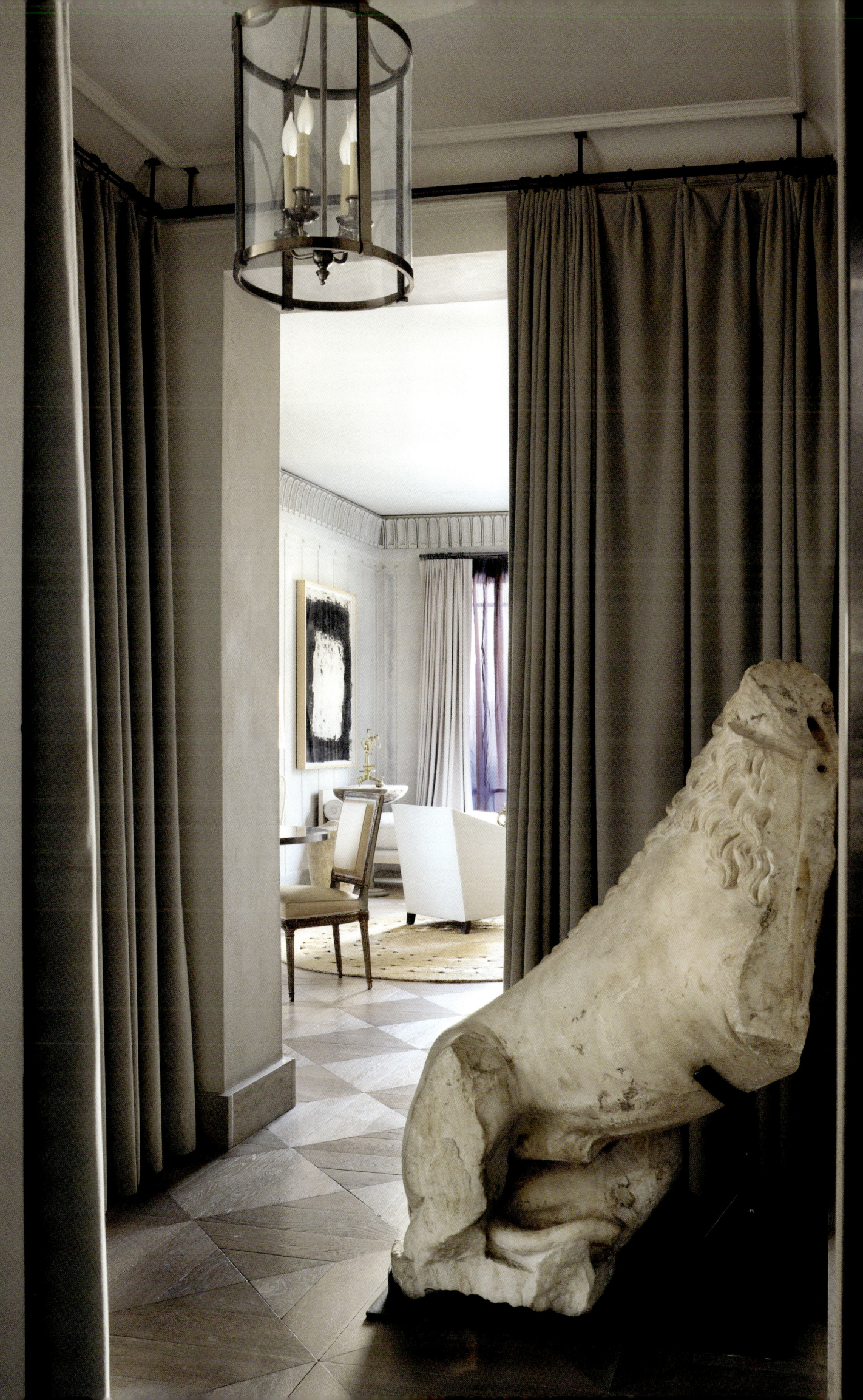

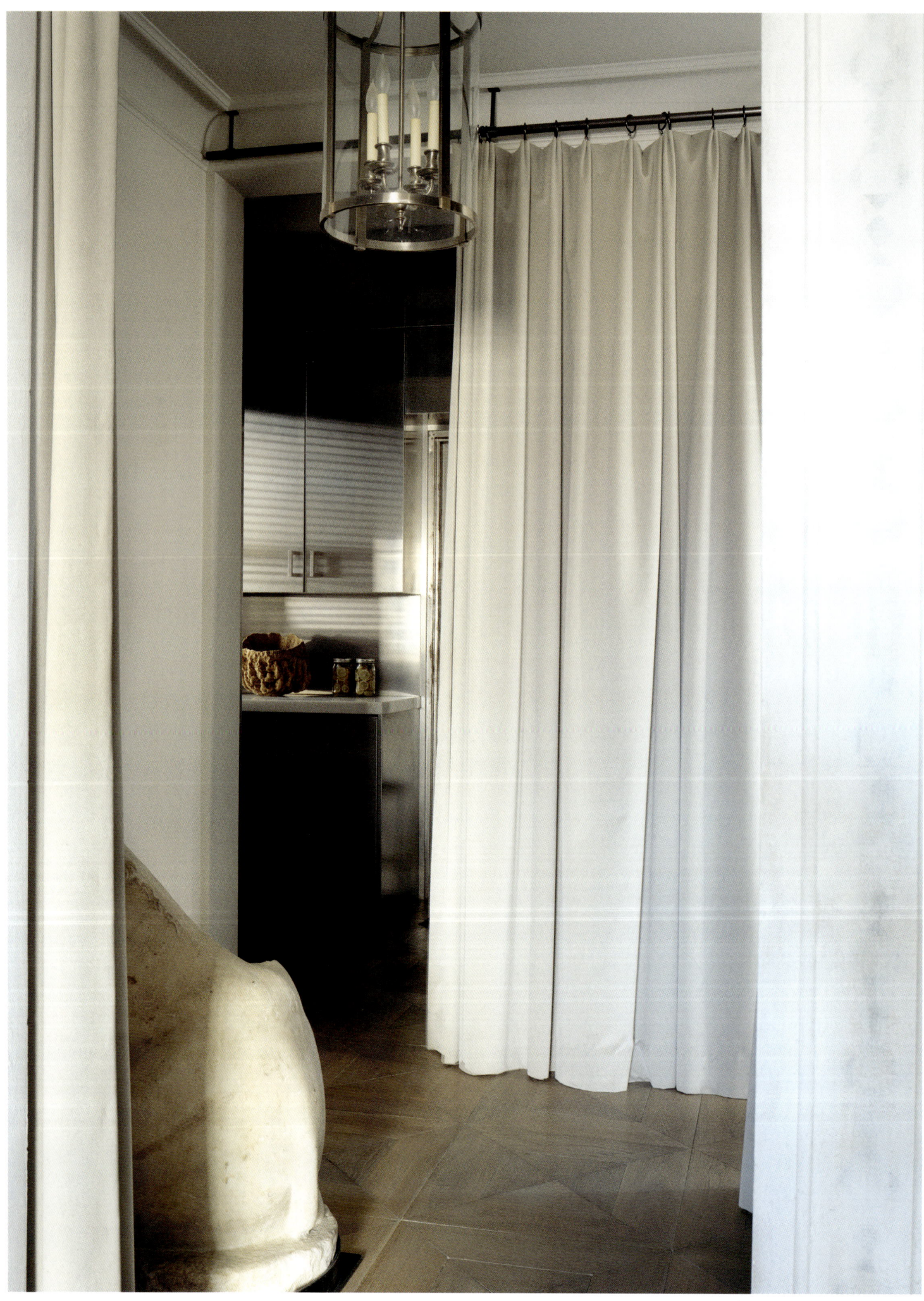

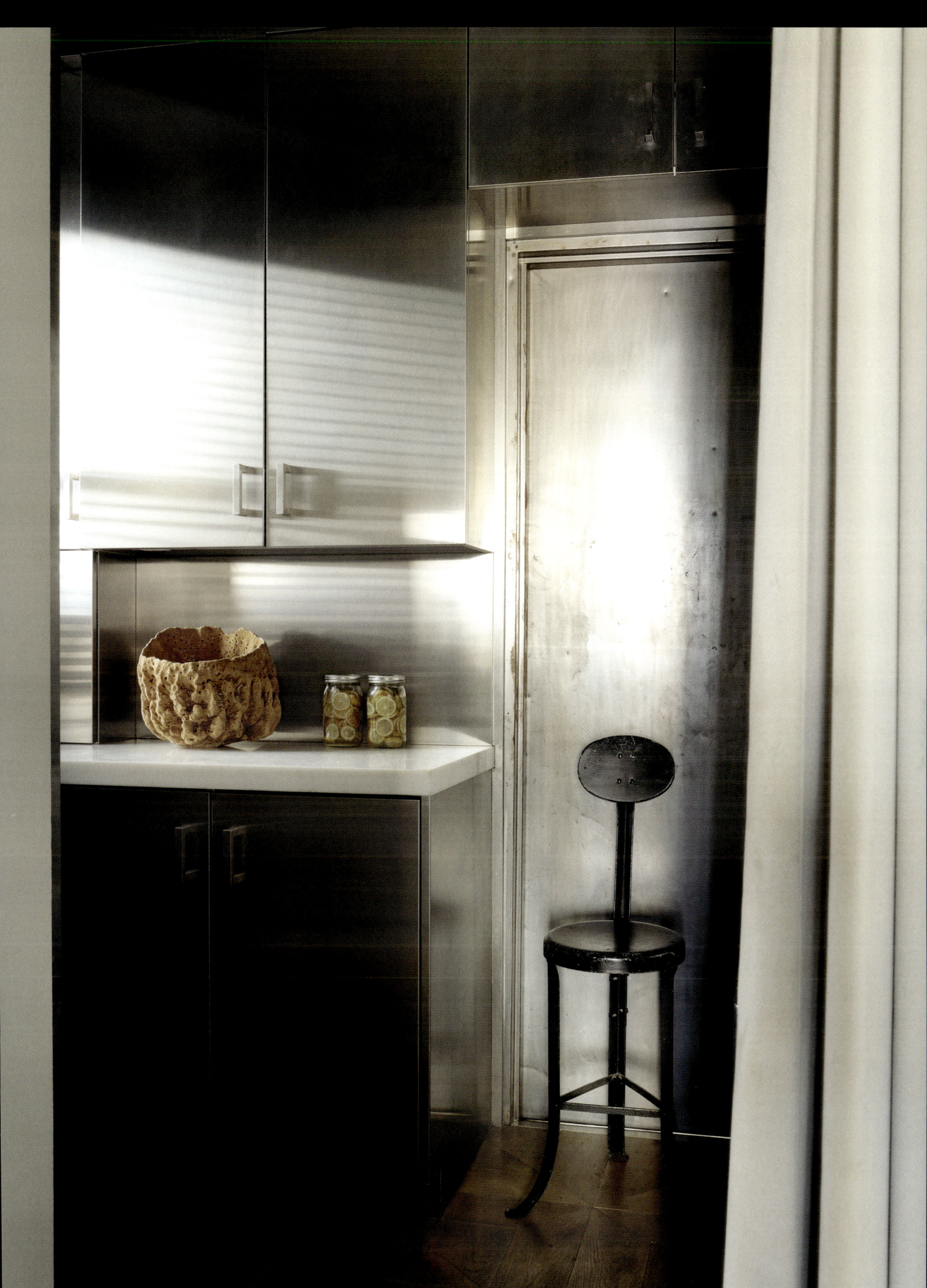

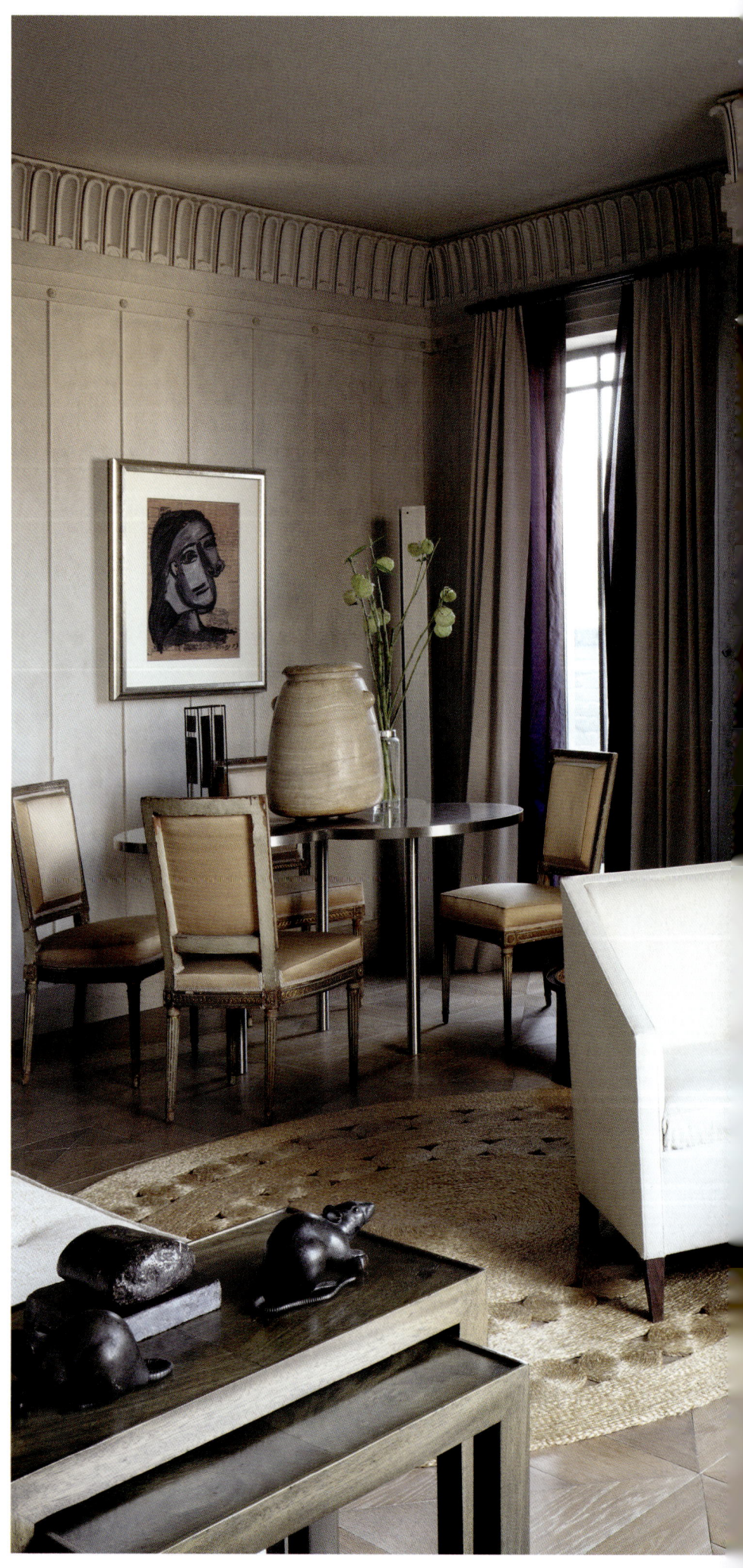

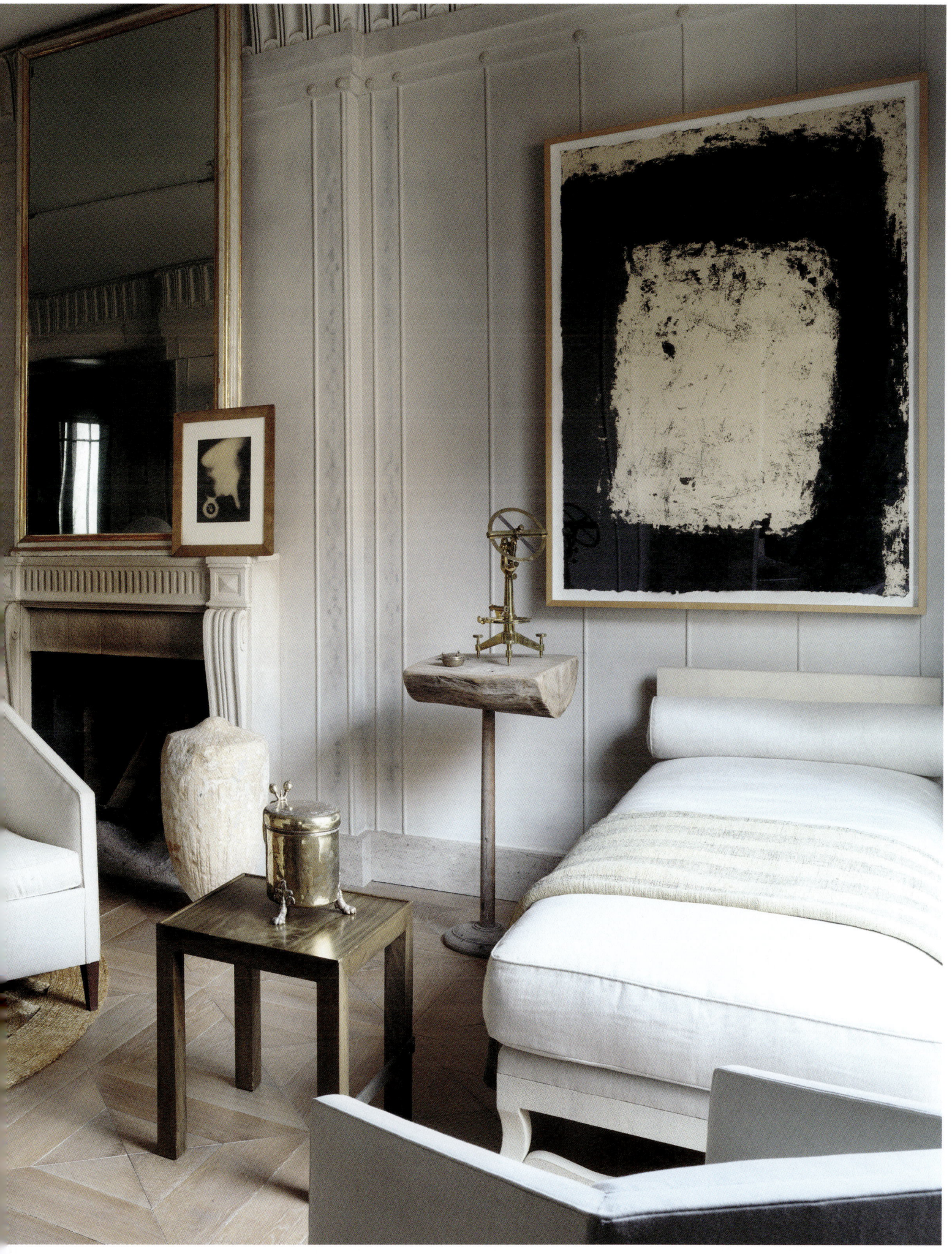

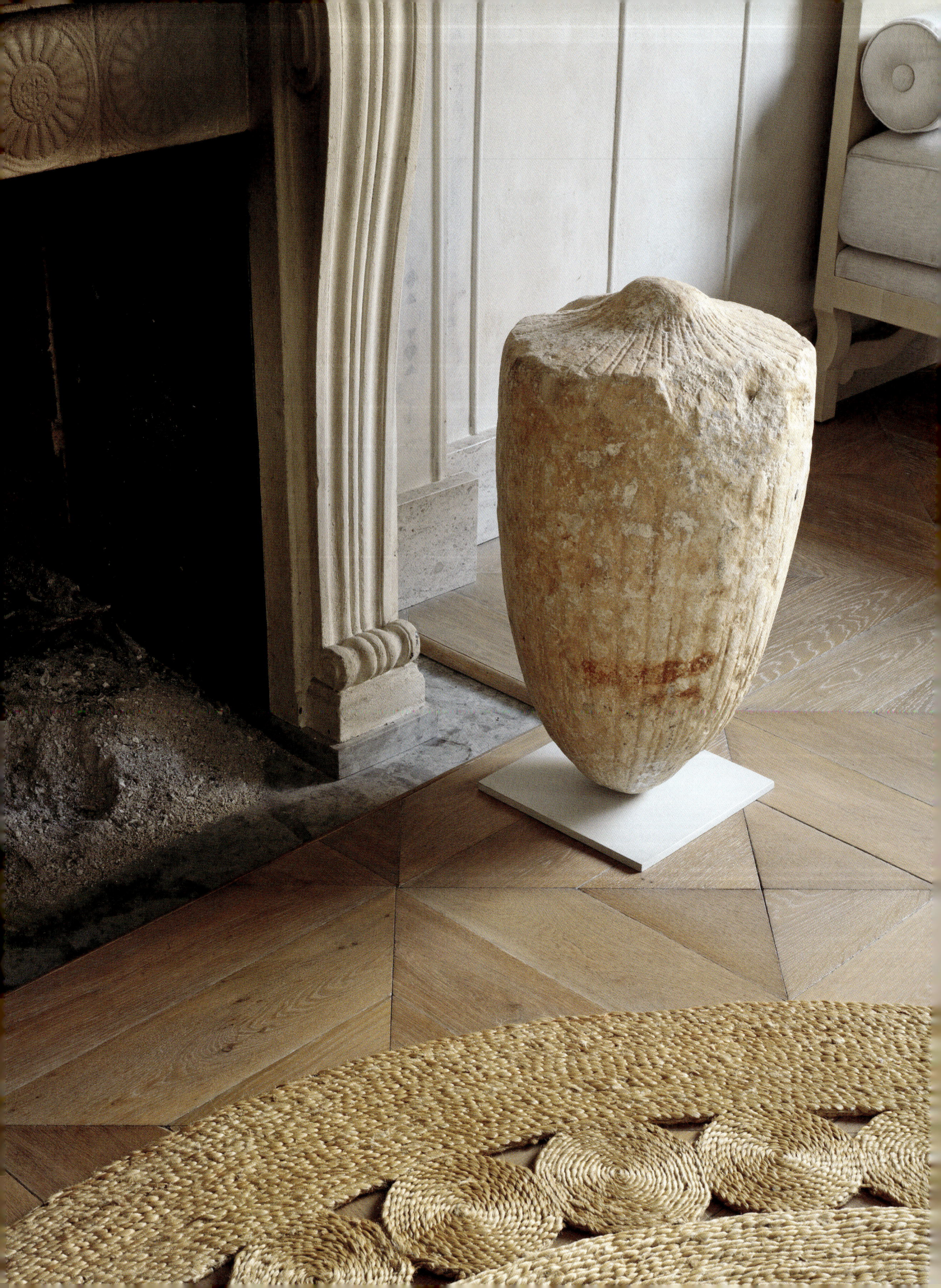

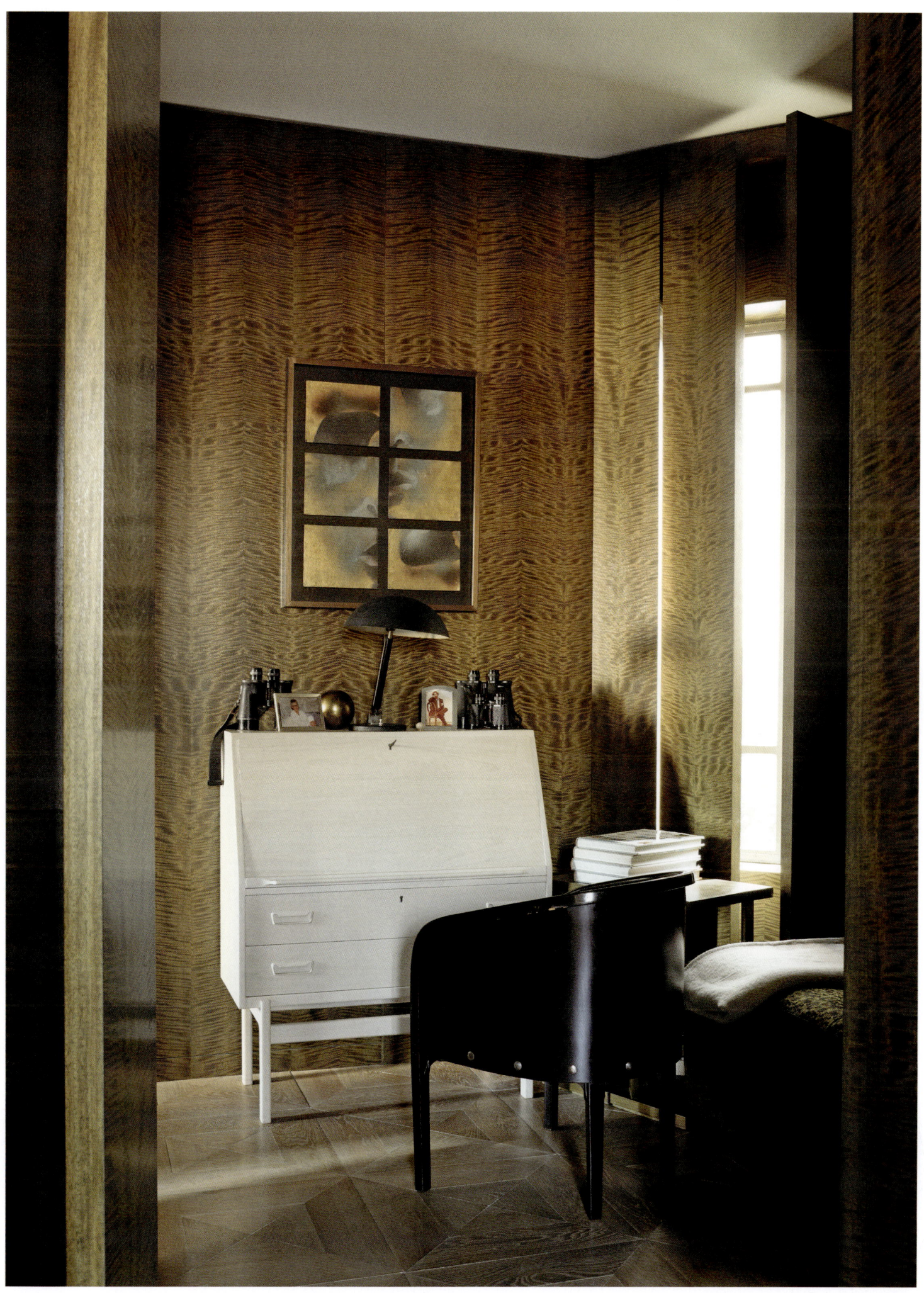

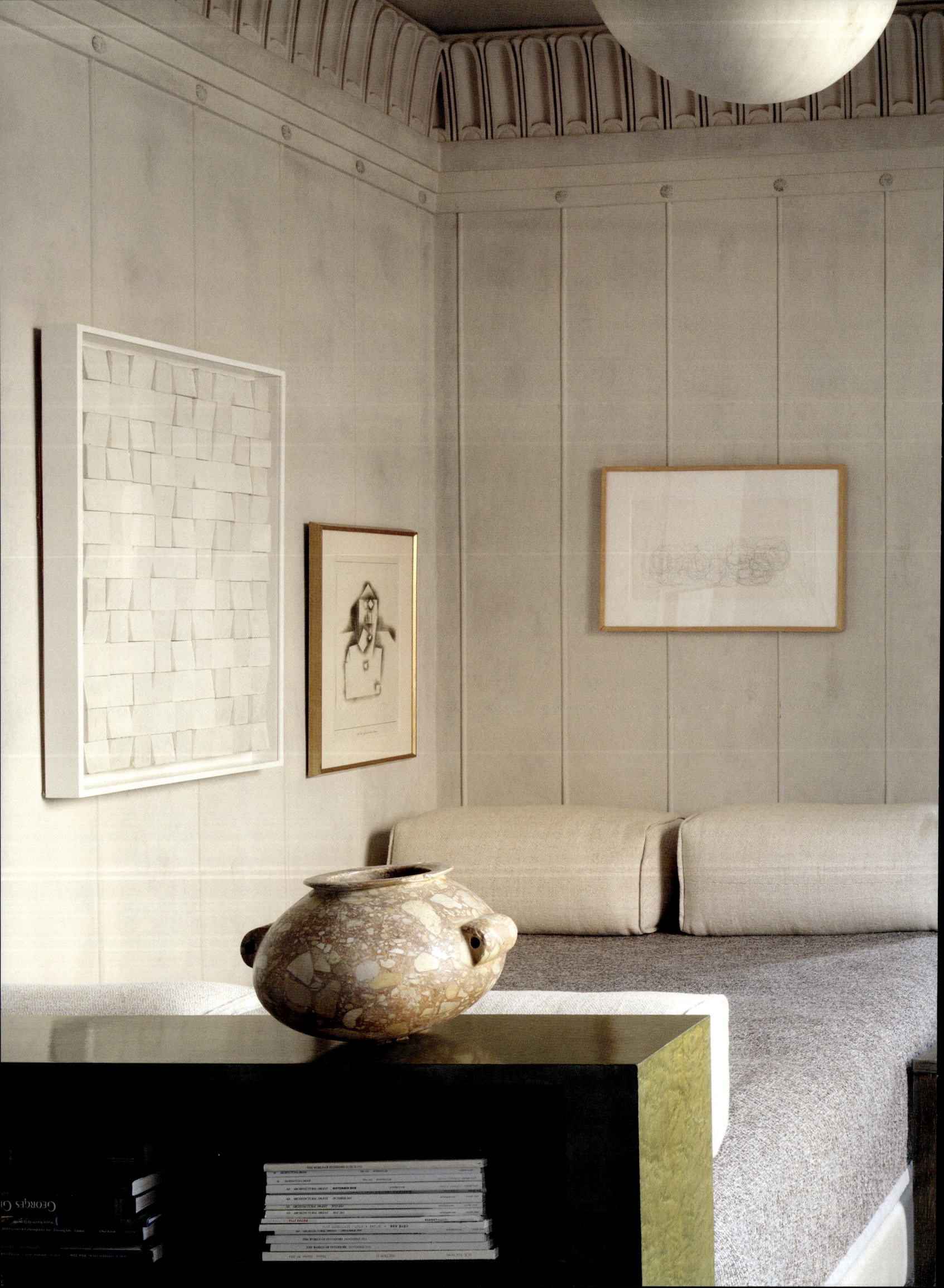

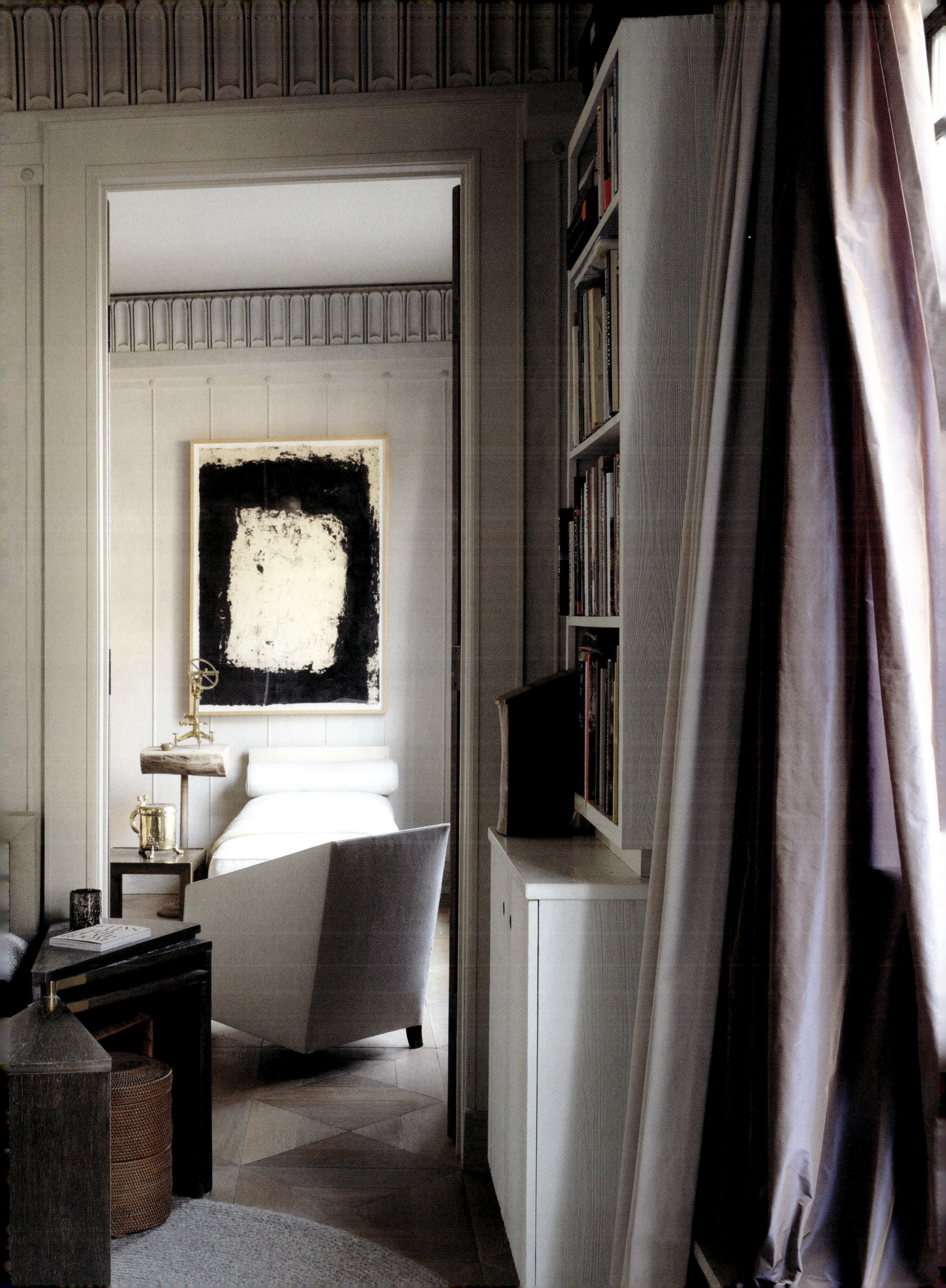

LET'S MAKE IT HAPPEN!

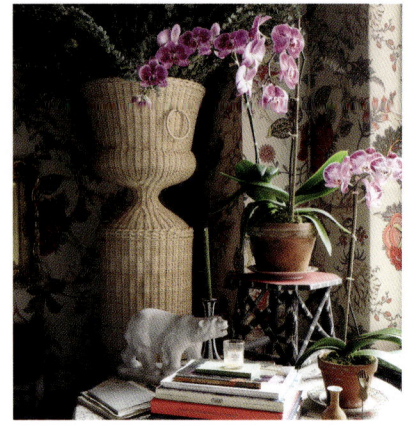

CARLOS MOTA

Constructed in the 1930s, my building was at the time of its creation the biggest rental apartment building in the world. I have lived here for more than 20 years and my one-bedroom apartment has the perfect layout for me. I spend much of my time traveling, so for the rare moments I am at home I want my apartment to feel as cozy and comfortable as possible. There are so many buildings in Manhattan that it is difficult to find the perfect apartment in New York City. When you do, you usually stay forever. Besides, I like the area—neither Uptown nor Downtown, but somewhere in between. So, instead of looking for a new apartment when I get bored with mine, I change or redecorate a room. This usually happens every five years or so. For an interior designer and decorator, the best project is normally your own home, so my apartment has become my mood board and a constant "work in progress."

As a Venezuelan, and pure Latin, I love entertaining at home. The smaller the apartment, the more people I used to invite, but as I have grown older my gatherings have become more intimate. Before I started traveling so much, I used to enjoy having people over, but I haven't entertained for a while now—I am just so seldom here. Perhaps this is why my favorite room is currently my bedroom—though it may also be because it's the most recent room to have been redecorated! I think of it as my "French old lady's bedroom," as it feels as if I am in Paris. I love it so much! My bedroom is a cocoon, which is why I covered the ceiling and the walls in this crazy French floral fabric, unearthed in a Paris flea market. I also love the green silk rug in my living room, which exerts a strong influence on the space—it's like walking on grass.

I am a professional shopper, not just for my clients, but also for me. My apartment is like a global bazaar or souk. I love anything exotic, especially orientalism, and my favorite painting (at the moment) is the large portrait in my bedroom, which I bought from the Kenneth Jay Lane estate. It would be this and my passport that I would rescue in case of a fire!

New York is not only a city that never sleeps—it is always changing and moving. Just like me.

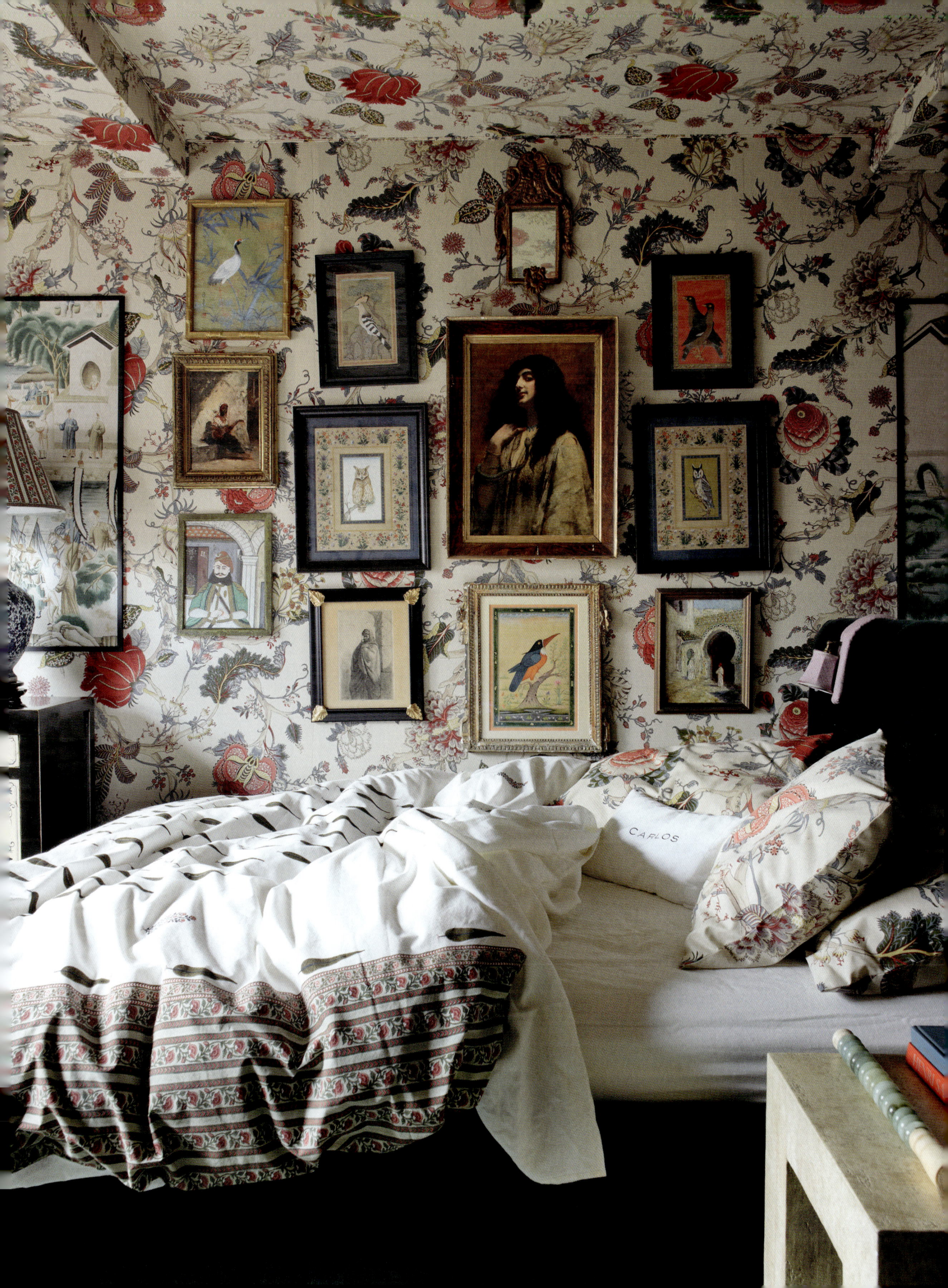

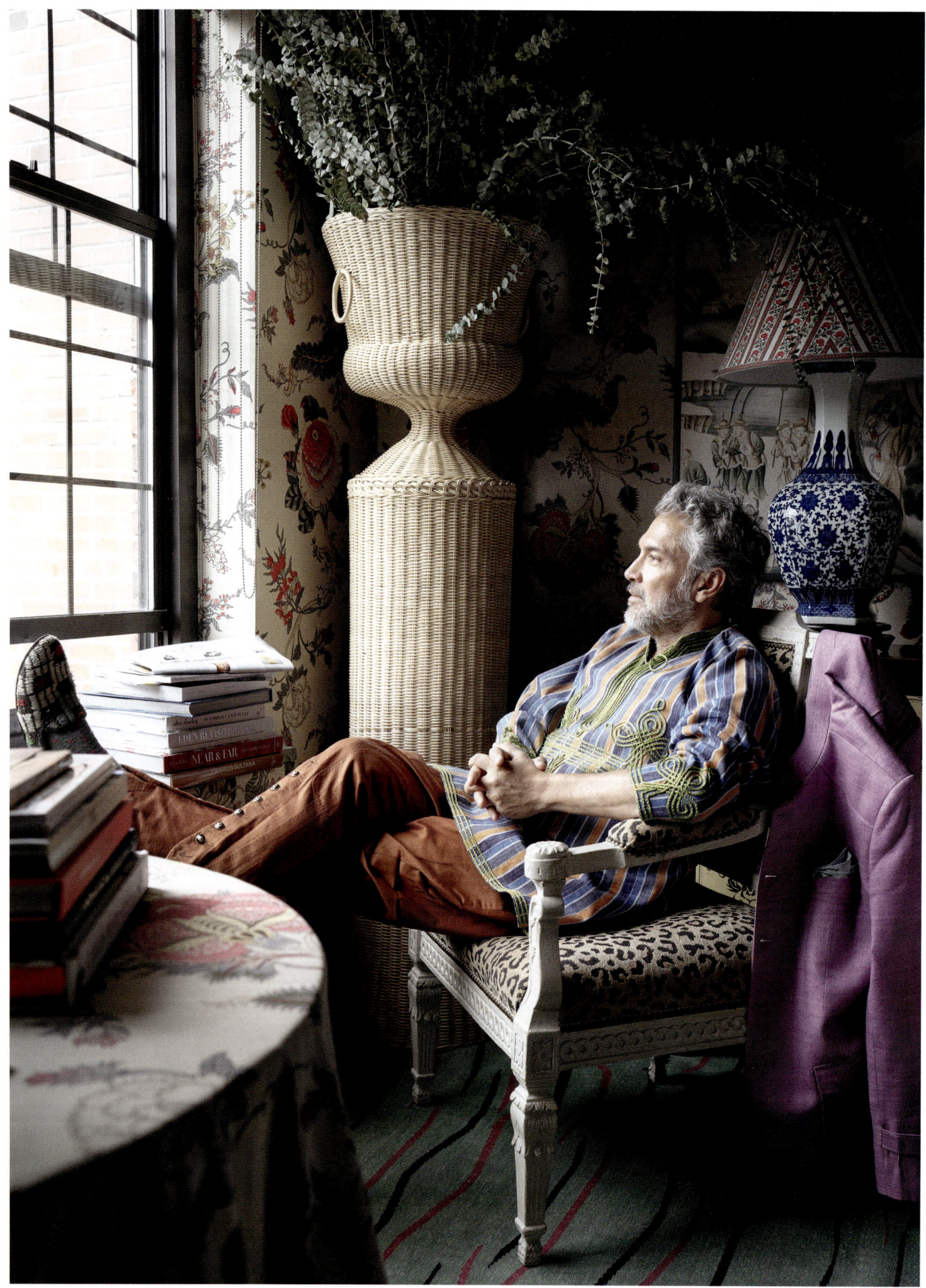

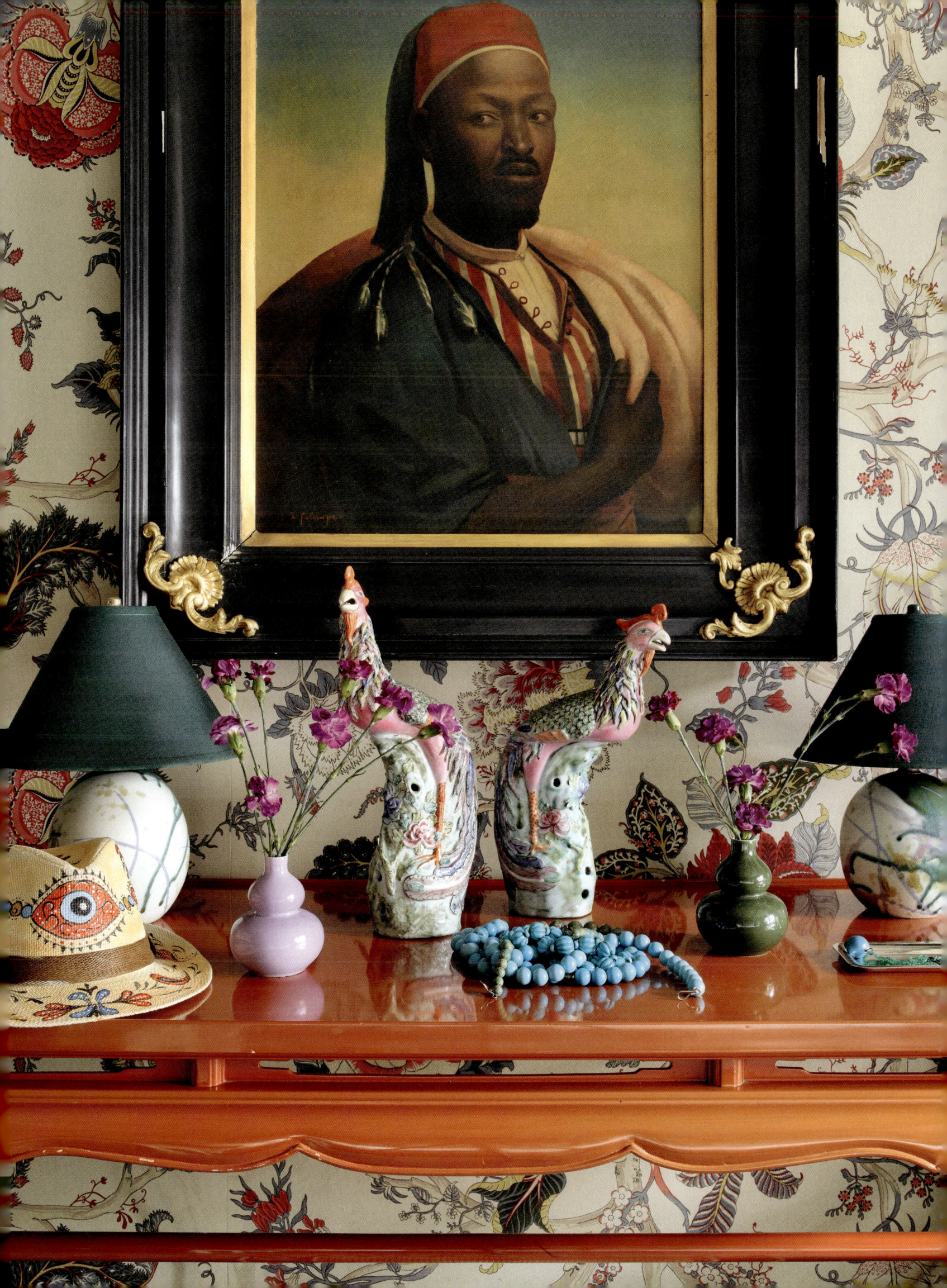

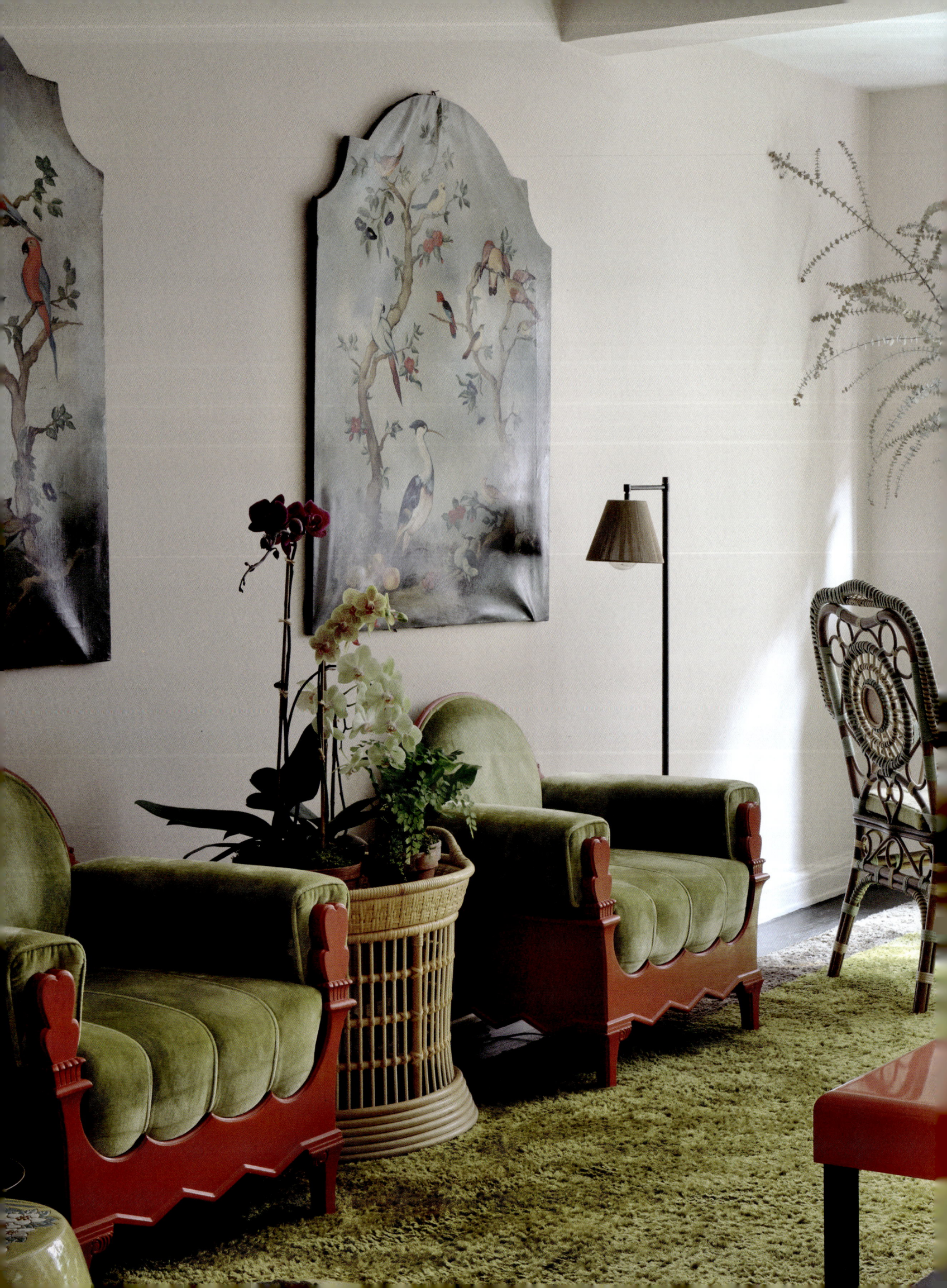

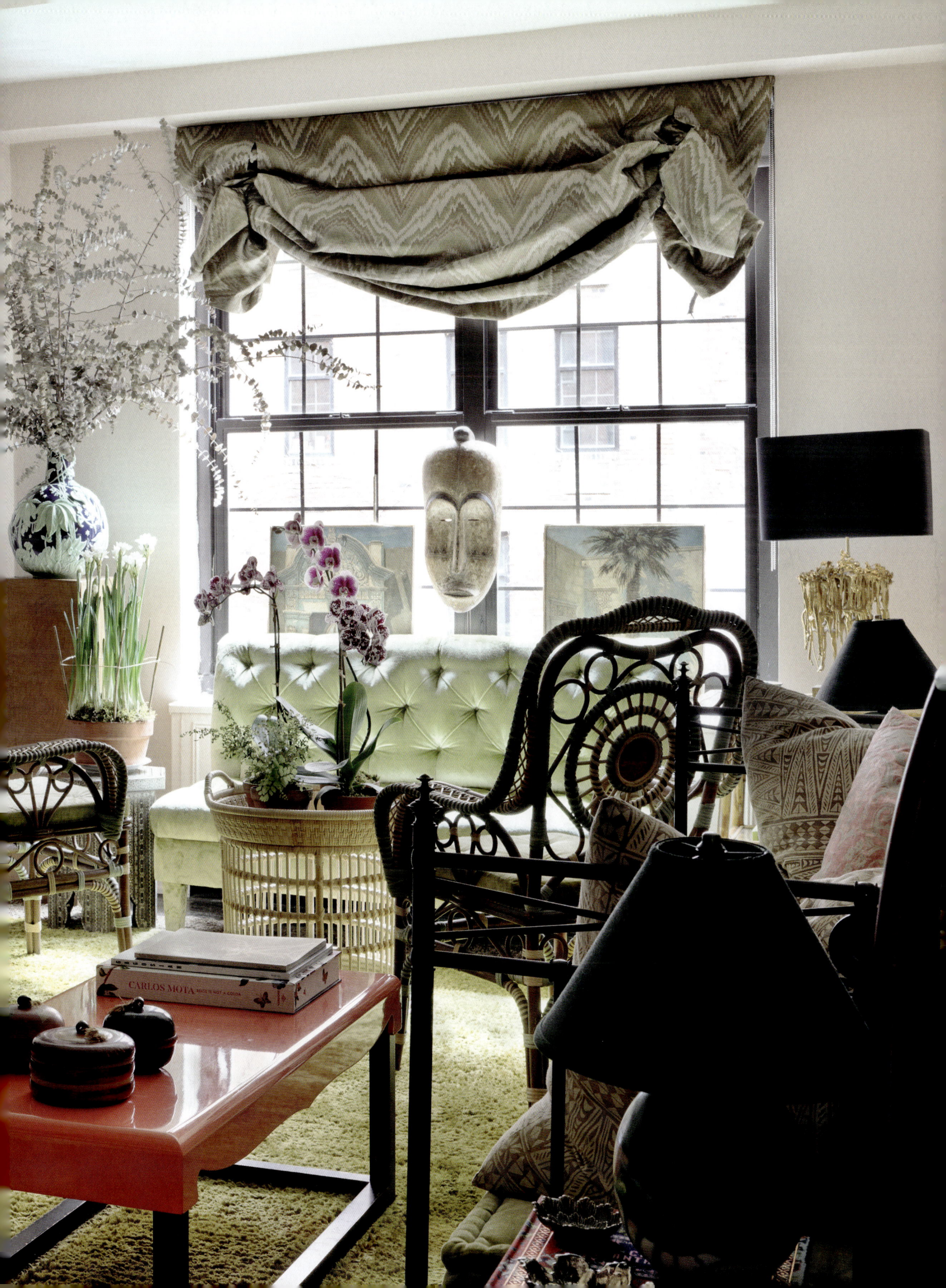

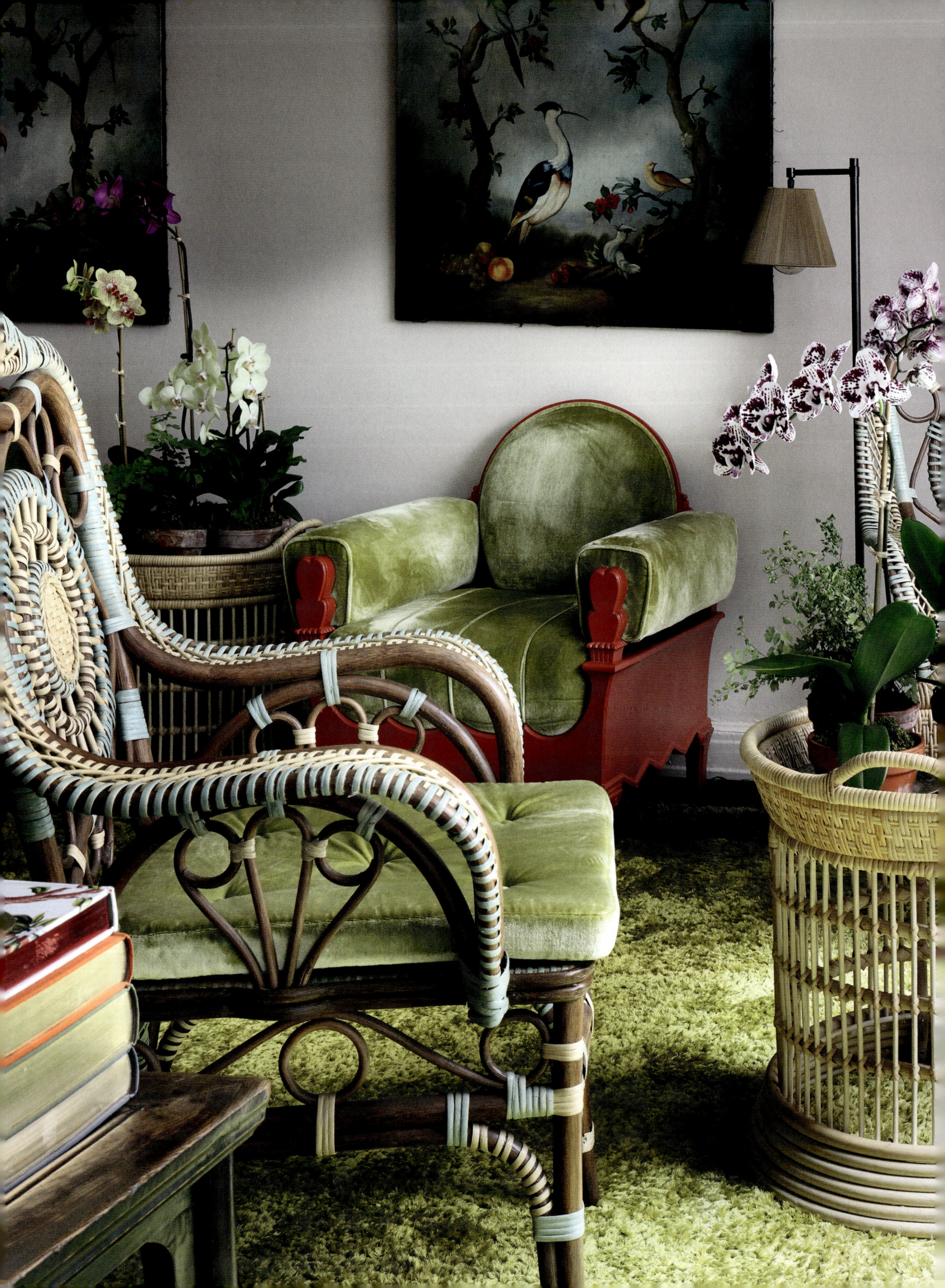

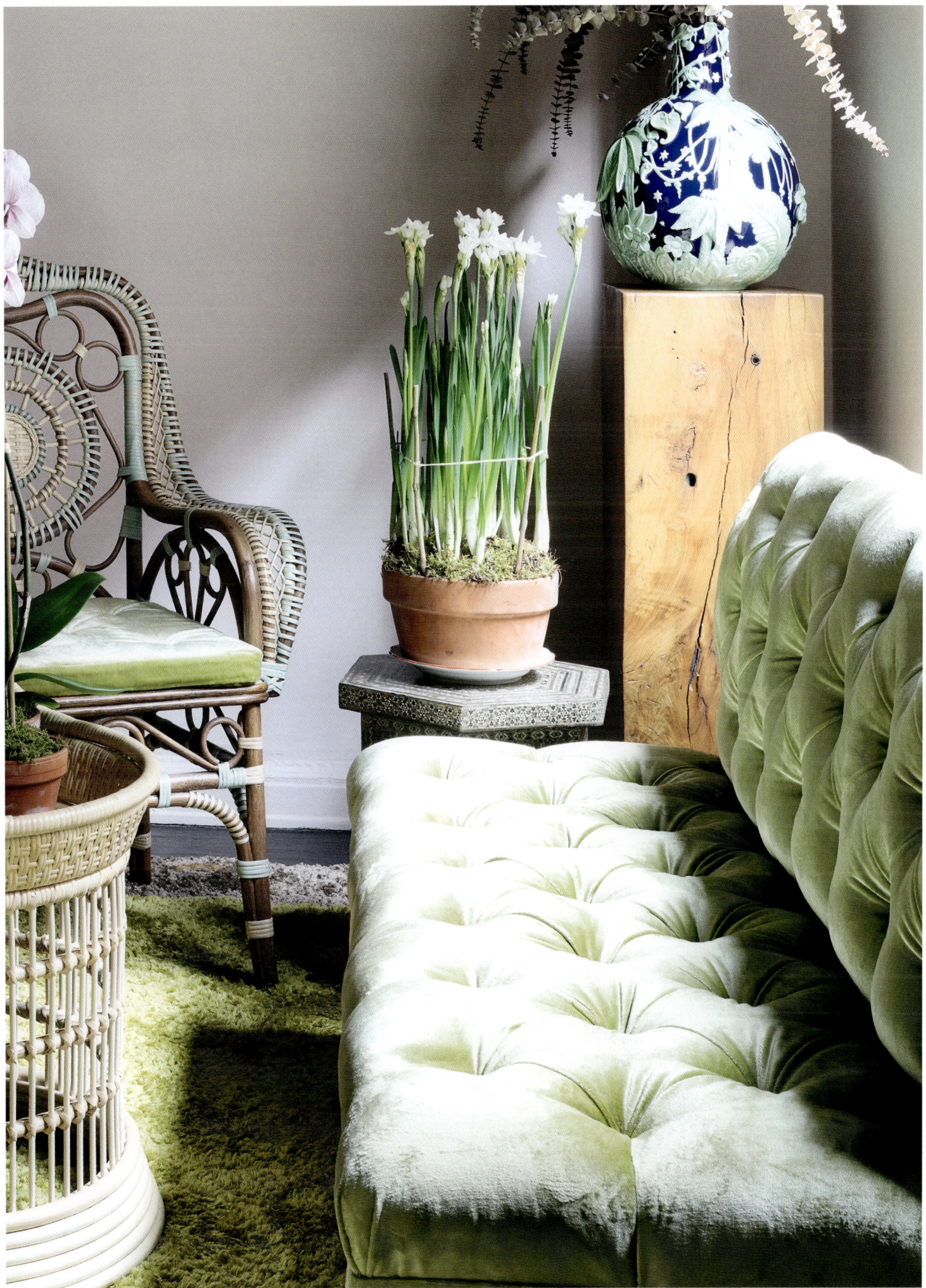

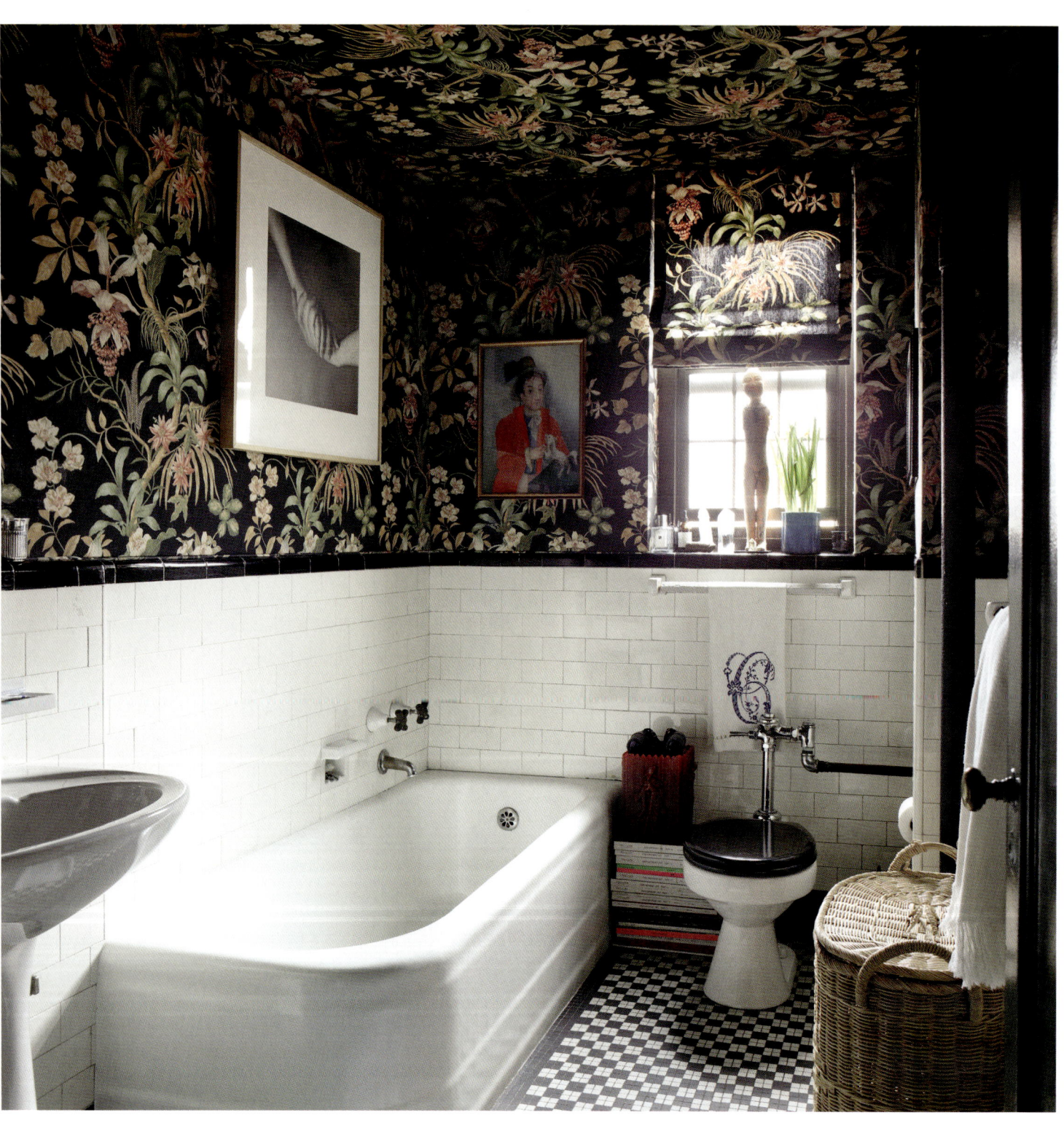

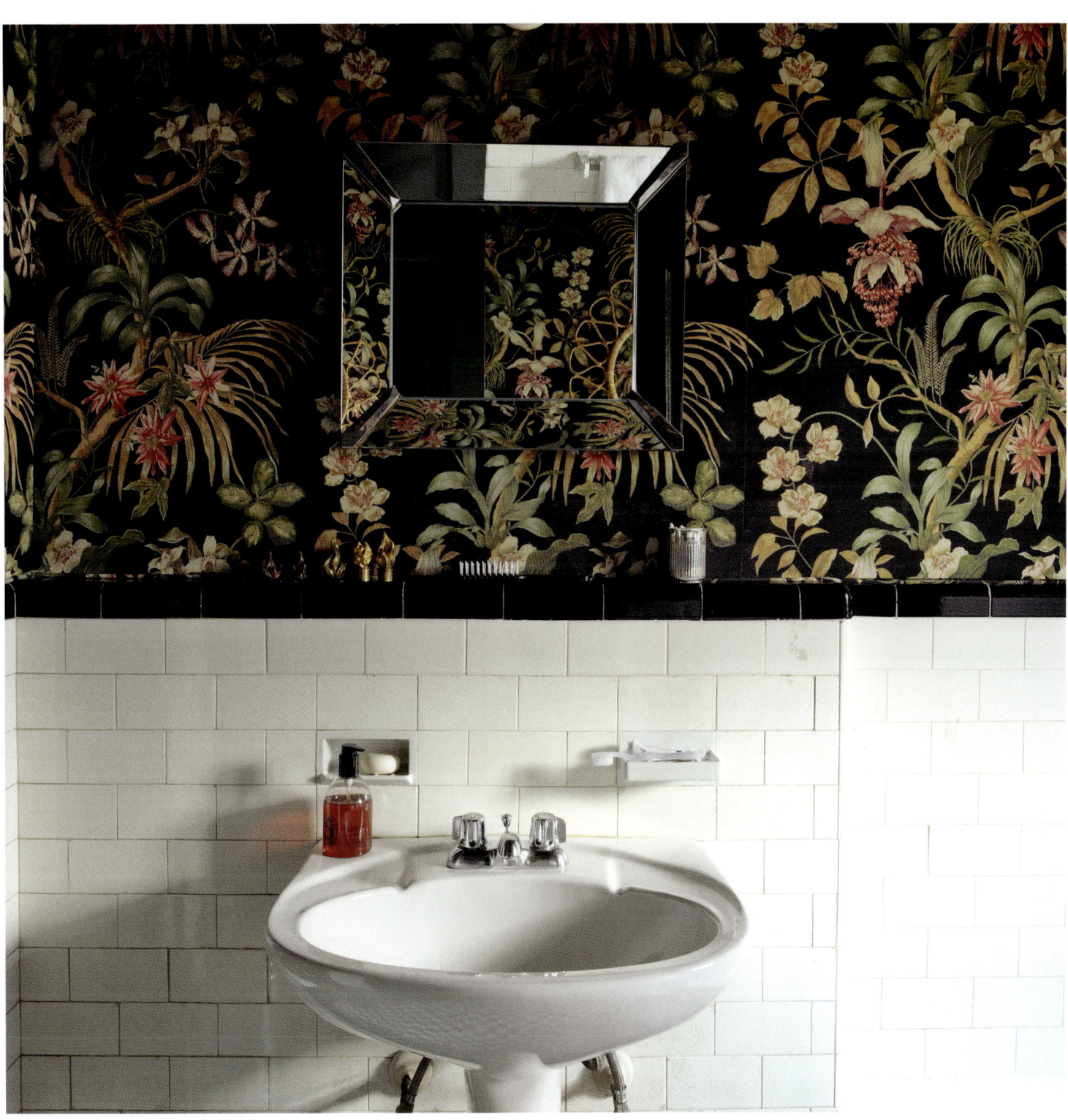

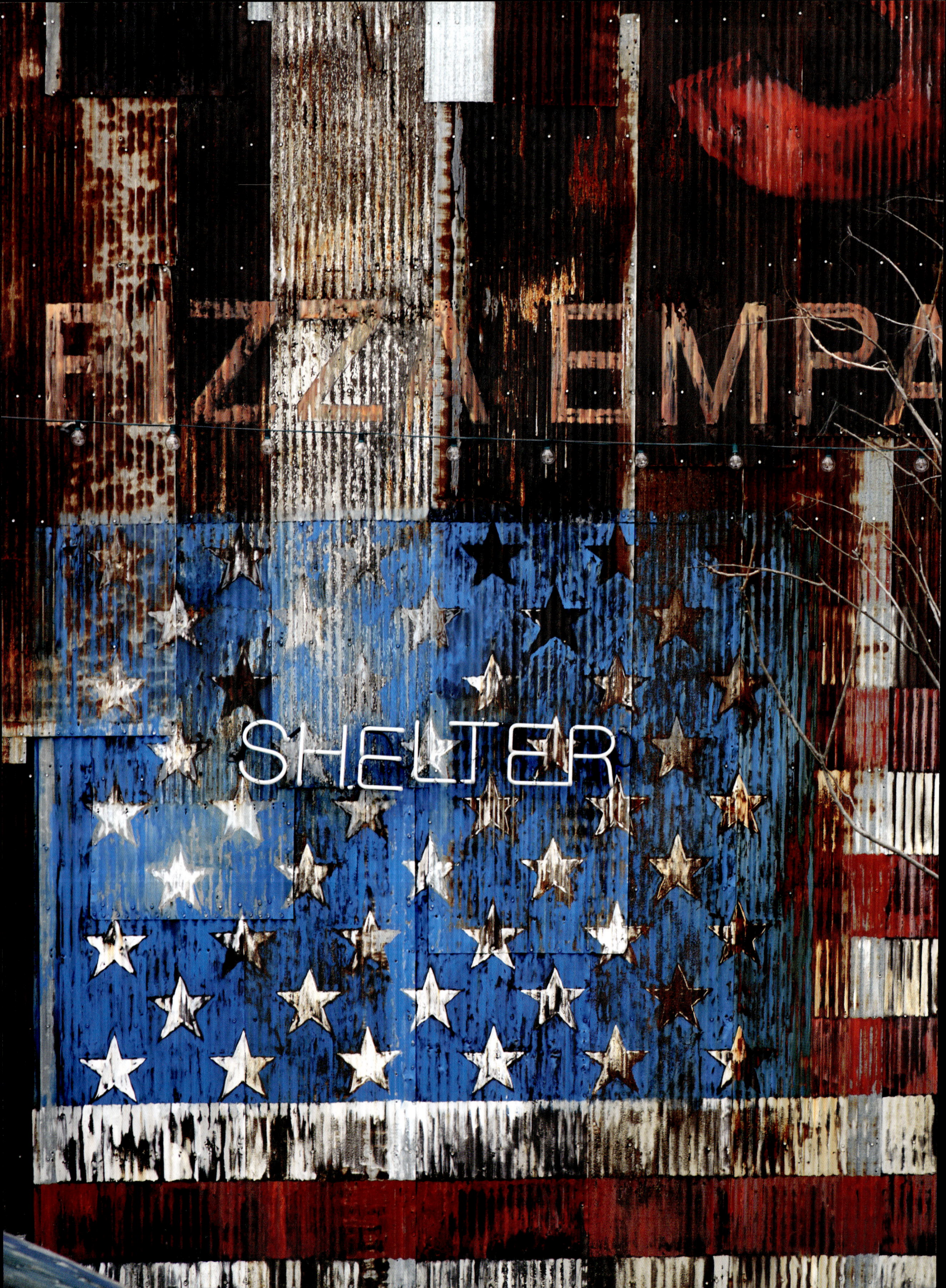

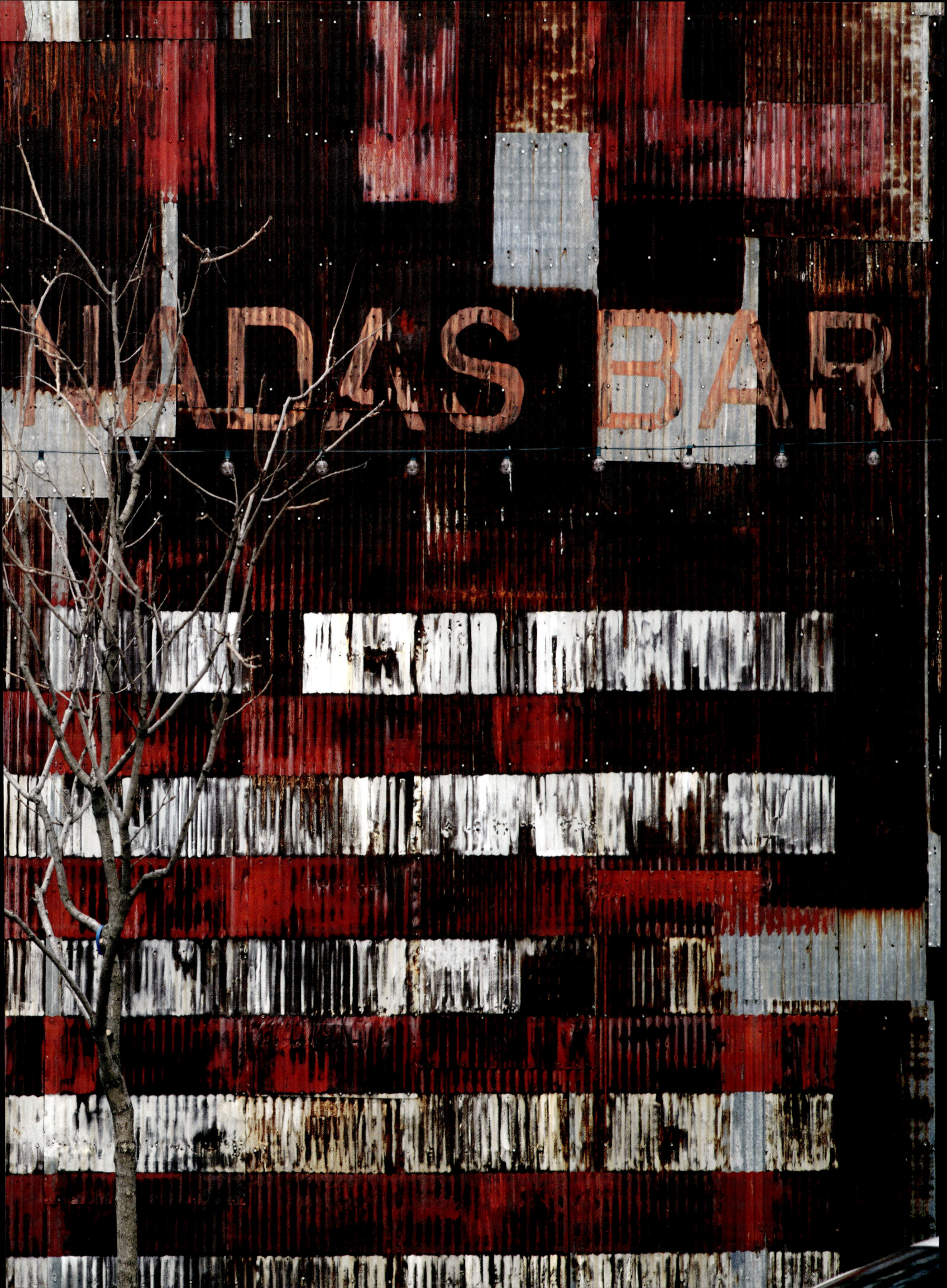

PERFECT PALETTE

NAN SWID

This is an apartment on a massive scale, located in one of the most amazing architectural buildings in New York – the epitome of old-world elegance. Nan Swid, an art collector, as well as an artist in her own right, has lived here for over 30 years. The apartment has been a work in progress for some time and reflects the interpretations of three architect designers in particular: Annabelle Selldorf, Stephen Sills, and, more recently, Kazem Naderi. Sills' legacy is still very much in evidence, in the spectacular entrance hall, with its marble flooring, elegant doors, and chandeliers, as well as a wonderful, rococo plaster, faux-wood console table by Jean-Charles Moreux, which he sourced originally for the hall and which now graces the living room.

Naderi has spent the last 10 years collaborating with Nan on her apartment, his main objective to address the proportions of this outstanding space and reinterpret it on a human scale, making the individual rooms both warm and inviting. This is less about redecorating and much more about creating a new backdrop for an important collection of artworks amassed over a period of 50 years.

I first visited the apartment in April 2017 and, prompted both by intrigue to discover how Naderi and Nan would work their collective magic and respect for their sensitive and gradual approach to the project, I returned two years later, twice more, each visit six months apart, in order to capture the subtle nuances of color and texture that were being introduced, as well as the editing and selection of each object and every piece of furniture that, ultimately, would transform the atmosphere of the apartment into a home for Nan, and less of a gallery.

It has been a rare privilege to revisit this apartment over an extended period of time and to update the visual record I began. The apartment's beauty, tranquility, and personality could not be rushed. Its soul has been revealed by Naderi and Nan in the steady evolution of its development. **SIMON UPTON**

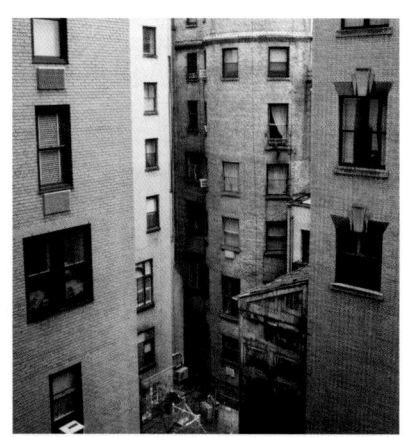

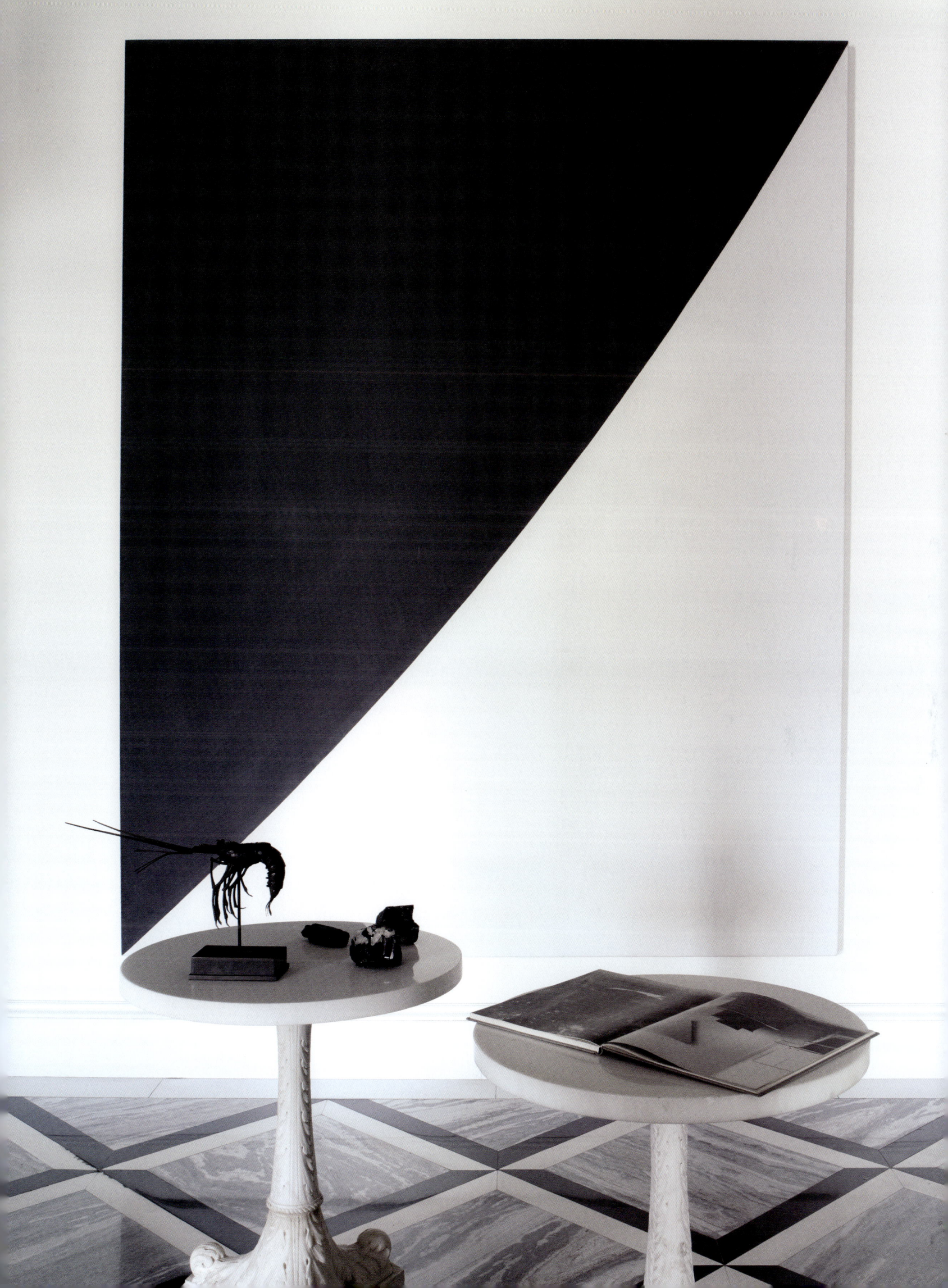

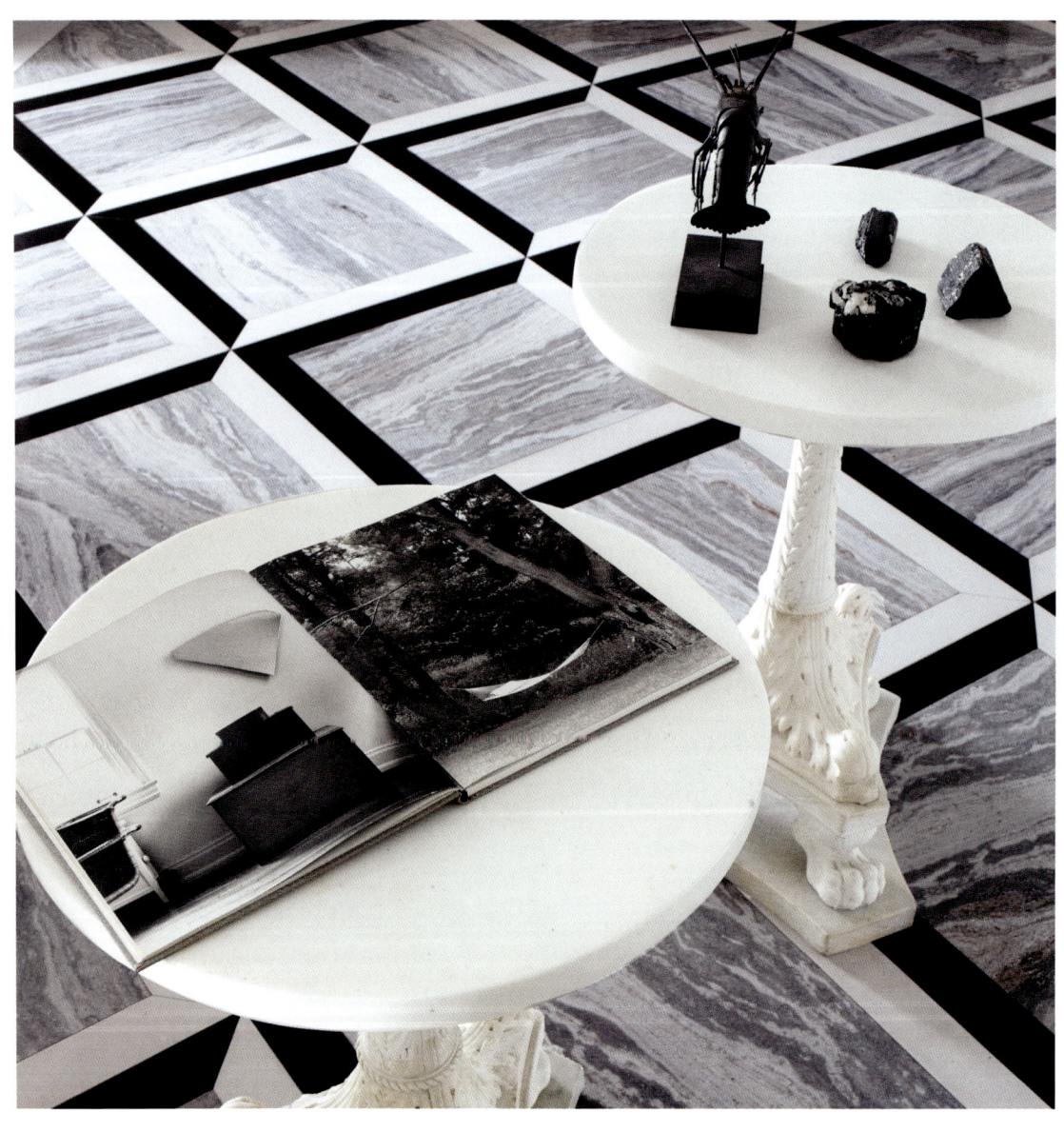

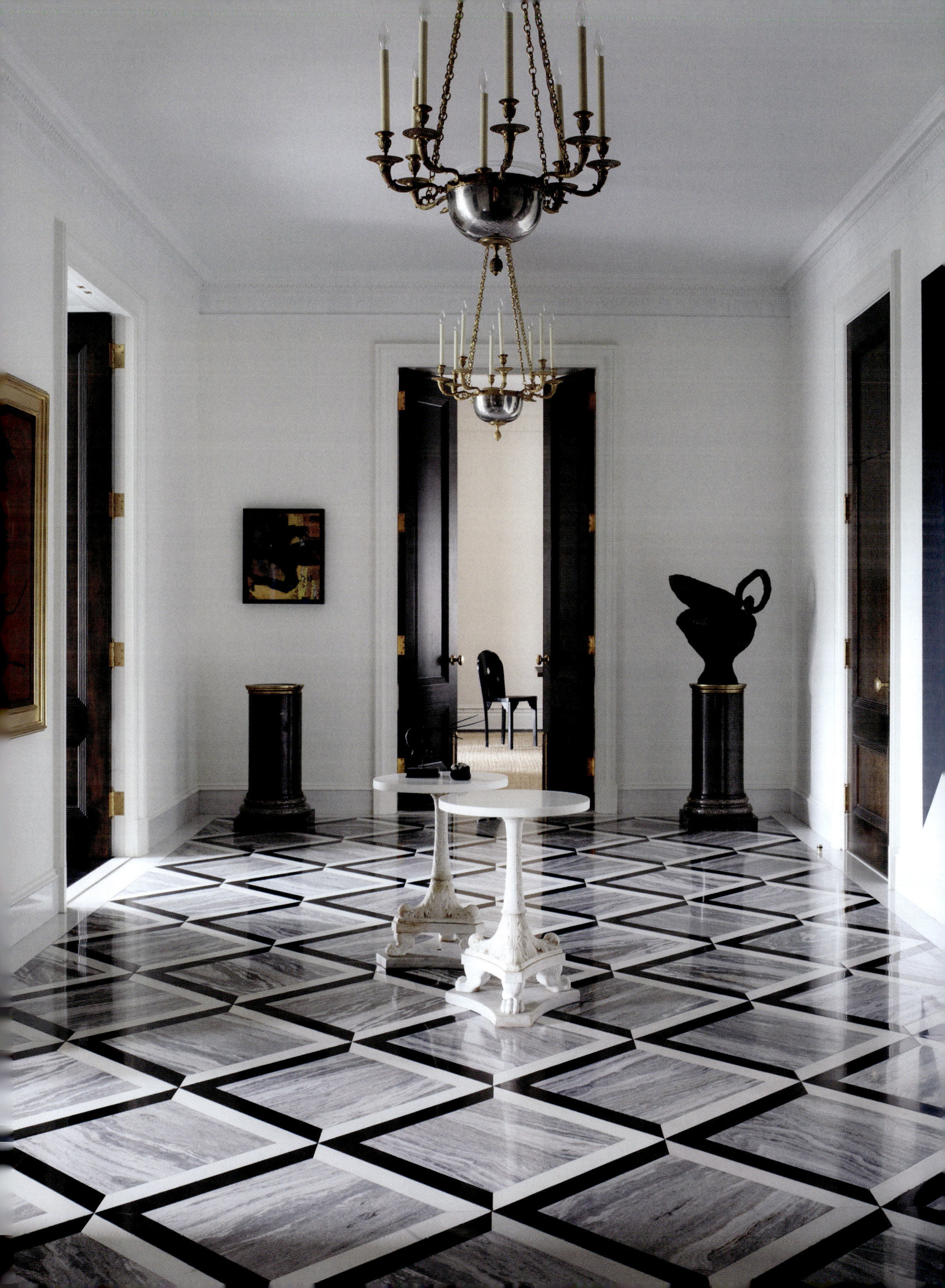

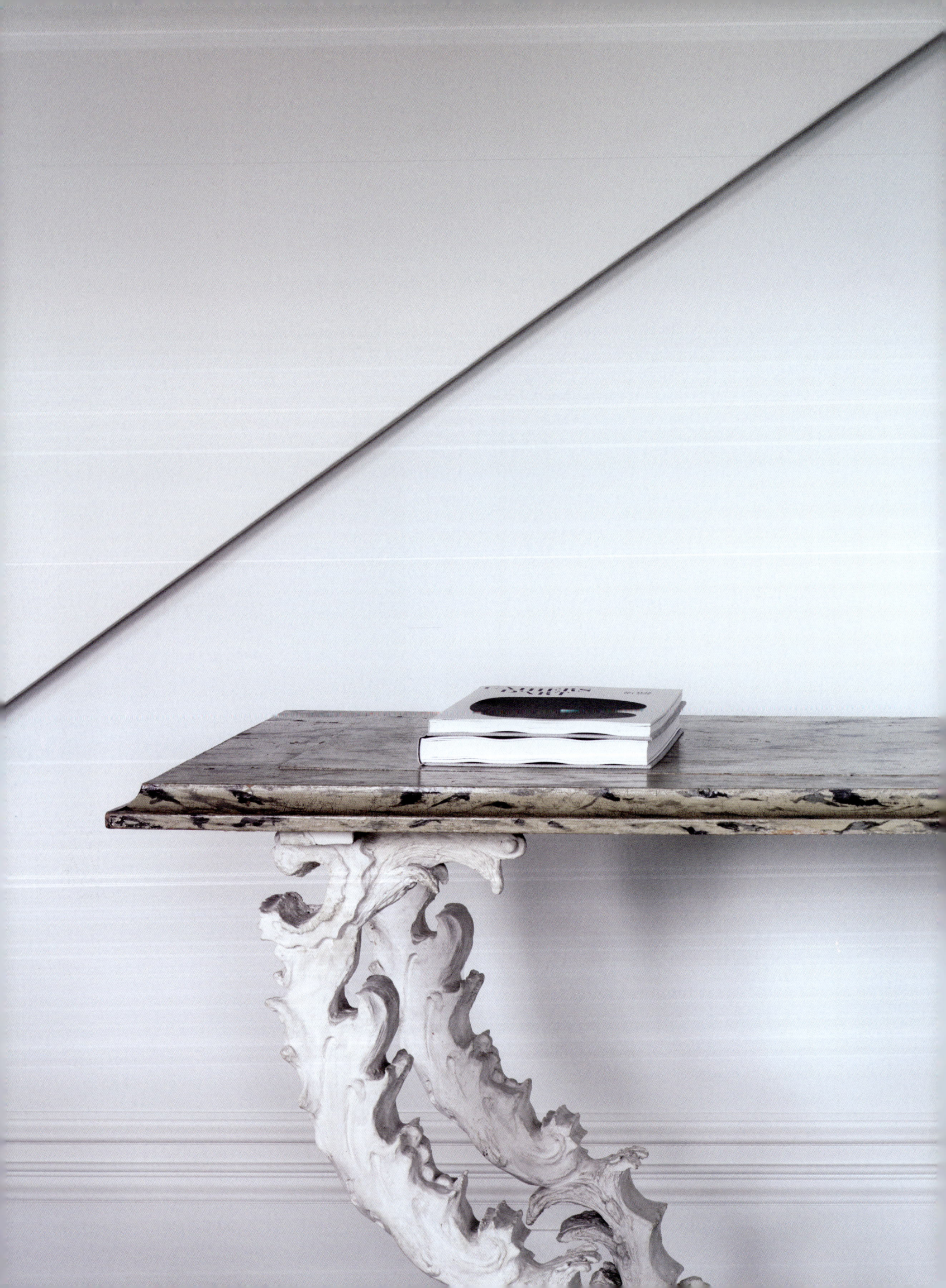

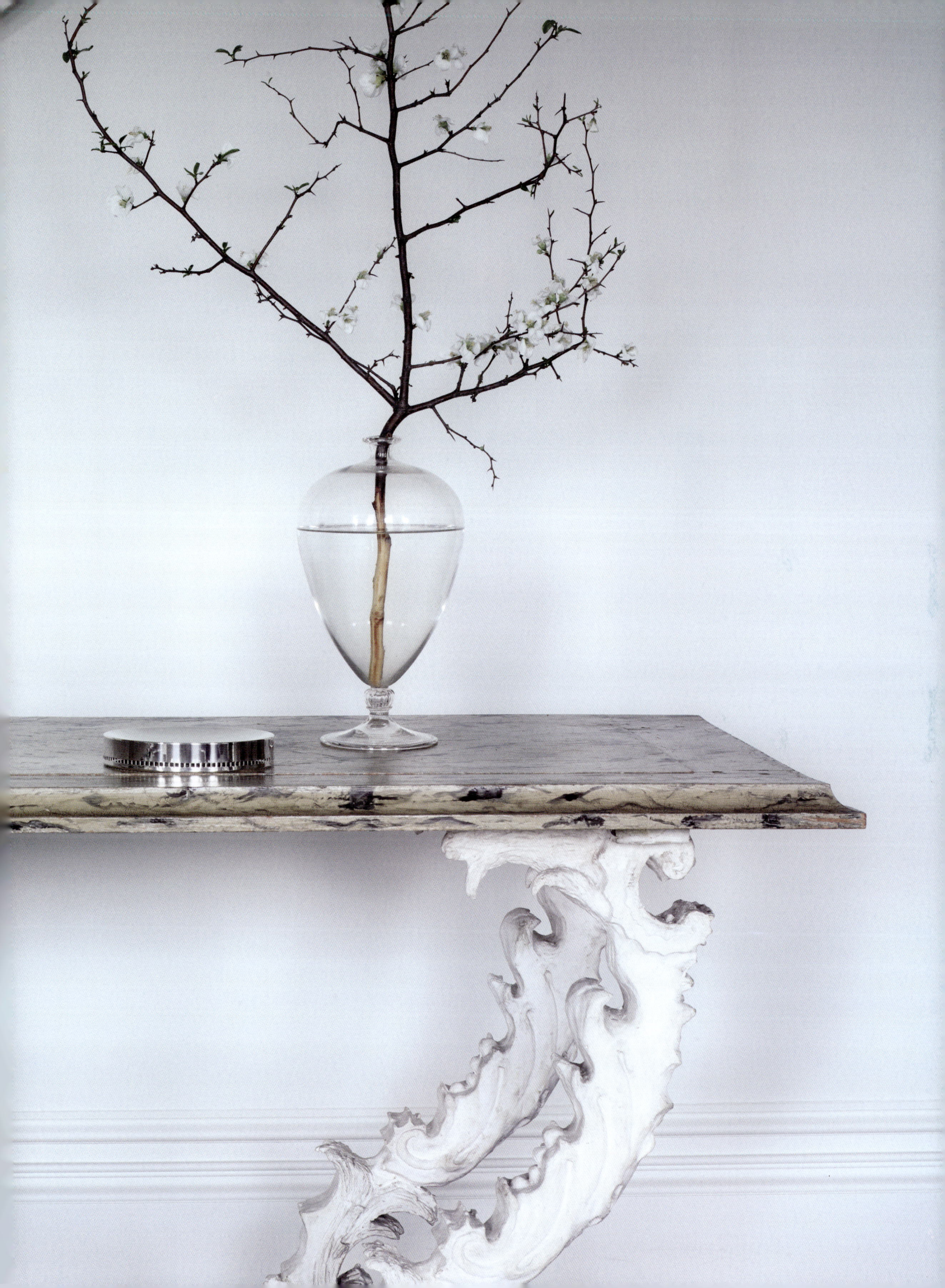

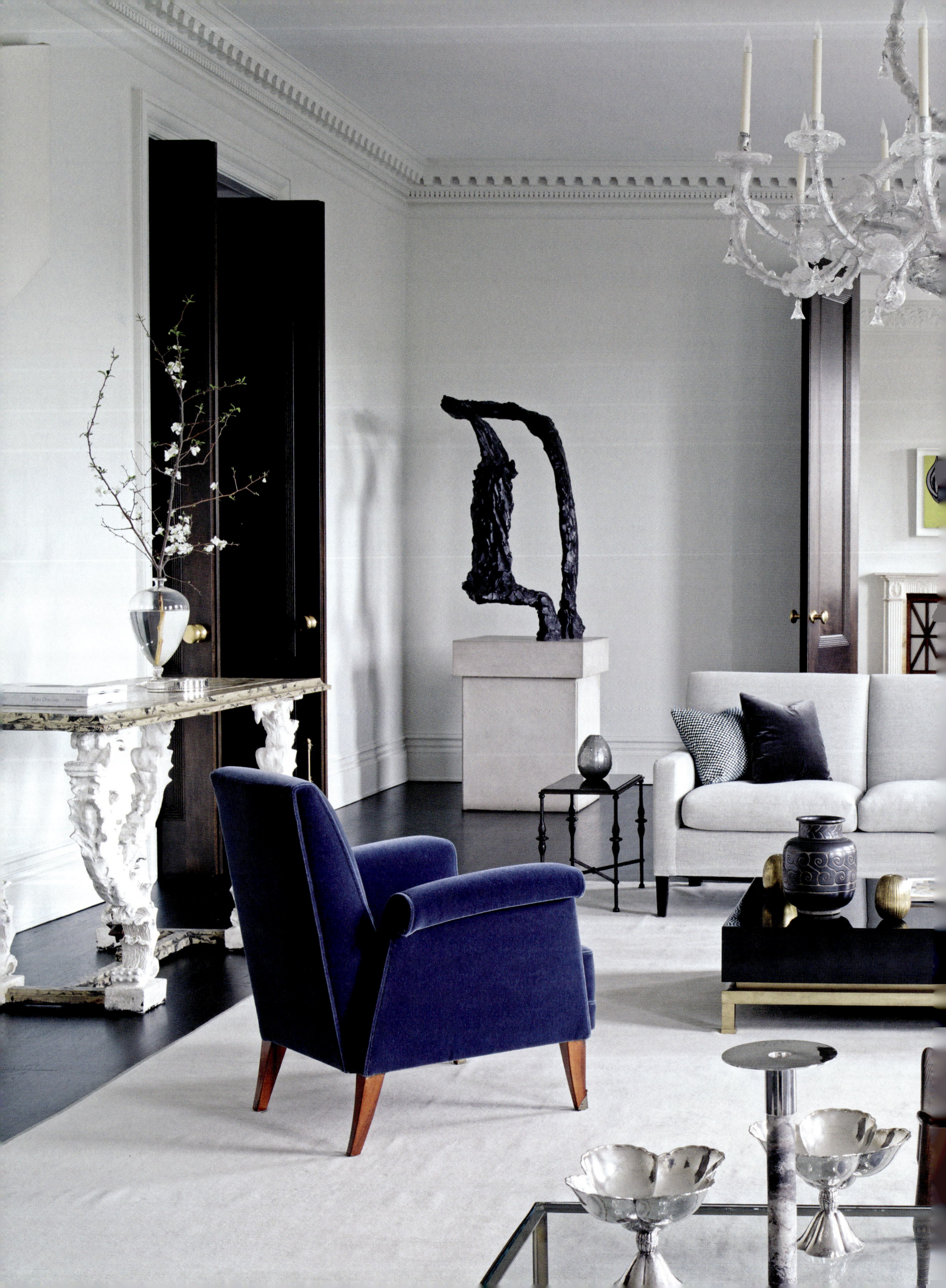

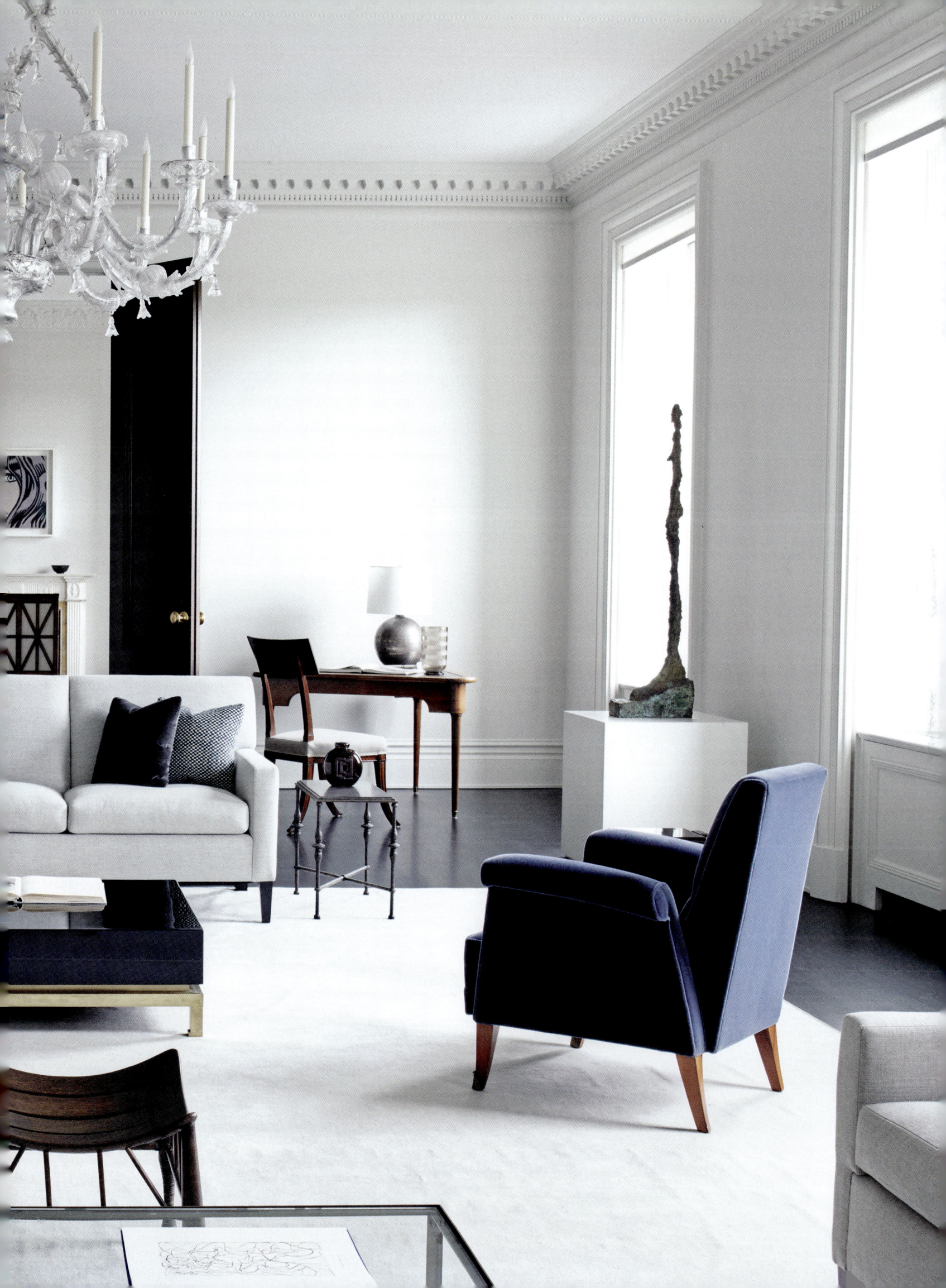

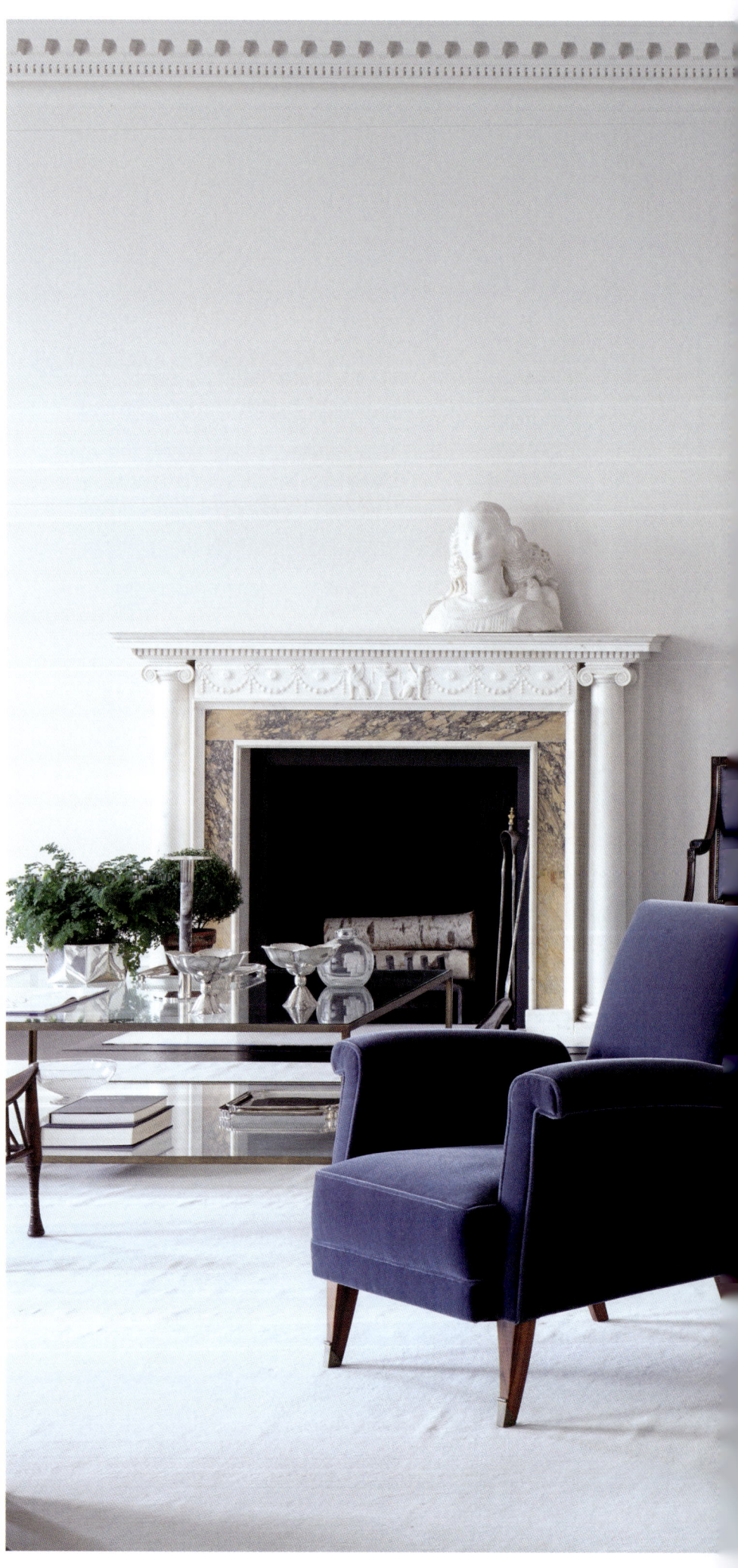

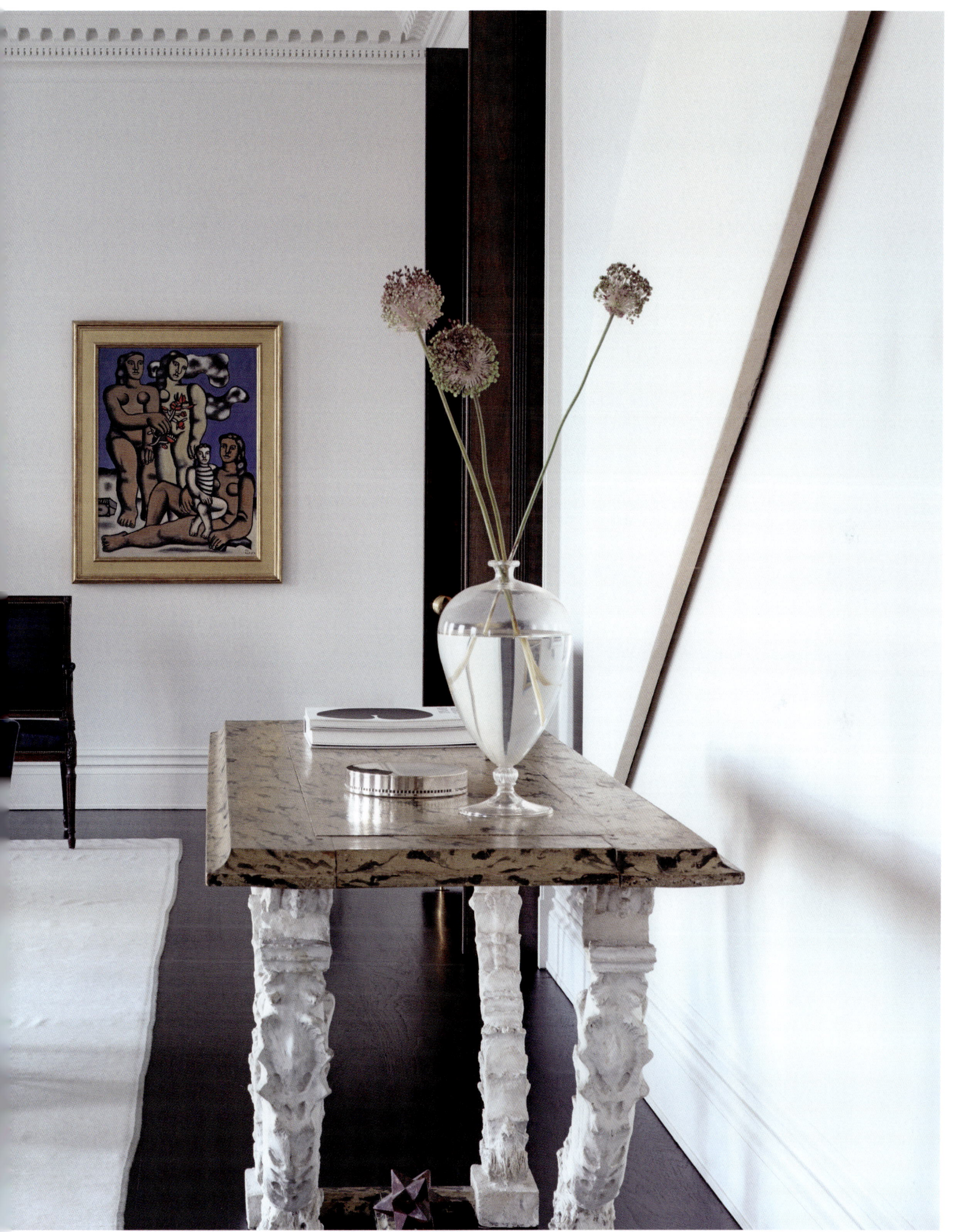

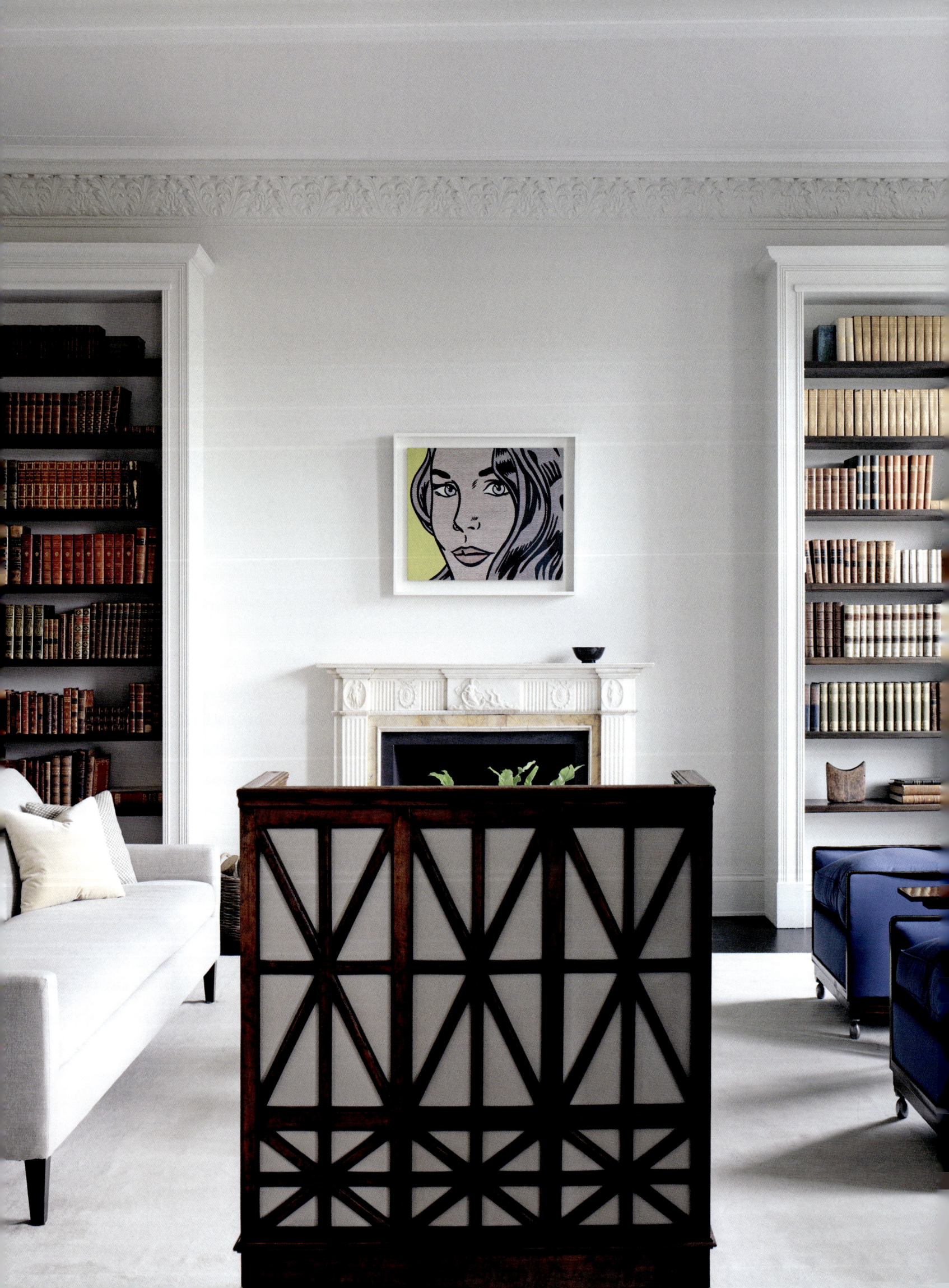

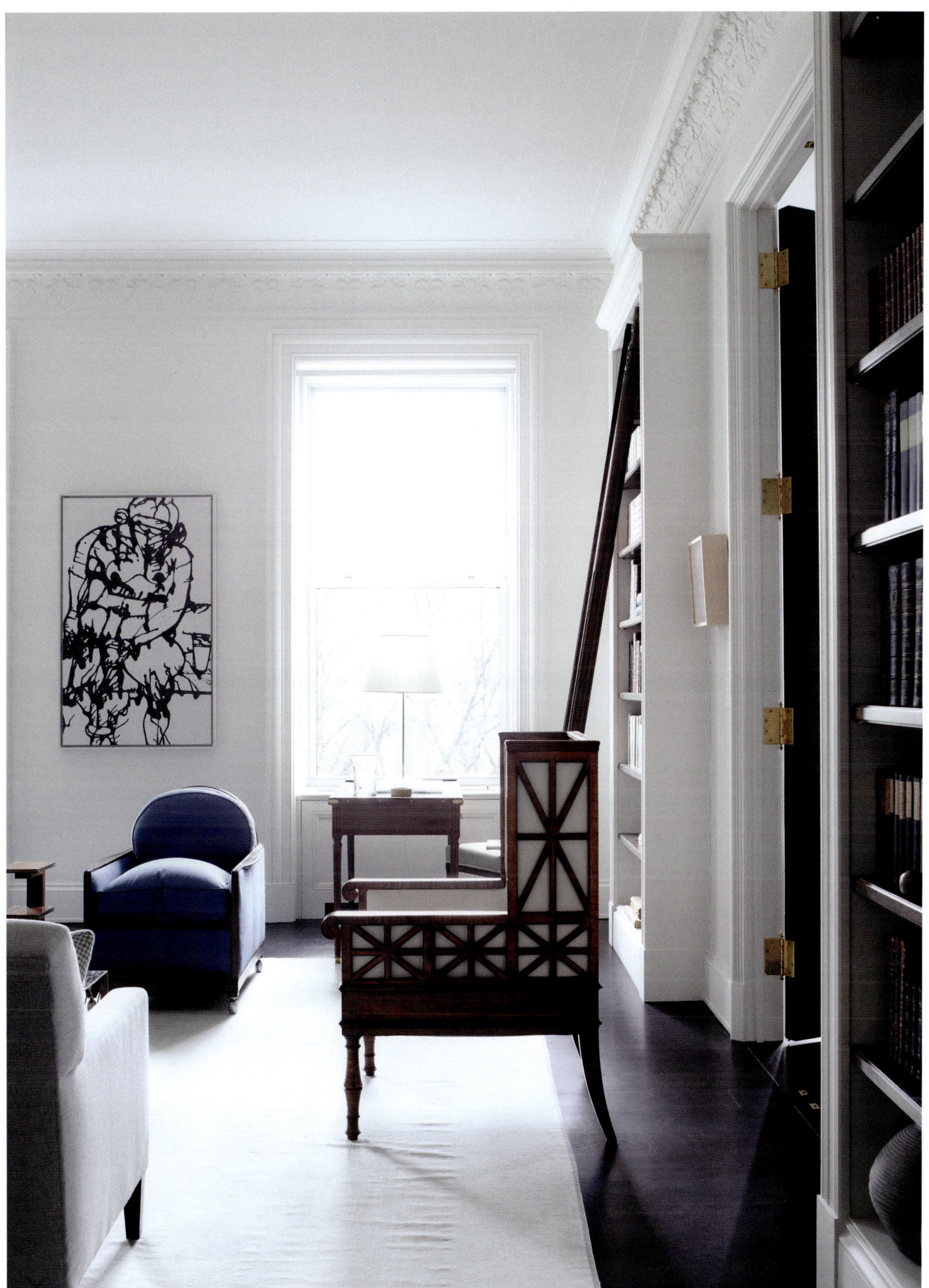

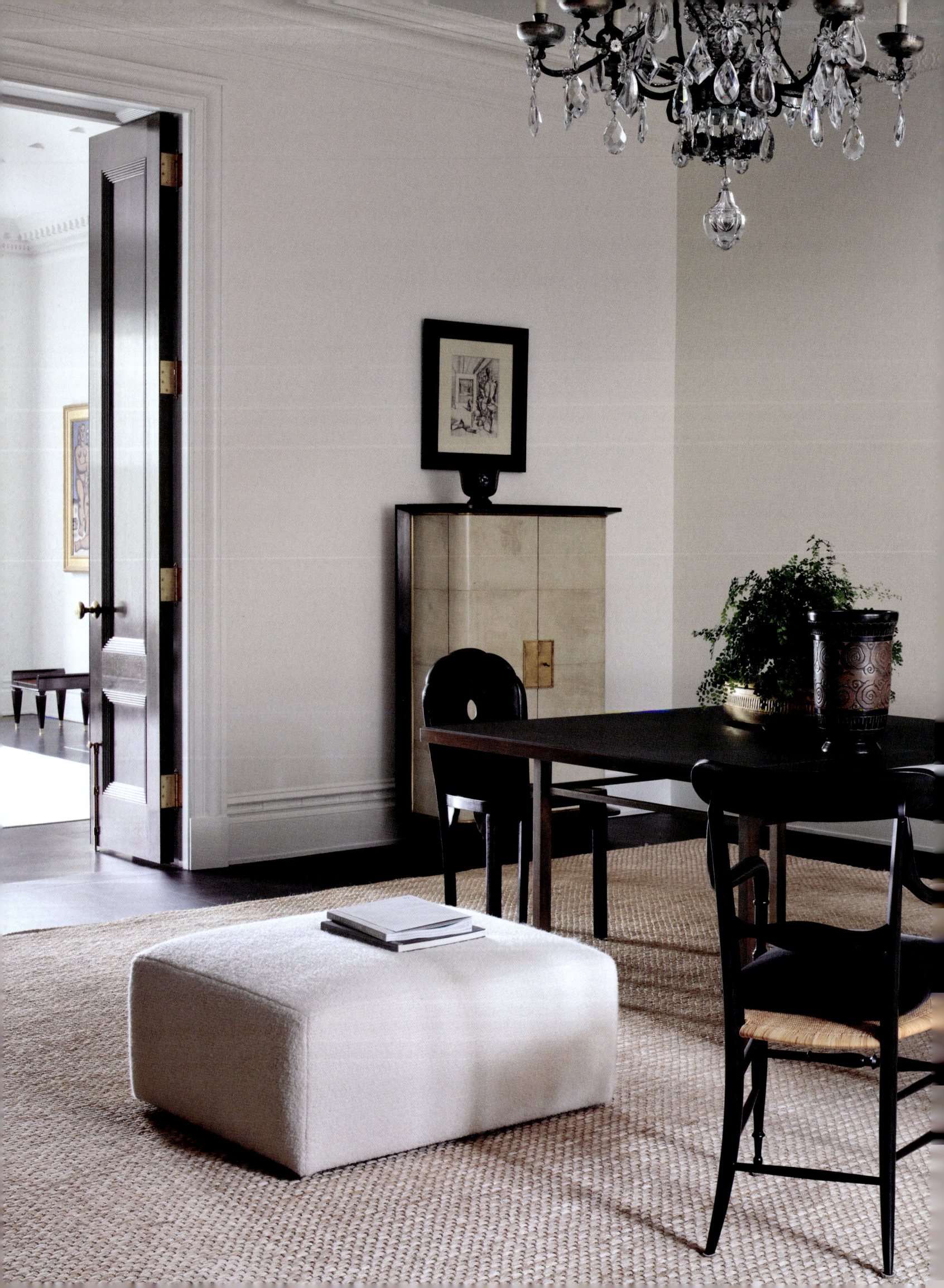

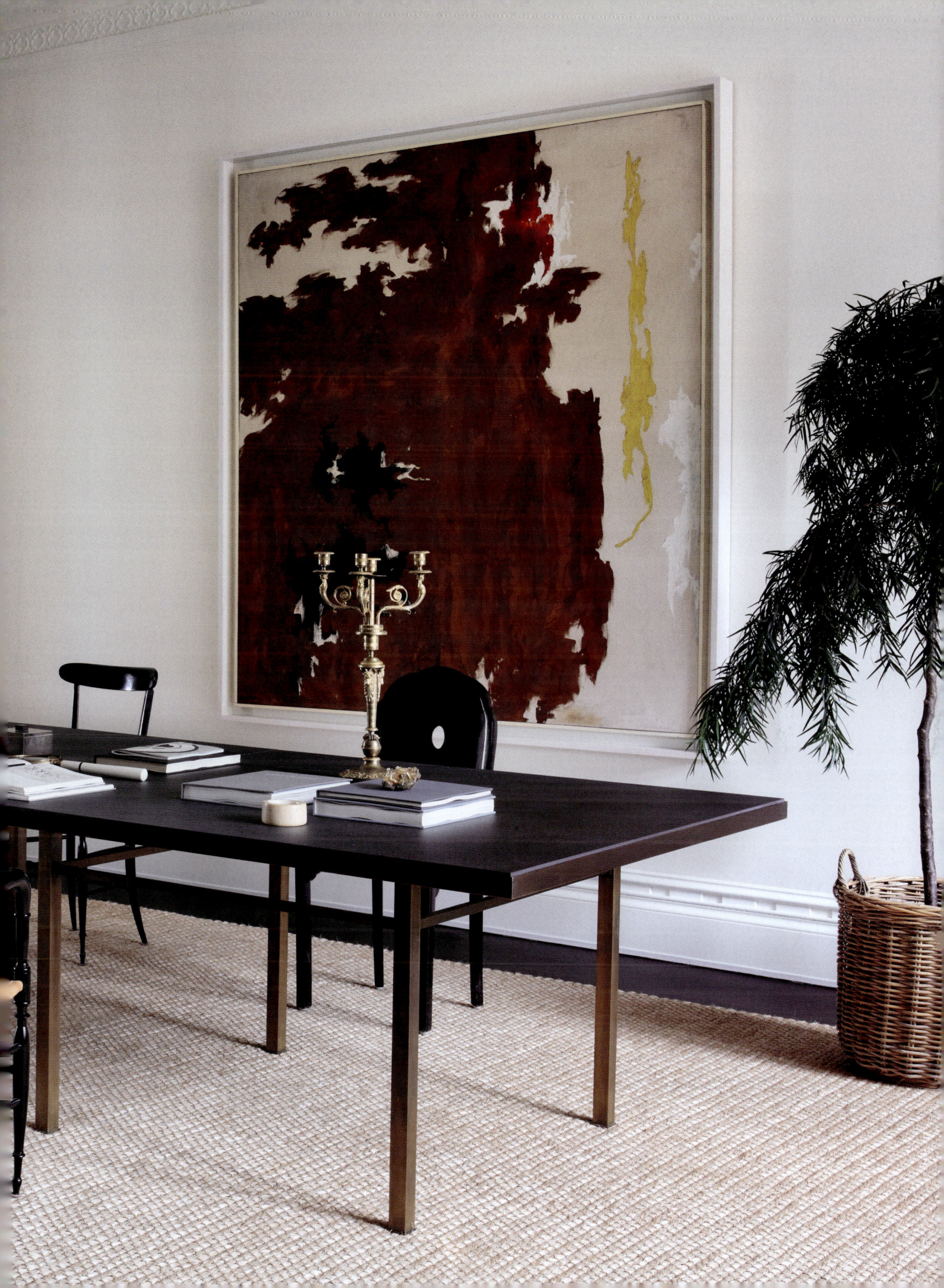

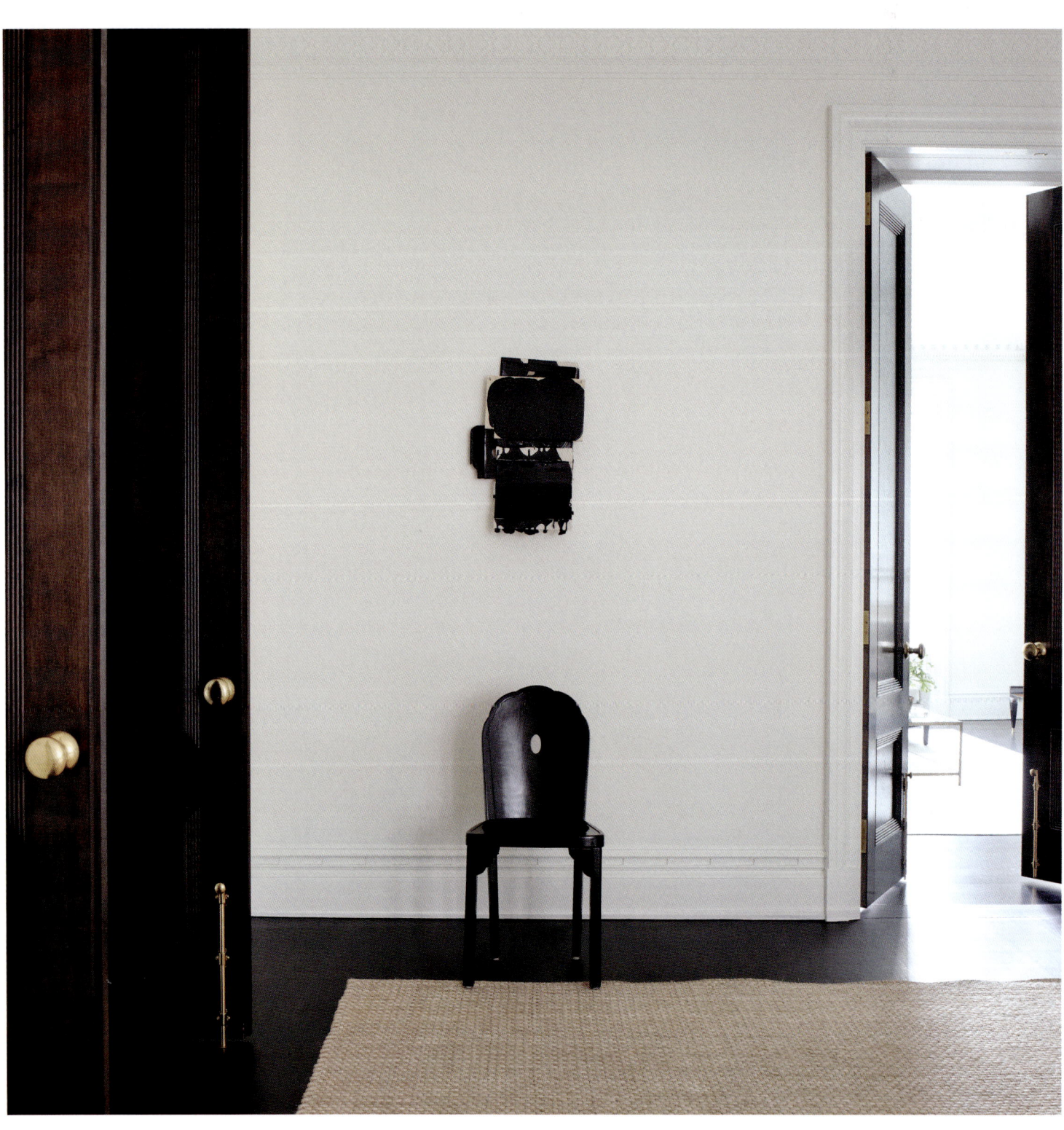

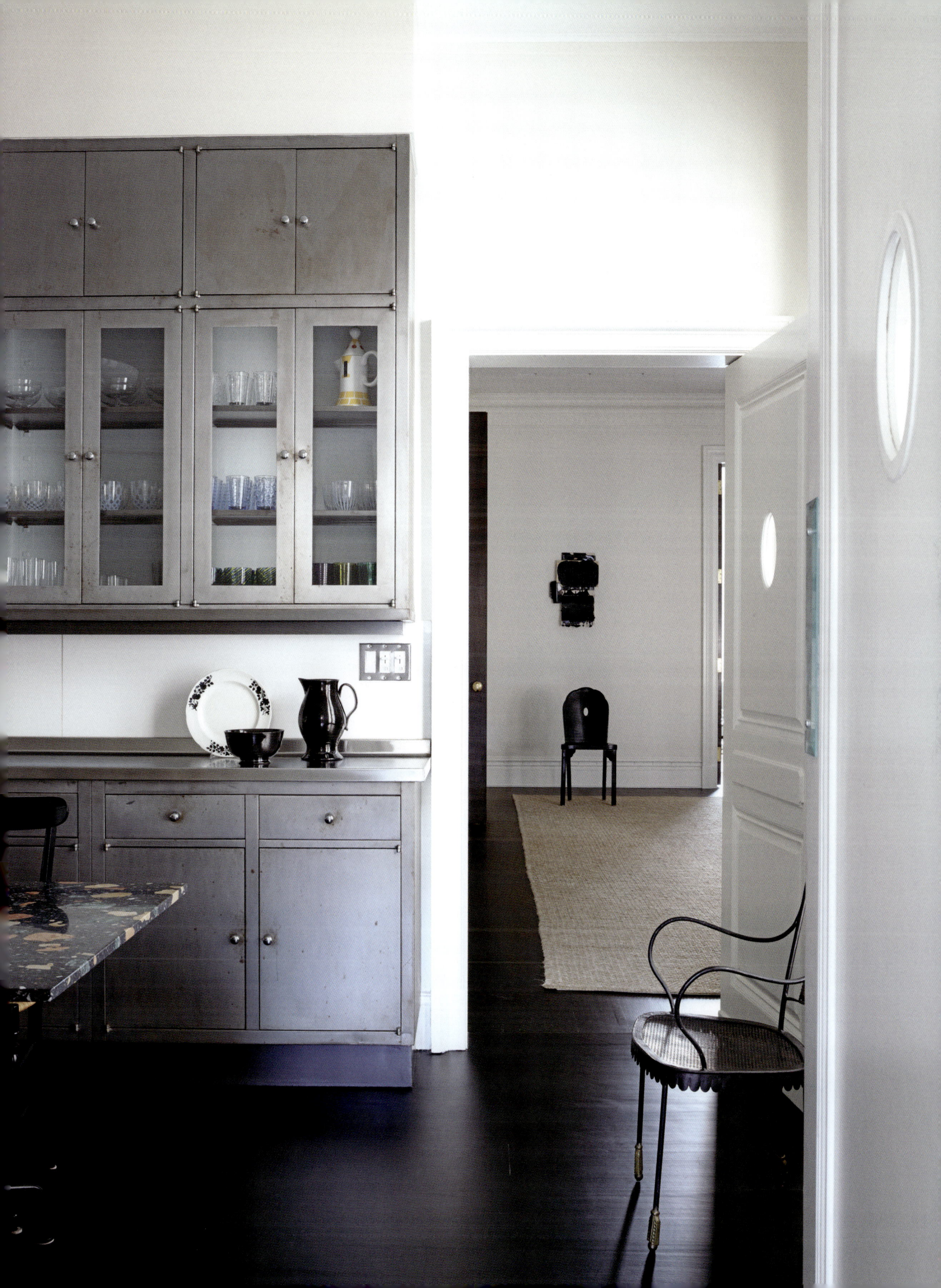

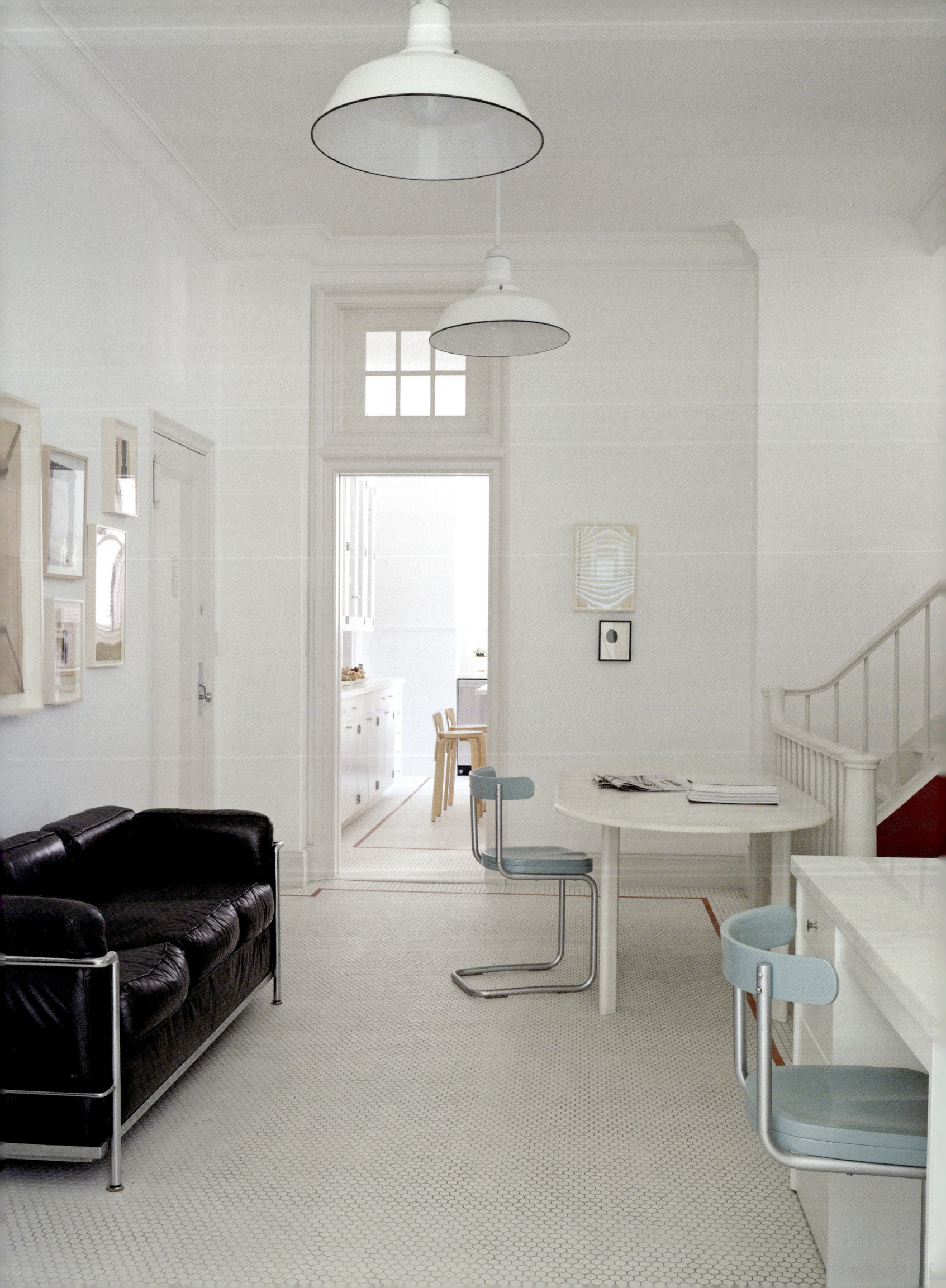

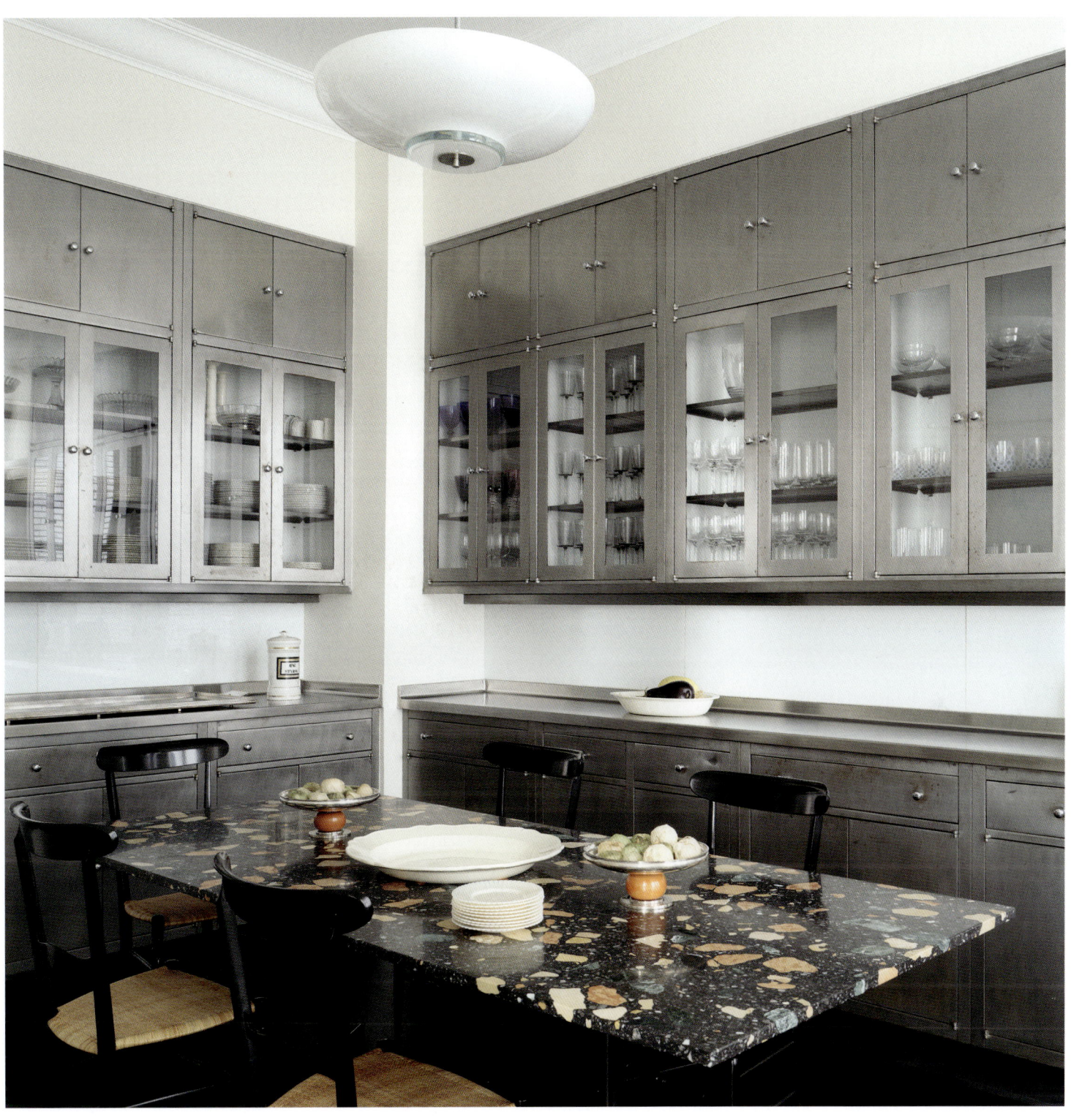

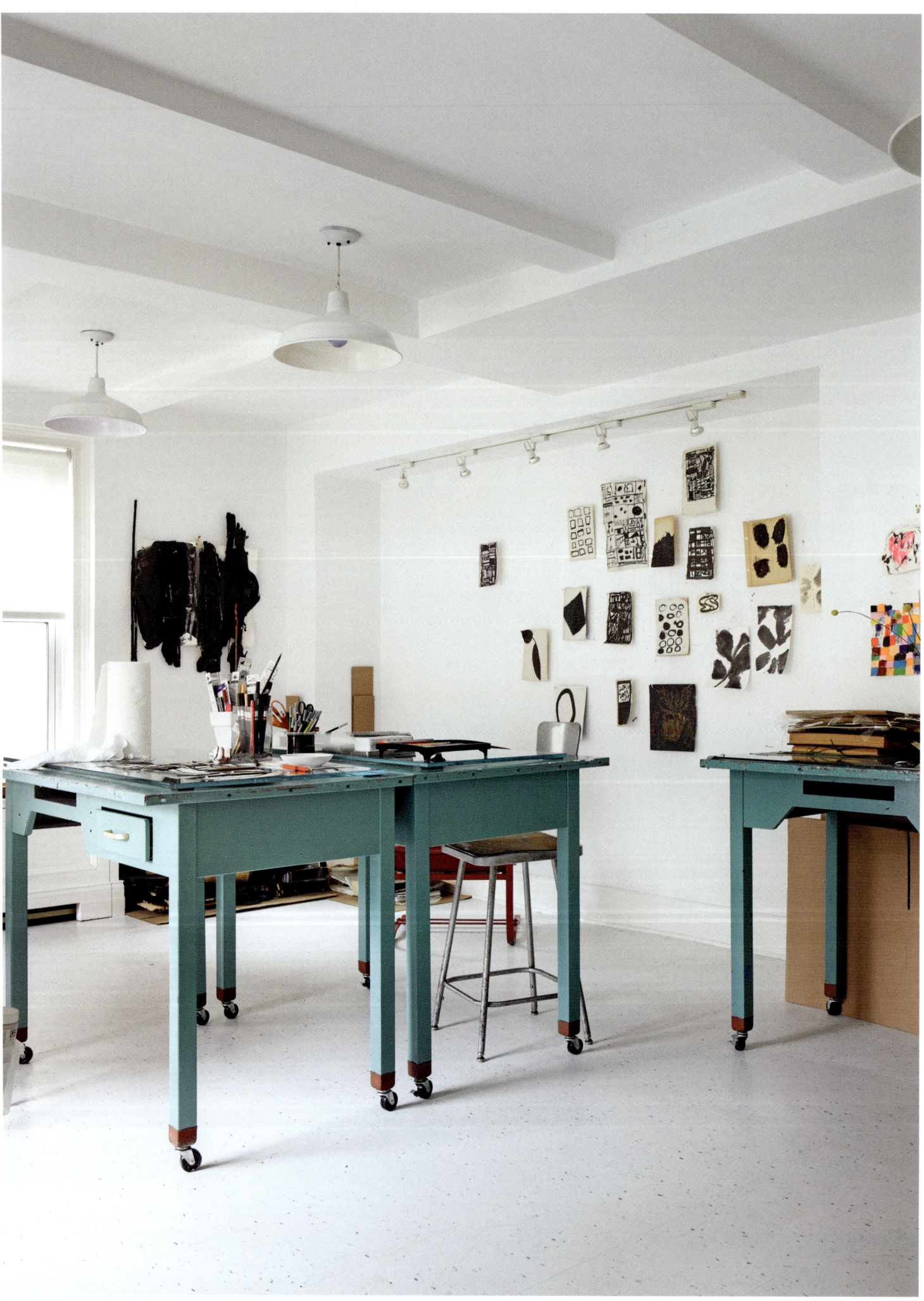

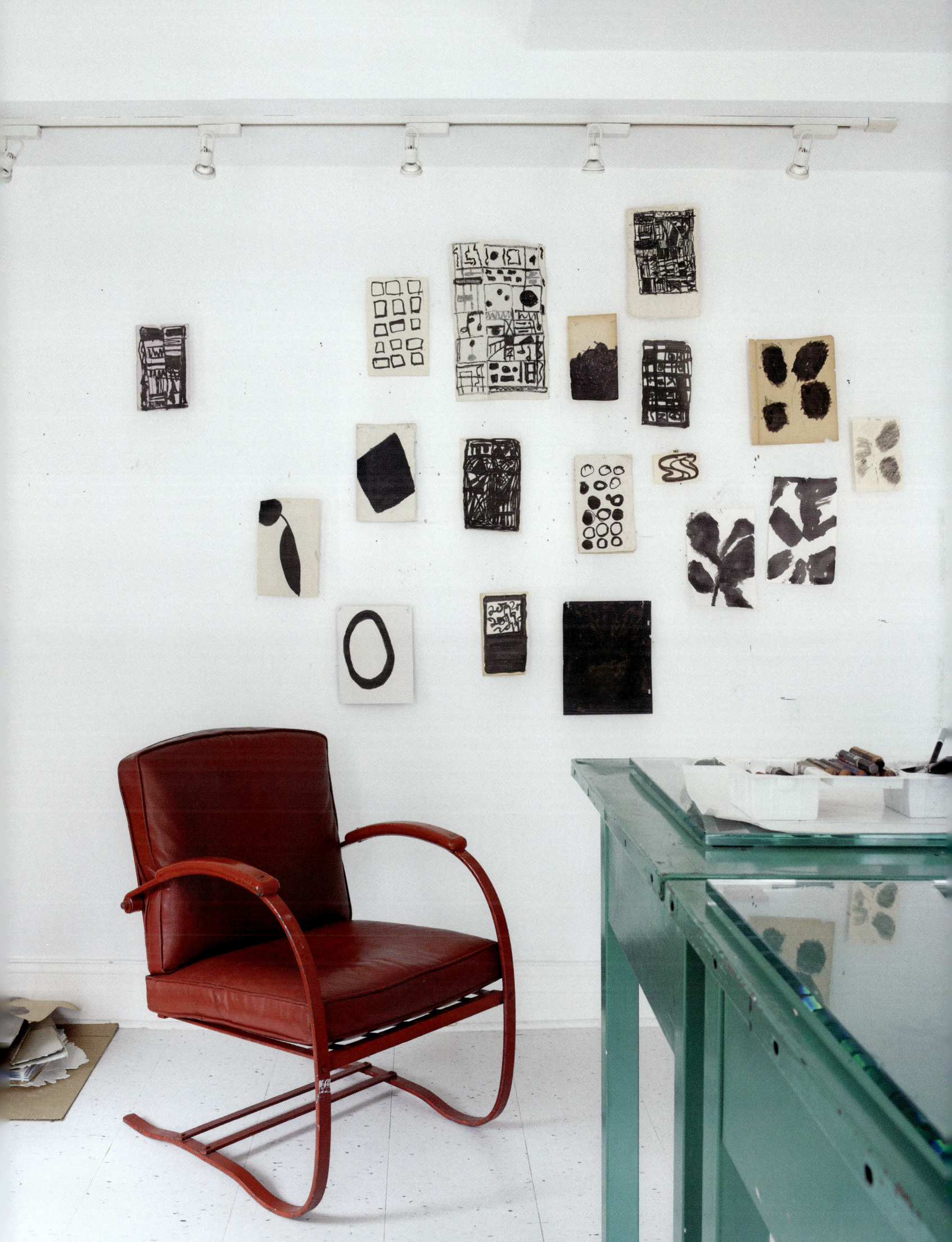

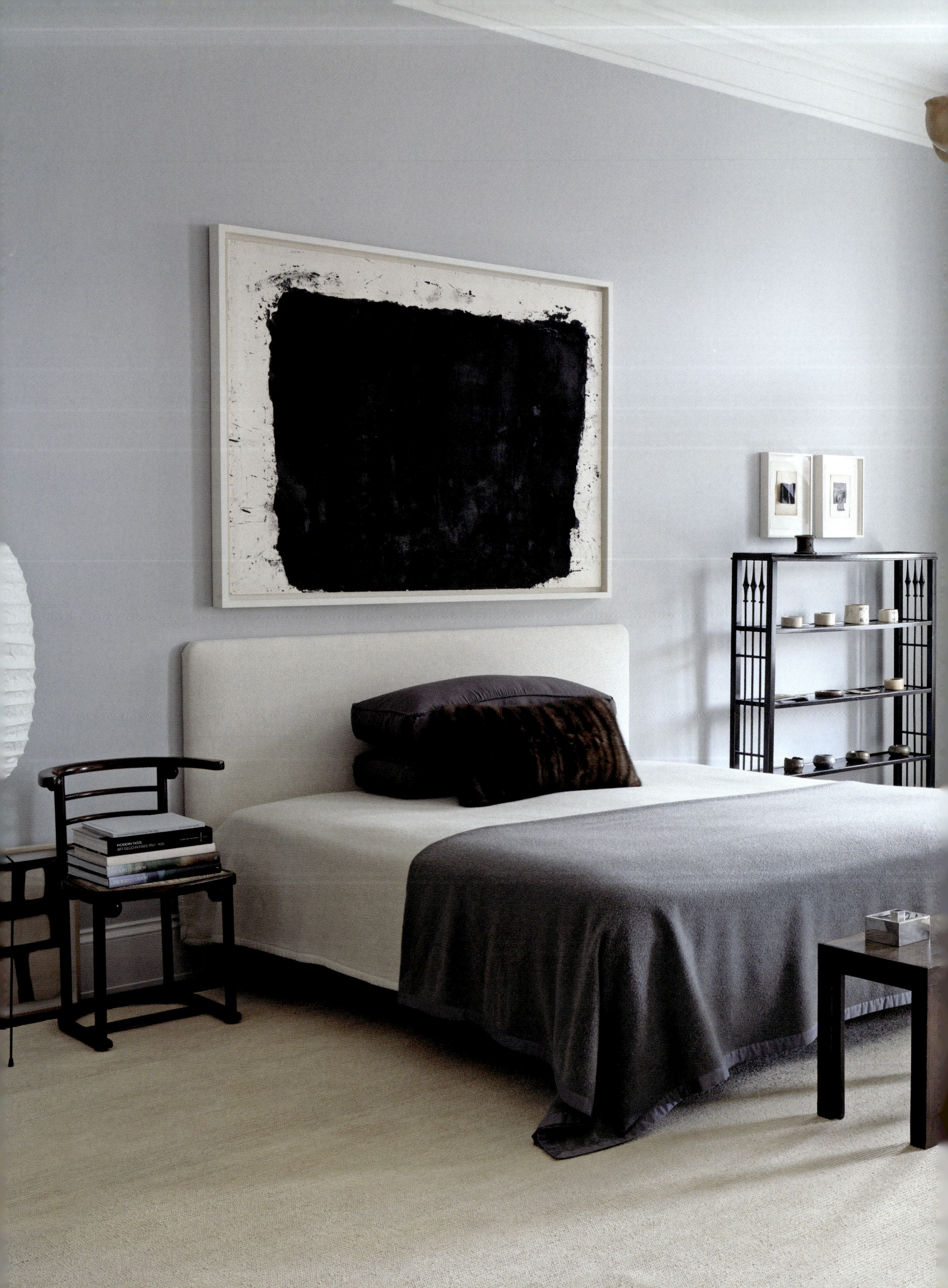

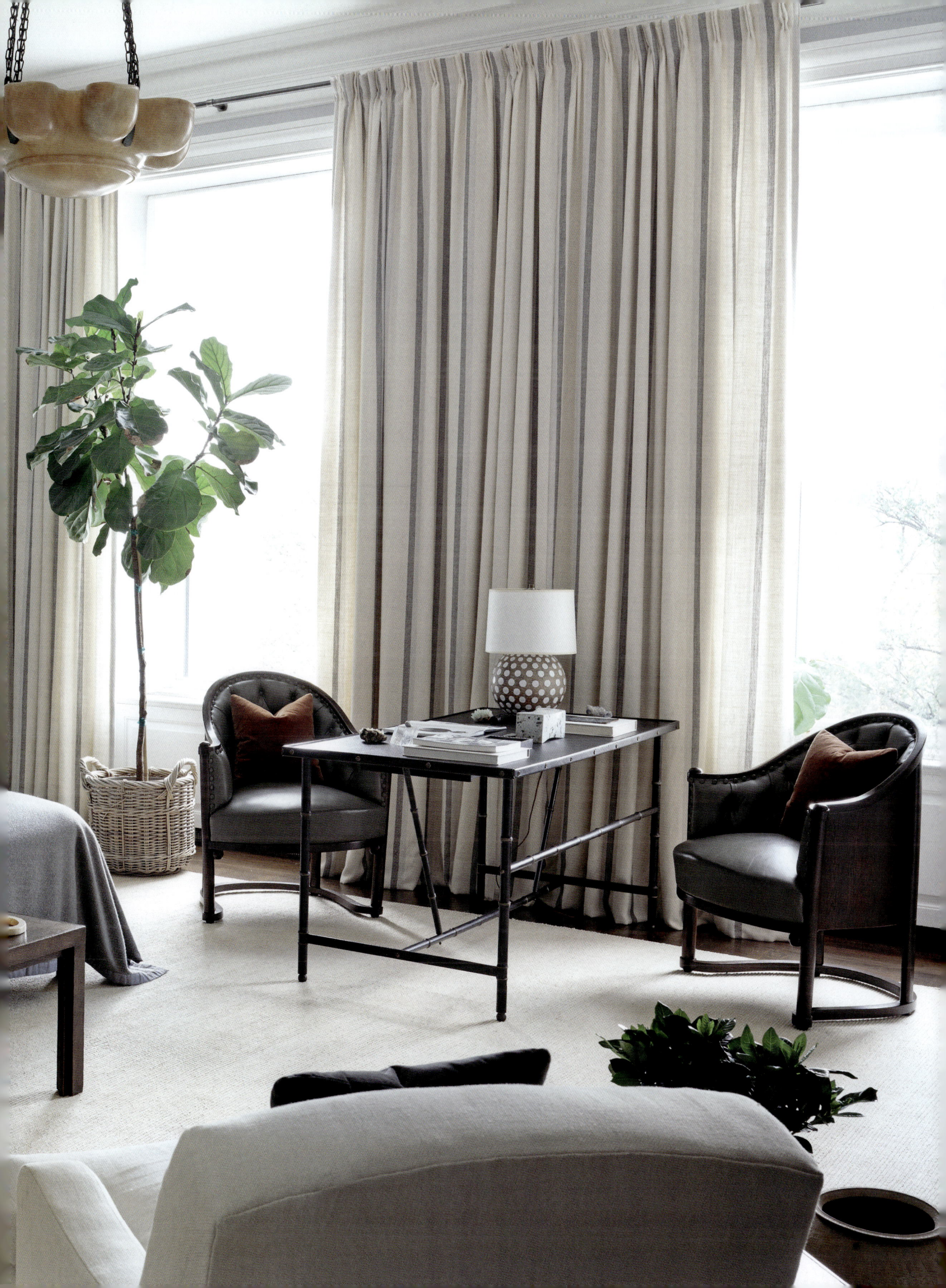

ARTIST

PROVOCATEUR

CARY LEIBOWITZ & SIMON LINCE

I'm a New Yorker but I grew up in the suburbs of Connecticut. I moved to New York in 1990, and have never left! I like New York—its messiness, its energy, and the happenstance of its architecture; its diverse food, art, and culture. New Yorkers are inherently nice people and I find it to be a friendly city generally.

I was living in Brooklyn, which in those days was not as cool as it is now, and must have bought the house over 20 years ago. My aim was to find the nicest architecture and greatest square footage for the least amount of money somewhere in Manhattan, and I ended up in Harlem. The house is a traditional New York, middle-class, turn-of-the-century brownstone situated between Hamilton Heights and Sugar Hill, and its "look" evolved over a period of three years. I had been buying things for what seemed like forever, longing to find somewhere to put them all, and the house has shown itself to be the perfect backdrop, with the staircase adding circulation. I would just love it to be twice the size, as I have hundreds of ideas and plans for it! For now, however, Harlem is taking a back seat. I met Simon a couple of years after I moved here and, although he likes it, he has always seen it more as my house, so these days we tend to focus more on our home in the country.

My favorite room is the main living room, which is covered in pink flowery wallpaper, discovered in a junk shop in Germany in the 1990s. I was so excited to use it at last that I was tempted to cover every room in the house with it! The living room has great proportions and now doubles as Simon's office. If I am allowed a second favorite, it would be the library upstairs, with its blue walls and ceiling and 1970s Nelson Mandela sofa, built from scratch in a Parisian "disco" style, with no arms. I even have a suit in the same fabric, which sadly I can no longer fit into. My most-loved piece of furniture used to be a glass Memphis dining table surrounded by Robert Venturi chairs, but it broke in half, so this accolade now goes to the three-piece faux Louis XV suite, which is upholstered in the Black Panther fist. I found the fabric in a flea market and the room took on a "salon" style.

A few years ago we had issues with falling plaster in a number of rooms, so I took the grown-up decision to move some of my more valuable artwork into storage—not that this means that the art still in the house is in any way secondary. My favorite pieces are probably all the Jonathan Borofsky *Dream* paintings, which are dotted about the house. They tend to move around a bit, but there is definitely one behind the Joan Collins desk in the living room at the moment … **CL**

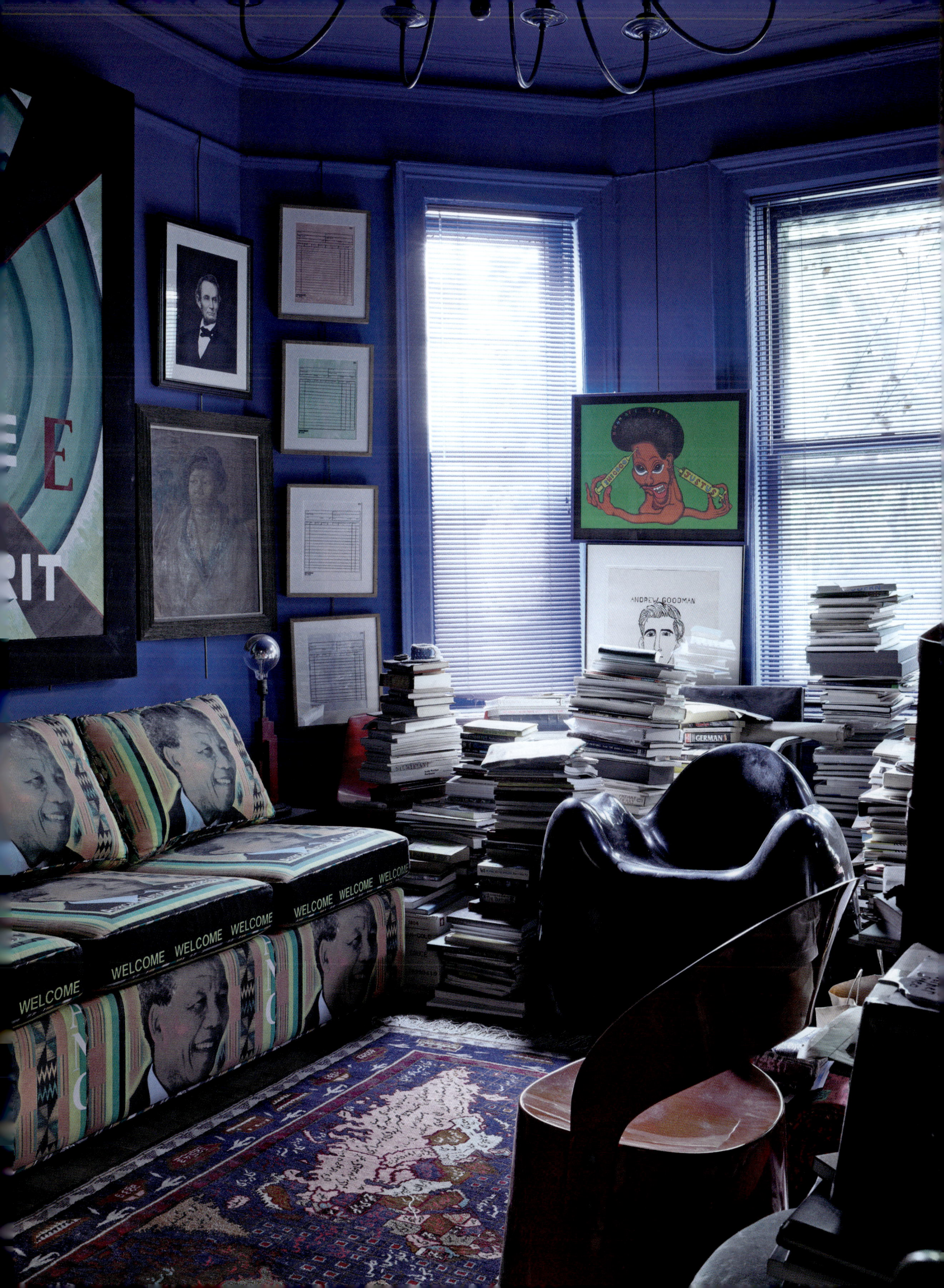

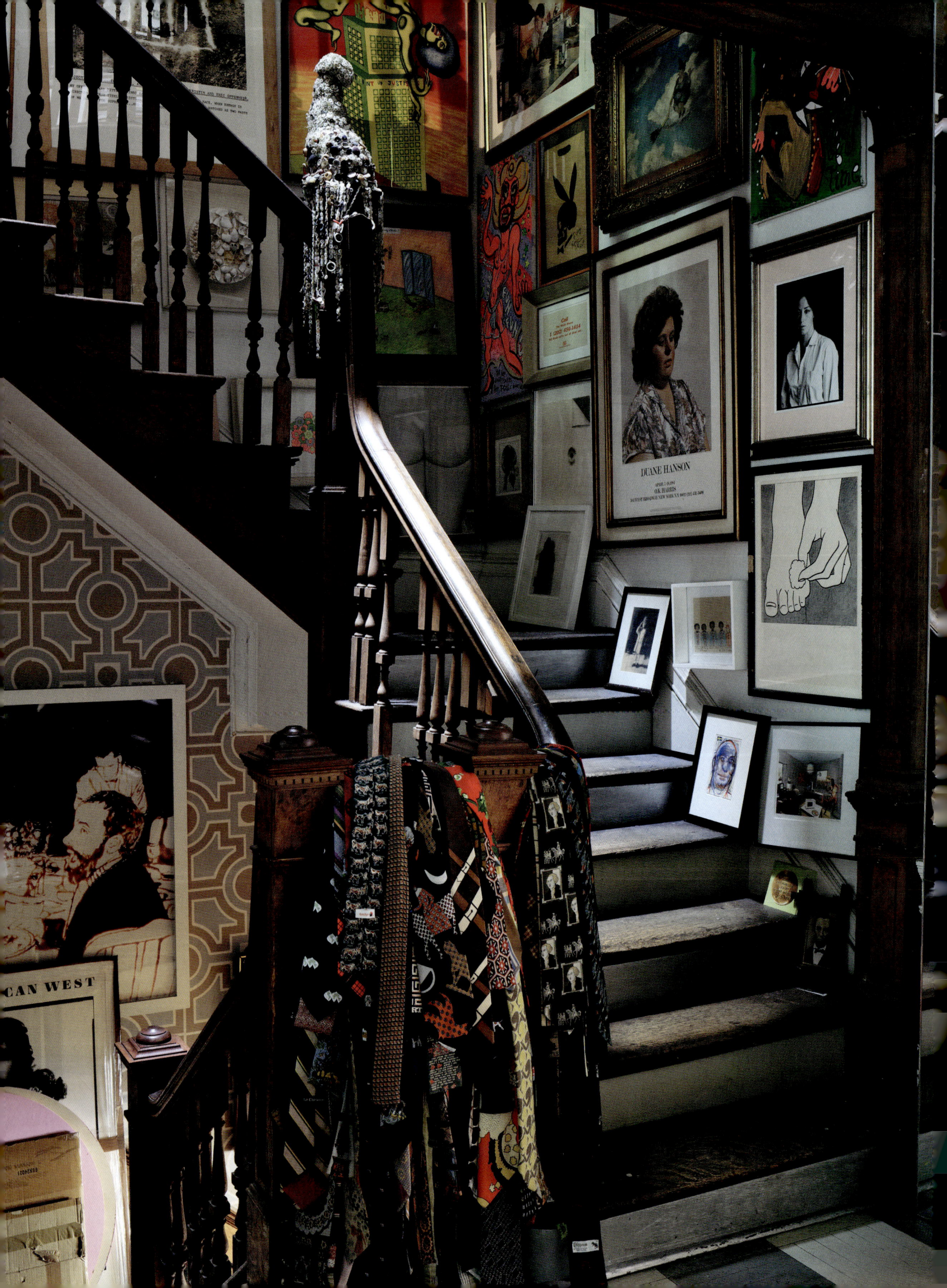

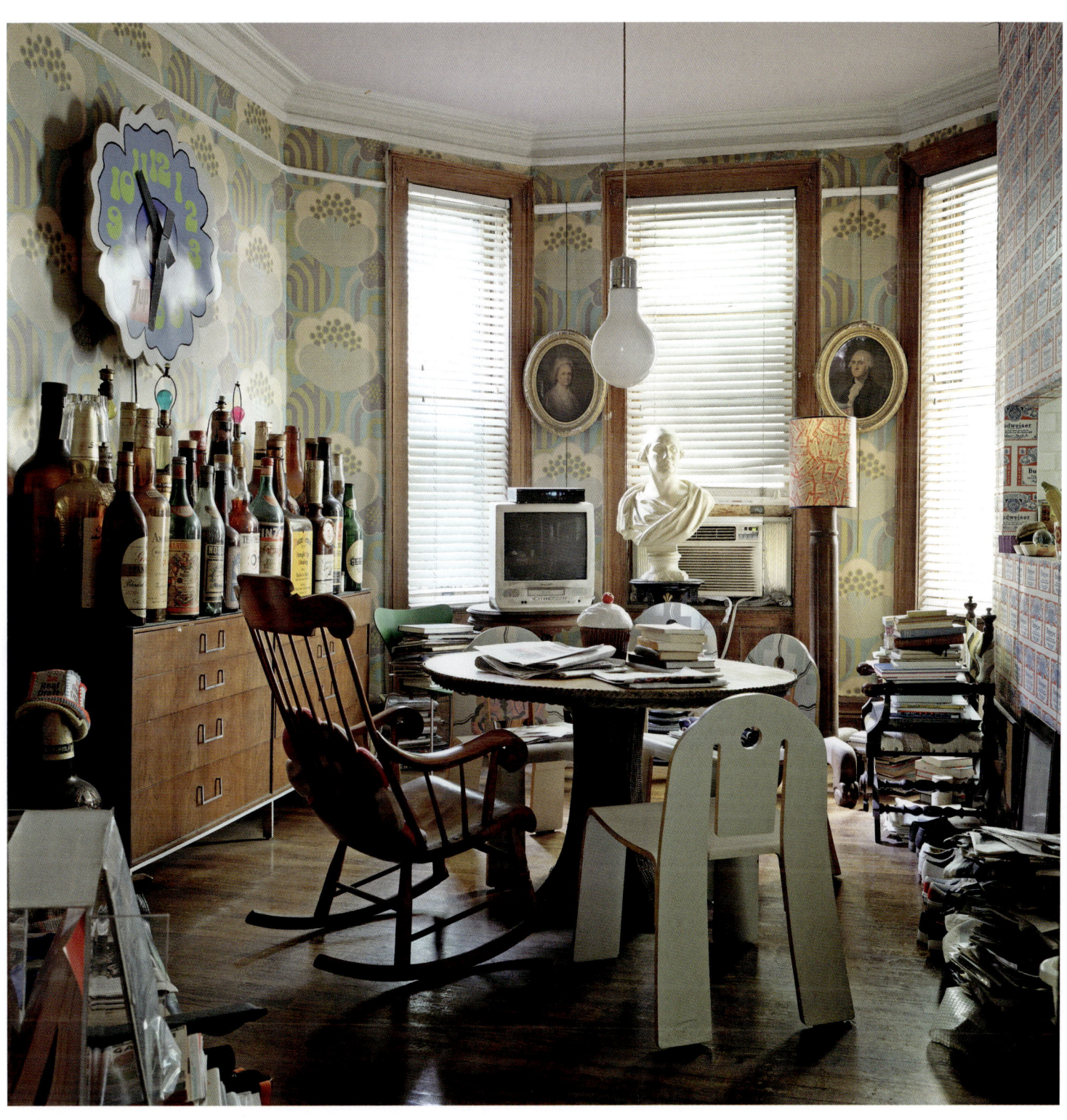

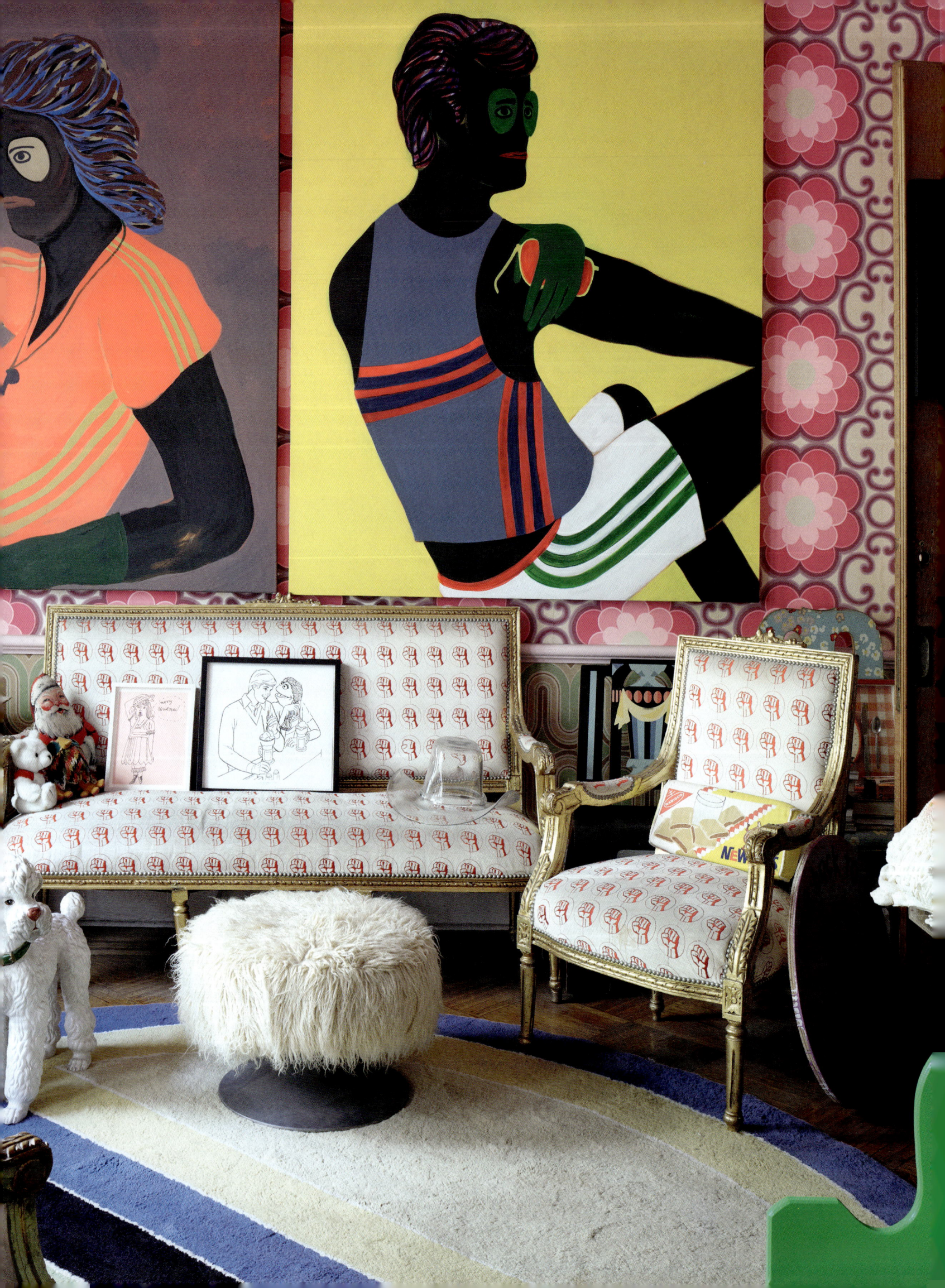

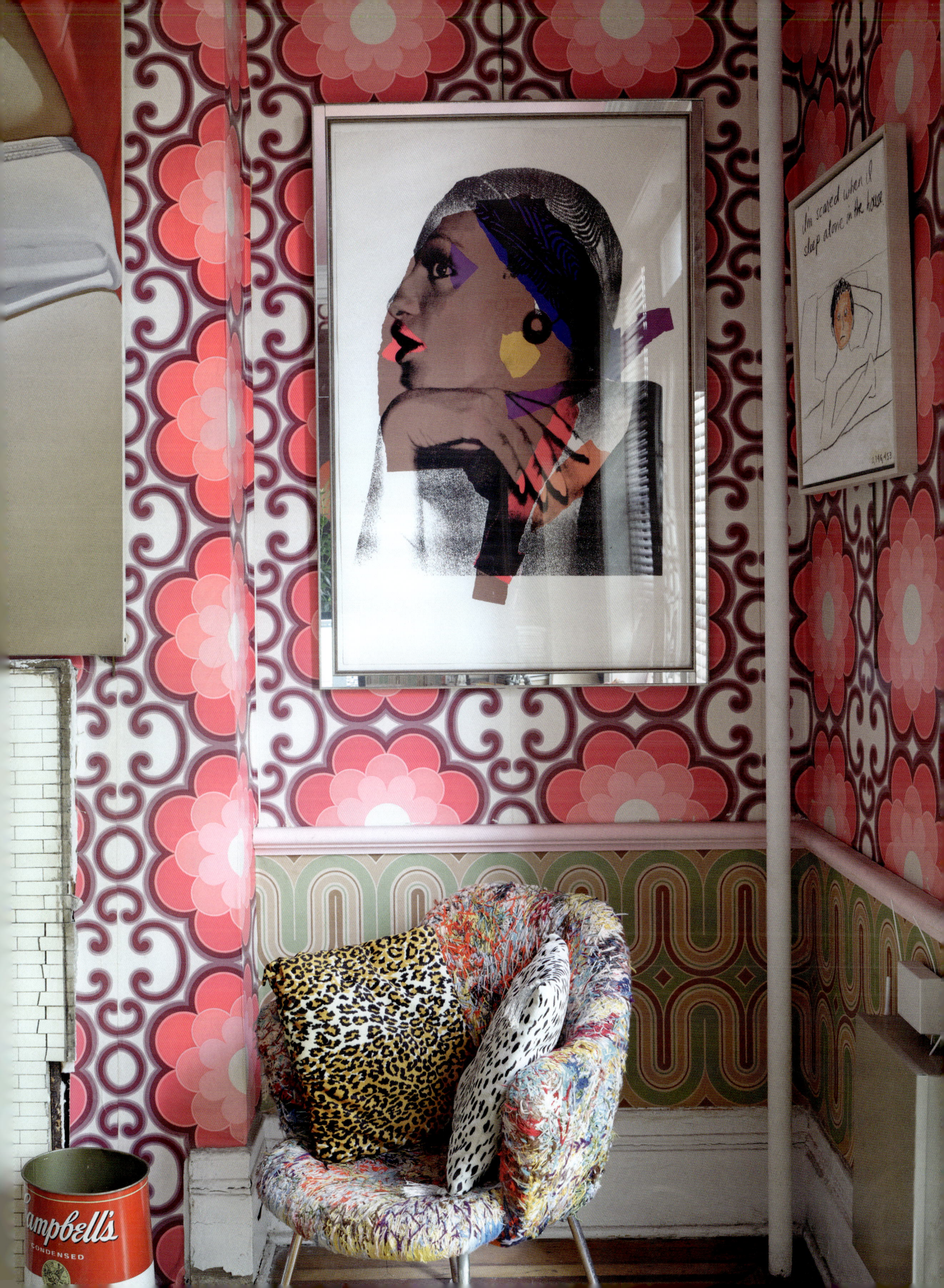

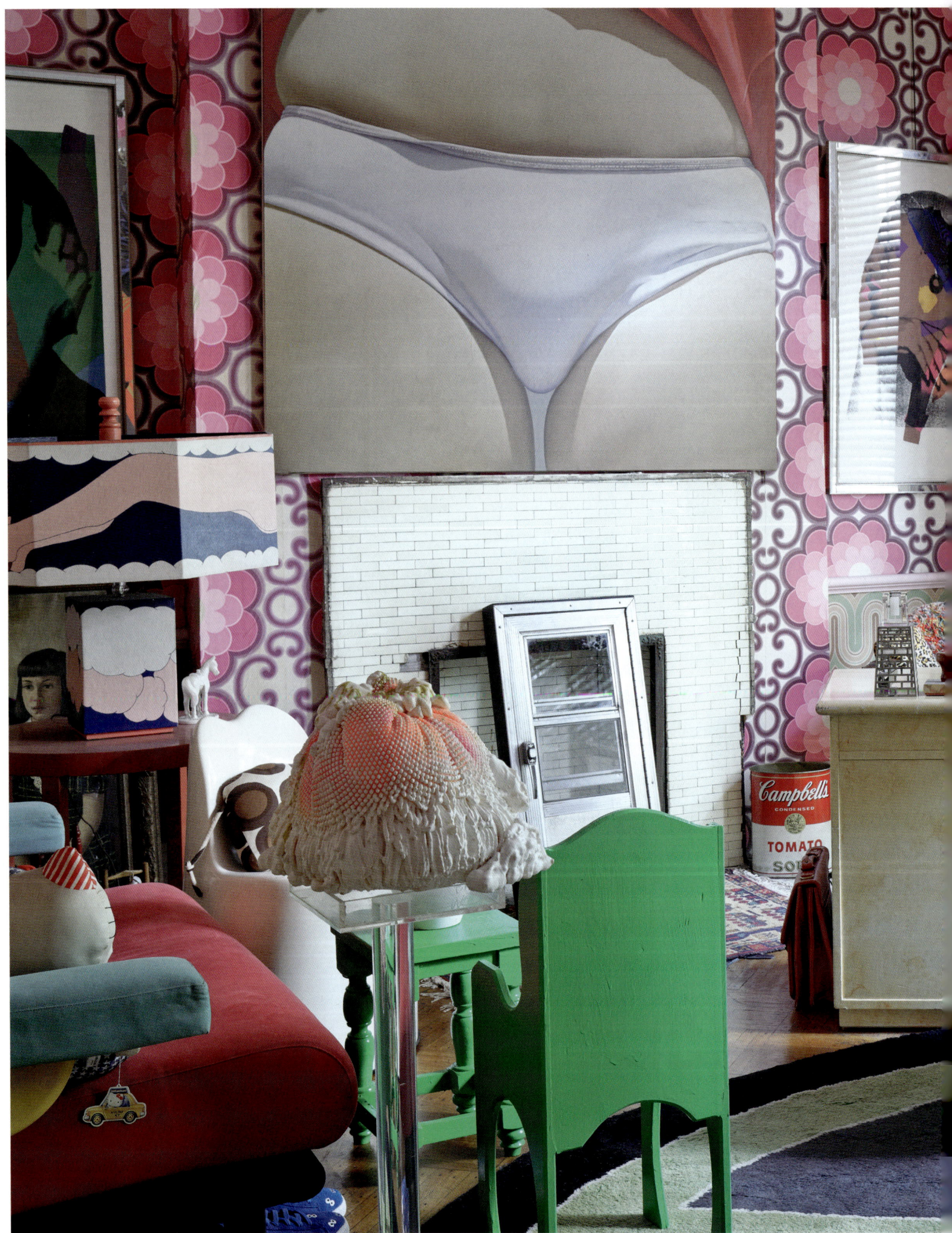

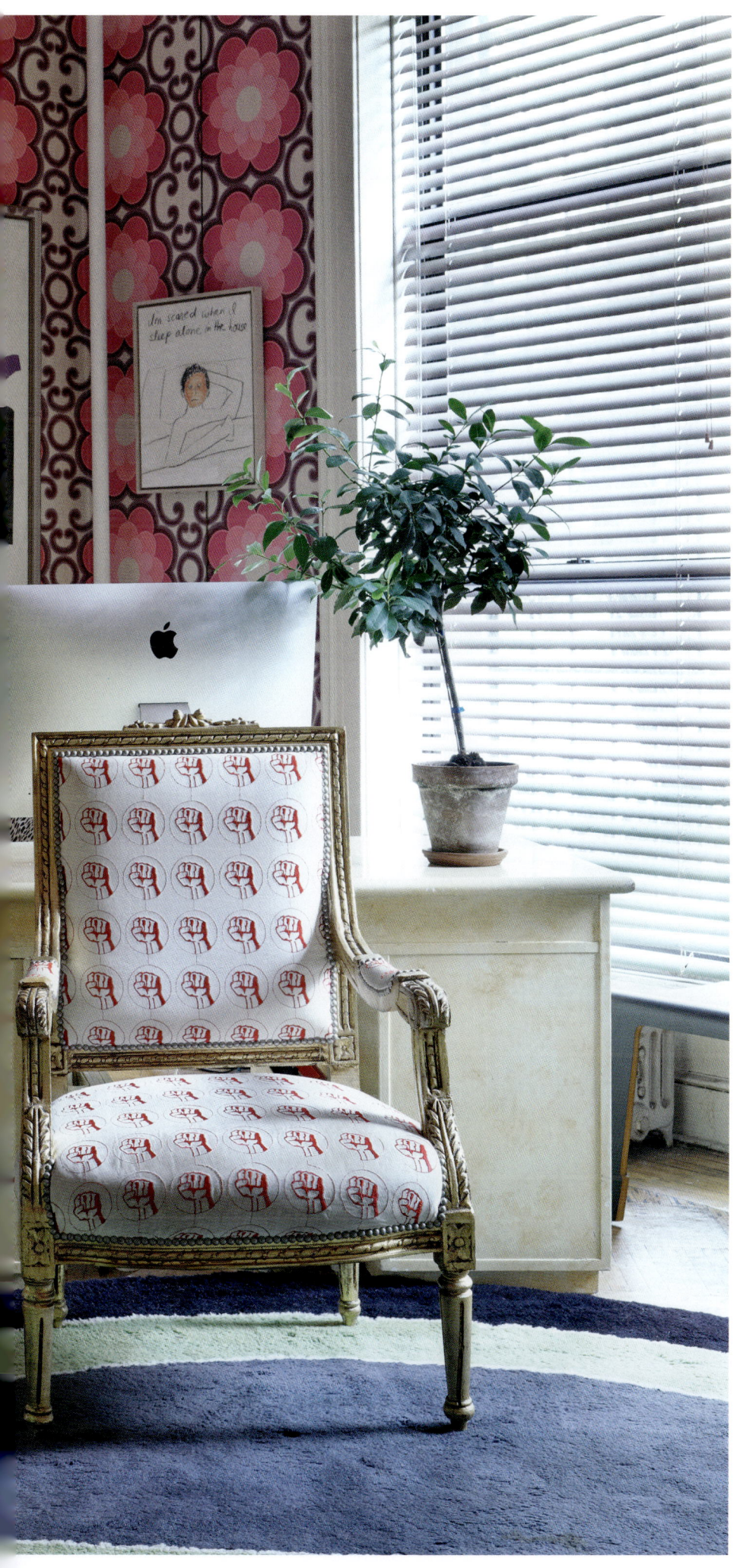

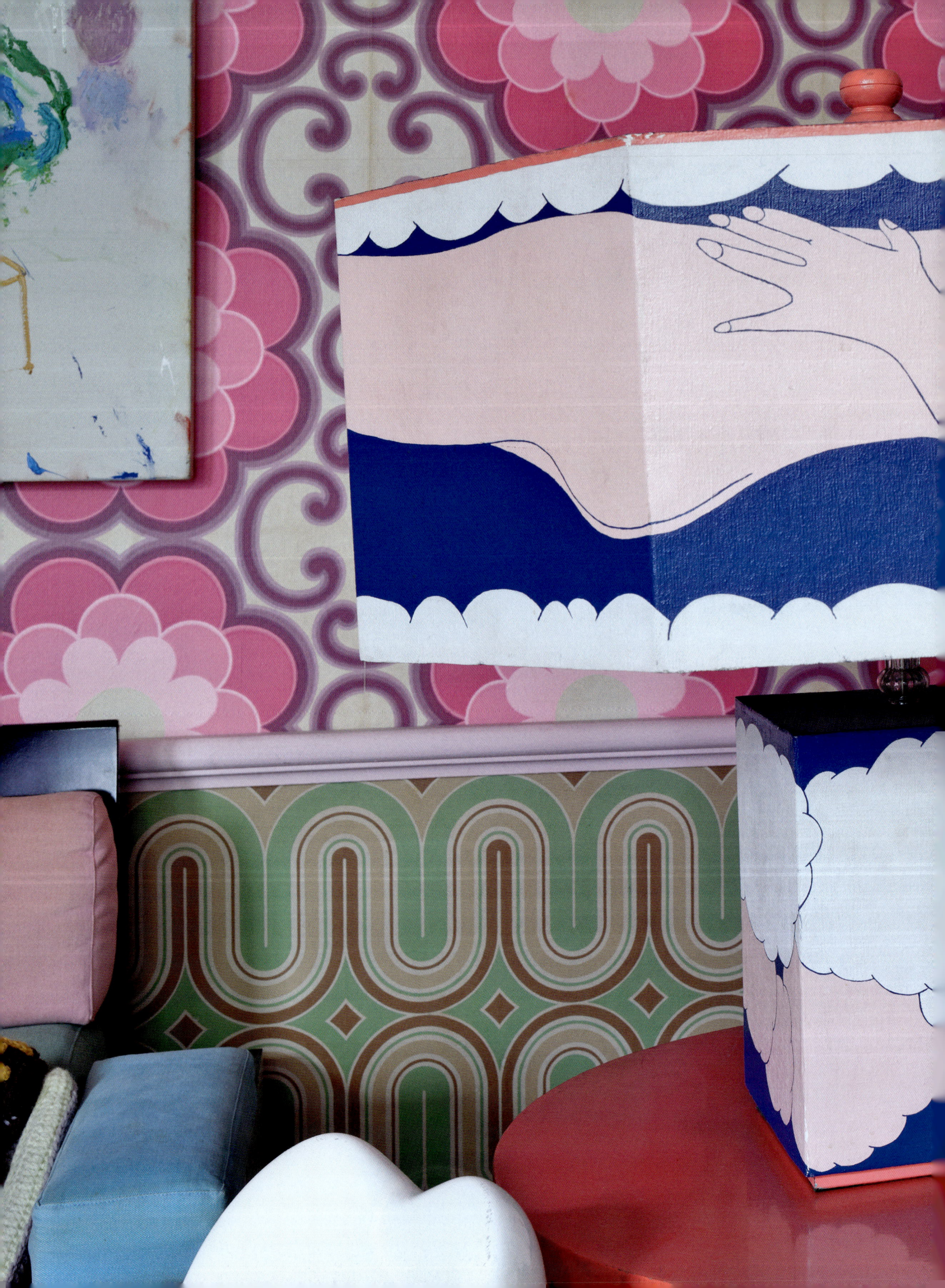

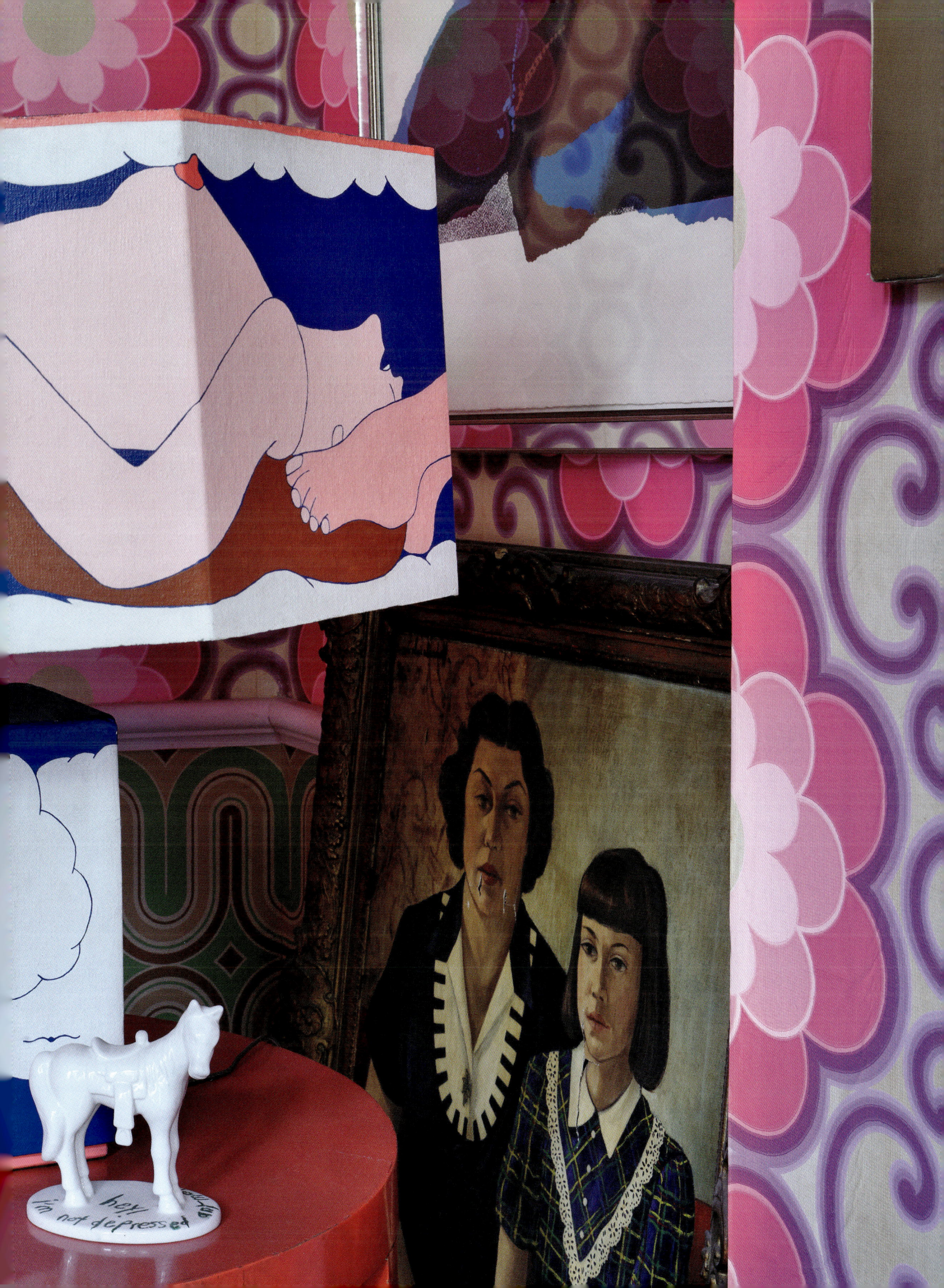

MODERN SENSIBILITY

LISA PERRY

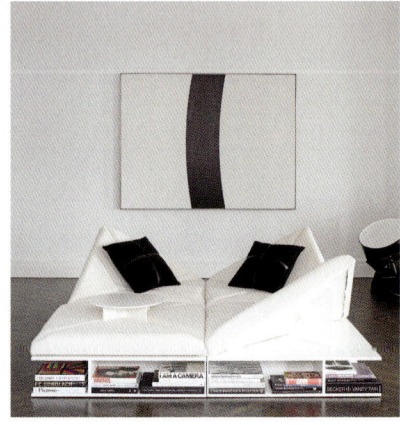

Sutton Place is a cozy neighborhood which runs from 53rd to 59th Streets, between First Avenue and the East River. Our first apartment is directly above this one, bought in 2001, just before 9/11. In the sadness that shrouded New York at the time, it felt like a safe haven, quiet and peaceful, and this area has become one that I love. It is rare for apartments to come up for sale here, so when this one did, in 2014, I just couldn't resist, in the hope that I might persuade my daughter, who lived in Boston, to move to New York.

The interior was of a classic Uptown, pre-war style, which I decided to renovate completely. I took down all the internal walls, retained the original fireplace, added moldings, and transformed it into a light and airy loft (by day the space is bathed in an extraordinary light reflected off the East River). I am a lover of color but for this space felt that I wanted to create a more serene environment than in some of my other homes, so I kept it pretty minimal with a big gray sofa and a dining table, and not much else. Today, I like to think of this space in constant transition, where a single piece of furniture can influence its entire feel and mood—and so it was when Simon arrived to photograph it for *The World of Interiors.*

The project came about thanks to my friend Benjamin Paulin, son of Pierre Paulin, the great furniture designer. Benjamin and his wife, Alice, had an exhibition in New York, in which they were showcasing prototypes of Pierre Paulin's work with the aim of bringing certain pieces back into production. The magazine was looking for an appropriate backdrop in which to photograph the furniture and my apartment seemed ideal, so it was a happy synergy for all of us. When Benjamin introduced the red piece, known as the "Flying Carpet" because it moves and undulates in all sorts of ways, its wow factor was undeniable. It transformed the space, not just physically but emotionally. I had to buy it, of course—and with it the Origami sofa that Benjamin had played on as a child, which has since become the perfect conversation piece, together with this great Alexander Liberman artwork.

I was born in Chicago but have lived in New York since the age of 21. It's my favorite city in the world! My design studio is in SoHo, an area which is creative and inspirational. I think I'm more of a Downtown girl at heart, but I love the contrast of coming Uptown at the end of the day and soaking up the view of the Queensboro Bridge, lit up as if with a giant string of pearls.

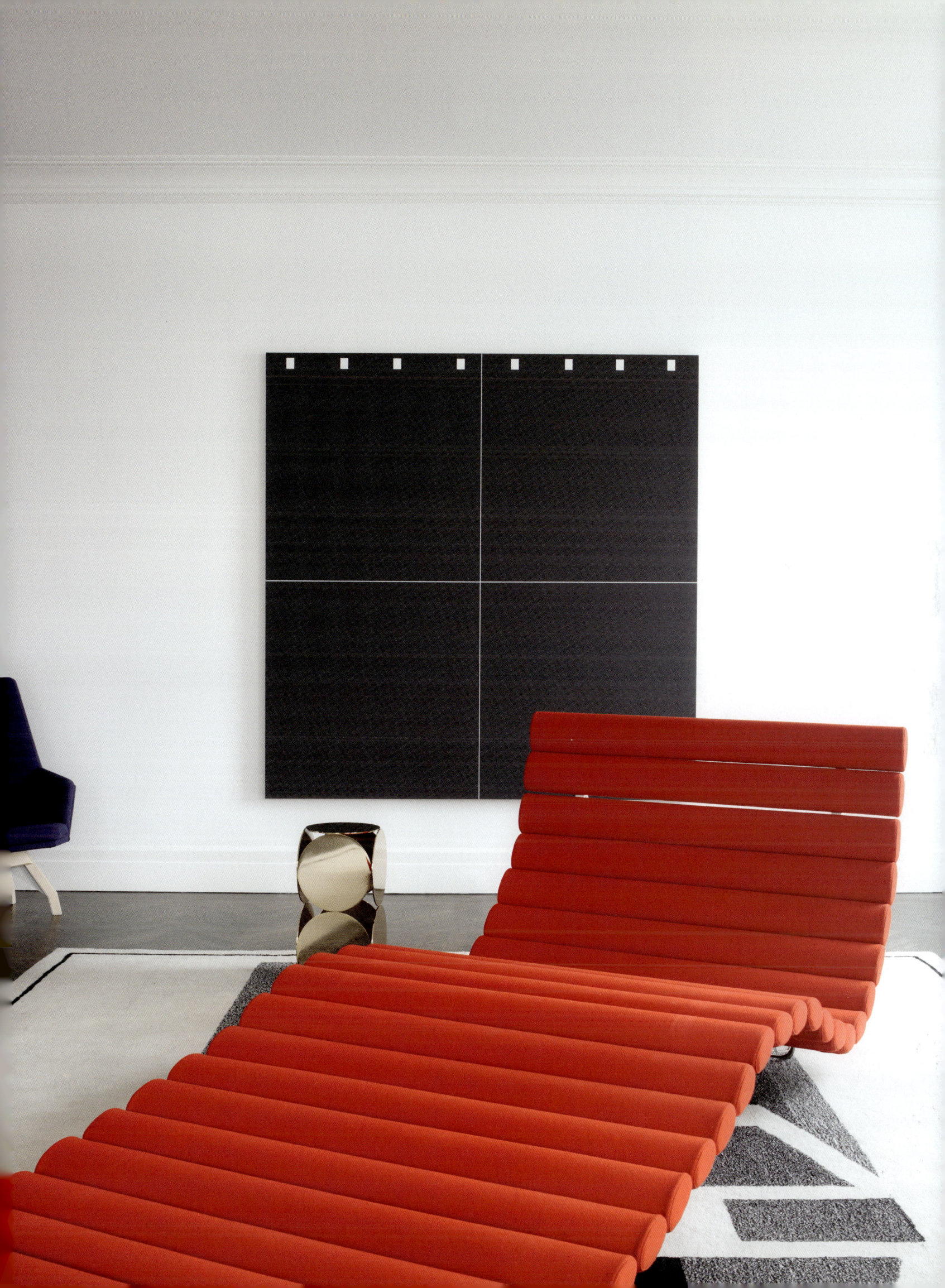

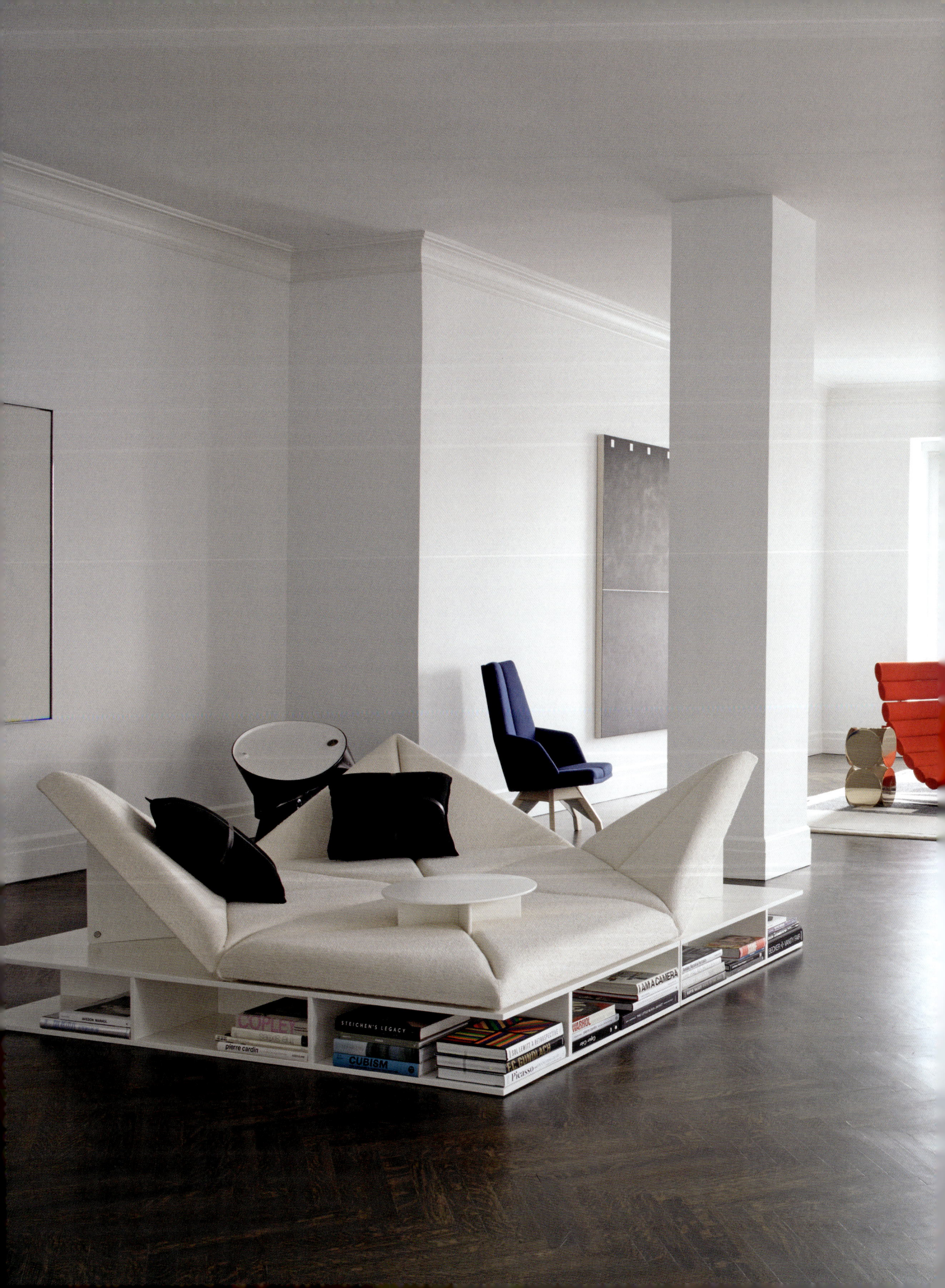

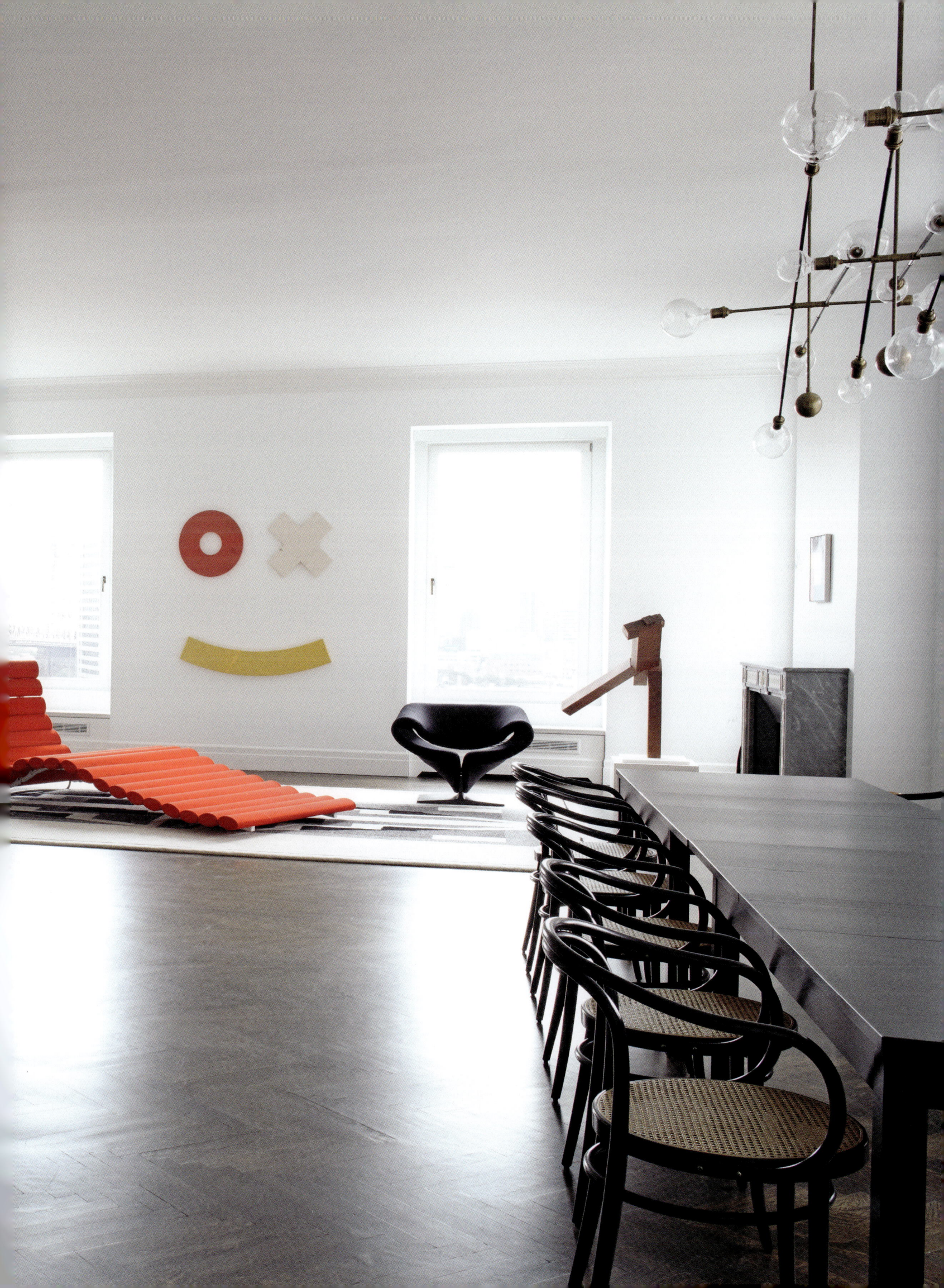

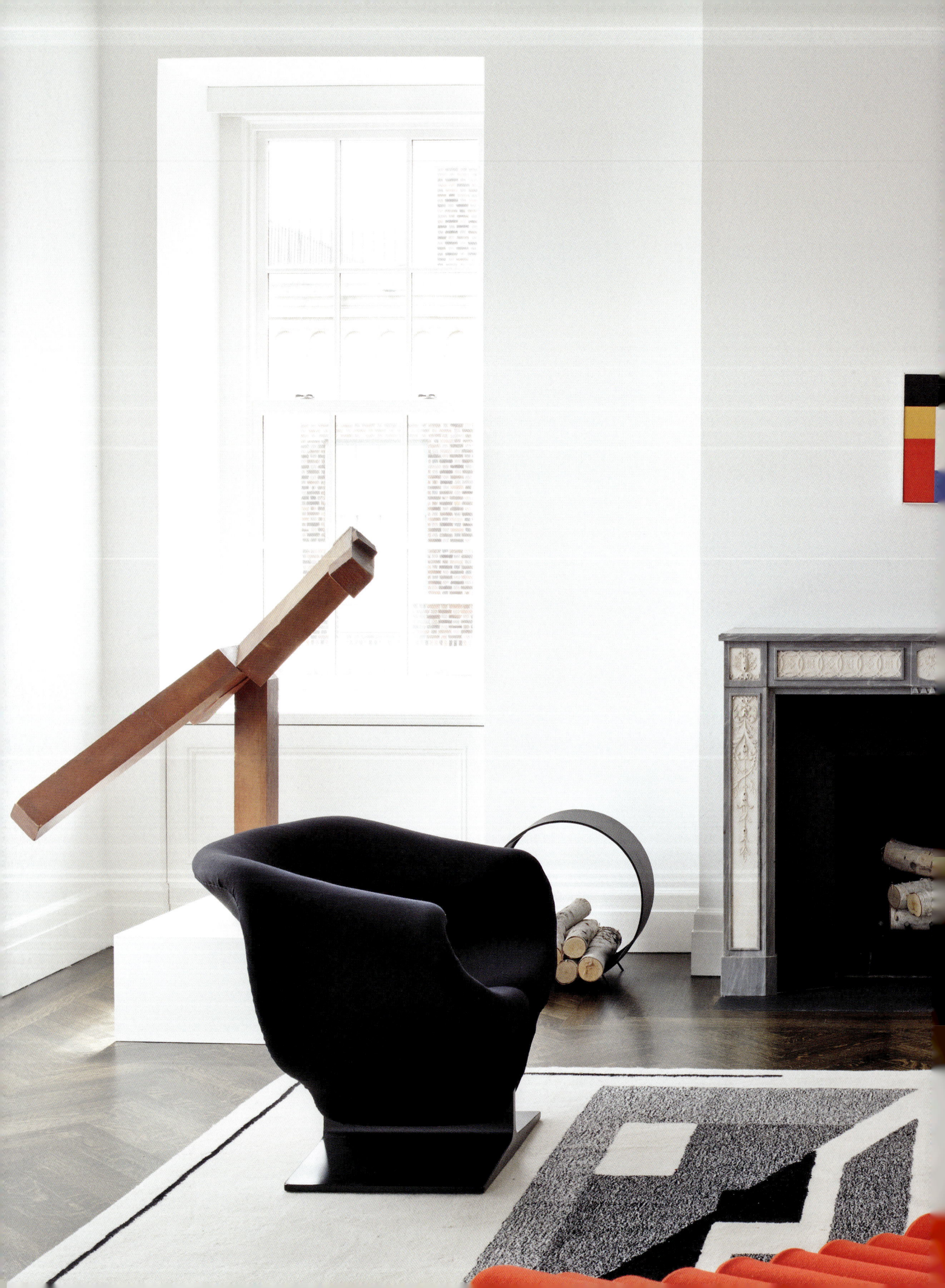

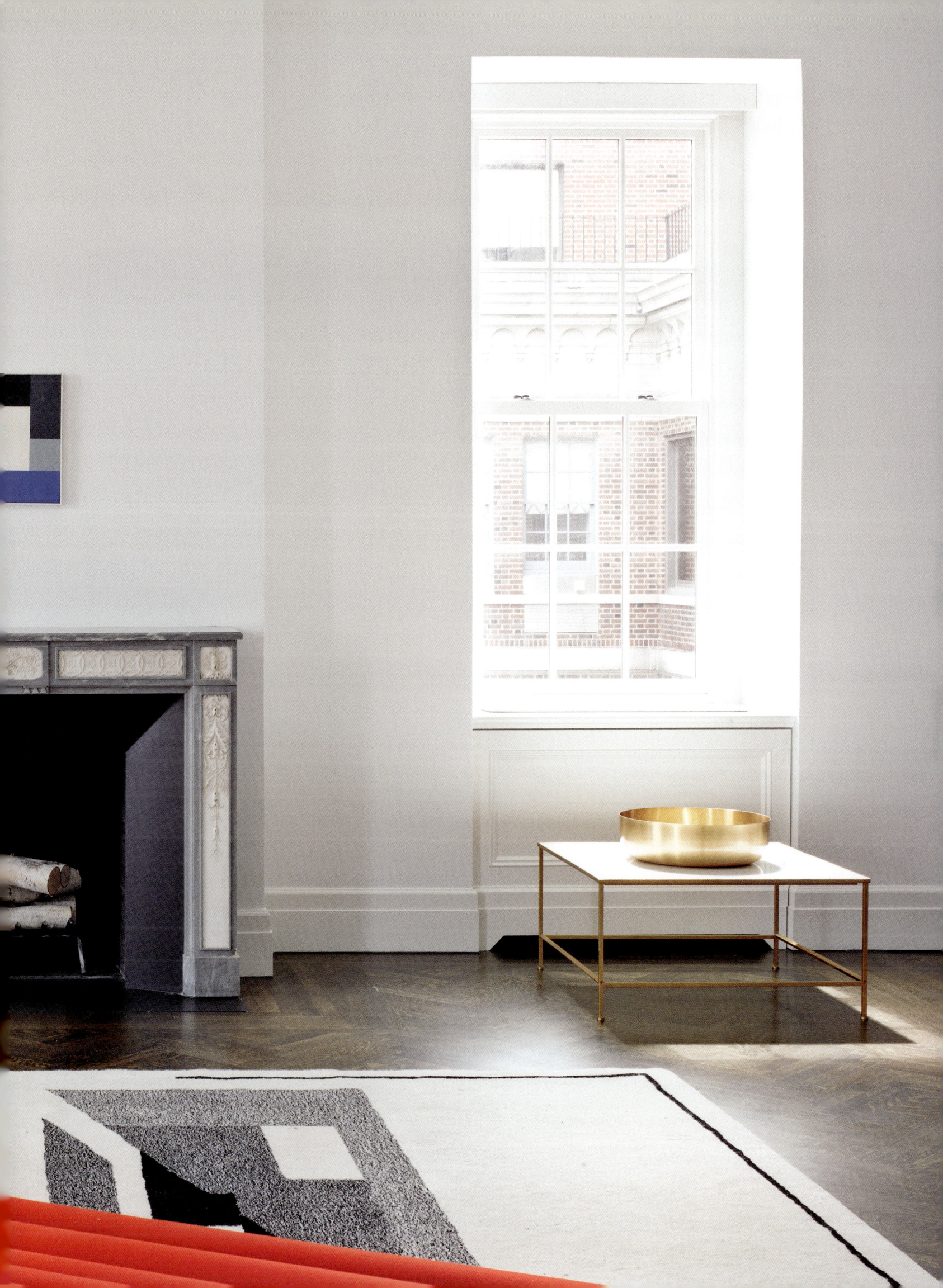

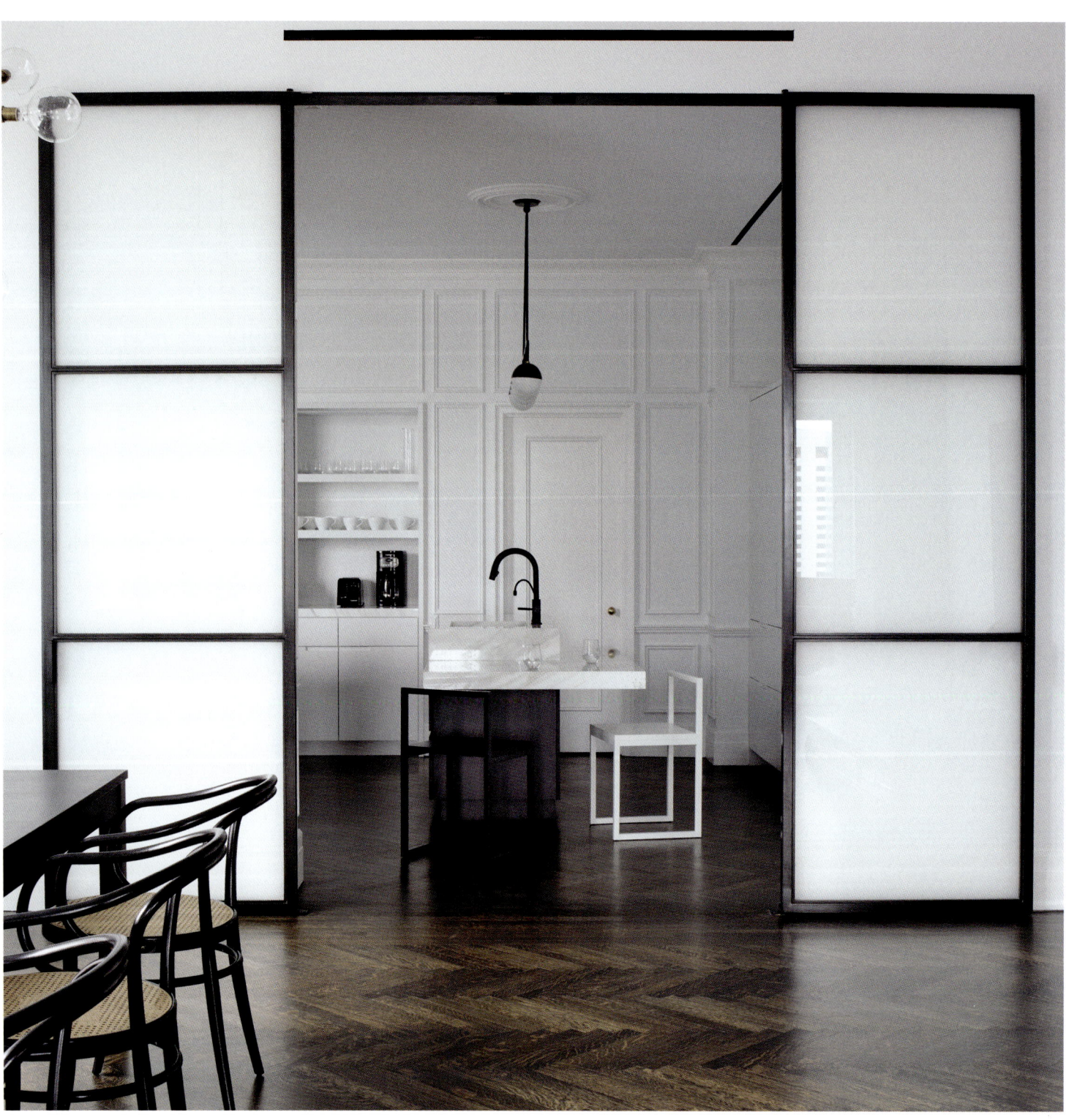

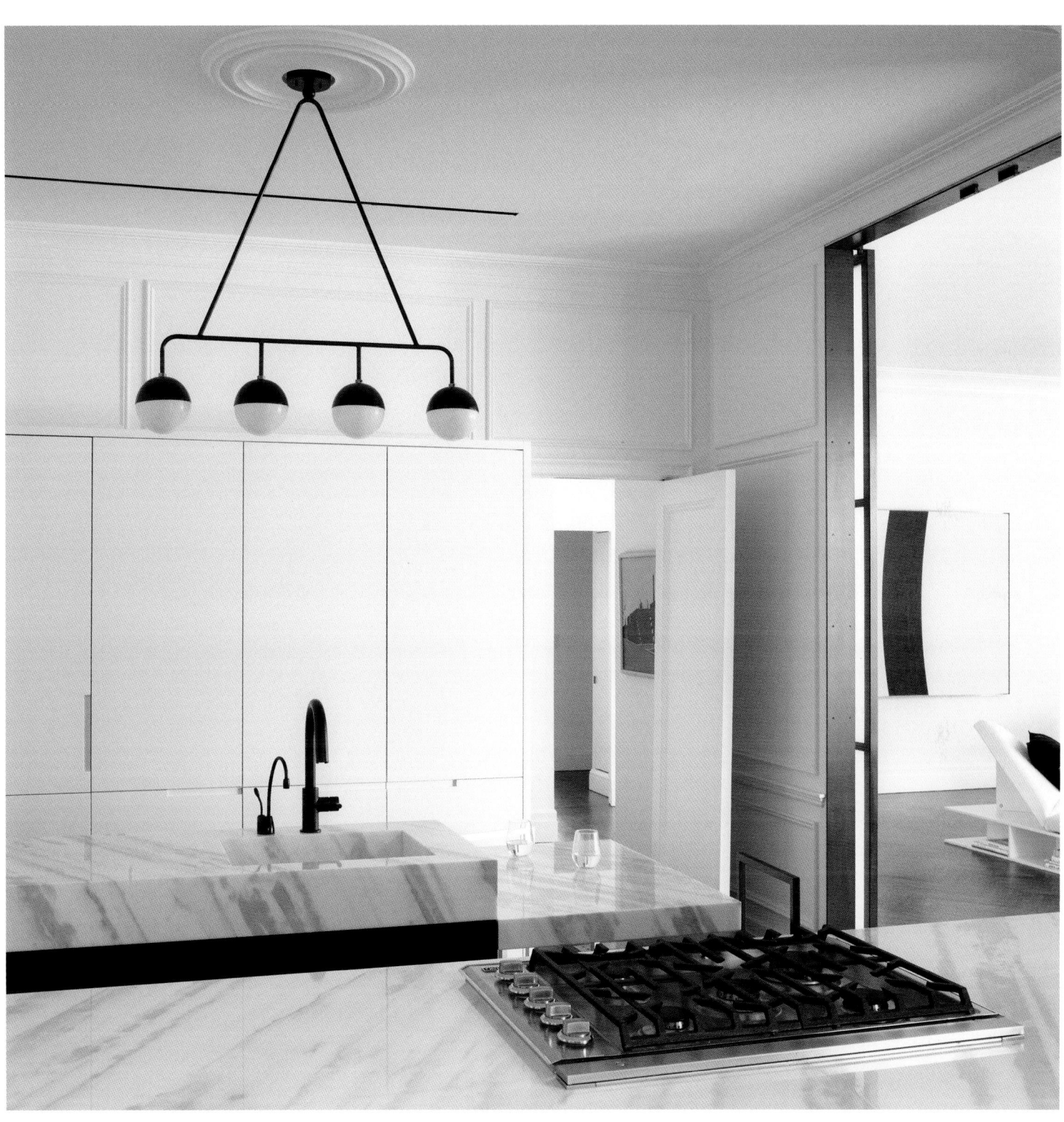

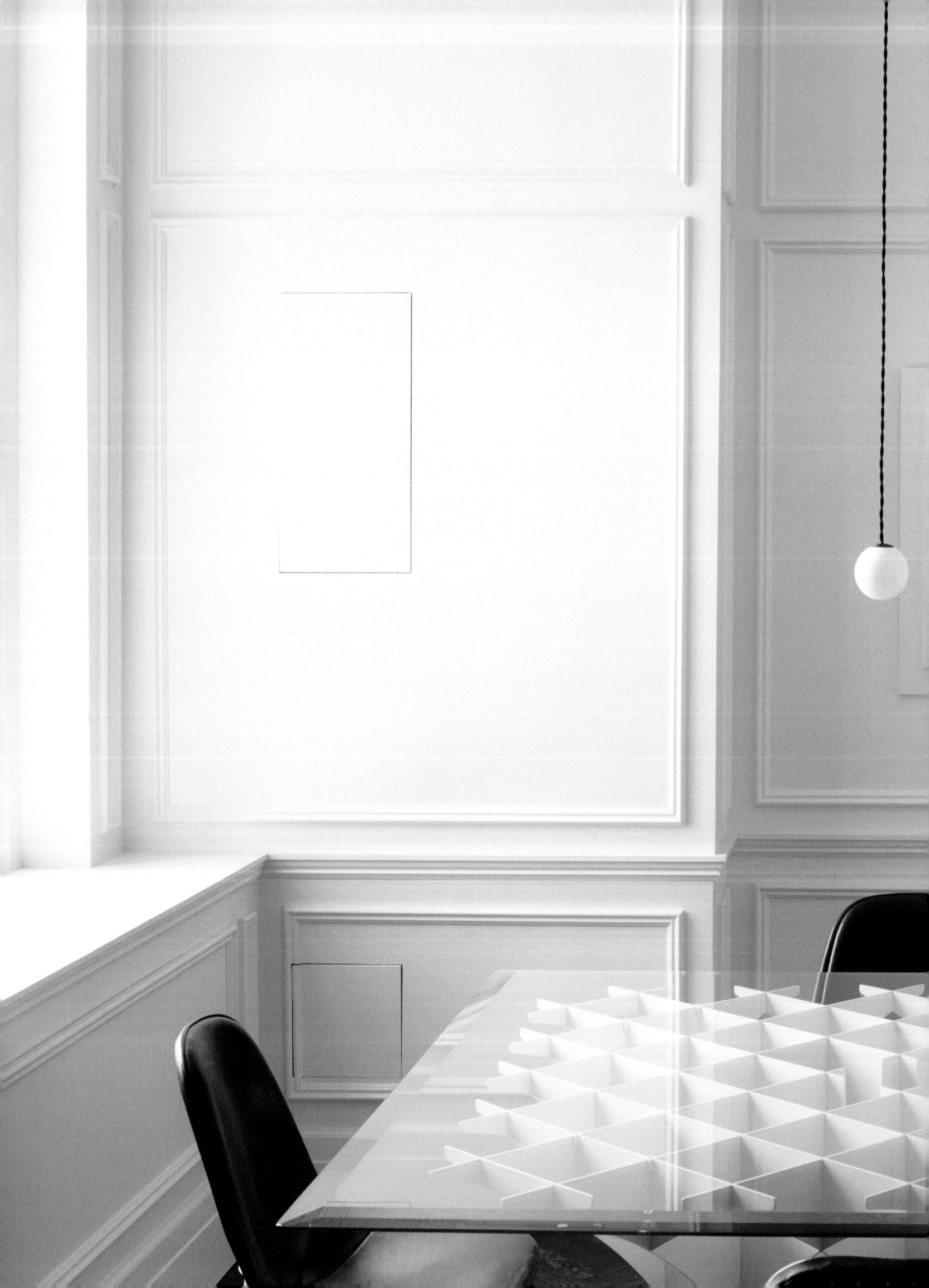

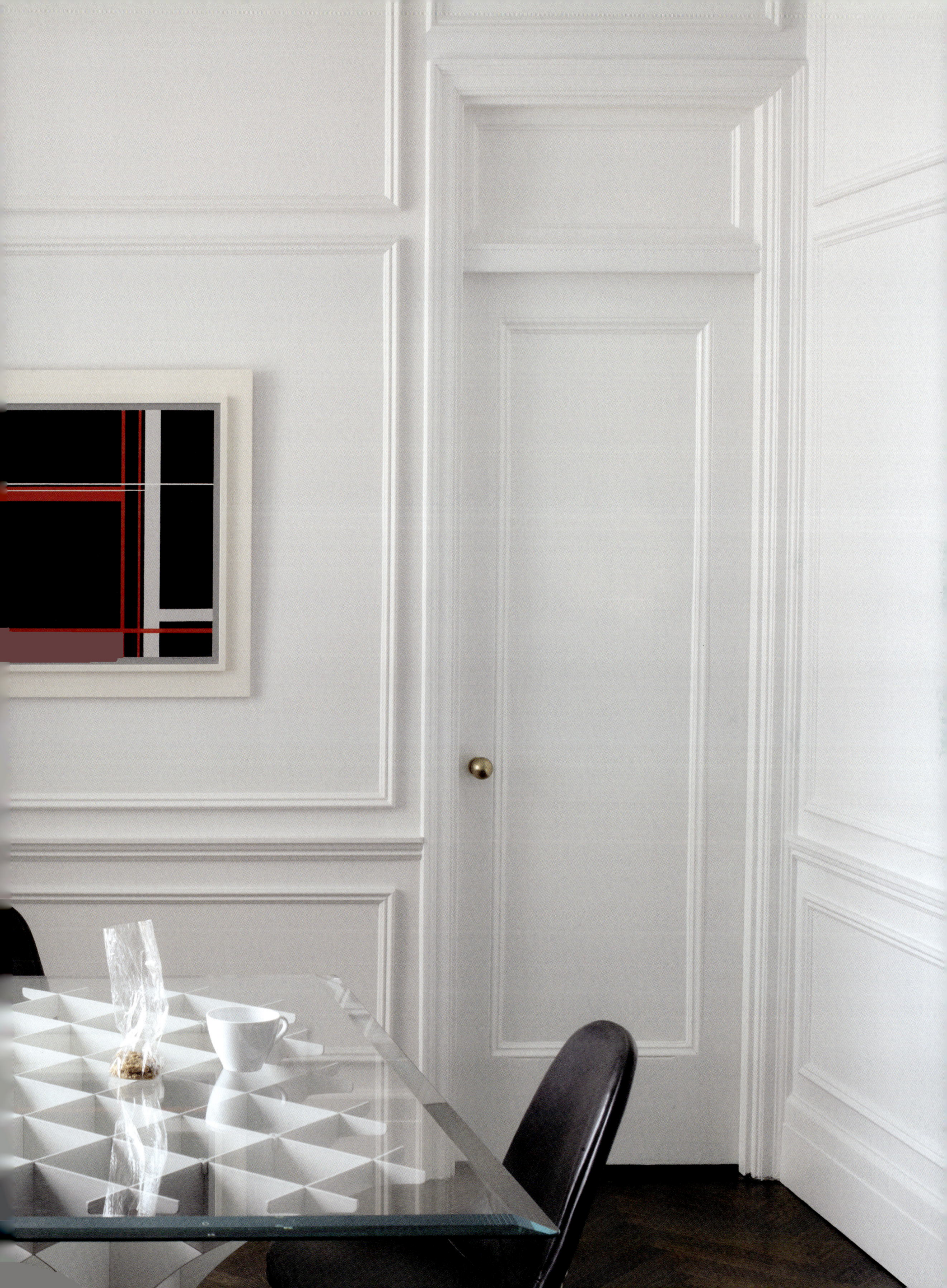

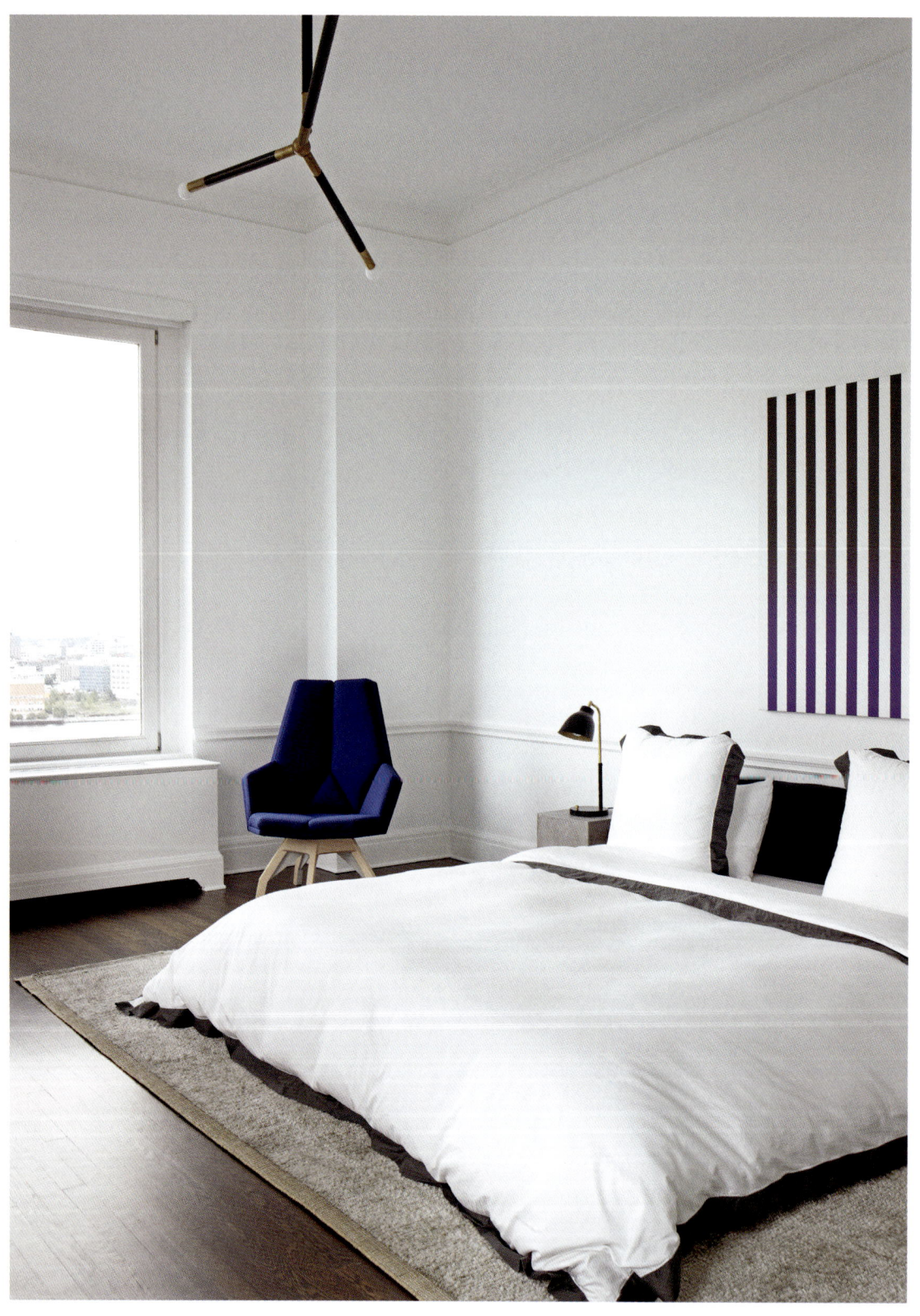

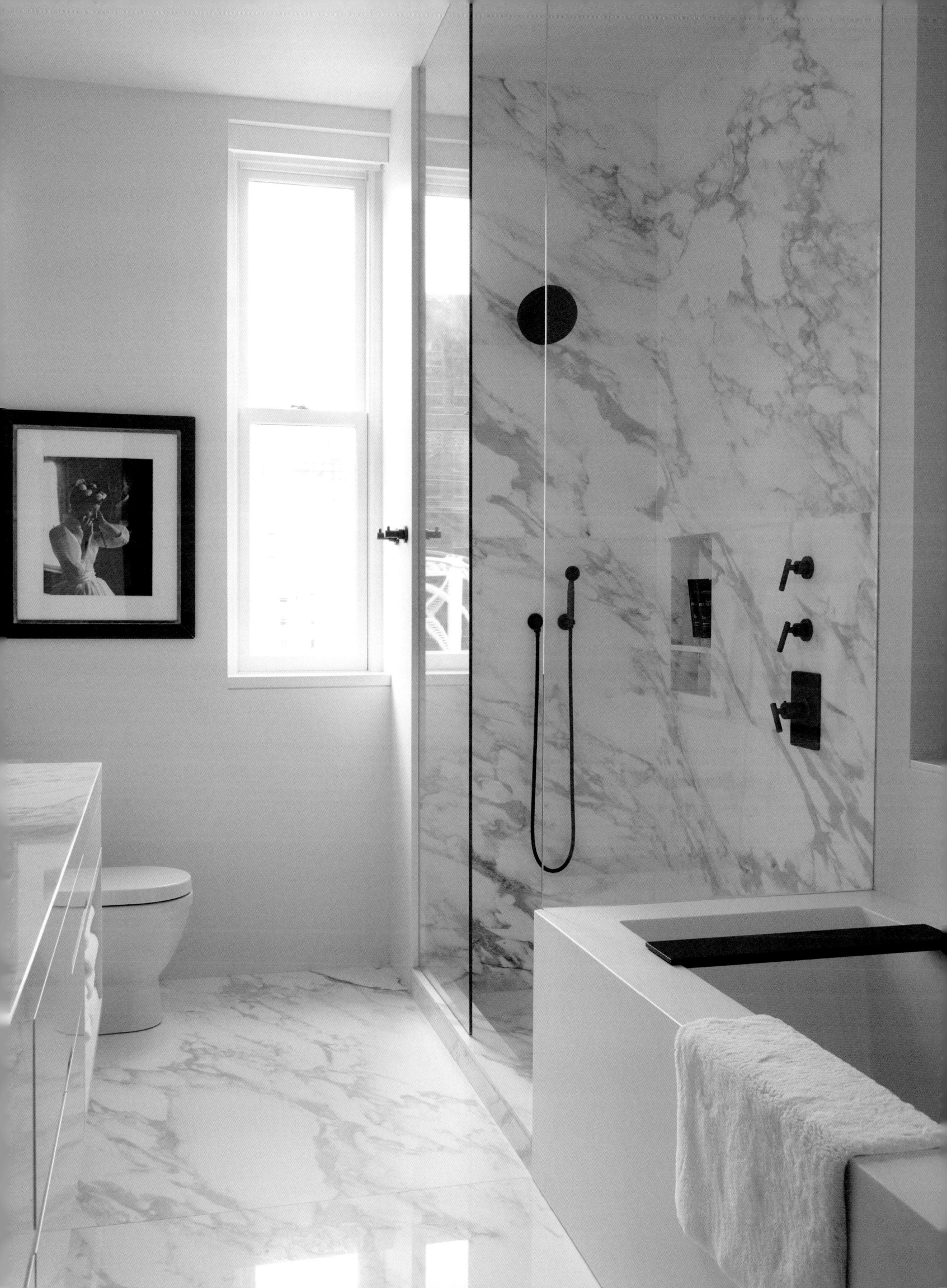

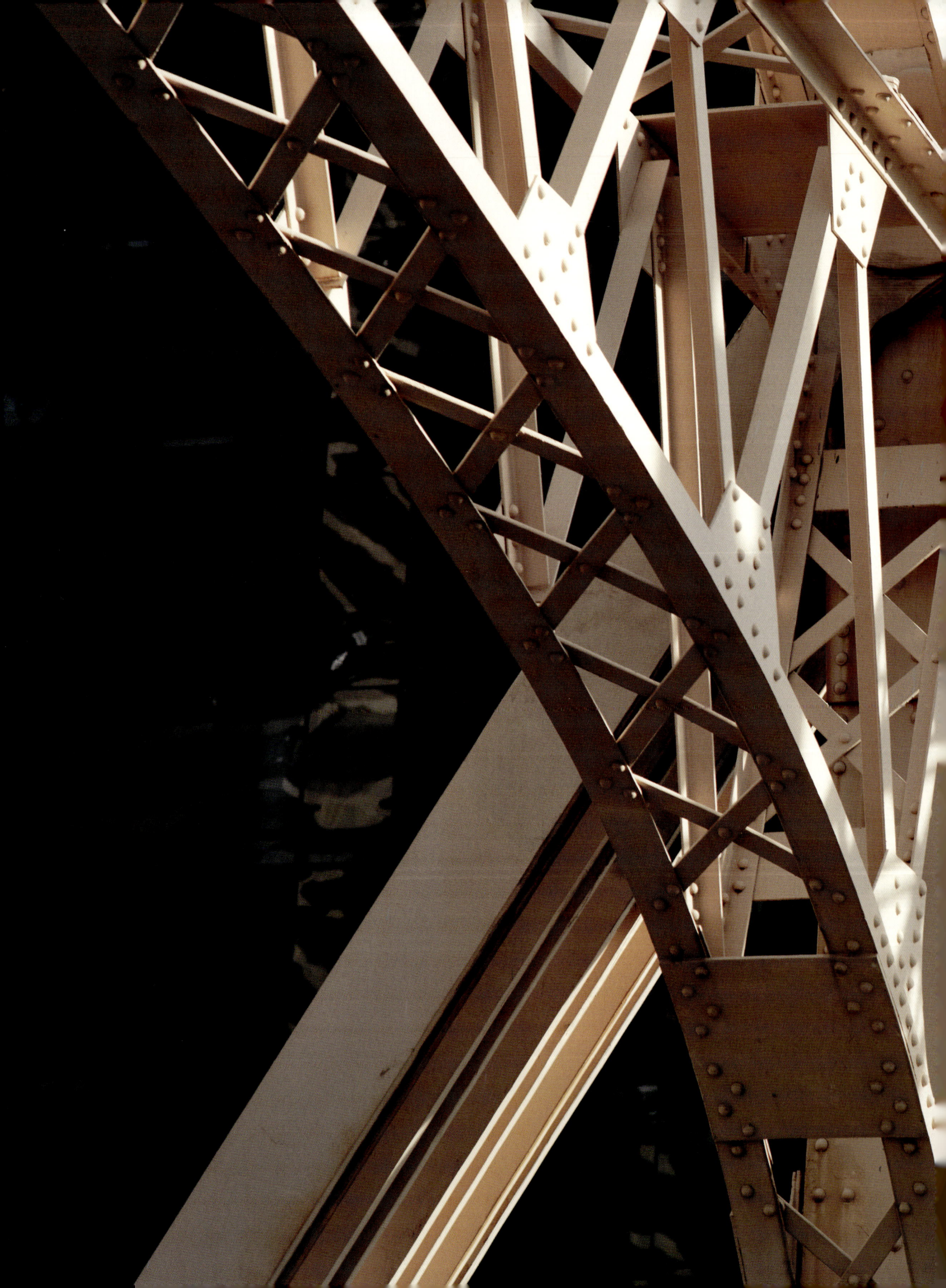

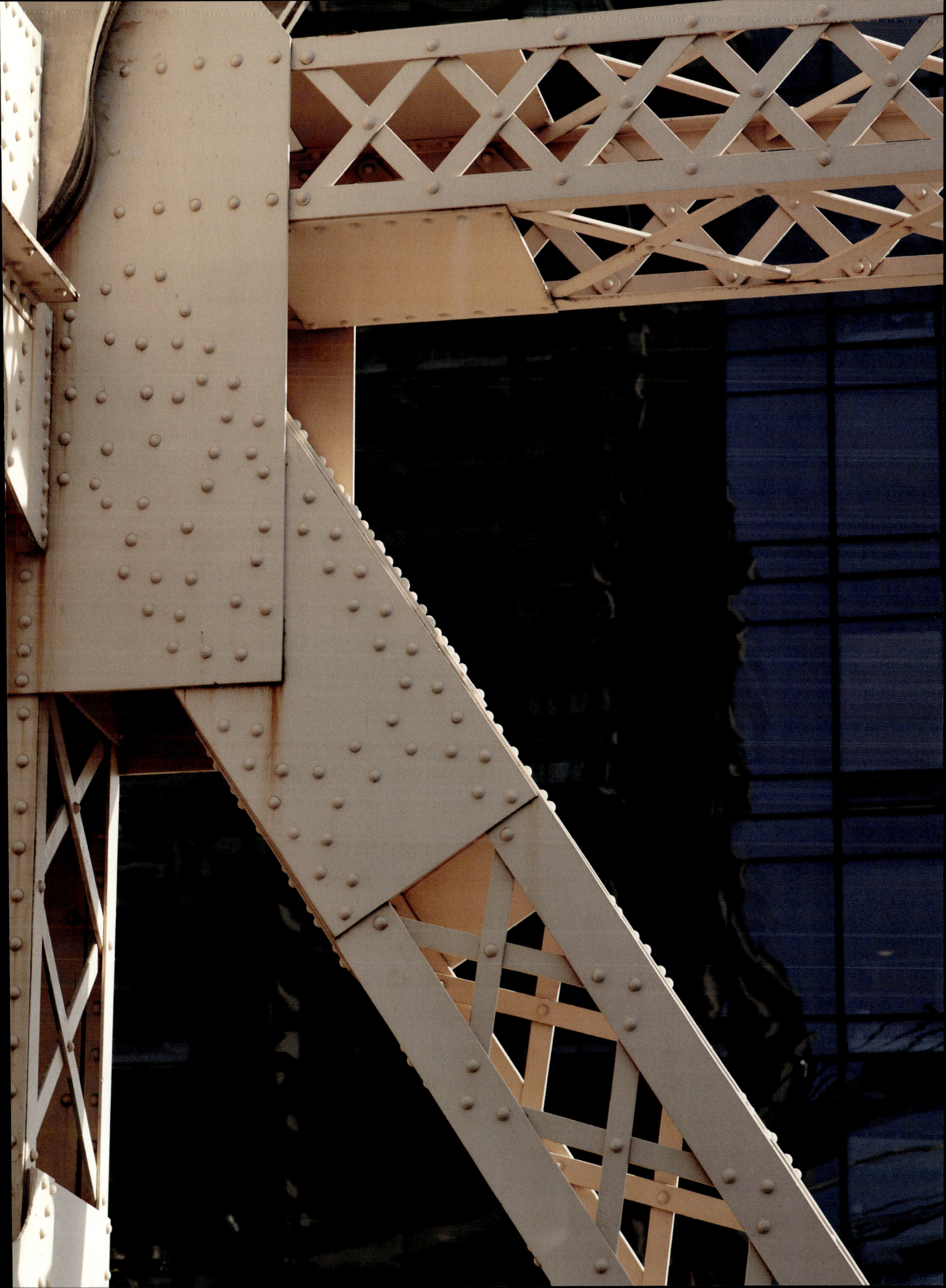

PARISIAN CHIC

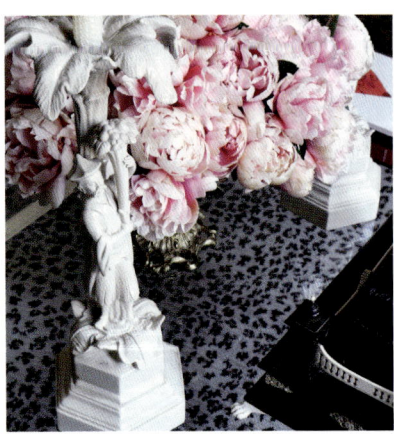

CYNTHIA FRANK

I had been using the apartment I had in Sutton Place before my husband Donald and I were married as a city pied-à-terre. By the late 1990s the children had grown up and left home and I felt such an overwhelming desire for a change of scene that Donald agreed to reverse commute to his neurosurgery practice, which was located outside New York City. I must have looked at 200 apartments with my real estate friend Patricia Patterson, and thought that I would never find the one for me. And then there was this one …

Situated just one block from Central Park, the building was constructed in 1907, at the same time as the Dakota building, and has an elevator that takes you up into each individual apartment. When the doors opened, the apartment literally spoke to me. I bought it that very same day! Today, all these years later, it very much reflects who I am: endless rooms with no apparent purpose, five working fireplaces, high ceilings, and original moldings, which I either restored or re-created, with support and advice from my great friends Timothy Haynes and Kevin Roberts.

I was barely 20 when I married and went to live in Paris. It was the 1960s and Paris was the most romantic and amazing place to be. It was there that I developed a love of antiques, already fostered by my father, and got to know all the flea markets. When I returned to New York a few years later, I got sucked into the fashion industry, working with *Harper's Bazaar*, and became a regular visitor to Paris for the shows. I had found my destiny!

I love entertaining and, while New York boasts so many wonderful restaurants, I prefer to invite my friends home, and do so as much as I can. "Glorious Food" is the go-to catering company for New Yorkers who entertain at home on a regular basis. I have used them for years and they know the drill by heart. I love flowers—roses are my signature—and I have elevated setting the table to a completely new level. I collect nineteenth-century Chinese porcelain and must have 500 different sets. I never buy anything new—it must always be antique, with patina and history.

As an enthusiastic host, the dining room has to be my favorite room in the apartment, with its original gothic paneling and the brass-legged Jansen dining table that I've owned forever. During the past year the room has become a "walk through," the pandemic depriving me of my greatest pleasure—to entertain my friends. I am also especially fond of the 1970s Ado Chale table on the mezzanine and the pair of vintage Serge Roche console tables in the entrance hall. For me, the apartment is more about the furniture than the art, but my most important piece hangs in the drawing room, a contemporary work by Albert Gleizes.

The apartment has turned out to be the happiest place in my world!

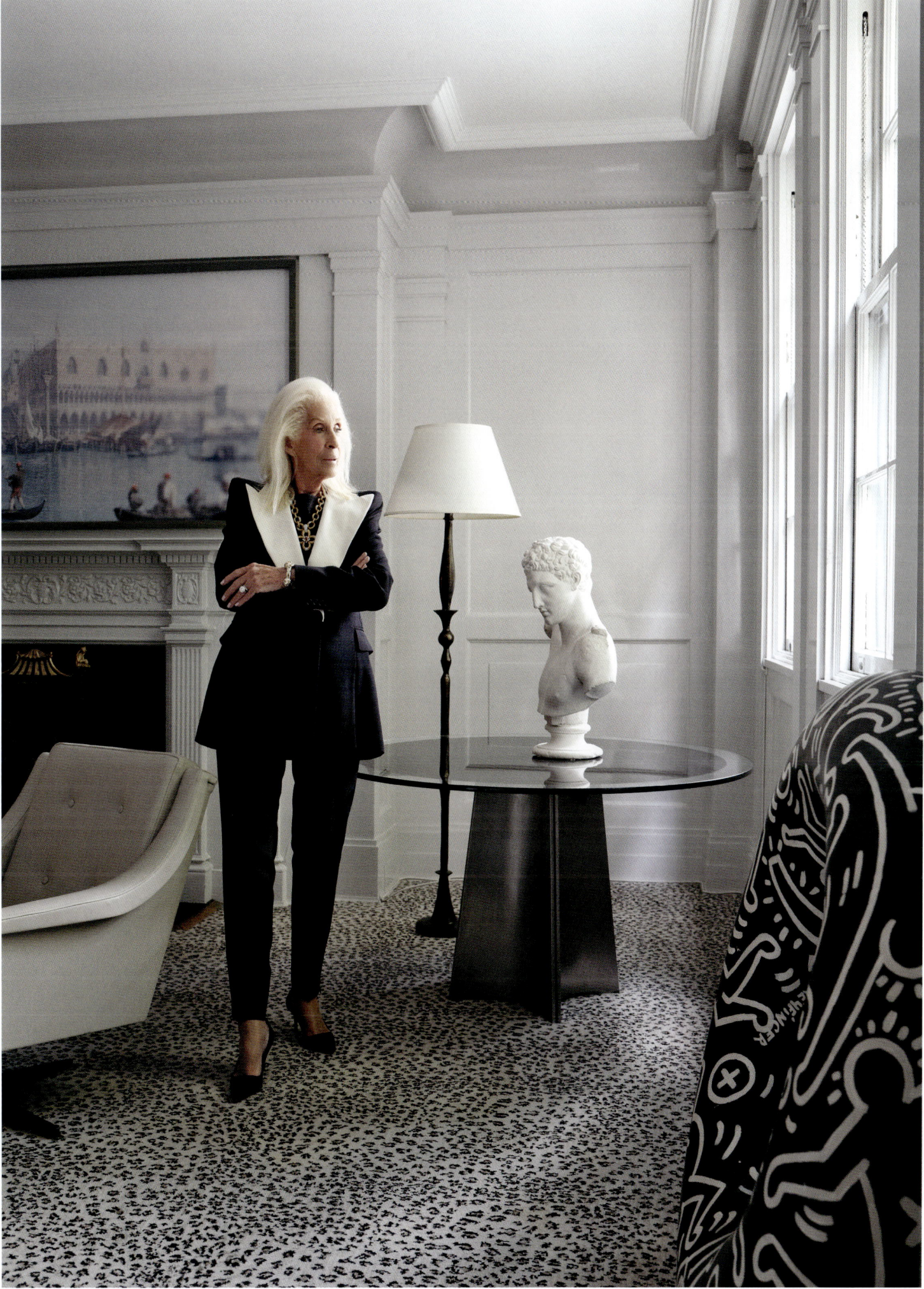

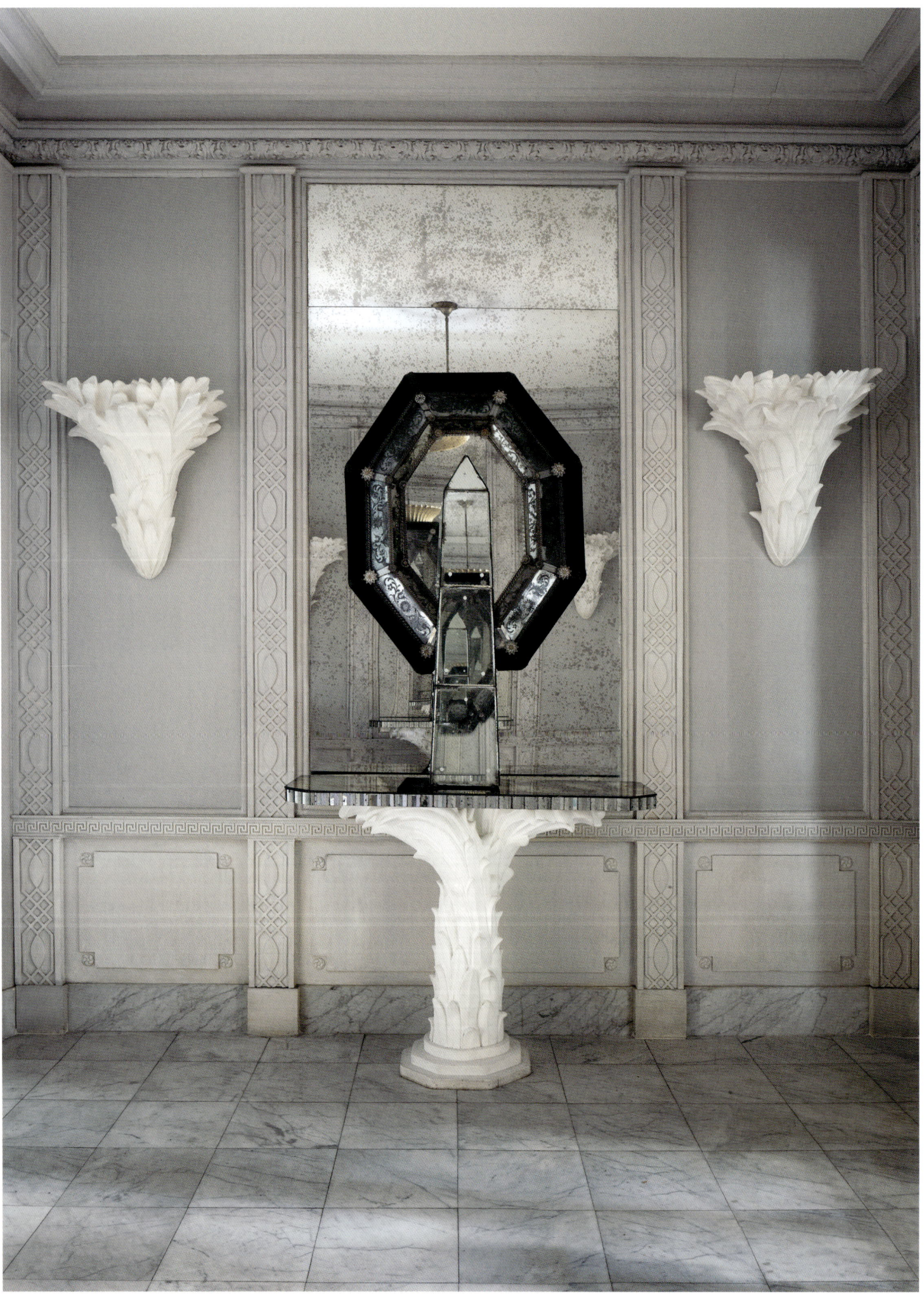

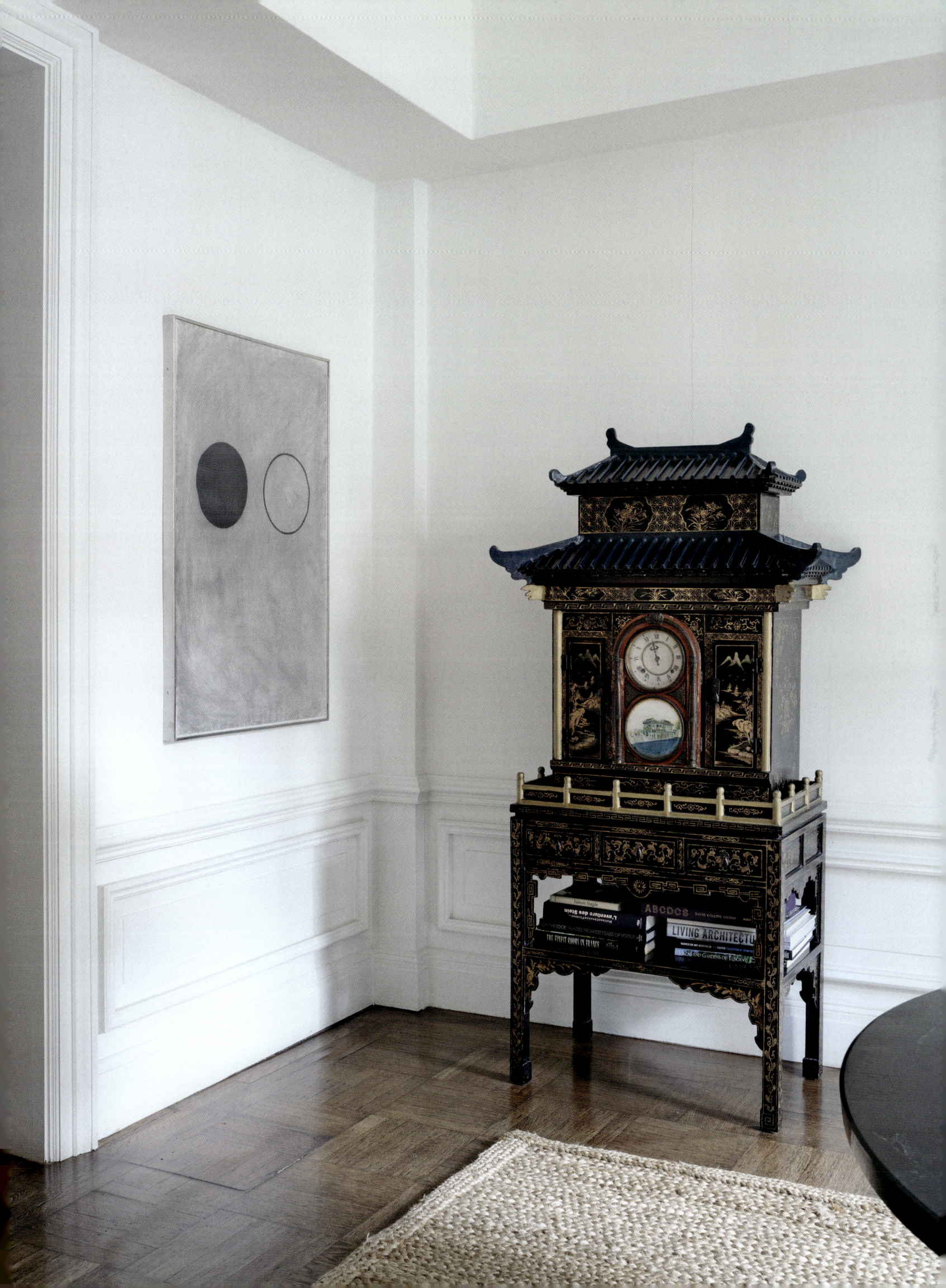

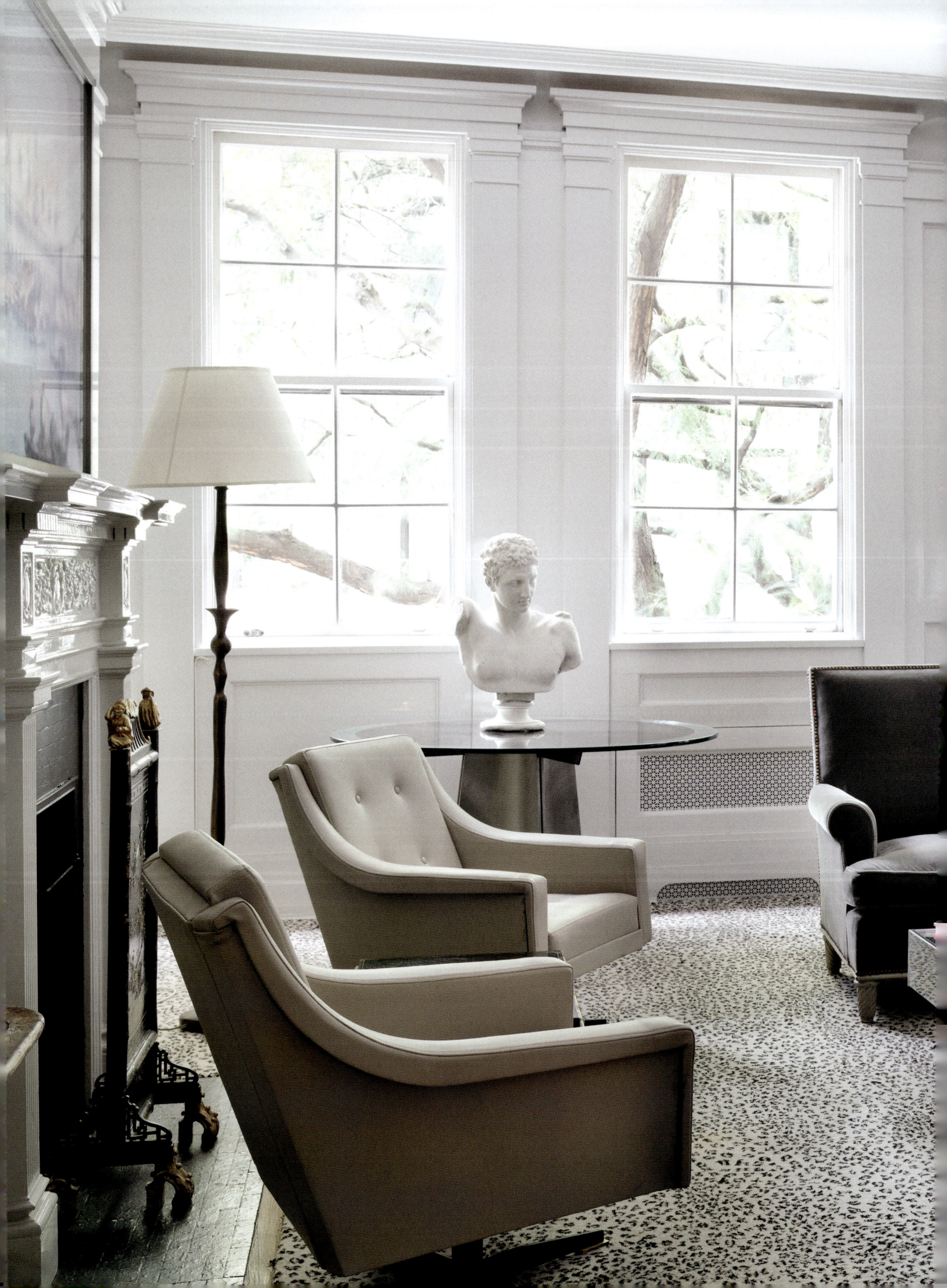

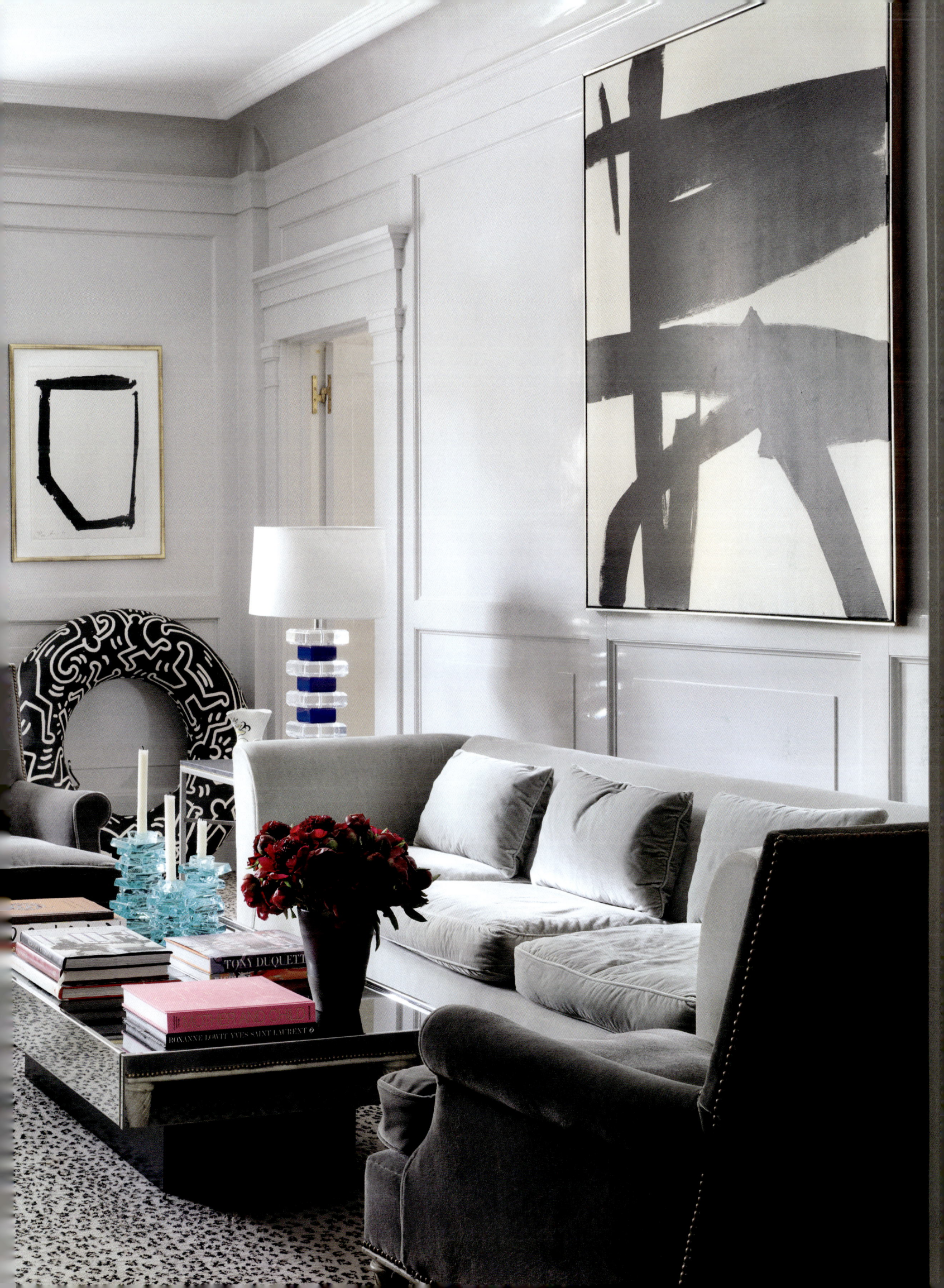

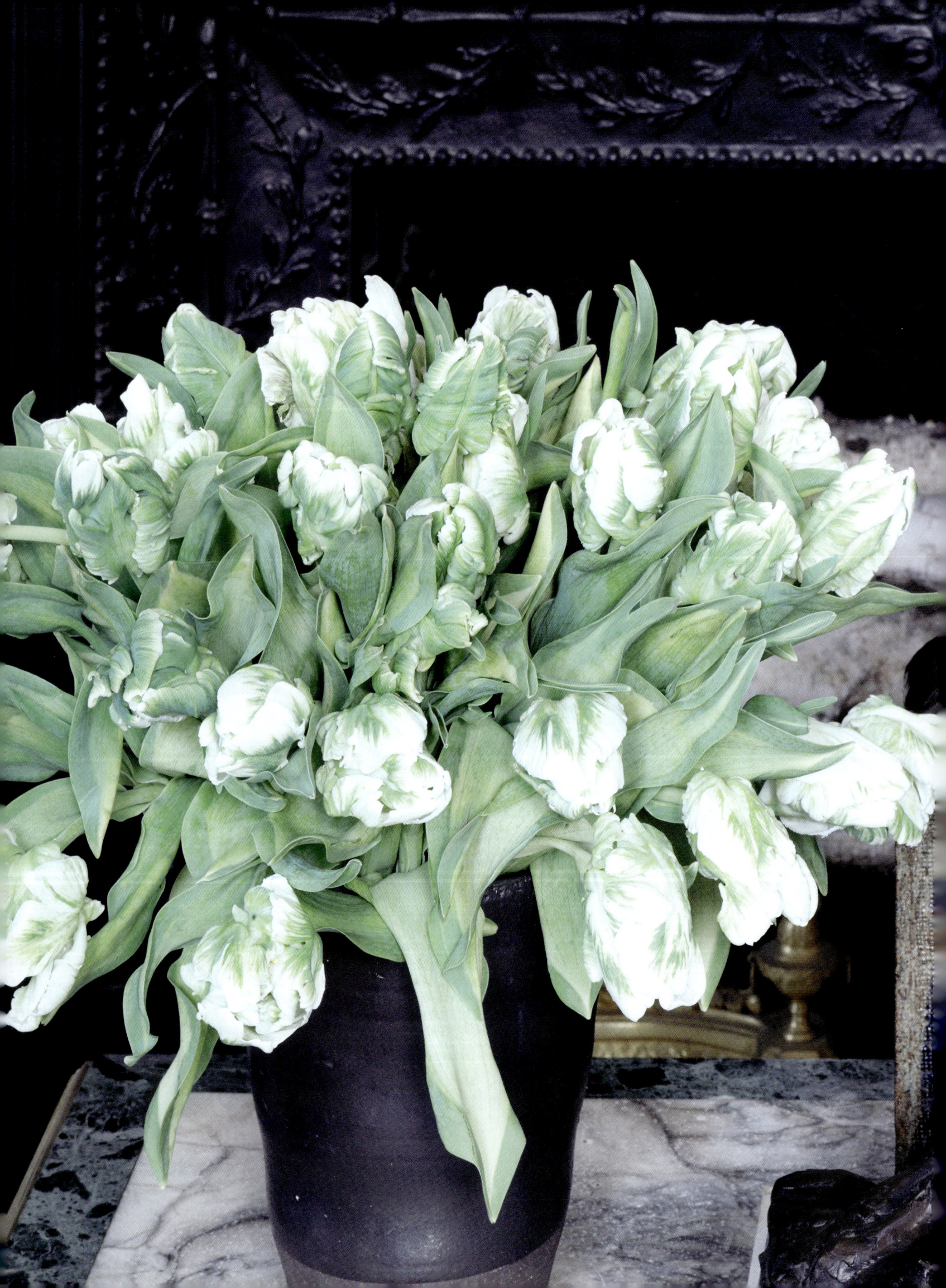

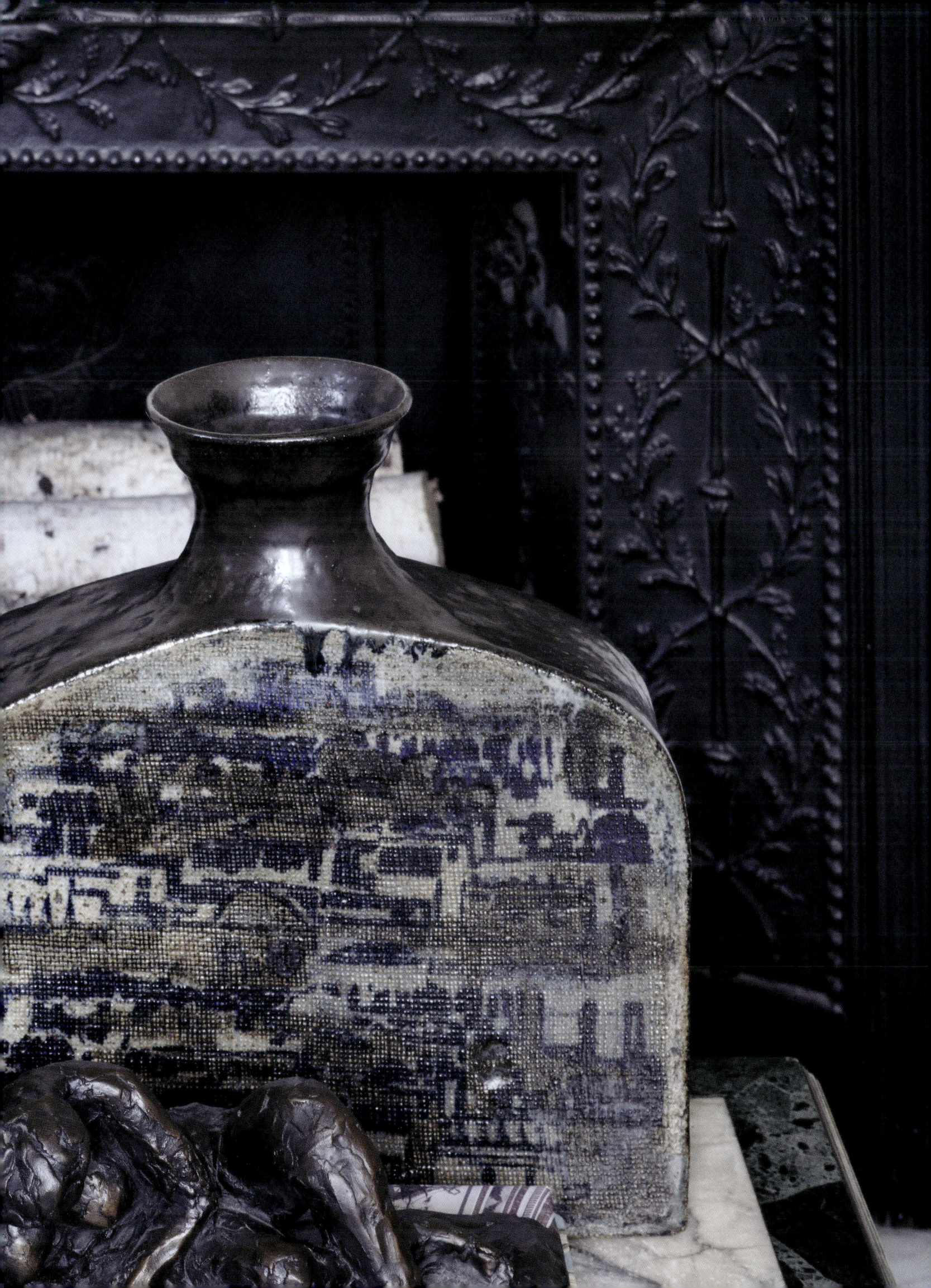

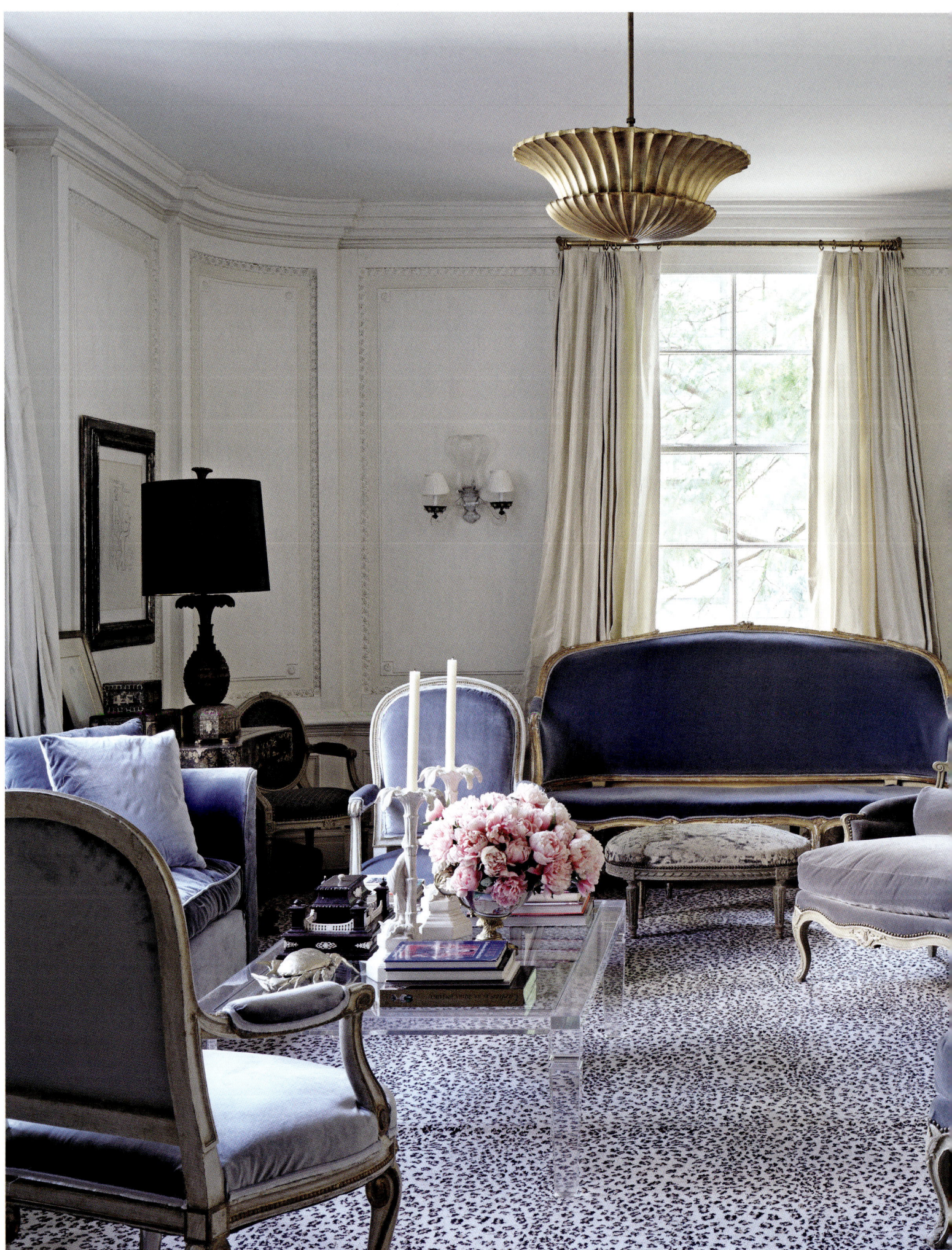

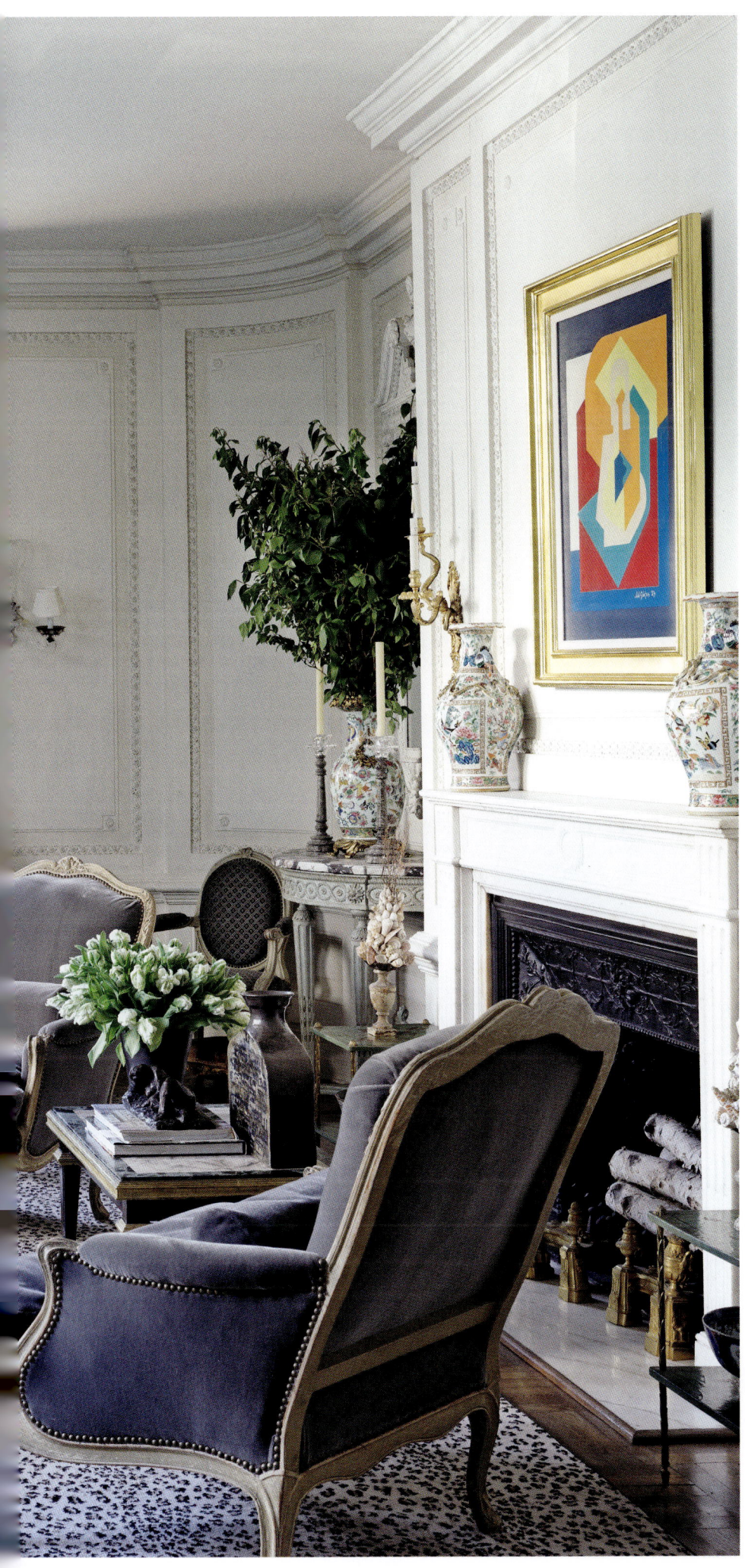

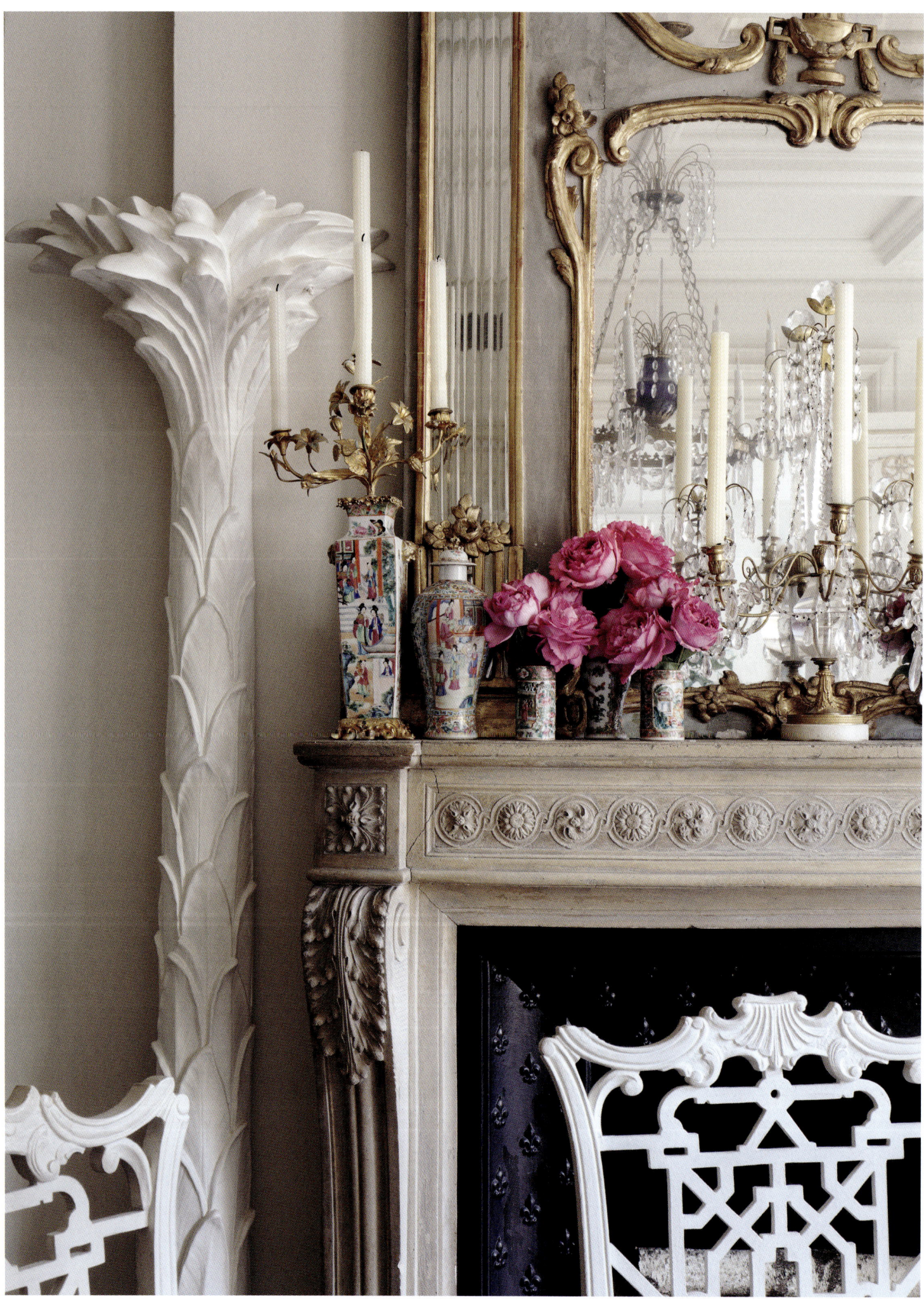

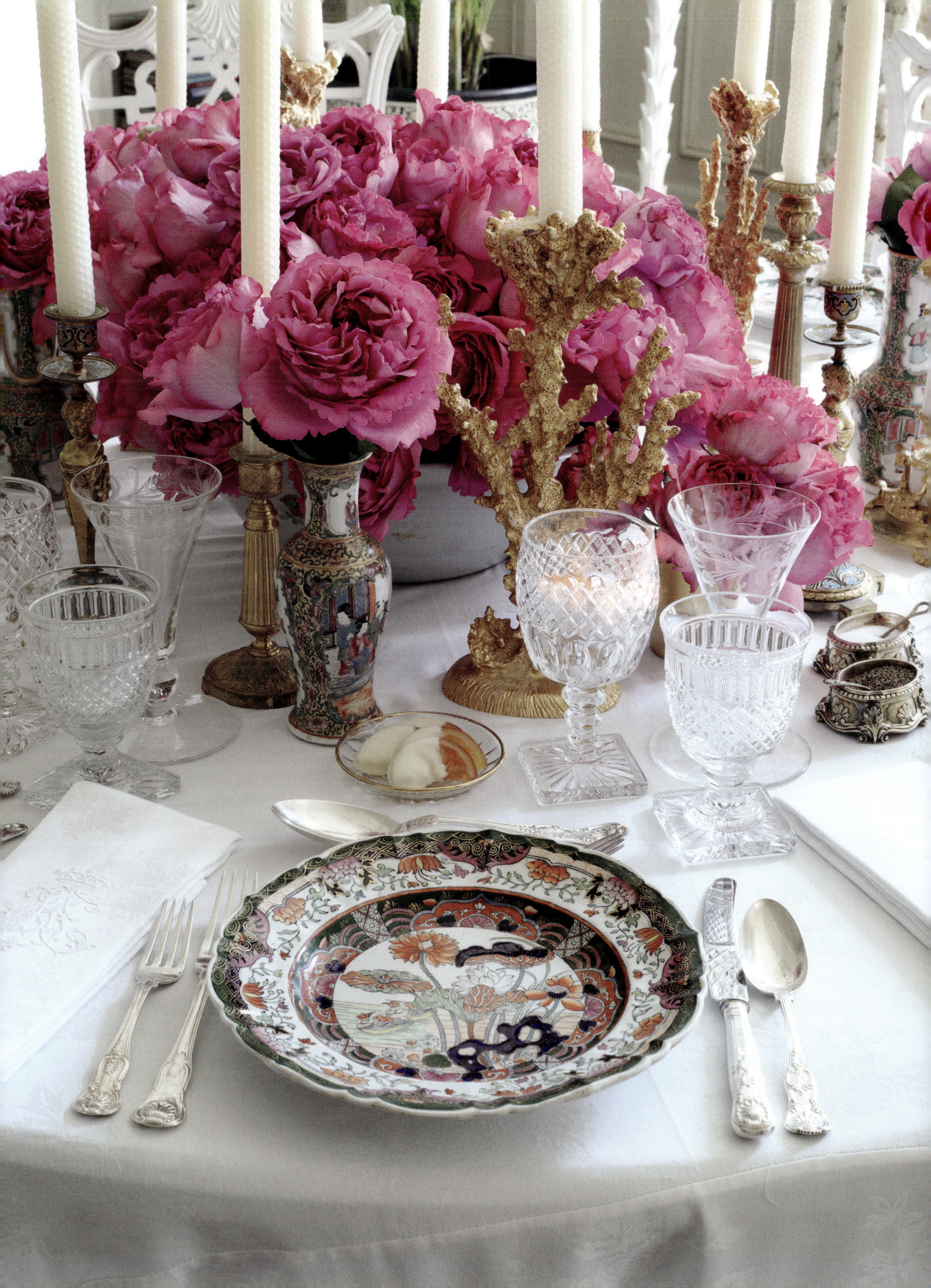

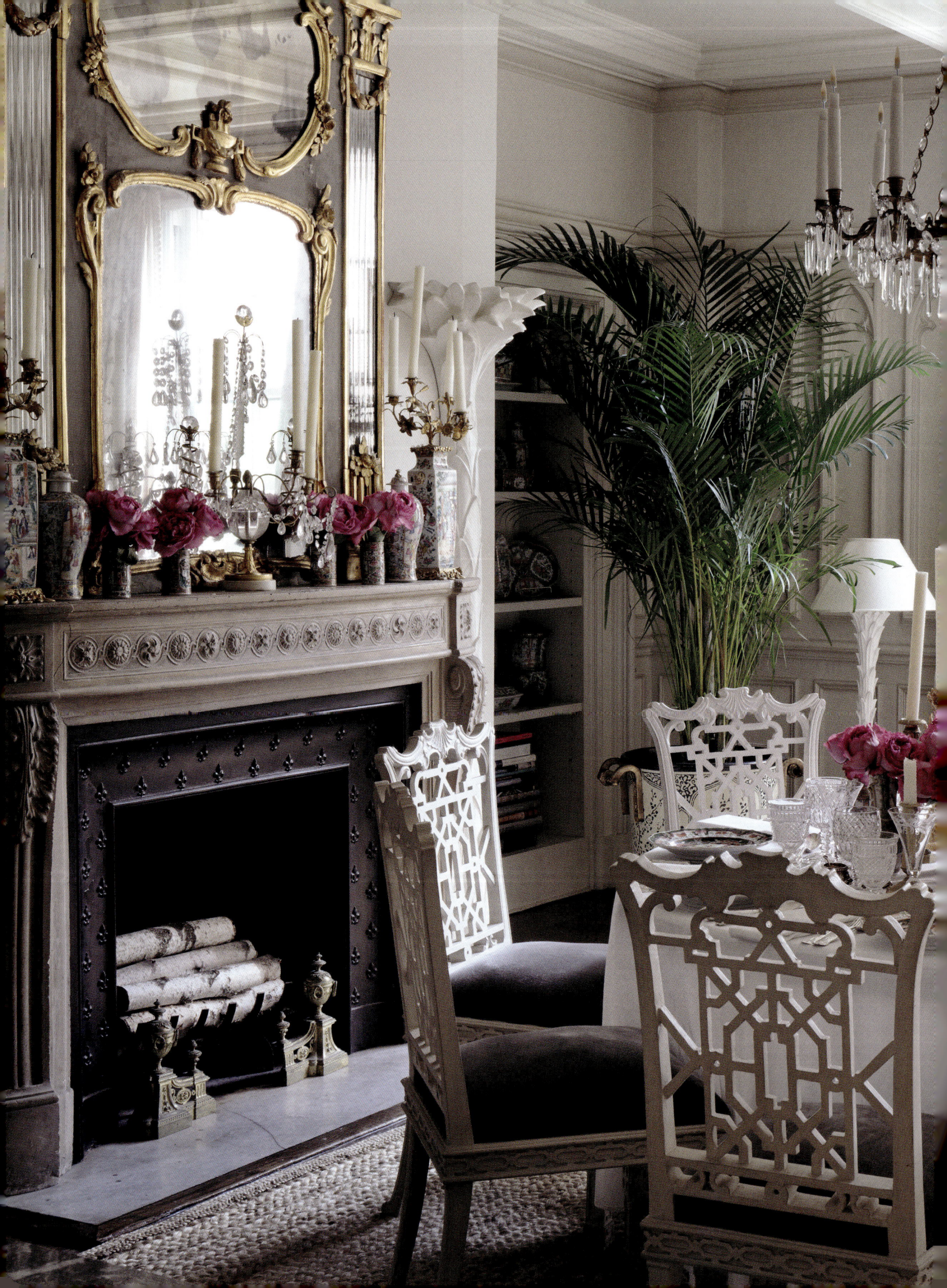

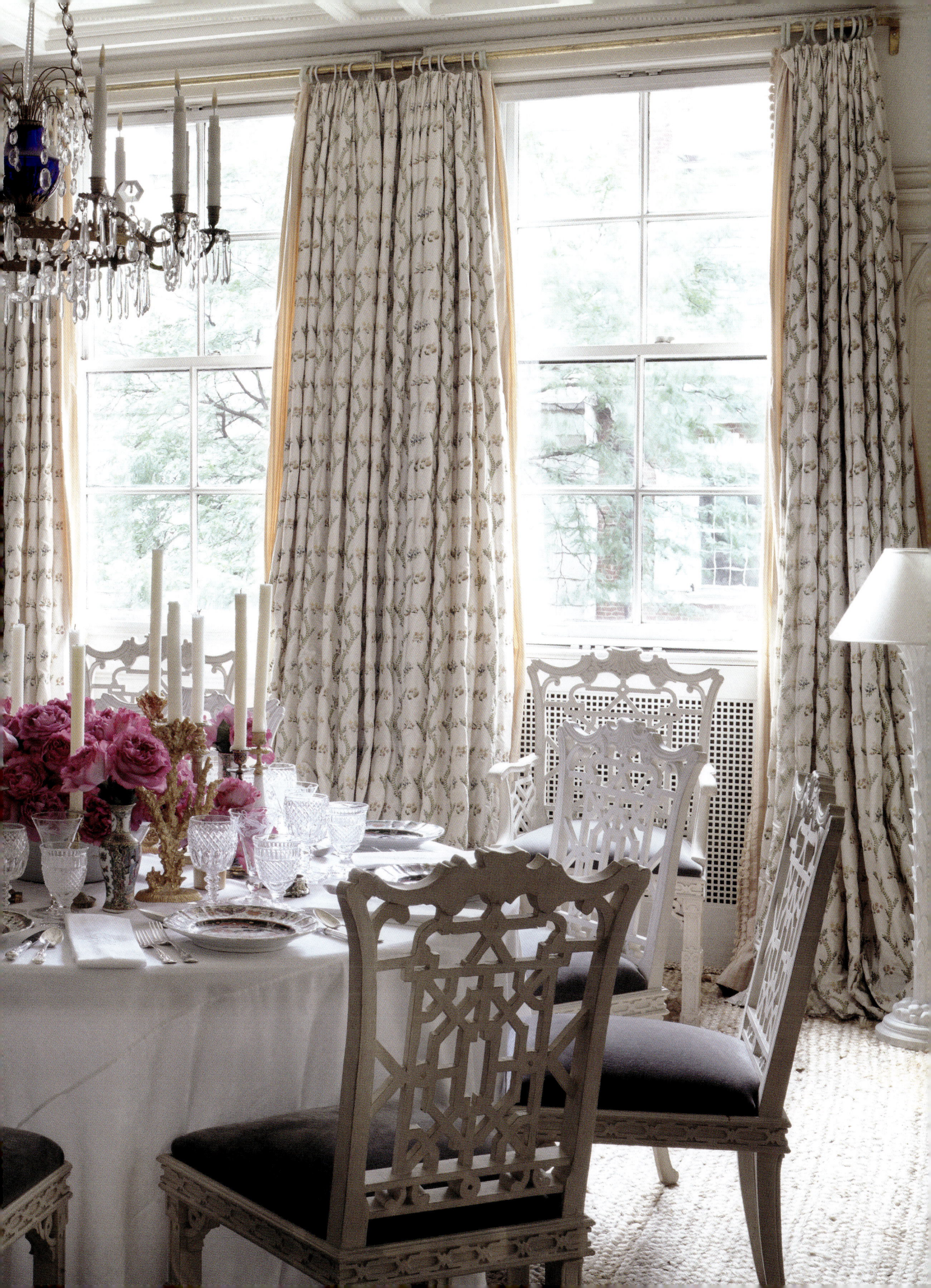

MAN ABOUT TOWN

WILL KOPELMAN

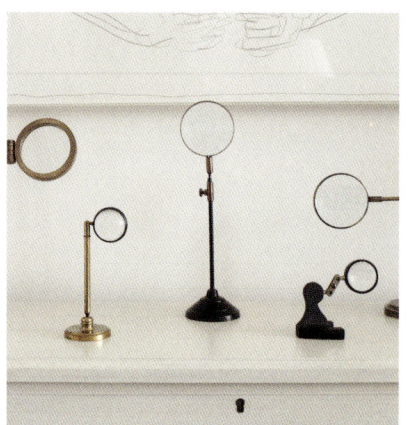

Many landmark buildings on New York's Upper East Side represent the early glory days of Manhattan, where the grand, pre-war condos were built in the economic boom of the 1920s, mostly by the five major architectural firms of the day. They were designed to be "contained homes," so architects didn't skimp on materials, ceiling height, or scale. This particular building was completed in 1918 and is a solid construction of steel, brick, and concrete, with great details and moldings throughout. As a result of this old-world construction, I don't hear my neighbors and they don't hear me (or the kids!).

Most New York apartments of this period had kitchens that were essentially the original service quarters; they are a small afterthought in comparison to the living spaces. Homeowners rarely cooked themselves; meals were staff-served to the dining room. All of this changed with the invention of the television, and suddenly families started eating in their living rooms to collectively watch TV programs. Now, many kitchens are designed to be the centerpiece of the home—mine included—and we spend a lot of time here. I love cooking, so a livable

kitchen/family room in the apartment was of the utmost importance, and I knew I wanted certain special inclusions, like a big La Cornue range and a wine cellar.

To facilitate this, I teamed up with architect Gil Schafer, who I had recently met at a wedding and we fast became friends; I have a huge passion for classic American architecture, and we are both rabid sticklers for detail. Gil and I worked to combine the existing kitchen, formal dining room, and laundry to create one big communal space. The floors are all original—a mixture of quarter-sawn oak, and the trim is a combination of cherry wood, oak, and pine—so I simply re-varnished them with a clear coat and then ebonized the rest. The metal-framed glass doors have become a significant design point in the apartment; I often work in the living room and wanted to be able to see the kids wherever they were playing.

I was born and raised on the Upper East Side and have always loved New York, but what carries the most meaning for me now is that my girls are playing in the same area of Central Park as I did when I was their age. My parents still live here, and my sister and her family too, and I moved back from LA and found this apartment about eight years ago. I fell for the soft whites and natural earth tones, and just added to it over time, trying to achieve a sweet spot between maximalism and minimalism. What is meaningful for me is utility … beautiful designs always have superior functionality, and that's always been the cornerstone of my approach.

In my work I love collaborating with people over their art collections. Every single piece should contextually reflect art that came before it or have significance that links to when and where it was created, so I prefer to look at collecting through a wider lens rather than focus on any one period. Buying objects you love should be instinctual. My instinct is eclectic for sure, but I wouldn't have it any other way. People like Albert Barnes understood that the sum is greater than its parts. I love old master paintings, folk art, outsider art, African tribal art, pre-Columbian, Greco-Roman, and Egyptian antiquities, Flemish tapestries … and I mix all of that with some of my favorite contemporary artists. I even have my old motorcycle in my living room—a 1977 Triumph Bonneville 750, made the month and year I was born. It holds a special place in my heart, so I keep it there. To me, if it has meaning, it stays.

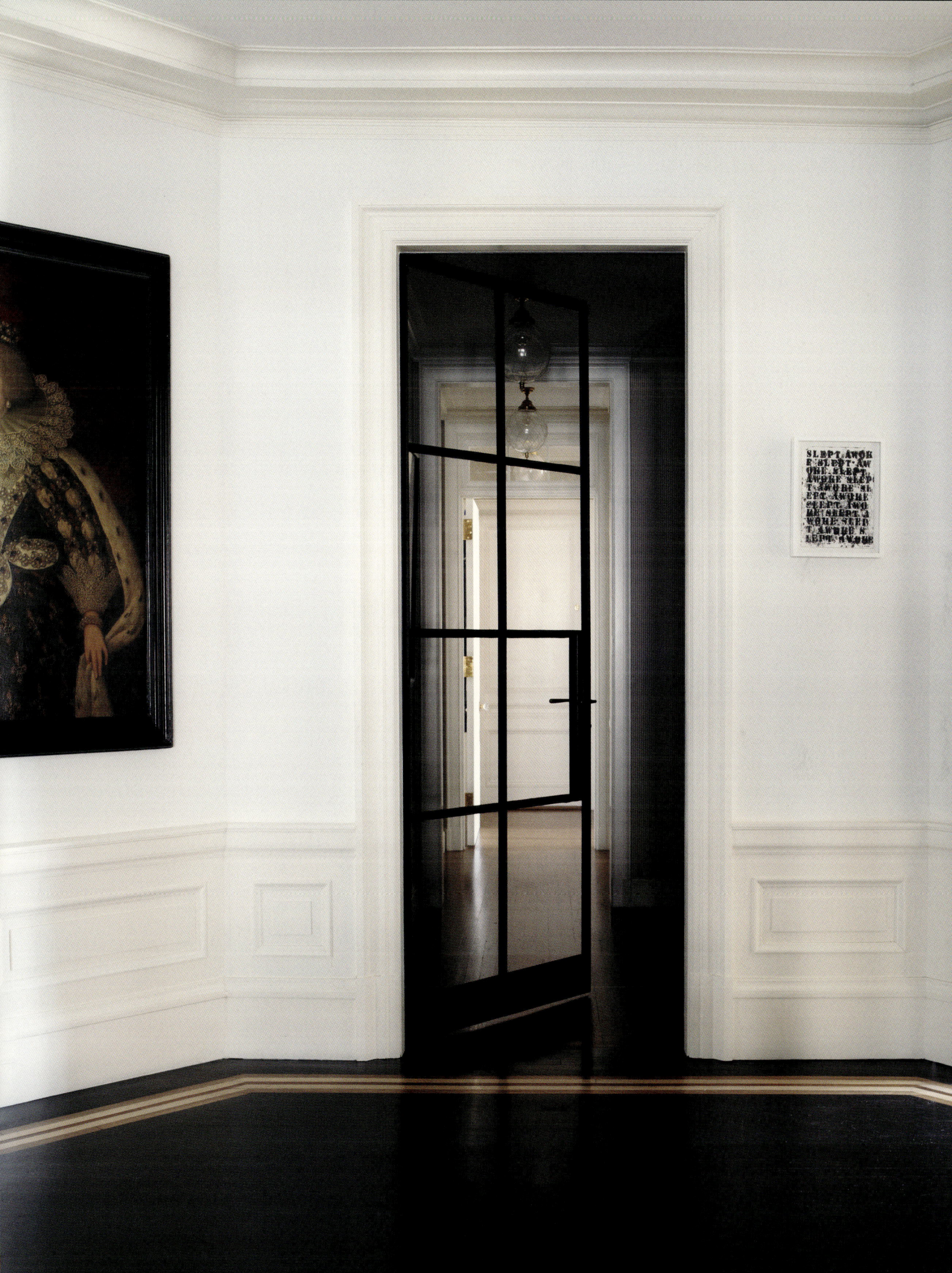

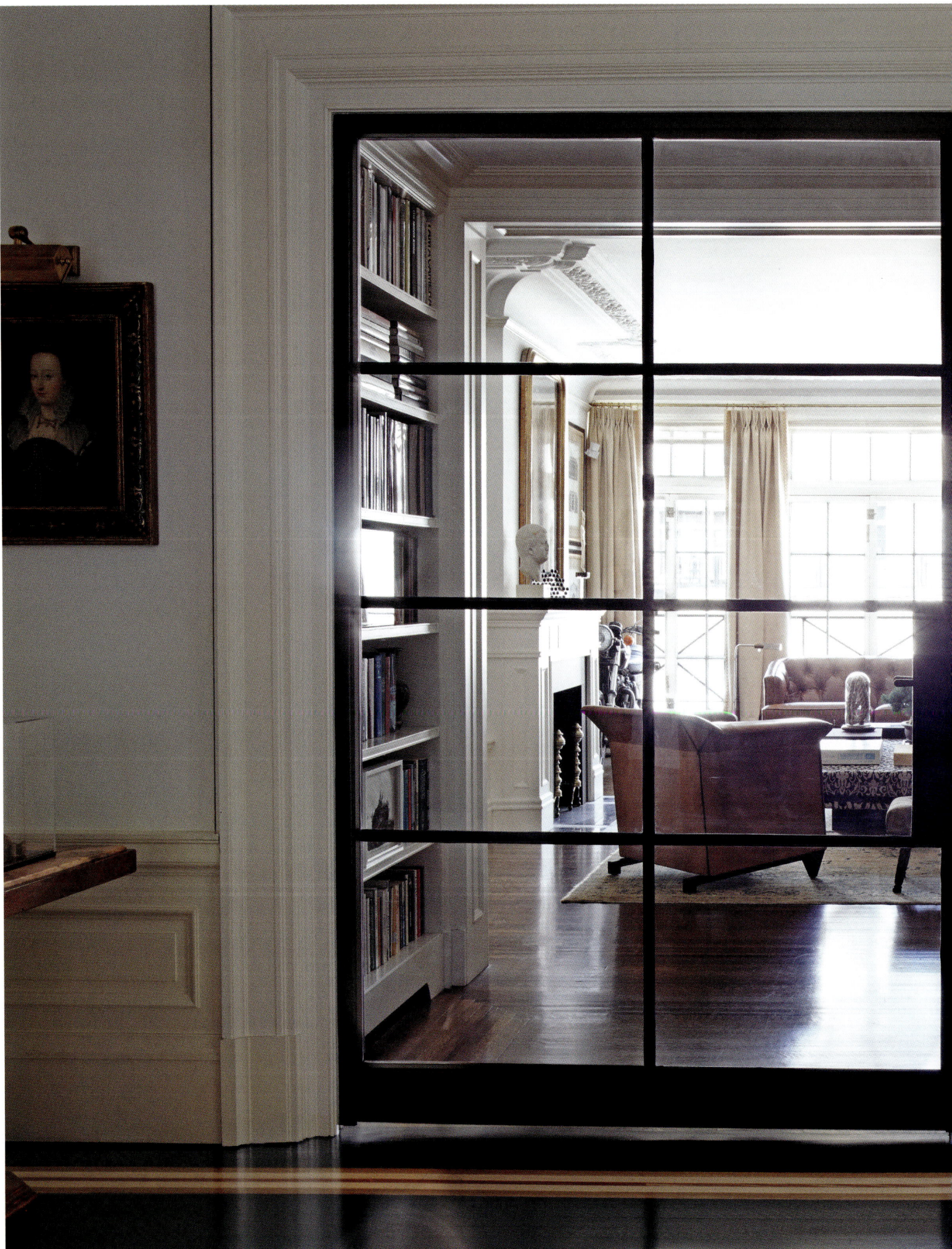

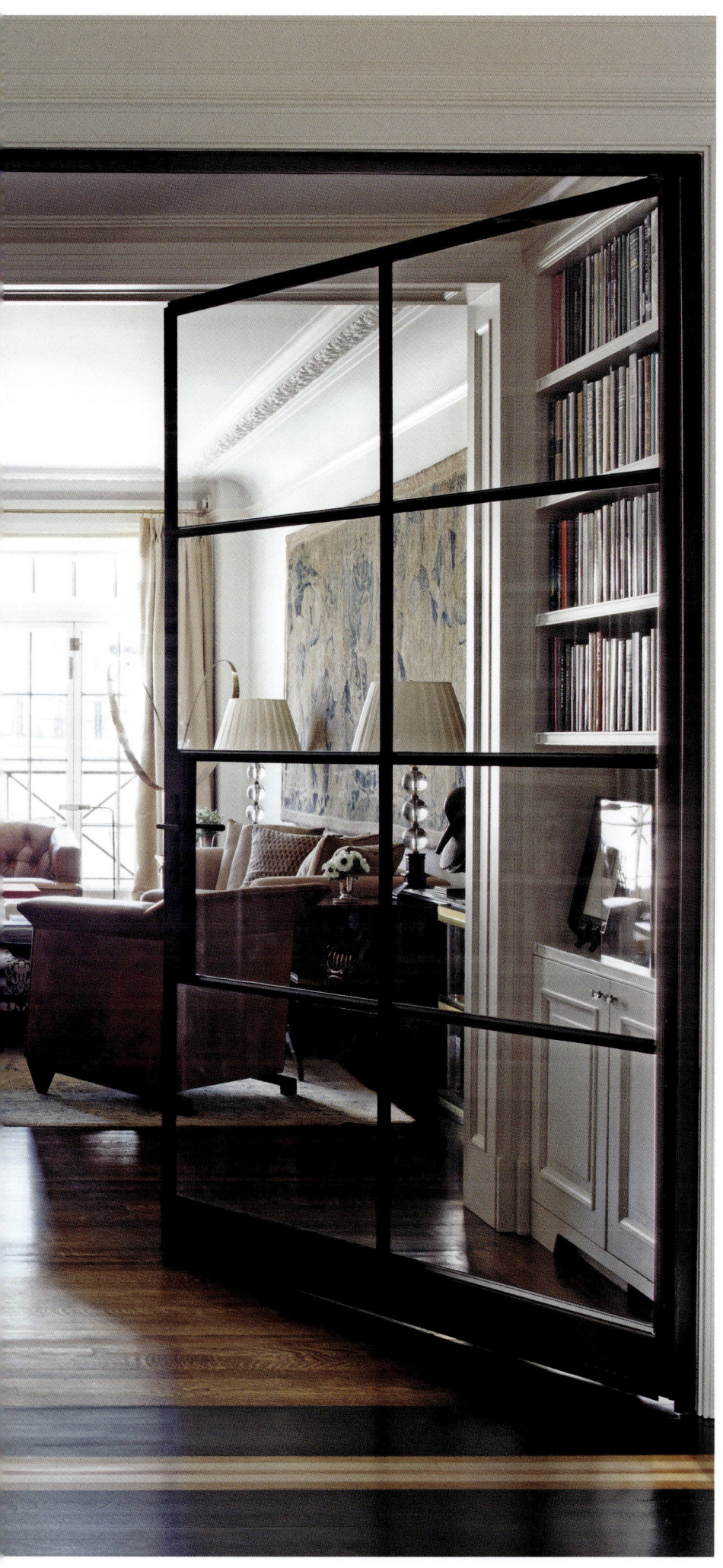

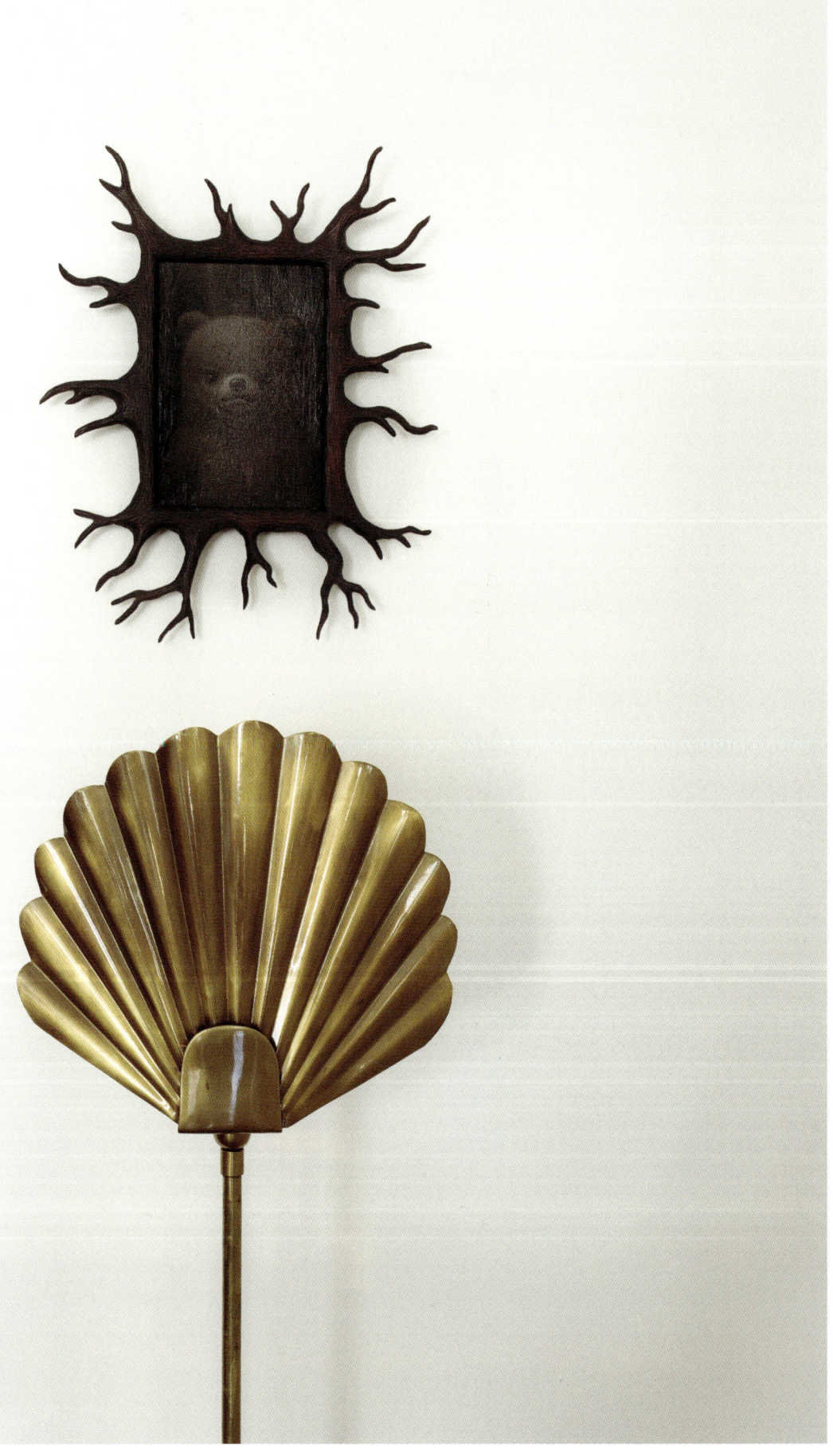

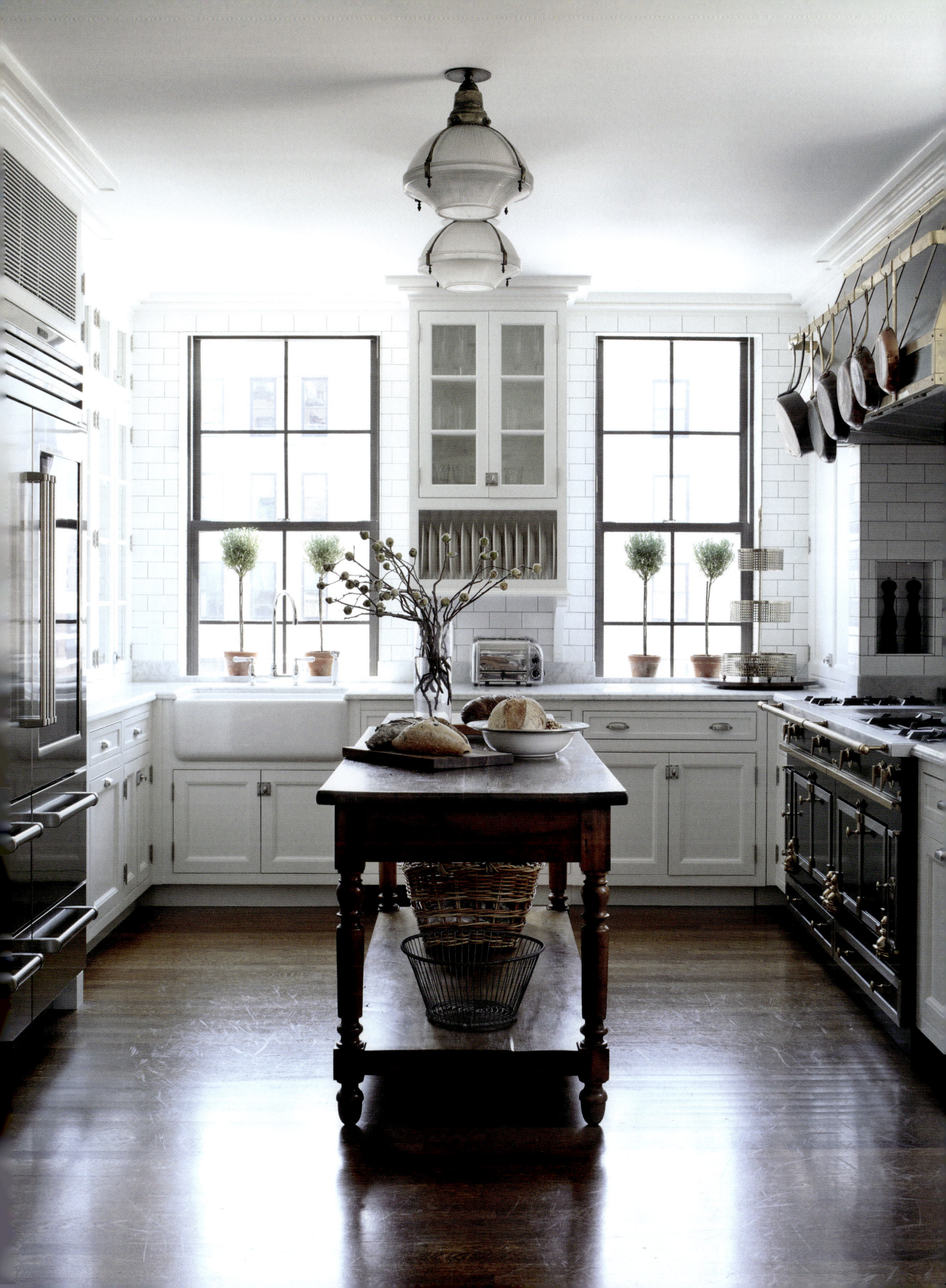

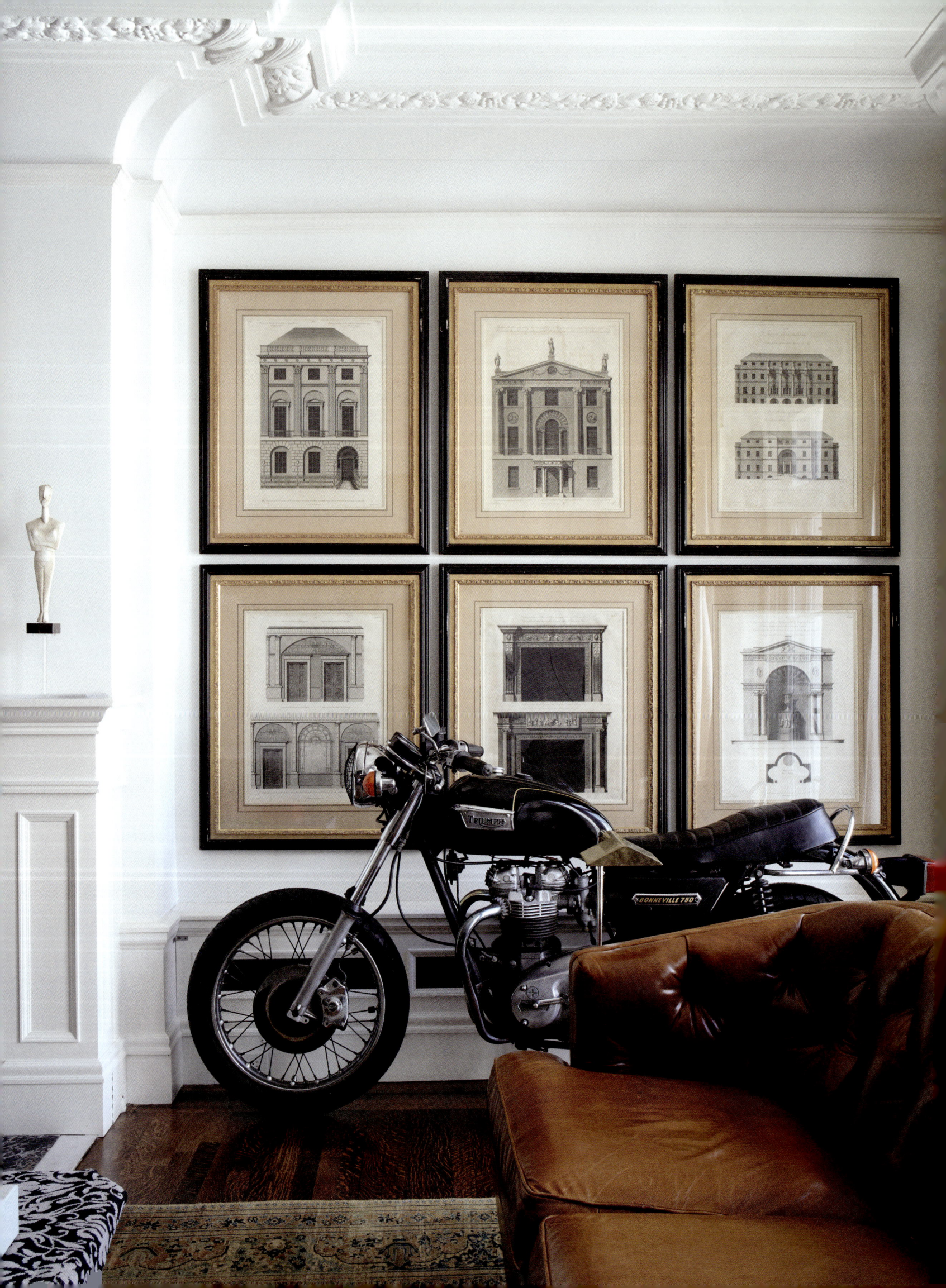

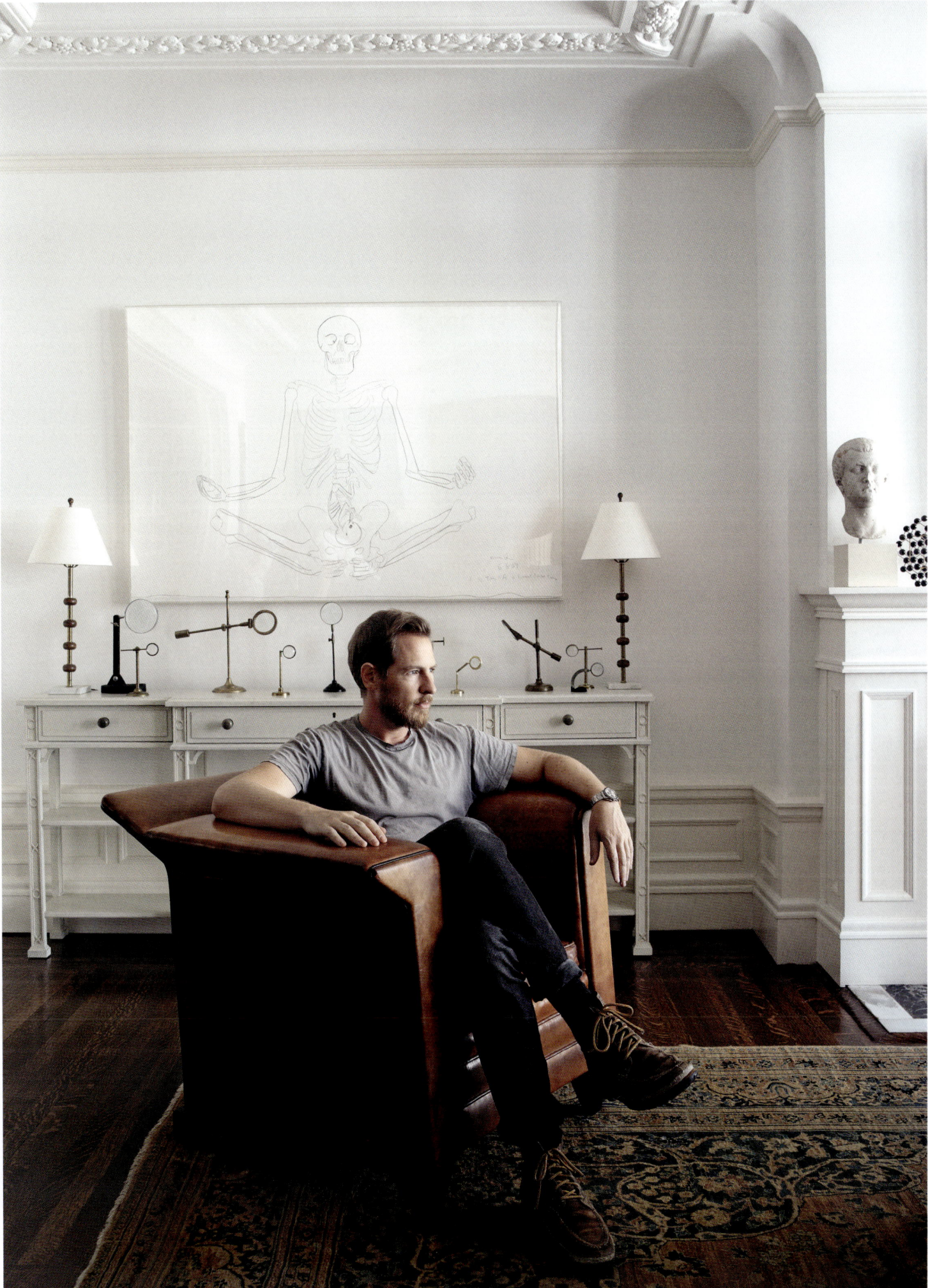

UNDERSTATED GRANDEUR

AERIN LAUDER

I have lived in New York most of my life and this city will always feel like home. Traveling with my parents as a child, and spending time in Europe in particular, opened my eyes to the fact that not everything is centered on New York, but also helped me to see America with a renewed appreciation whenever we returned. All the moving around reinforced in me that importance of home.

The first time I set foot in this apartment, sunlight was streaming through the tall casement windows and I fell in love with its old-world New York charm. For me, light is the most important element in any space. It brings warmth and life, while the play of shadows, as the light moves around a room, introduces a constantly changing energy. Back then, I felt I could be happy here, and that was over 20 years ago. We are still here.

I was fortunate enough to work on our apartment with one of my favorite decorators, Jacques Grange. I love the way in which he is able to create an environment that is clean, inviting, and livable, all while utilizing the room's underlying structure. Jacques has the ability to incorporate color, fabric, and texture to make a space look personal, comfortable, and effortlessly chic, which has made our apartment the special place it is today.

I adore entertaining friends at home; in candlelight, the dark, velvety walls of the dining room set off the gilded furniture and transform the room into a jewel box. While eating out at my favorite restaurants—Majorelle, J.G. Melon, Sette Mezzo—is always a treat, as a family we tend to hang out in the kitchen.

I have always lived with a blue-and-white palette—my grandmother Estée's favorite combination. I love it in every way, shape, and form! The Yves Klein in the sitting room takes center stage as my most-loved artwork because the color blue is so special, while my dressing room is my secret garden. The walls are covered in hand-painted Chinese wallpaper from Gracie—a direct reference to my grandmother.

I still get a thrill every time I walk to the office and see the American flags waving just outside my window and all those skyscrapers lining the streets. It's one of those quintessential Manhattan views. I am here, in the heart of New York, with all this energy around me!

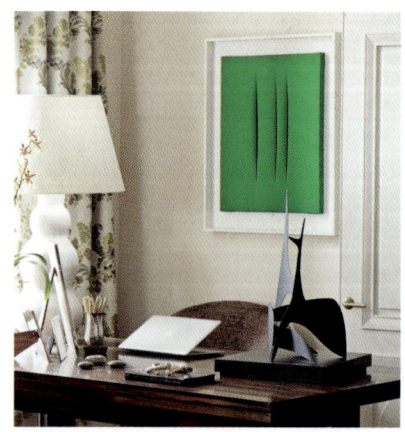

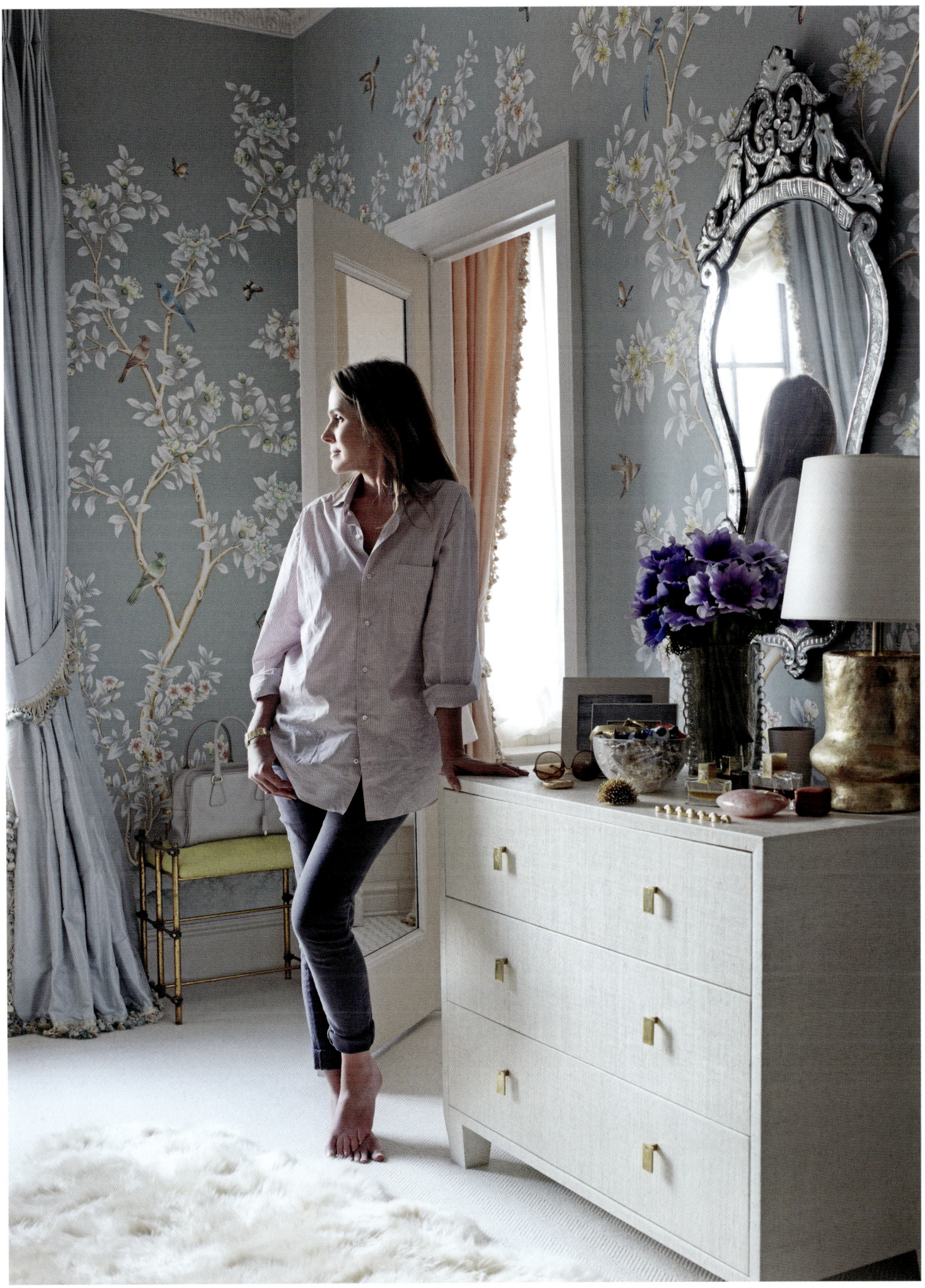

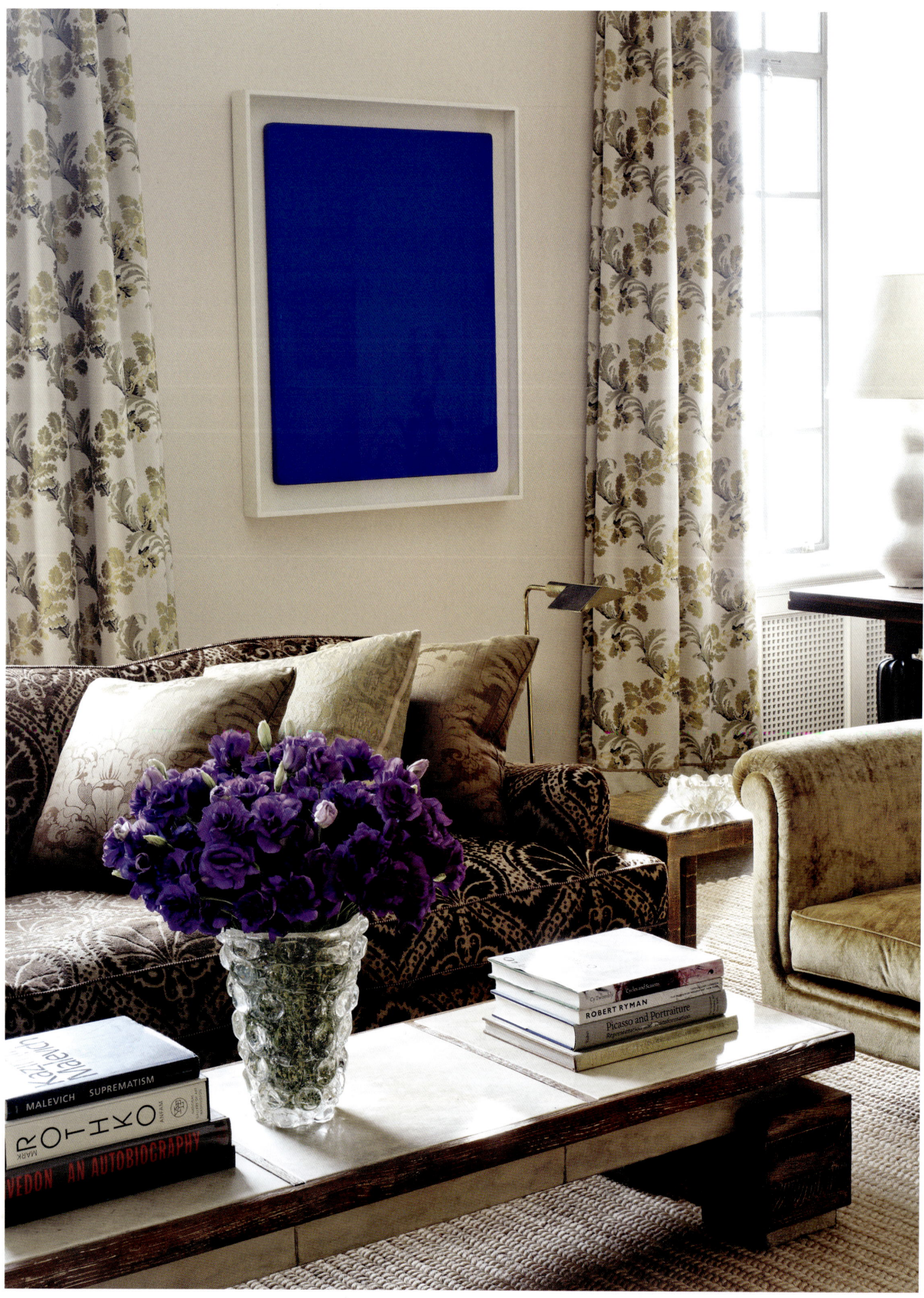

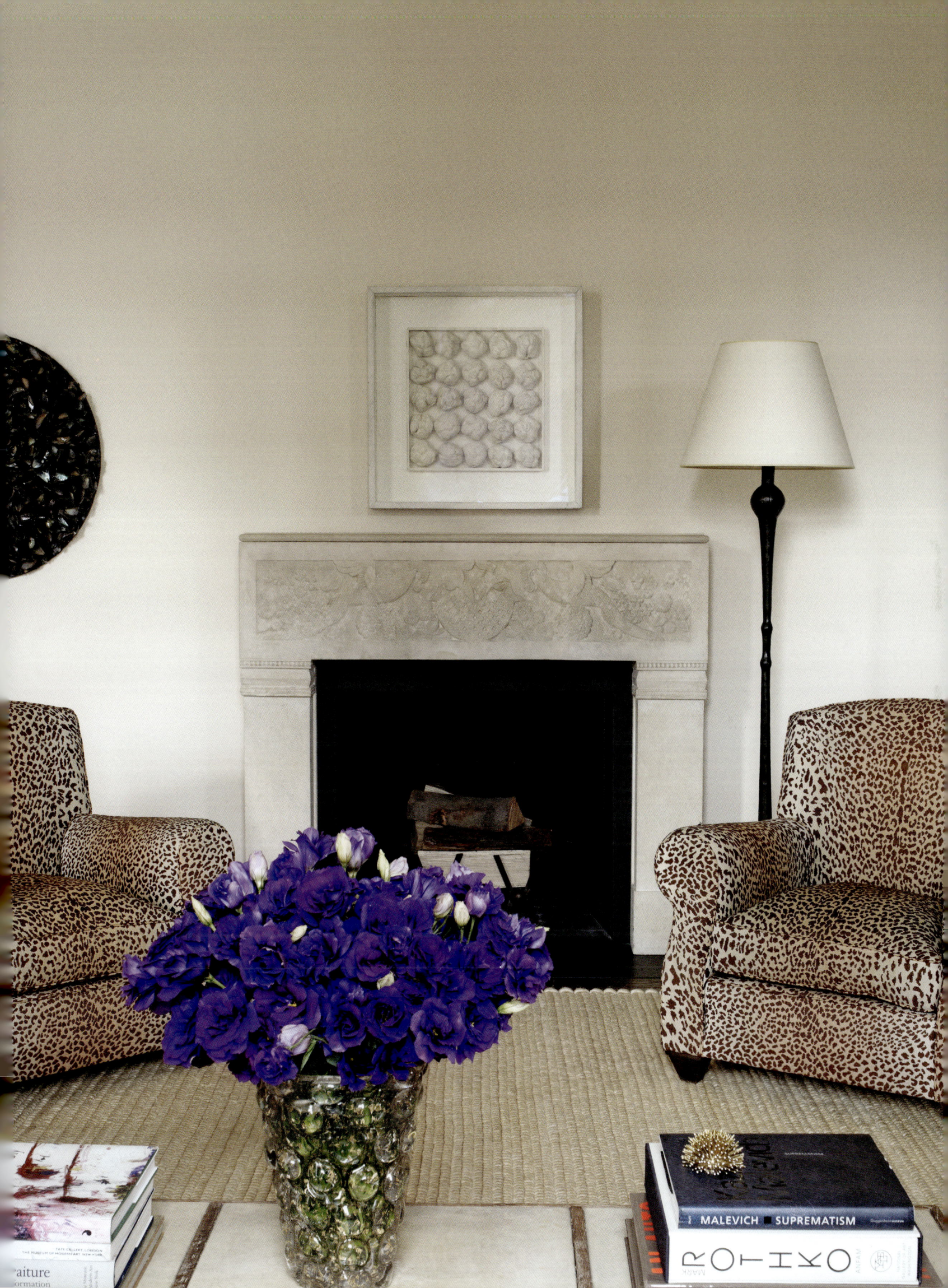

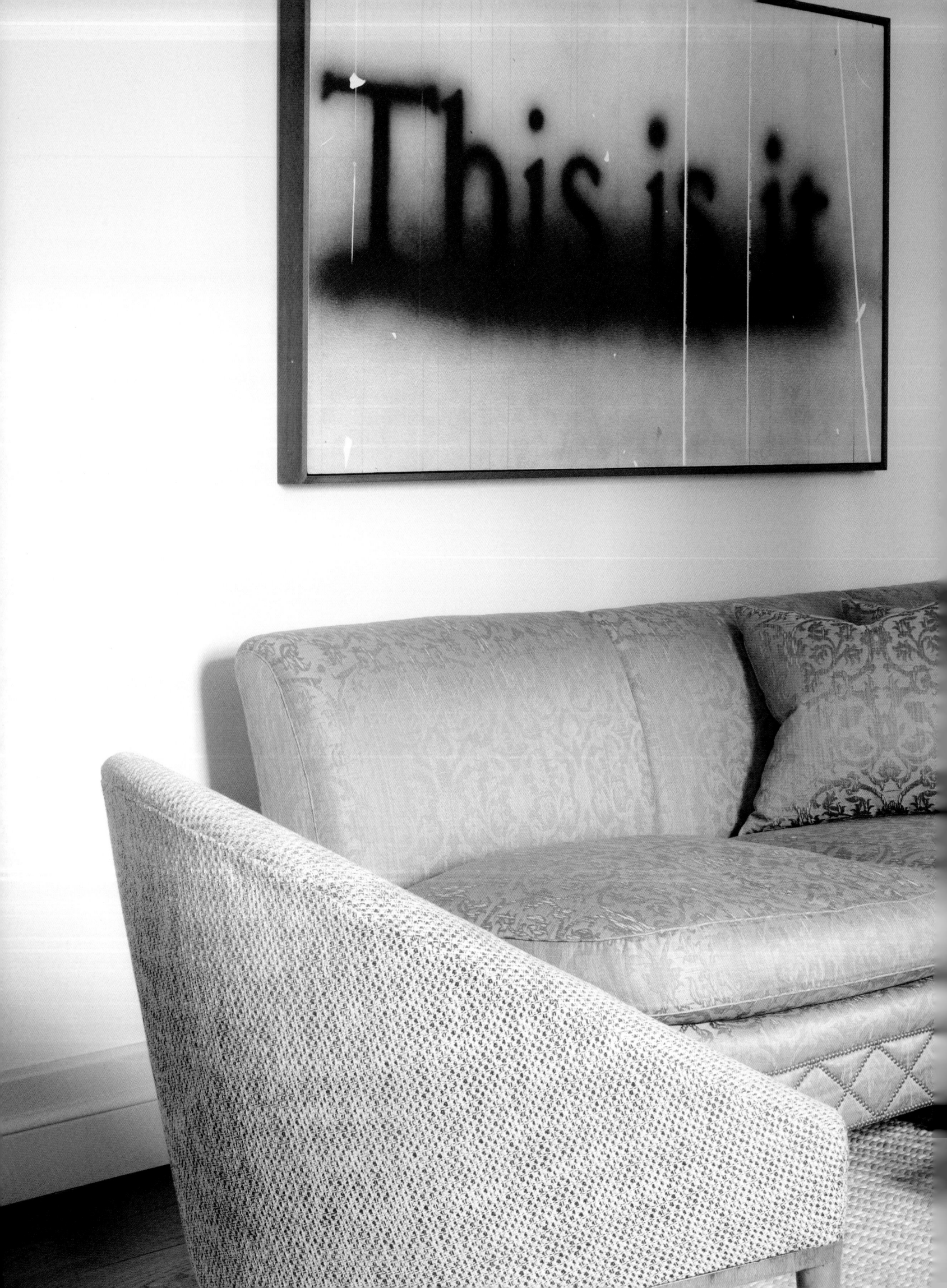

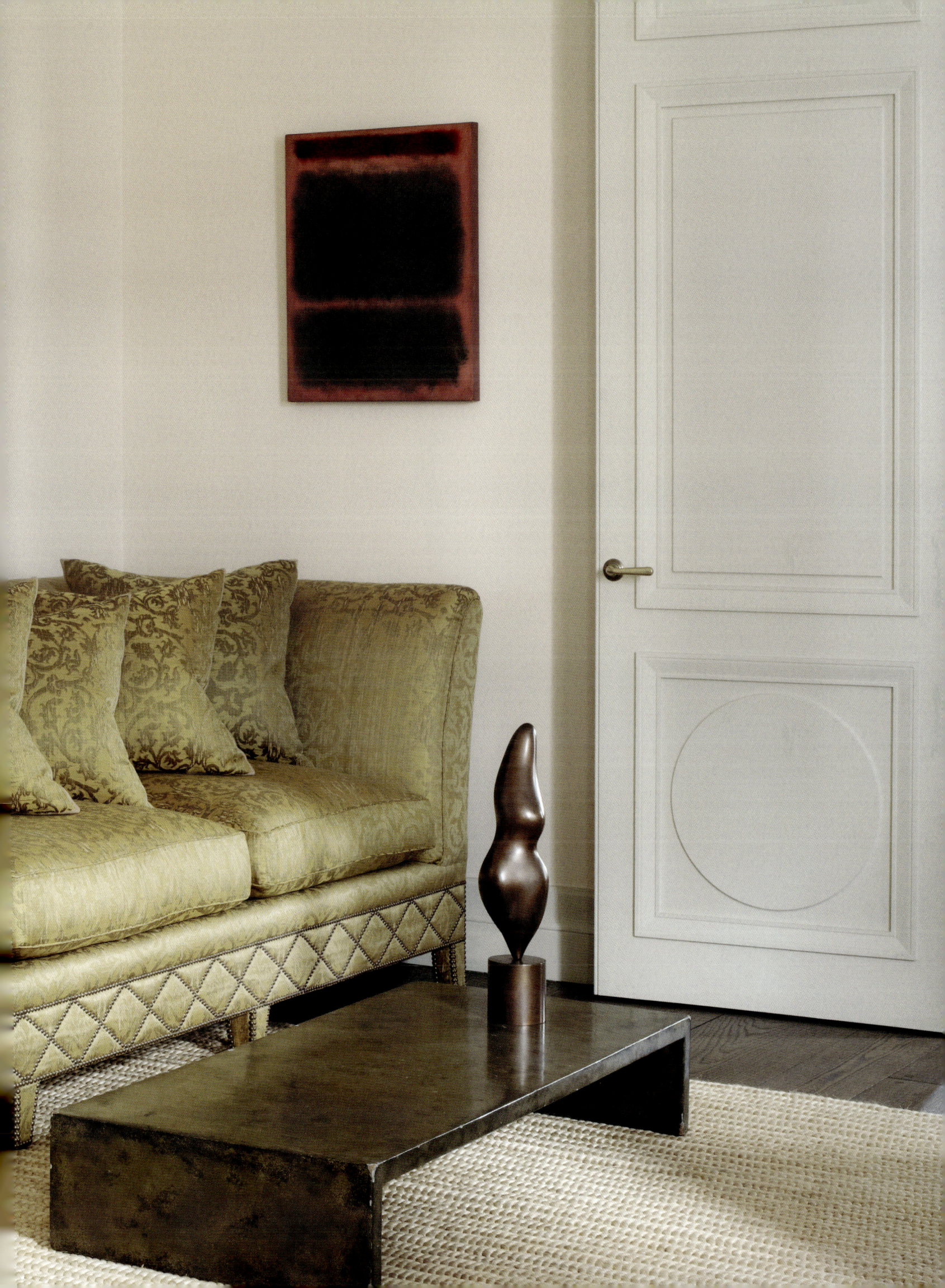

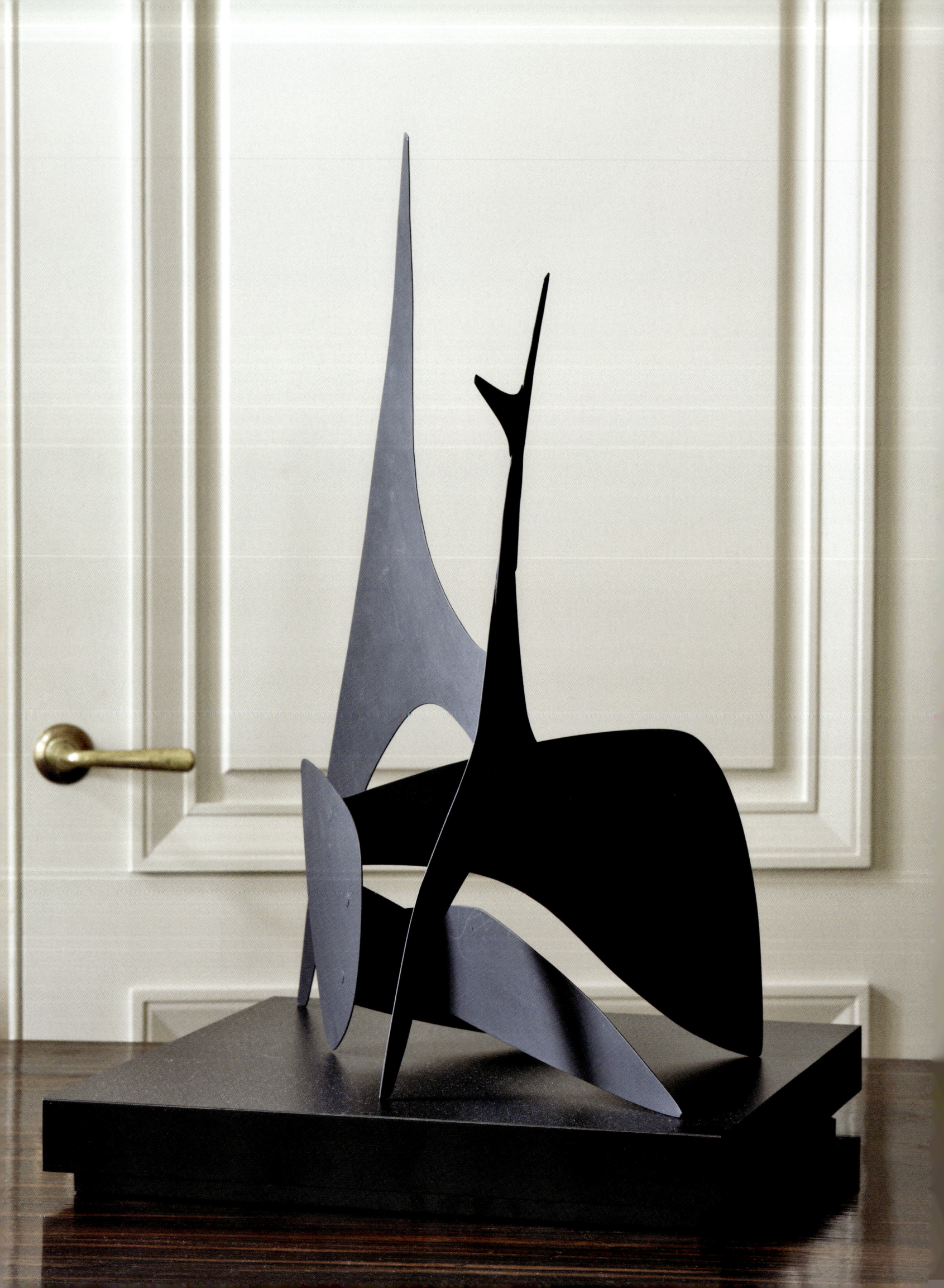

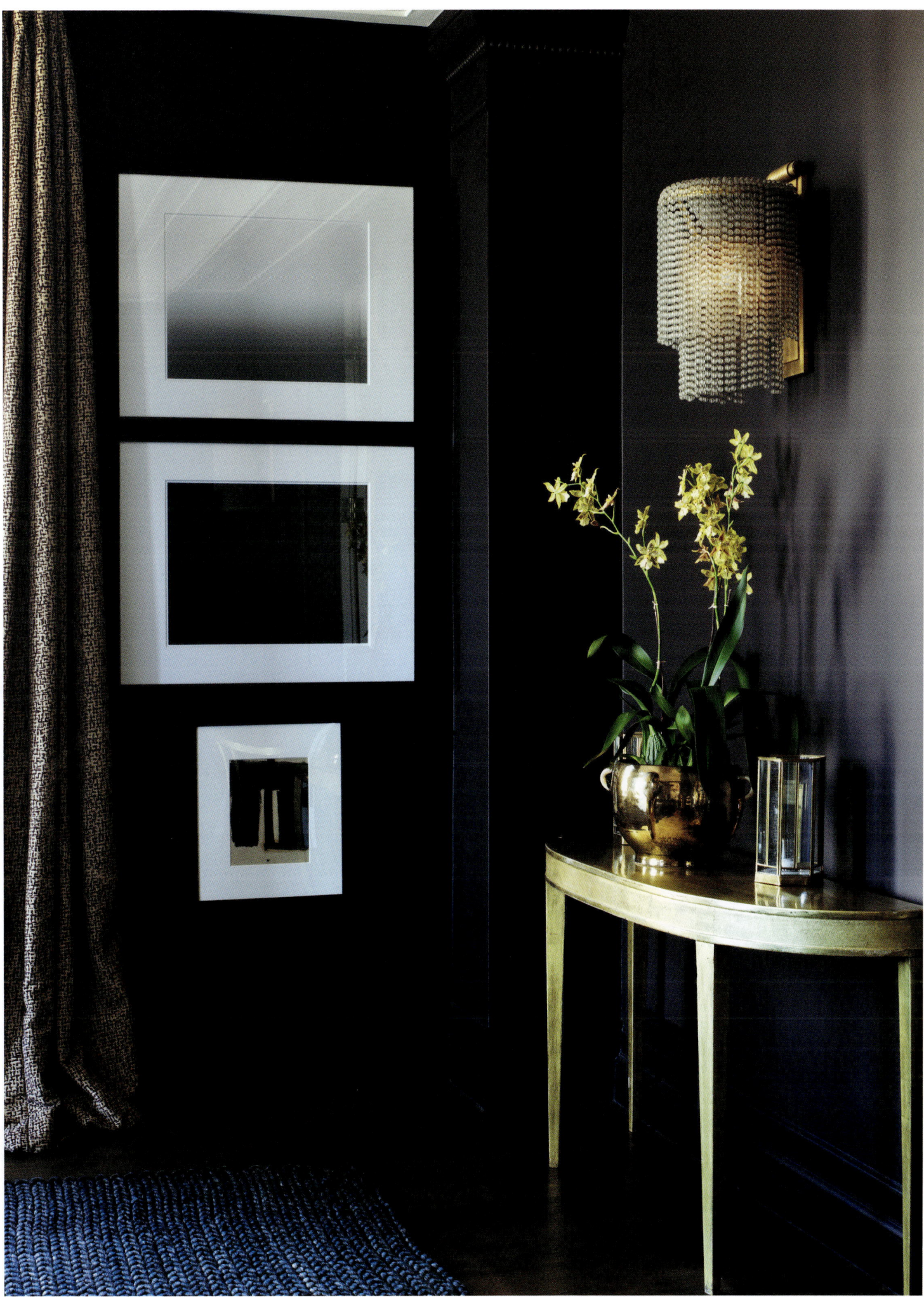

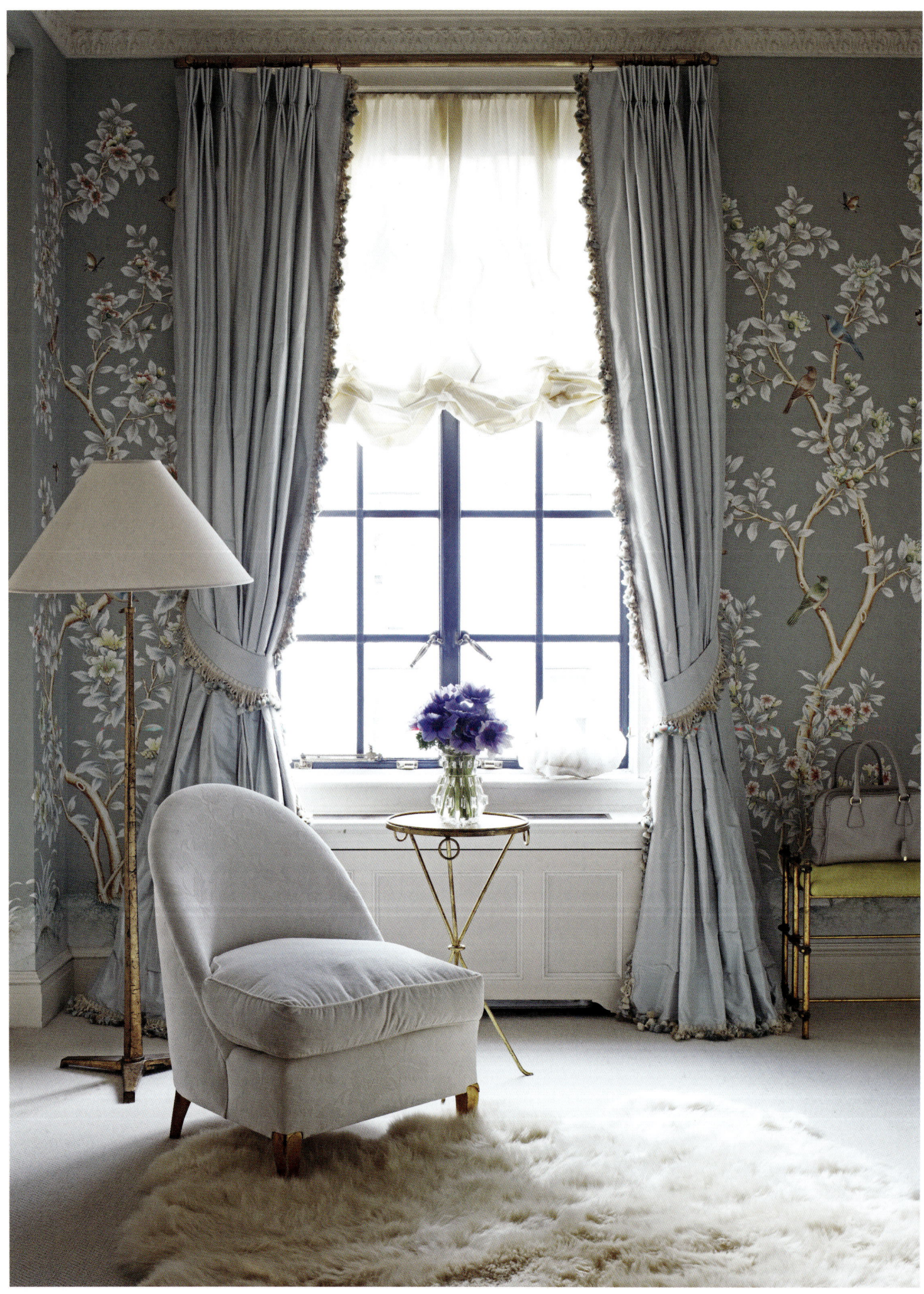

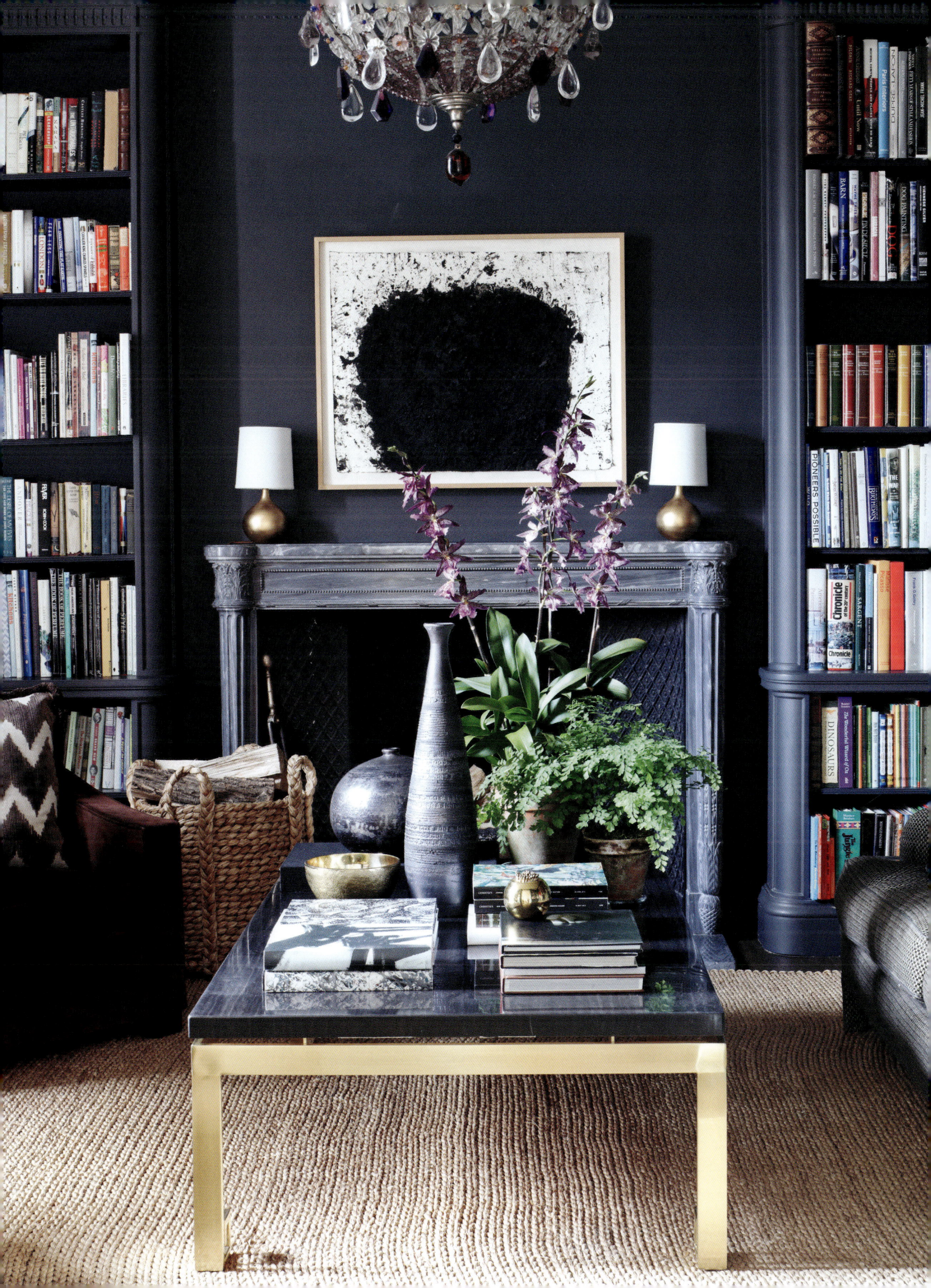

LOFT LARGESSE

TIMOTHY HAYNES & KEVIN ROBERTS

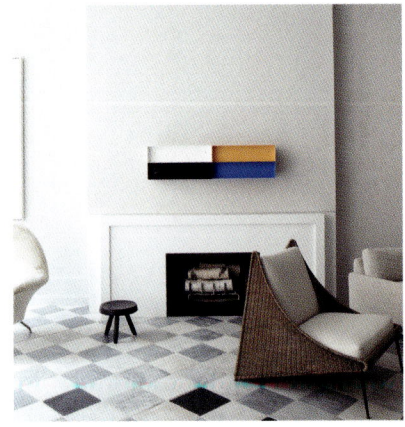

We had been living in a loft in Tribeca for over 20 years, a former factory floor with pigeons flying around, that we transformed with eighteenth-century furniture and 12-foot-high glass French doors. I loved it there, but we really needed more wall space. We are both interested in the history of art and how the architecture and interior spaces of every home we design influence the overall composition of a room. The dialogue we are able to create between art, furniture, and objects is a passion that has a huge impact on our work.

It was inevitable that our ever-expanding art collection would eventually prompt our next move, but trying to replicate a wider version of our Tribeca loft in Downtown Manhattan proved more difficult than we had anticipated. A solution ultimately turned up in the shape of a floor for sale in a historic six-story cast-iron building on Mercer Street in SoHo, built in 1910 and converted in 2000. Tim thought it had definite potential; I wasn't so sure. But there was nothing else on the market at the time that would provide the amount of wall space we were looking for, so we ended up putting in an offer, and planned an extensive gut renovation.

While our names may be synonymous with some of the fabulously luxurious properties that we have been privileged to create for clients, our approach to our own homes has always been quite restrained. We are, neither of us, particularly interested in decoration for decoration's sake. We have a reputation for being sensitive to the character of any location, and our attitude toward our own loft on Mercer Street was to be no exception.

The "gut job" began by taking the loft back to its bare bones, redefining the original architecture of the space and restoring its historical integrity. Tim didn't want to transform the loft into some ultra-modern space, as the exteriors of these cast-iron buildings have period details, like columns and fluting. So, we opted for rough, textured eighteenth-century floorboards, salvaged from a Pennsylvanian farmhouse, contrasting with a unified expanse of floor tiled with antique marble.

Our furniture spans three centuries and ranges from eighteenth-century antiques to twentieth-century classics. Essentially, our loft has become an understated backdrop to our life as collectors, in which the furniture—and more particularly the artwork—takes center stage.

And yet, once again, eight years later, we have reached another watershed moment, when Mercer Street is to be replaced with something new and different. Our collection of art and furniture is to have a further change of scene; perhaps this time the wall space will prove to be sufficient— but for how long? **KR**

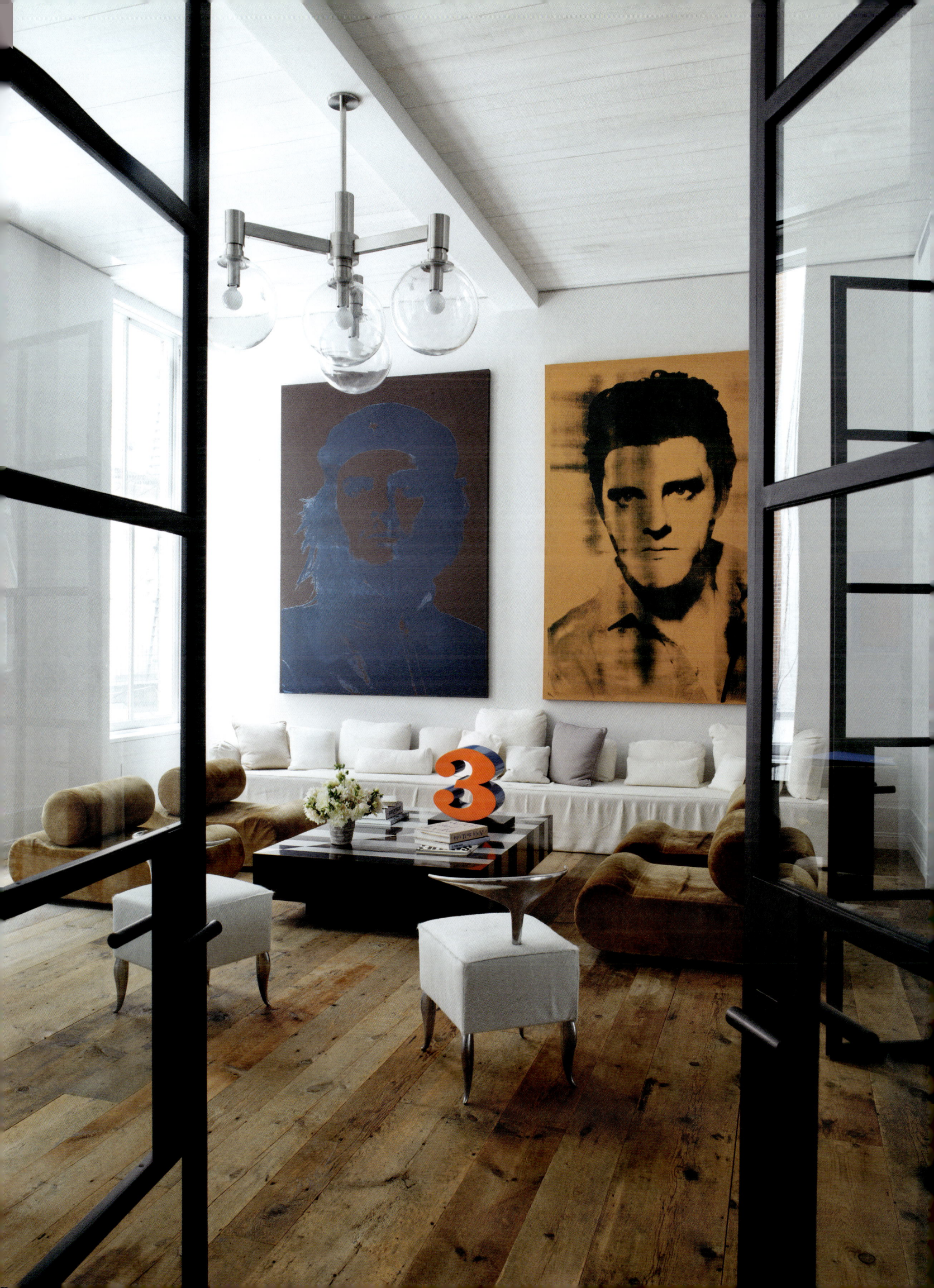

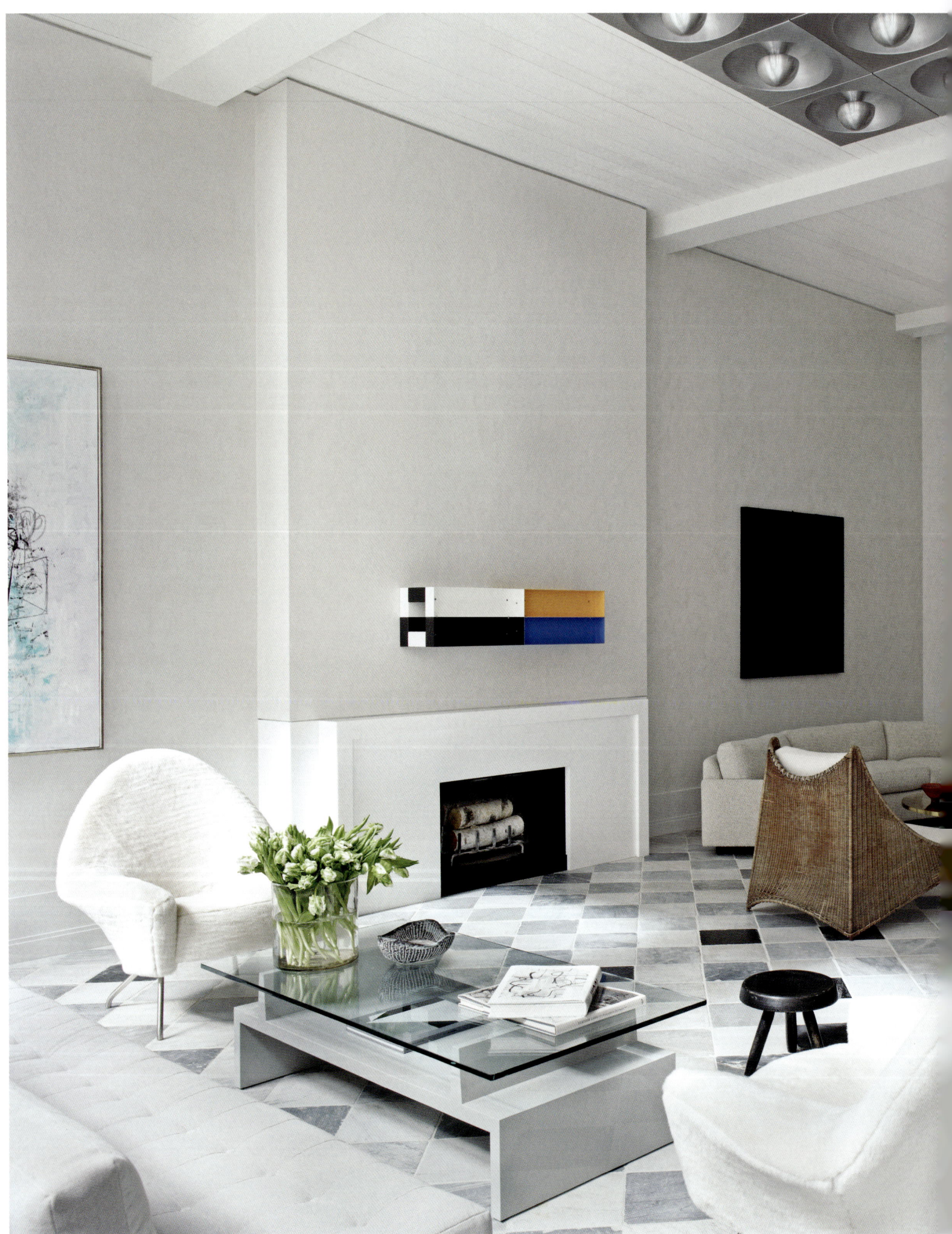

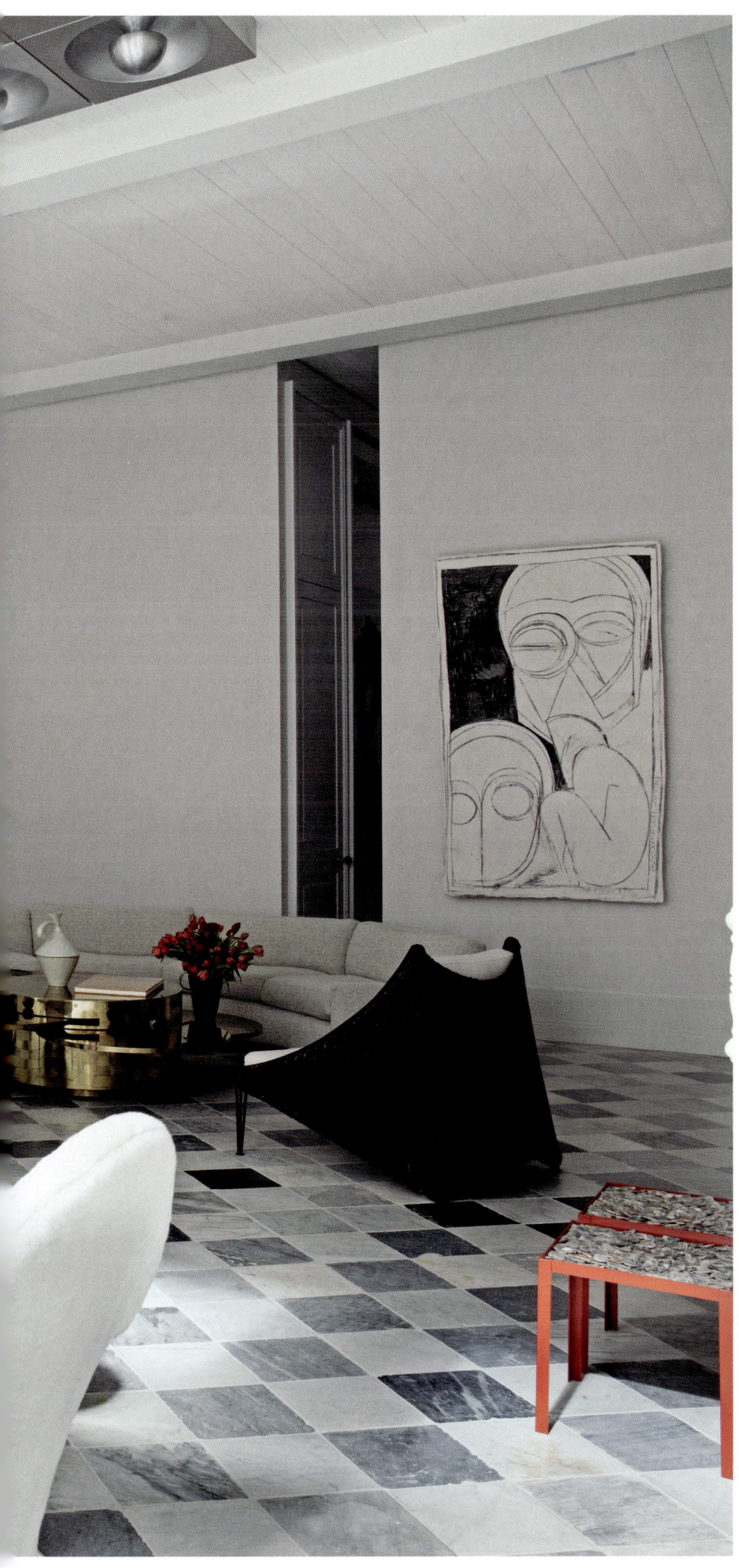

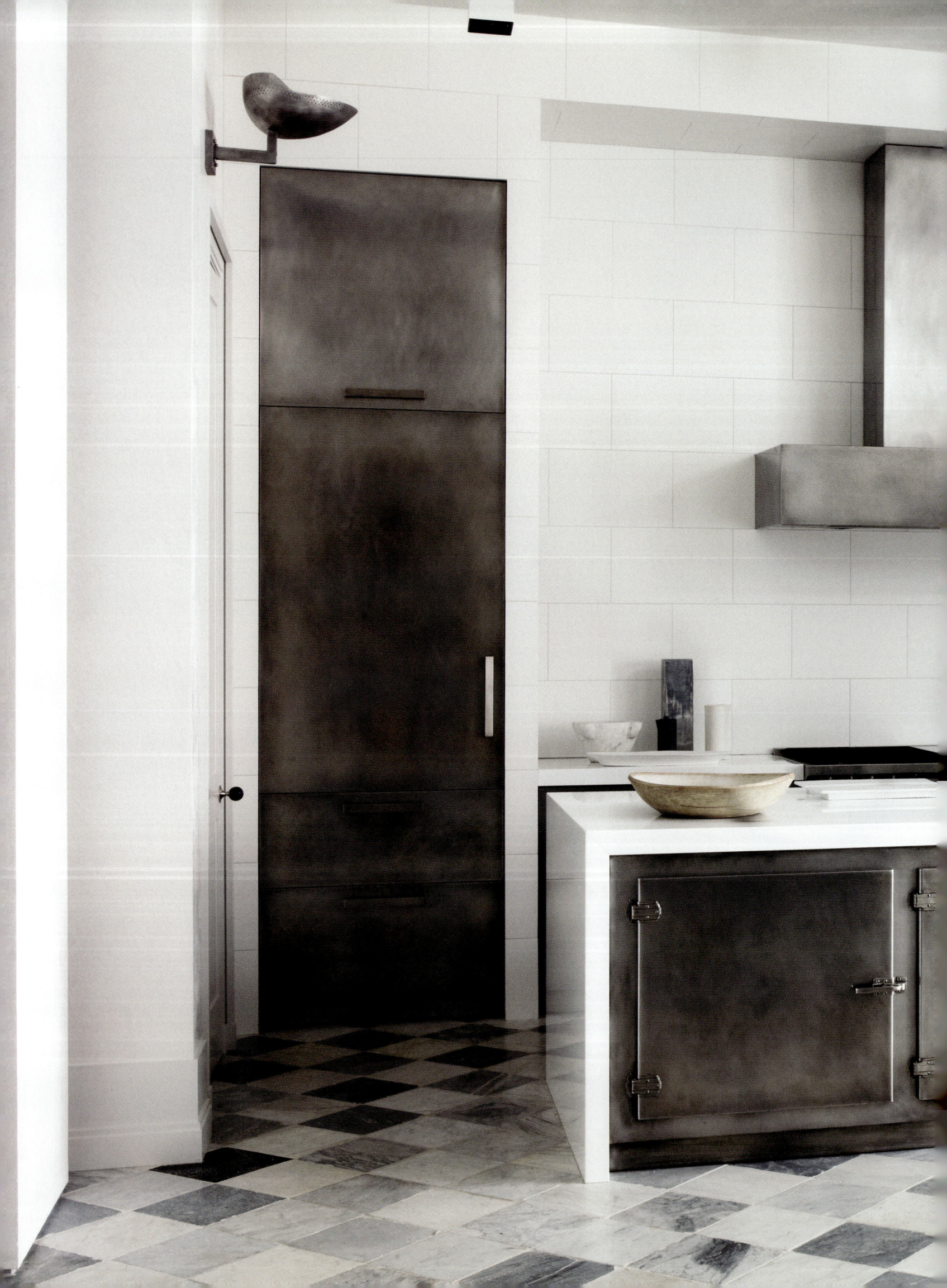

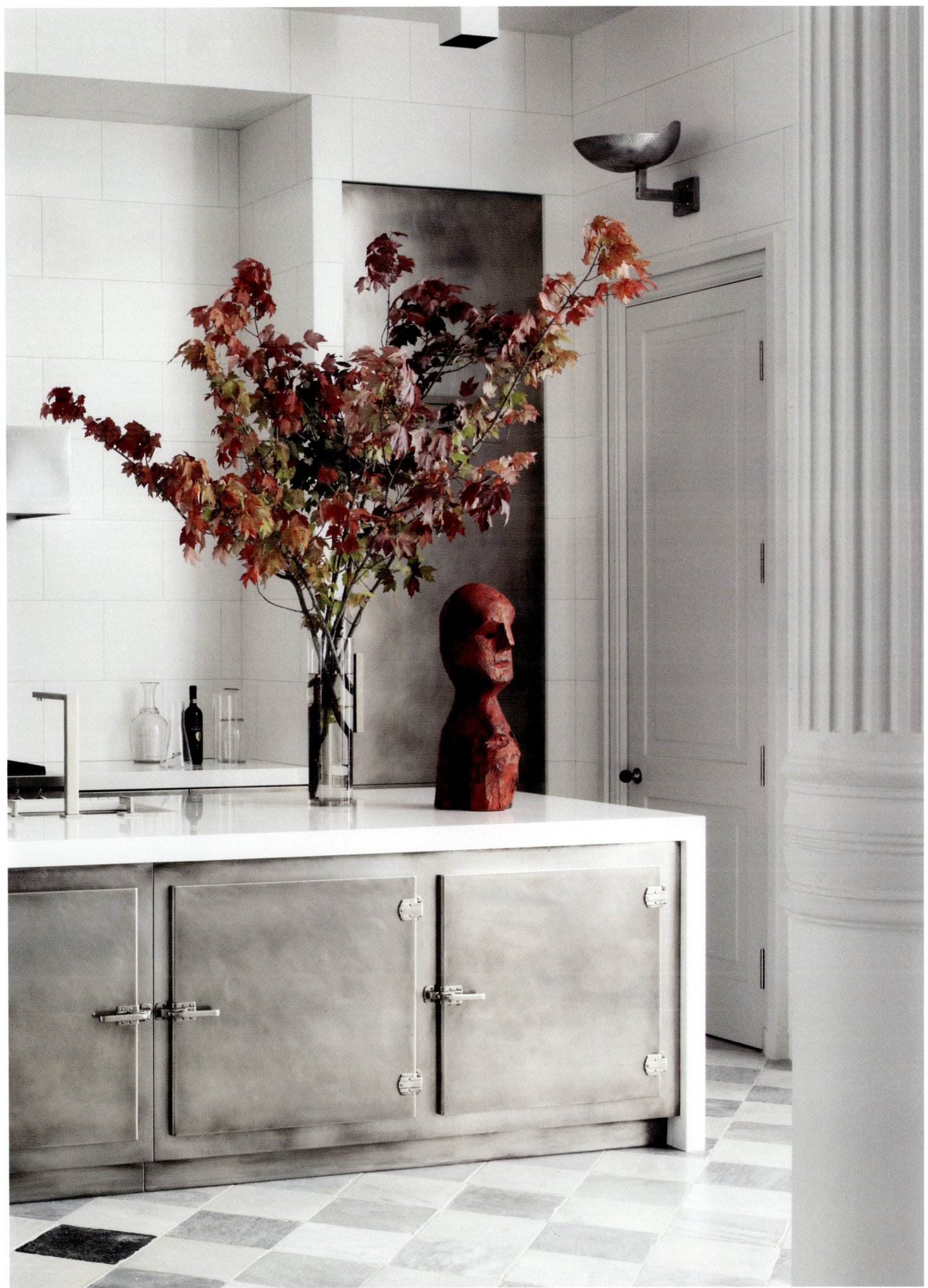

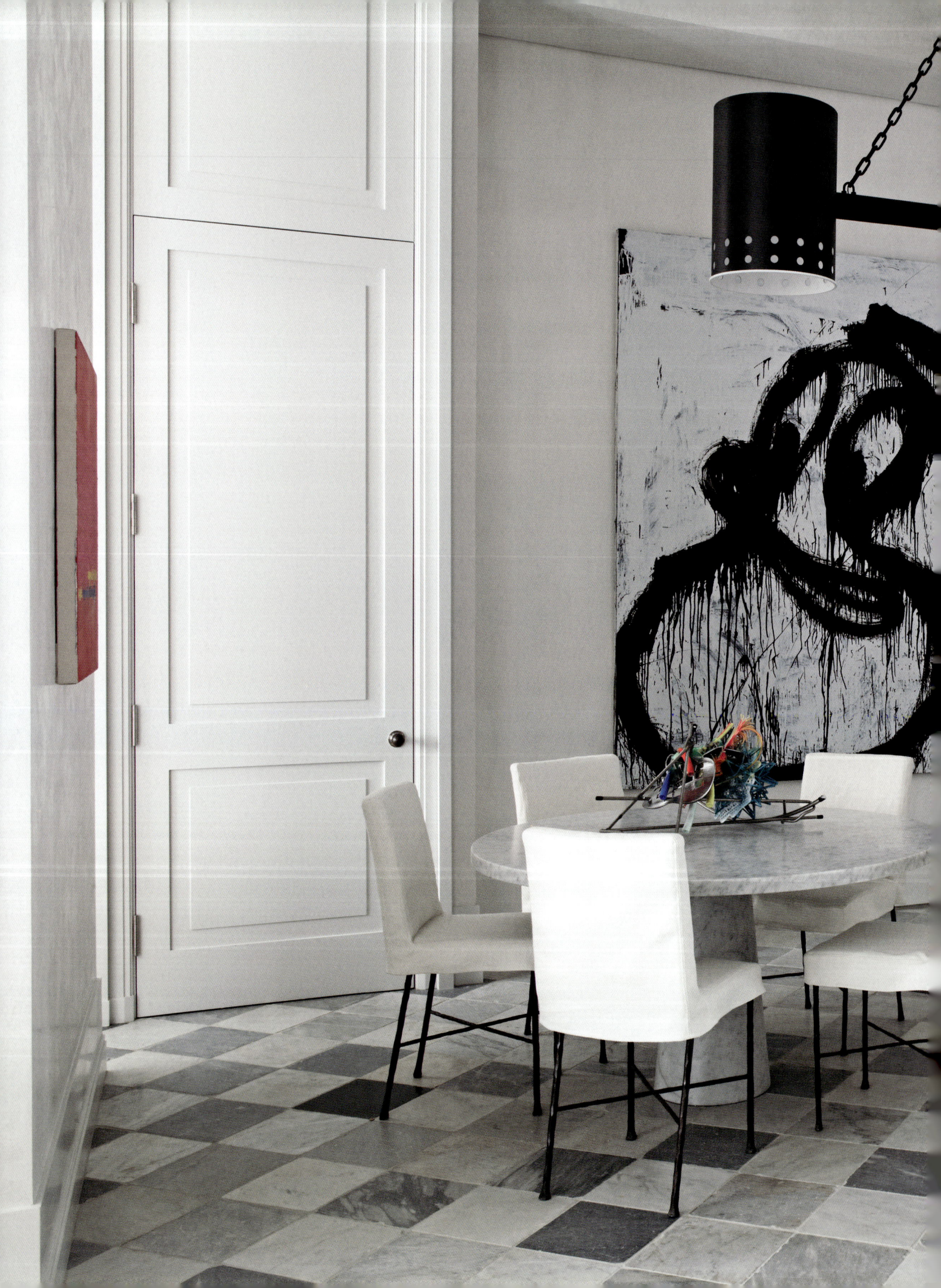

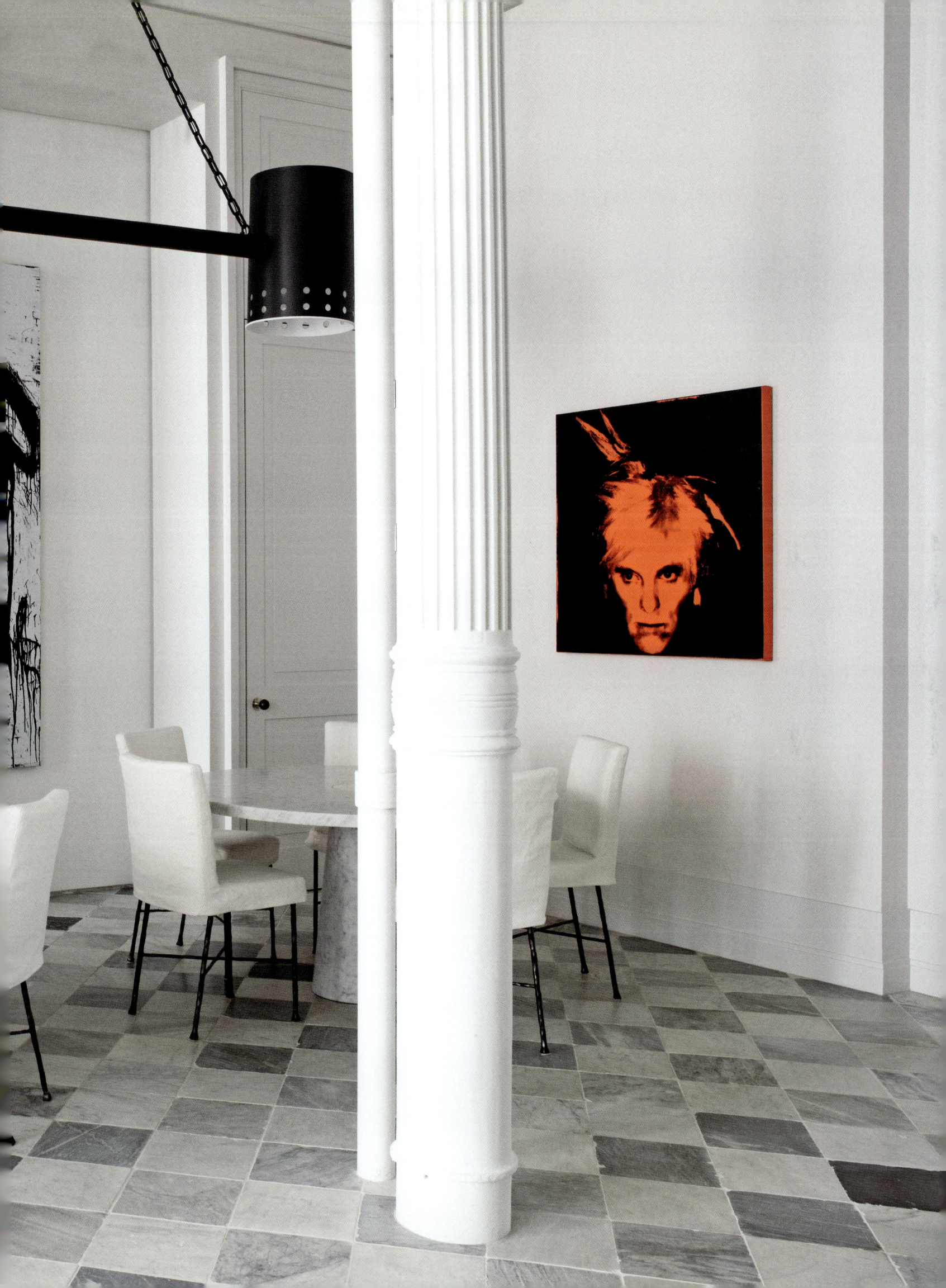

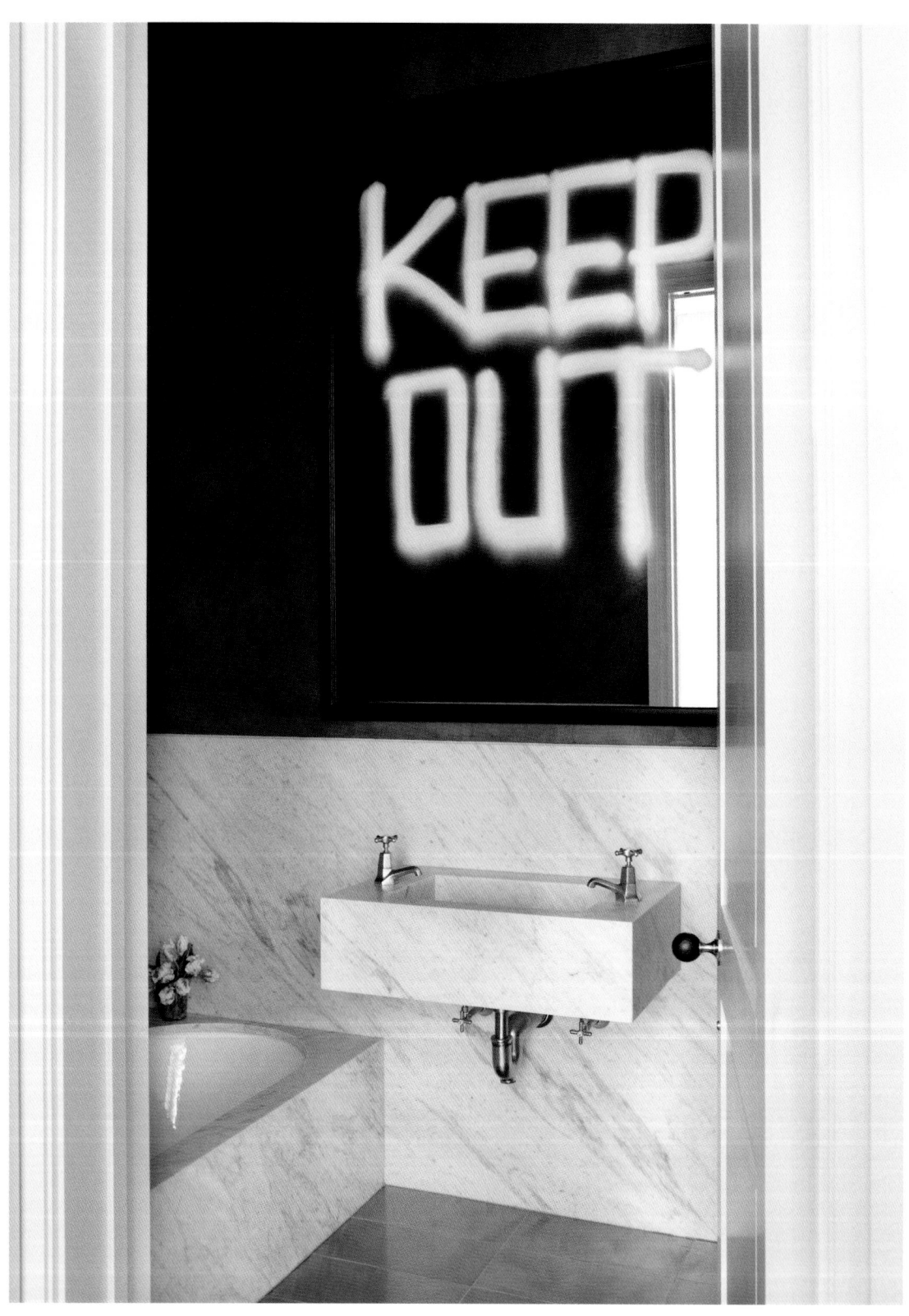

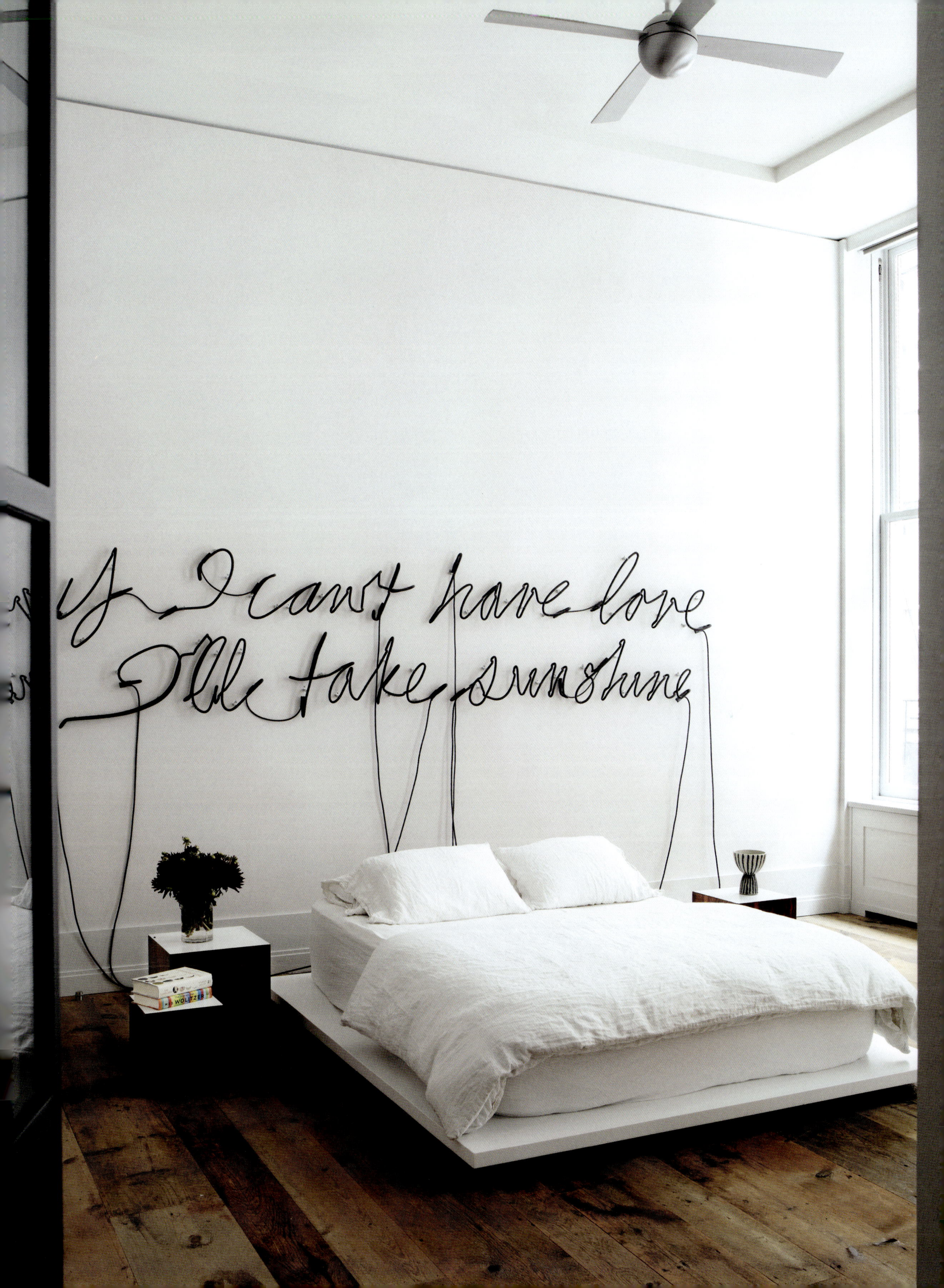
I can't have love
I'll take sunshine
WOLITZER

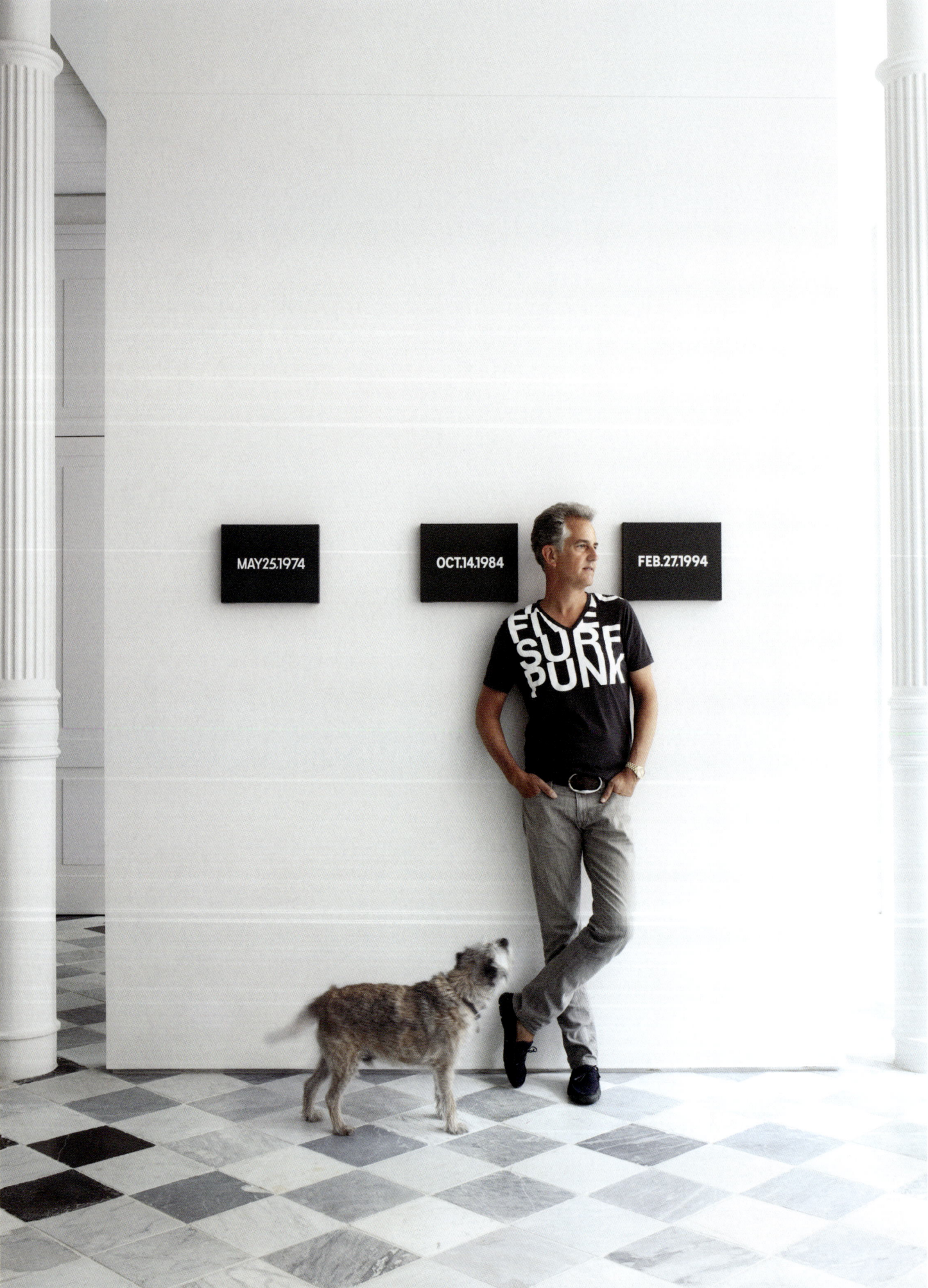

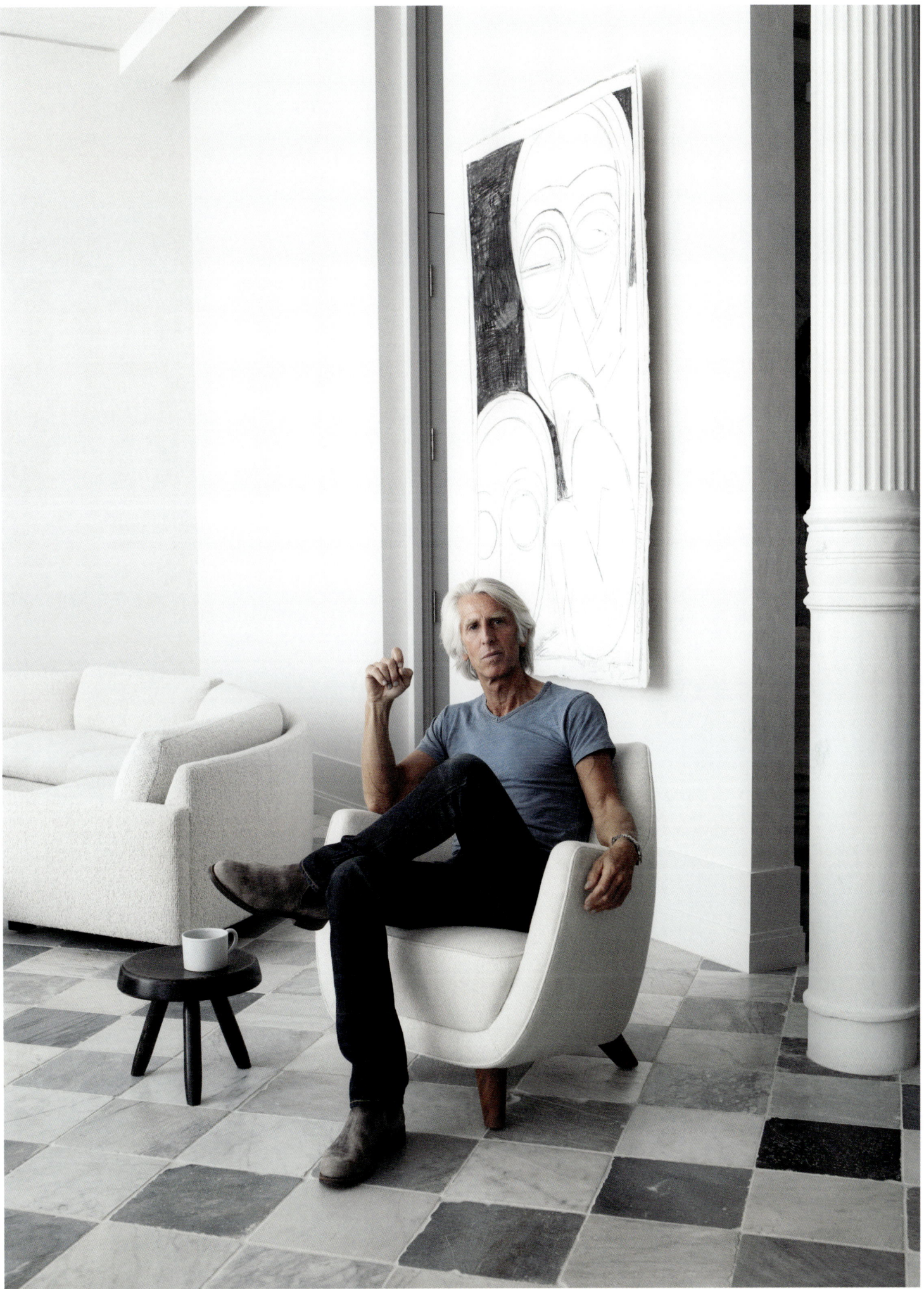

PENTHOUSE PIED-À-TERRE

MICHAEL S. SMITH

I was born in California and grew up around the movie business. Although I have lived in several areas of New York, the Upper East Side is the neighborhood I've always identified with the most, with its sense of history and numerous references to films by Mike Nichols and Nora Ephron. It is also where most of my clients are.

About 10 years ago I had been working on a project for a client across the street, when I spotted this duplex penthouse. It had a beautiful terrace garden and looked interesting, with

real personality, and I had always wanted an apartment with outdoor space. The terrace had views stretching all around it, including one framed by a church spire, lending it a real cinematic sensibility. The penthouse itself was luxurious in its sequence of spaces: you could see green out of every window, so atypical for New York and more representative of something you'd see in a movie, where everything is beautiful and there are no backyards or dingy light wells. Between the 1930s and 1950s, French chic and *boiserie* were considered to be the ultimate in taste and worked well with the New York architecture of the period, and this influenced my desire to do something decidedly French with the interior, particularly since I had a lot of furniture and lighting from Paris.

My favorite room is the bathroom, lined from floor to ceiling in Carrara marble. It represents an idea I had always hoped to distill and references the bathrooms in The Ritz Hotel in Paris, yet somehow has managed to exceed even their grandeur. It has a skylight and a view of the Carlyle tower from a side window, which also overlooks the terrace. It is a prism of luxury Frenchness, boasting an immersive tub, steam shower, heated floor, and hidden TV! Of all my furniture, I am especially fond of the black lacquer desk in the living room—sculptural, simple, and rather pleasing—and then there's the eighteenth-century hand-painted Chinese wallpaper that adorns my dining area … It is the holy relic of Elsie de Wolfe—an interior designer who I admire more than any other—and all that remains of the original paper that was used in the dining room she created for Condé Nast's penthouse apartment in New York.

I only spend about 20 percent of my time in New York, and the penthouse is a real luxury. In my imagination it's a classical late-eighteenth-century pavilion—a sanctuary of pleasure and privacy.

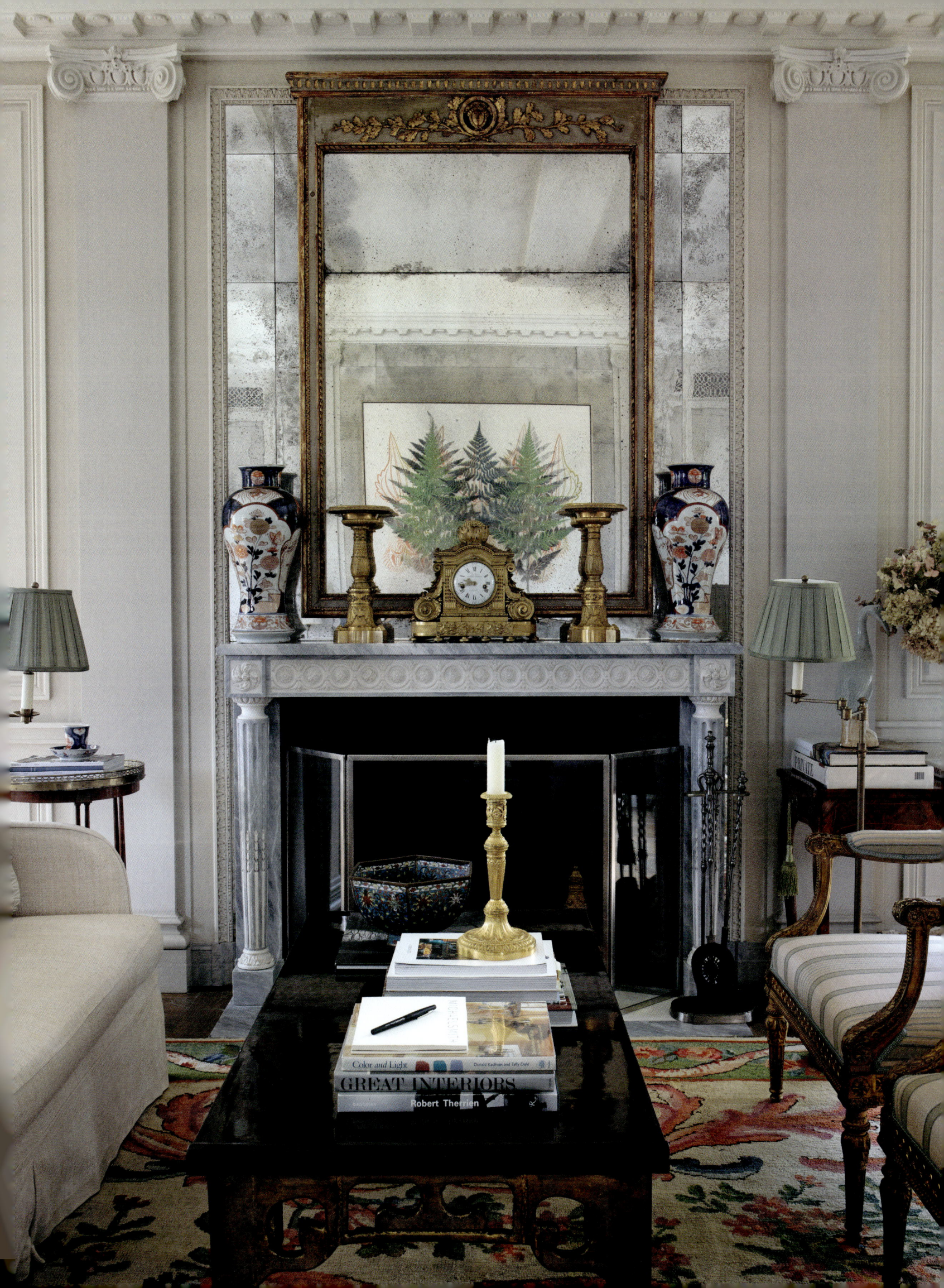

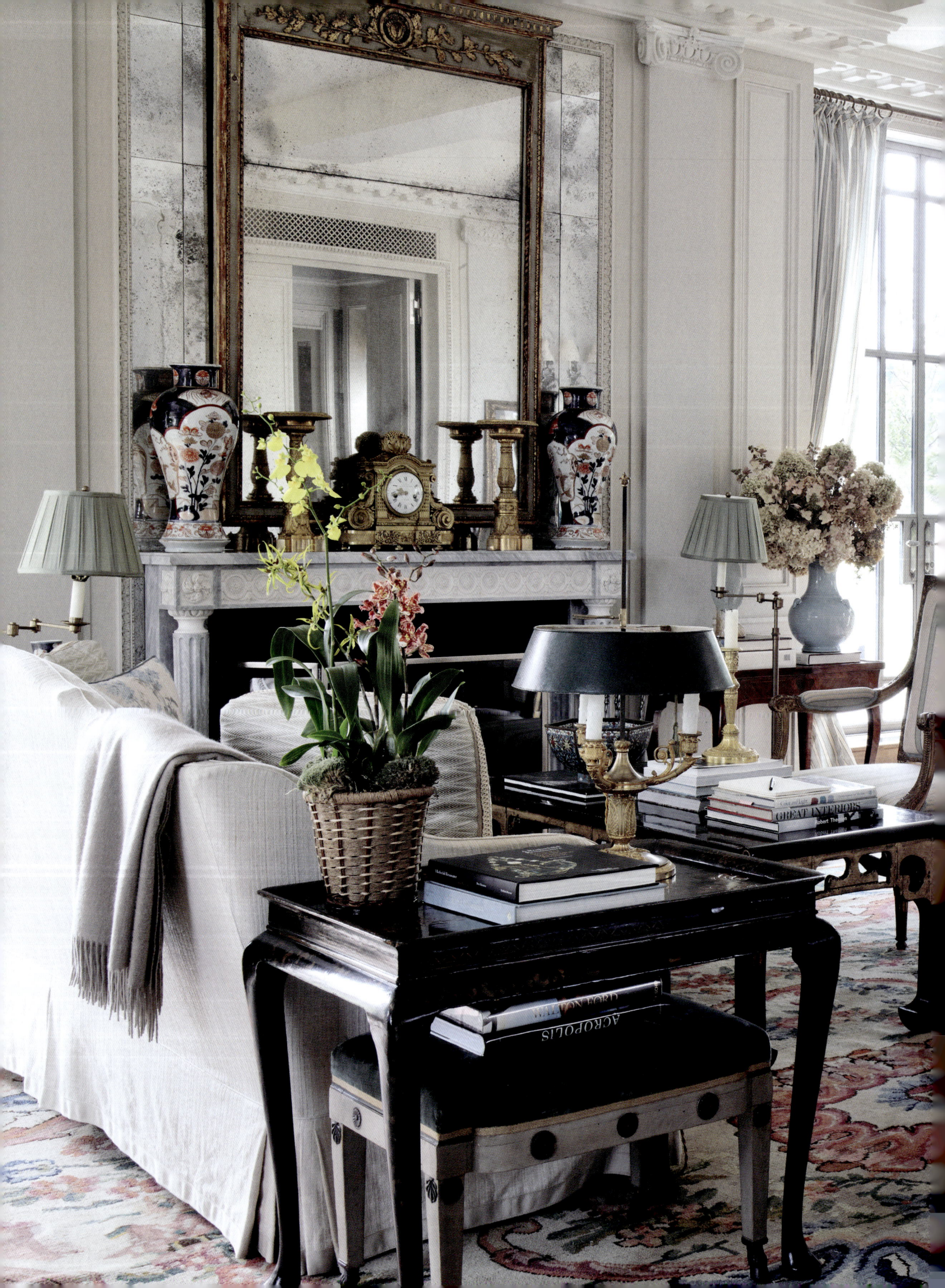

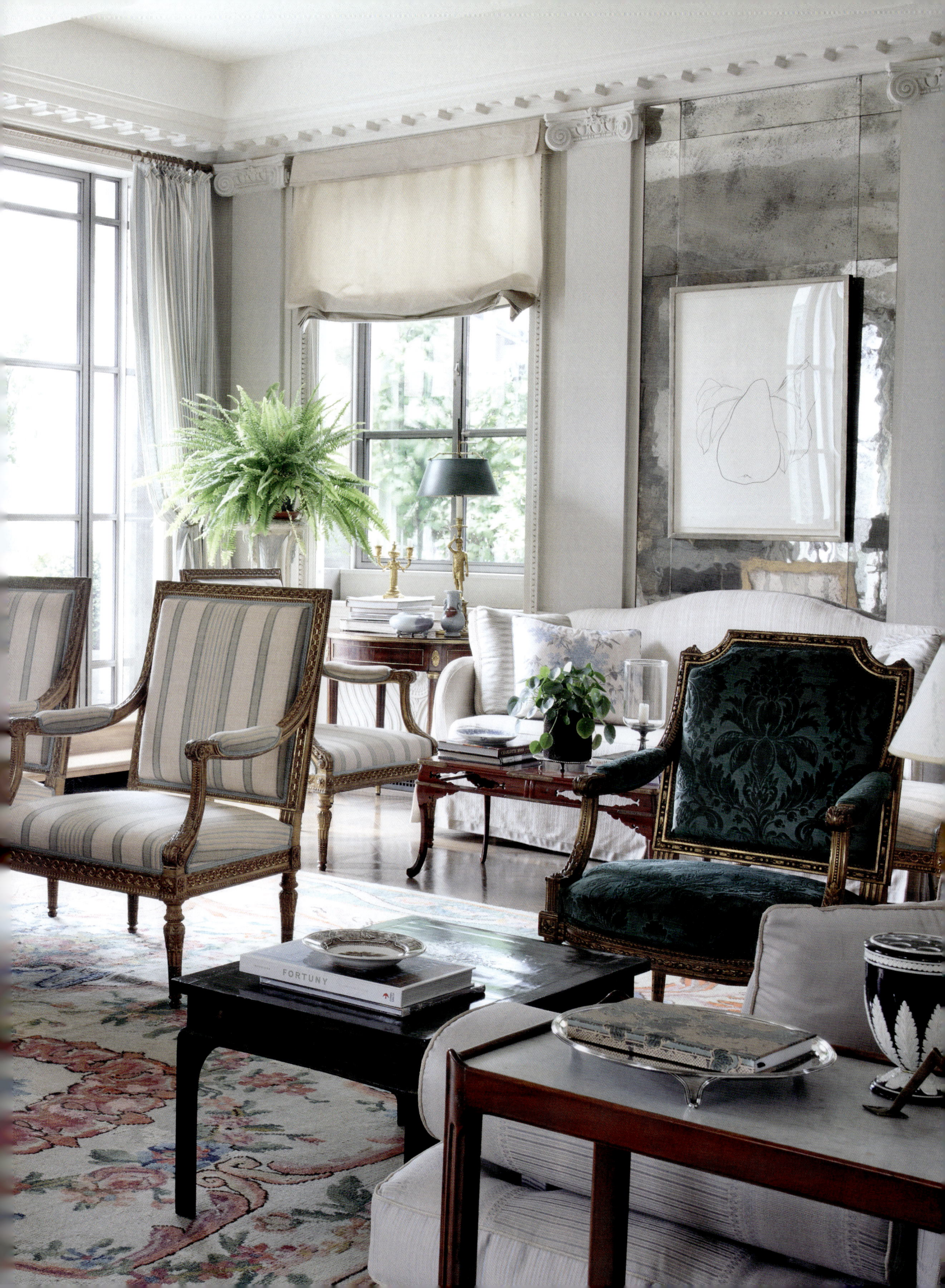

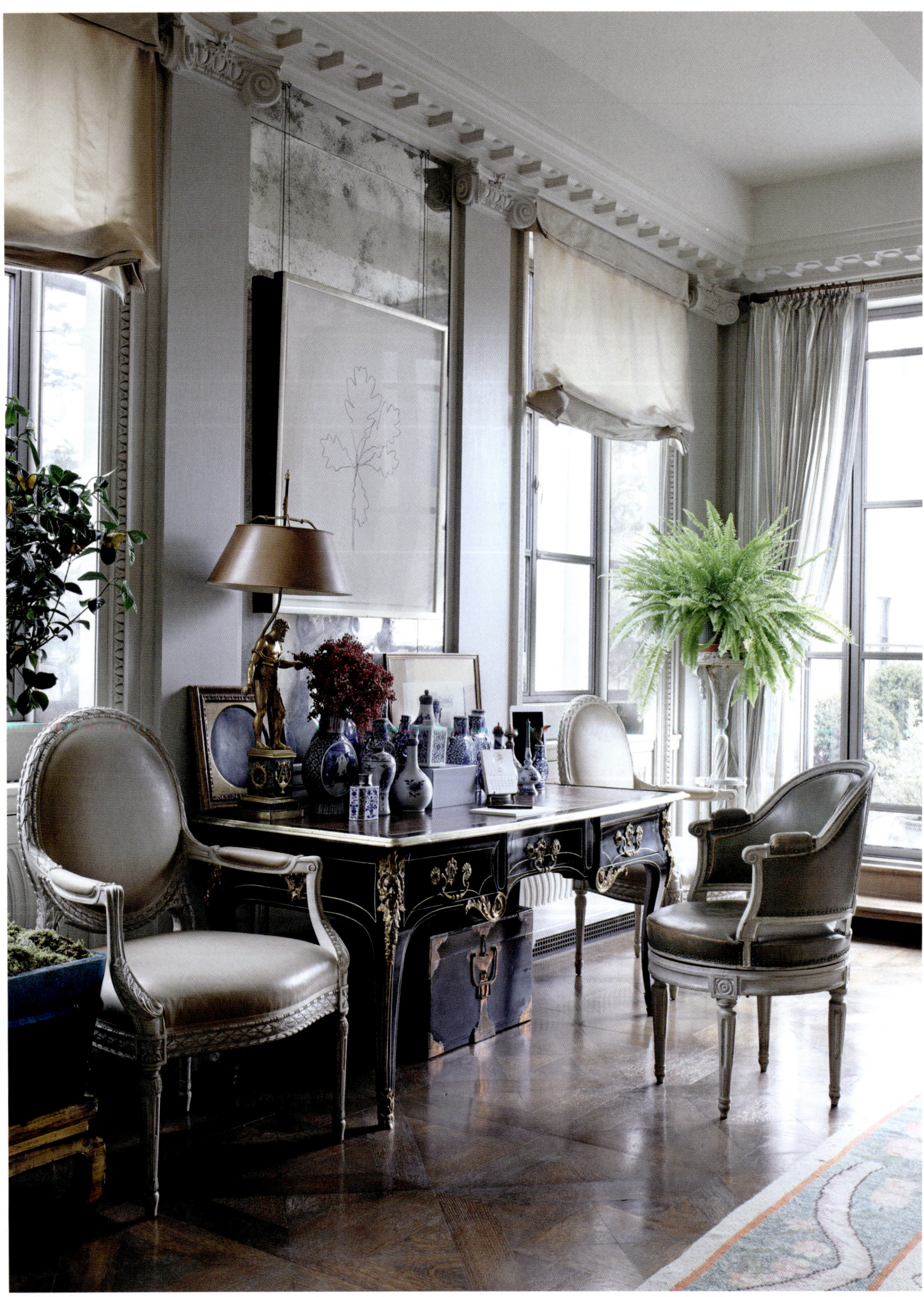

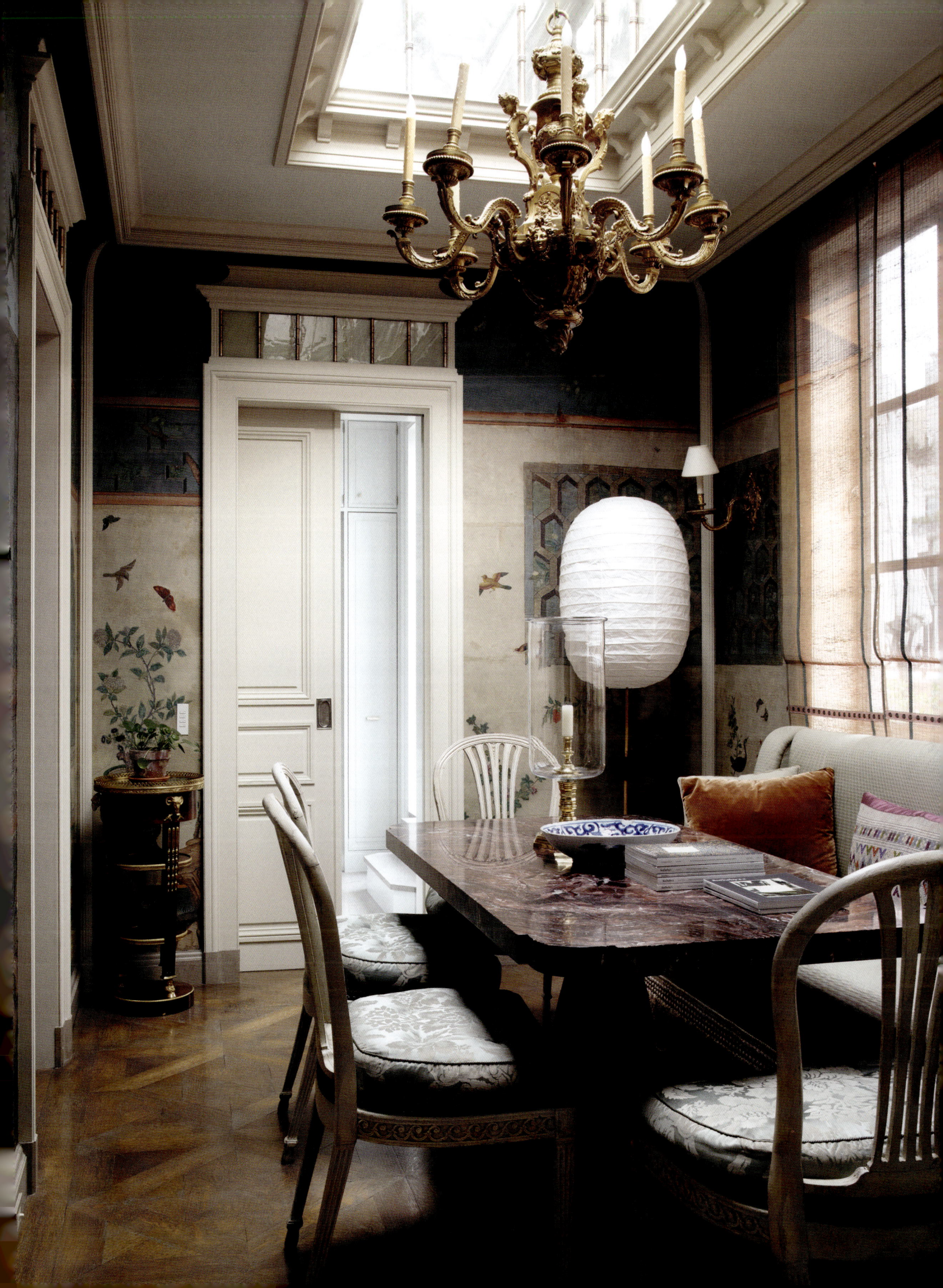

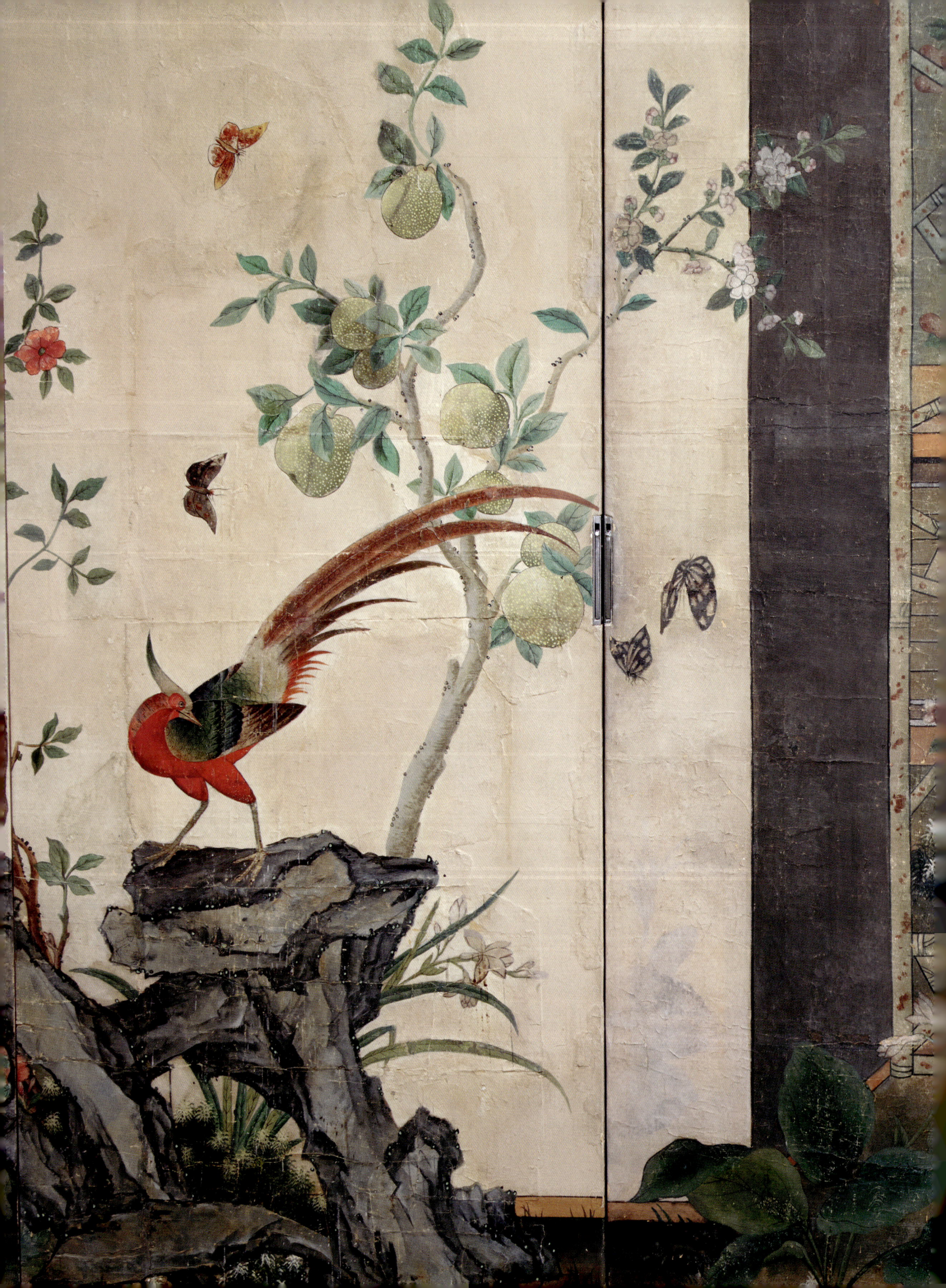

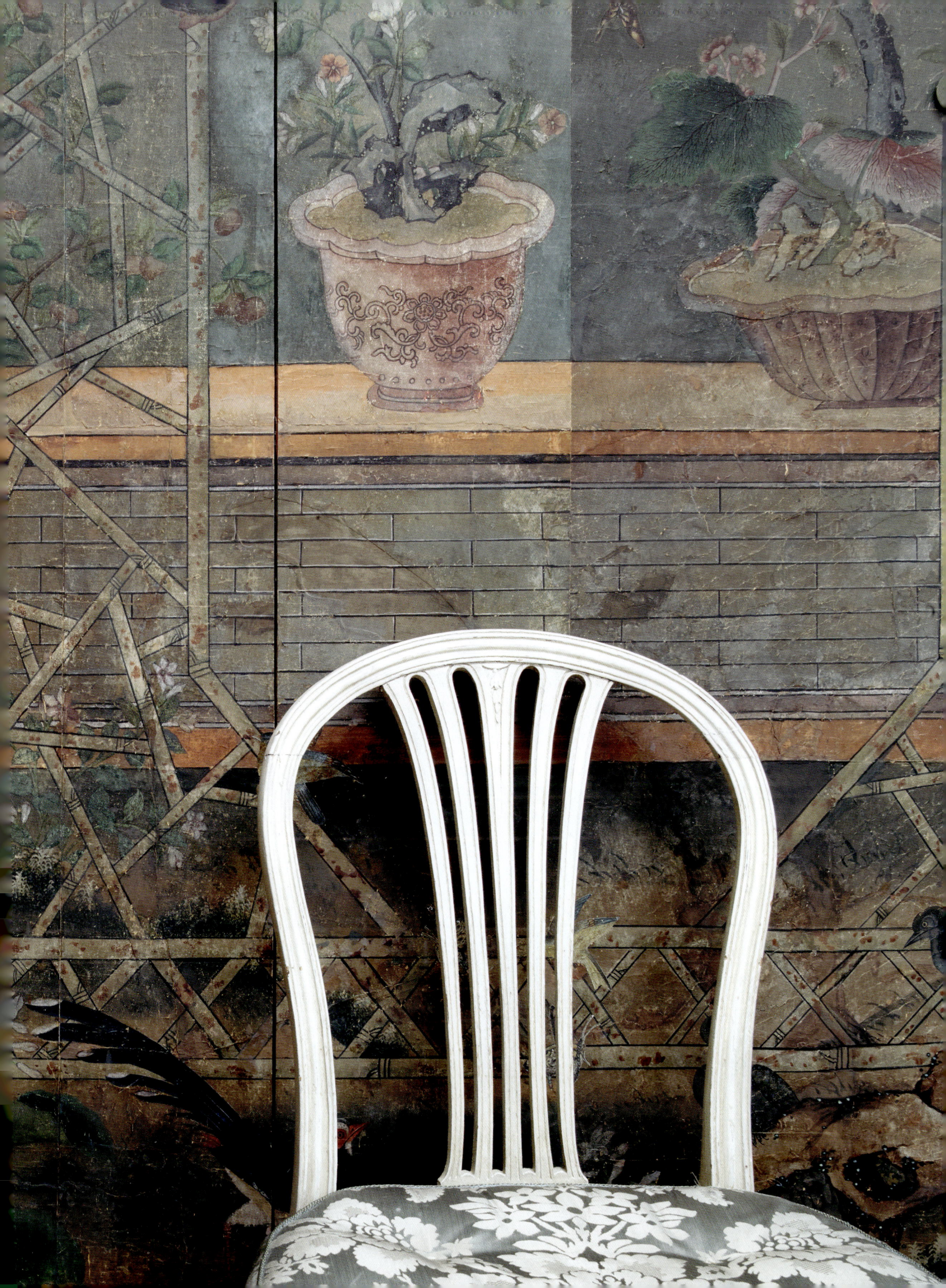

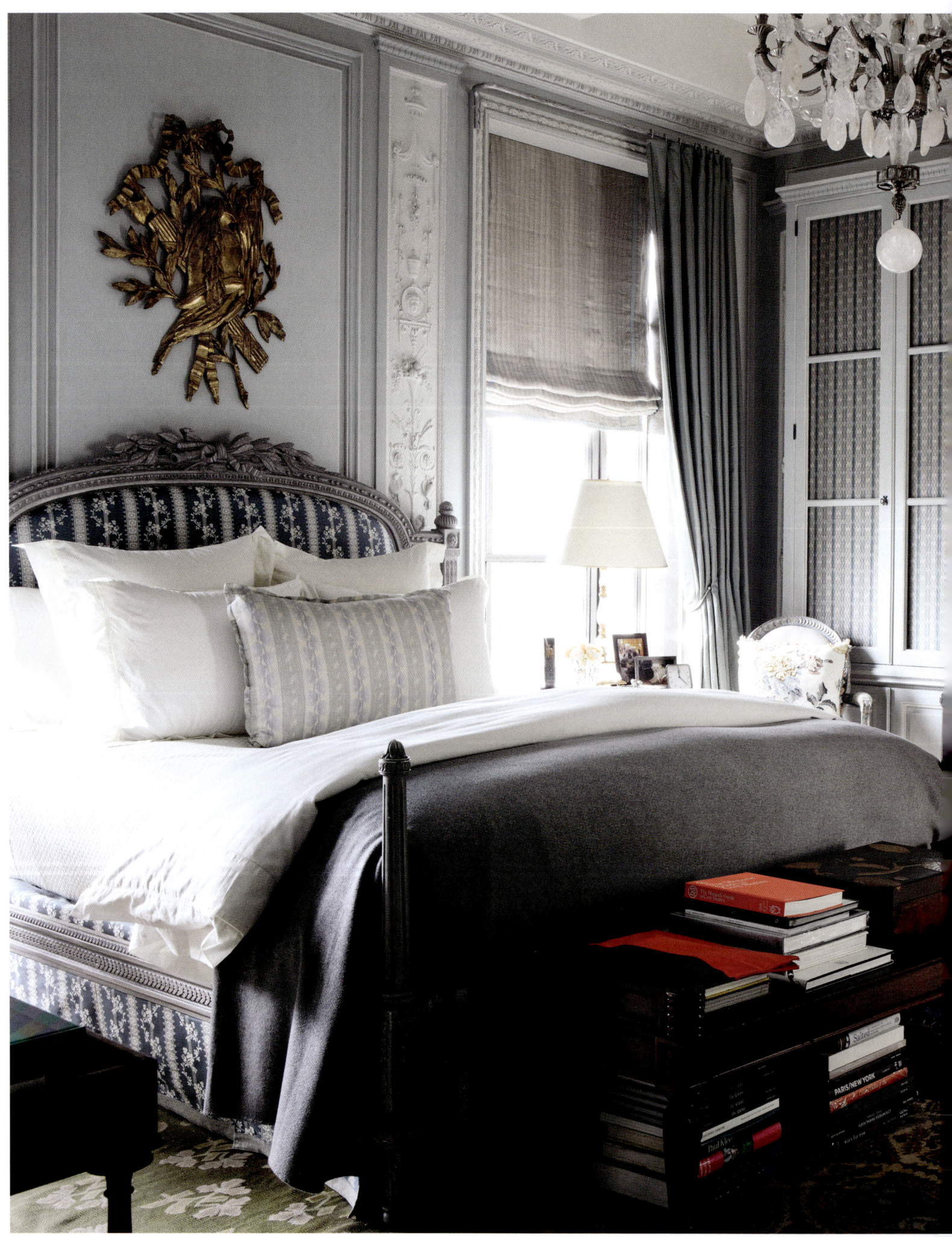

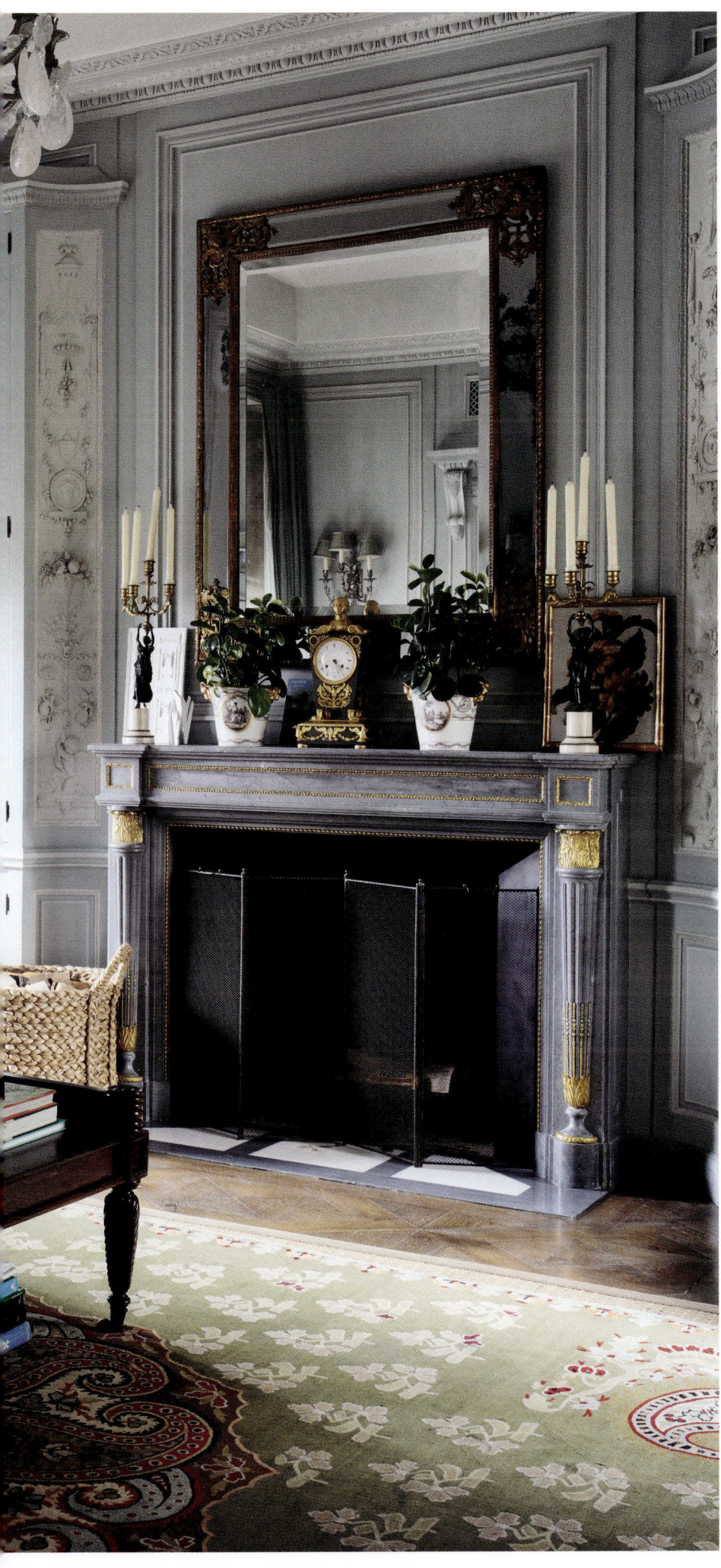

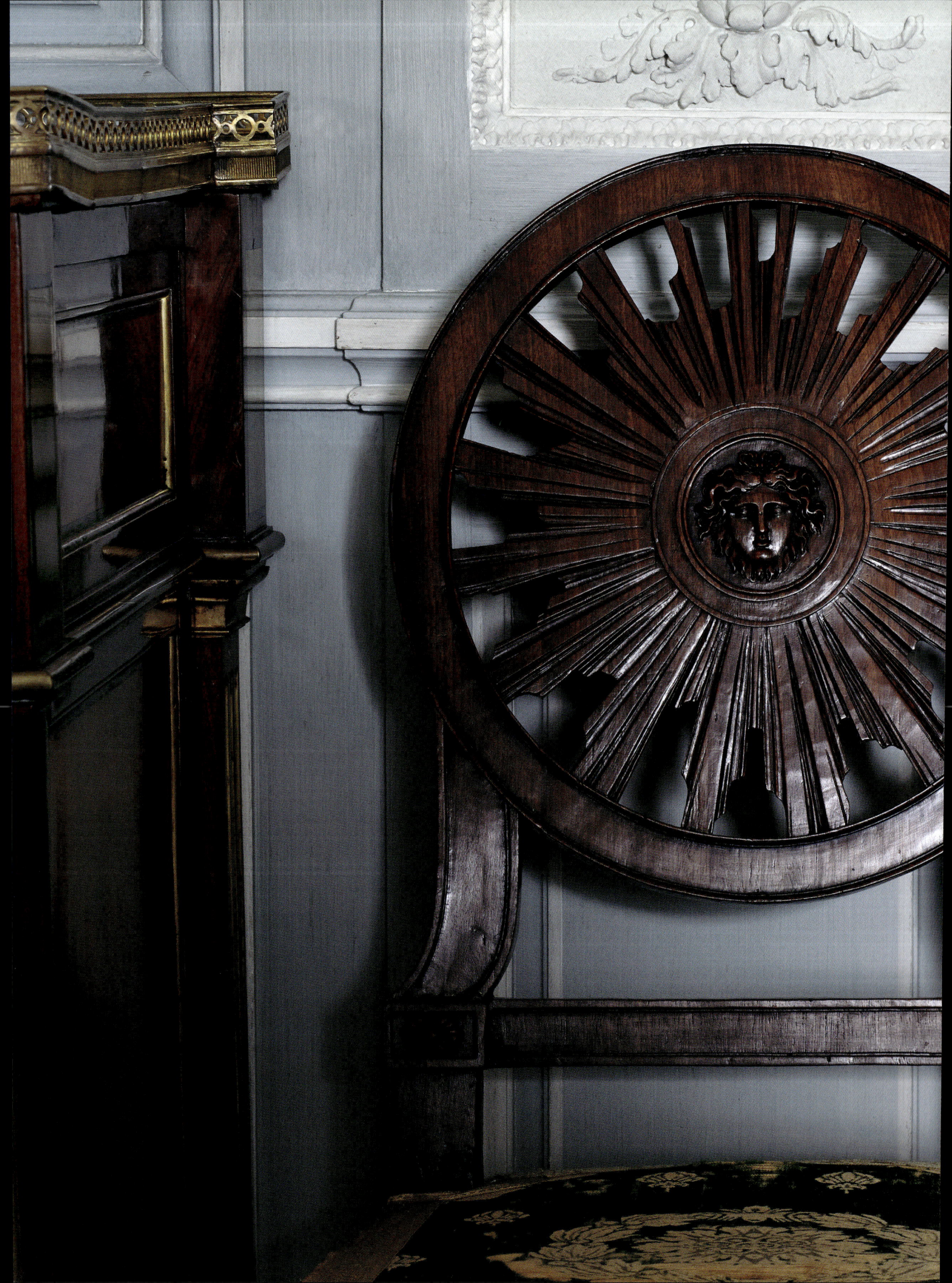

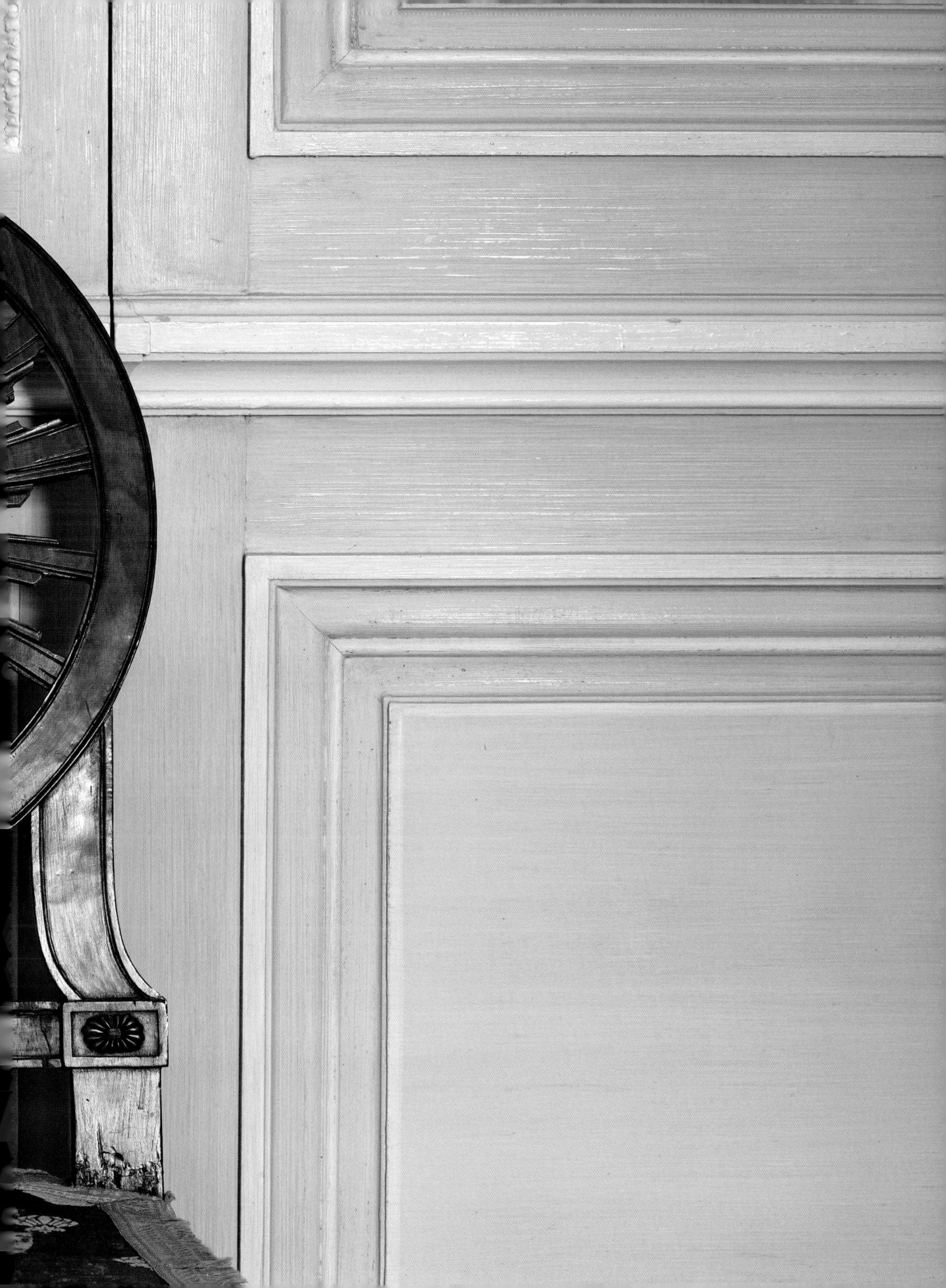

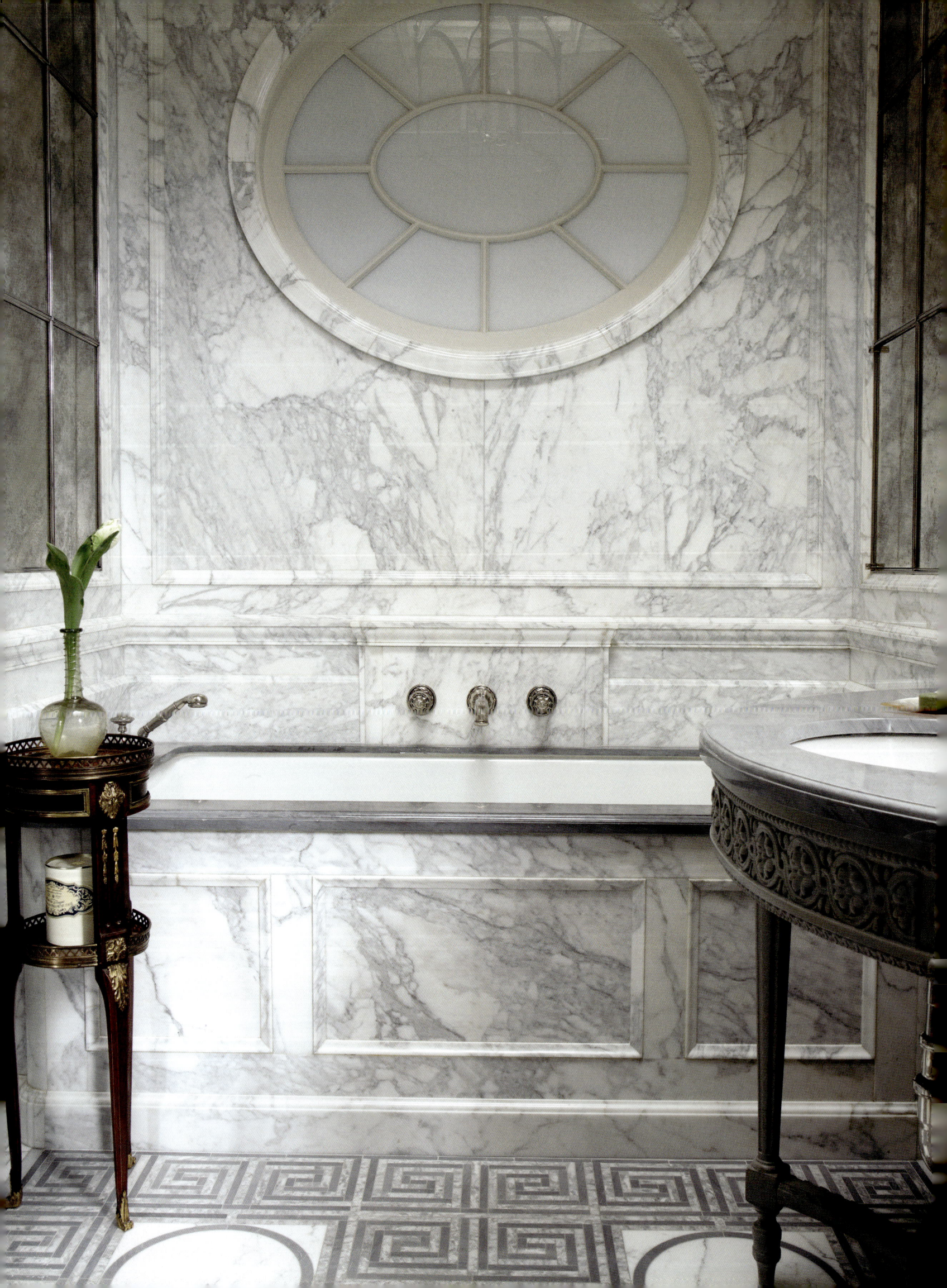

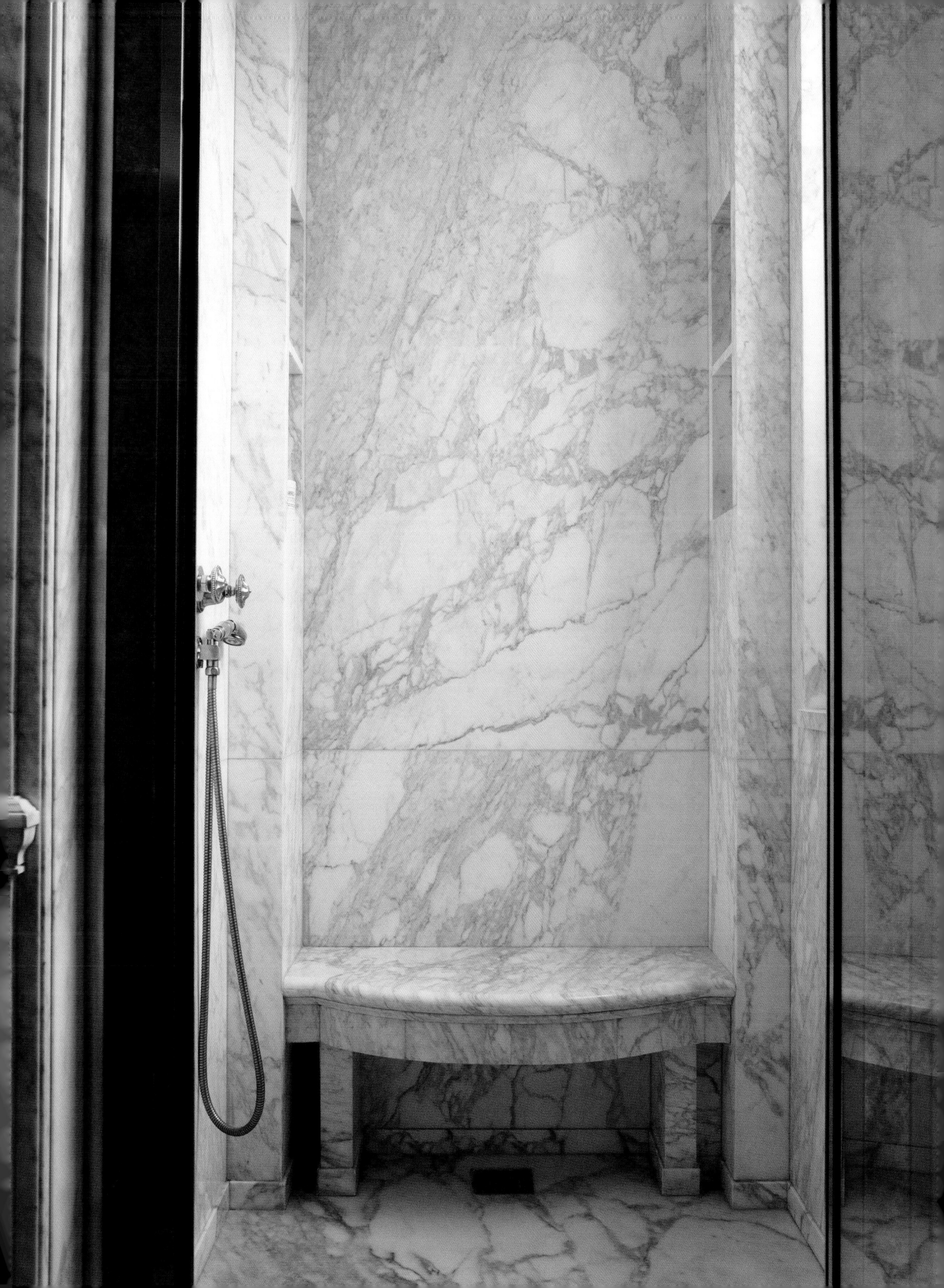

ROOM WITH A VIEW

NICKY HASLAM

New York in the 1960s was a mix of shiny confidence and elegant past. To be part of the heady whirlpool that was Manhattan at the time was utterly magical. I had an exciting and interesting job at *Vogue* and met and became friends with a wonderful cross-section of people. In those days New Yorkers had grace and spirit; people dressed properly and wore gloves at lunch. It was a stylish time—a moment of unsophisticated sophistication, when the city was still theirs, in the sense that they all knew and loved its various idiosyncratic areas. Today, there is barely anything left of "old New York" and, sadly, it is no longer high on my list of favorite places to visit. The city has lost its girlish laughter and become the place to go and get things done, and Diana Vreeland's "youthquake" of 60 years ago is but a distant memory.

Working on this Manhattan apartment in 2010 brought back all the memories of that decade, when I actually lived in the city. Talking to plasterers and builders was as much fun as going to a restaurant! (My local favorite, incidentally, was undoubtedly the Marea, an Italian seafood place in the basement of the adjacent building.) Located on the 73rd floor, overlooking Central Park from Columbus Circle, the apartment made you feel as if you were standing on the roof of the world. The vistas stretched from Long Island Sound to the torch of the Statue of Liberty, and the Upper East Side seemed as miniature as an architect's model city. I have this thing about views and, while the apartment has an undeniably staggering one, as Gertrude Stein once wrote, "I like a view but I like to sit with my back to it."

Film decoration has always been a strong reference for me. I love the drama and sense of space that can be introduced to any interior, and when decorating this apartment there were a lot of ideas I sucked out of the past, including the whiteness of Philip Johnson's apartment, where I lived for a short while. It was a challenge for me to decorate somewhere modern, and I wanted to bring back a touch of the old New York glamour that I found to be so missing in the city's contemporary interiors. In order to make the rooms appear taller and more relevant to the incredible view, I created a series of free-form double cornices below the existing ceilings. The effect is almost futuristic. The only construction column is clad with Doric flutes and paired with a second, which conceals a bar, while shiny floors reflect the sky and the lights at night. Bold gestures, whether in shape, color, or texture, are a requisite of good design.

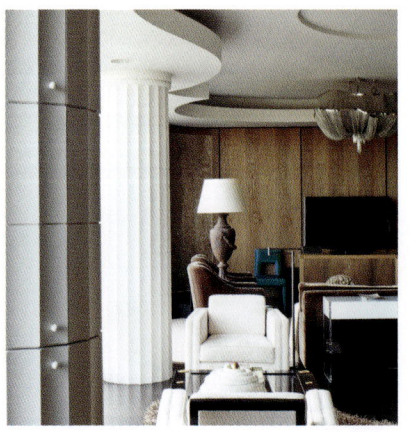

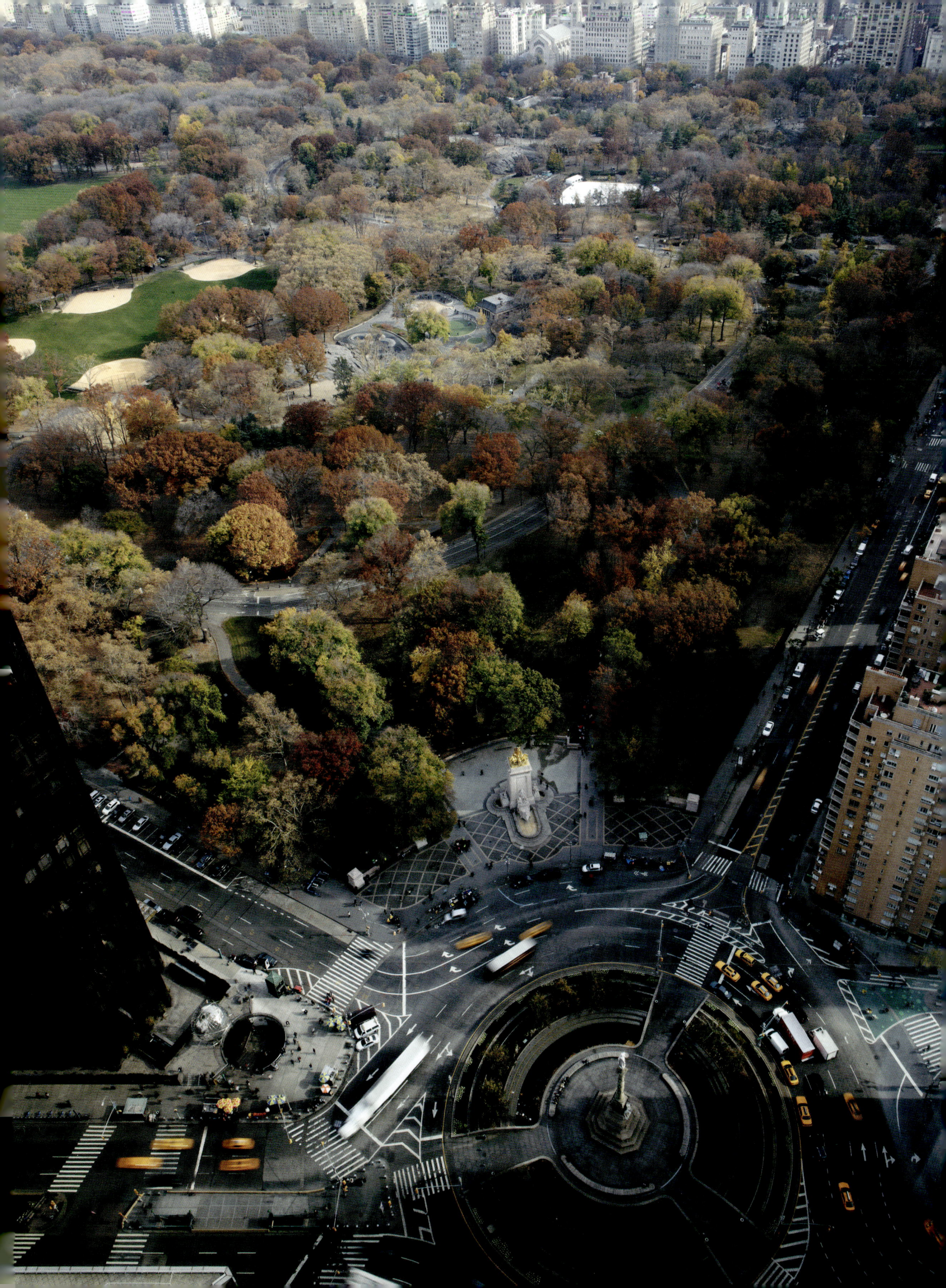

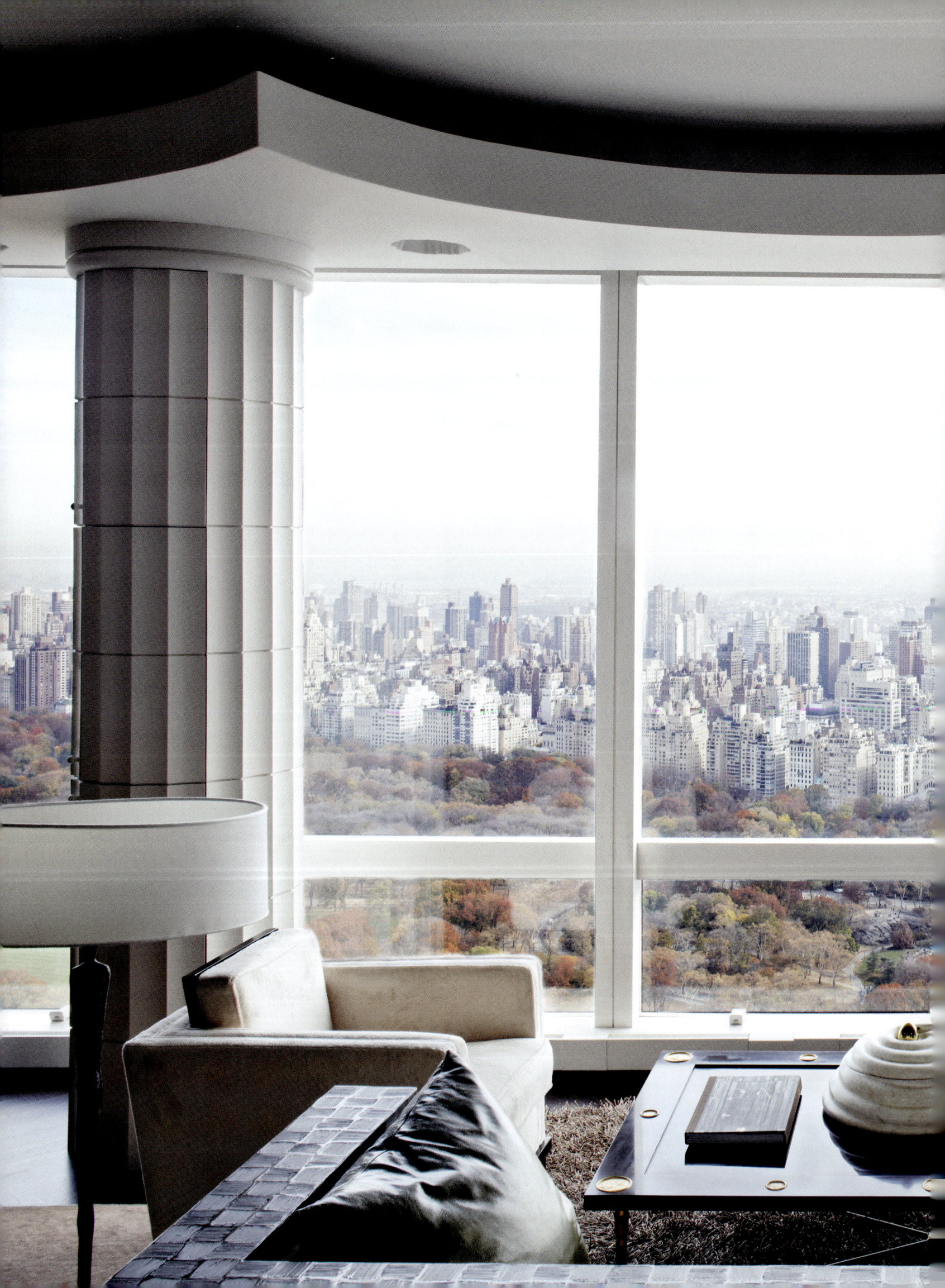

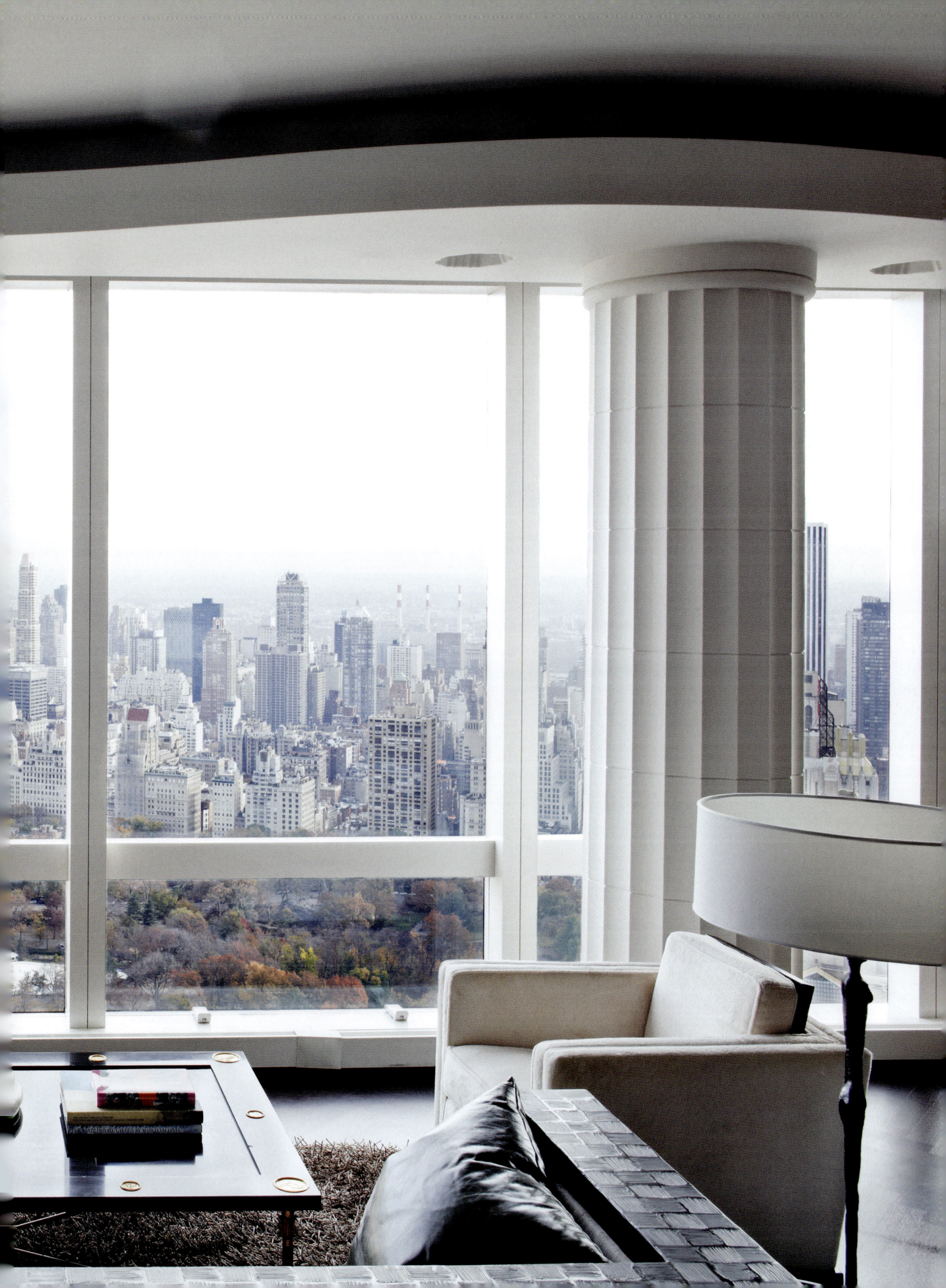

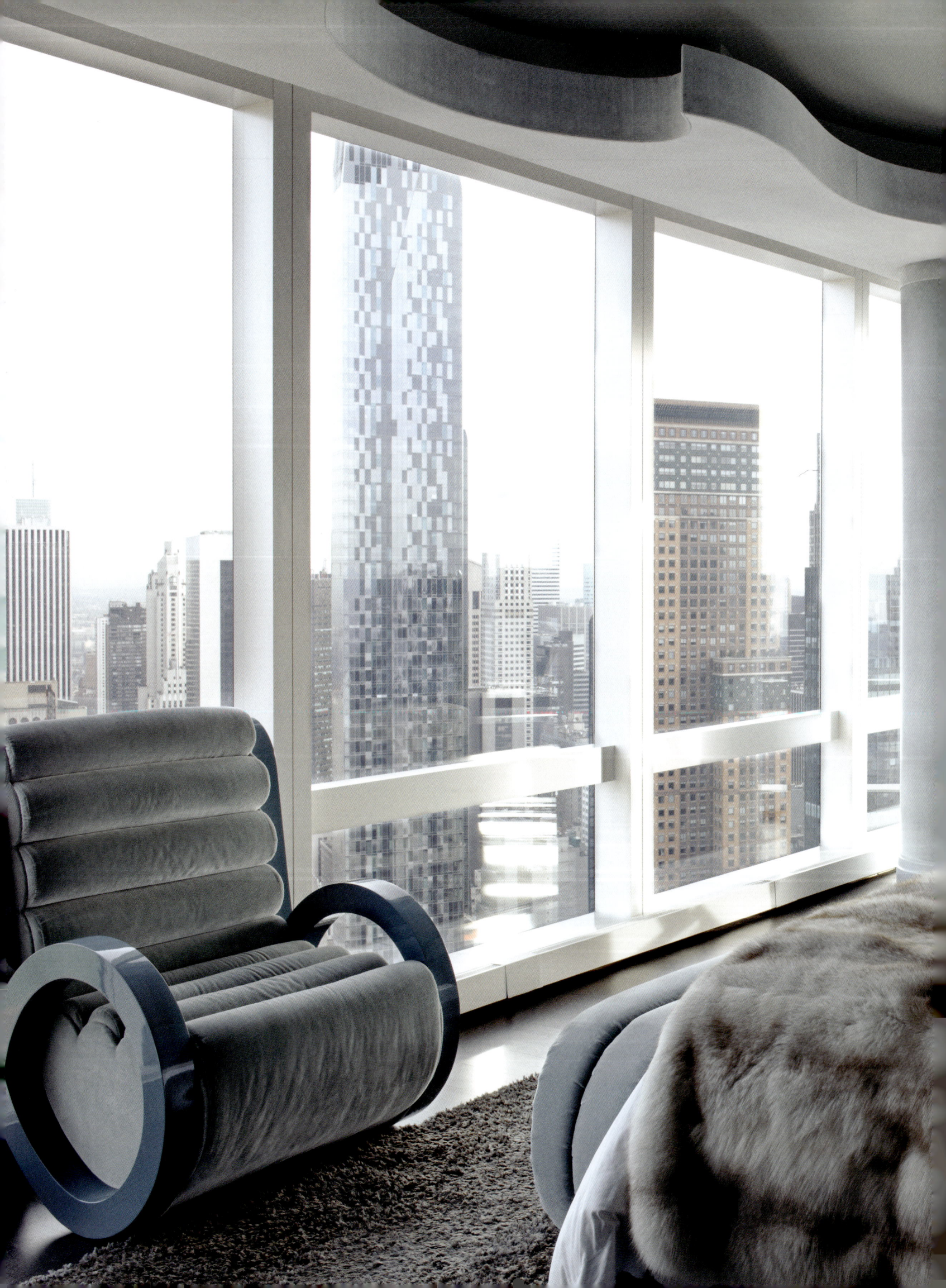

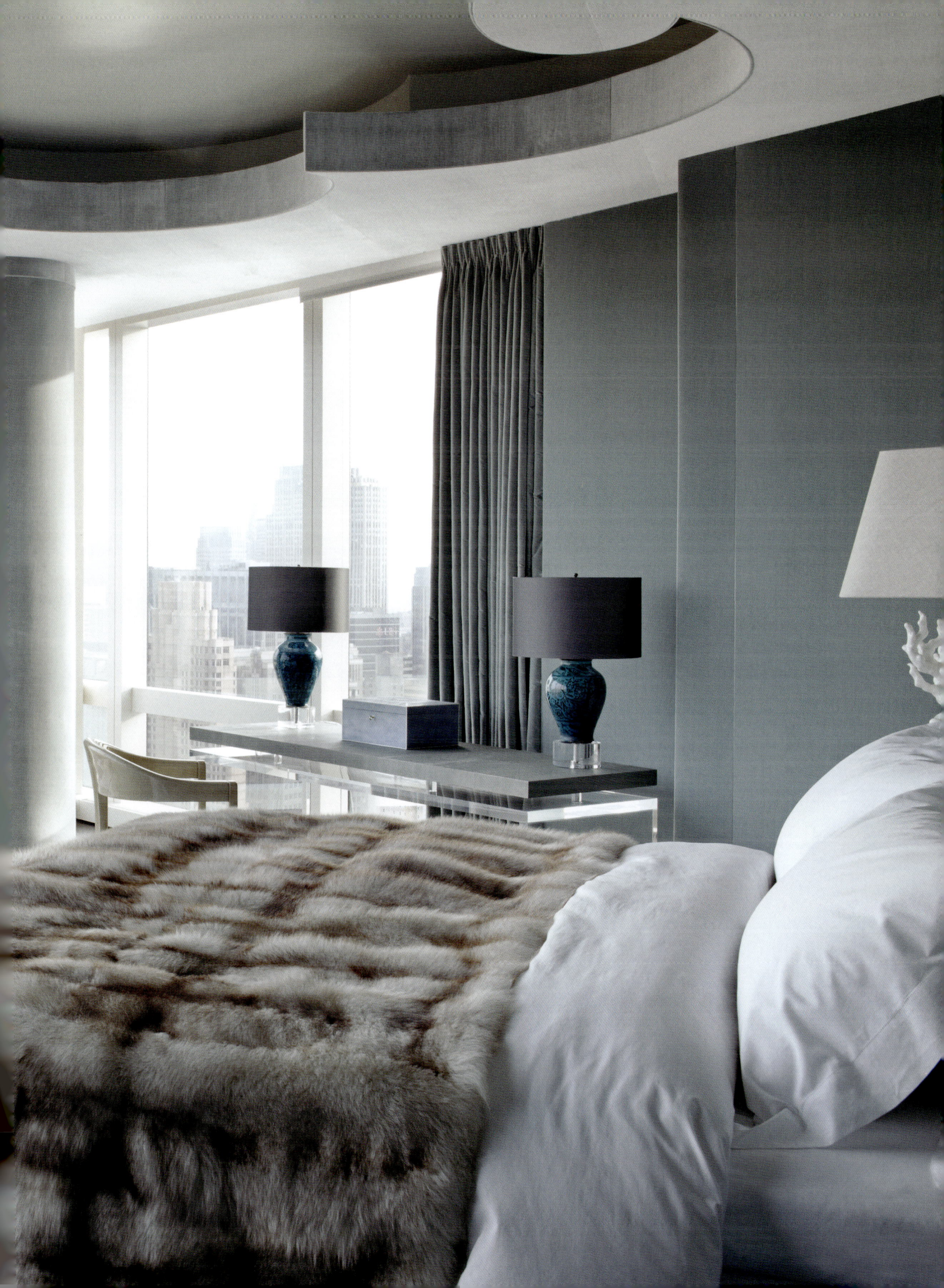

A TOUCH OF RED

NIAN FISH

I was born in Kobe, Japan. My father was an American soldier and we traveled a lot and had little to live on. I arrived in New York in the 1950s, a time when the city was defined by eclectic artists, writers, and musicians—people living on the edge and struggling to make it. I first discovered the West Village back in 1967, when I was still in high school and rents were little more than $50 per month. I then moved for a while to the Upper West Side at a time when the area was "cool," but it was the Village that eventually called me back, with its pre-war, four-story brownstones, abundance of trees, and, for me, a vital view of the sky. Sadly, it is now an unaffordable district for those that originally gave it life.

My apartment is in a building that dates from 1929 and is one of four coveted properties by architects Bing & Bing that were aimed at the luxury market of the day, with sunken living rooms, wood floors, and working fireplaces. The building has a communal rooftop garden—a rare thing in New York City—from where I can see the sea and the sky.

The apartment became available back in 1999, so I have lived here for 22 years, have never moved on, and don't mind admitting that I would be happy to die here. I am the worst cook in the world and only use my kitchen to boil tea. The West Village has everything I need within a four-block radius: bodegas, delis, parks, trees, and restaurants. I could not be better located!

In my bedroom I have an eighteenth-century Ming dynasty desk. It is high, so I need a tall stool. Sometimes I work there until four in the morning, in front of a wall of paintings and artworks that I have acquired from flea markets and garage sales, and one I found literally thrown out on the street. I remember, as a child, that the walls of our homes were completely empty—not a single poster or postcard. I was fascinated by illustration and would often tear off the scenes on shampoo bottles, or labels I found pretty, and make a collage to put on the wall. I think that perhaps my career path was defined by these moments in my early youth. I have never spent more than $100 on an artwork, with one exception: the painting in my bedroom that cost me considerably more!

My favorite piece of furniture is a Victorian deep red velvet lounge chair, covered in a pink Indian fabric, which stands proudly in my living room. The ceiling of my bedroom is a jade green, the walls a combination of glazes—cinnabar rubbed with ochers and browns to create a special red, and black stained floors. I live surrounded by color in a colorless city—the perfect backdrop.

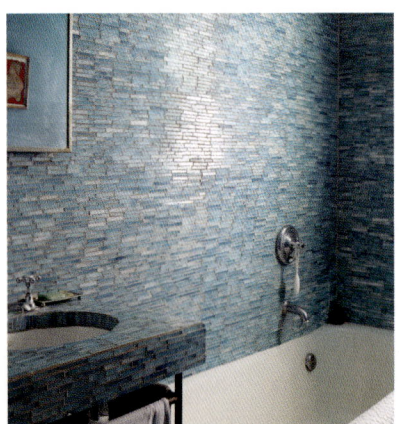

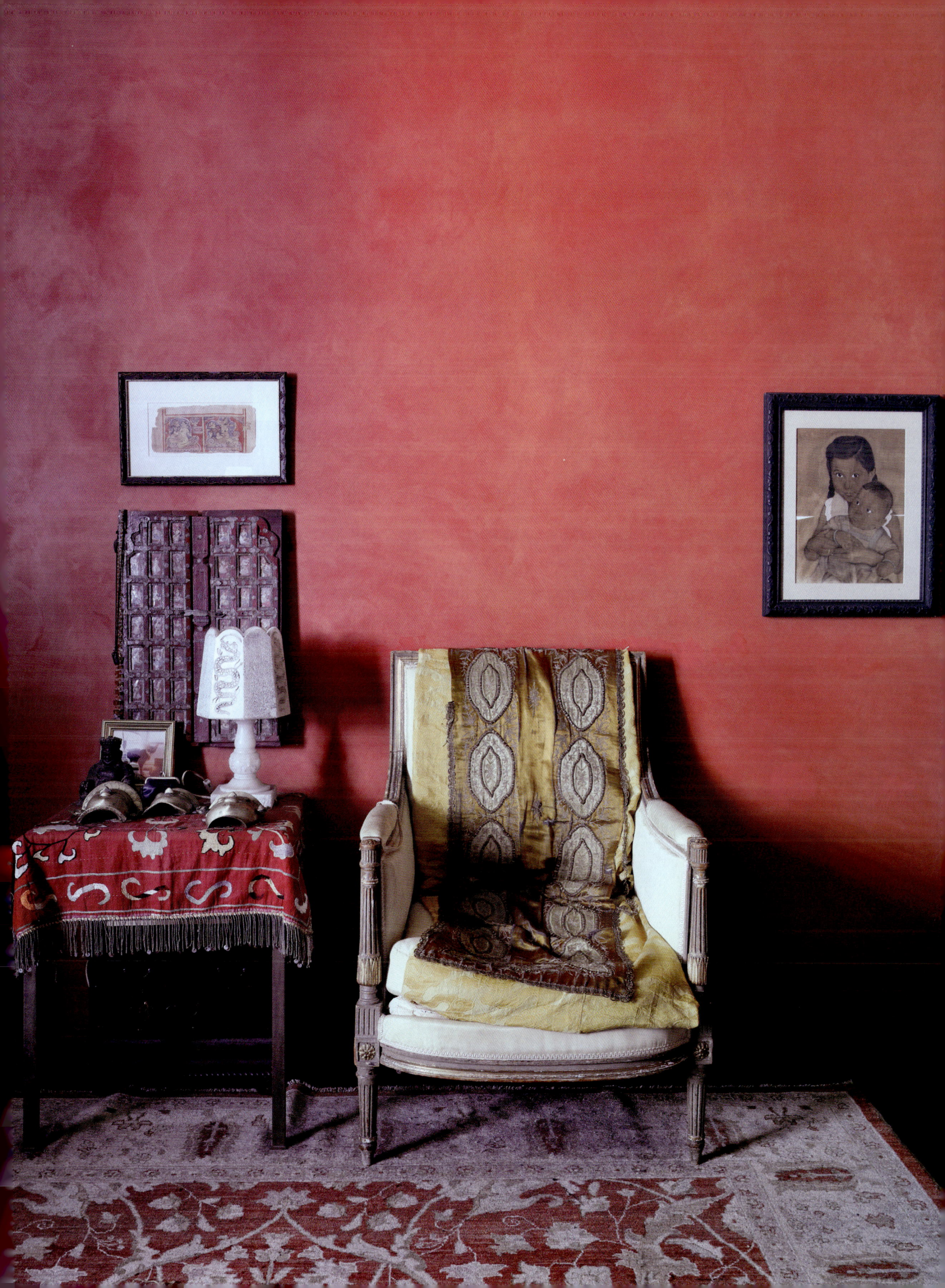

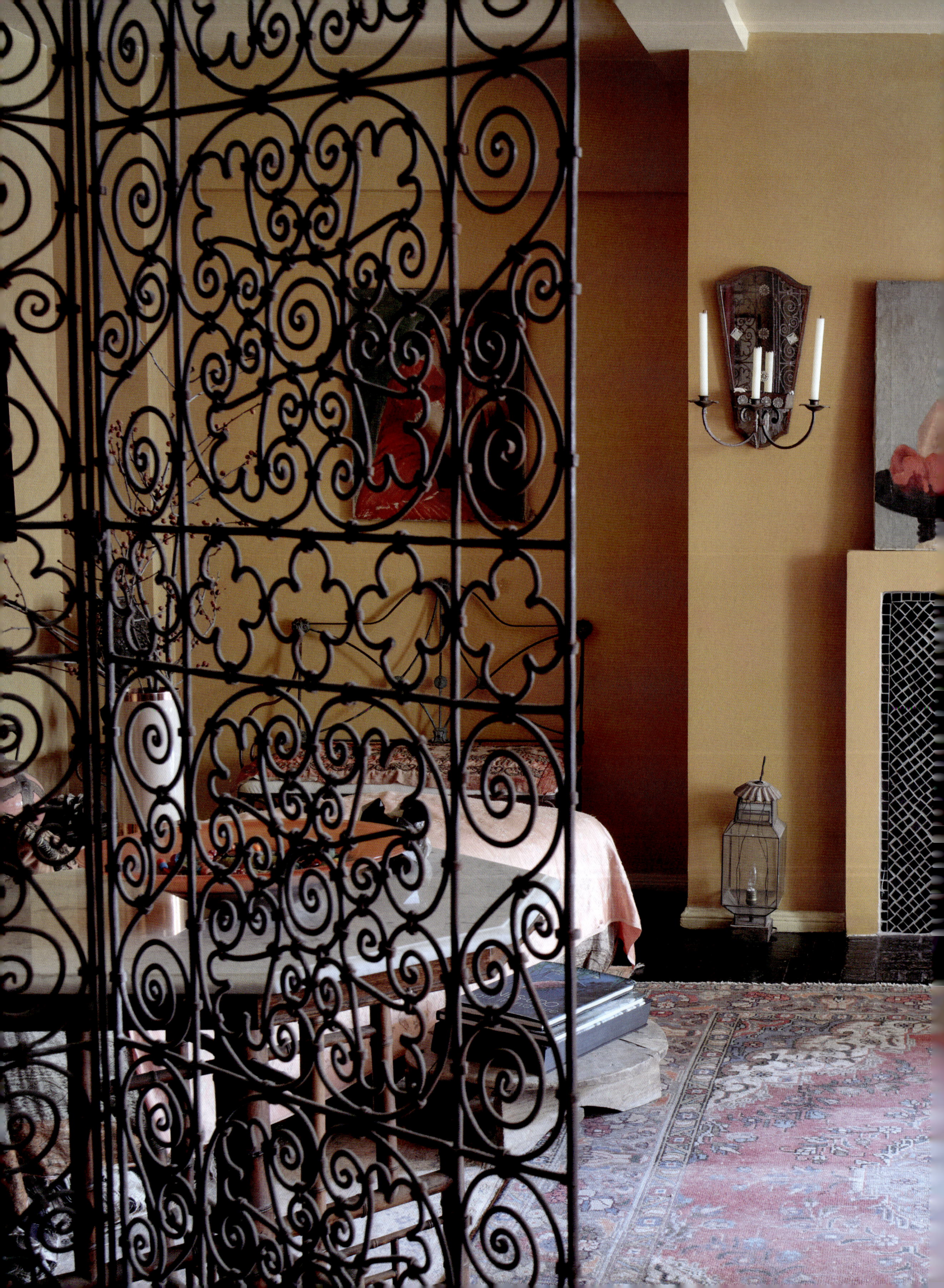

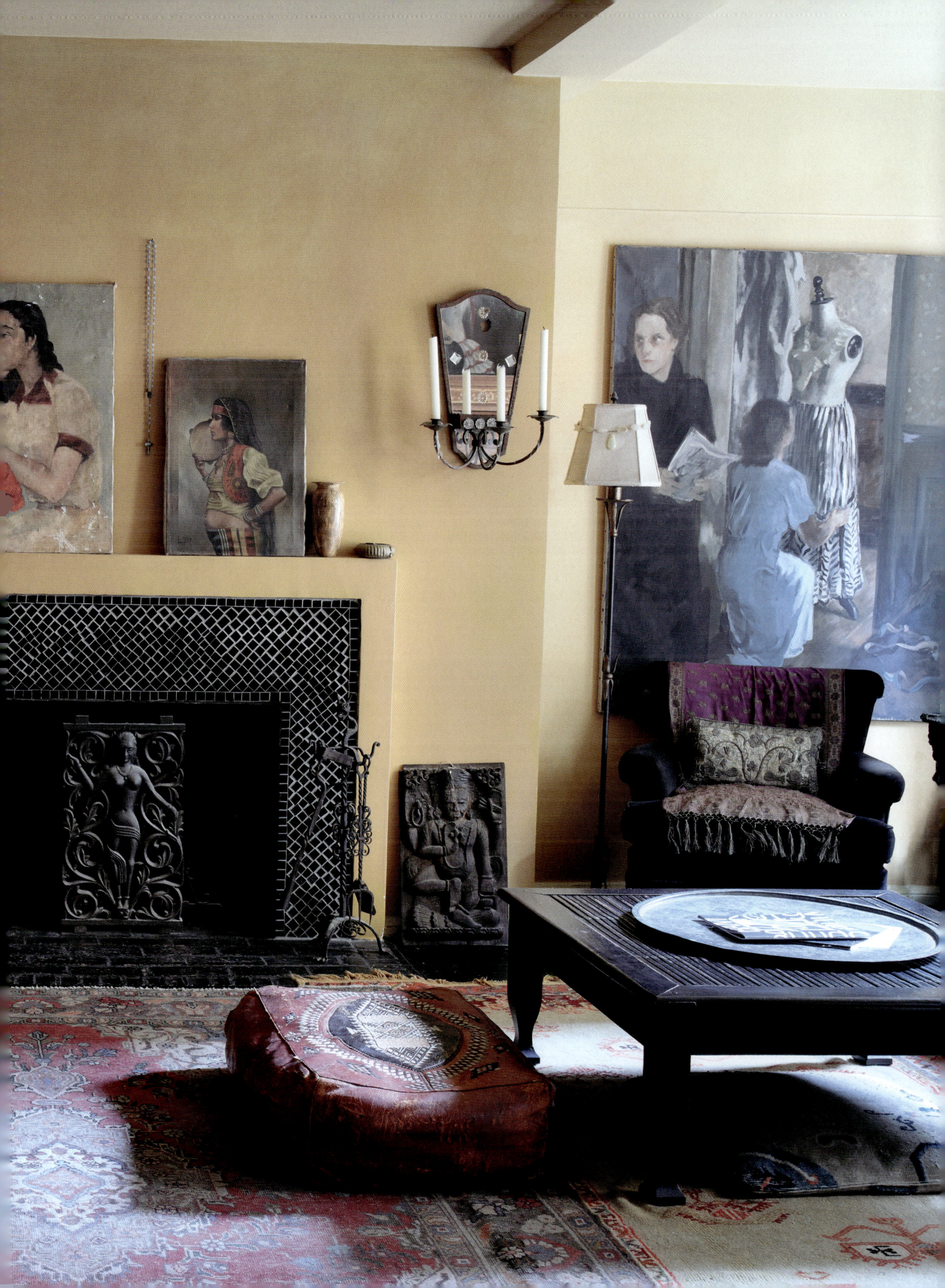

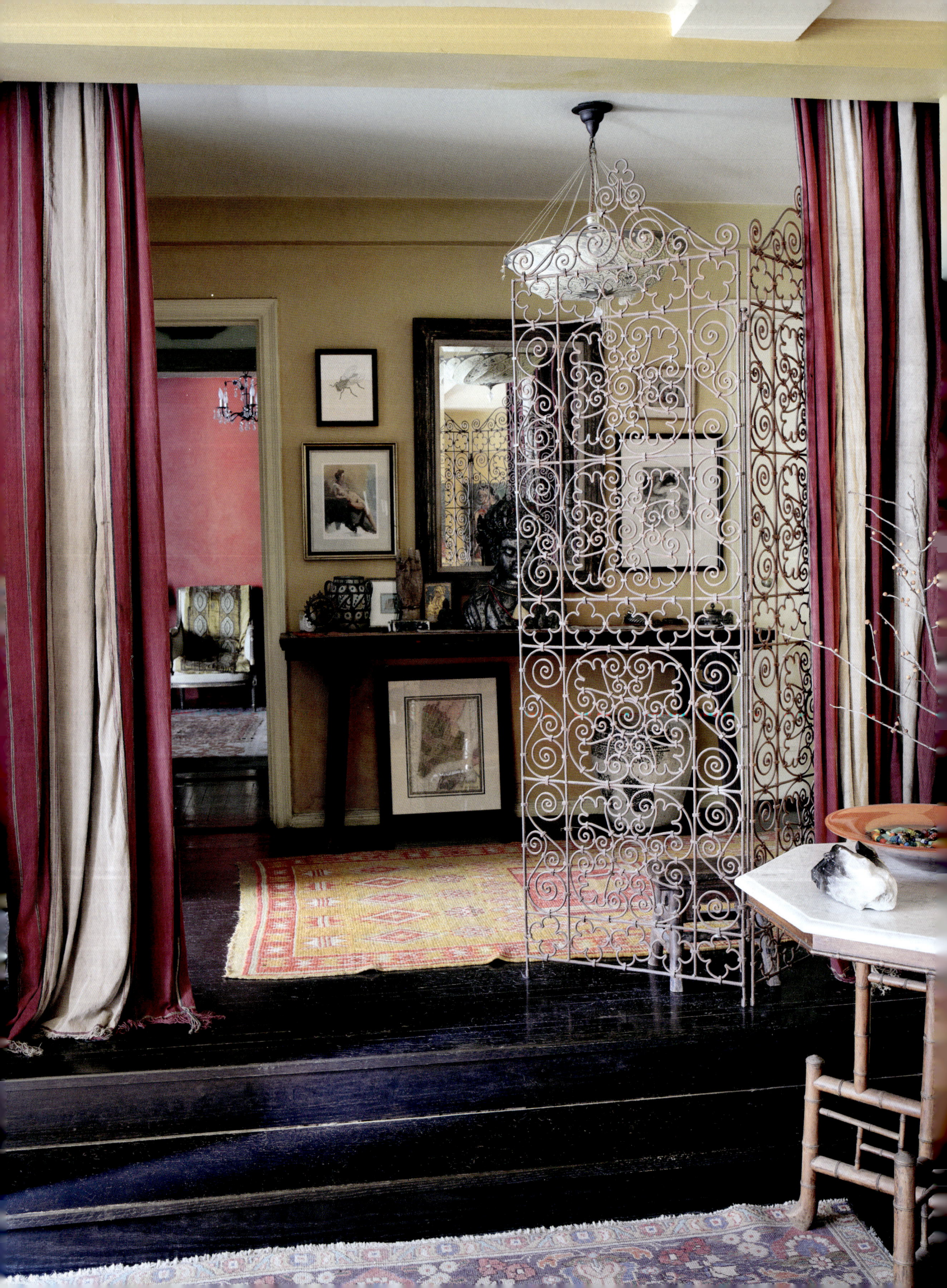

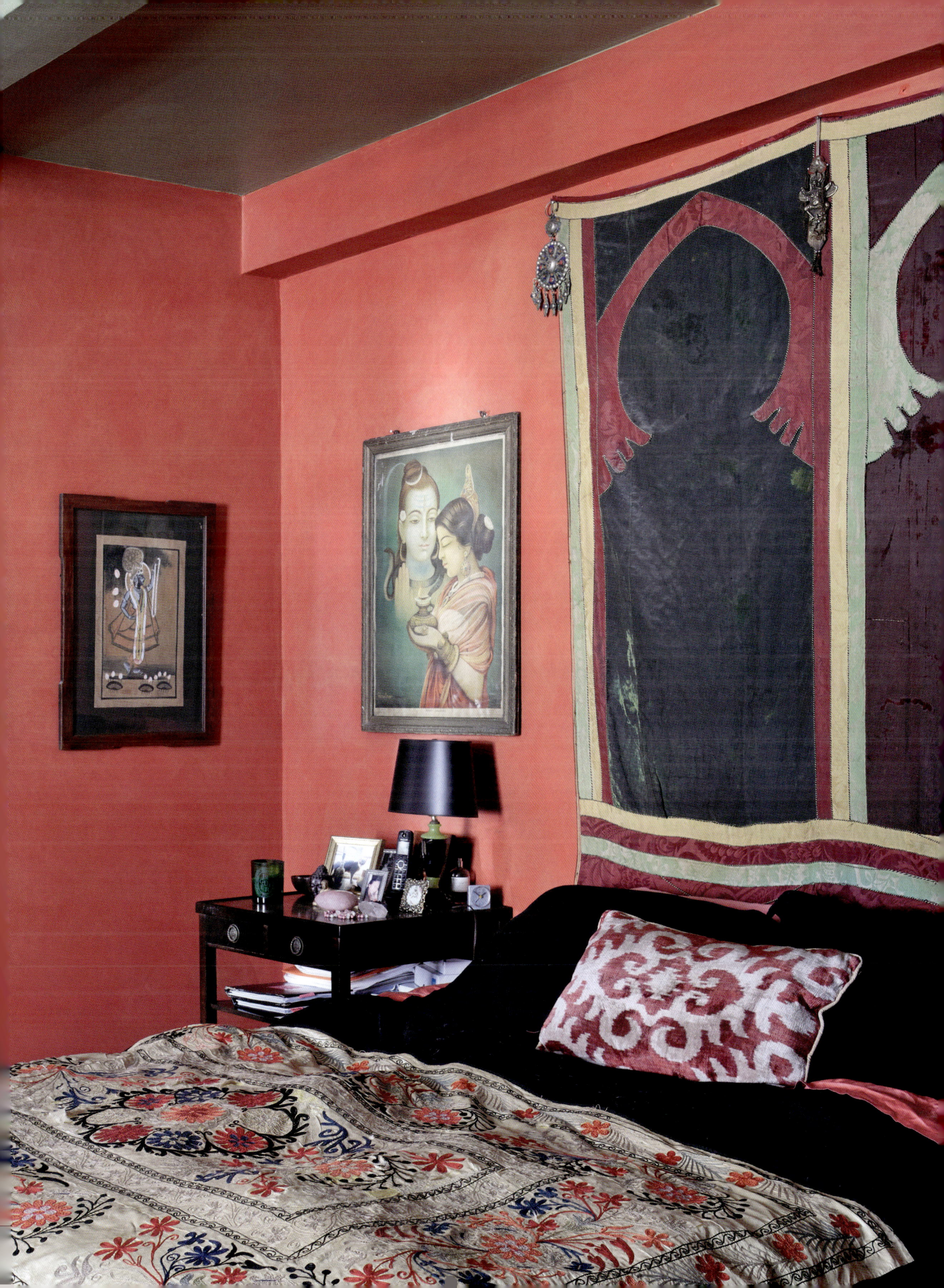

SOPHISTICATION

JULIE HILLMAN

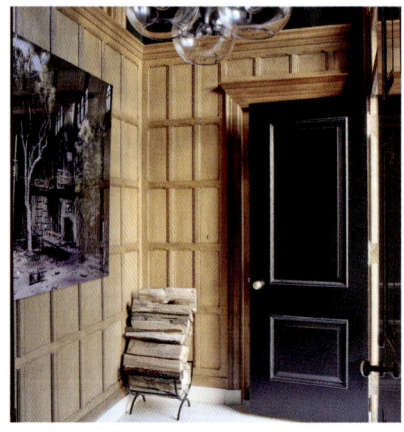

It must be nearly a decade now since my client was in the process of purchasing this extraordinary home and I was invited to get involved. A maisonette on Fifth Avenue, right opposite The Metropolitan Museum, is a very rare thing. The building was the first luxury apartment block to be built on Fifth Avenue between 1910 and 1912, and the architect was encouraged to incorporate as many embellishments as possible to attract the attention of America's wealthiest families. We are a small interior design business and take on only a handful of clients at any one time, so, at first, I thought we wouldn't be able to fit the project into our schedule. That was before I paid the property a visit, a place the like of which I have never seen before in this city. New Yorkers are quick to demolish or repaint and it is almost impossible to find anything preserved, which made the house all the more unusual, with its pre-war wood paneling and original light fixtures. The project was the opportunity of a lifetime!

I didn't plan on doing very much to the property, as so much of the original design simply could not be improved upon. My client collects contemporary art, and this set the parameters around which we were to create and design furniture and fittings. The goal was to fashion as harmonious an environment as possible. Many of the rooms were dark, so the lighting

needed to be updated. The bathrooms required modernizing and the kitchen refurbishing and, while we were at it, we introduced a library and swapped out a few rooms. The living/dining room was huge, with windows at pavement level. It was a strange sensation, from the tranquility of the interior, to feel the urgency of people hurrying past, going about their daily lives. I loved the size of the room and its sense of space, but felt it did not work for this dual purpose. By removing the dining table we were able to create a series of seating scenarios, which introduced a different energy.

This left us without a dining room, and with a vast, unused entry hall. We designed a fabulous table made up of five separate pieces of marble supported by bronze bases on castors made by Eric Schmitt. By day, the table is pushed back against the hall's original wood paneling, and by night it is pulled forward and used as a dining table, with place settings to accommodate 25–30 people. But my favorite piece of functional furniture has to be the daybed. It grounded the living room and gave it soul, separating and spacing the other seating groups. I also love the chandelier, which hangs above it; made of paper plates, it was put together in situ by the artist, Christopher Trujillo.

I originally come from Chicago, and moved to Manhattan in the late 1980s to study at Parsons School of Design. I have been here ever since, living and working in the city. I am honored to have worked on a home that is so uniquely "New York," and am glad it was captured so beautifully by Simon.

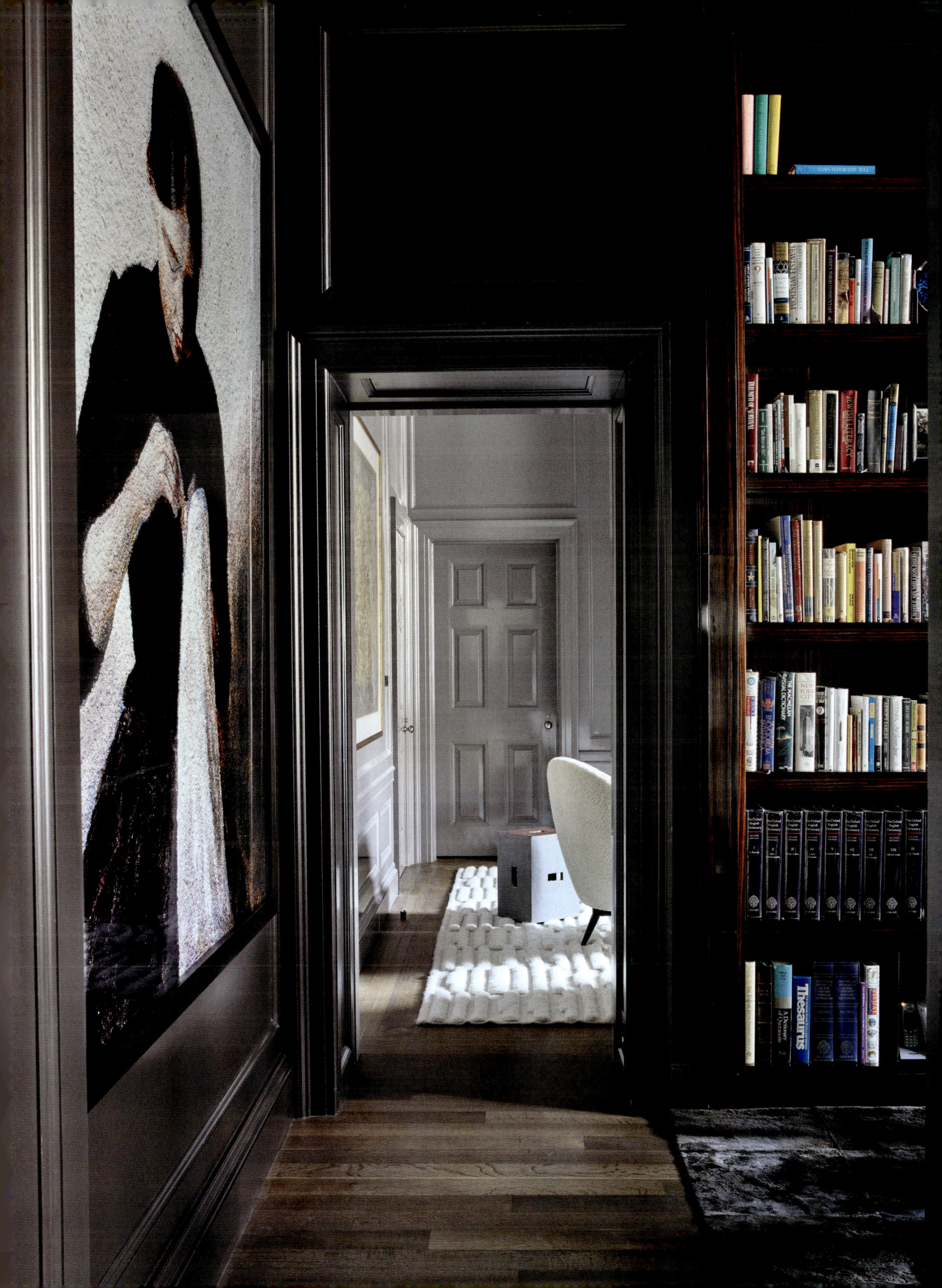

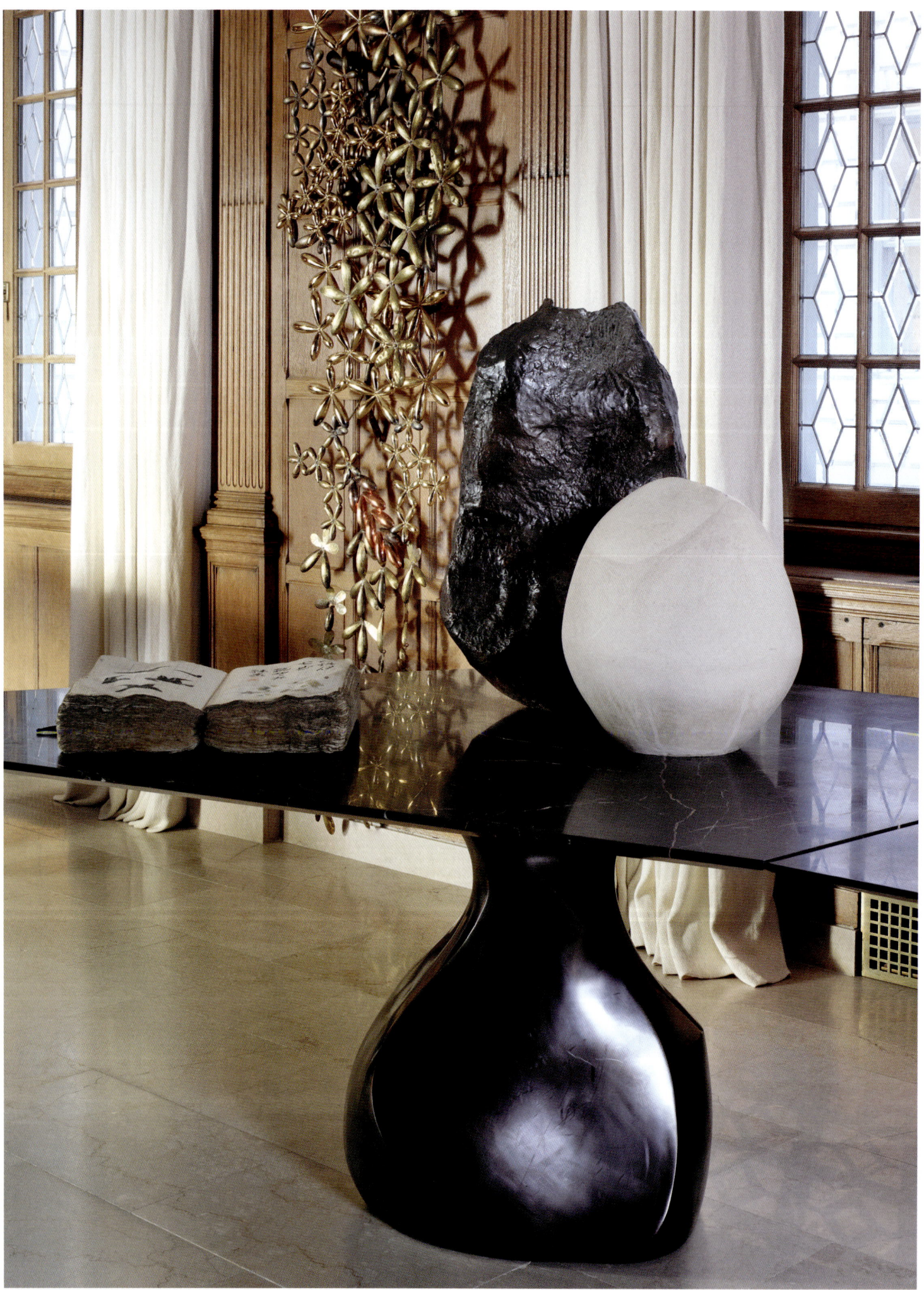

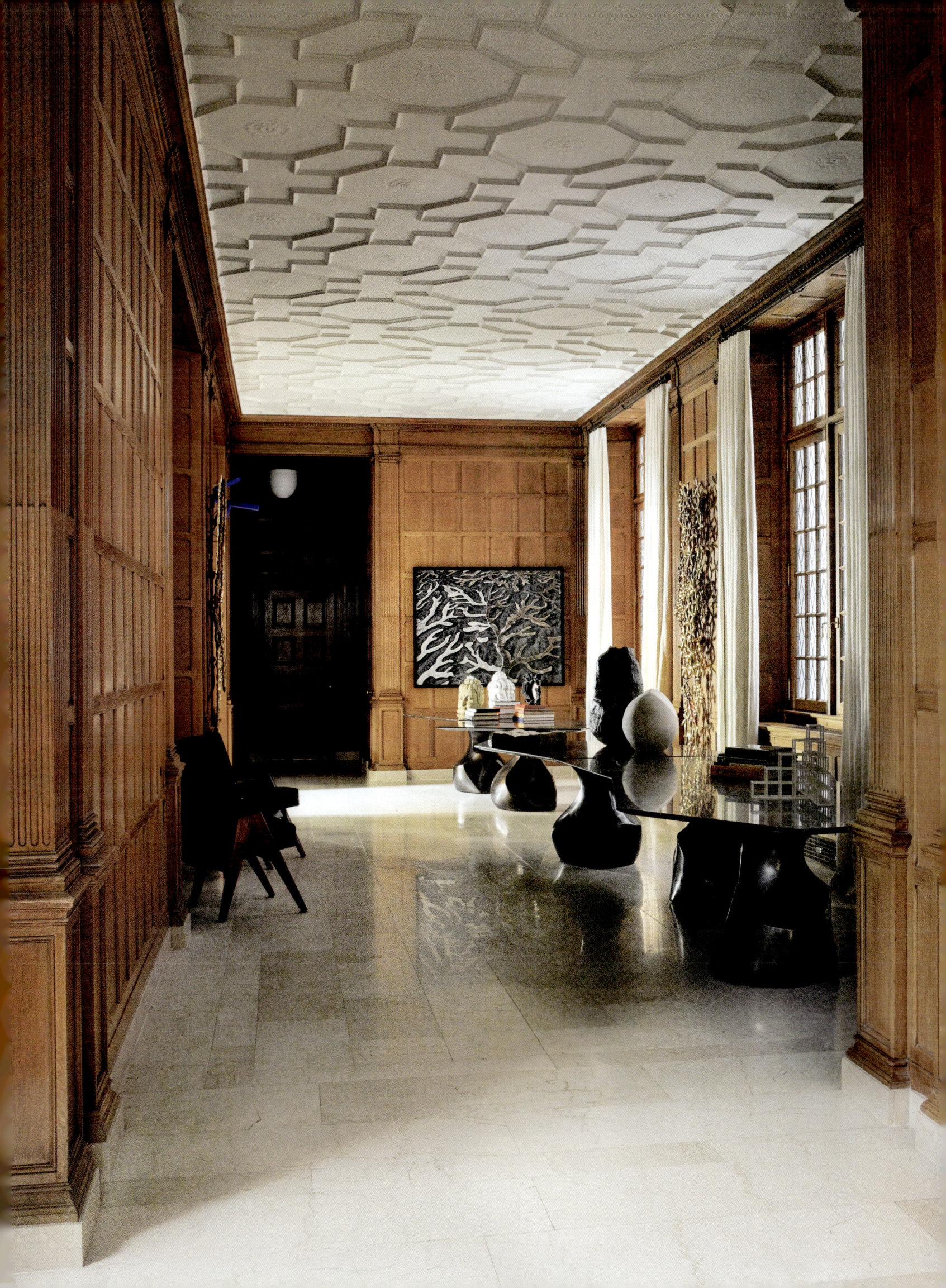

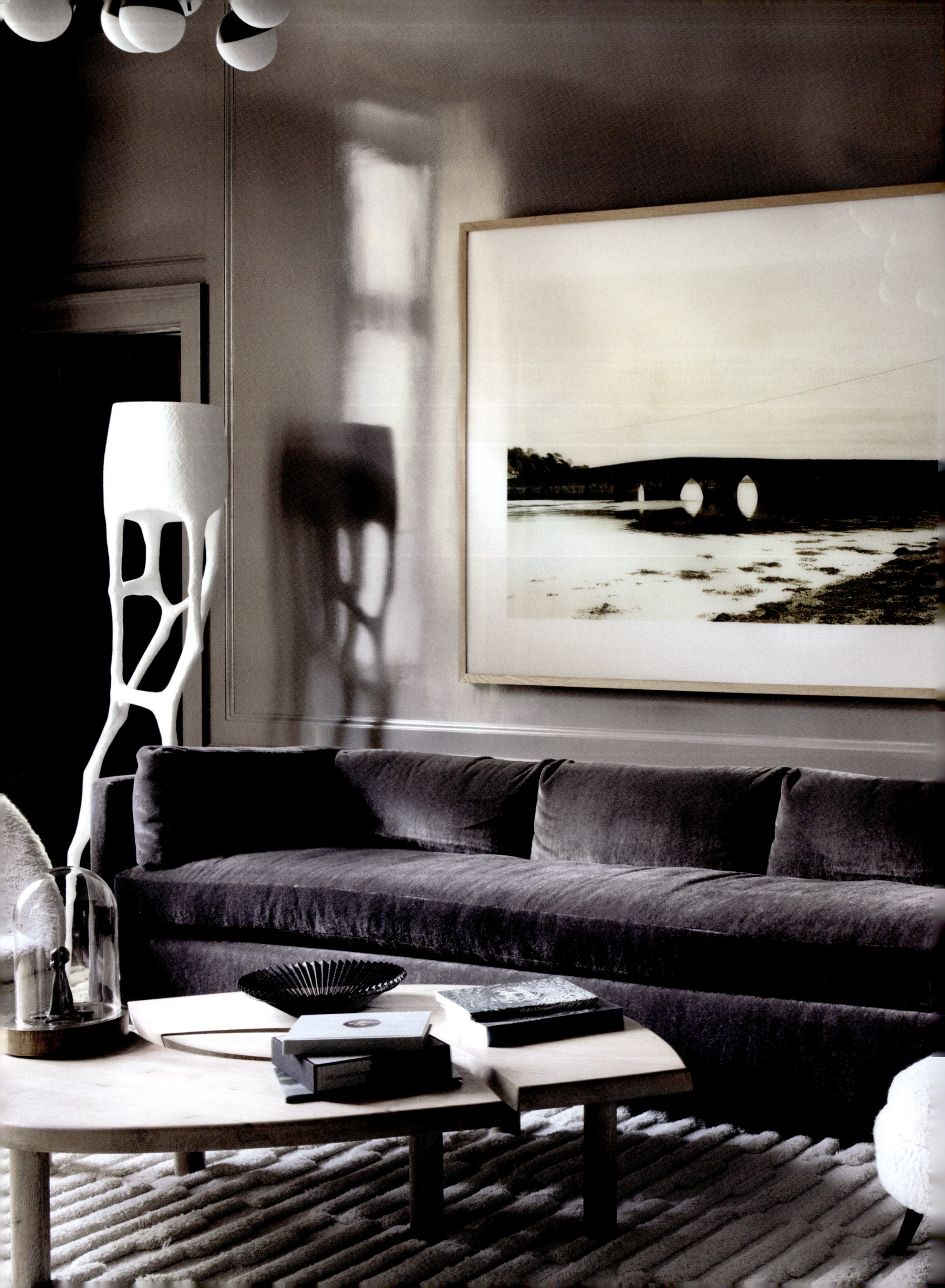

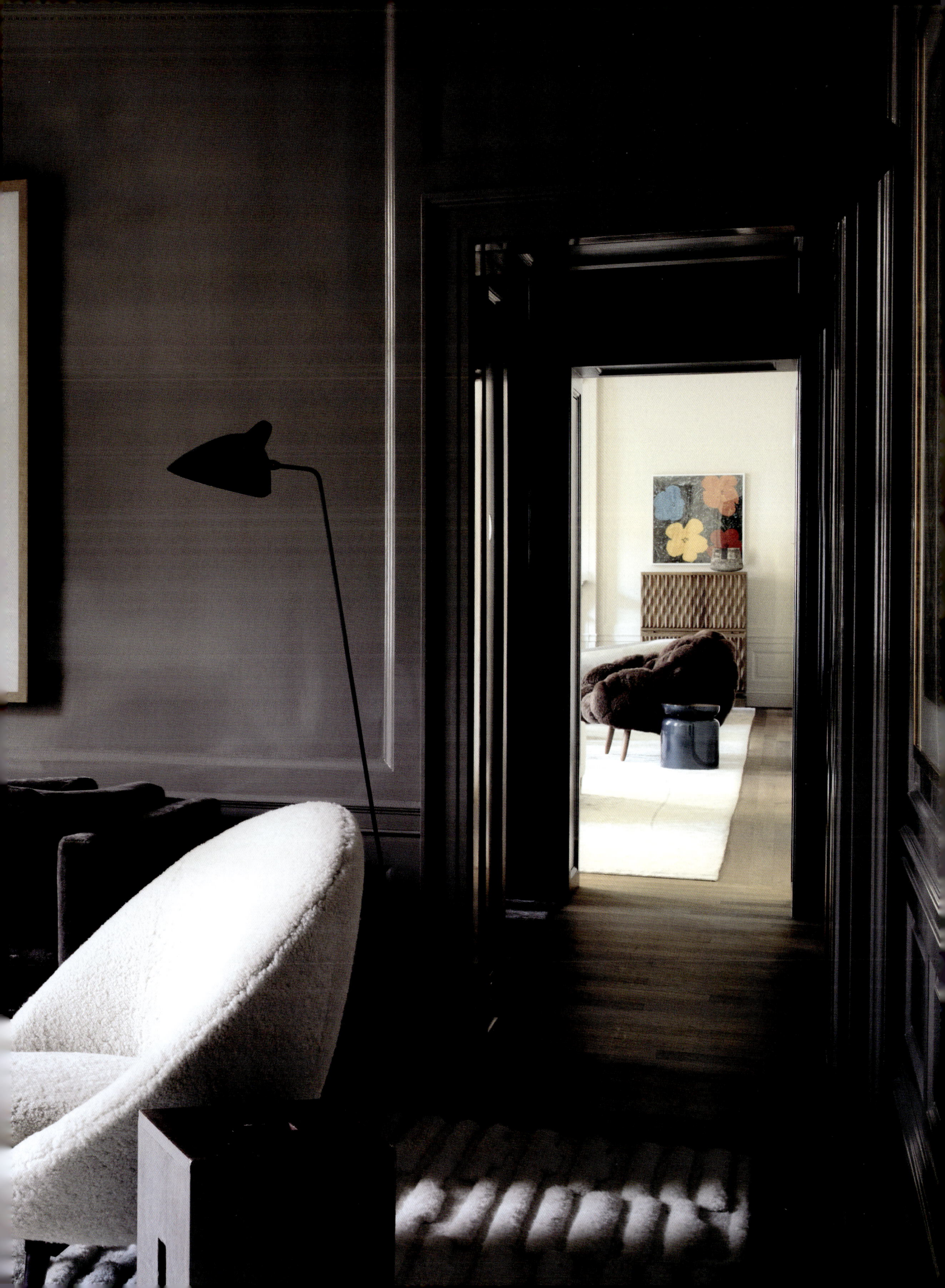

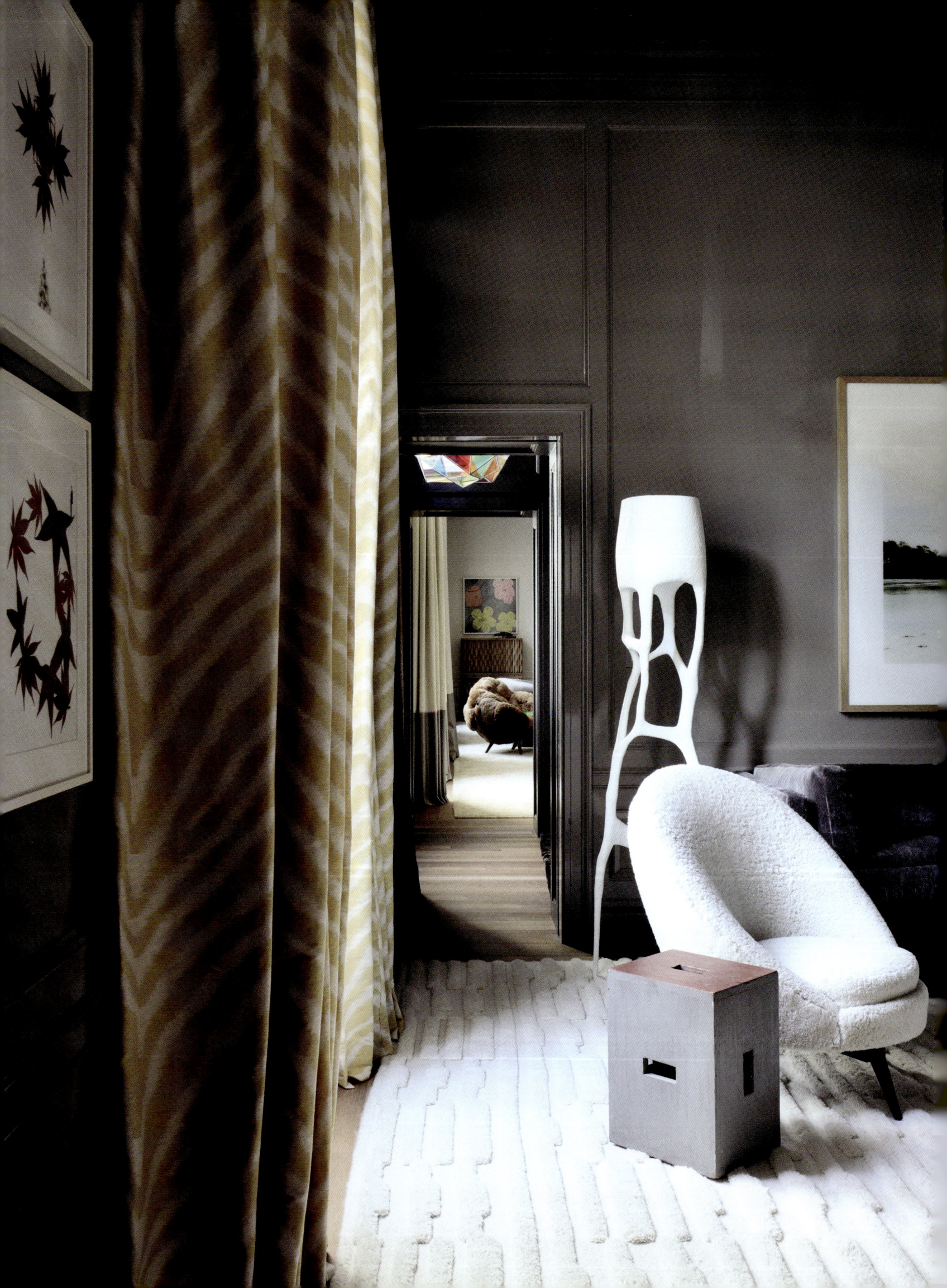

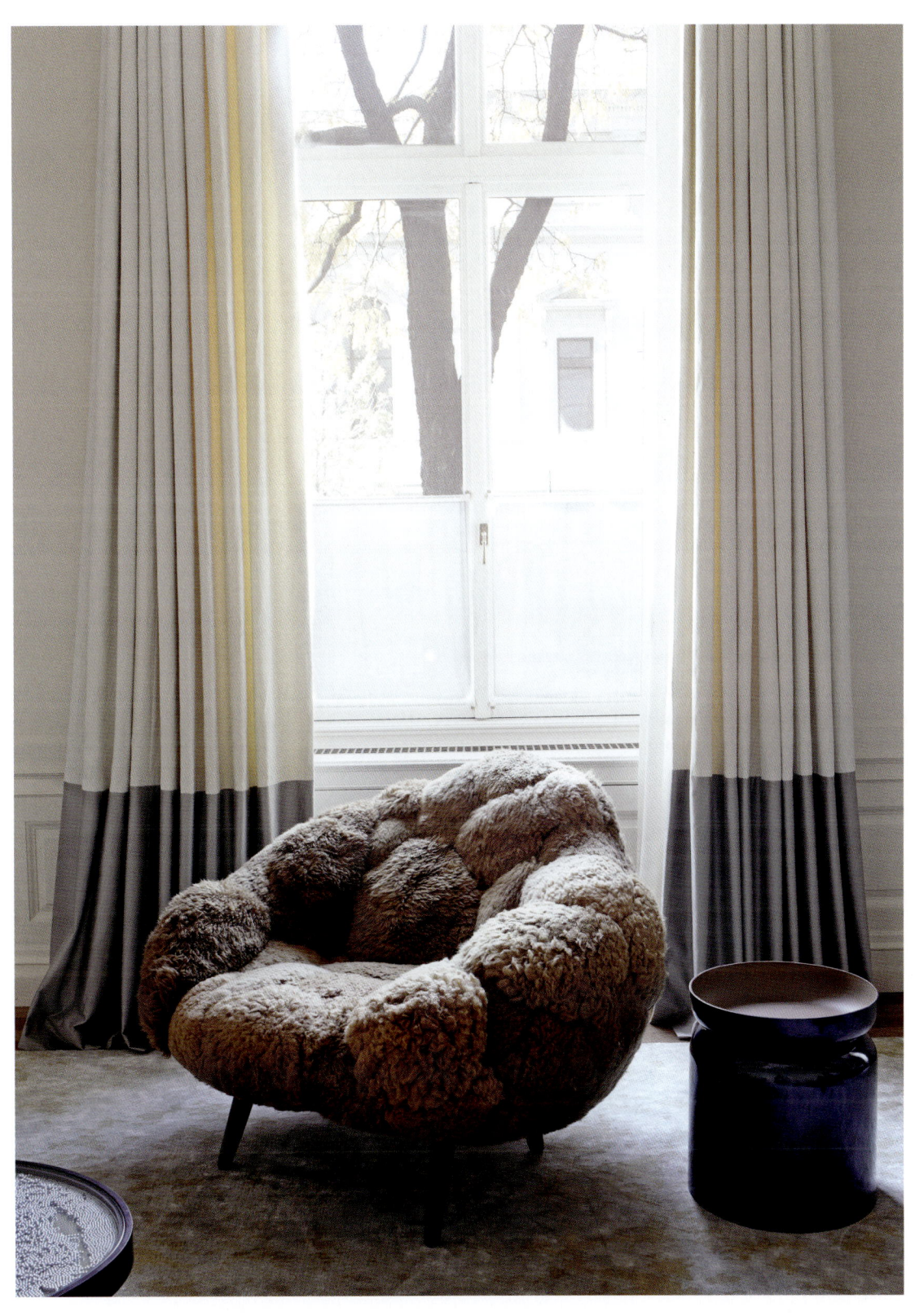

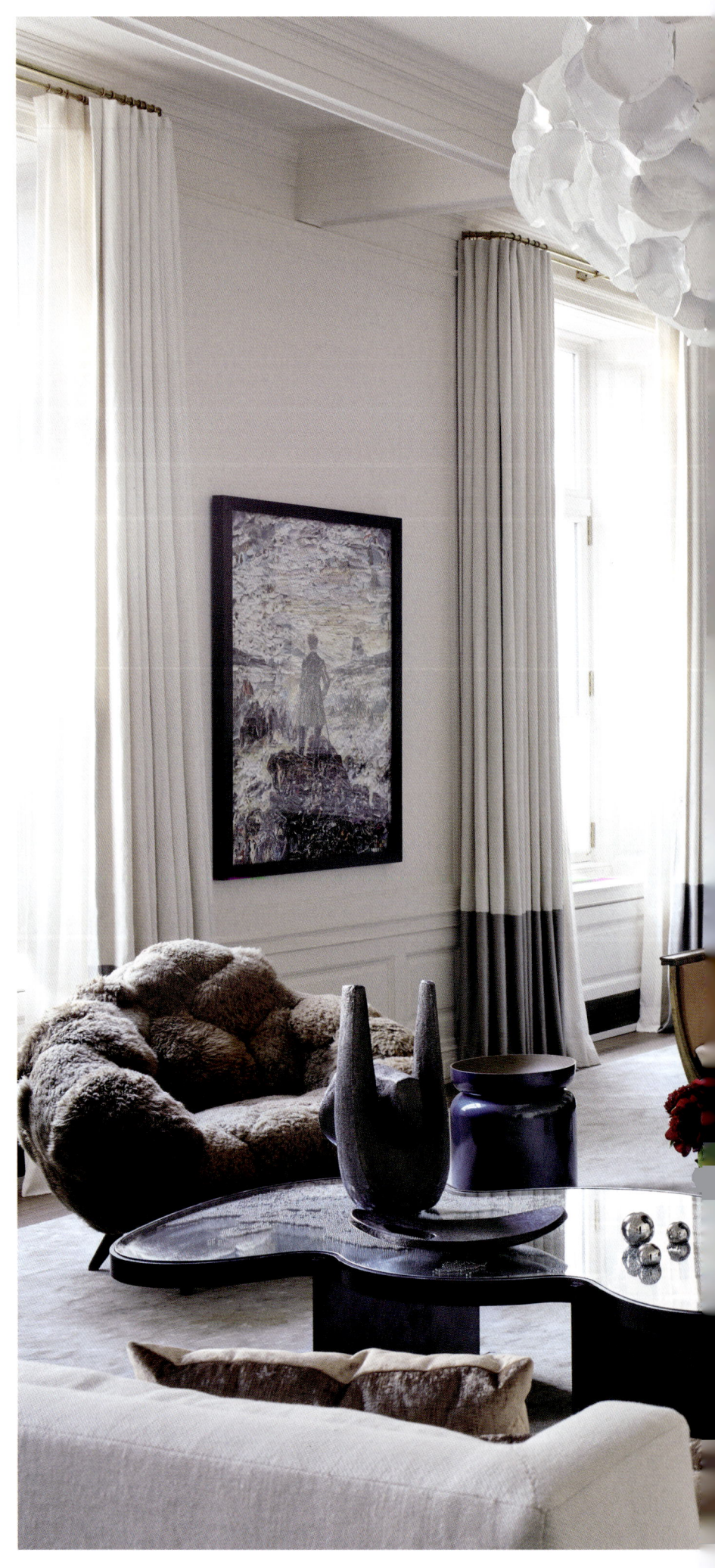

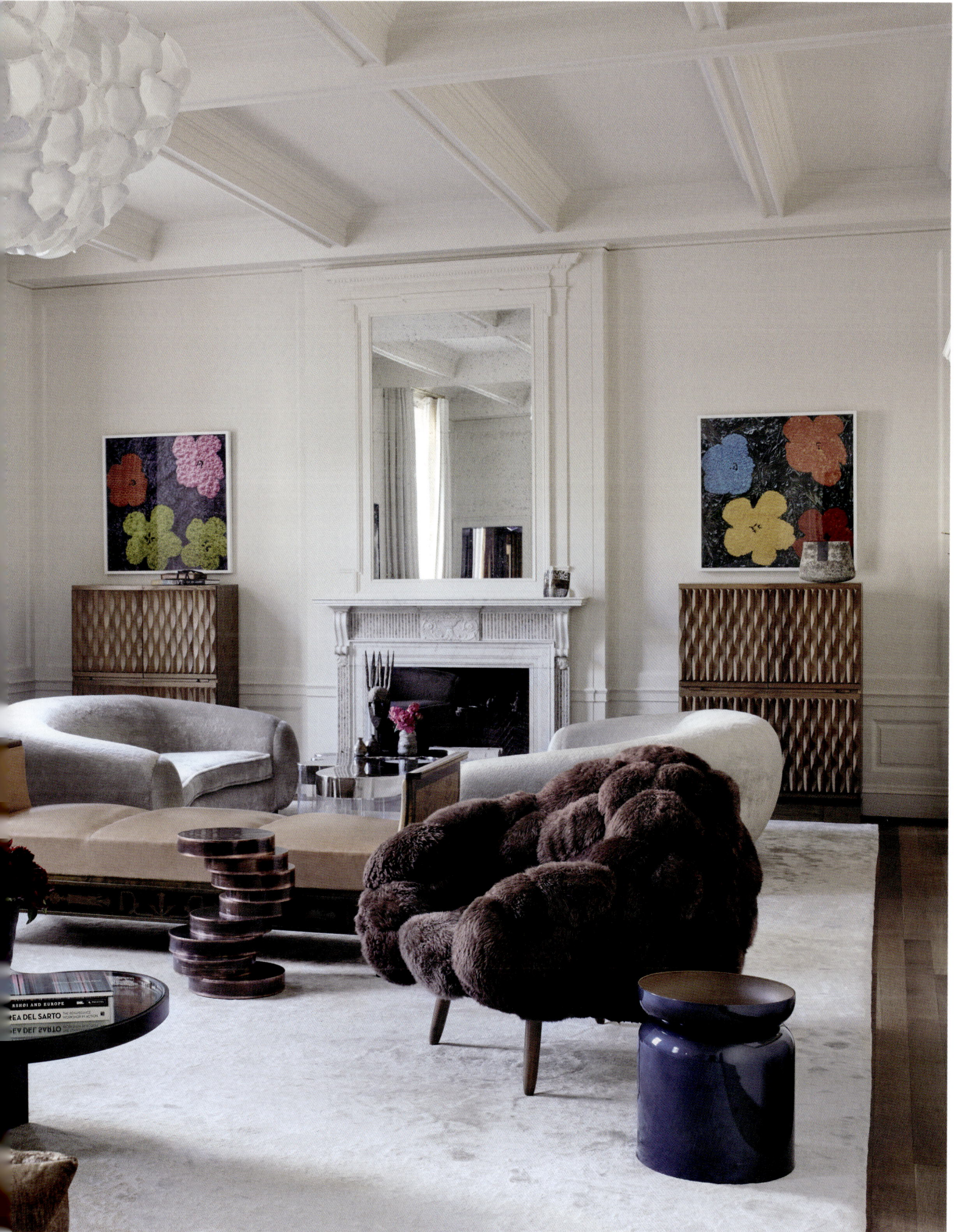

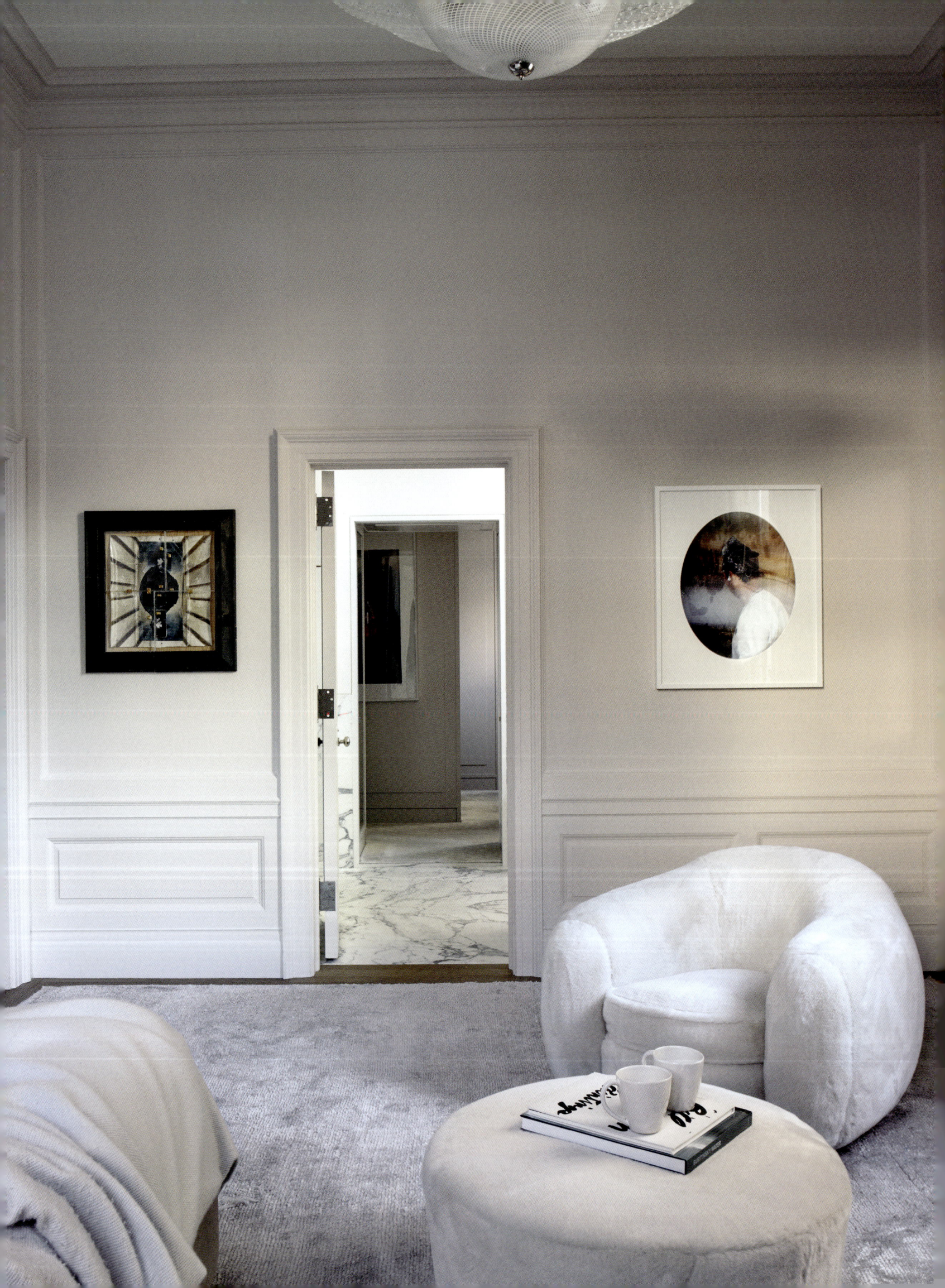

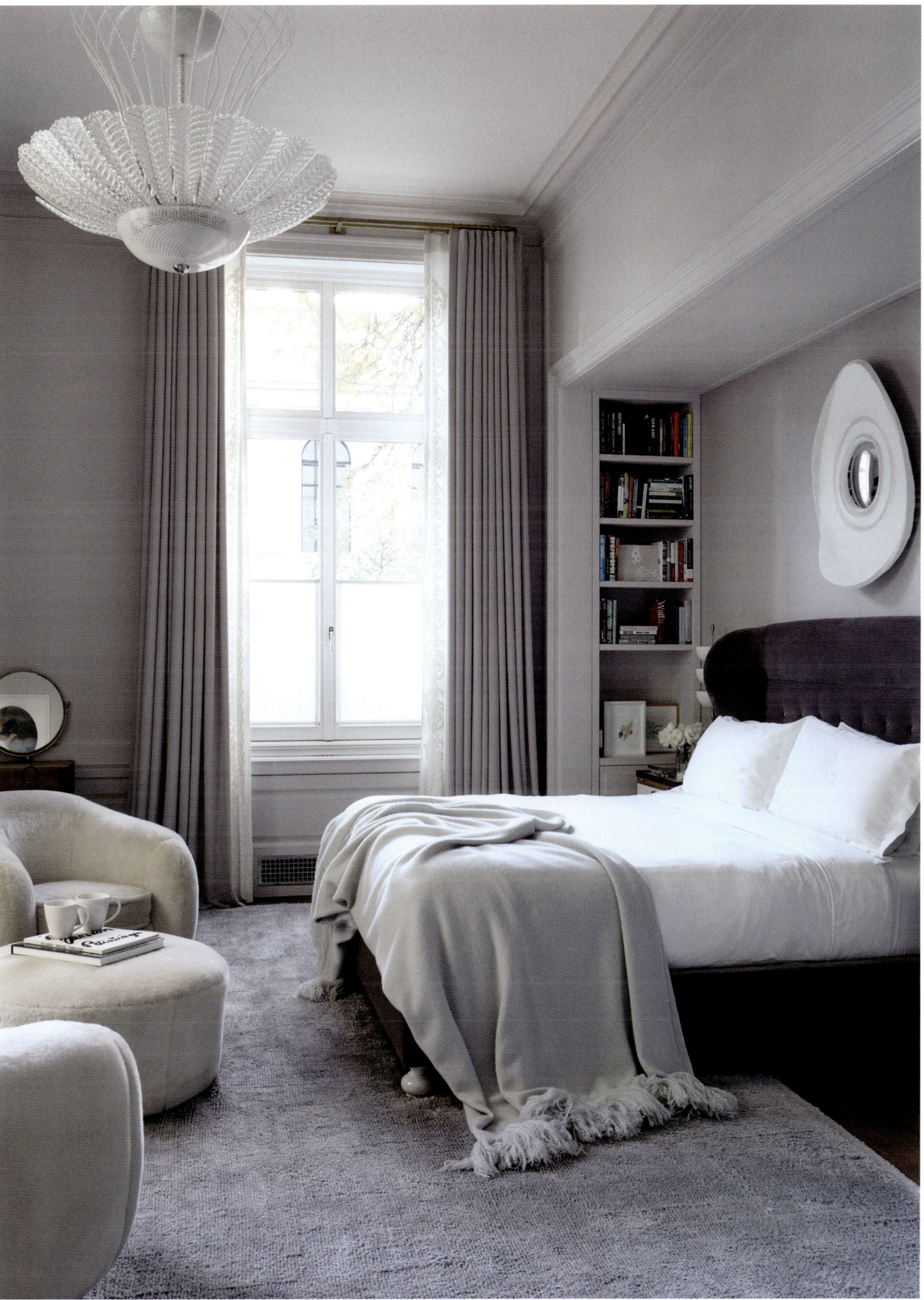

LIVING THE DREAM

MARTIN BOURNE

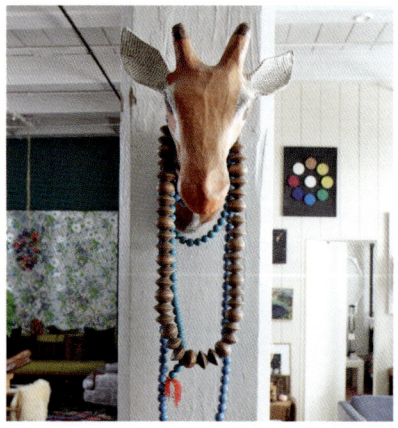

I moved to New York from London about 25 years ago and, with nowhere to live, was told of a place in Dumbo. That place turned out to be a vast nineteenth-century building in the Victorian warehouse district, with huge windows and lots of light: *the* New York dream loft space. I didn't stop to think whether I could afford the rent—I just moved in. As a prop stylist, it suits me perfectly: a space in which I can work, as well as store all the things I buy or use in the magazine industry.

Dumbo used to be a very "artsy" part of New York, and when I first moved here I would see the famous 60s model Veruschka cycling around the neighborhood looking like the proverbial bag lady. It was a rough-and-ready district, and not unusual to find the wreck of a burned-out car down the street. Nowadays, the once abandoned park under the Brooklyn Bridge is a super-cool place to hang out, and the previously transient population—who would buy an apartment and then flip it without moving in—is now becoming a community in which we actually know one another.

The loft divides naturally into three main areas simply by the placement of furniture. The living area is defined by a fuchsia pink sofa and armchairs, the dining or "party" table occupies center stage and is where we do all of our making, drinking, and chatting, and then there is my desk and "creation" area against one wall, which is an ever-changing tableau of found things. My favorite piece at the moment (I am always changing my mind) is a bright red Vladimir Kagan swivel chair with two ottomans, which I found at the 25th Street flea market back in the day.

There are two artworks that really stand out for me. The first relates to my husband, Leilin Lopez, who is a big fan of Gloria Vanderbilt and used to follow her on Instagram. They struck up a friendship this way, and he started to "like" her paintings. One in particular was a portrait of a flame-haired woman, naive and quite bonkers. One day a car drew up outside and Gloria's housekeeper got out with an enormous package. It turned out to be the painting, fully framed, and with a note from Gloria. It now forms the centerpiece of a wall of miscellaneous artworks. The second piece of art I am especially fond of is a weird Ashley Hicks totem that complements all the other quirky things that populate the loft.

I enjoy being a foreigner in New York. Being English, Americans think we have an innate sense of history and provenance—that unique characteristic which enables us to mix things up and live in a jumble of periods. If Americans have learned something from me over the years, I have certainly learned from them the importance of exuberance and enthusiasm, and grand-scale extravagance. They never do things in a small way. Everything can be as fantastic as they please, as long as it is the best it possibly can be.

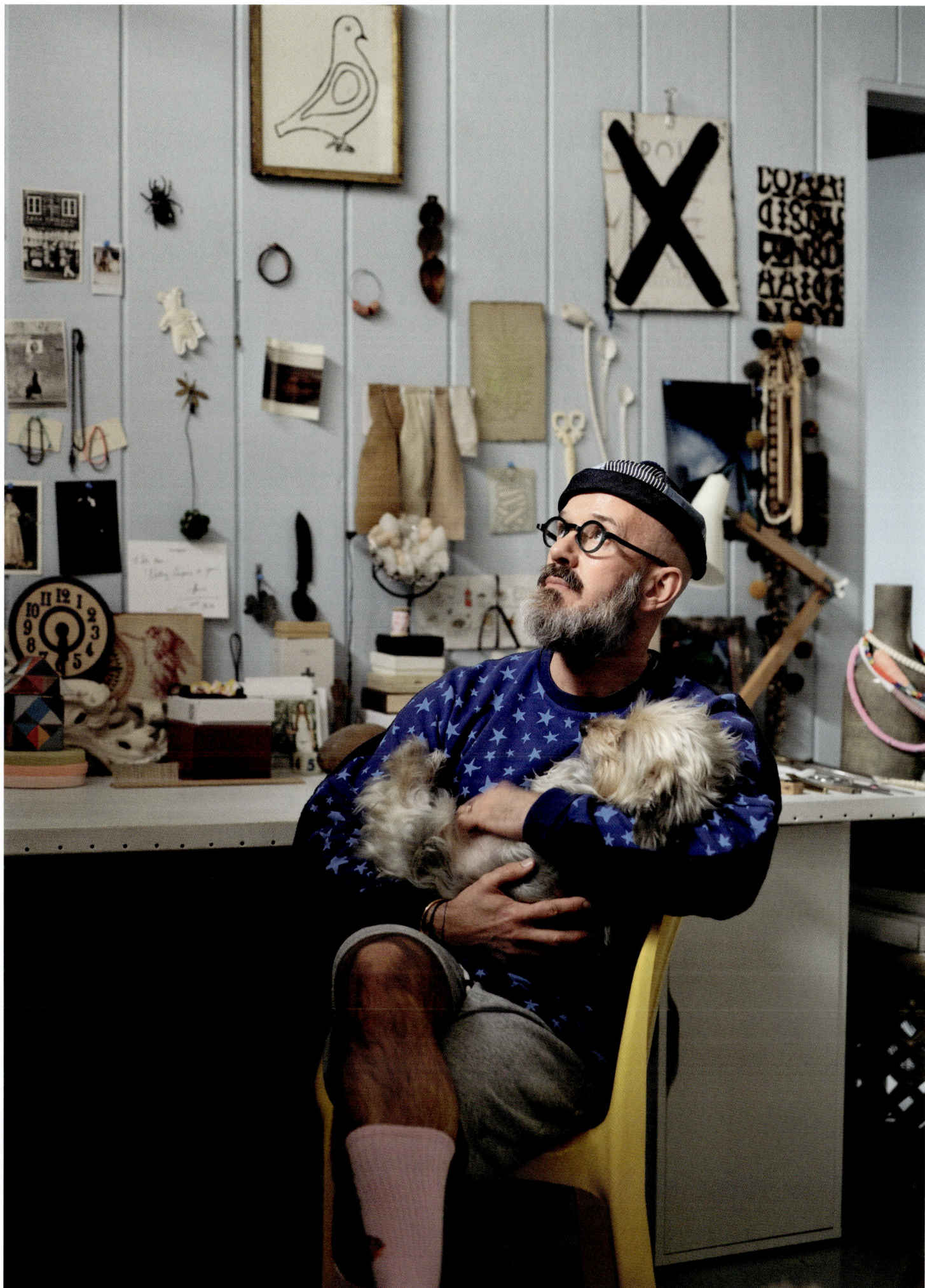

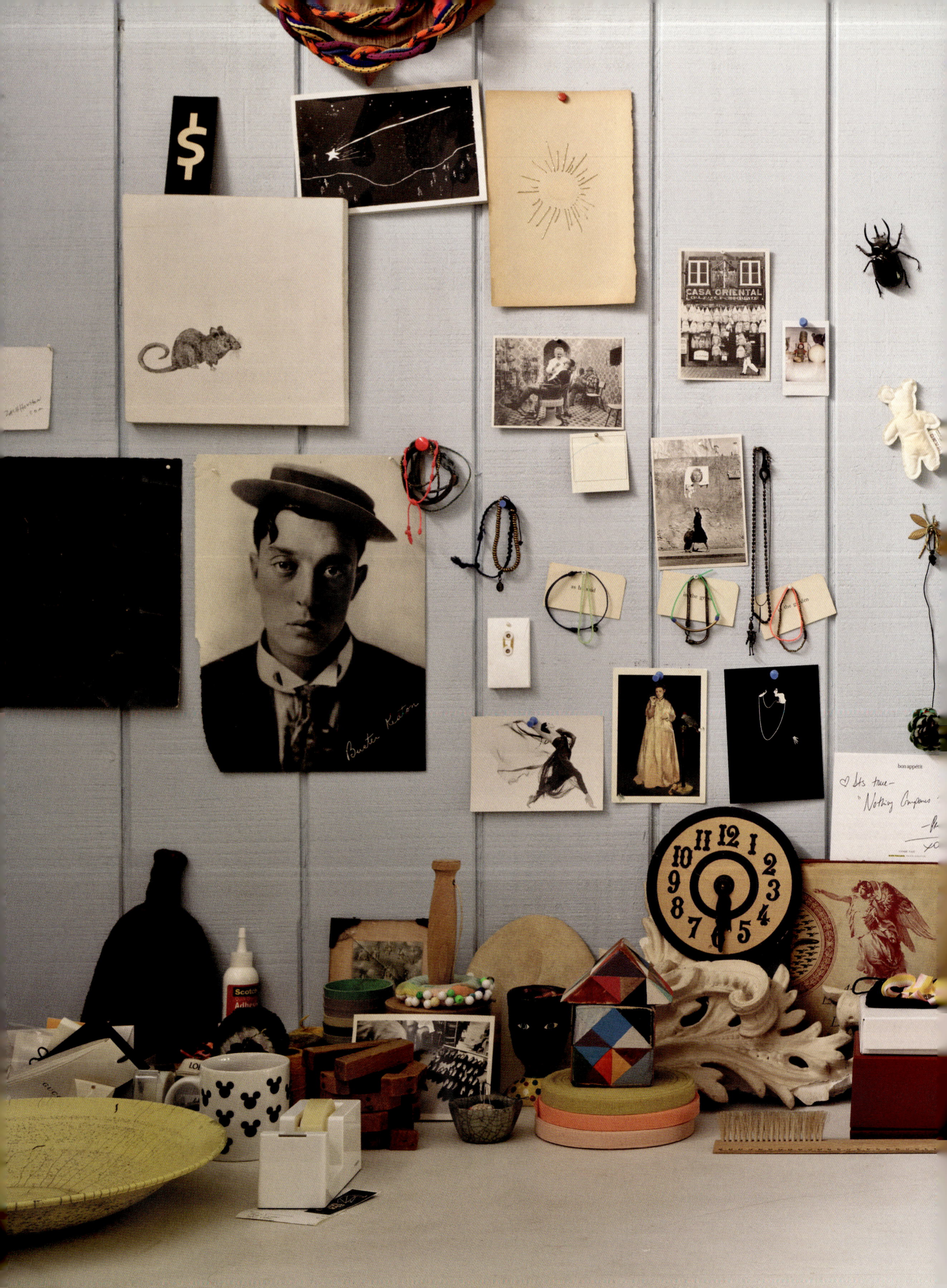

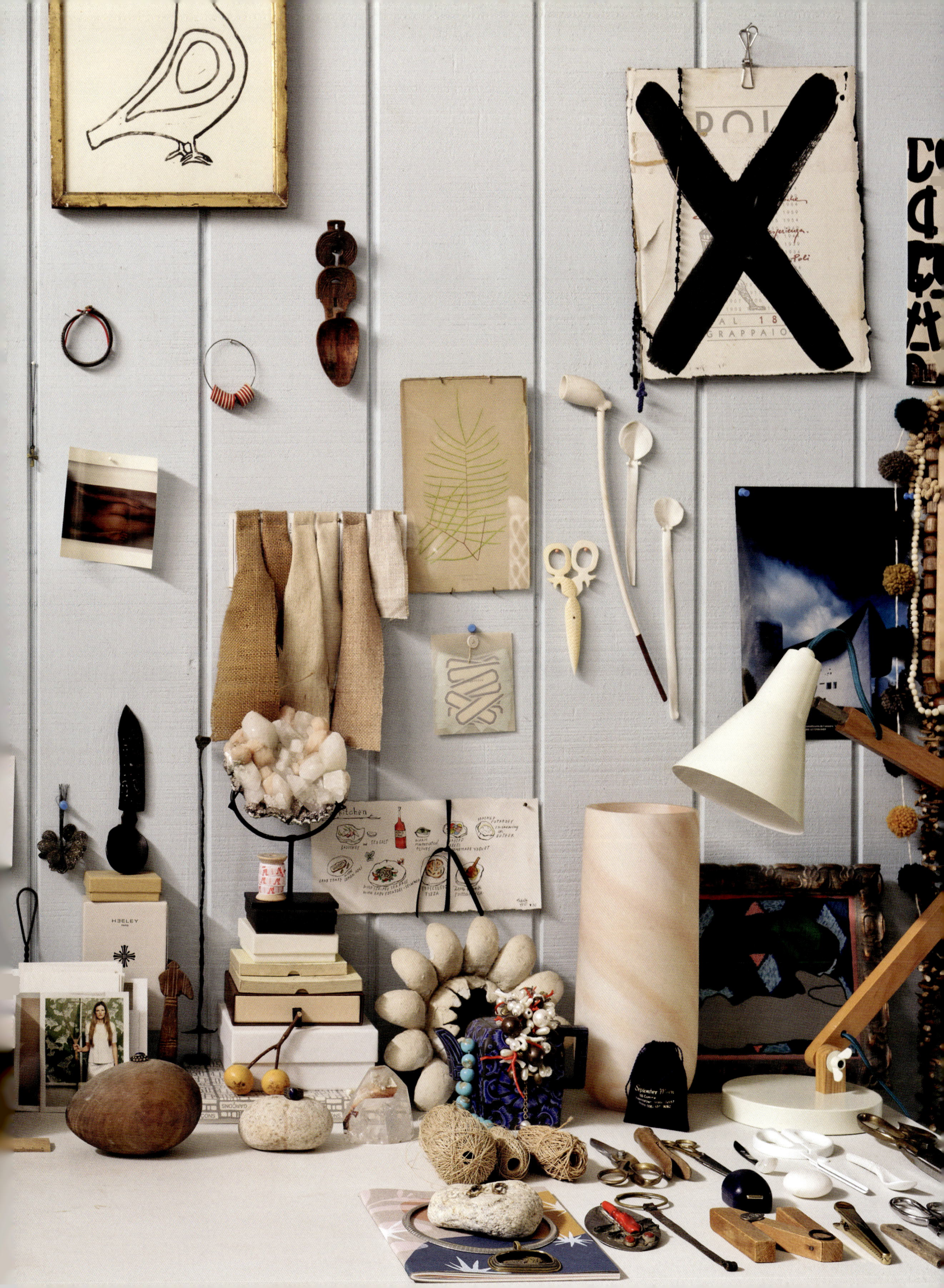

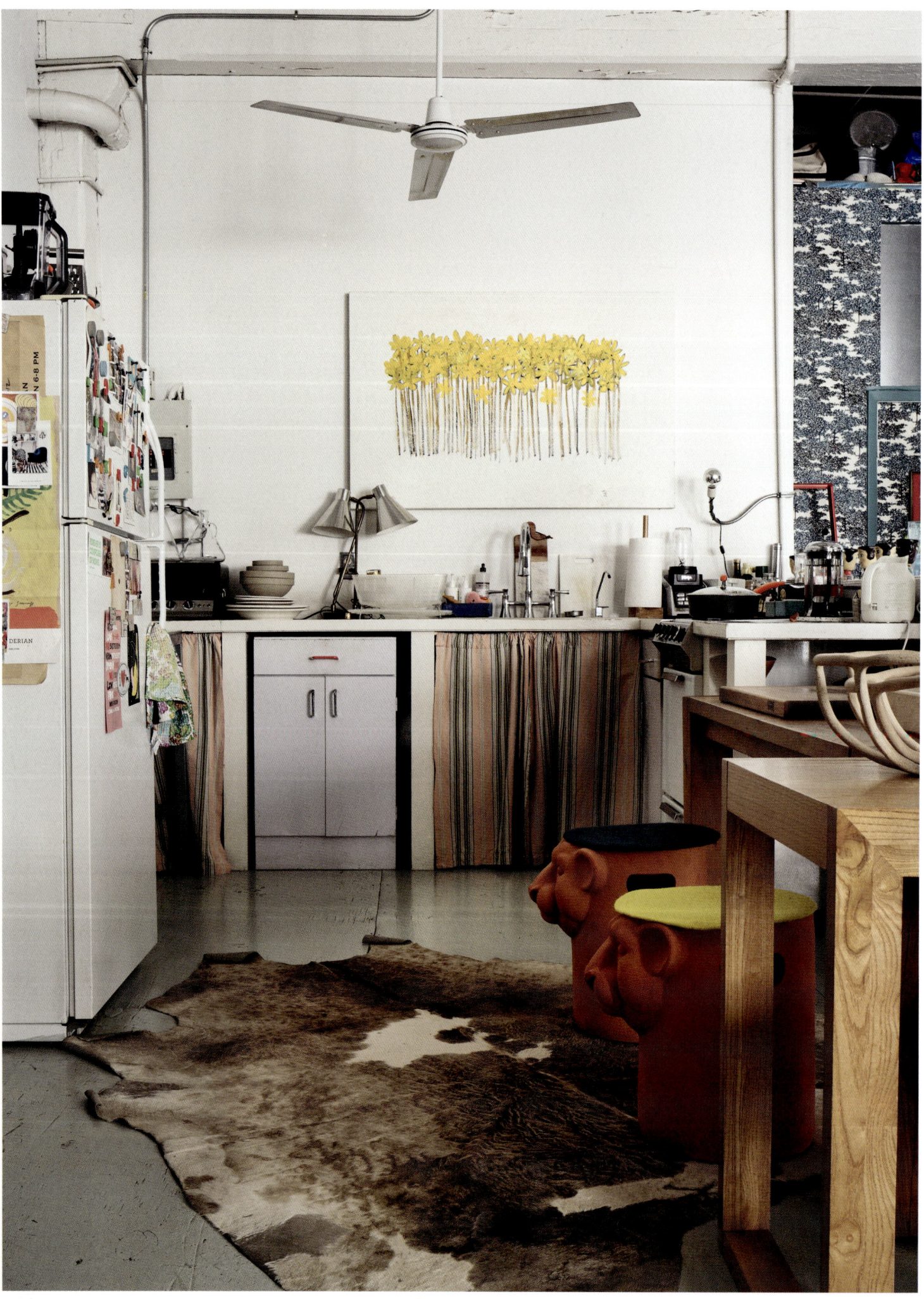

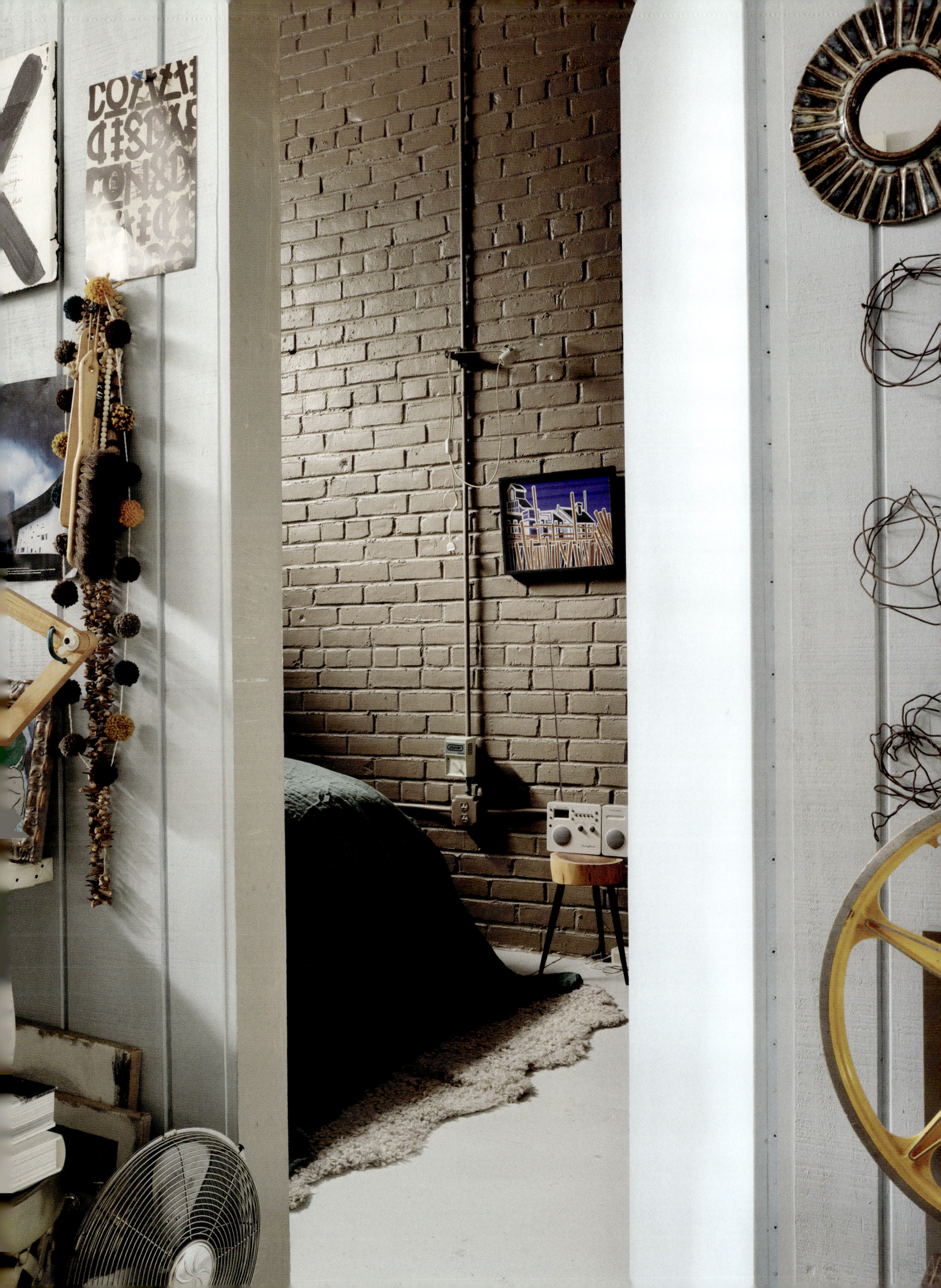

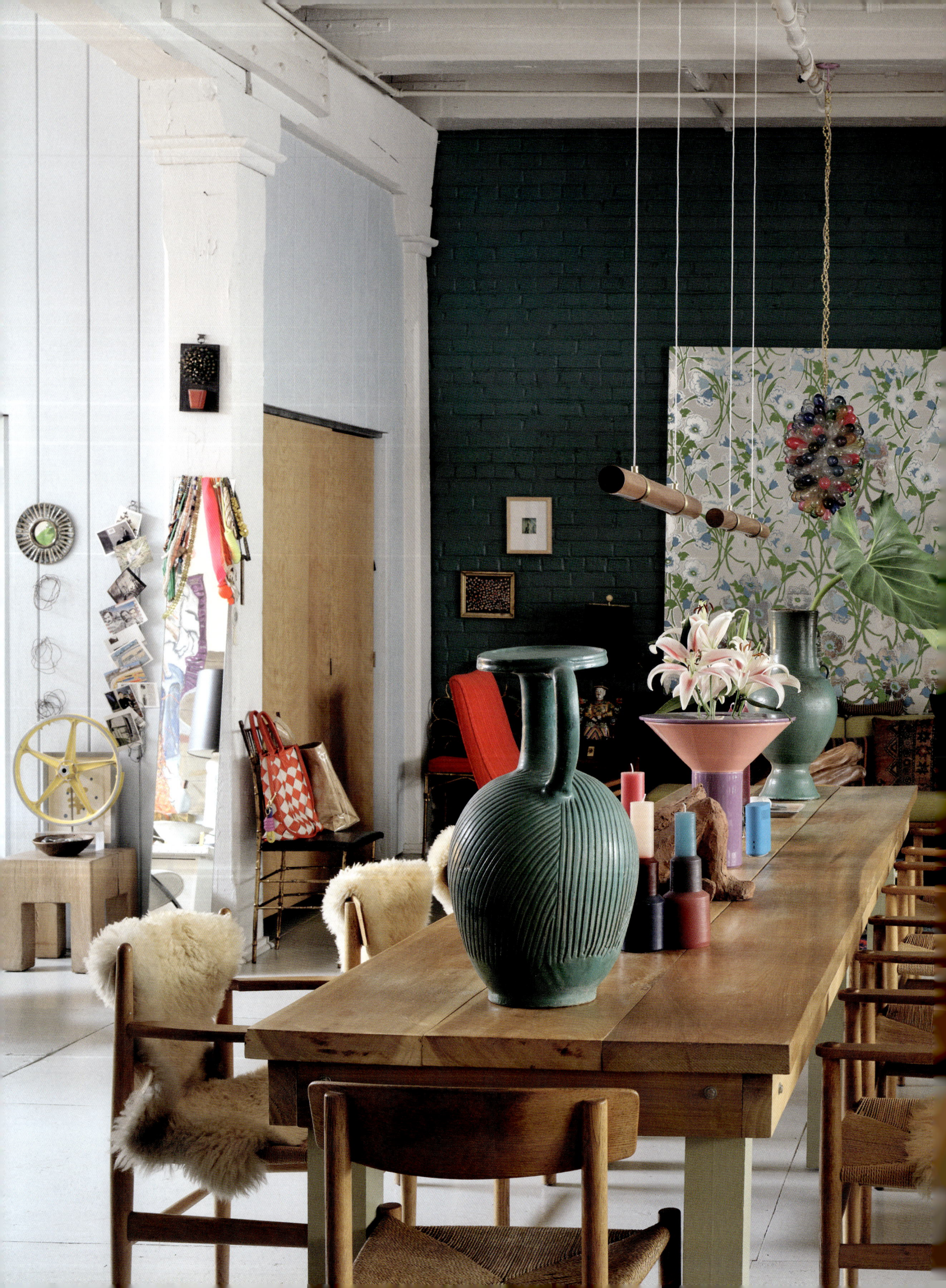

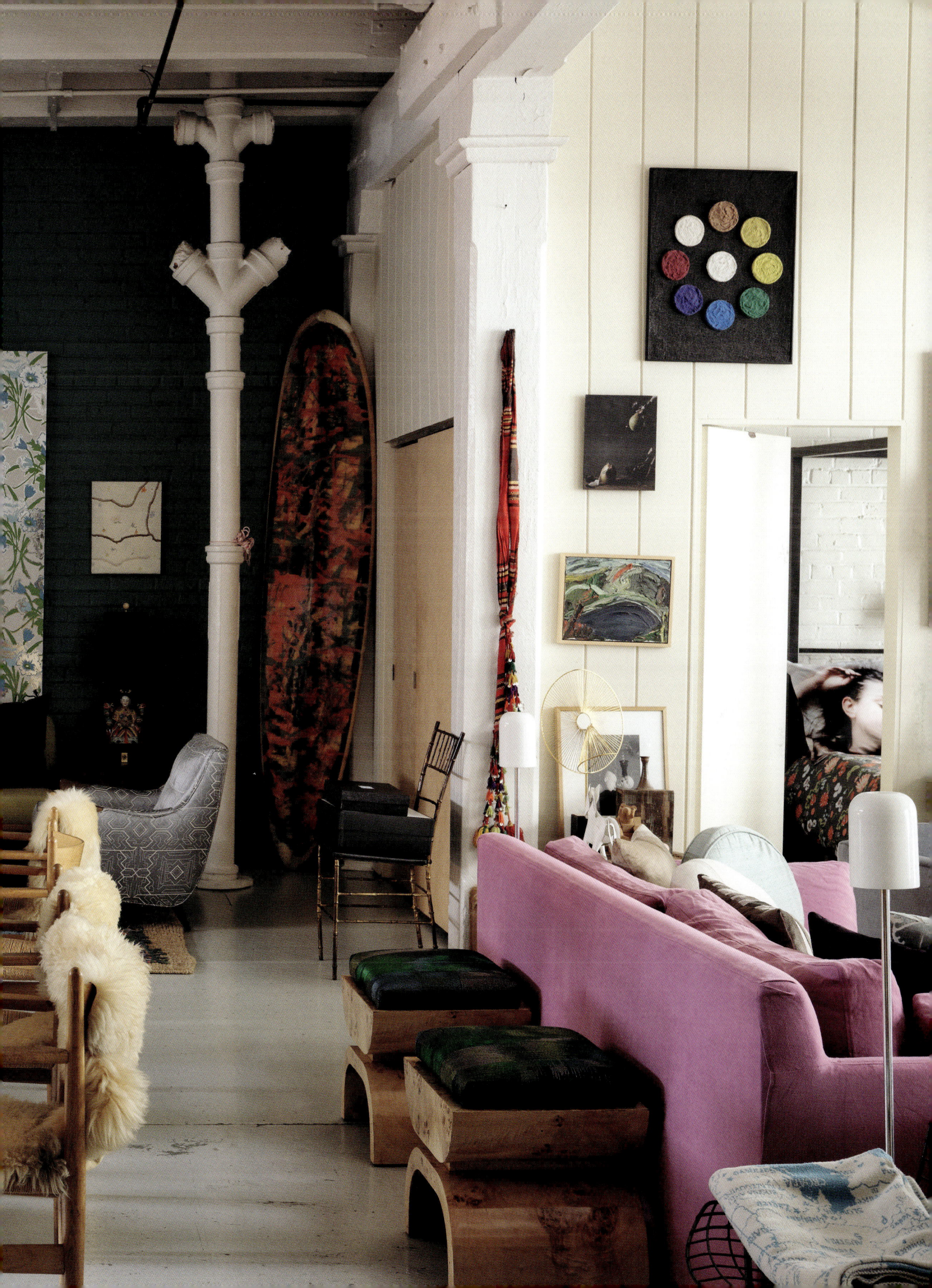

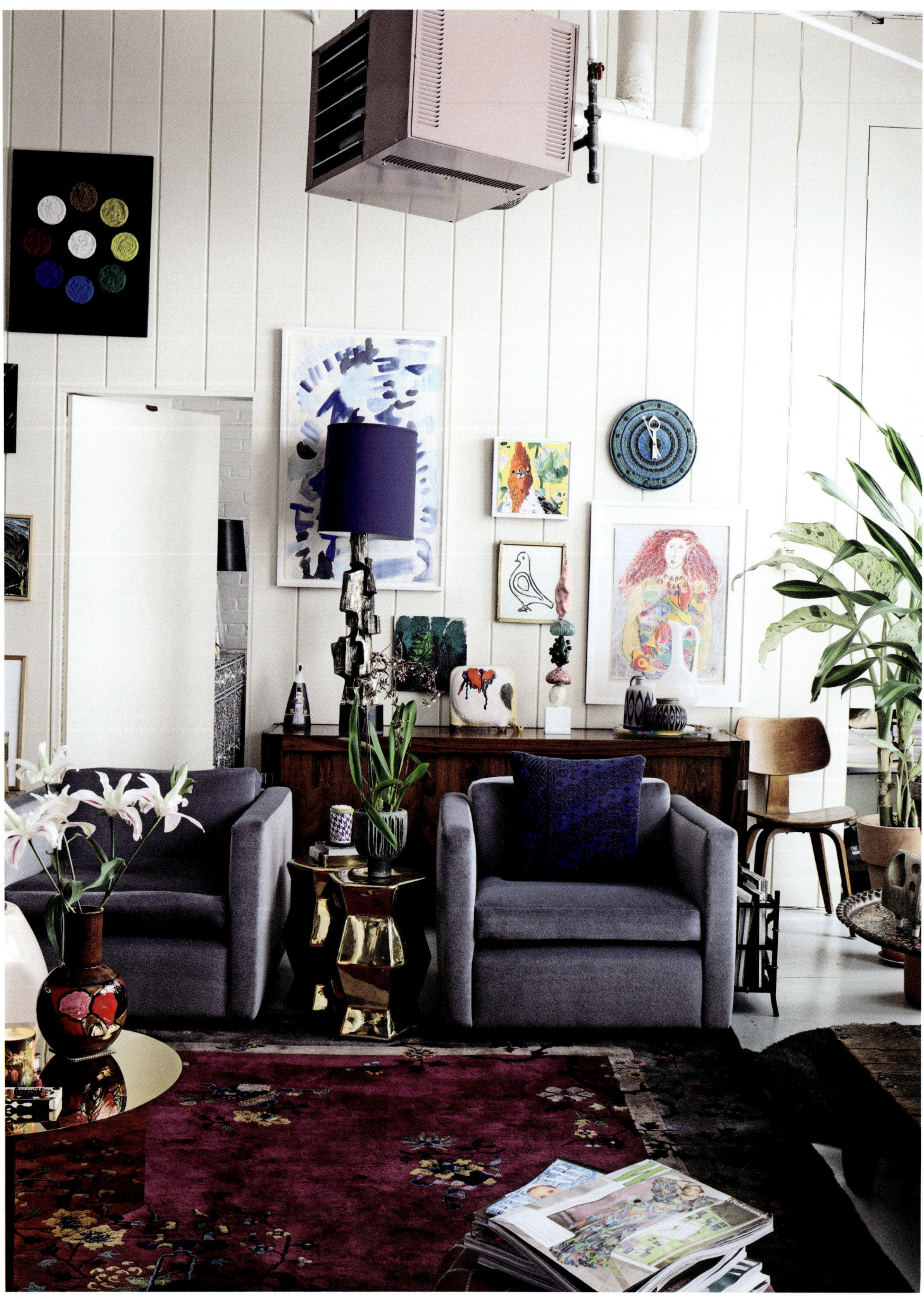

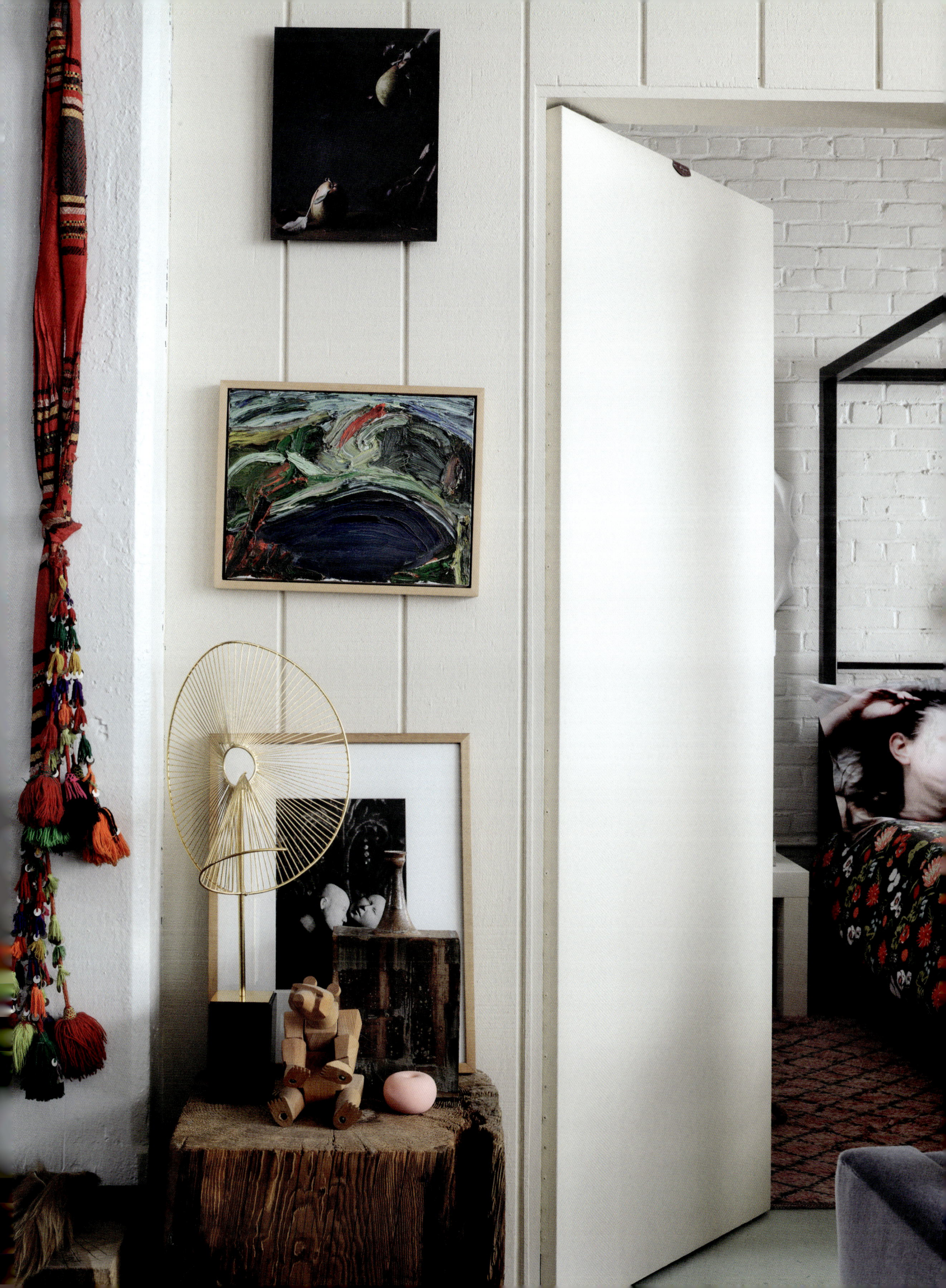

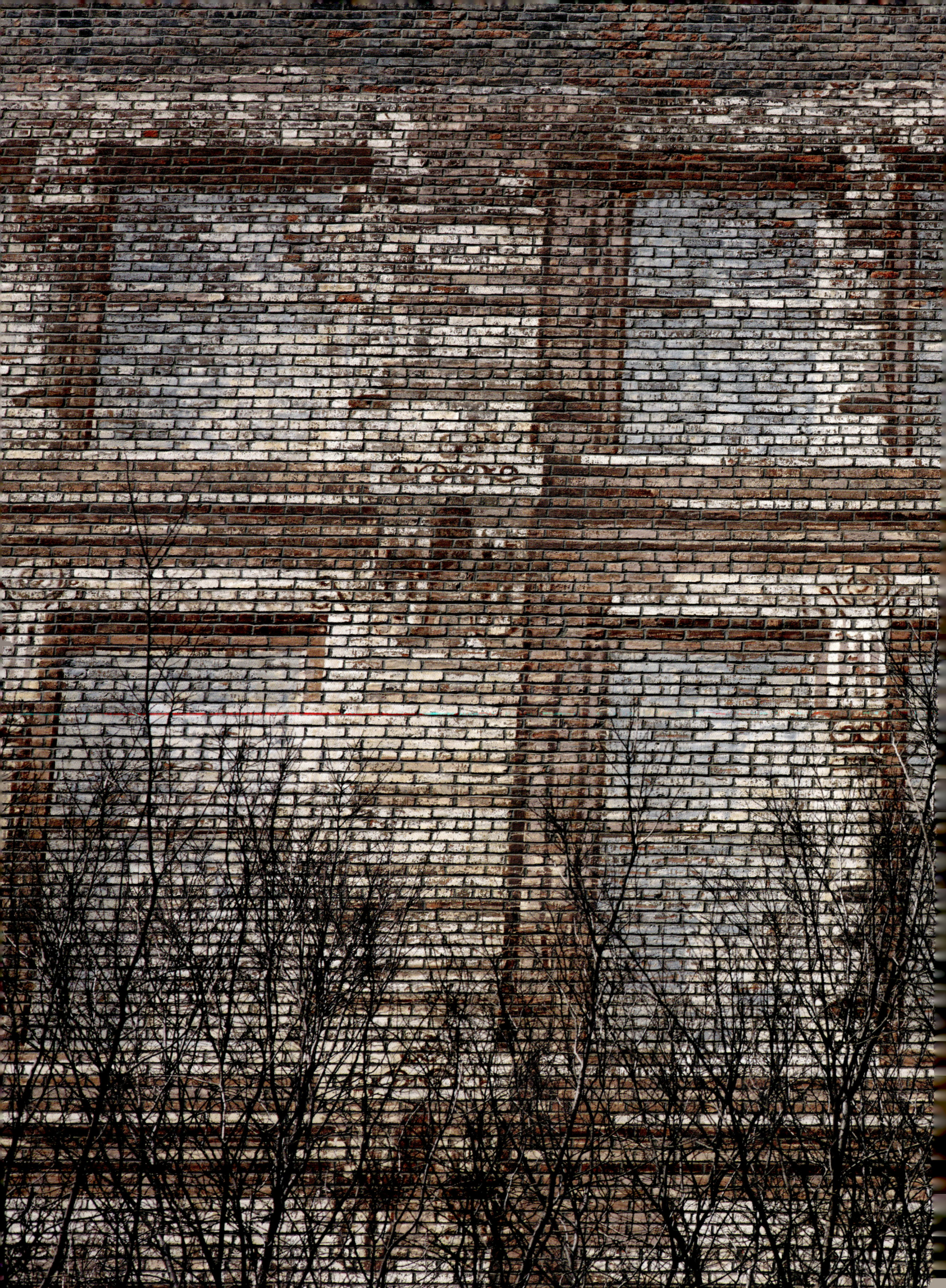

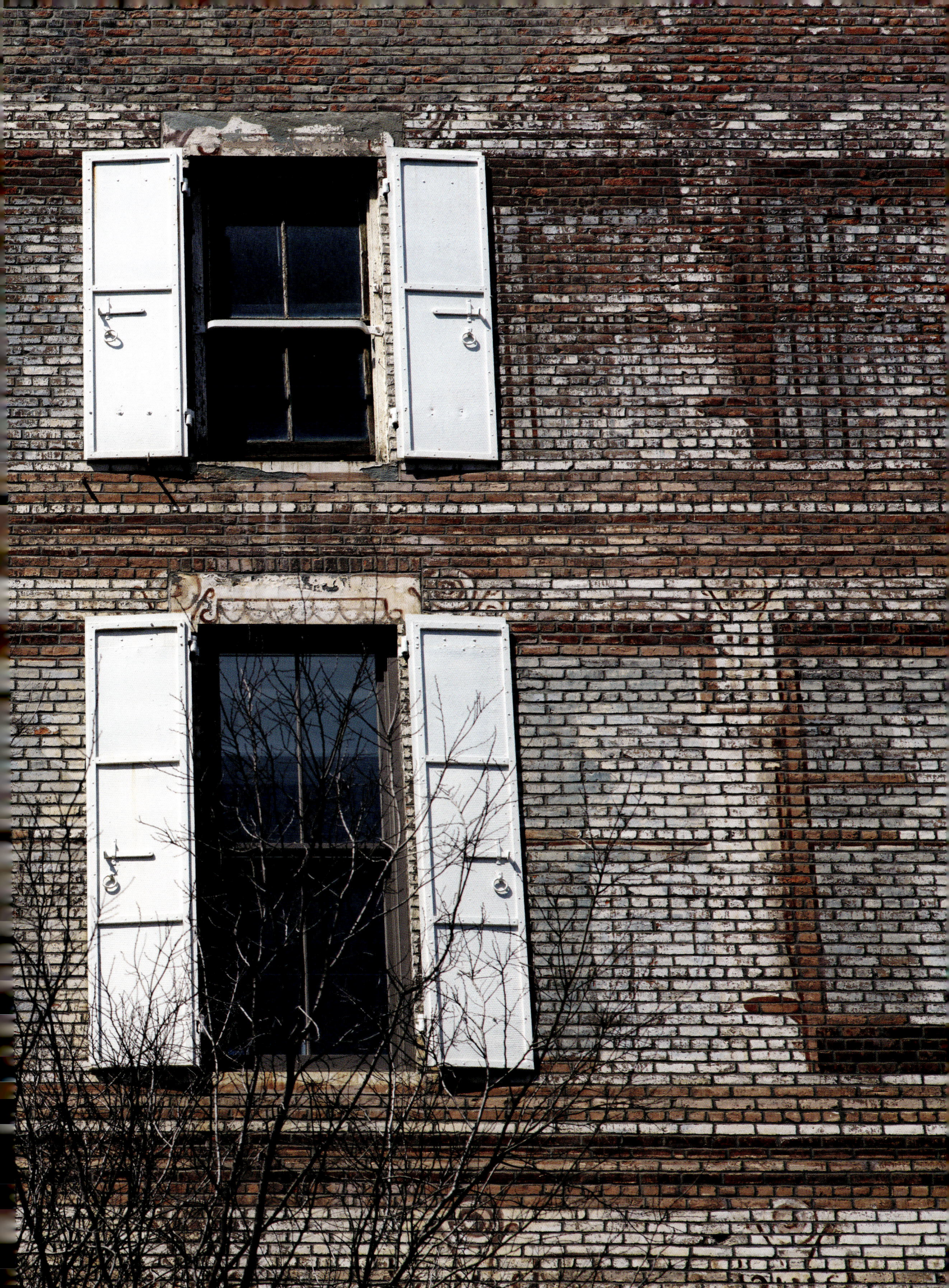

MANHATTAN REFUGE

ANNE BECKER

Once referred to as Alphabet City, the East Village is a mixture of low-rise, nineteenth-century townhouses and early twentieth-century former tenement blocks. My apartment was located on the ninth floor of a special pre-war building near Tompkins Square Park, which is shaded by rare elm trees. It had views on three sides, and I would watch the sun rise over the East River and set behind the trees in the park to the west. With no air conditioning, my windows were always open to the elements and I experienced some epic thunderstorms.

I bought it back in 1998. It was a somewhat ordinary two-bedroom layout, but with the help of friend and designer Gregory Bissonnette, we combined the two units and made the apartment so much more spacious. I lived there for 10 years and over that time I saw a lot of changes. The area started to trend upward, buildings were refurbished, and it became more gentrified. We benefited from locally owned restaurants, independent retailers, and a vast assortment of ethnic food, so eating was amazing! We had yoga studios, grass-roots theaters, and a thriving underground music scene, but with the introduction of new bars and restaurants, the nature of the neighborhood changed.

My Dad's family were born and raised as New Yorkers, so I guess that's what I consider myself. Having a dog helped me to connect with nature. I didn't have my own getaway at that time, so at weekends my Labrador Otis and I would often go and stay with friends on Long Island or in Woodstock.

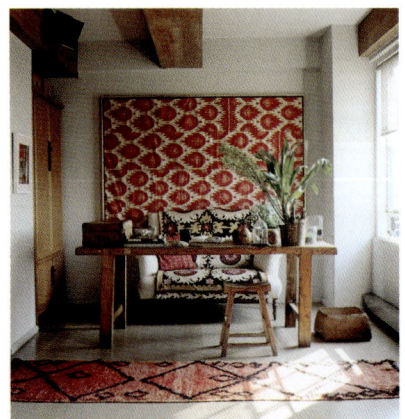

Sometimes we even drove as far as Bear Mountain in Upstate New York so Otis could enjoy a proper swim. During the week, there was always Central Park as an immediate antidote to the city's intensity.

I loved the kitchen/living area in the apartment, especially Greg's settle, with the wooden kitchen table in front of it. I also adored the disco ball hanging in the corner of the living space! It brought the room to life and made it sparkle. It now hangs in my living room back in Devon, England, where my husband Simon and I continue to enjoy its joyful twinkling. Greg's sensitive style influenced me greatly. The way in which he would integrate color, furniture, and objects reflected the manner in which I like to paint: blending until there is a contrast. I filled the apartment with textiles and bits and pieces that I had collected over the years, and which all held special meaning. It was comfy, cozy, and safe.

It was my sanctuary—my "getaway" in the bustling heart of Manhattan.

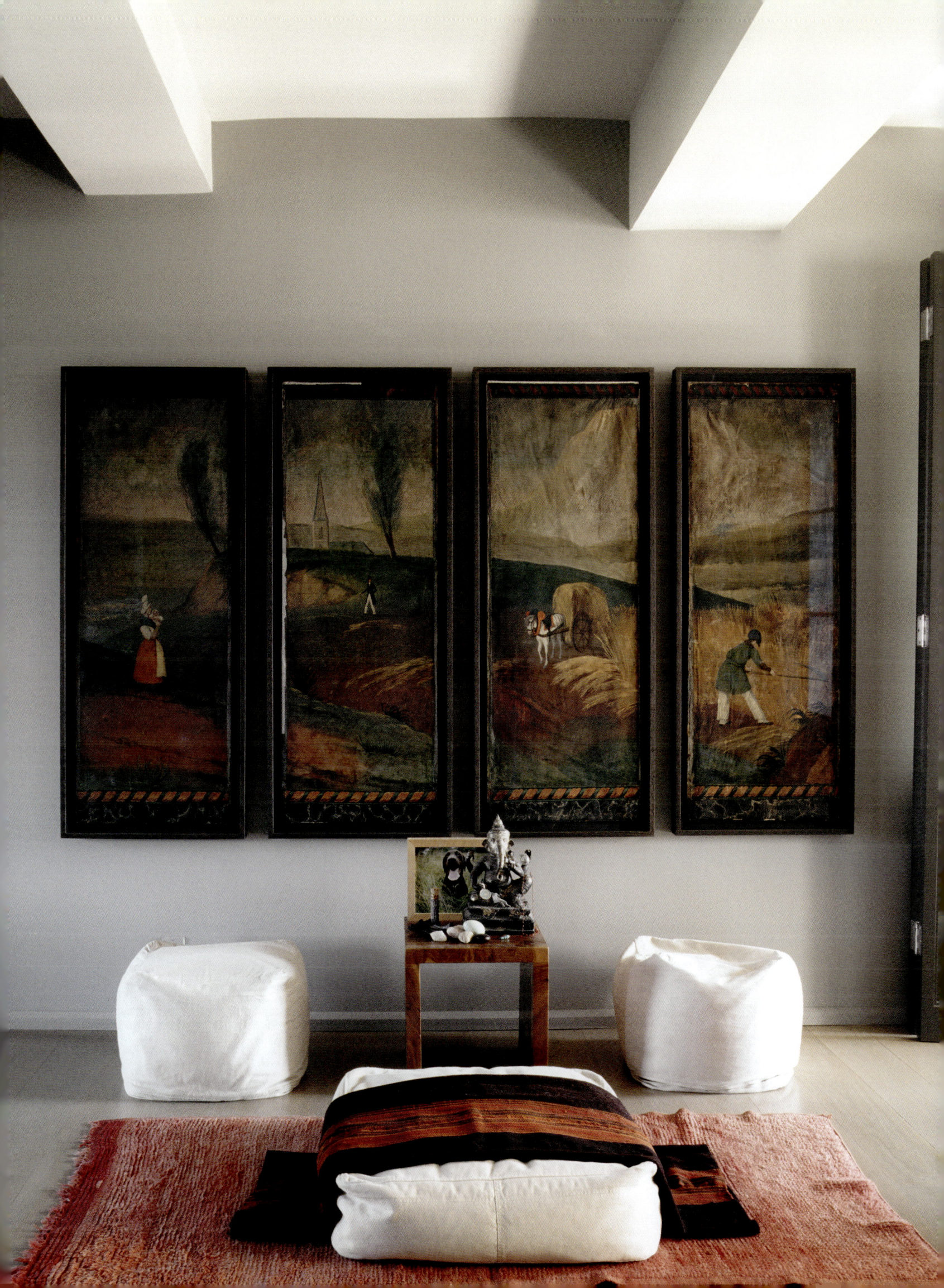

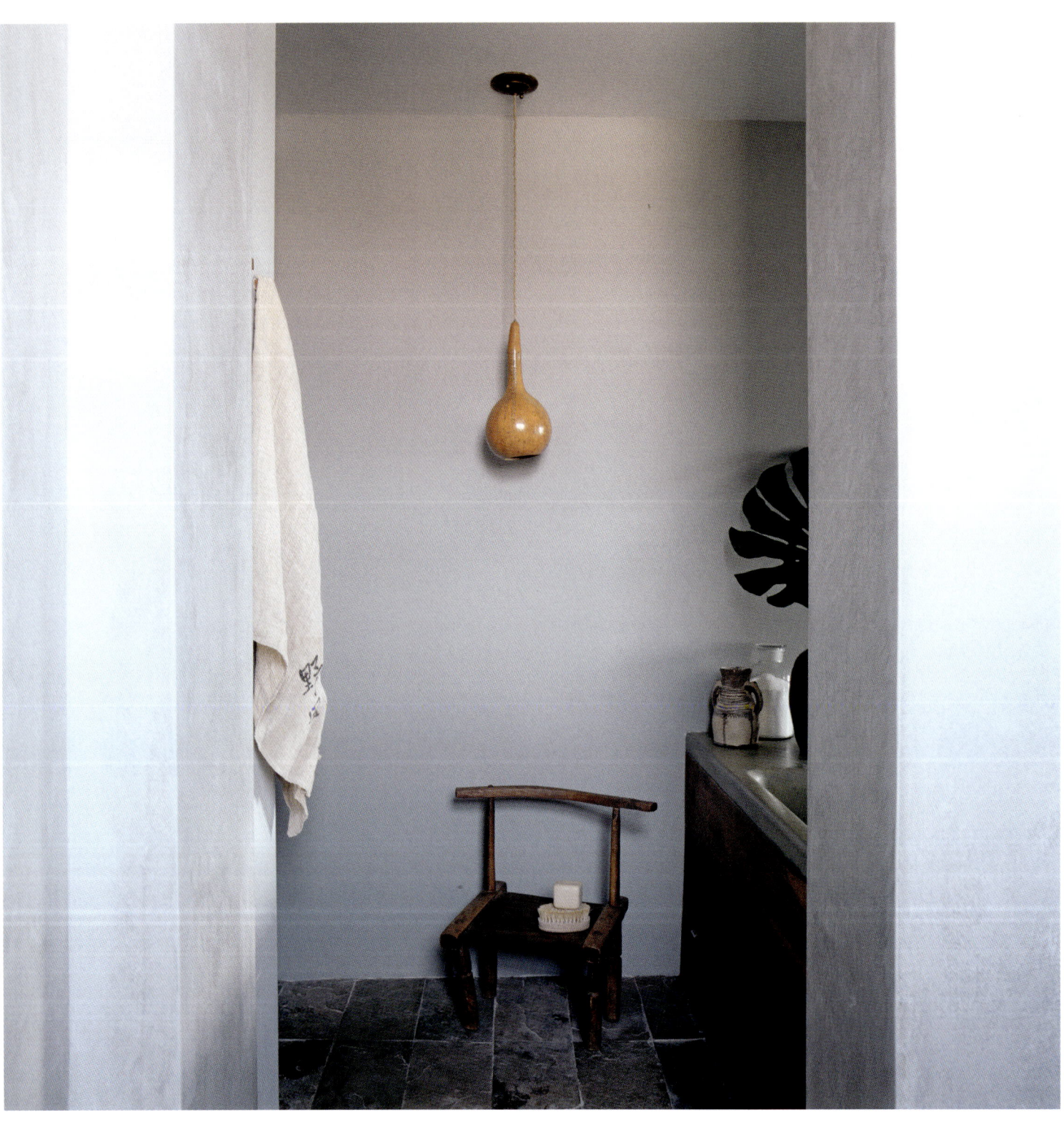

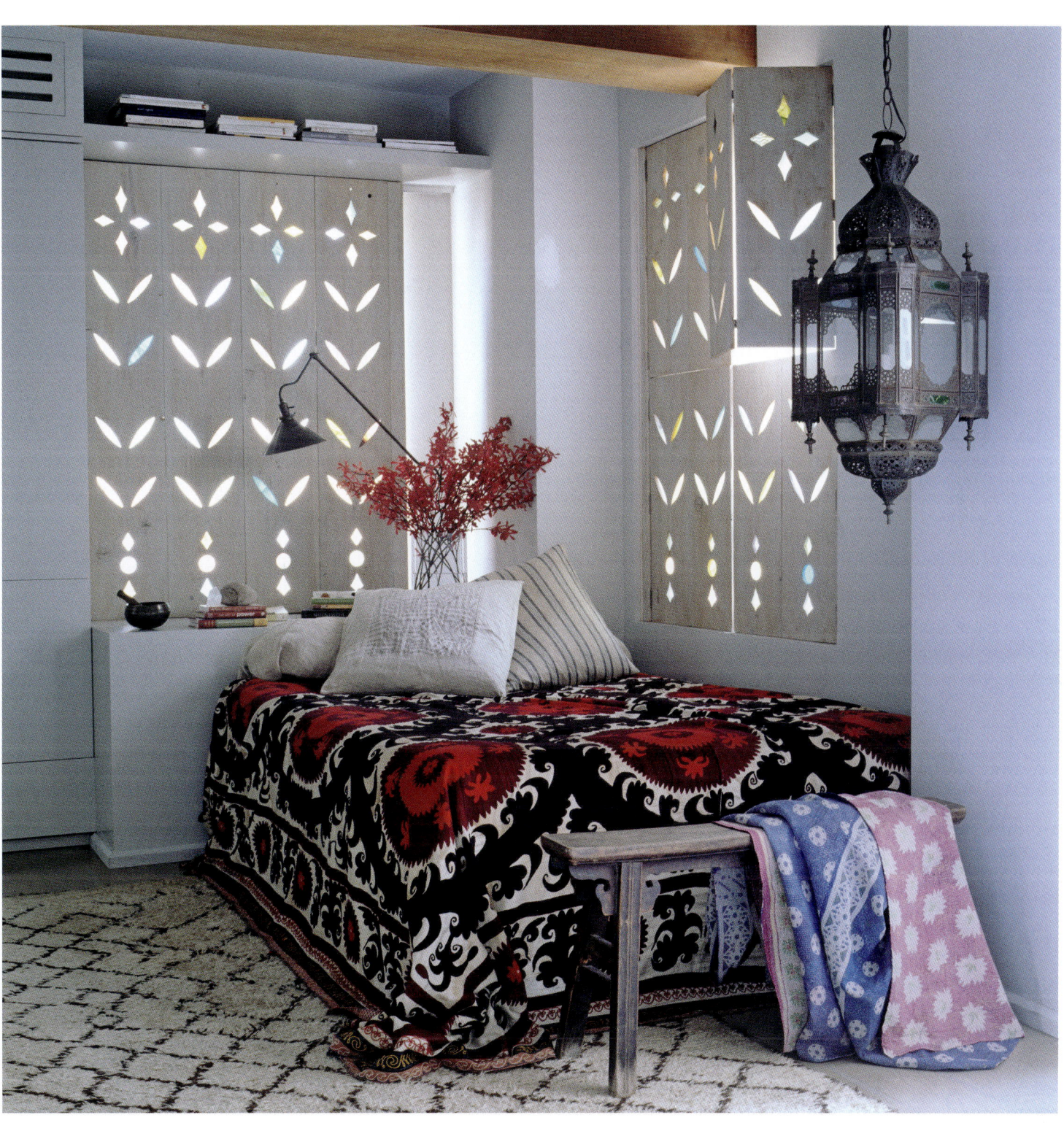

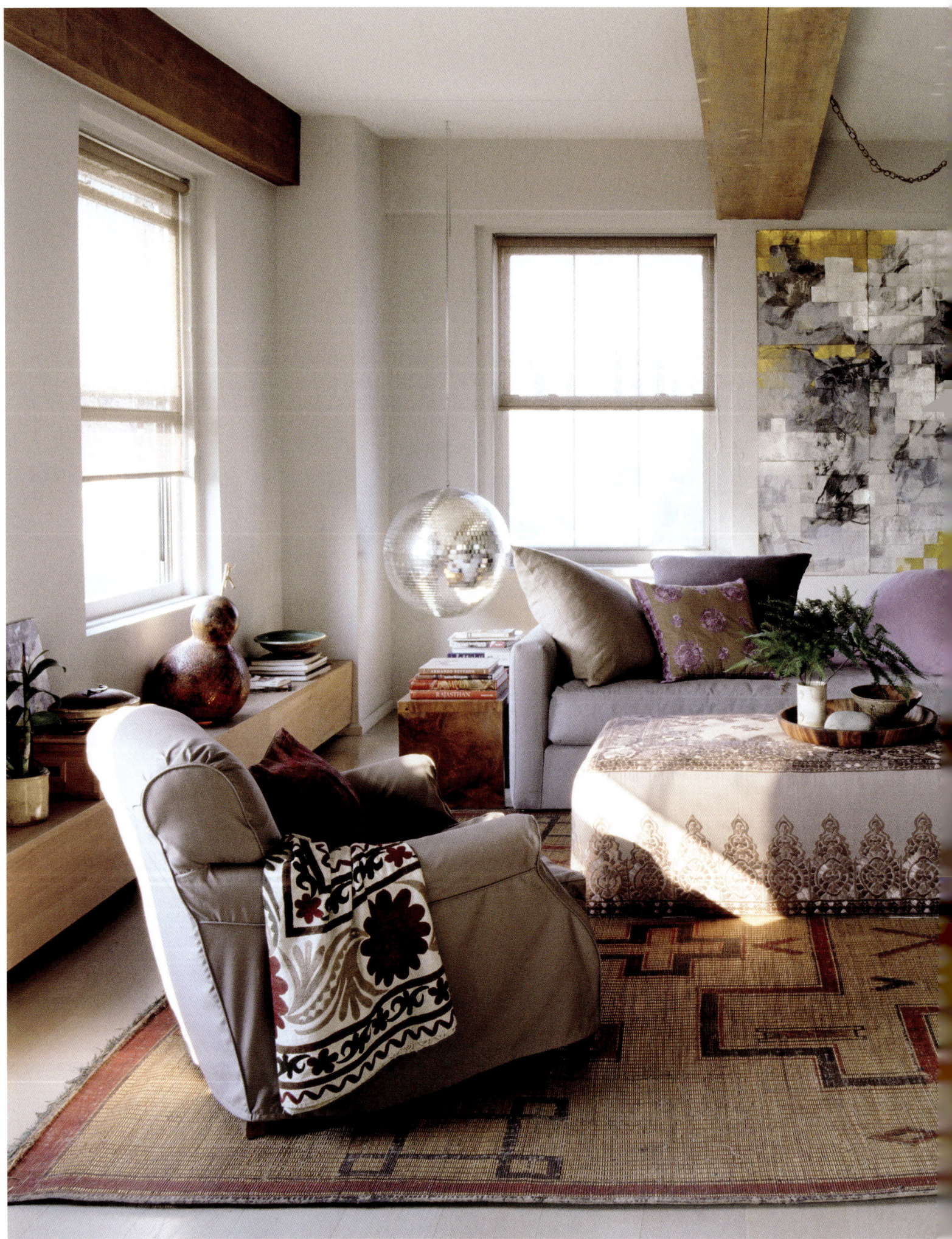

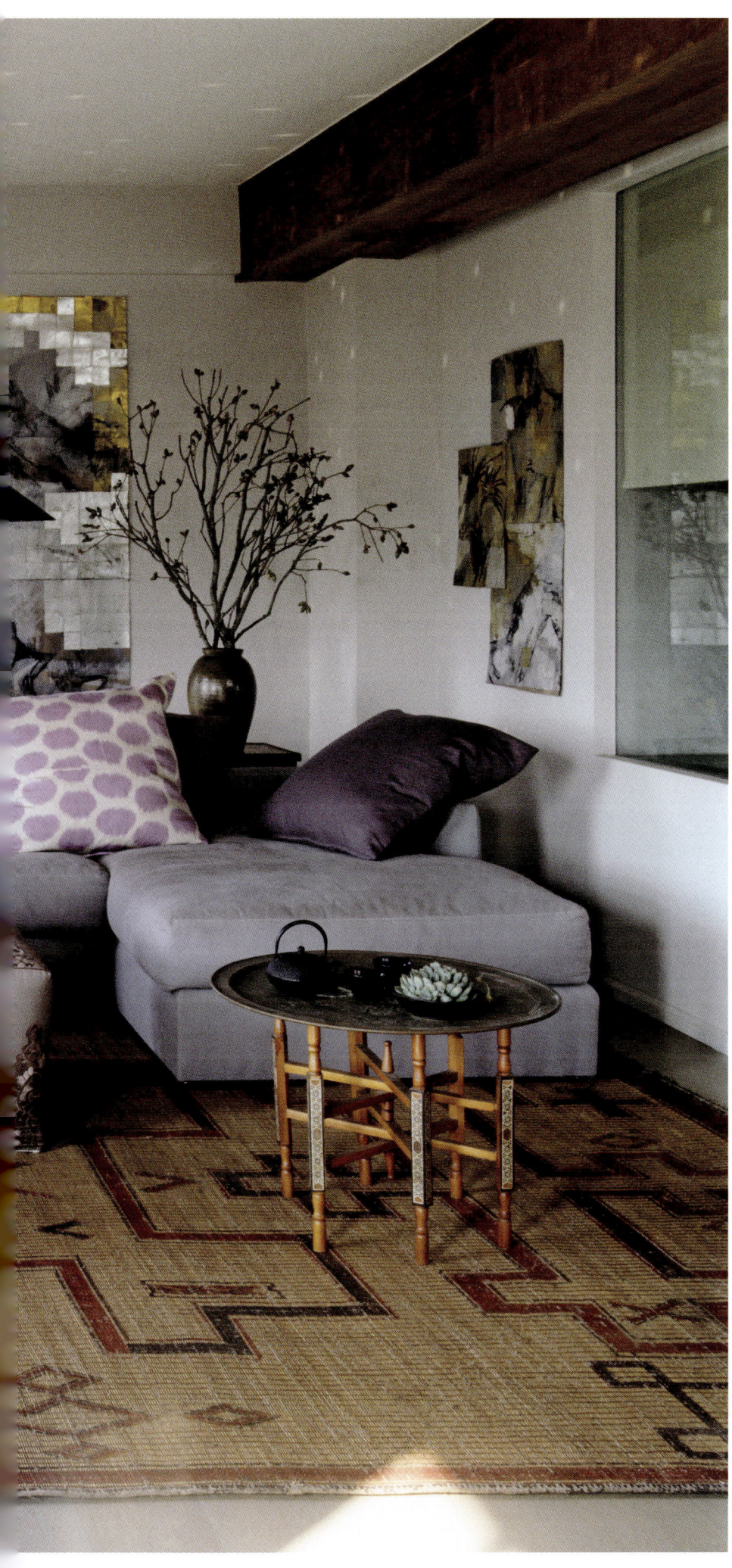

NOD TO NEOCLASSICSM

CAROL PRISANT

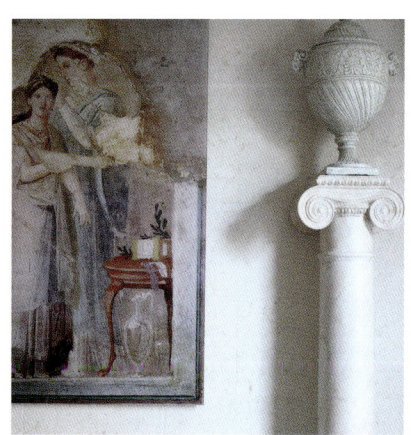

I was born in Pittsburgh, the "gateway to the Midwest" (although we never thought of ourselves as Midwesterners), and first came to New York in 1956 to go to college. In those days New York was a man's world. The Harvard Club had a separate door for women, and we were not allowed to wear pants!

Having spent most of my married and family life away from the city, I moved back to New York five years after my husband died and took on a massive apartment on the river, determined to keep up appearances. But it was isolating and lonely, so I decided to look for somewhere smaller and more central—and the Upper East Side is as fancy as it gets! My new apartment is close to Central Park, quiet and genteel, and Bean, my look-alike Gremlin Miki, has made lots of friends, which forces me to socialize and gets me out. It may be a swanky address, but when I first viewed the apartment it was a total mess, complete with a dead 'roach in the living room—which for me, sealed the deal! The apartment was completely remodeled, and I asked the lovely David Mann, architect extraordinaire, to help me reorganize the space. The rest—the pretty part—I did myself. Originally it had three bedrooms; now, it's down to one, with a pantry and laundry room occupying one of the others. I am

no foodie, so we got rid of the kitchen, which has become my den, and I have a twin-burner gas hob and a microwave, which serve the purpose. (If I have to entertain, I invite friends to one of two clubs of which I am a member. I don't think I have been to a local restaurant since the day I moved in!)

My husband and I lived in a period house, redolent with history, yet I have been buying up neoclassical bits and pieces for years. By removing walls and opening up this albeit small space, David Mann has allowed me to live this particular dream, in which I can happily accommodate my neoclassical collection. My inspiration? The classical rooms at The Metropolitan Museum, full of sunlight and marble—yet my sculptures are all plaster imitations, the floor is painted plywood and the walls are just wallpaper. Having been an antique dealer for 25 years, it somehow goes against the grain to be surrounded by fakes but, as I have got older, I now find I value beauty over authenticity.

While I love the loft-like space of the apartment since the walls were removed, my bedroom is also very close to my heart. Rupert—my boss and editor of *The World of Interiors*—refers to it as "very grand granny." It is the third iteration: same wallpaper, same bed. No changes whatsoever!

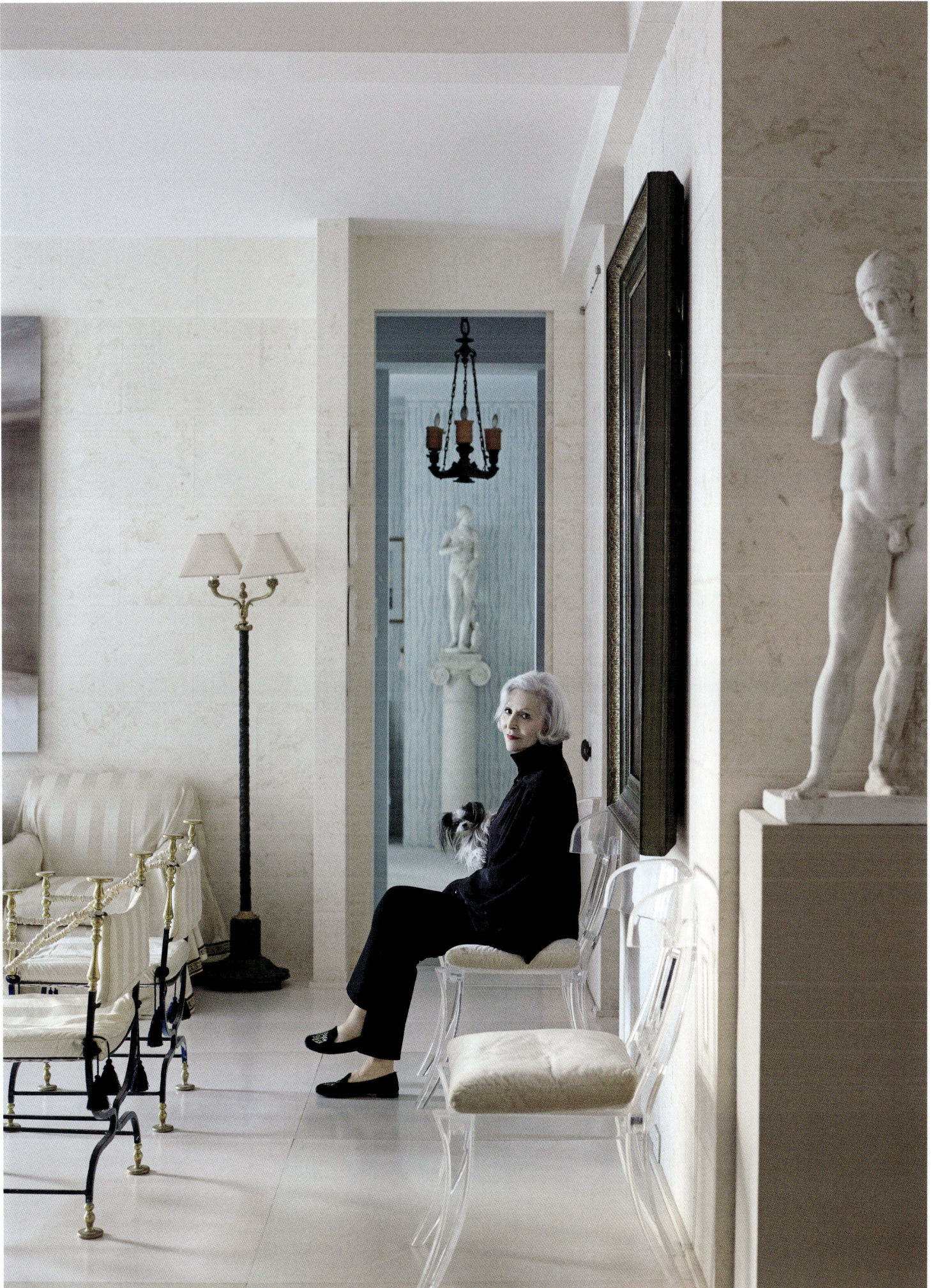

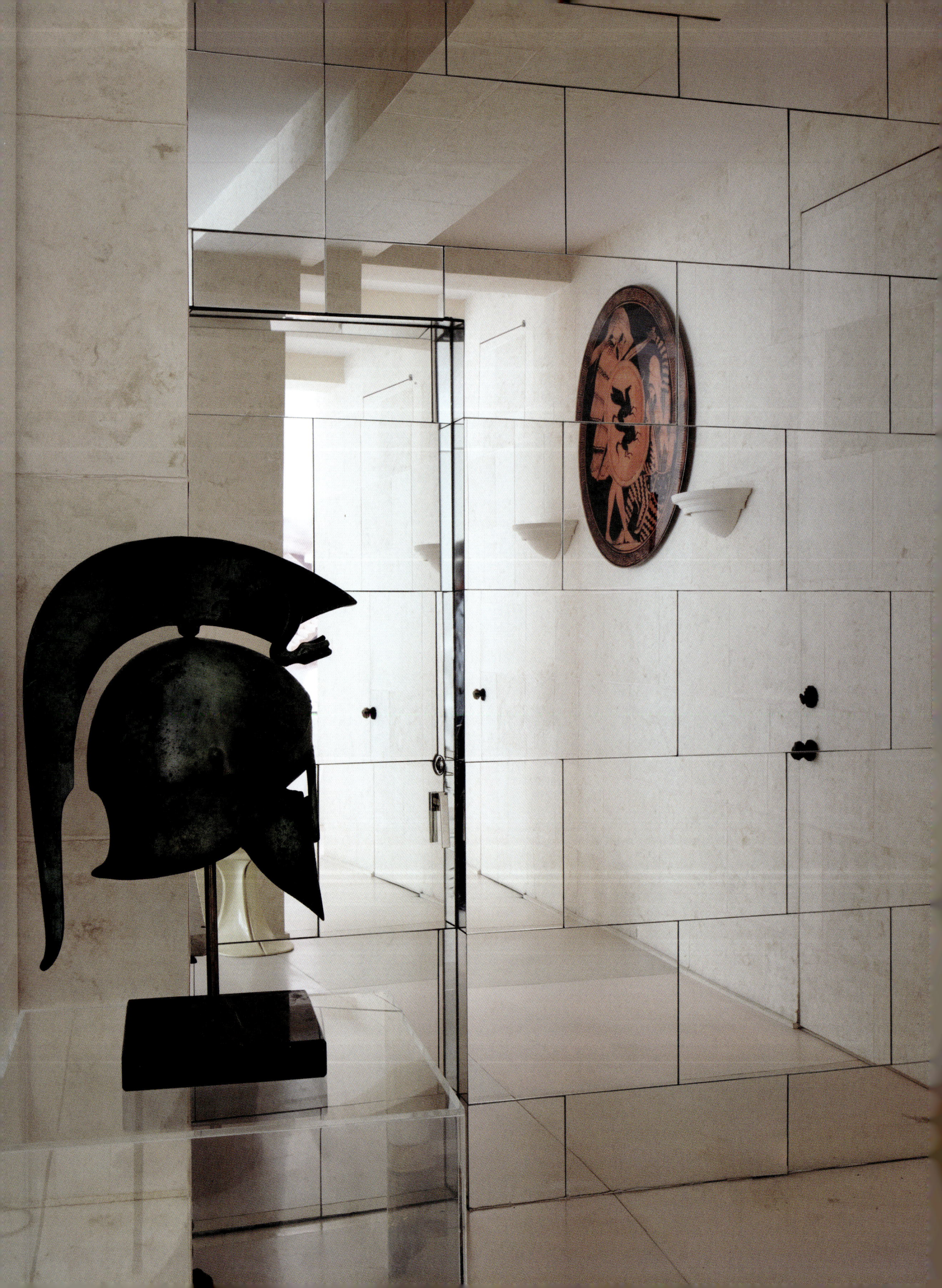

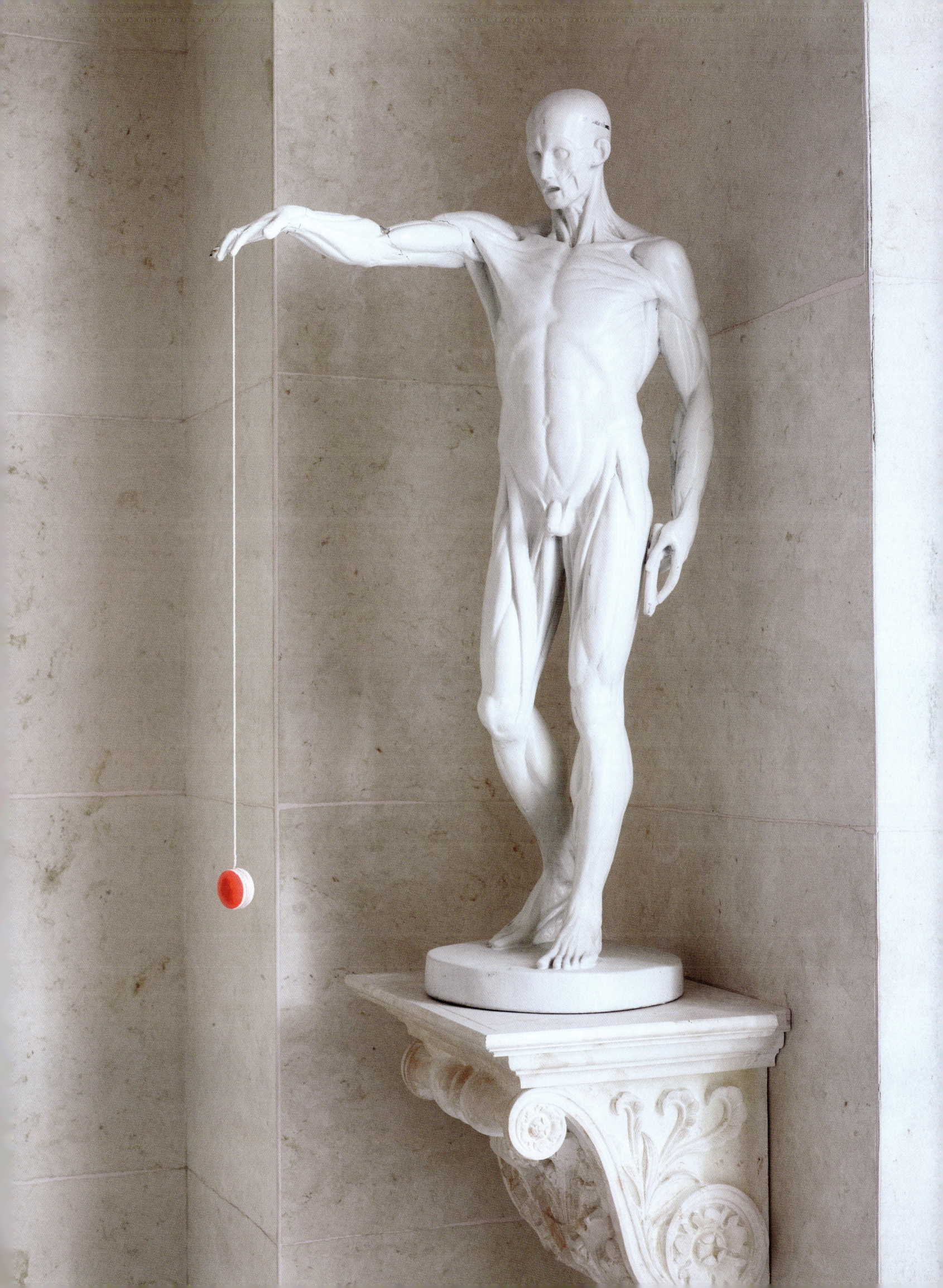

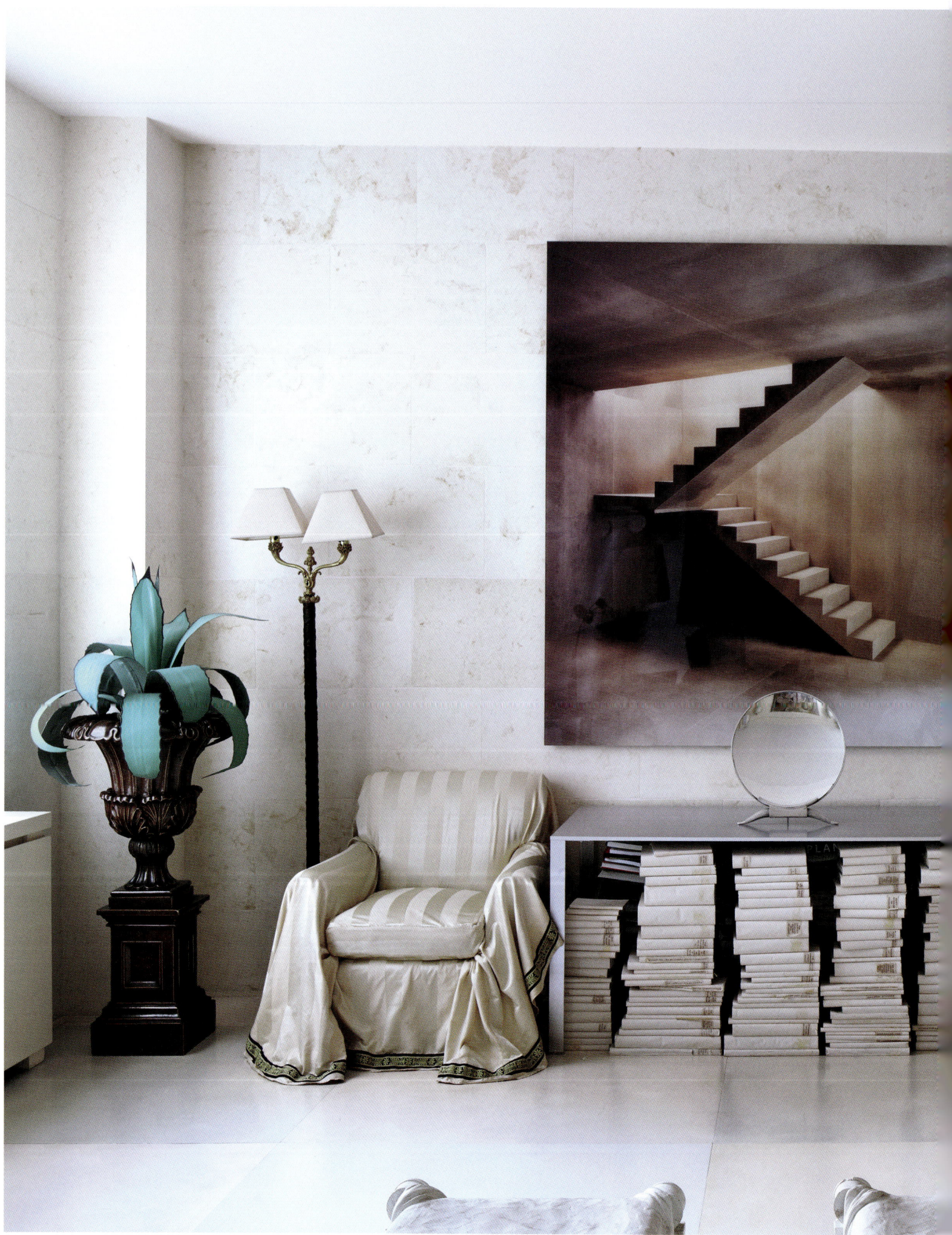

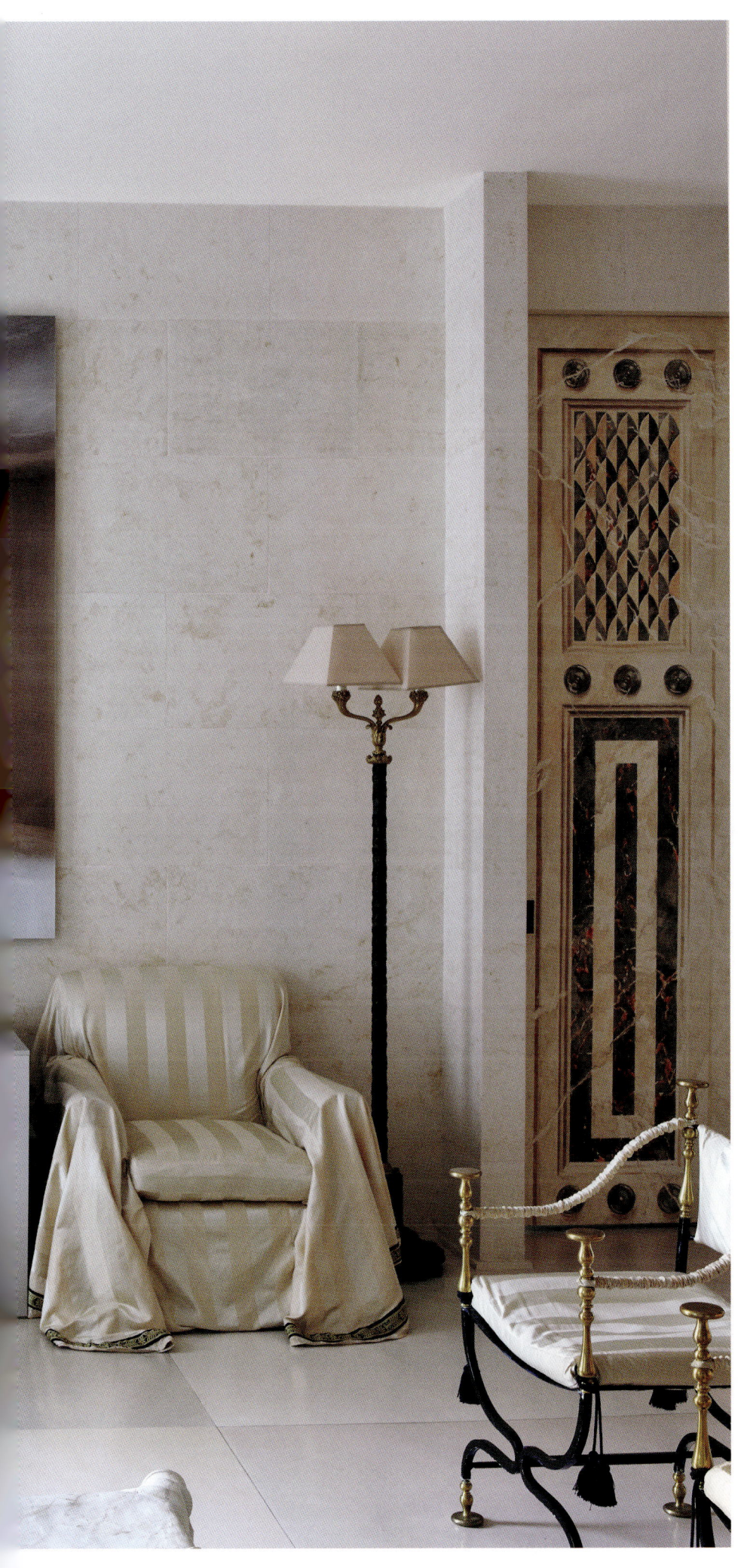

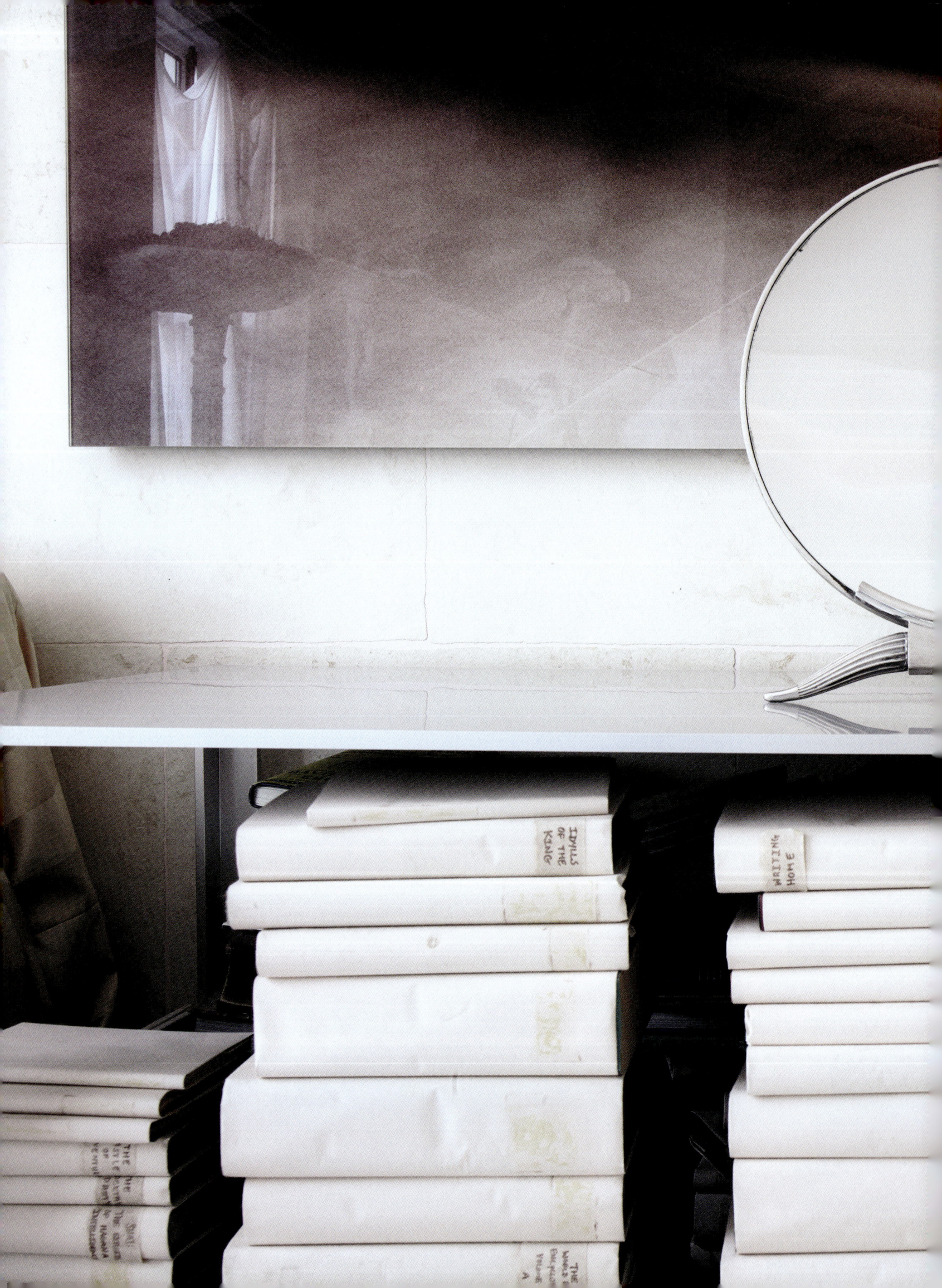

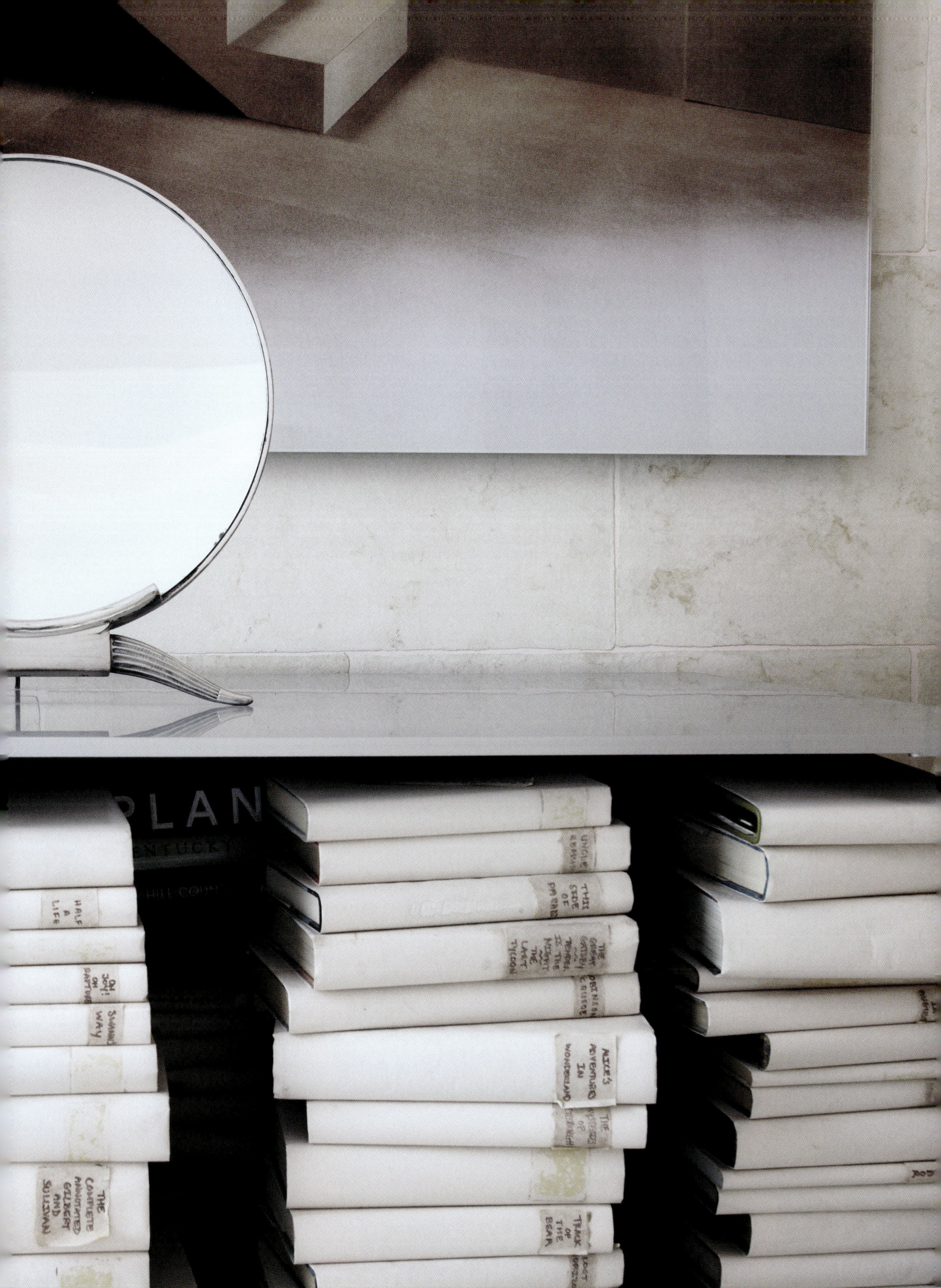

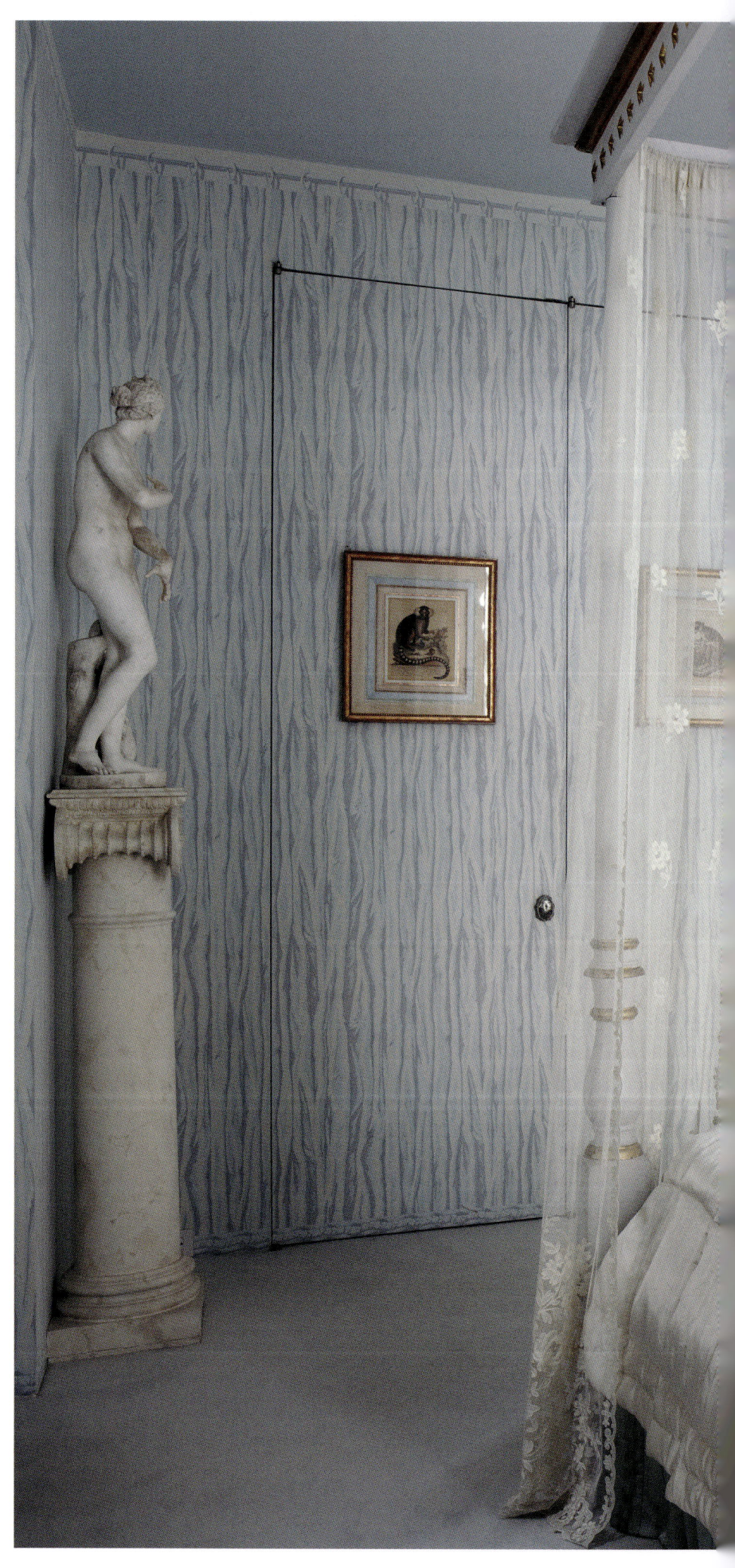

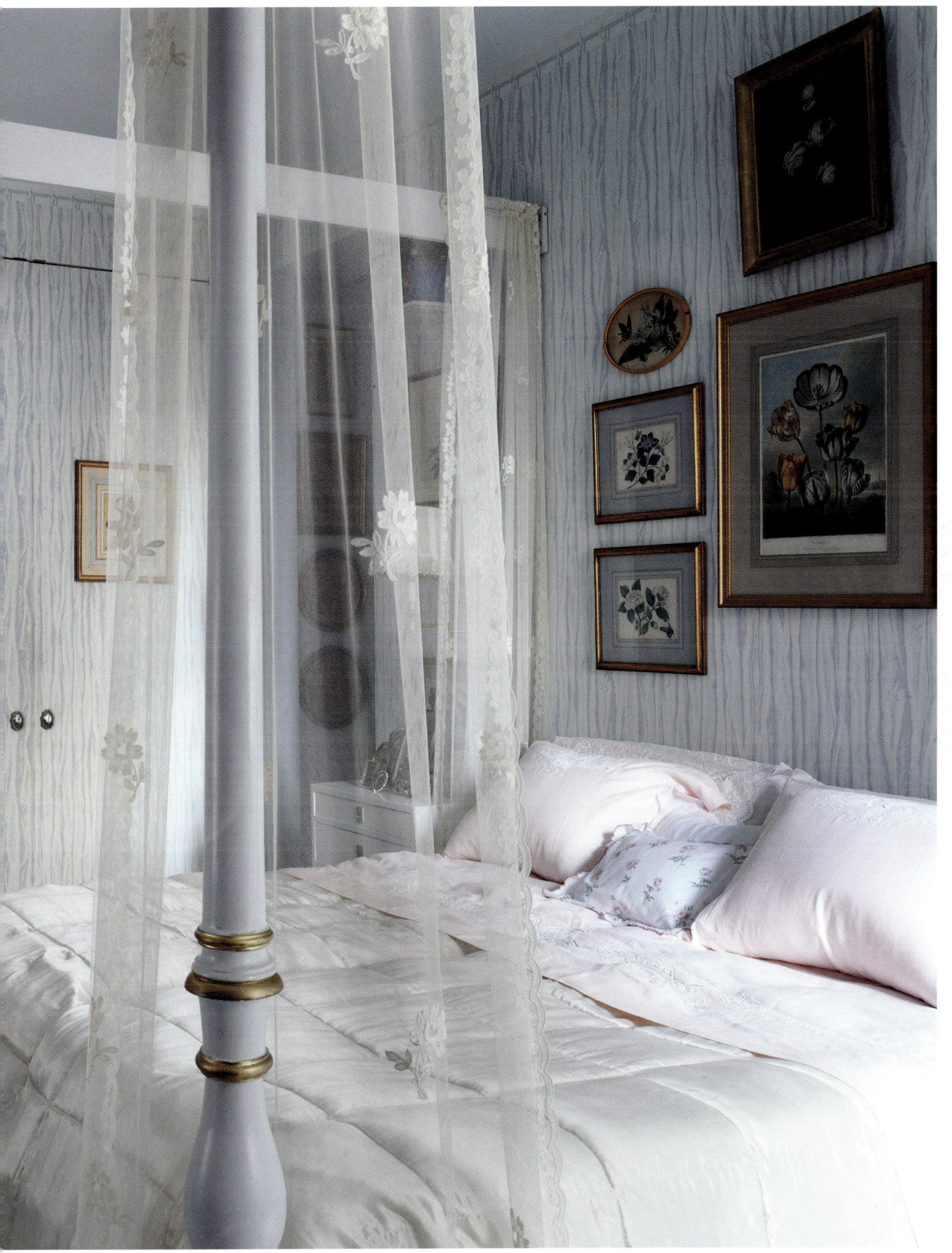

GLAMOROUS FANTASY

MILES REDD

I am originally from Atlanta, but I think most Americans have a chip inside them that makes them move to New York at some point in their lives. Mine went off at about the age of five!

I live in Nolita, a neighborhood that combines a Downtown lifestyle with a cozy and quaint atmosphere. It's charming and picturesque and, I guess, back in the day, would once have been considered part of Little Italy—hence the name ("North of Little Italy"). My home is a small townhouse—there are not many here—and was a blank slate when my sister and I bought it together in 1998. The idea back then was that I would live at the top and my sister and her family at the bottom. It was a real family house and retains lots of happy memories—we all love this house so much. As the family grew up, the house just got too cramped, so they moved out about five years ago.

With no obvious background history, the interior suited my purpose perfectly, and over time—it took me at least two years, and I am constantly refining it—I was able to transform the house into what you see today, which is something more French in feeling. As a designer, I like to shake things up, and to step away from traditional taste and expectation. Essentially, I just buy things I like and push them around until they work. For me it is all "in the gut."

Nolita is a place where you know your neighbors, with plenty of restaurants and bars, and a local life to enjoy and be a part of. Eating out is so much fun—being able to revel in a different atmosphere, and be served something delicious and then walk away! But I also love eating at home, and feel very fortunate to have the best of both worlds in New York City.

My bathroom and bedroom are where I live when I'm at home. My bathroom I discovered in a salvage warehouse. It came from the Lester Armour House, designed by David Adler, in Lake Bluff, and I put it back together in my townhouse. It is by far the biggest room and, from time to time, doubles as a dining room. With a bathroom like this, I needed a bedroom that would compete. It is a design borrowed from Serge Roche and made for me by John Rosselli. I like to sleep in a darkened tomb, so my bedroom has spectacular satin curtains and features a canopy bed. I love canopy beds because they give a bedroom presence and drama; mine certainly takes center stage.

A good decorator plans carefully, thinks about the whole puzzle, and makes it flow, but that doesn't mean you can't keep adding!

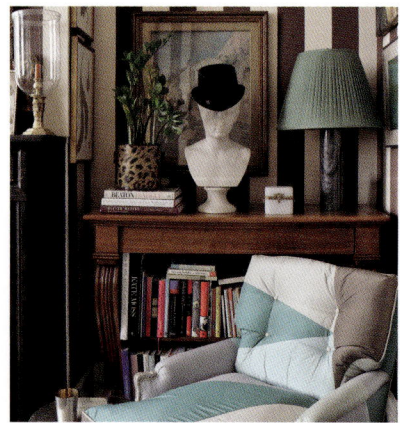

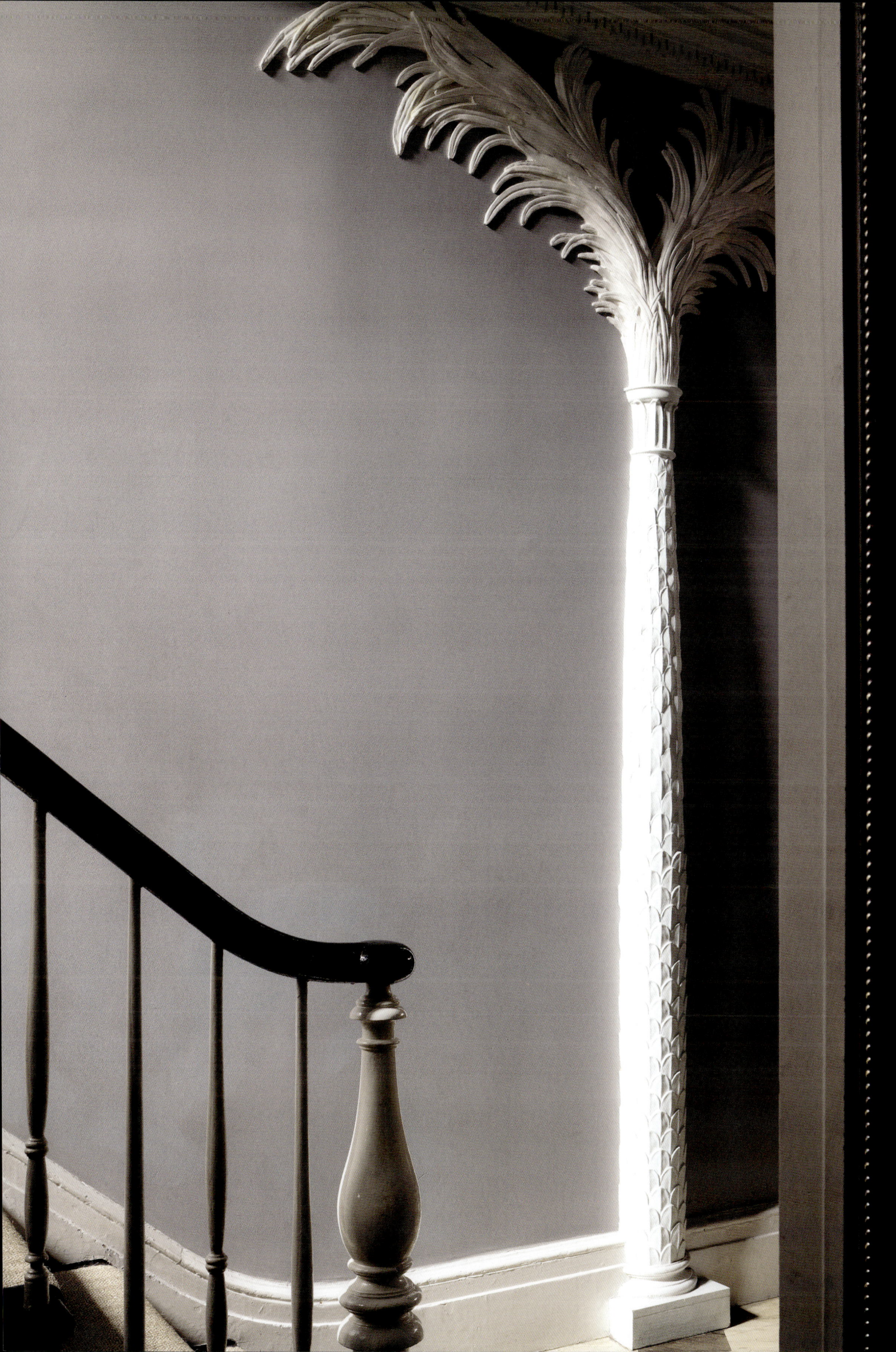

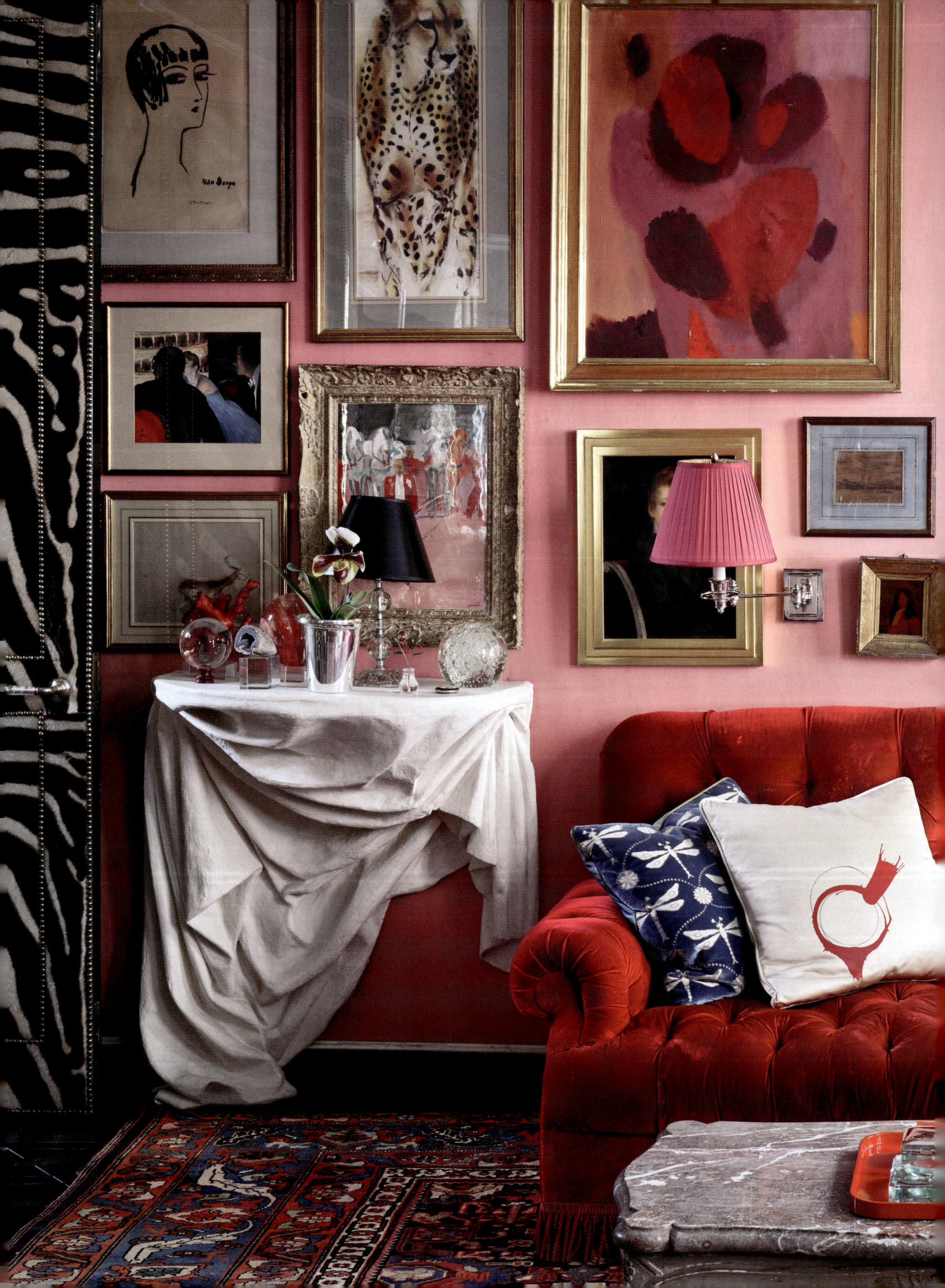

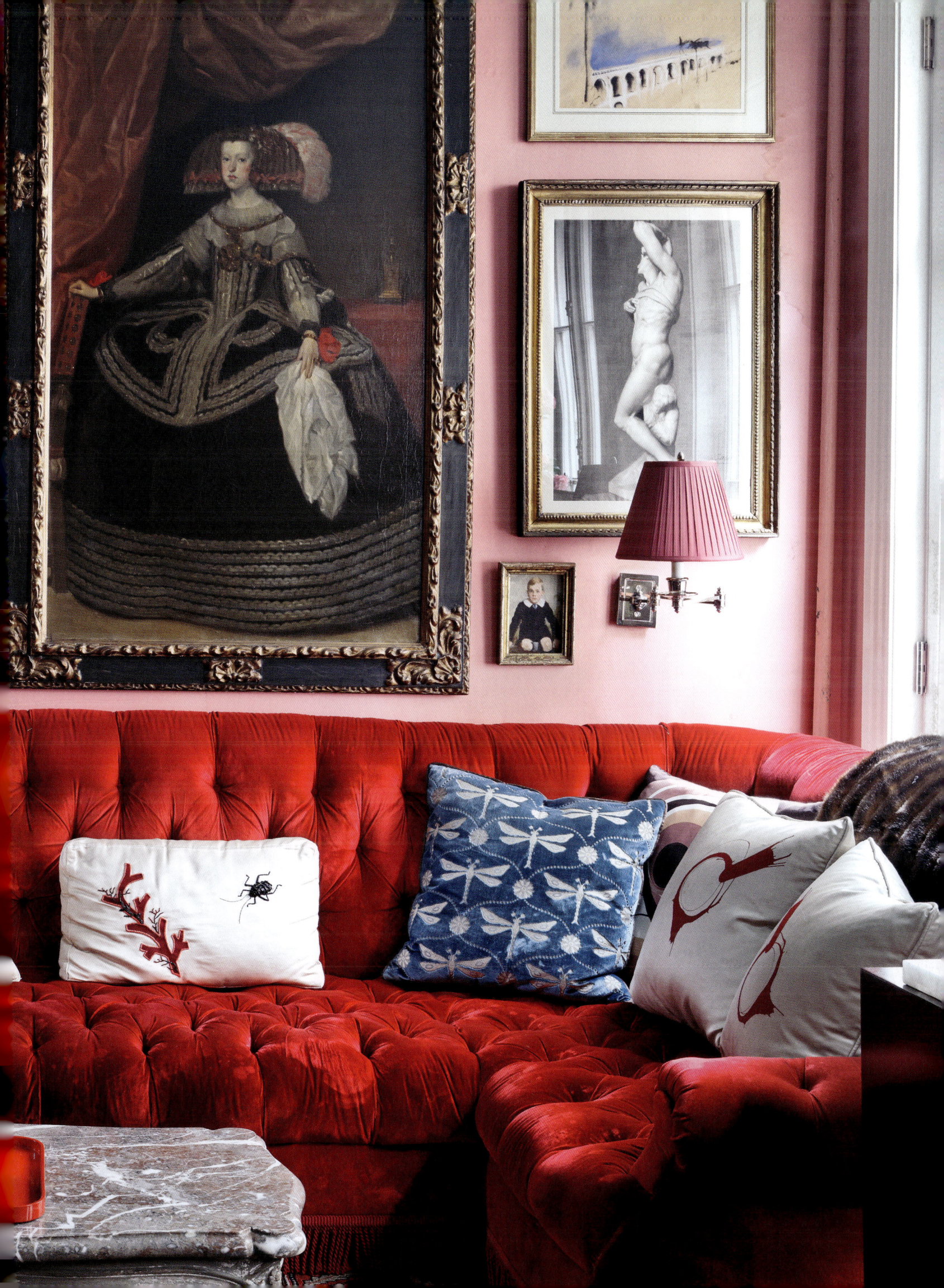

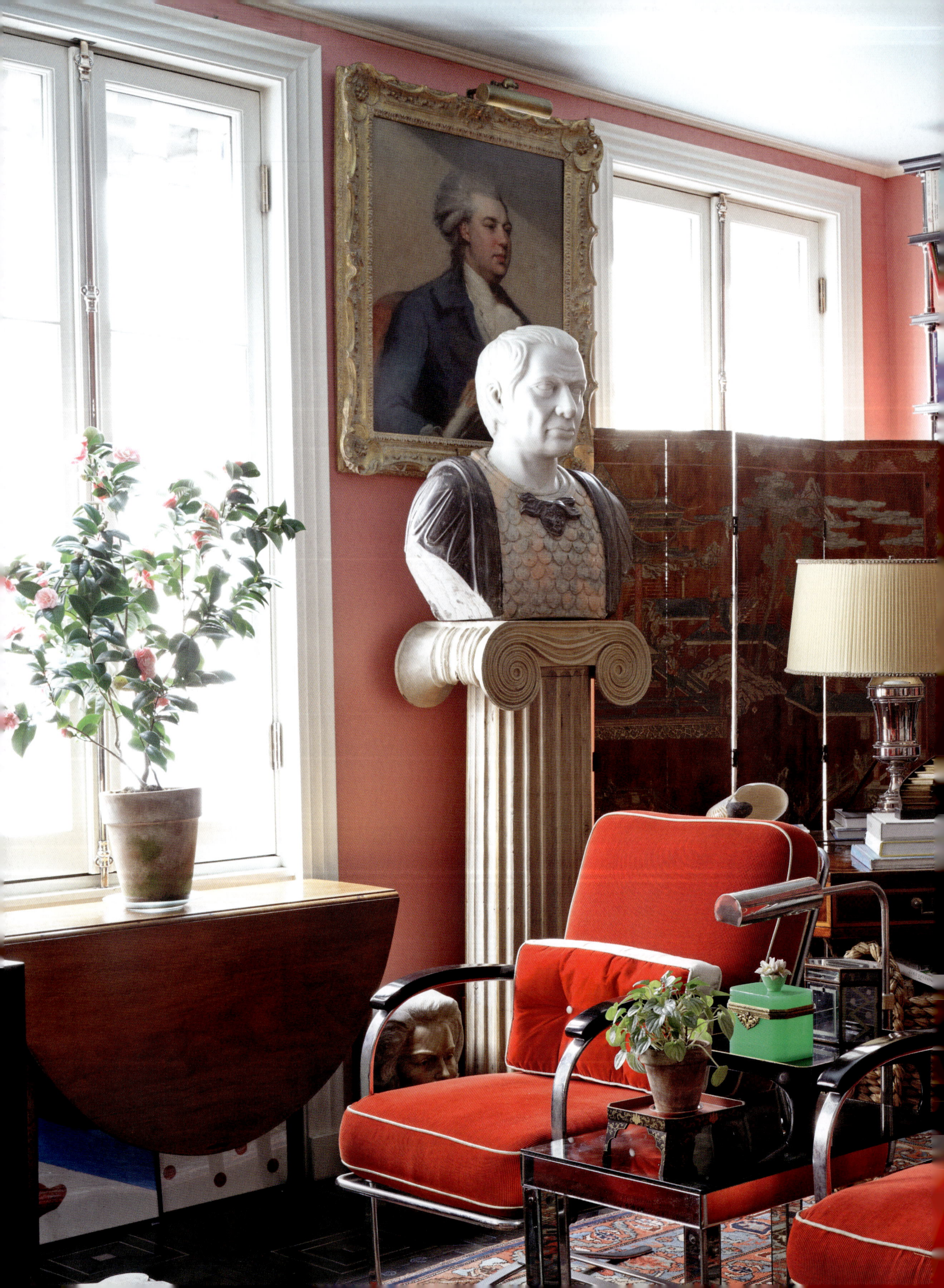

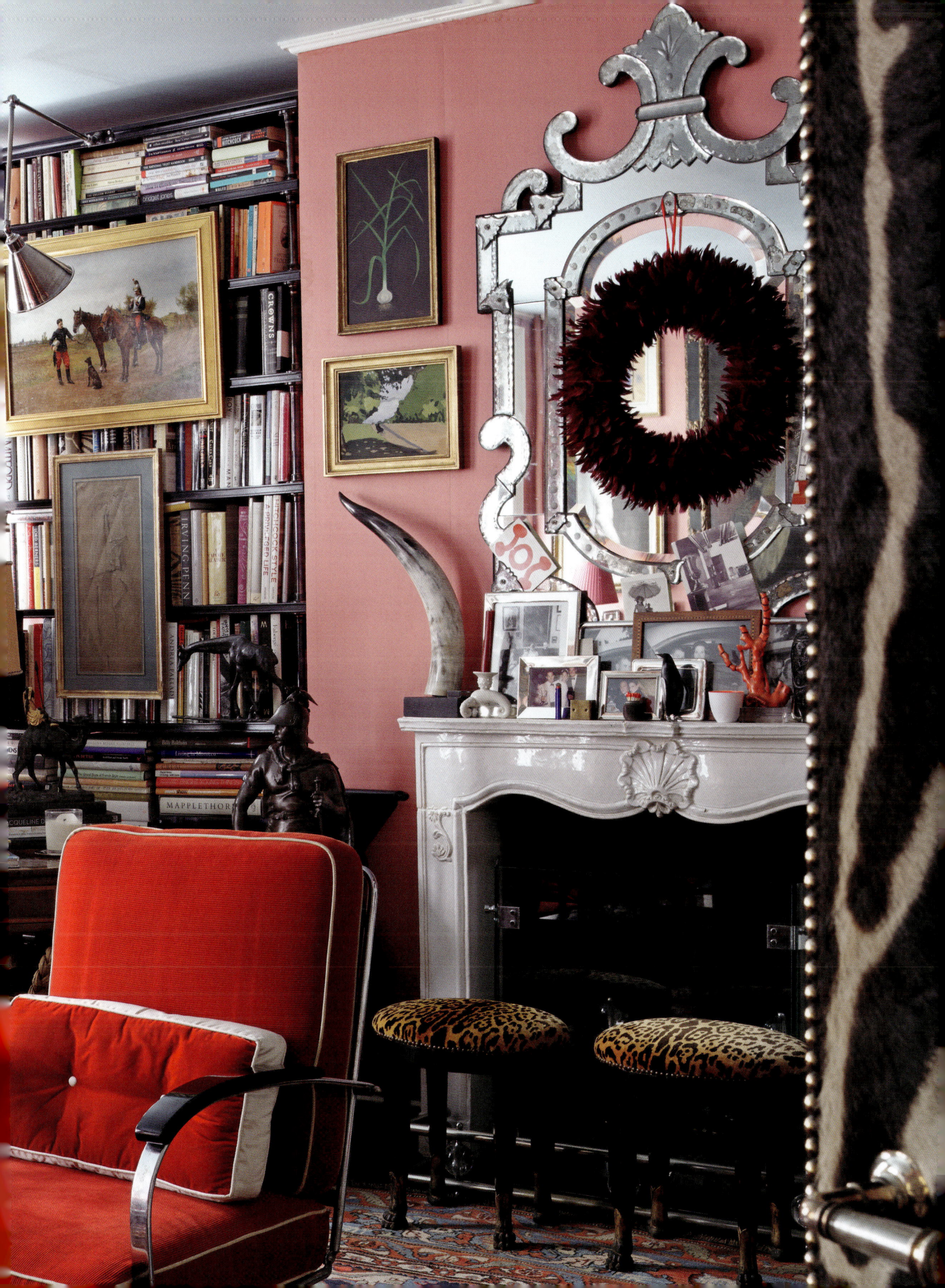

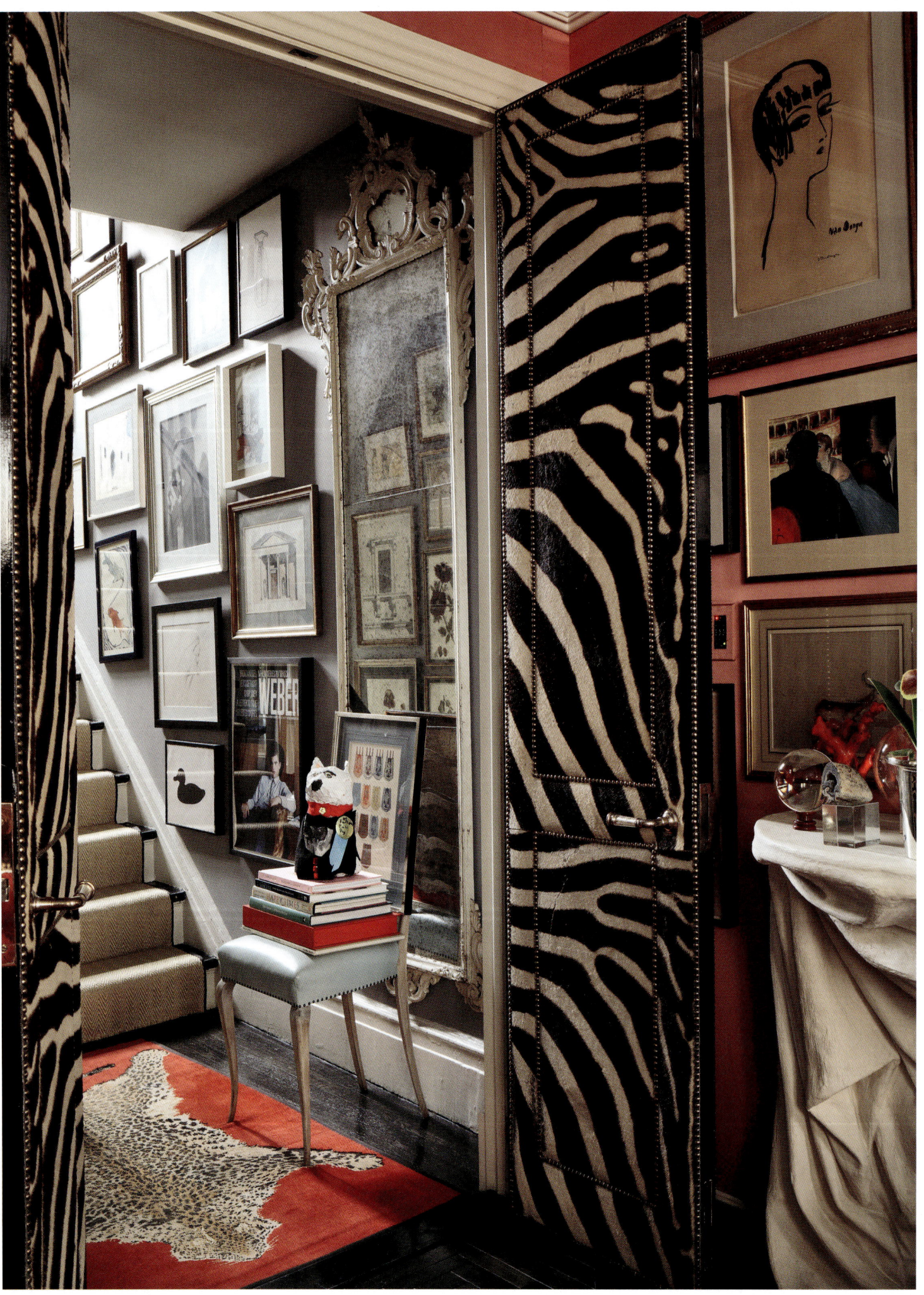

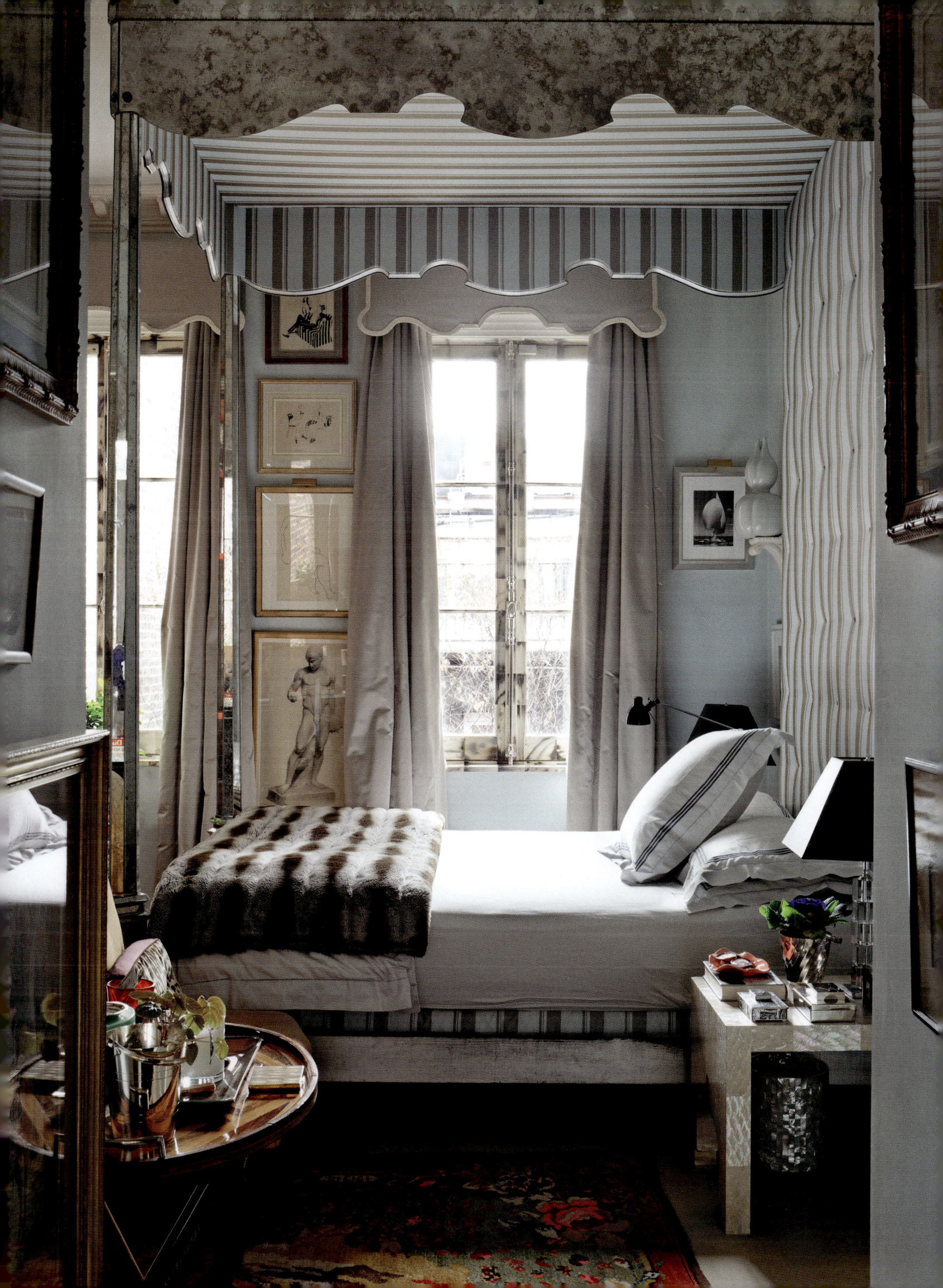

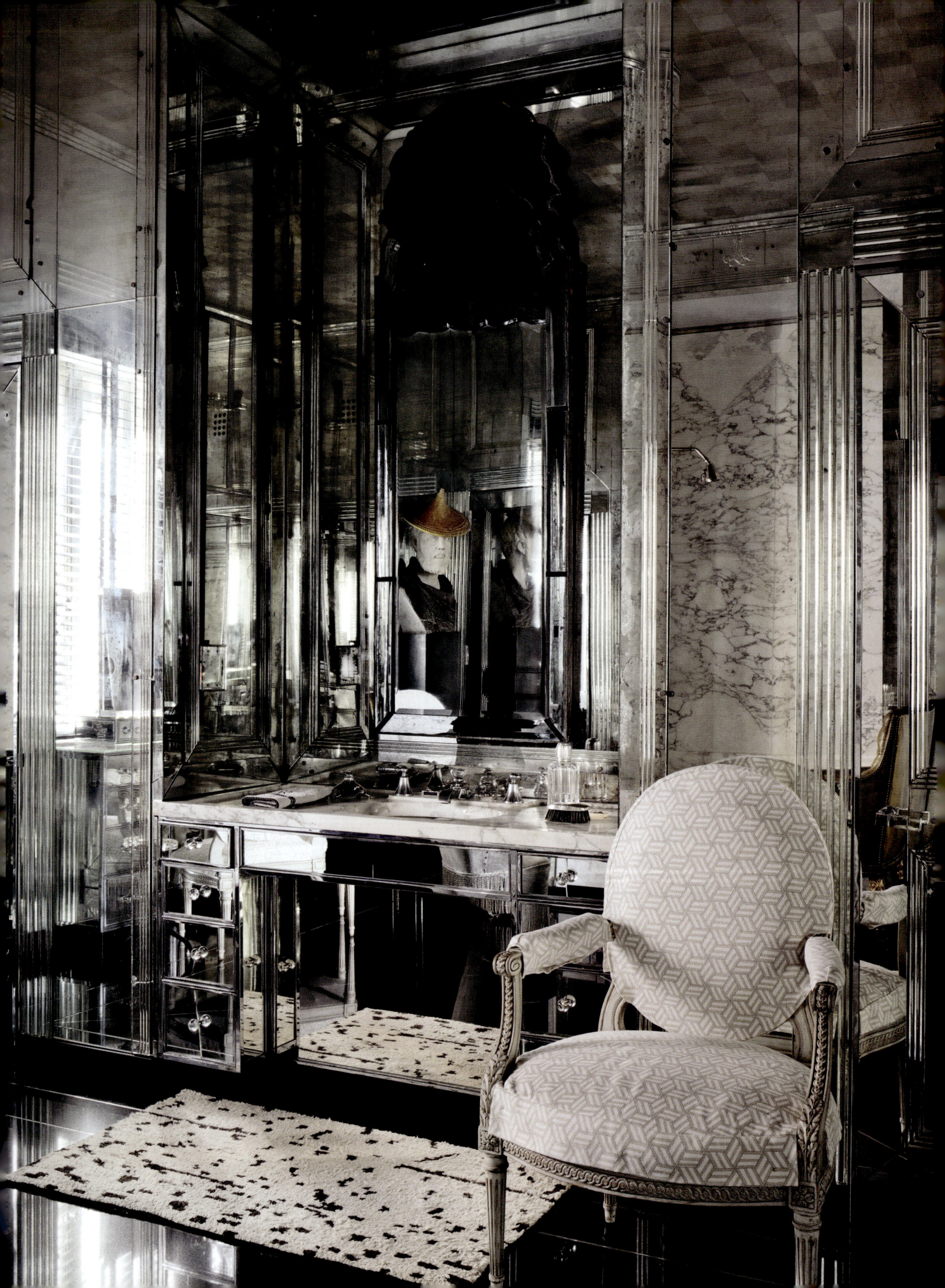

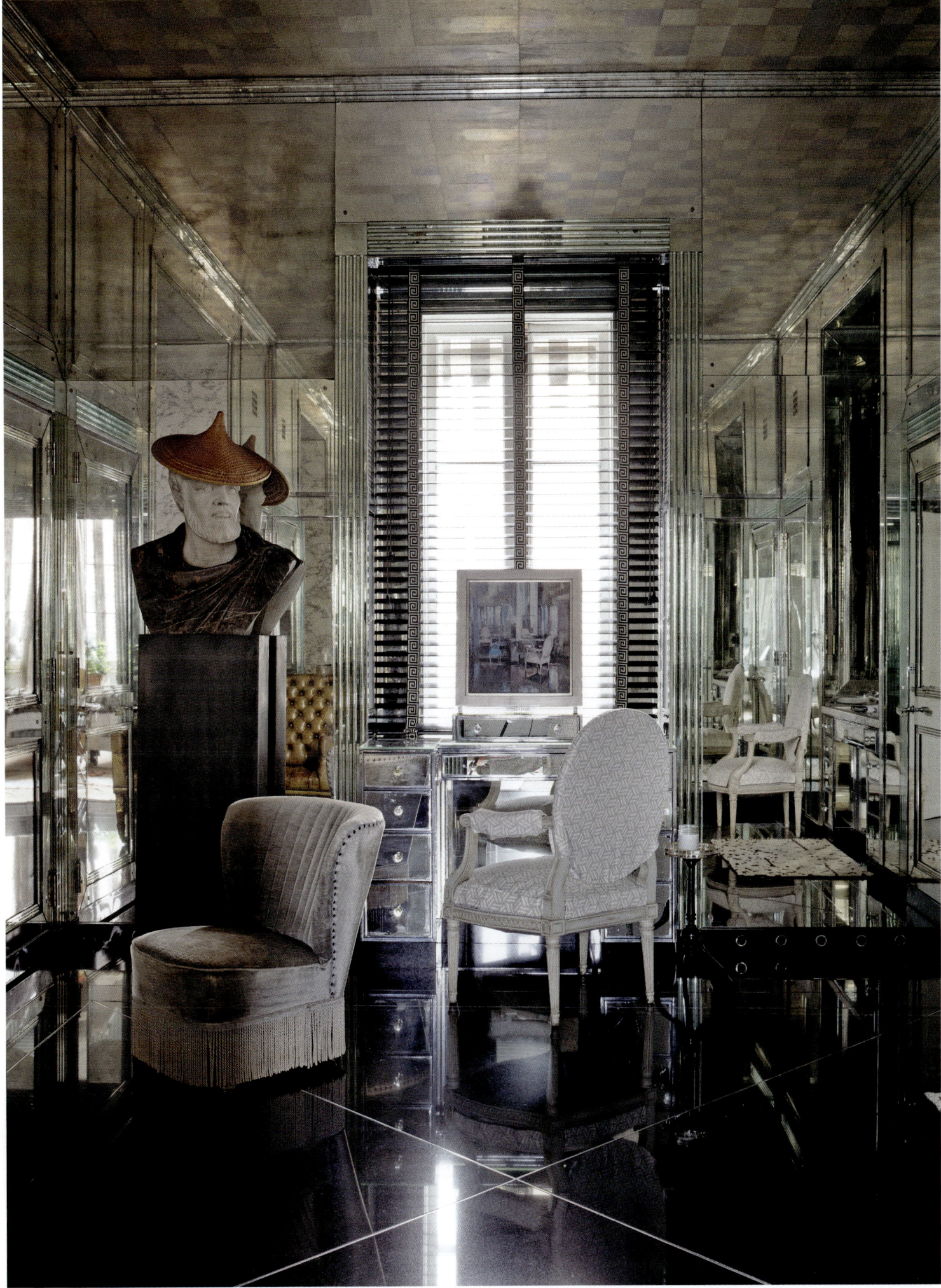

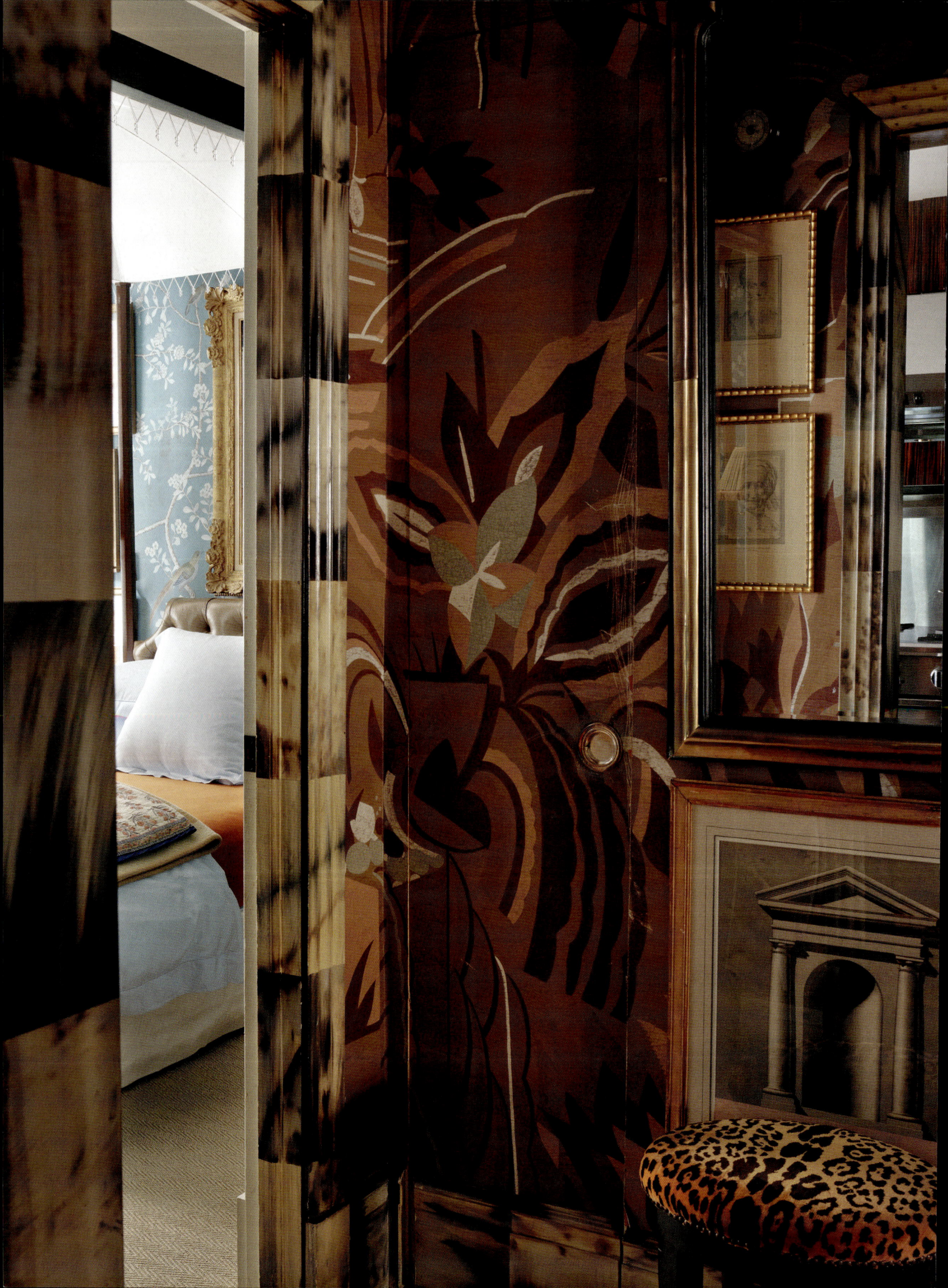

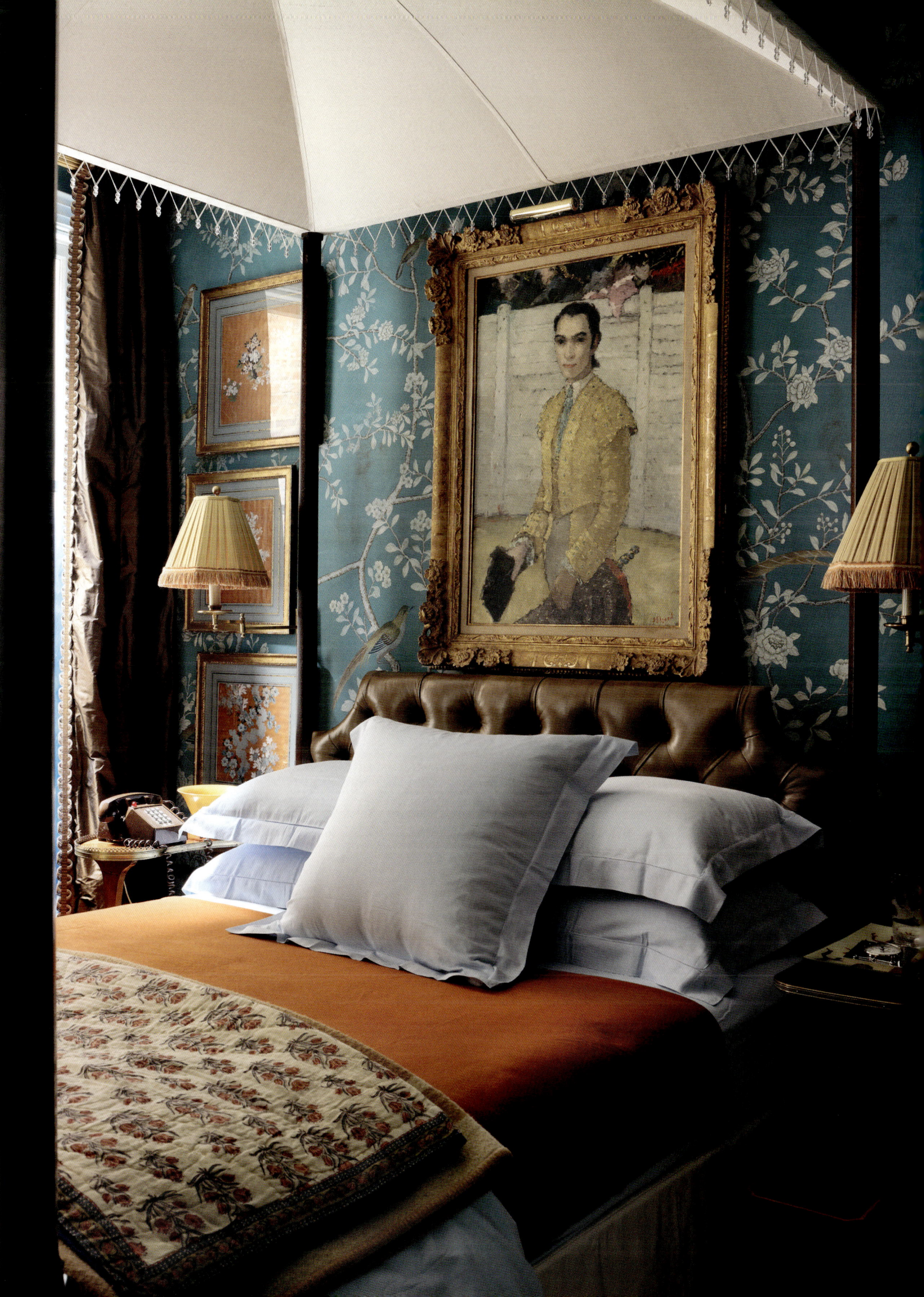

LOFT NONCHALANCE

GREGORY BISSONNETTE

East Williamsburg is situated between Bushwick and Williamsburg, neighborhoods that have been discovered and transformed first (of course) by artists, then by a younger generation of people working across the rich, unique, creative fields of NYC. Over the past decade, the development has resulted in many apartment towers replacing older structures and vacant lots, but the creative character remains strong. I had been living in the East Village with my dear friend Anne Becker. She was soon to be moving to London to marry Simon, so I needed to relocate. My acupuncturist had a loft space that he offered as a stopgap until I found my new place. It turned out to be so perfect that, six years later, I'm still here.

The building dates back to 1920 and the high ceilings in the loft are what made me fall in love. The loft is a quirky space, with one large L-shaped room that I have visually divided into three areas: Living, Sitting, and Working. My home is clean and simple, unfussy and open, which allows me the visual and mental space to create my work as an interior designer and stylist for a clientele that spans a spectrum of tastes and needs. Here, I can paint and create without concern about any mess I might make (I particularly like the slop sink in the kitchen).

The clarity and openness of the space free me. I've surrounded myself with only my most-loved personal possessions. The school desk was a gift from my mentor, Zack, who was the creative director at Calvin Klein in the 90s. He encouraged and helped me to understand and believe in myself as a young artist at the time. A vintage drawing table is where Simon chooses to work when he comes to stay. The African bed was a gift from Anne and is where my Labrador, Seymour, likes to while away his day. The French settee and chair were a gift from the estate of a long-time client, and are pieces we had found together in Paris. My collection of flea-market finds, artist friends' work, and family heirlooms—photographs going back to my Canadian great-grandfather in the 1800s—are all special to me.

I was born in Connecticut, which makes me a New Englander by birth, but I am definitely a New Yorker by choice. I have lived here all my adult life—the energy and diversity are essential to me. When I need to reset, I return to nature at my remote cabin in Vermont—sadly, a bit too far as a weekend getaway. The simplicity there restores me. I spend time in my field or on the back porch with the constants: the birch tree that's been there my whole life, showing her seasonal looks; the turtle emerging from the pond, the way he has every summer for 30 years. After time here, I can return to my home in the city, recharged and grounded, ready to create.

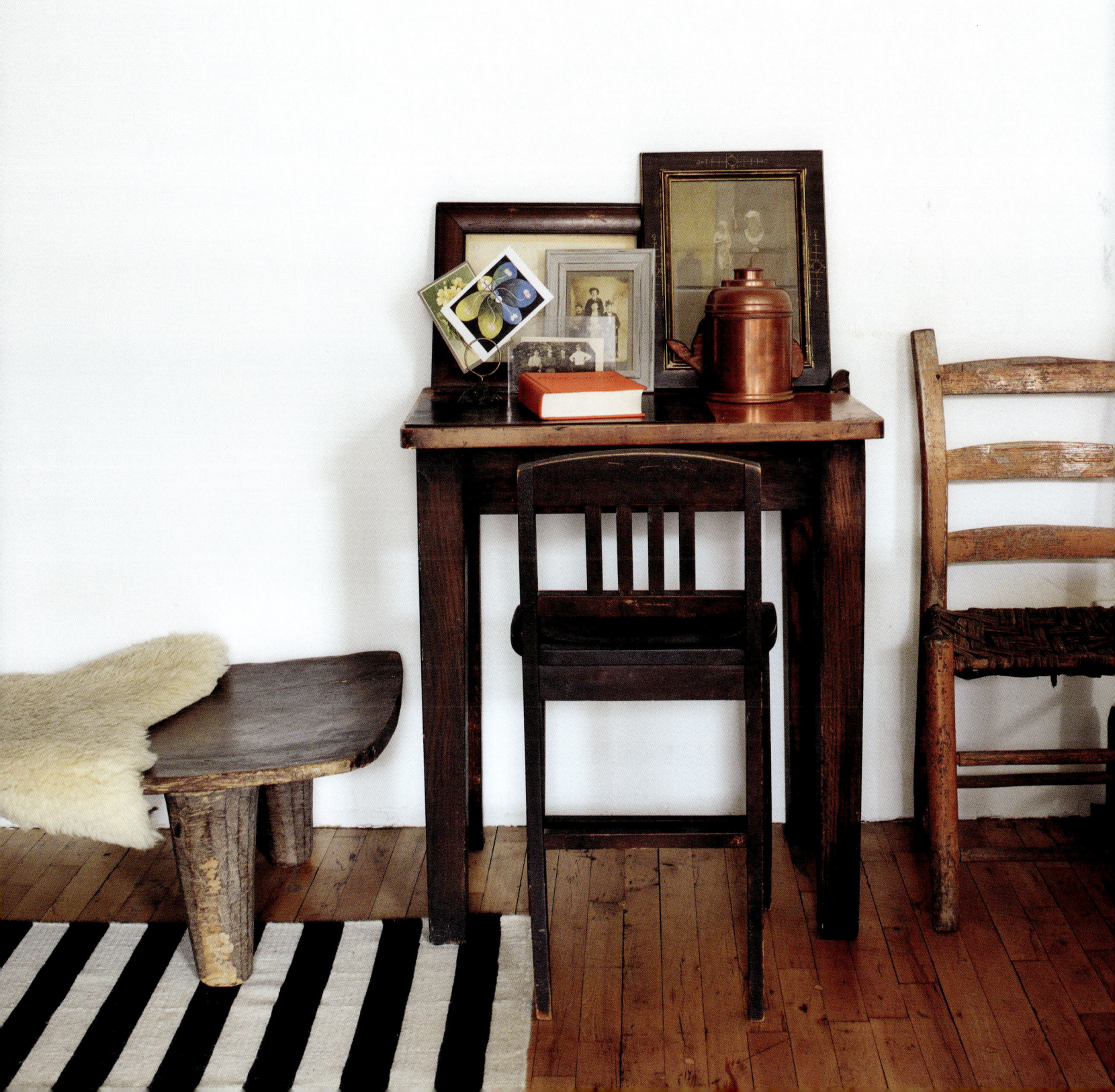

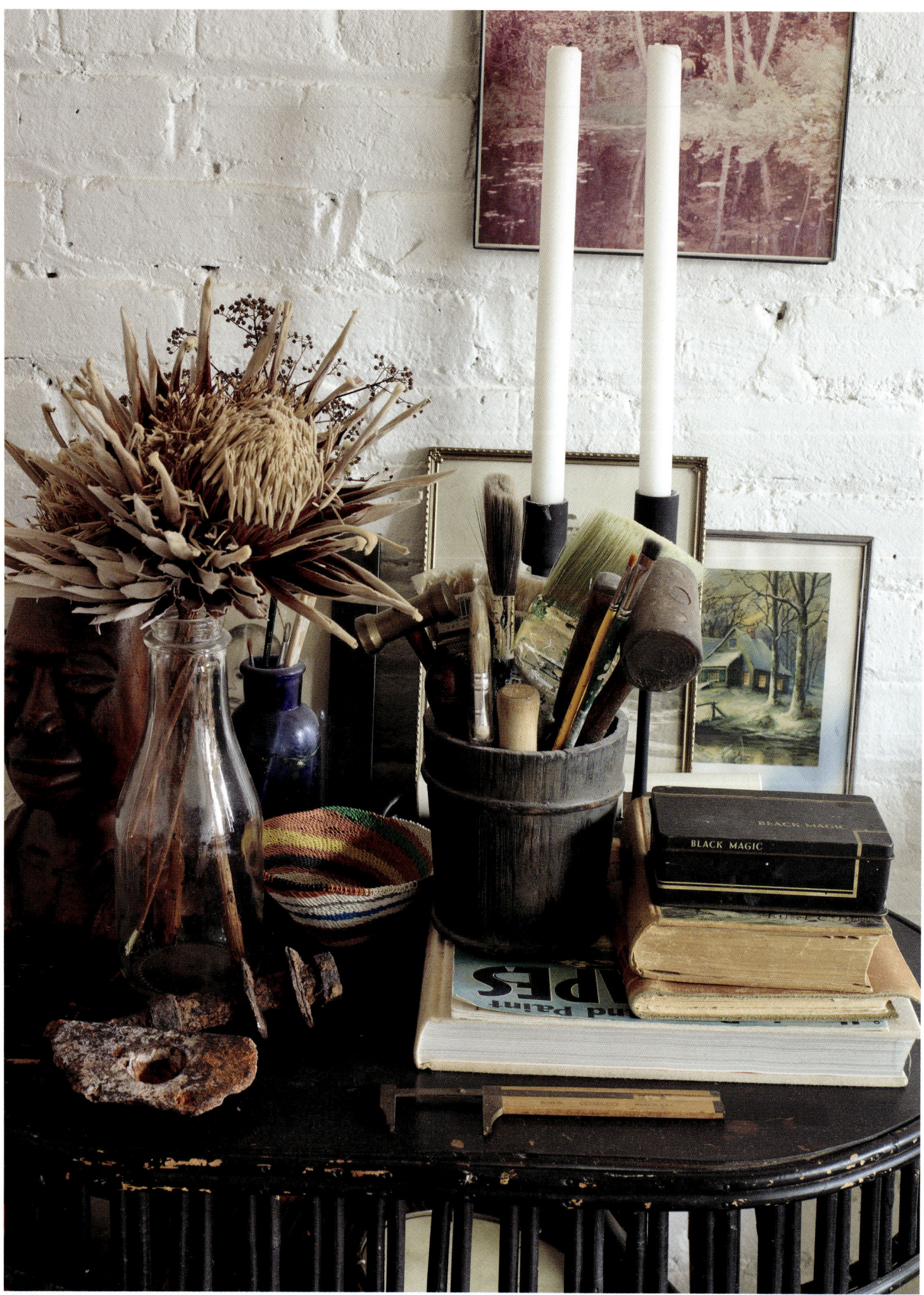

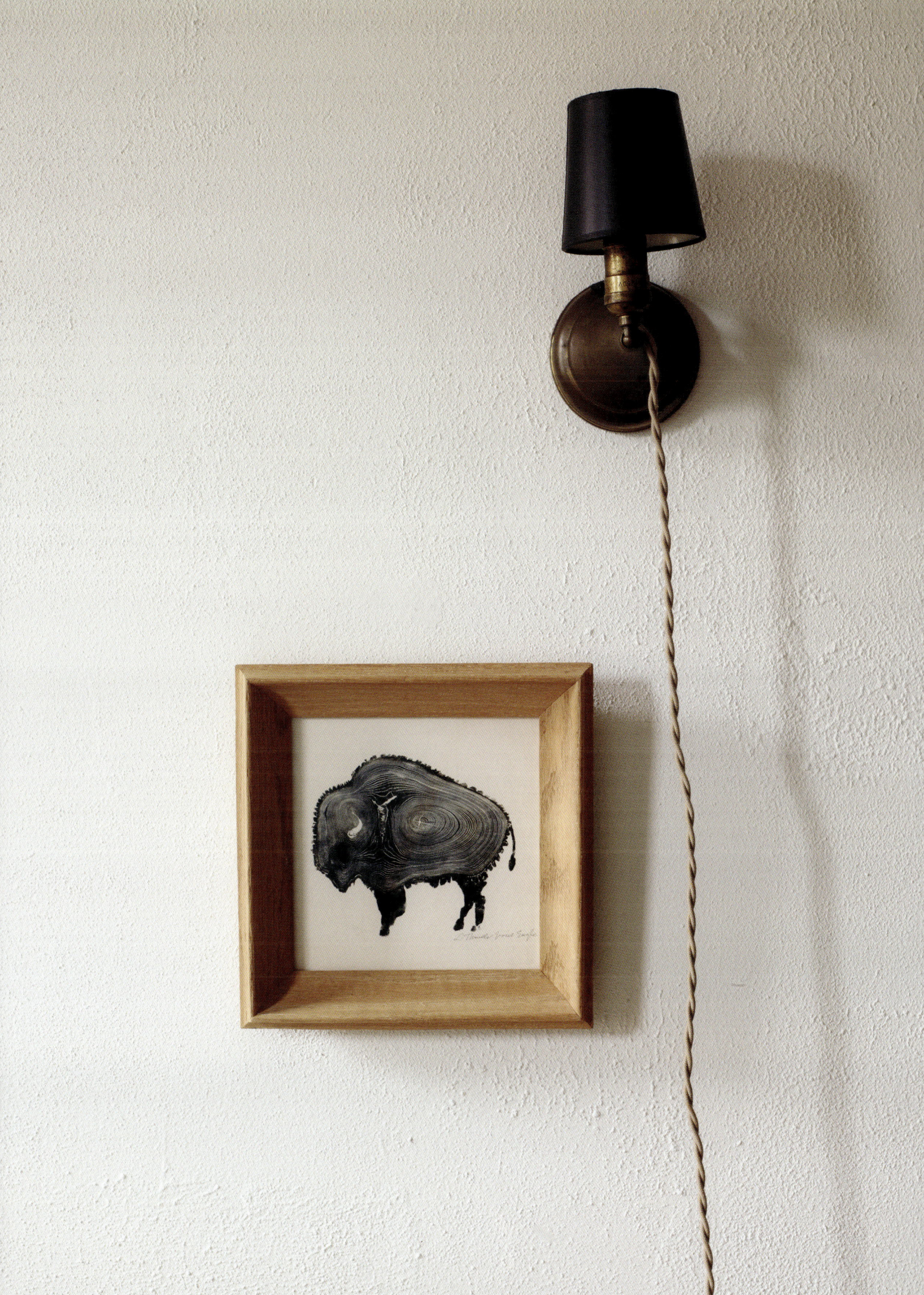

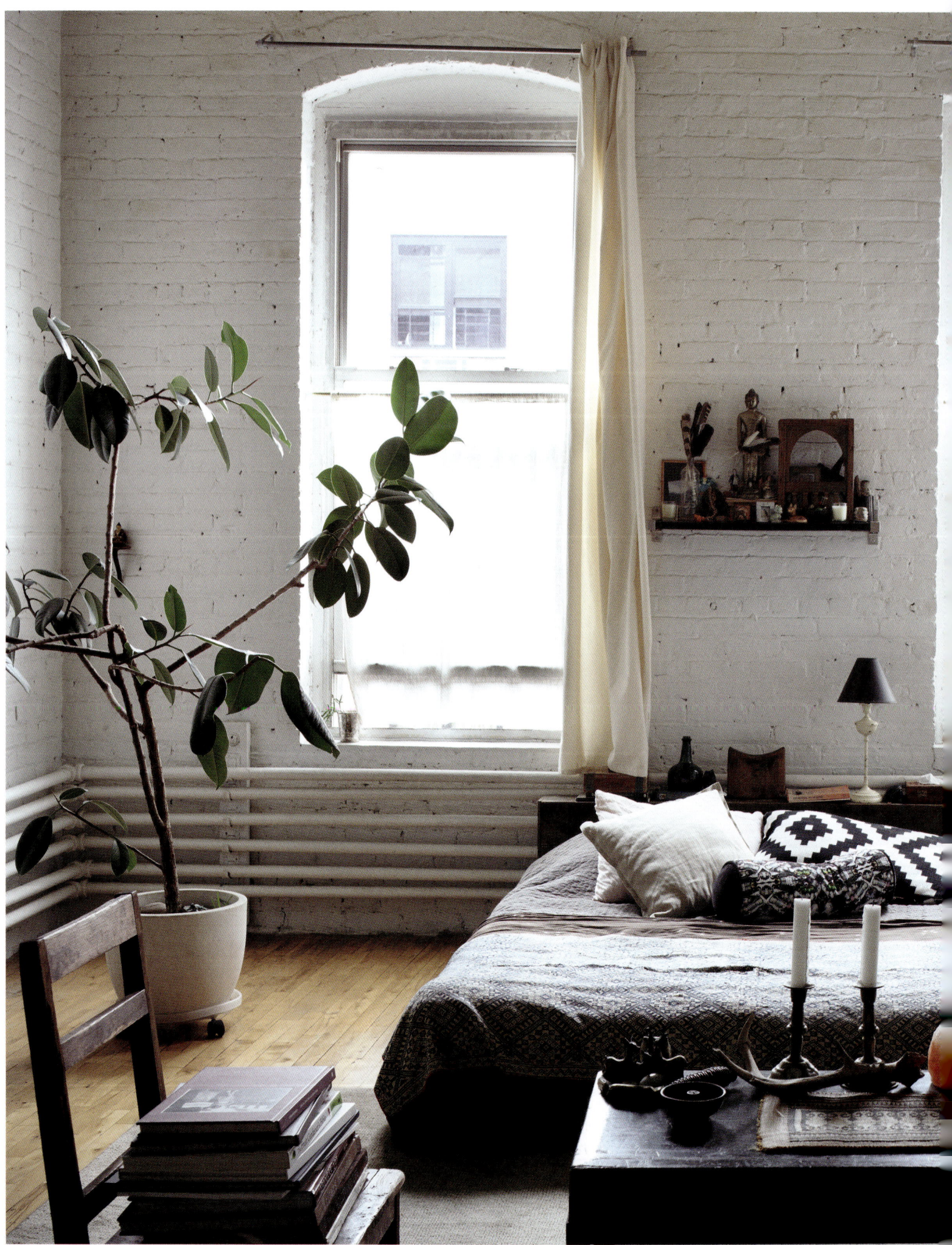

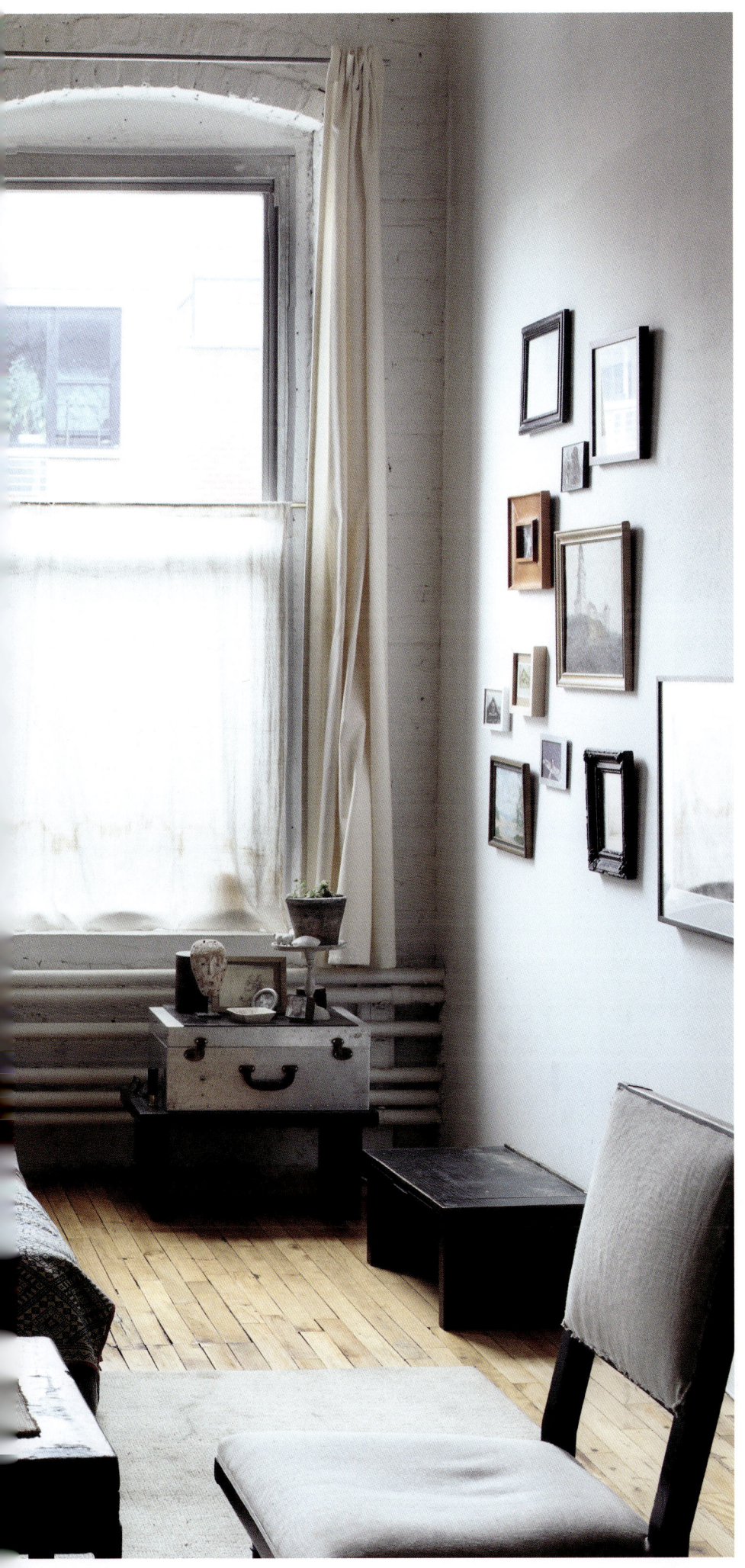

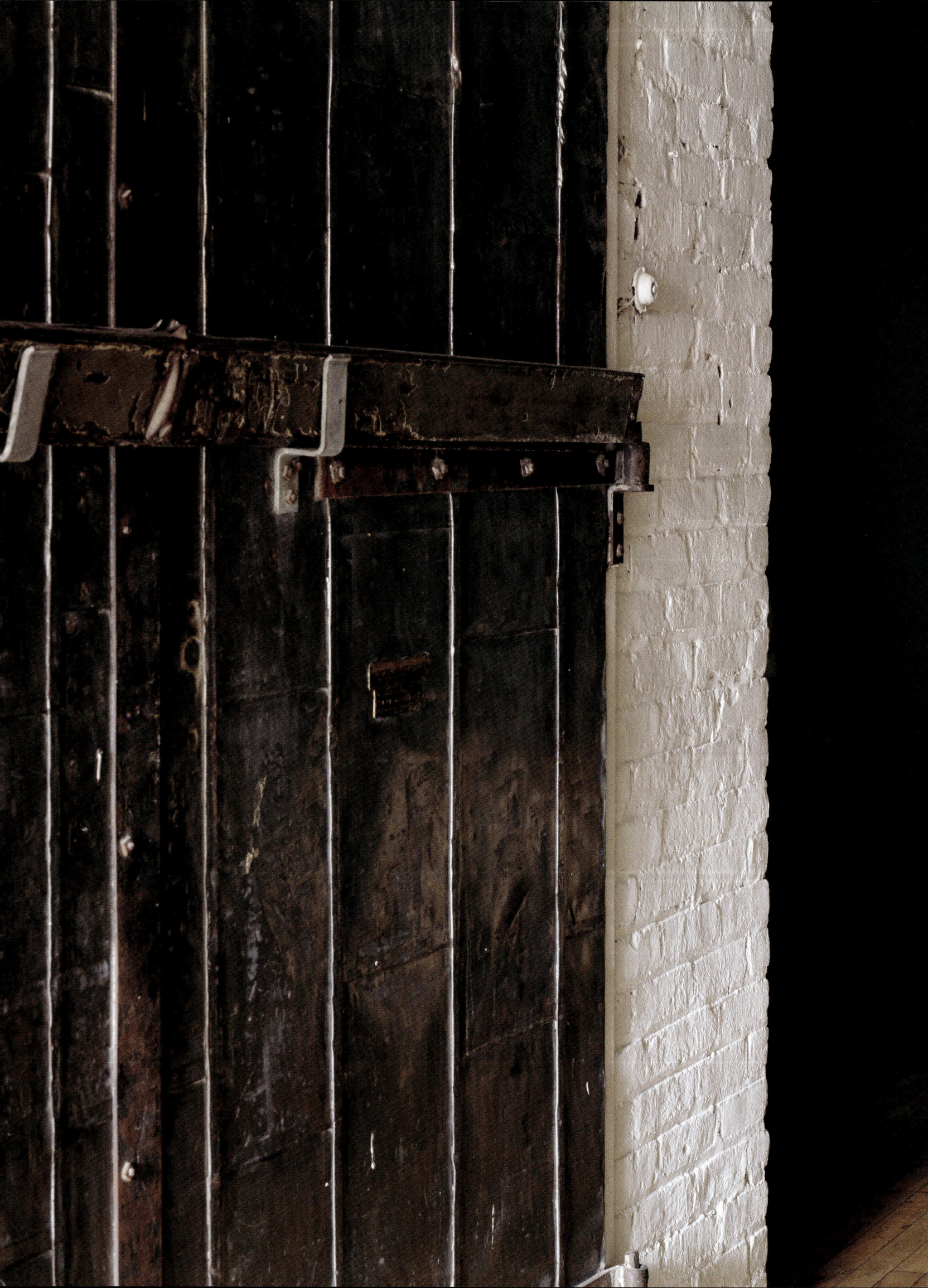

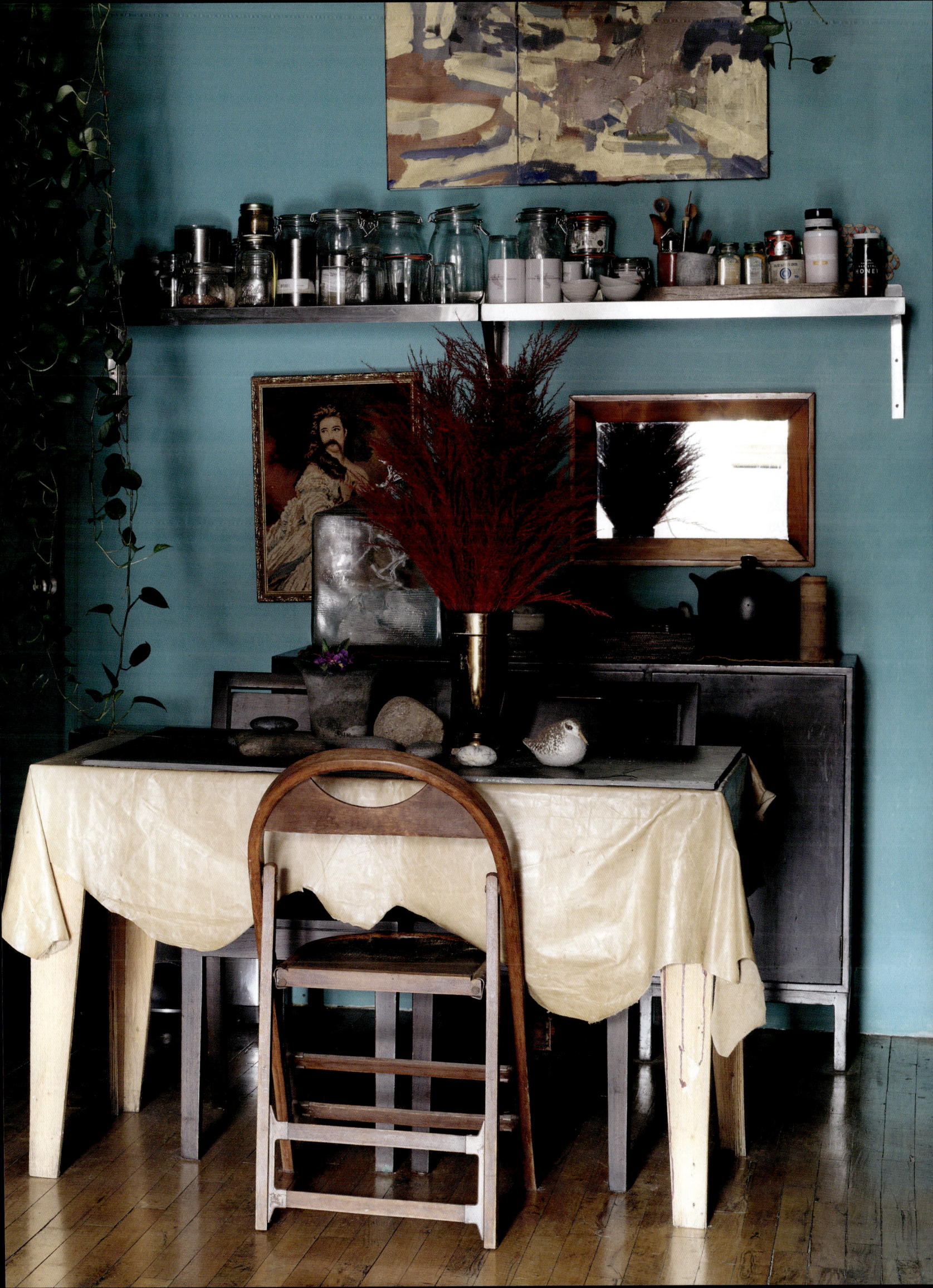

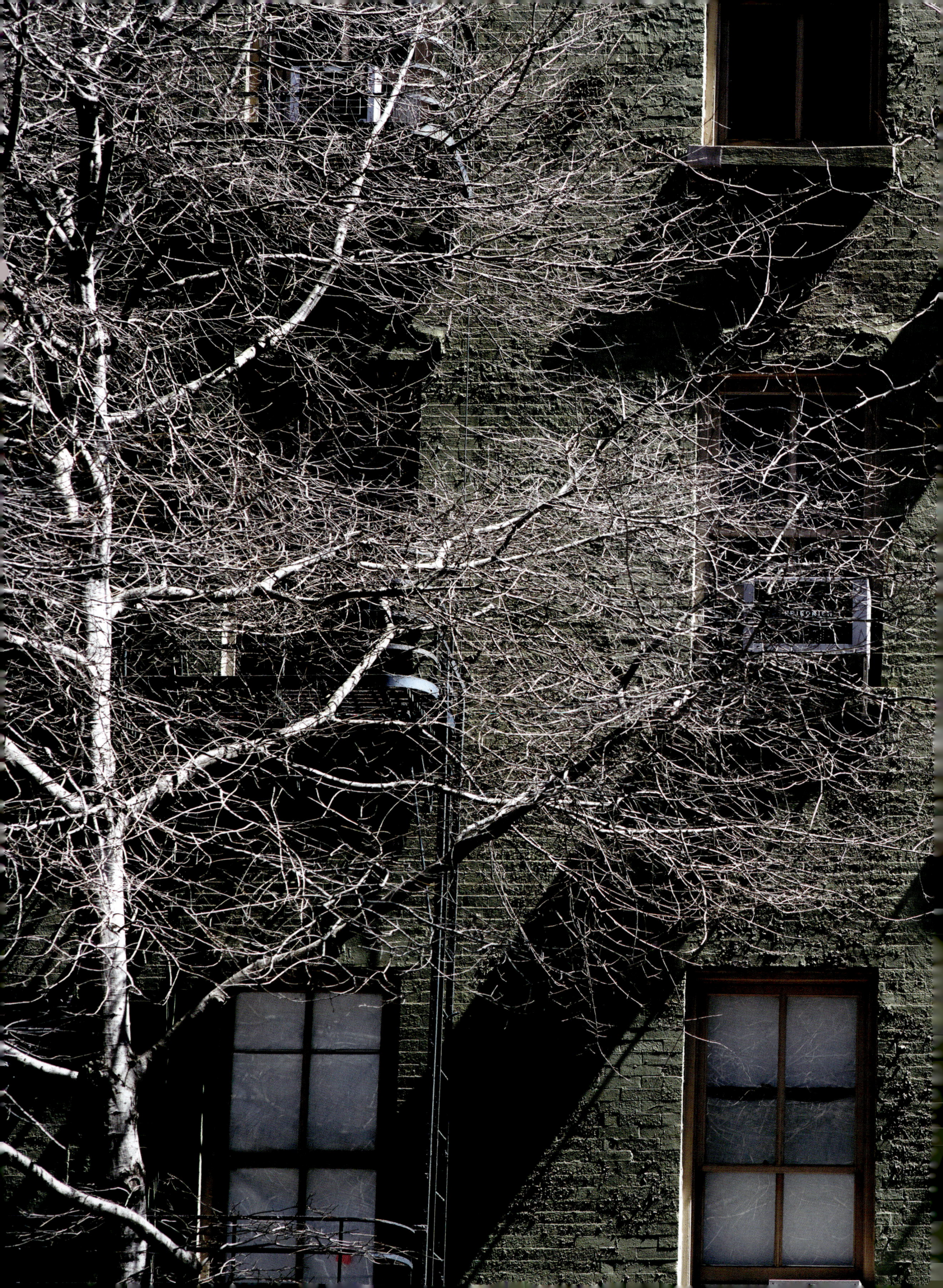

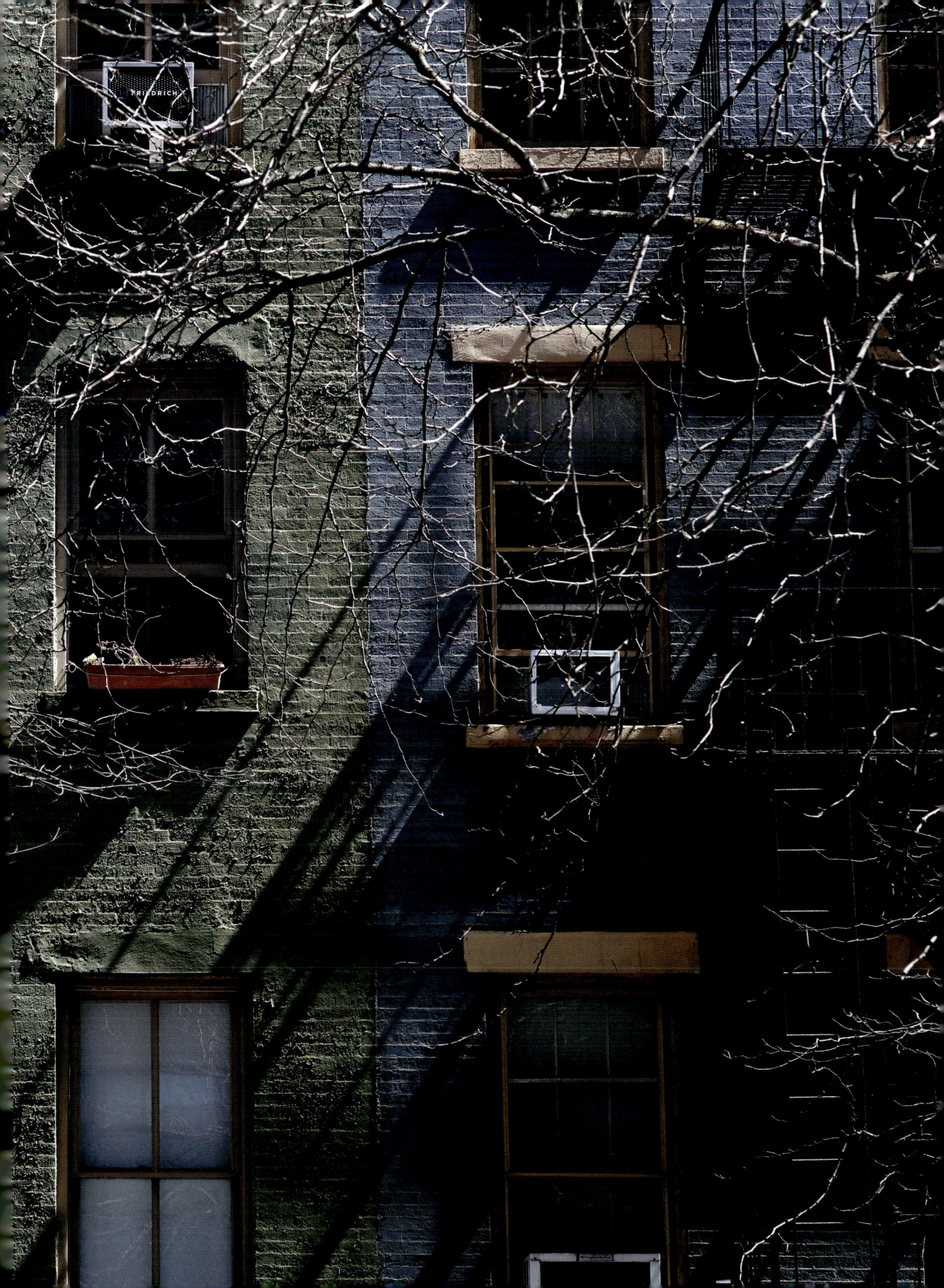

CABINET OF CURIOSITIES

MICHAEL REYNOLDS

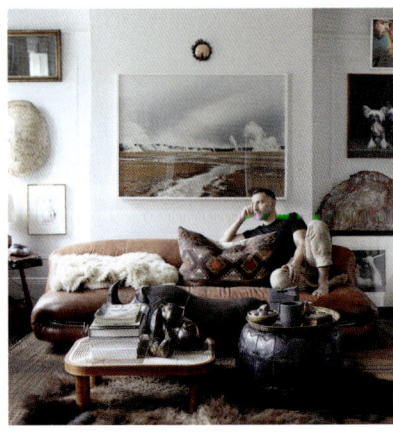

Rather unusually, I live in the same building I was born in. My grandparents lived here their entire lives, then my parents and aunt had apartments, and I recently inherited my mother's share of the property, which I hope will safeguard its future. I live on the second floor, at the front of my building. There is a fig tree in the back yard, which my grandfather planted.

The East Village has always been a hotbed for artists—Jackson Pollock among them. Popular with hippies in the 70s, it later became the center of the punk movement. Over the years it has remained untamed, and has somehow managed to retain its own identity as an impenetrable neighborhood and community, less glamorous than other districts, maybe, but edgier. Historically, it was an area inhabited by immigrants such as my family, and the boom in construction of tenement buildings in the nineteenth century gave rise to the affordable housing—low-rise, constructed on silt—that still characterizes the East Village today.

I moved away for a while, but essentially I am a homing pigeon, drawn to the culture and history of the East Village—and, more particularly, to this building—and in 1987 I returned. For the past 20 years or more I have lived in the apartment with my partner, Eric Hoffman, yet I also get the sense that I am living with ghosts; I feel the positive energy of the various members of my family, who have all now passed away. When I decorate, I don't feel that I'm doing it alone. When I move things around, change the color of a room, or introduce a new piece of furniture, I sense their influence. Of all the spaces in the apartment, I have a particular fondness for the dining nook, which is cave-like, dark, and intimate. When I have friends over I can squeeze up to five around the table. The apartment still houses my grandmother's original kitchen; I always light a cinnamon candle (I buy them from a witchcraft shop around the corner) when I'm cooking, and the scent and ritual reminds me of my grandmother, so she is always there beside me.

While none of the pieces furnishing my apartment are of particular value, I love them equally, as each reflects something about me. My home is filled with crystals that resonate deeply and personally with me, and the wall of my bedroom is lined with framed artworks. Reflected in the mirrored cabinet on the opposite side of the narrow space, it feels as if I am sleeping in a gallery, which is really rather wonderful, I think.

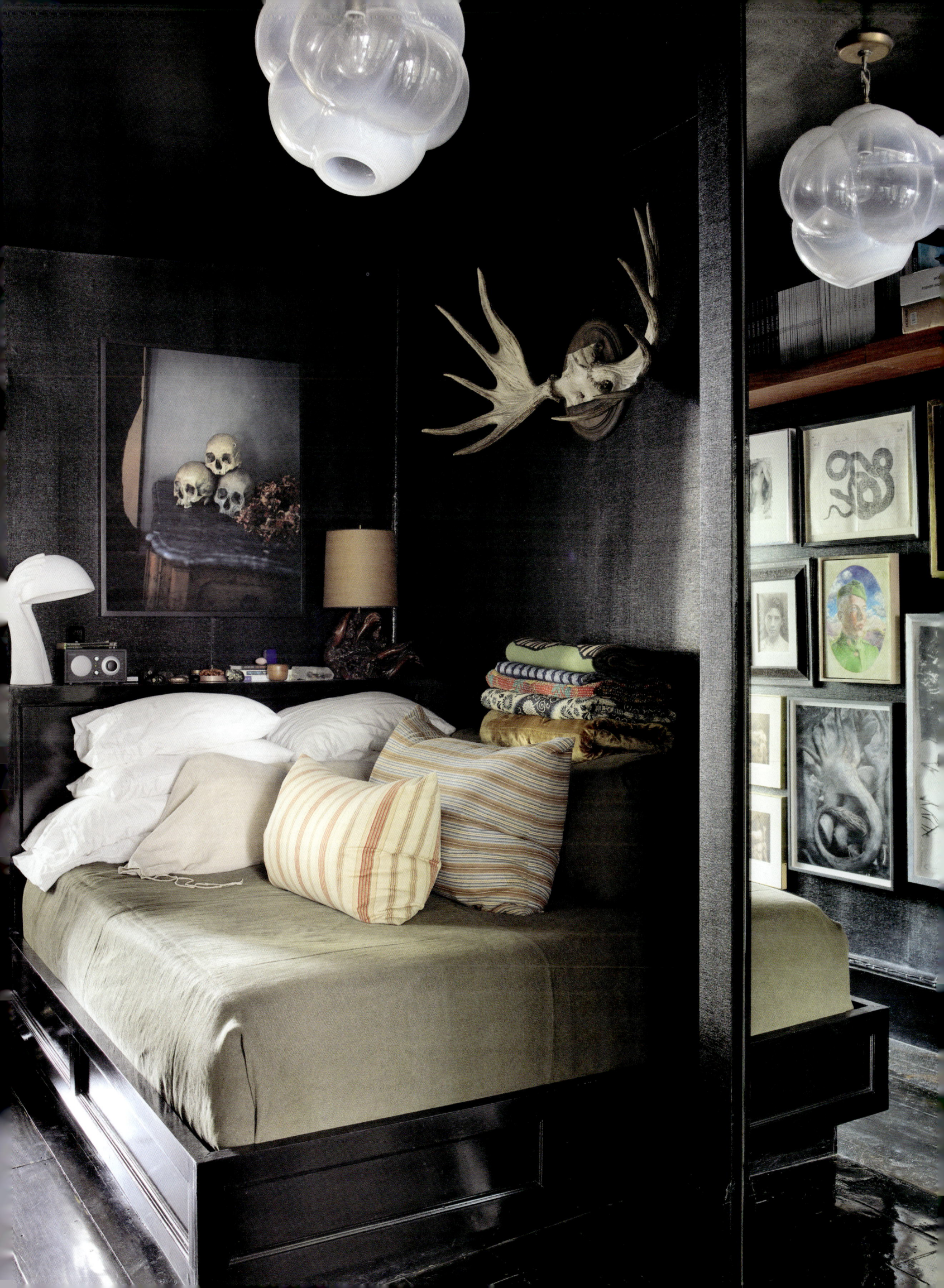

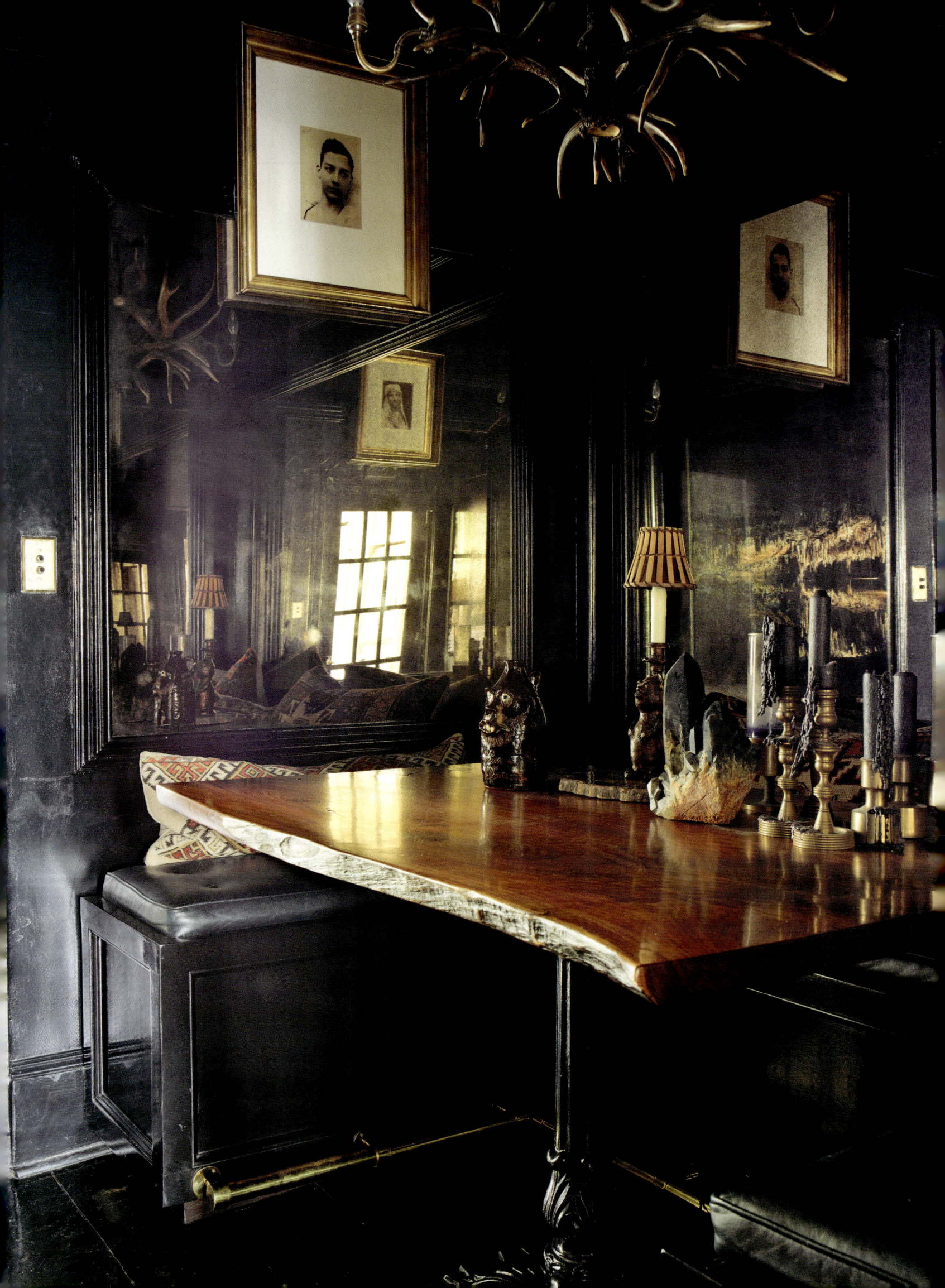

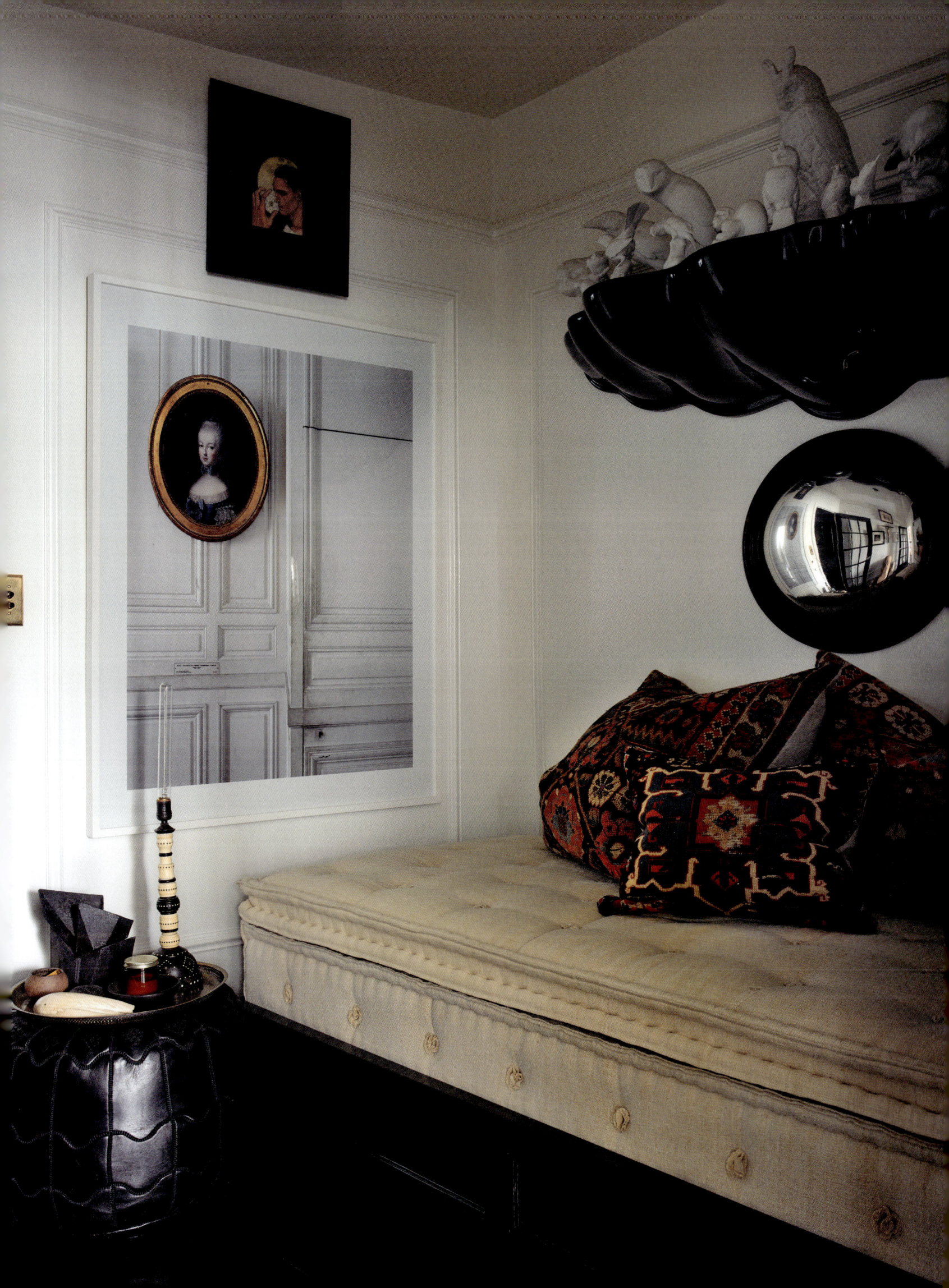

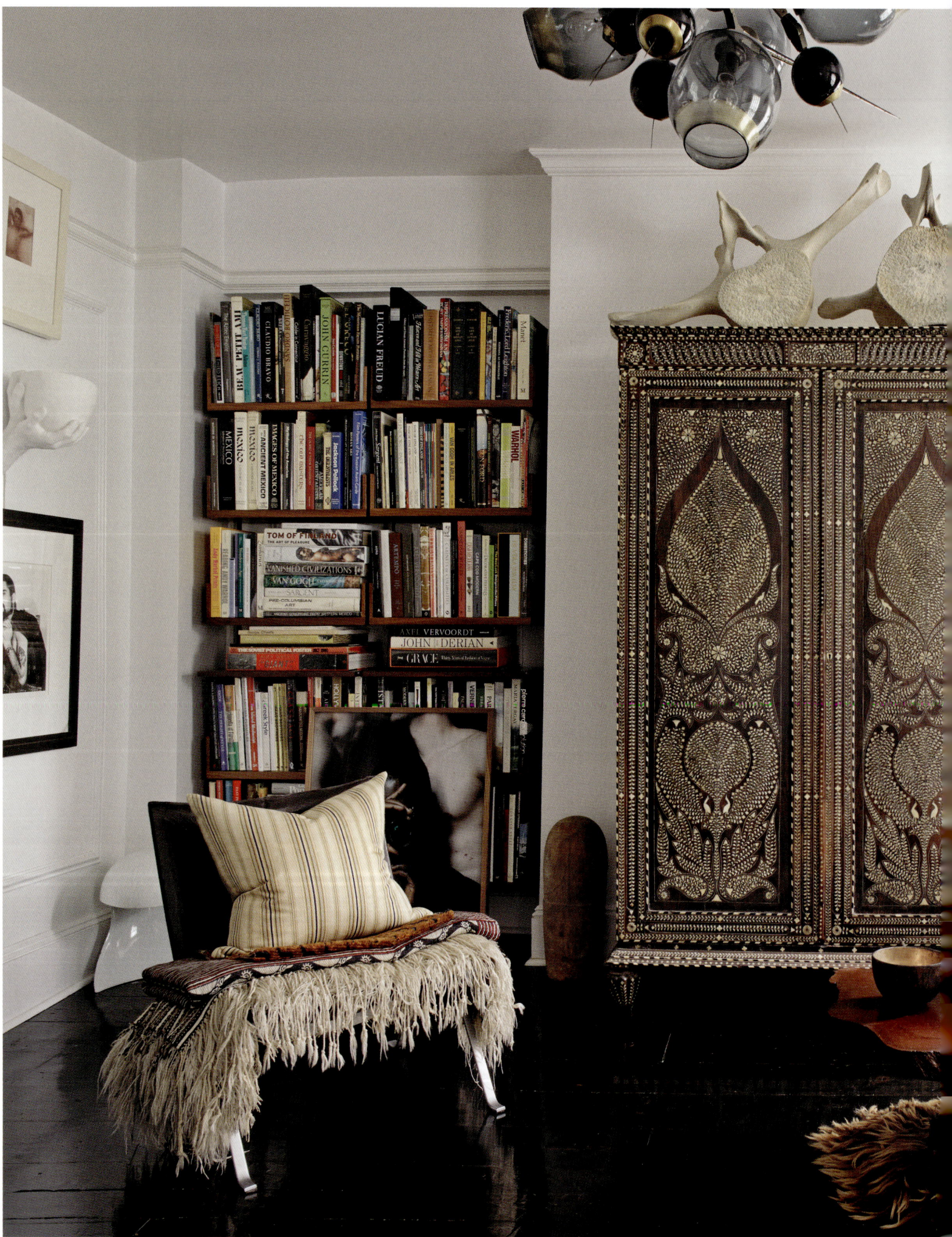

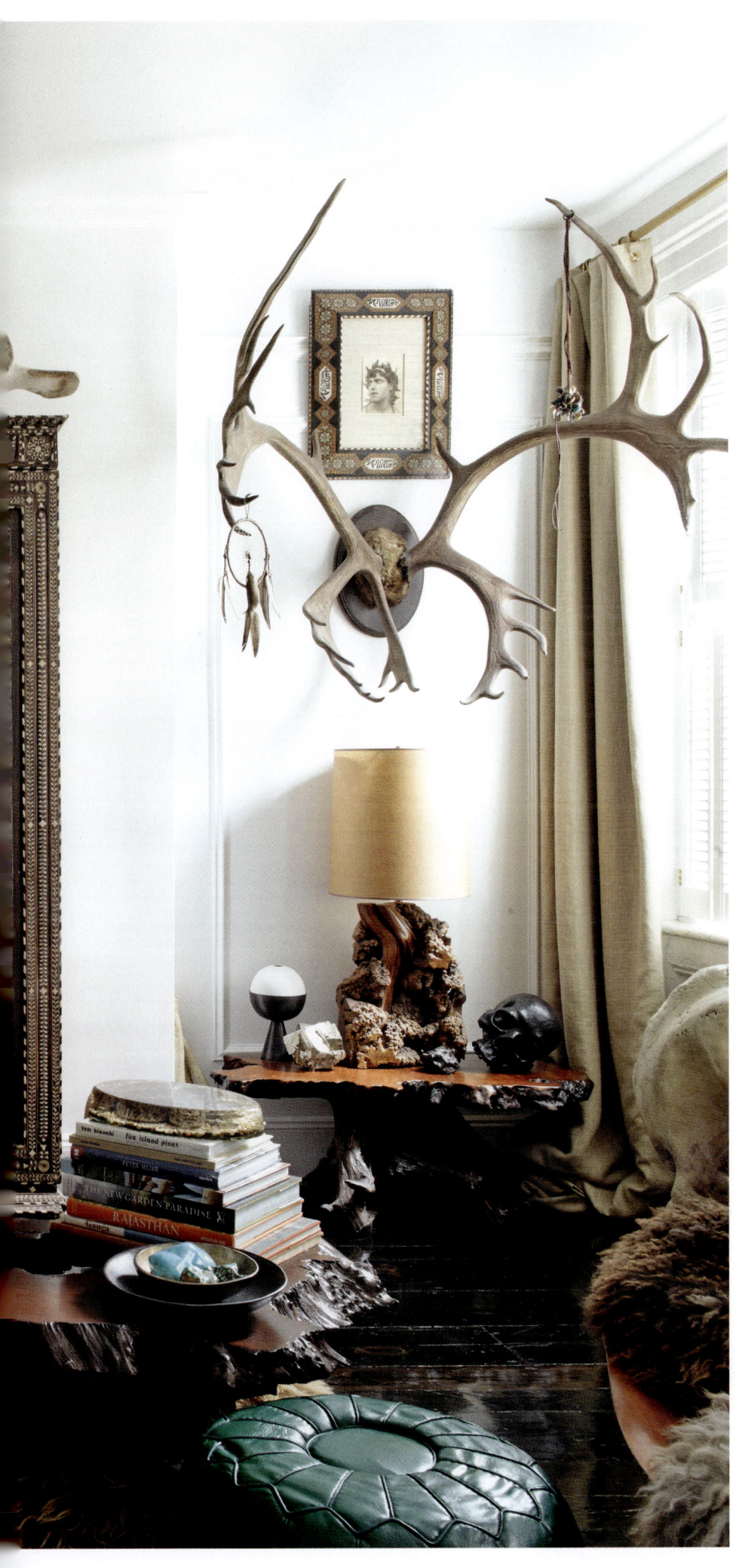

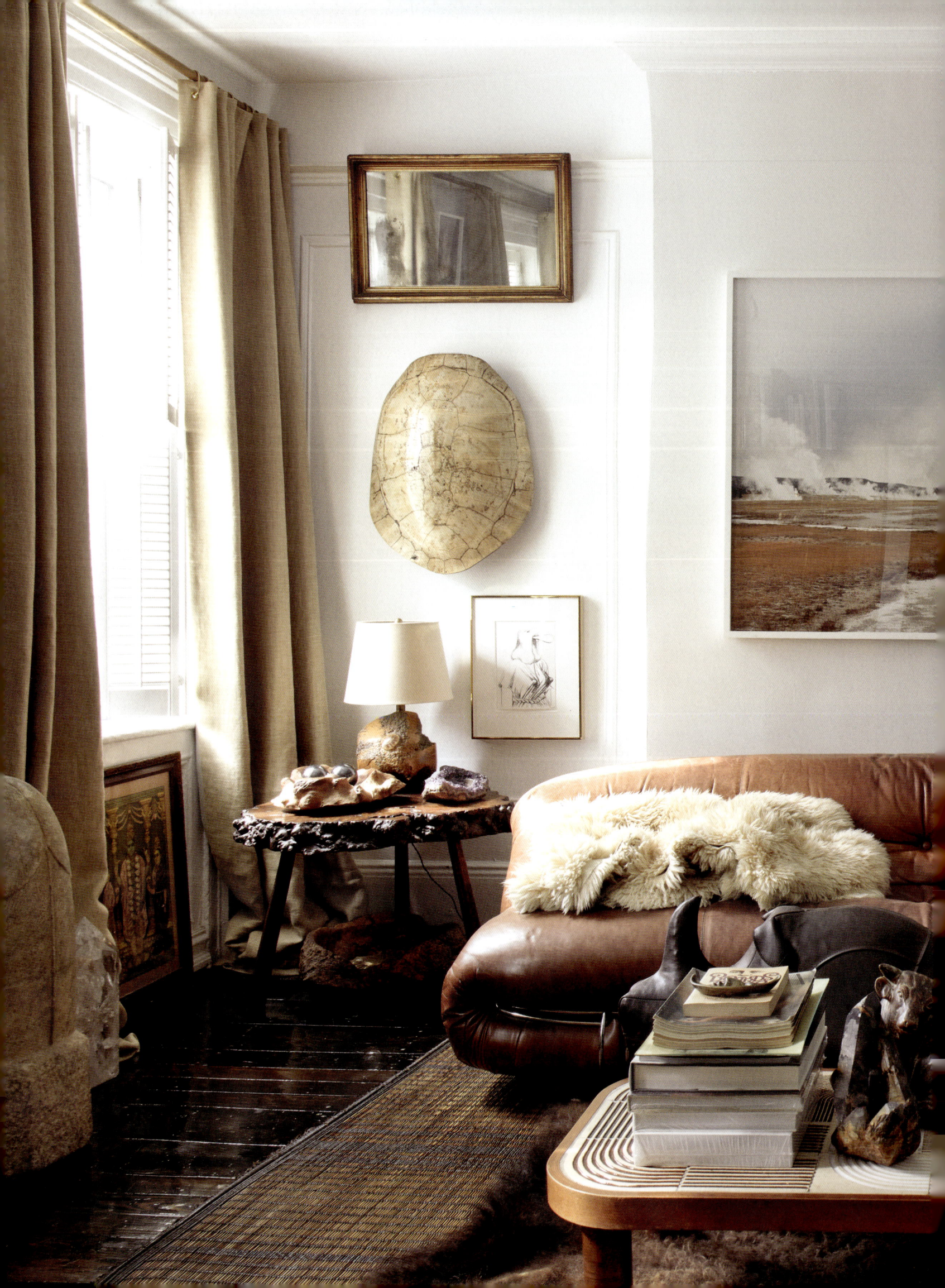

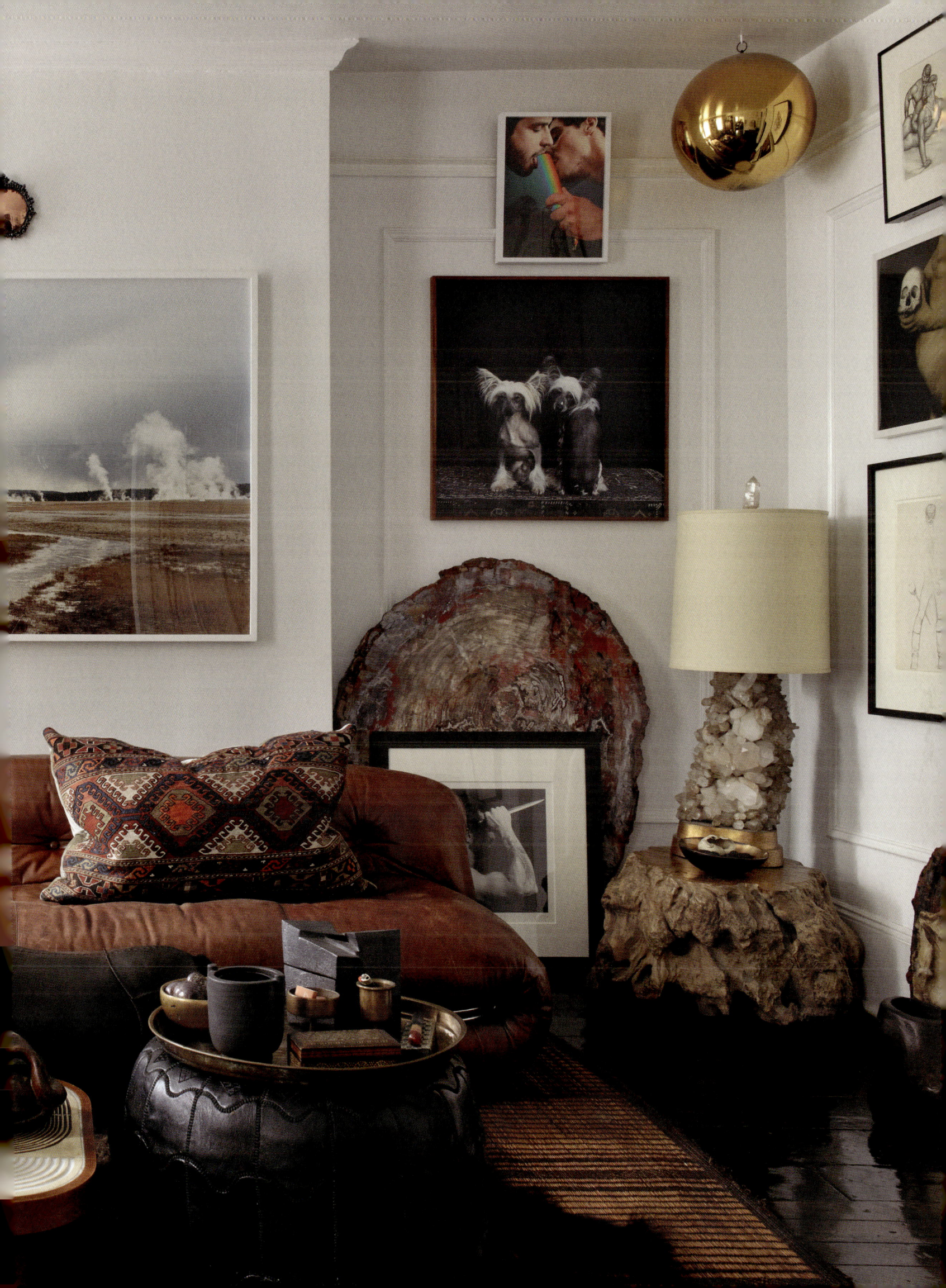

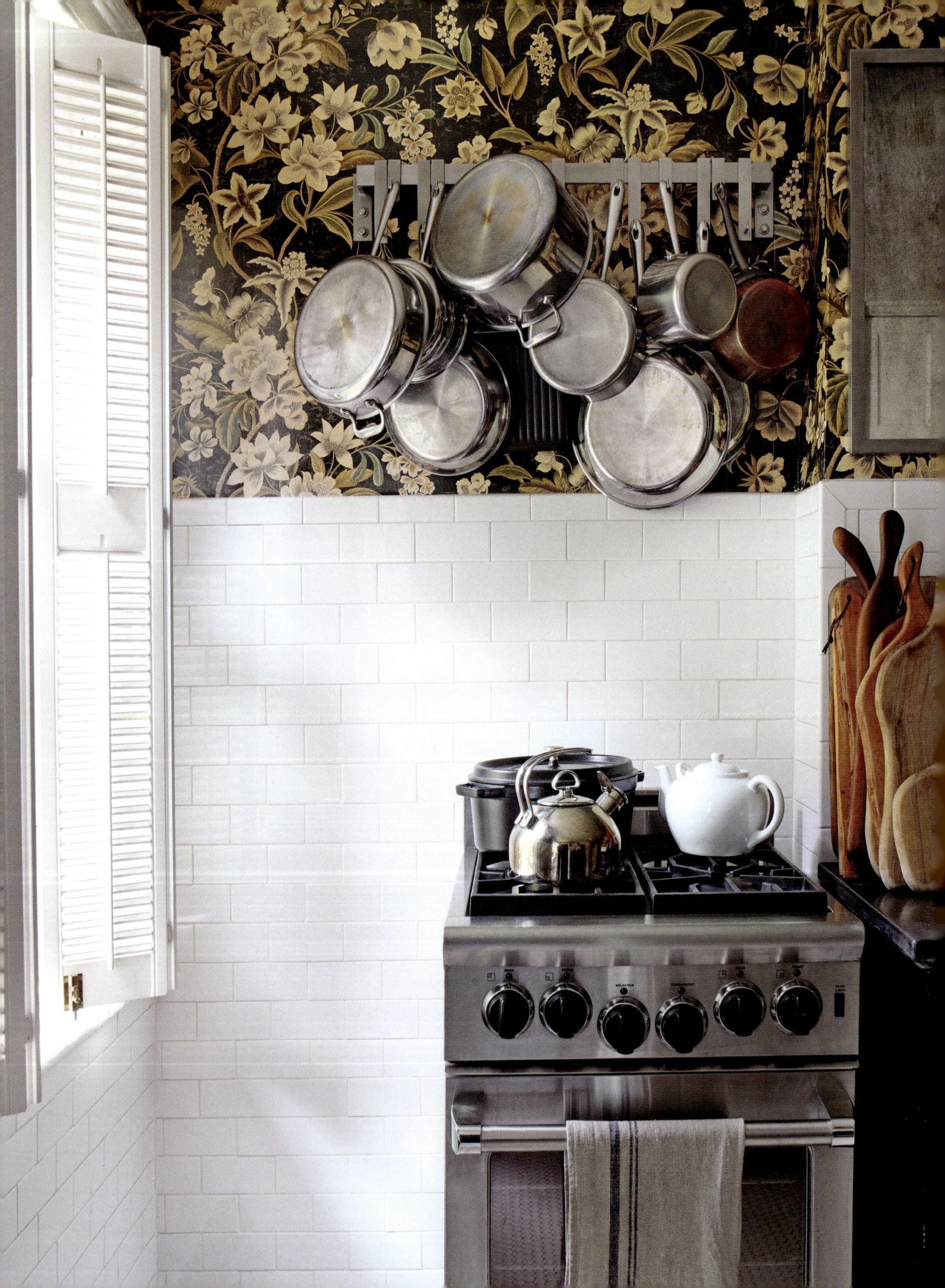

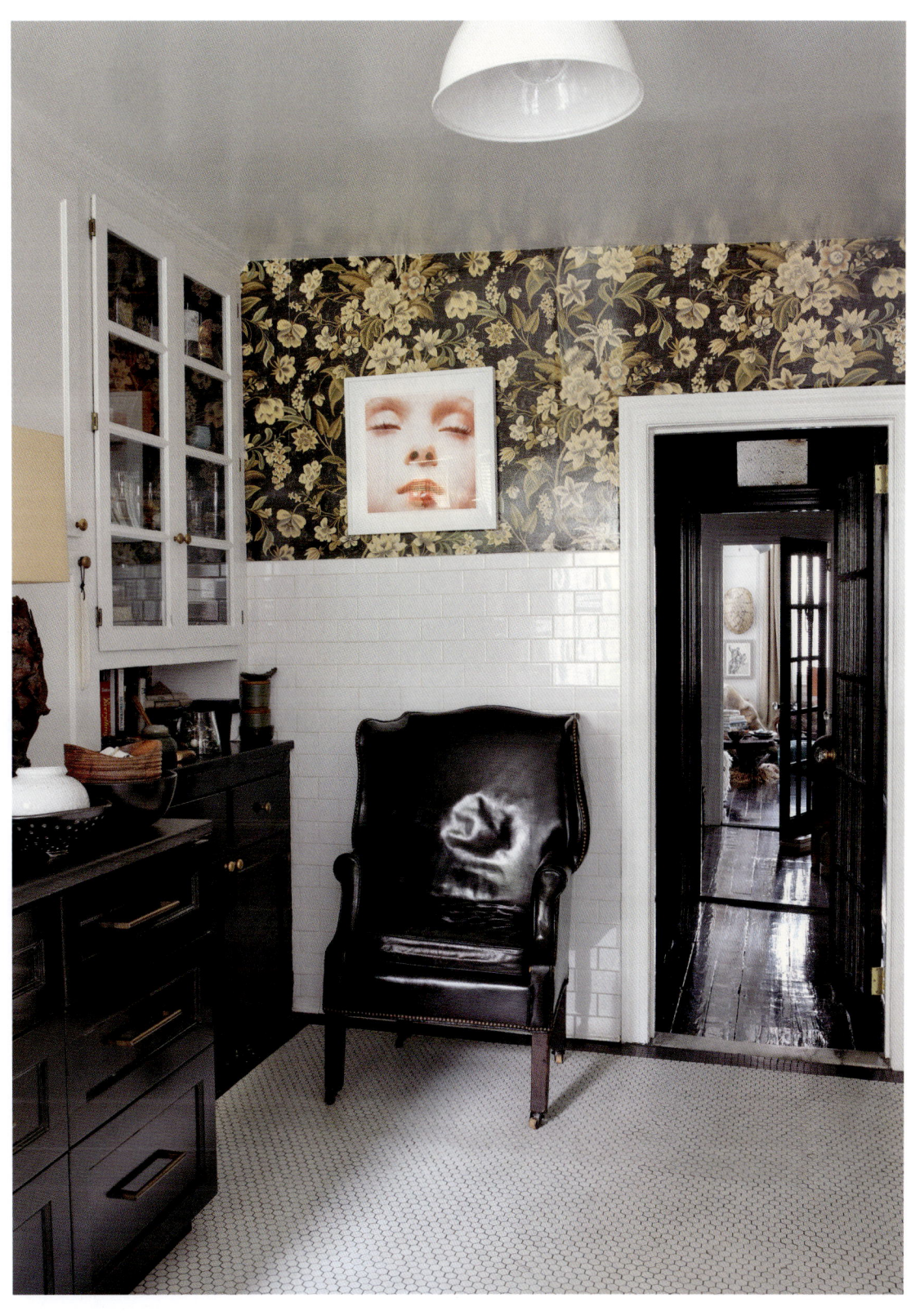

PERSONAL GALLERY

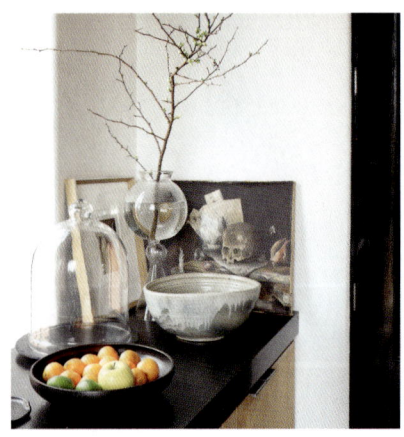

ALFREDO PAREDES

For years, I lived in Tribeca, and though I loved all the old industrial buildings there, it never felt like home. So, after 10 years, I started looking around. I found this place in 2009 and it really captured my imagination. It had been renovated a decade or more earlier and needed lots of work, but there was just something special about the place—I couldn't stop thinking about it. I came to see it four times over several

months before making an offer. It wasn't just the 14-foot ceilings, the abundance of natural light, and the large terrace that got me (though they were big selling points). Somehow, I saw a long *future* here.

It took about 18 months to pull it all together; basically, I took the place down to its concrete shell and started over. While I wanted to create the overall impression that the apartment had existed in its present form forever, much of it is brand new, including the stone staircase, the casement windows, and the distressed oak walls. In other areas we used salvaged materials, such as the fireplace mantel sourced from an old residence on the Upper East Side, and the wood for the beamed ceiling, which came from an old barn, and which we stained a darker color. I worked on the structural side with Michael Neumann Architecture, but the vision for the space is entirely my own, with inspiration from the work of Axel Vervoordt. Given my background at Ralph Lauren, I'm accustomed to creating evocative environments, but this was the first time I'd really been able to do it in a major way for myself and my family.

Even though there are loads of great places to eat in the East Village, almost immediately my husband and I found it more fun to eat at home, inviting friends to gather around the long table on the terrace or the circular table in the parlor. It doesn't hurt that my husband's a great cook! Now that we have two young children, meals have become more of a family affair. We've lived here for more than 10 years and I still love everything about the apartment, and the space inspired me to acquire some of my all-time favorite pieces, like the console table against the wall in the living area, and the glorious Pat Steir artwork—*November Rain*—that hangs above it. When we moved in, I never imagined it would accommodate not just us and our two dogs, but our two children as well. Today, it's become the heart of our family life.

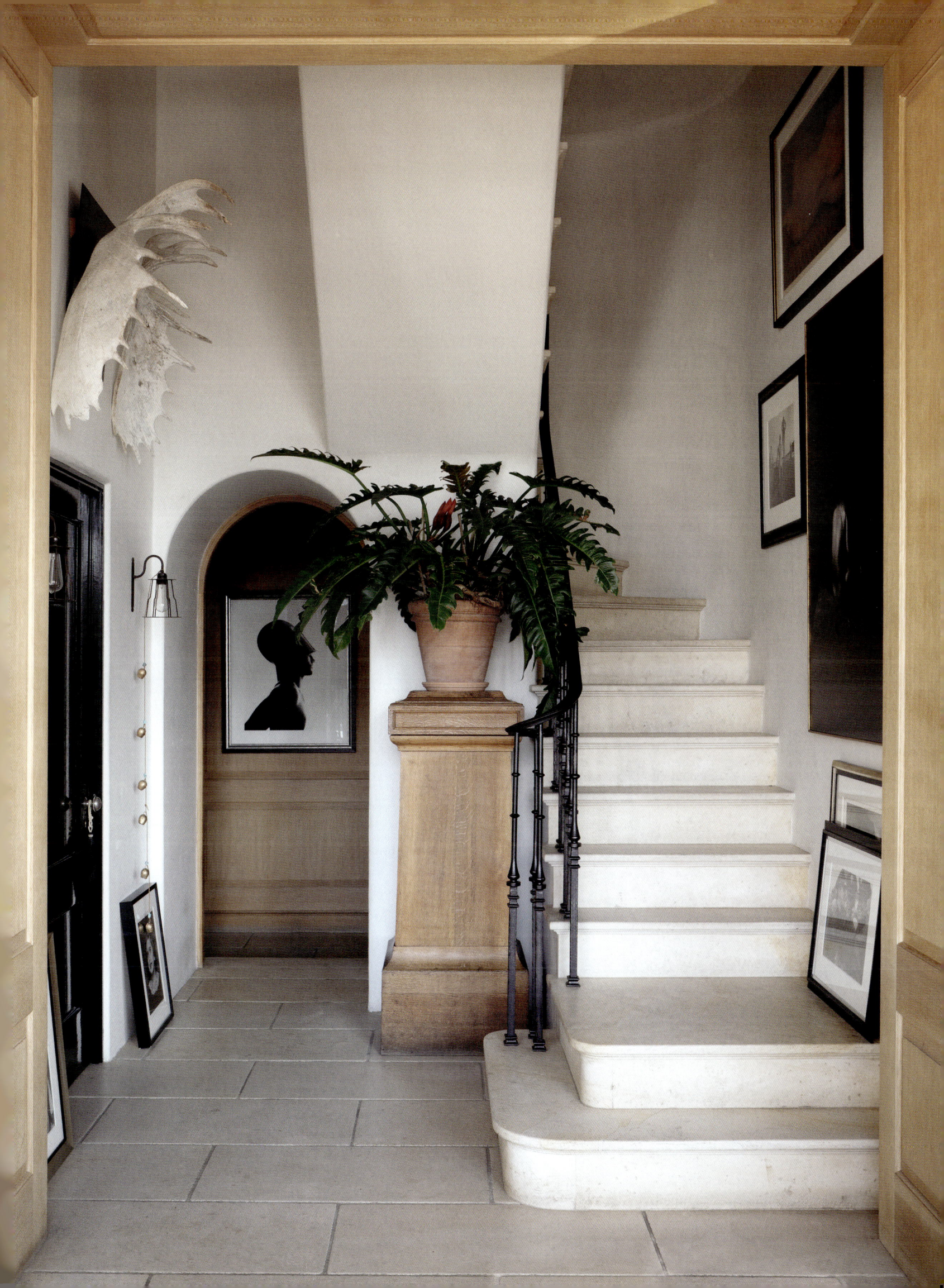

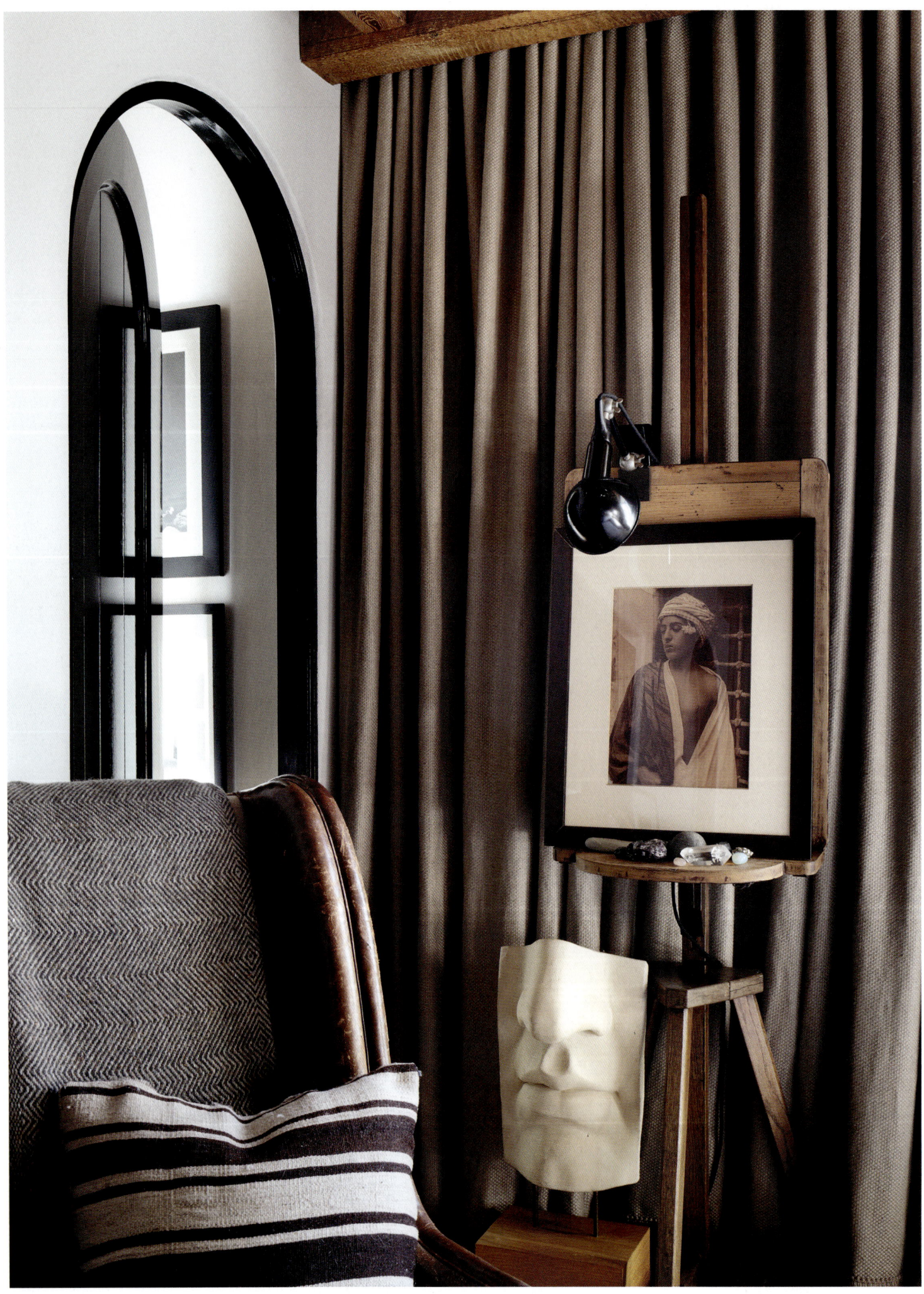

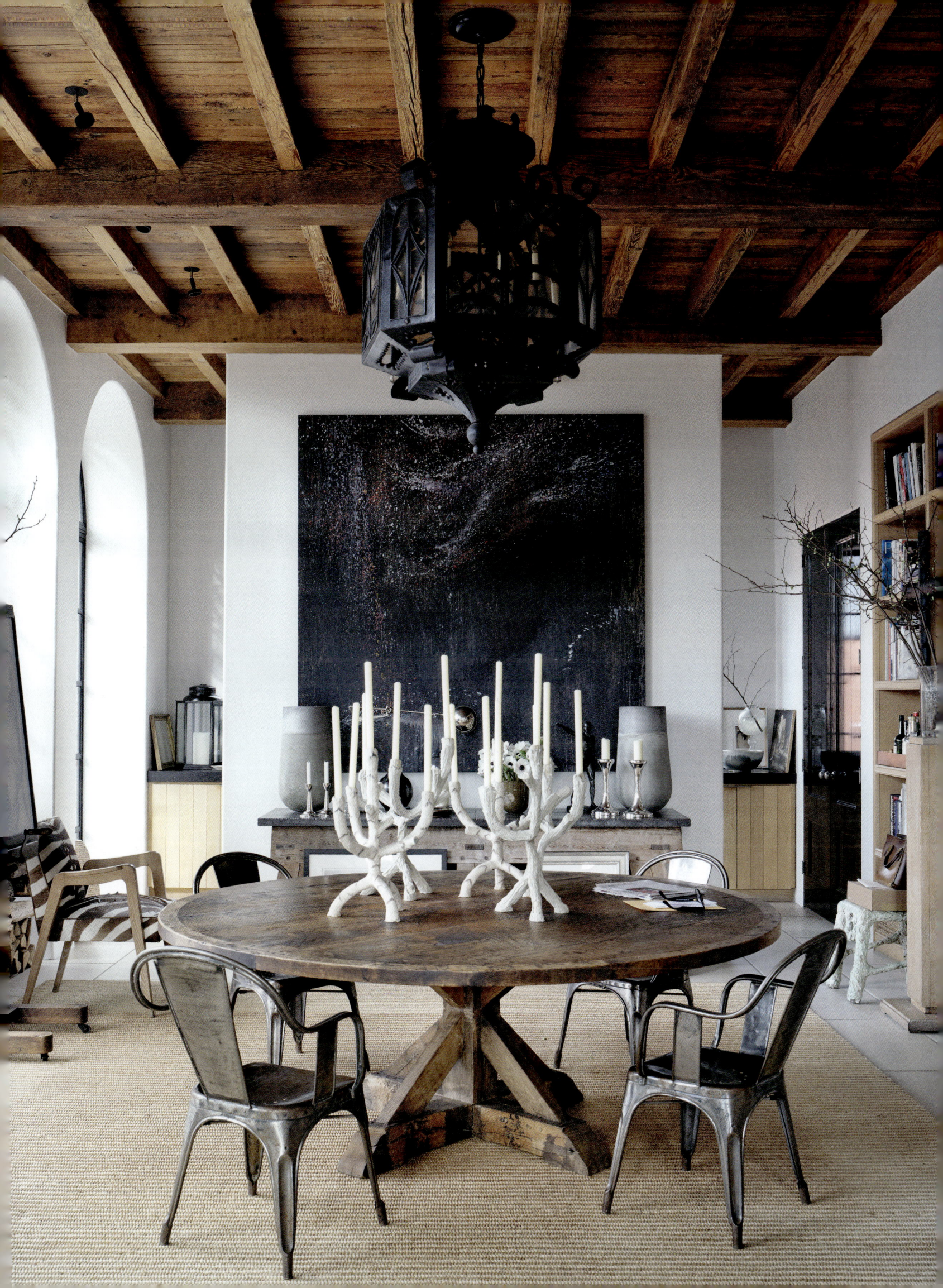

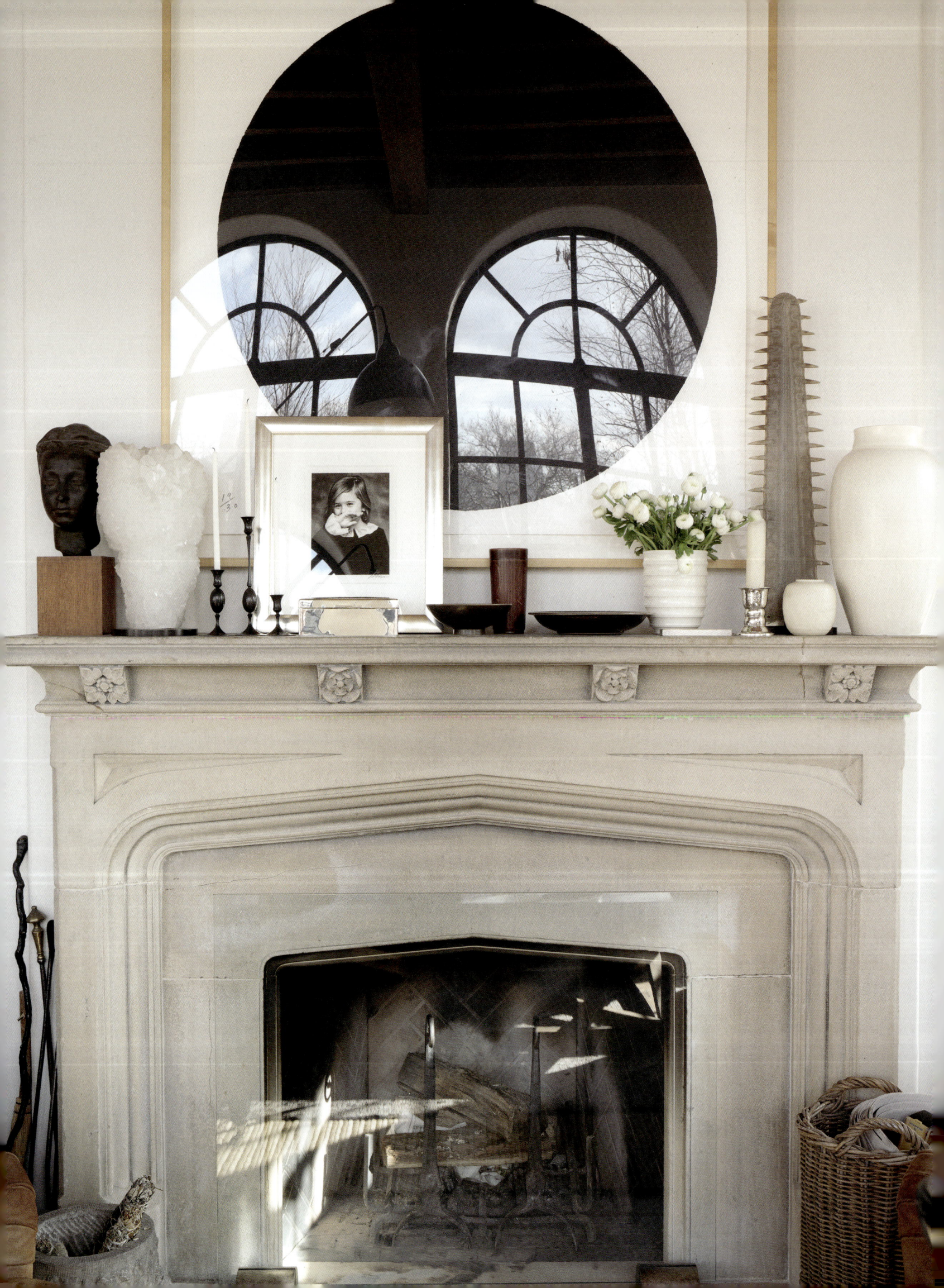

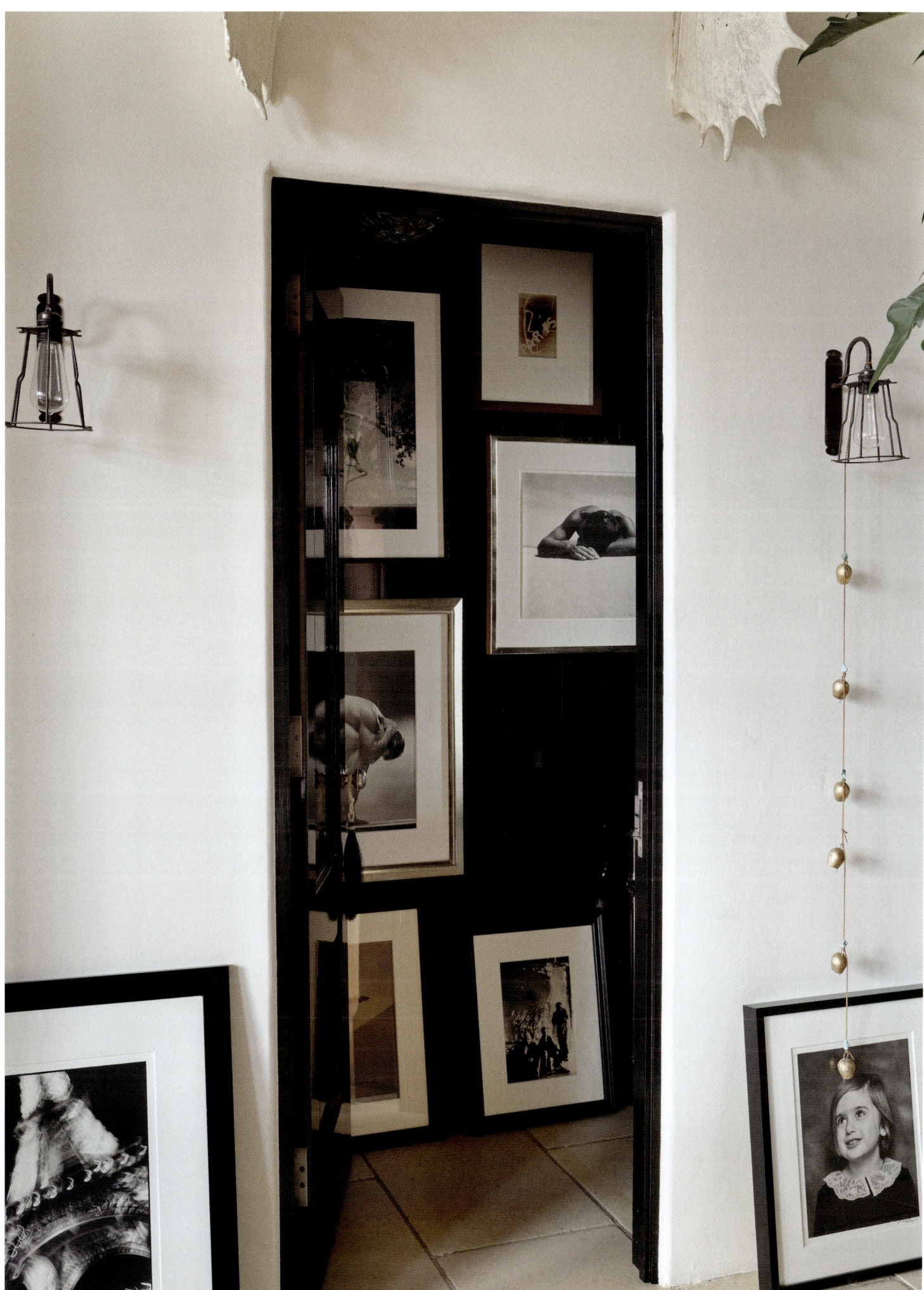

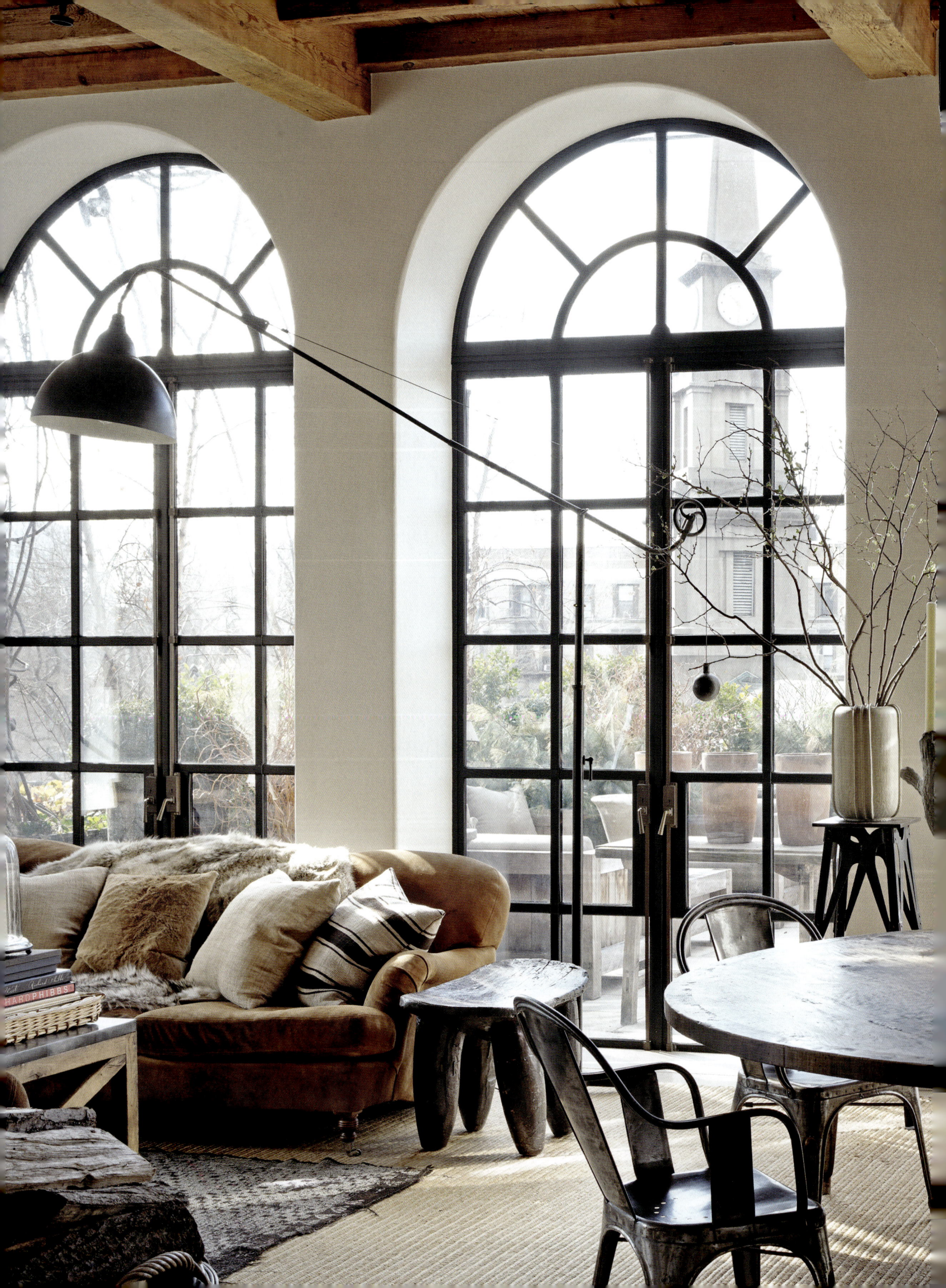

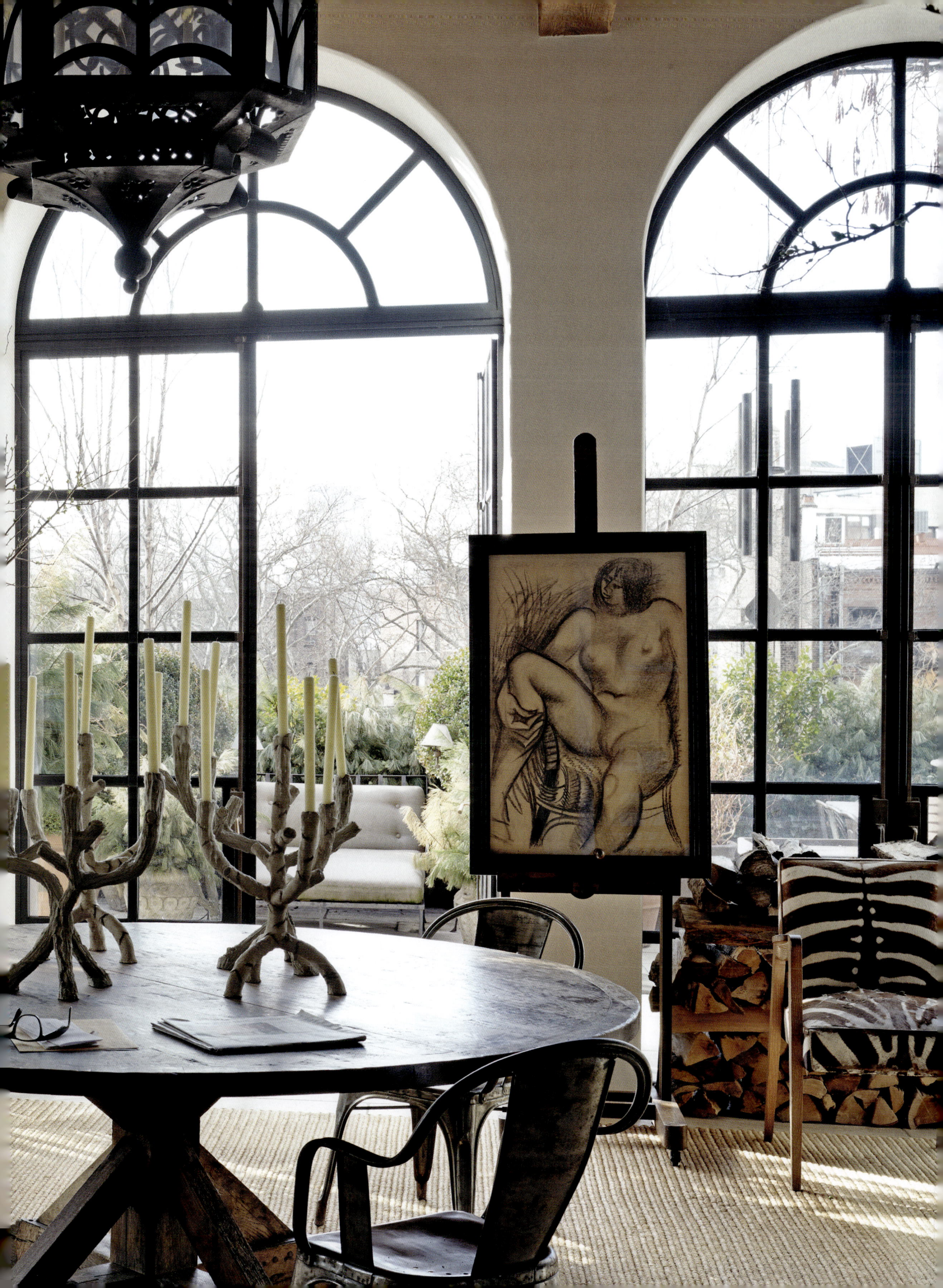

GETAWAY

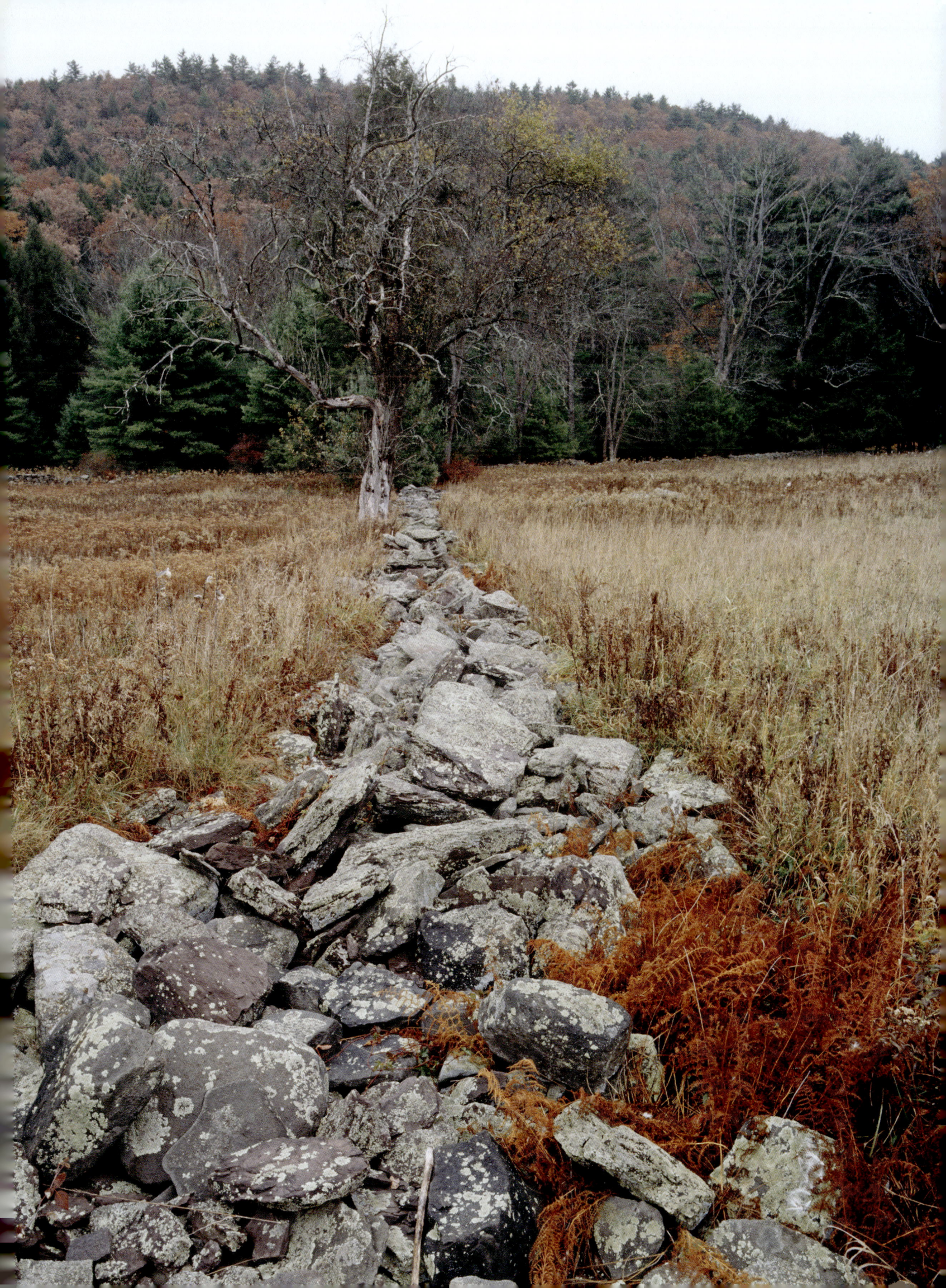

FOR ME, "GETAWAY" IS A STATE OF MIND—

an innate sense of urgency to escape the relentless daily treadmill of the city, and in particular that of New York, and to exchange its concrete intensity for the beauty of nature. It is perhaps not so much about recognizing a need for relaxation as for re-identification. A city, any city, but particularly New York, needs its counterpoint. Call it getaway or destination, those of us who live in the city and are fortunate enough to have found a "refuge"—whether as owner, tenant, or simply with friends at weekends—is how we survive.

"Getaway" is beyond New York's commuter belt: the Hudson Valley, Long Island, Shelter Island, Oyster Bay, Cape Cod, The Hamptons, Nantucket, Montauk, Sag Harbor, Claverack, Connecticut, Massachusetts, and even more remote places such as Maine and Vermont … as long as visits are regular and, at best, every weekend. As you leave New York, suddenly the trees seem taller, the sea larger and wider, and nature reaffirms its importance in our world.

When I first met my wife Anne, we would walk her dog Otis on the odd bits of shoreline around the city or The Palisades just across George Washington Bridge. If we had more time, or it was a weekend, we would rent a car and drive up the Hudson River to the spectacular Bear Mountain State Park, or down to the estuary and marshy islands of Jamaica Bay. Our ultimate getaway was our friend Greg Bissonnette's small, off-grid cabin in the mountains of Vermont—the ultimate proximity to nature, and which we would share with the local black bear and red deer.

Country house, cabin, surfer's shack, whatever it might be, is not just a refuge from the city, but also a destination— a place at which many will arrive on a Friday evening and not leave until late on a Sunday. A place to recalibrate, to detox, to entertain friends, and above all to sleep, away from the city that never sleeps.

MILDRED'S LANE

J. MORGAN PUETT

I don't think of Mildred's Lane as a getaway but more as a *destination*. During the summer months it is definitely so. Mildred's Lane is an art residency, a school, a retreat, and my home. I organize events, workshops, and lectures each year; in collaboration with my friends and colleagues, we create landscape projects, installations, and events, questioning concepts around the environment, relationships, labor, dwelling, and creative domesticating. Everything I do here becomes part of the landscape, and I enjoy sharing this new contemporary art site with others.

The pleasure of Mildred's Lane is to create spaces and outbuildings for people to stay in—to give them a room of their own in which to regenerate, think, and feel. Over the years the landscape has become my art practice, growing into a 94-acre installation. There is a deep history here, with colonial settlements on the border between New York and Pennsylvania from the 1750s. There are records of Native Americans living here for thousands of years. By the 1830s, the settlements developed into a string of industrious villages—now called the Upper Delaware River recreational corridor, and one of the cleanest rivers in America.

I had been looking for something like this property for years and, while renting my brother's cottage a few miles away, I heard of an abandoned farm deep in the woods. It felt perfect. I bought Mildred's Lane with friends and my partner at that time, Mark Dion, in 1997. Mark is still a beloved family member, collaborator, and very much involved in the Mildred's Lane Project. We spent the first several years rebuilding one of the original barns, then started to save the homestead, while renovating and creating art installations in the other shacks and sheds, even moving some small building art projects on-site.

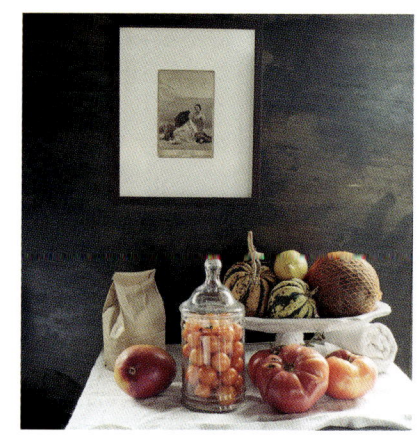

I always wanted to collect vernacular architecture in this way. These projects are scattered throughout the landscape; conceptually, rather than a static sculpture in a park, Mildred's Lane attracts artists, writers, students, and visitors from all over the world. I also have a studio and gallery on the other side of the river in Narrowsburg—a small, exciting culture and society.

I was born in rural South Georgia and arrived in New York from Chicago in 1986, after graduate art school. But I hated living in the city. It was essential to commute to the country, between my art and the fashion world in New York City, barely 100 miles away. I left the city behind after my son was born in 2000. Although I still travel a lot for work, Mildred's Lane is my permanent residence, art project, and primary focus. I live close to the bone here in the landscape, and enjoy being here by myself. My favorite time of day is "the blue hour," or twilight—that time when the sun is setting. I make a fire and listen to the sounds of the land and the life in it: "*bewilderness.*"

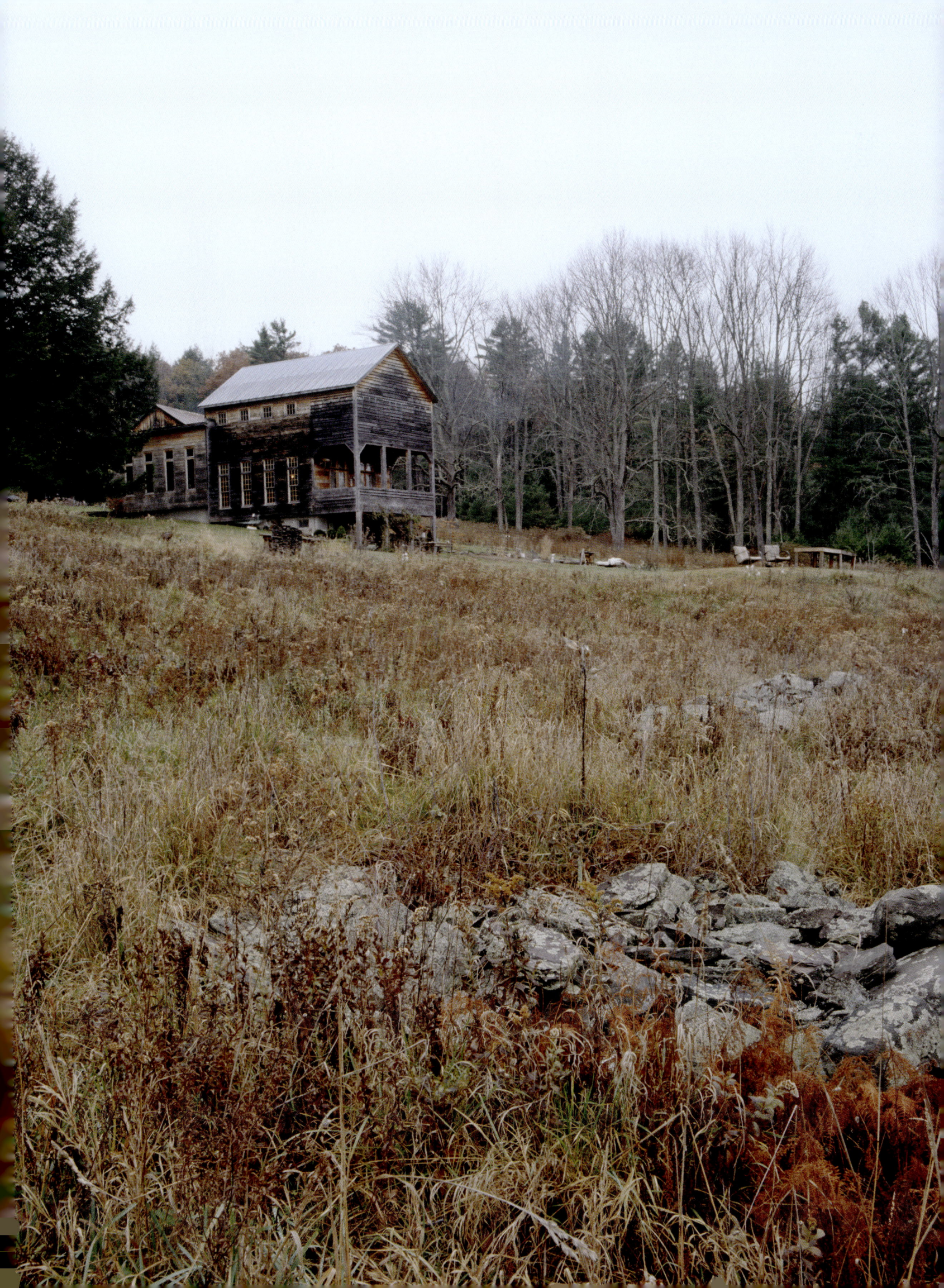

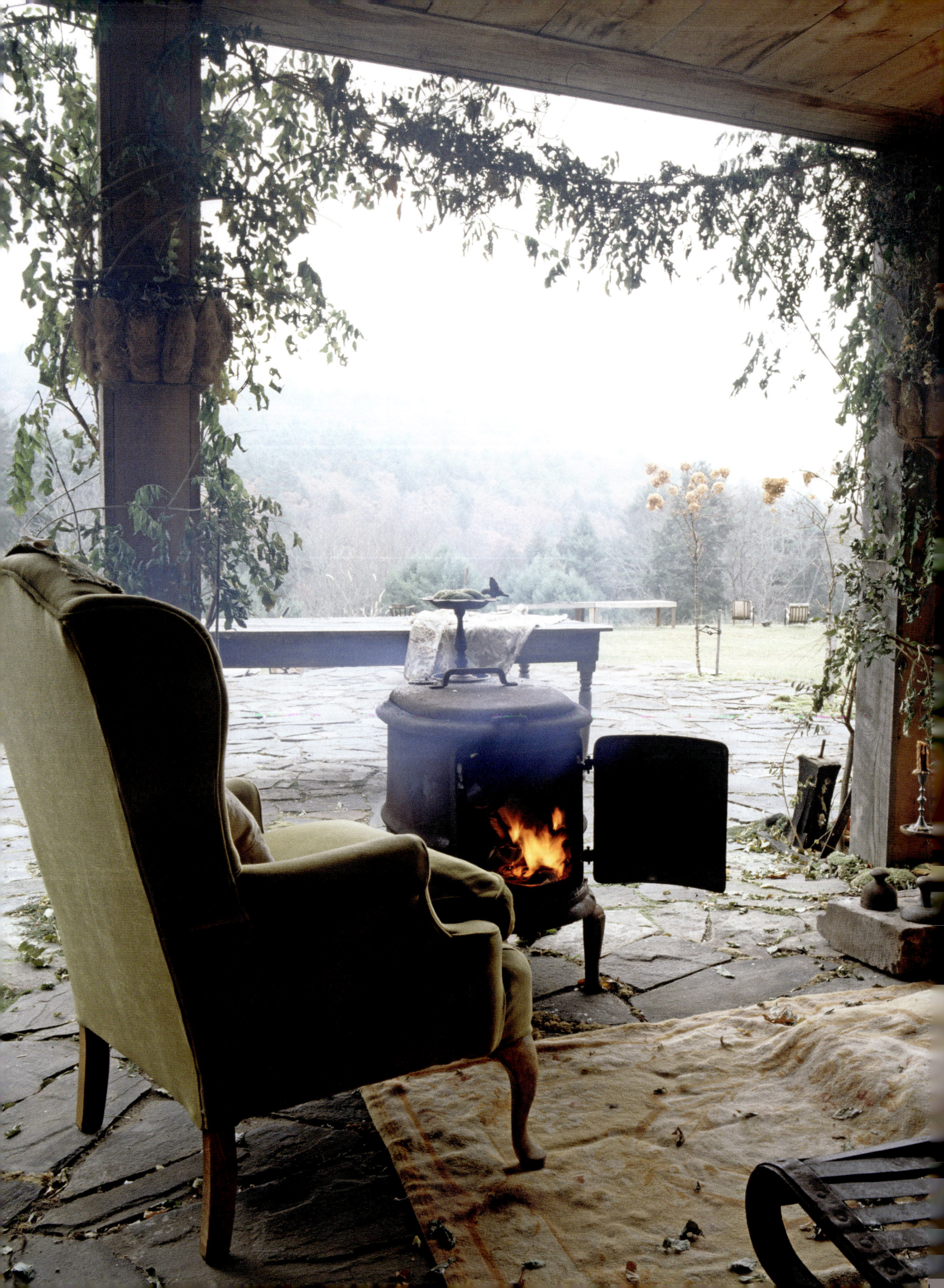

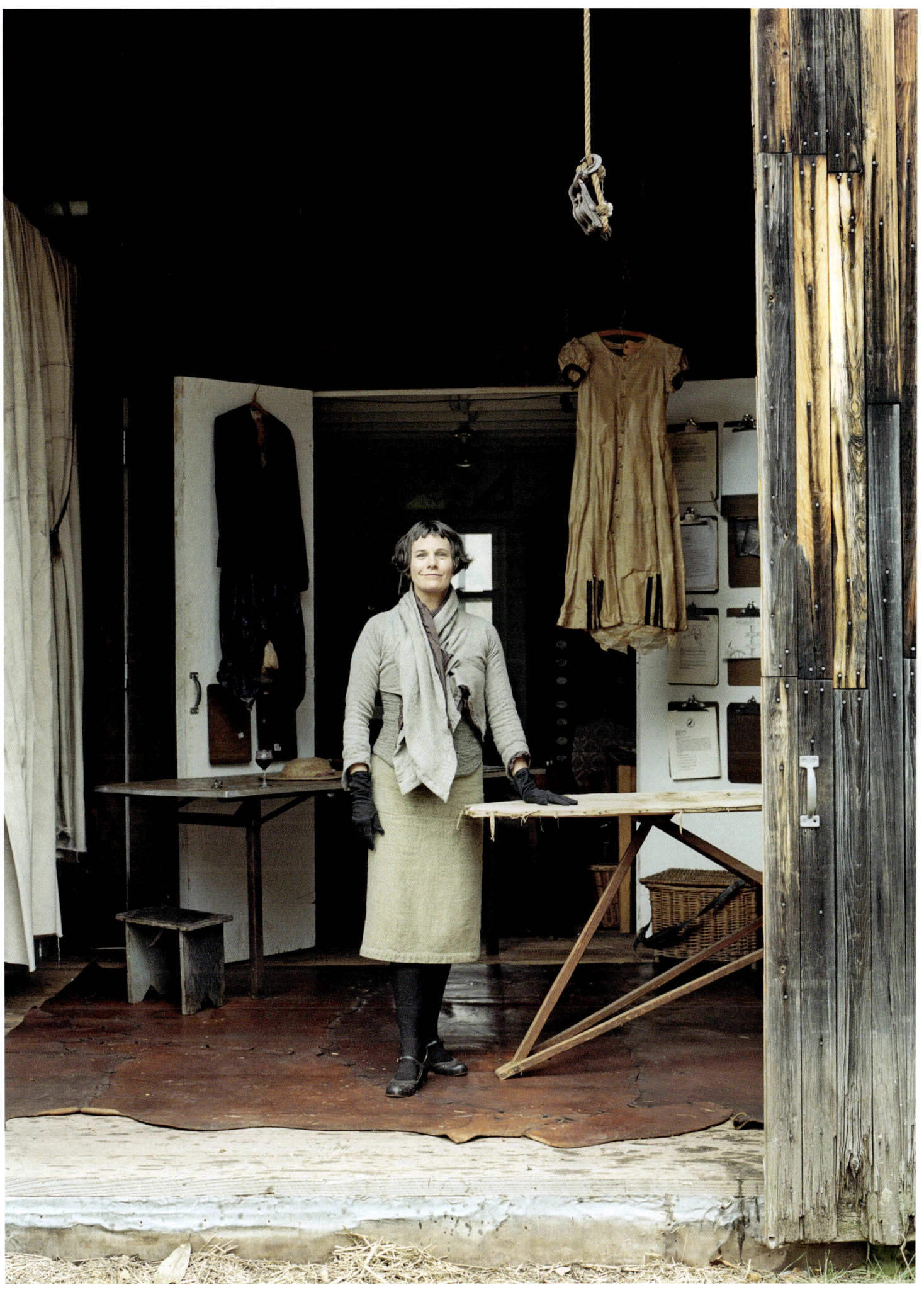

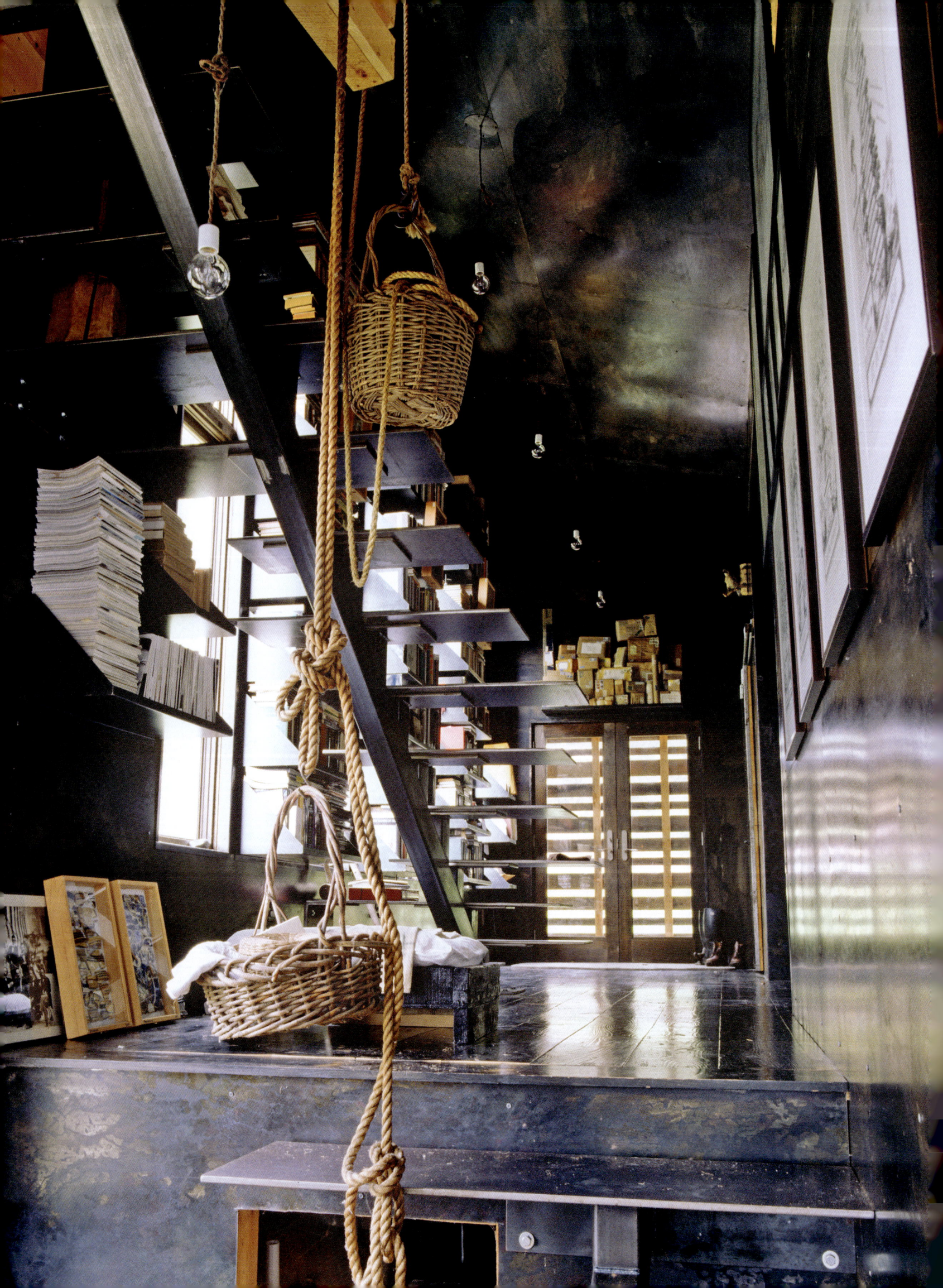

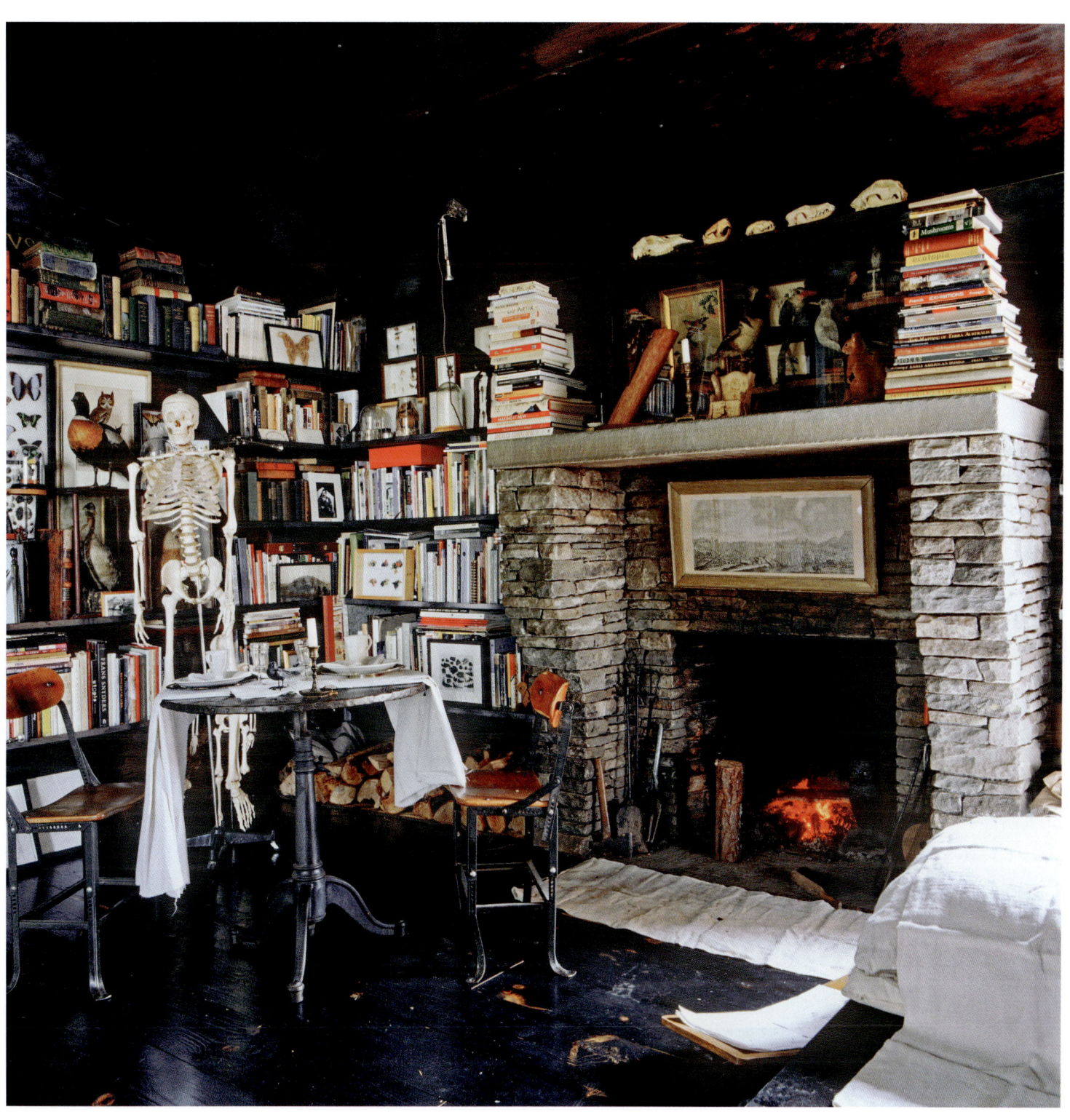

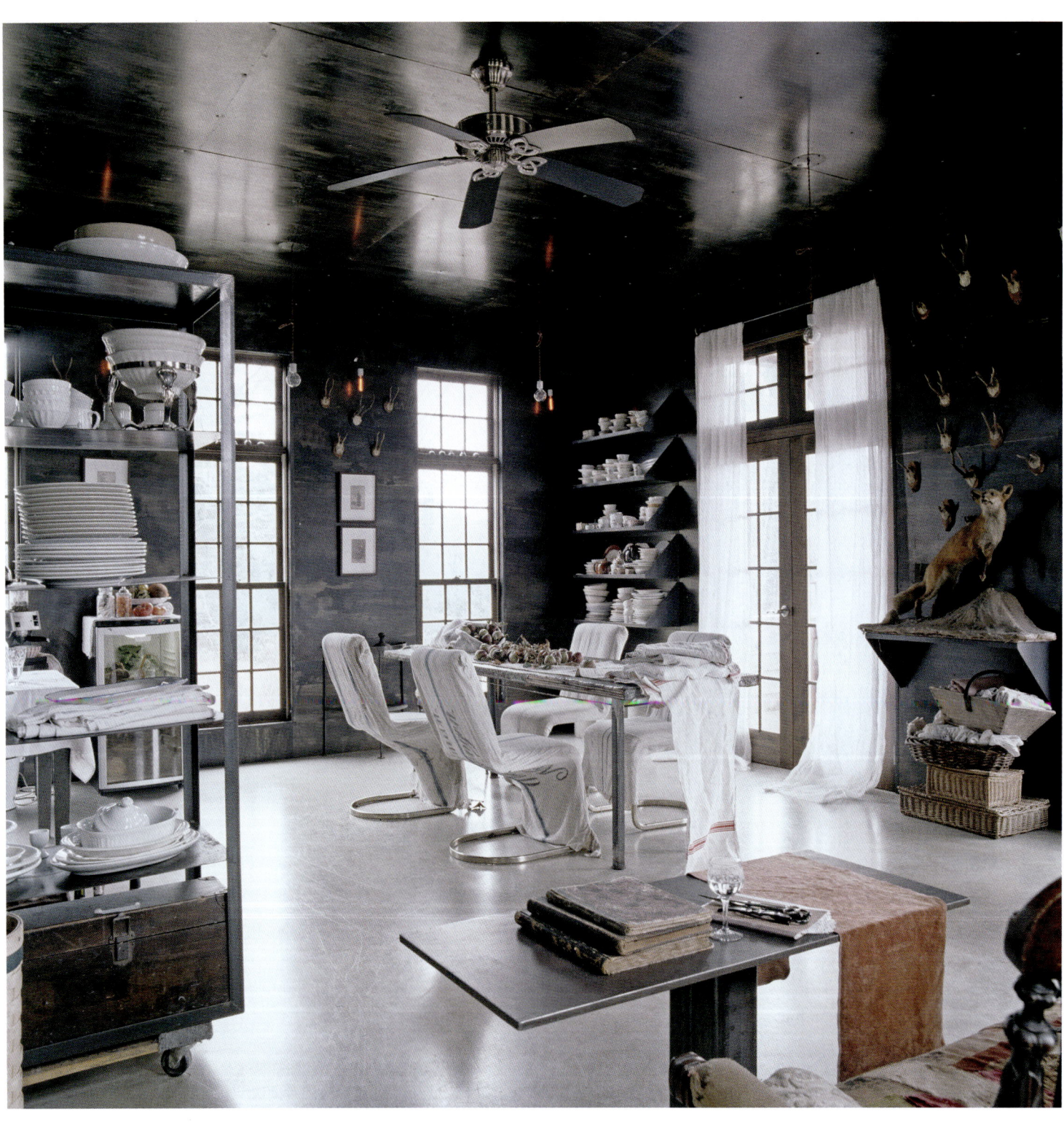

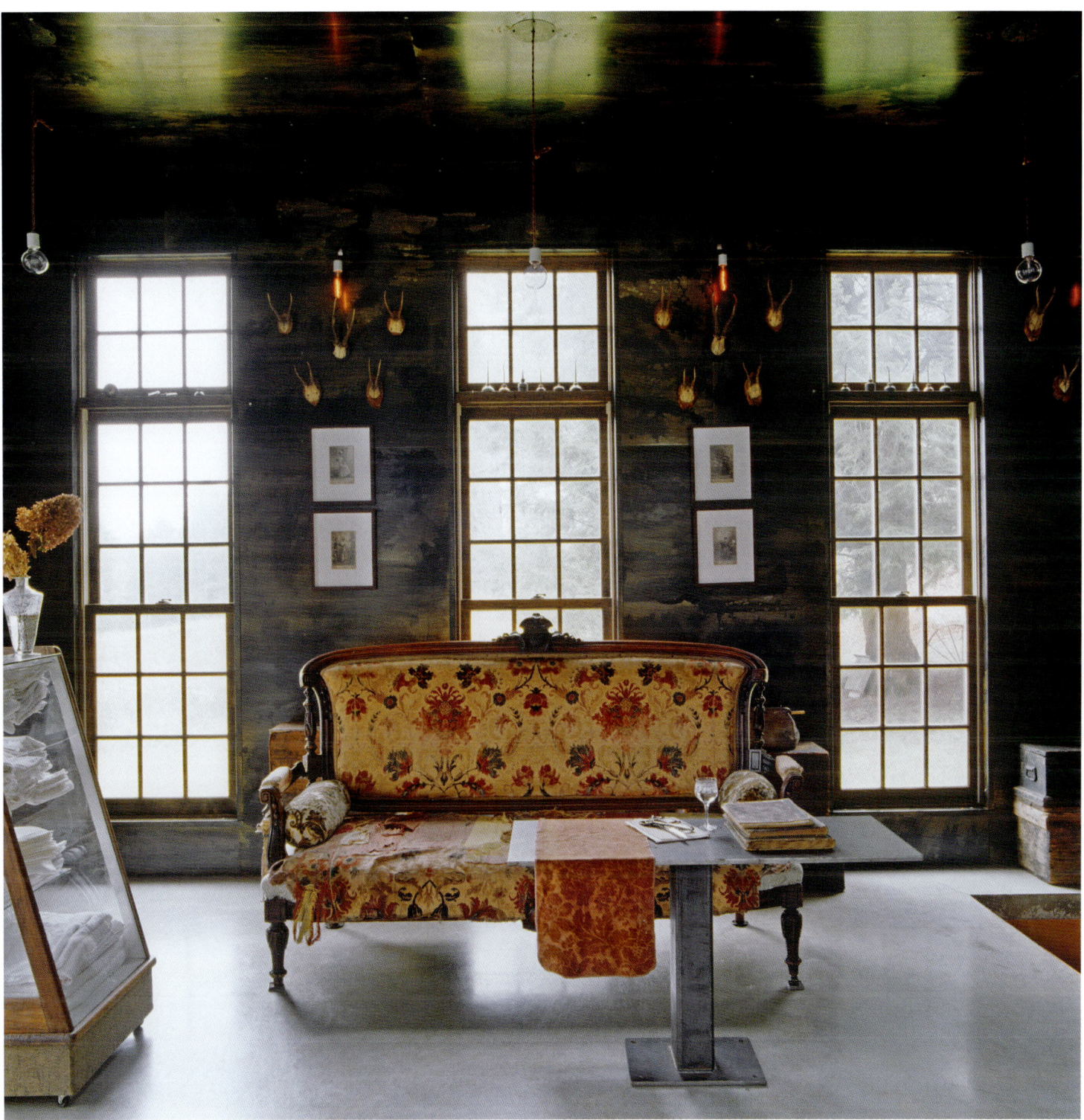

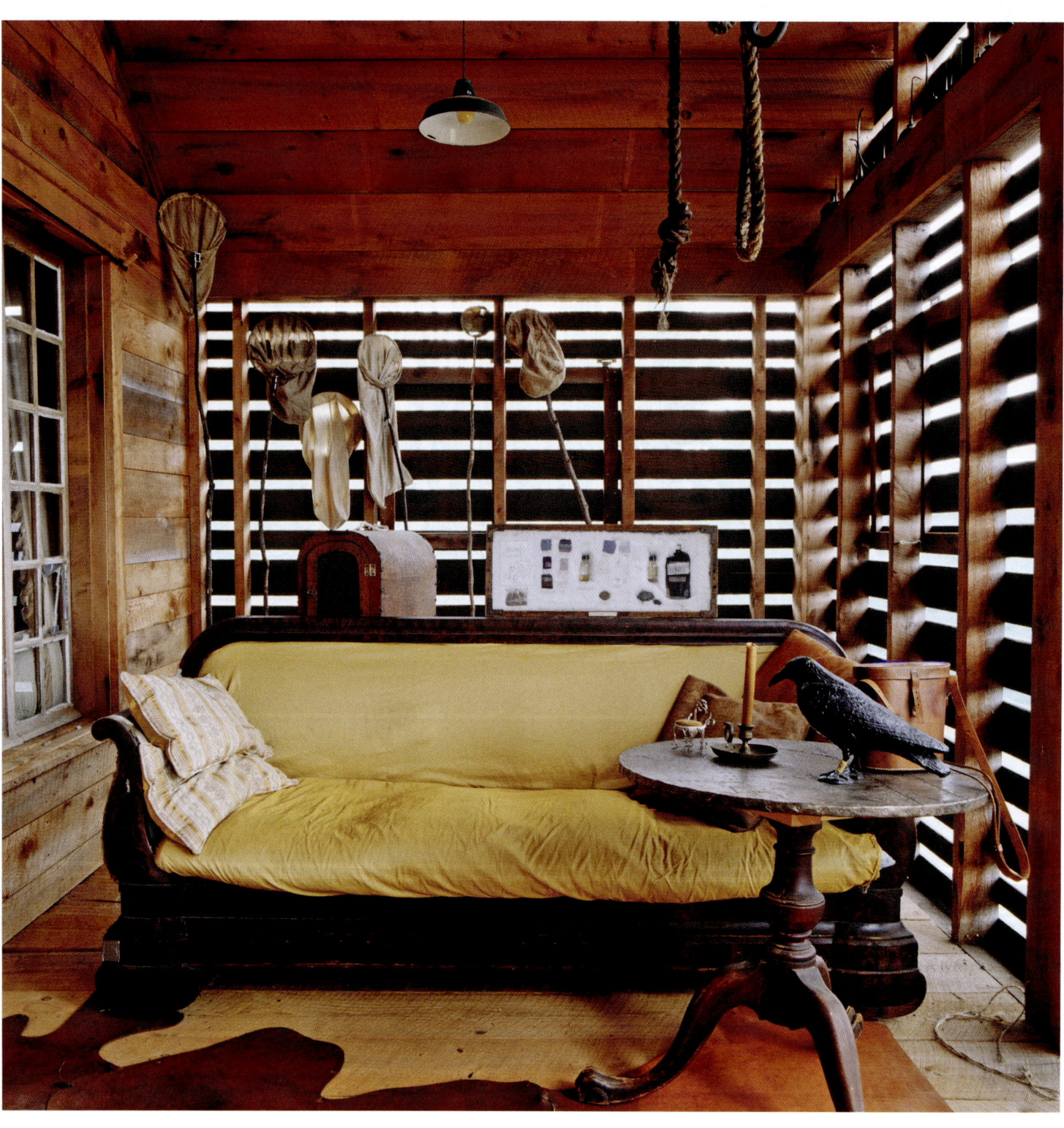

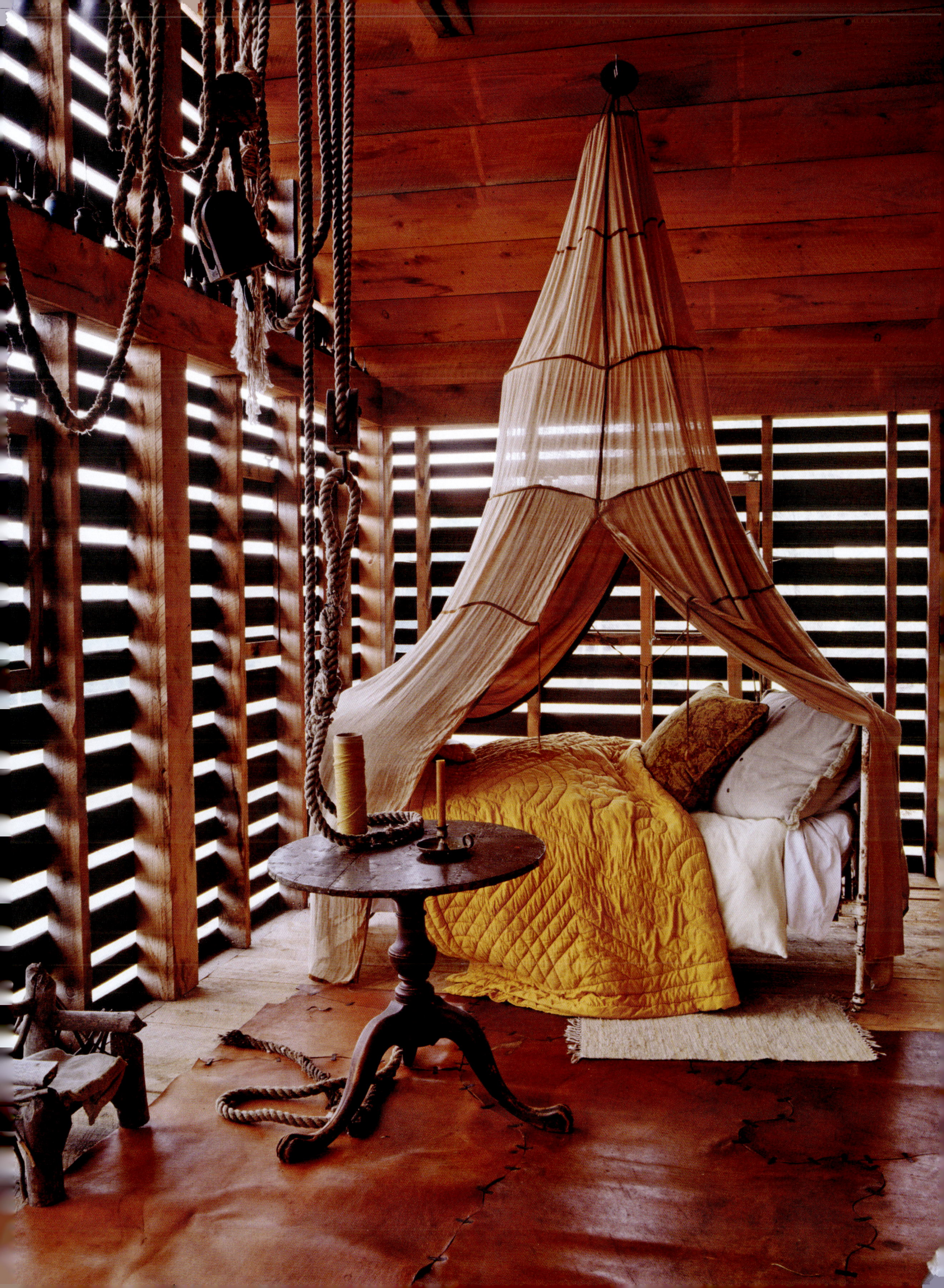

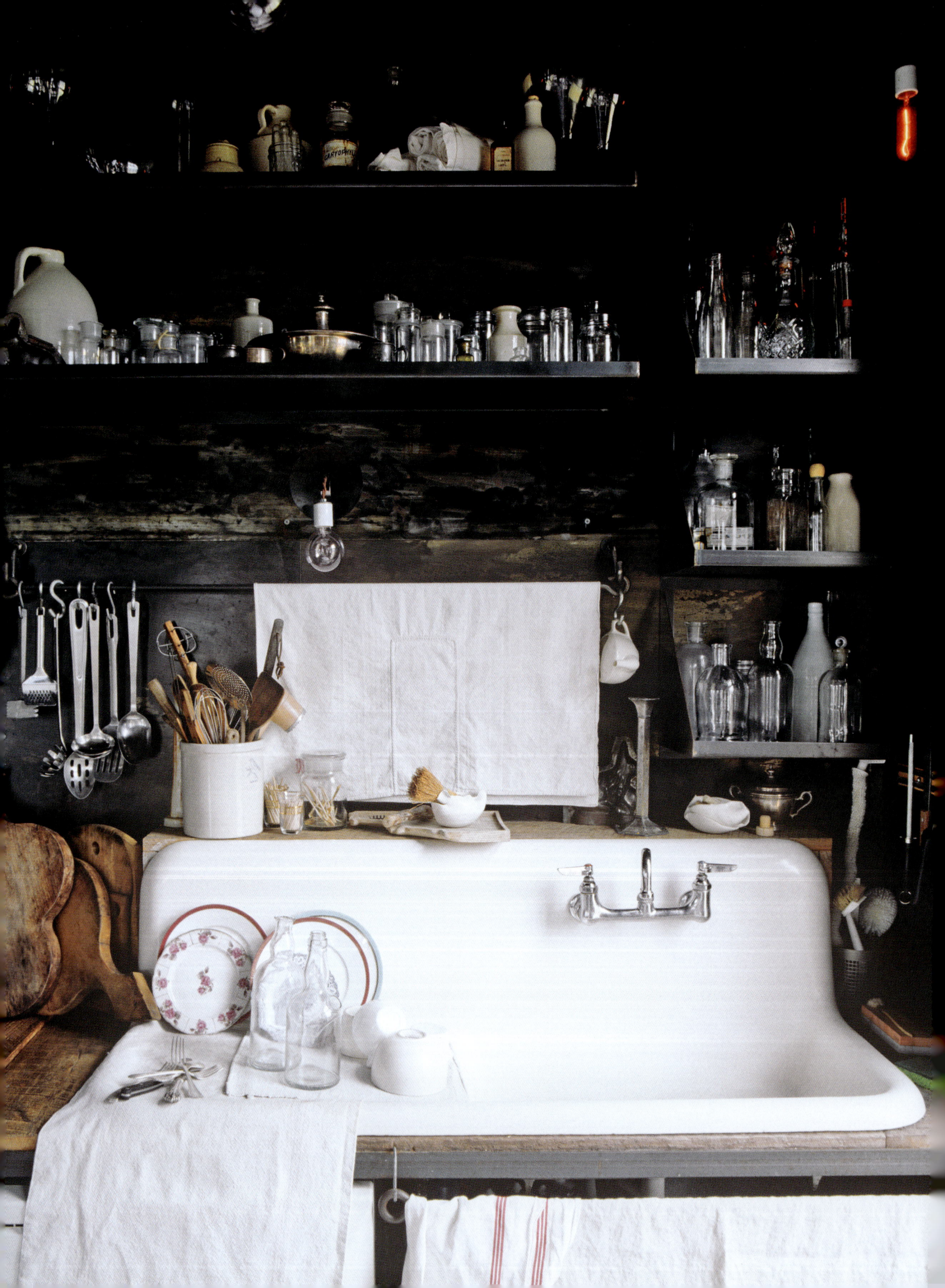

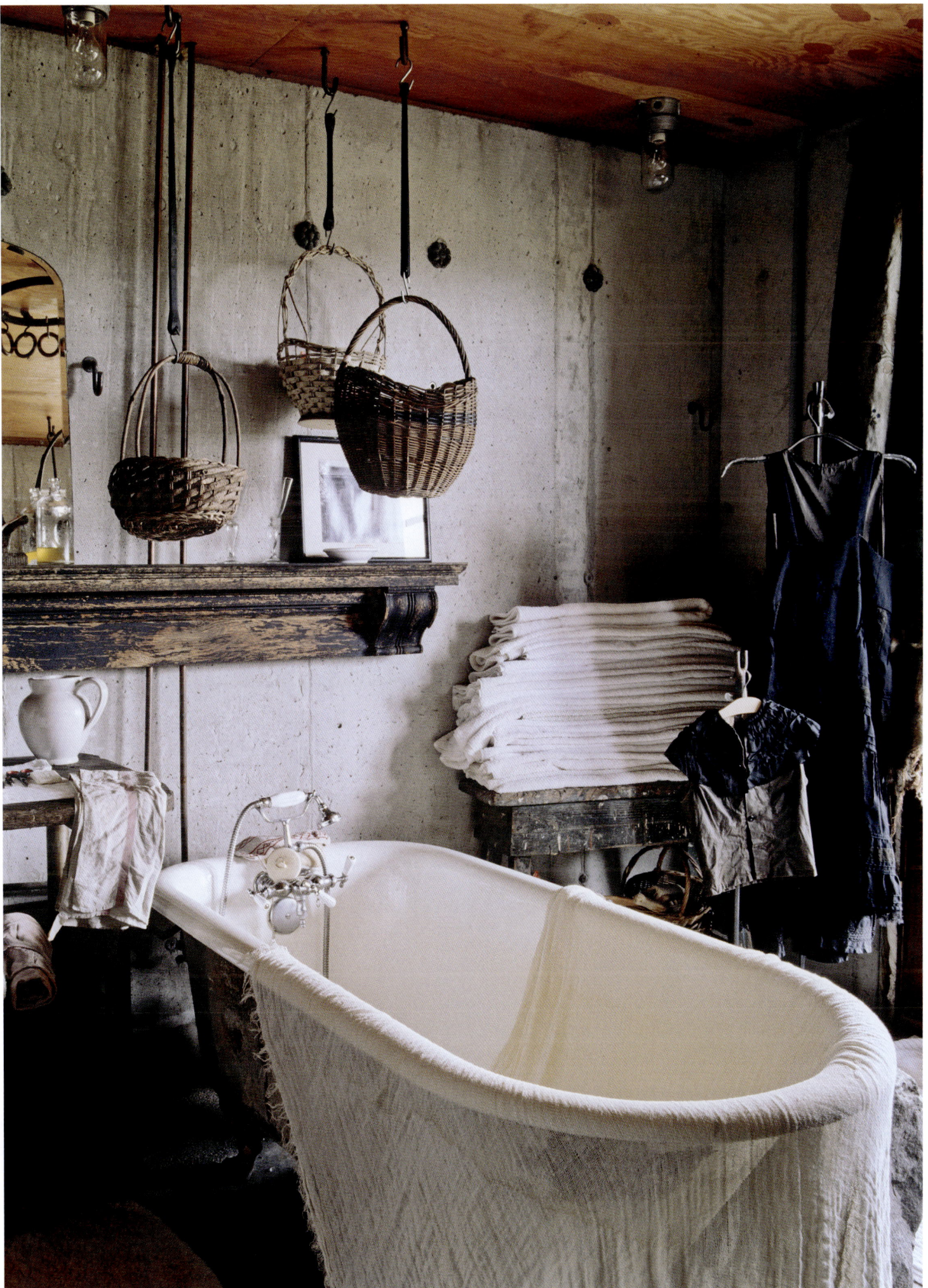

COUNTRY MANNERS

STEPHEN SILLS

I discovered this place while visiting a friend at a retreat out here in Westchester County back in the early 1990s. Driving through the countryside, I came across the eighteenth-century village of Bedford and was struck by just how beautiful it was. Over the months that followed, real estate agents must have shown me at least 50 properties, none of which was quite right. And then there was this one: an almost derelict house, sitting

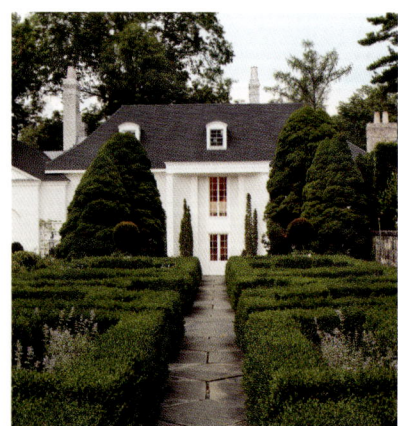

alone on some 20 acres of land, with trees growing through the garage. I knew immediately that this was the house for me. I bought it three years after Dad gave me the New York penthouse.

For me, the country is all about space. Growing up in Oklahoma, I spent most of my childhood outdoors. I learned about gardening from my parents; my mother grew flowers and my father vegetables, and I raised trees from seedlings. After the purchase, I was delighted to discover that the property had once belonged to the renowned American gardener and botanist Helen Morgenthau Fox, and that she had planted all the wonderful specimen trees that make this garden so special. The house may well have been in ruins, but I inherited the great trees she planted and one stone wall. I made the commitment to develop it and introduce my own ideas. I am neither a horticulturalist nor a landscape architect and have worked with the same gardener for the past 26 years. I learn as I go, and have picked up many ideas from visits I have made to some of the great estates in Europe. Together, we have created something which I feel is a combination of English, Italian, and American. Sometimes I feel Helen's presence in the garden, guiding and advising me. I think she is pleased with what we have created.

Bedford is only 45 minutes' drive from New York, so I try to spend as many weekends here as I can. While I have completely restored the 1920s colonial house on the property and transformed the ruined garage into a guest cottage, it is the garden that remains the big attraction for me. In the same way I approach the design of an interior, I have created a series of rooms and spaces in the different areas of the garden and fitted them together. By creating structure and visual sculpture, from the stone terracing to the parterre of box hedges and lavender, I believe I have added to Helen's original layered design.

In New York, I never really switch off. The closest I get to relaxing is out here, puttering around in the greenhouse.

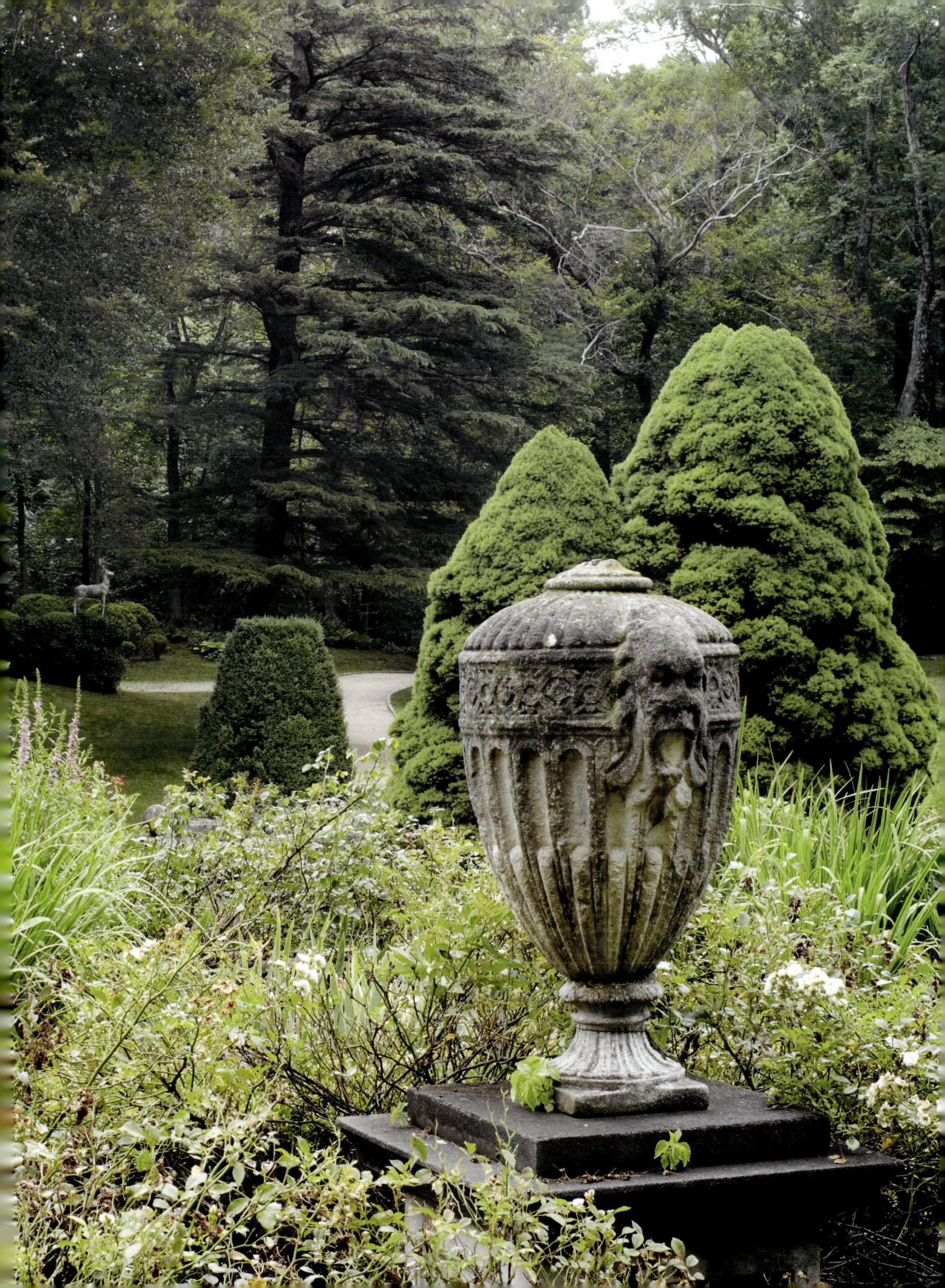

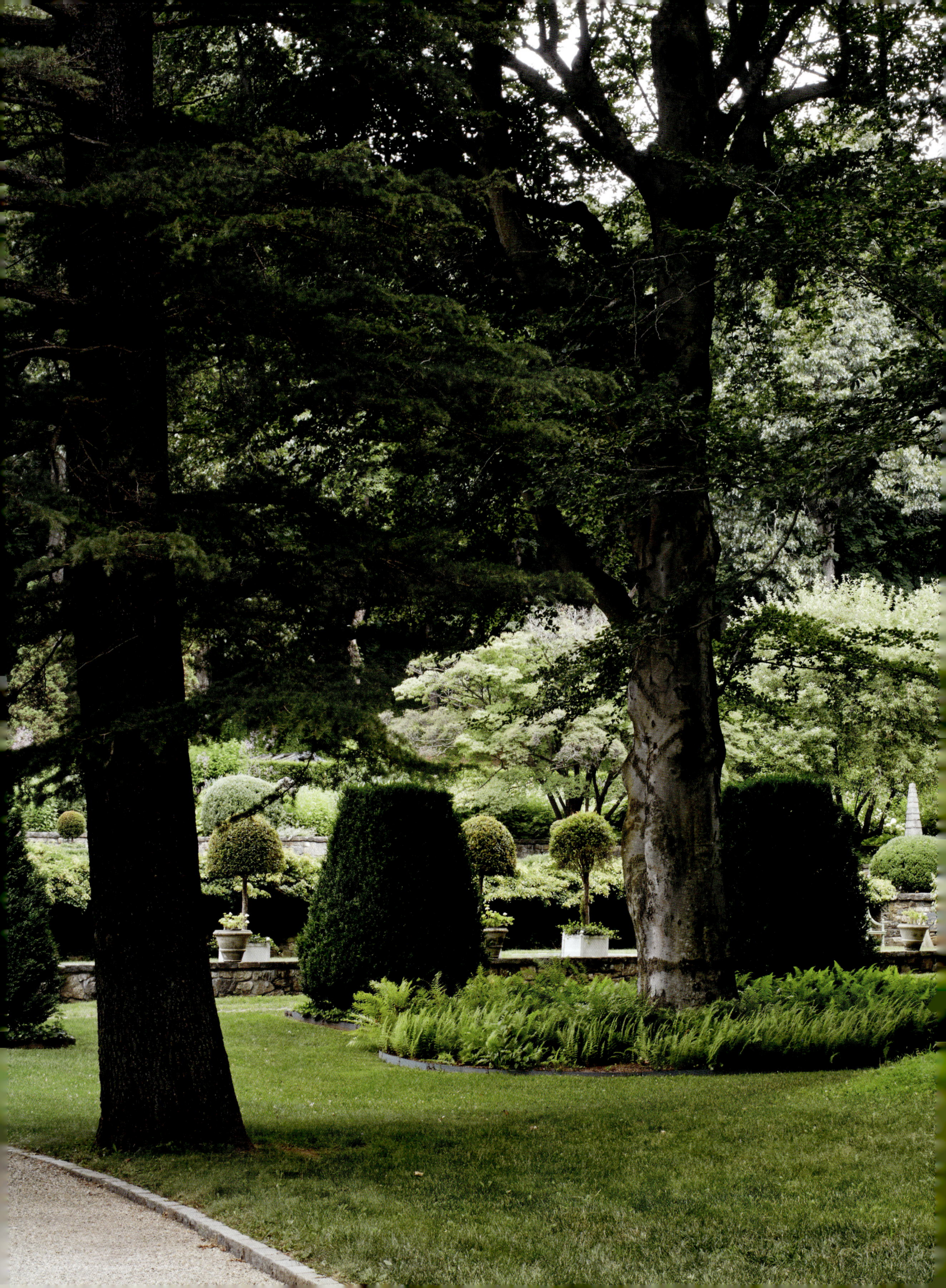

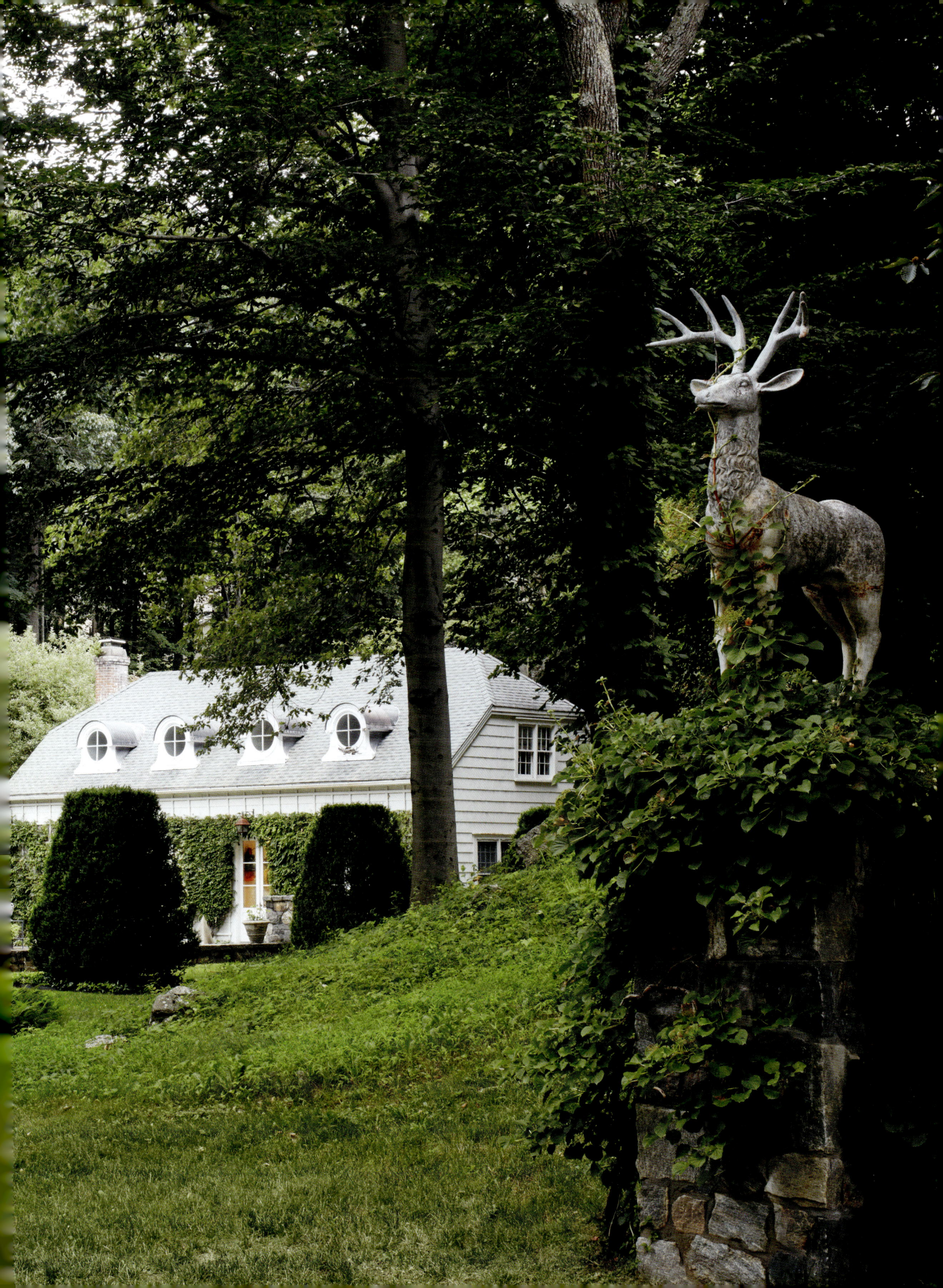

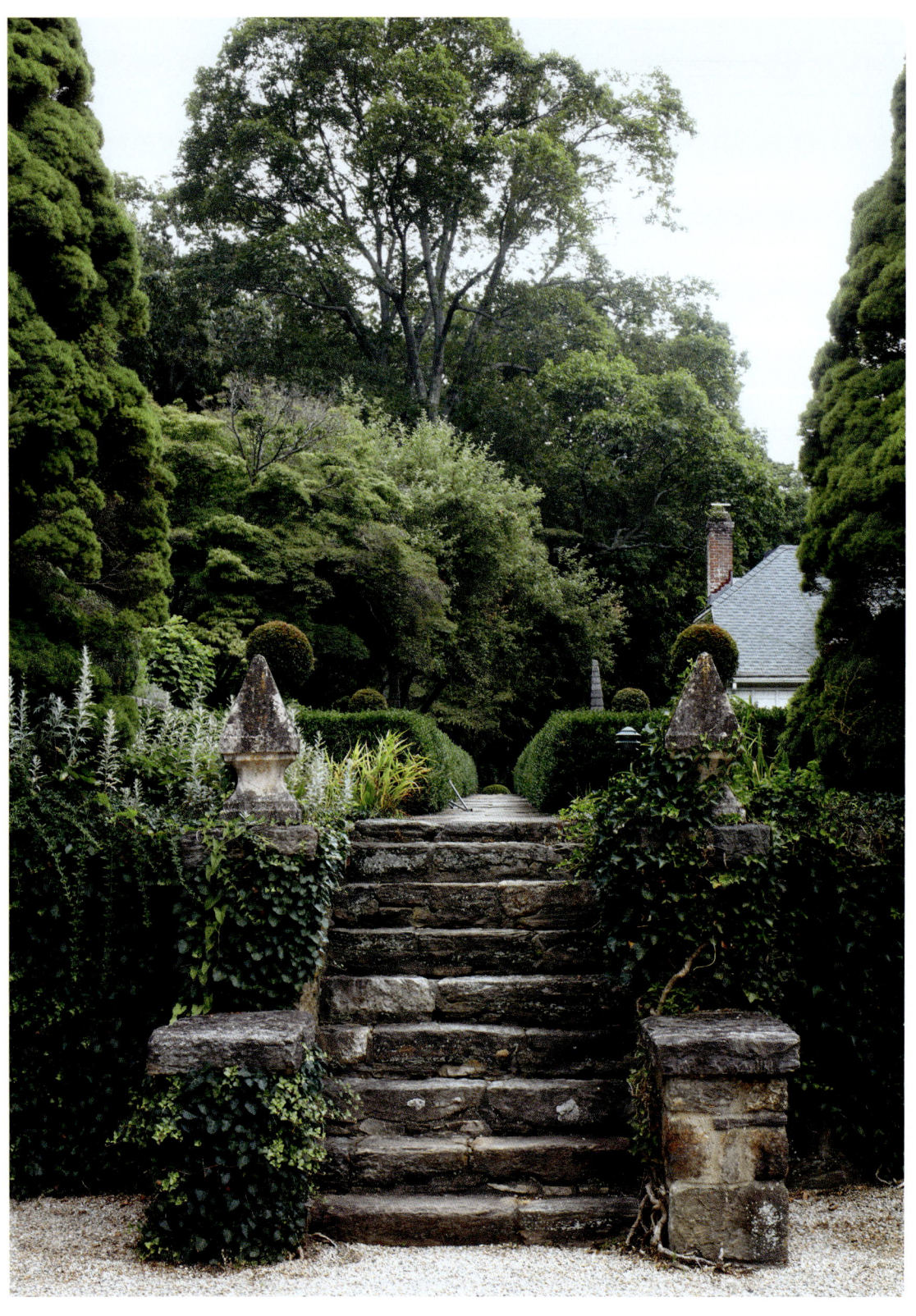

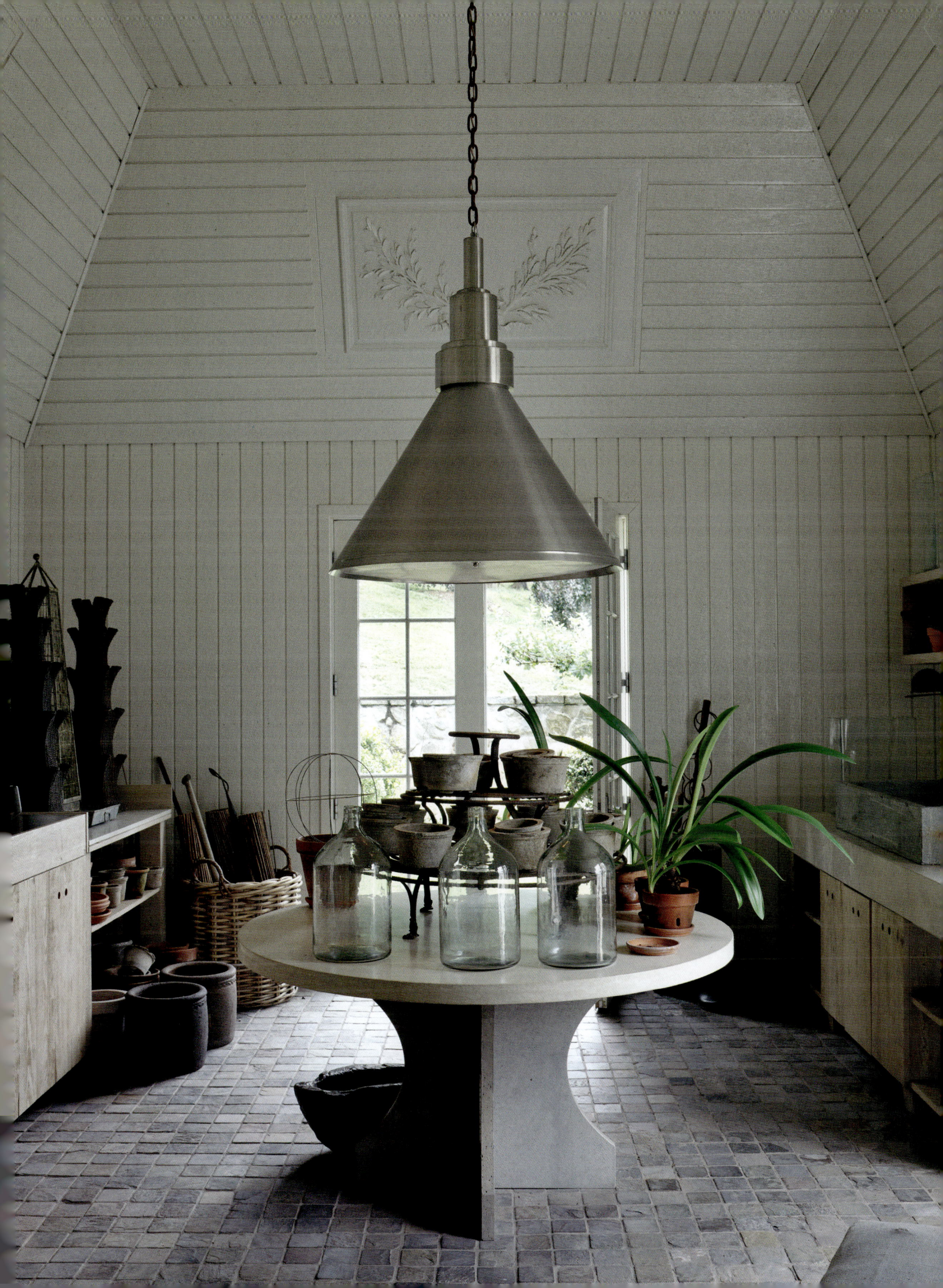

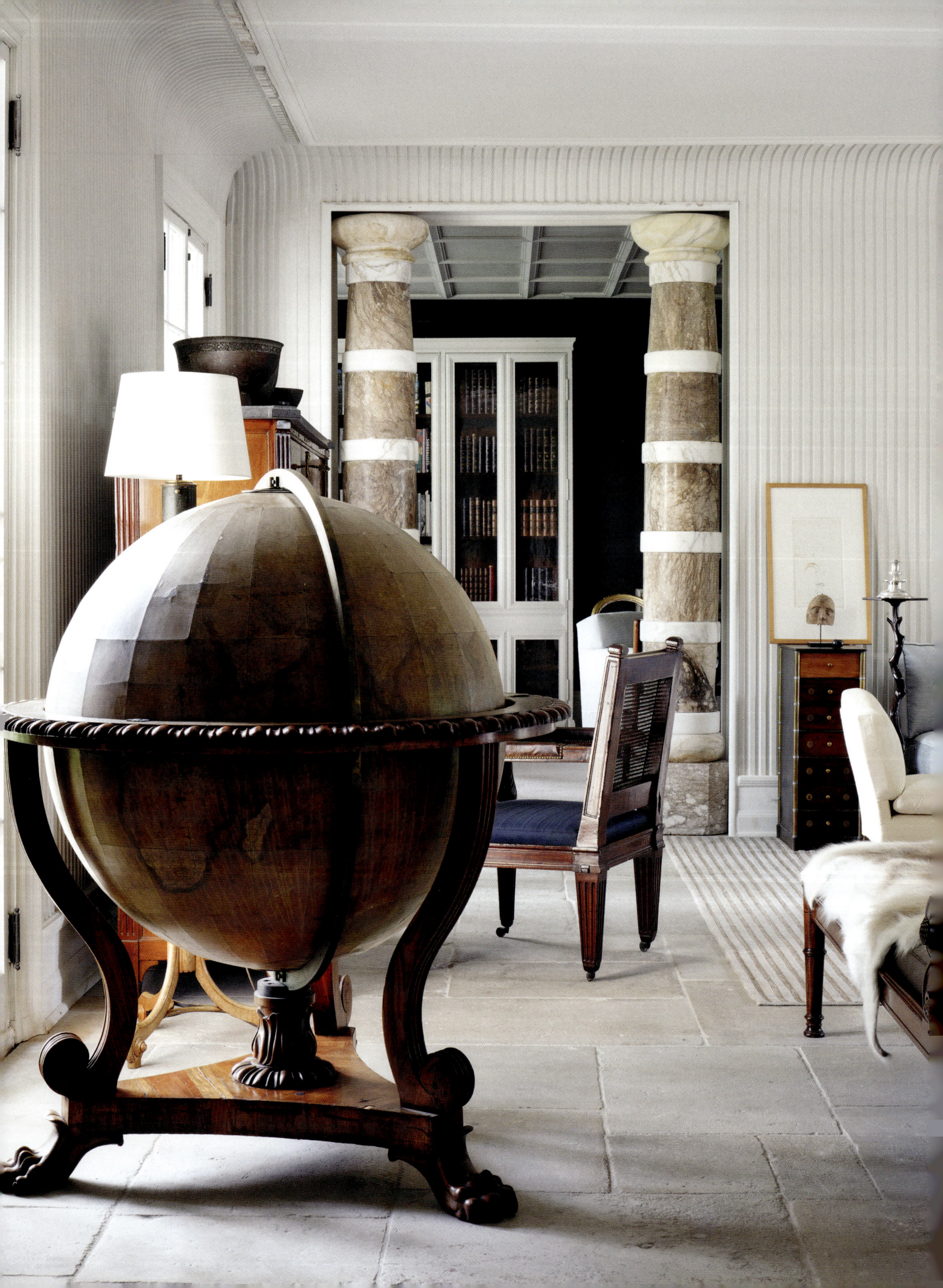

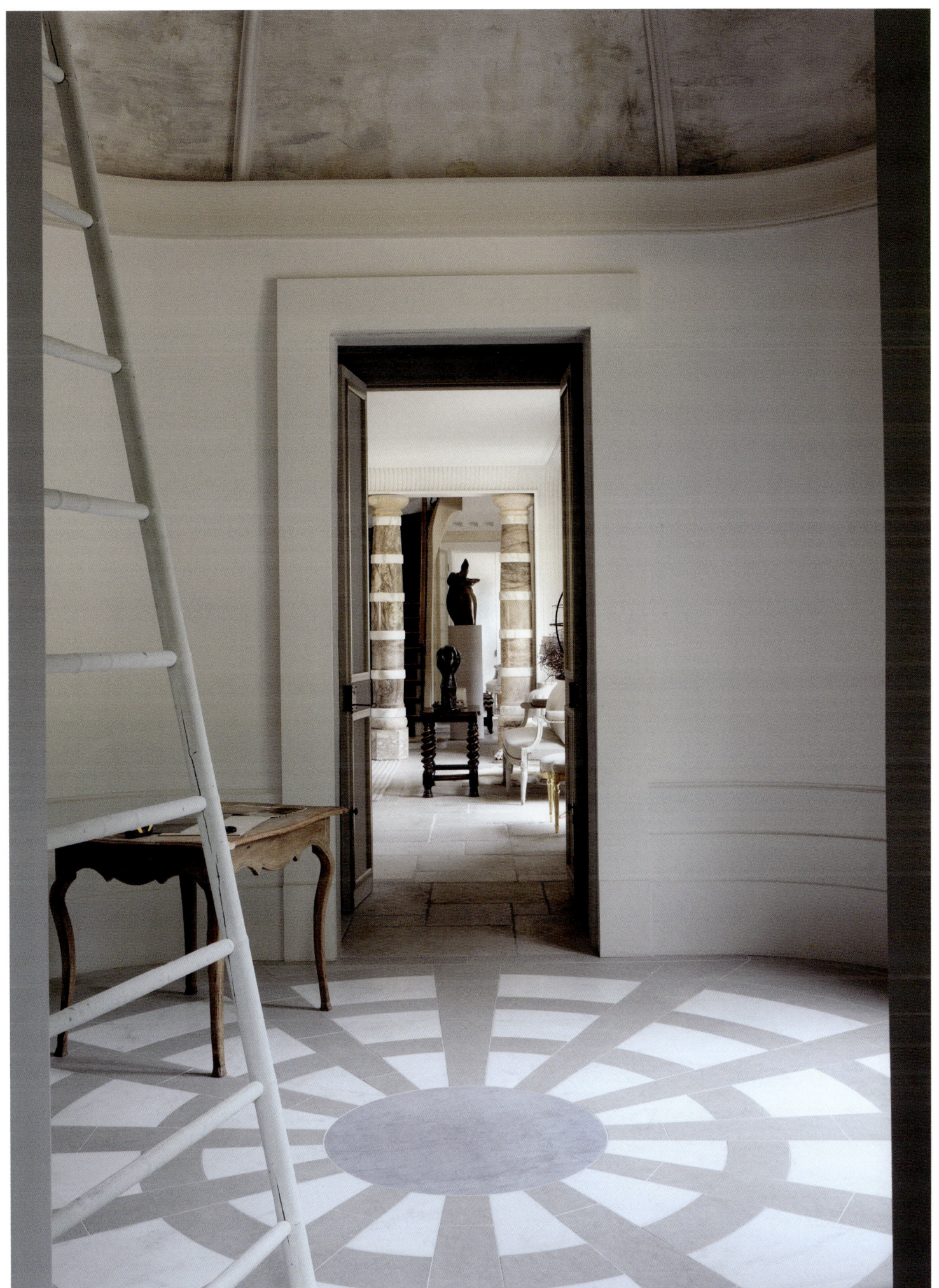

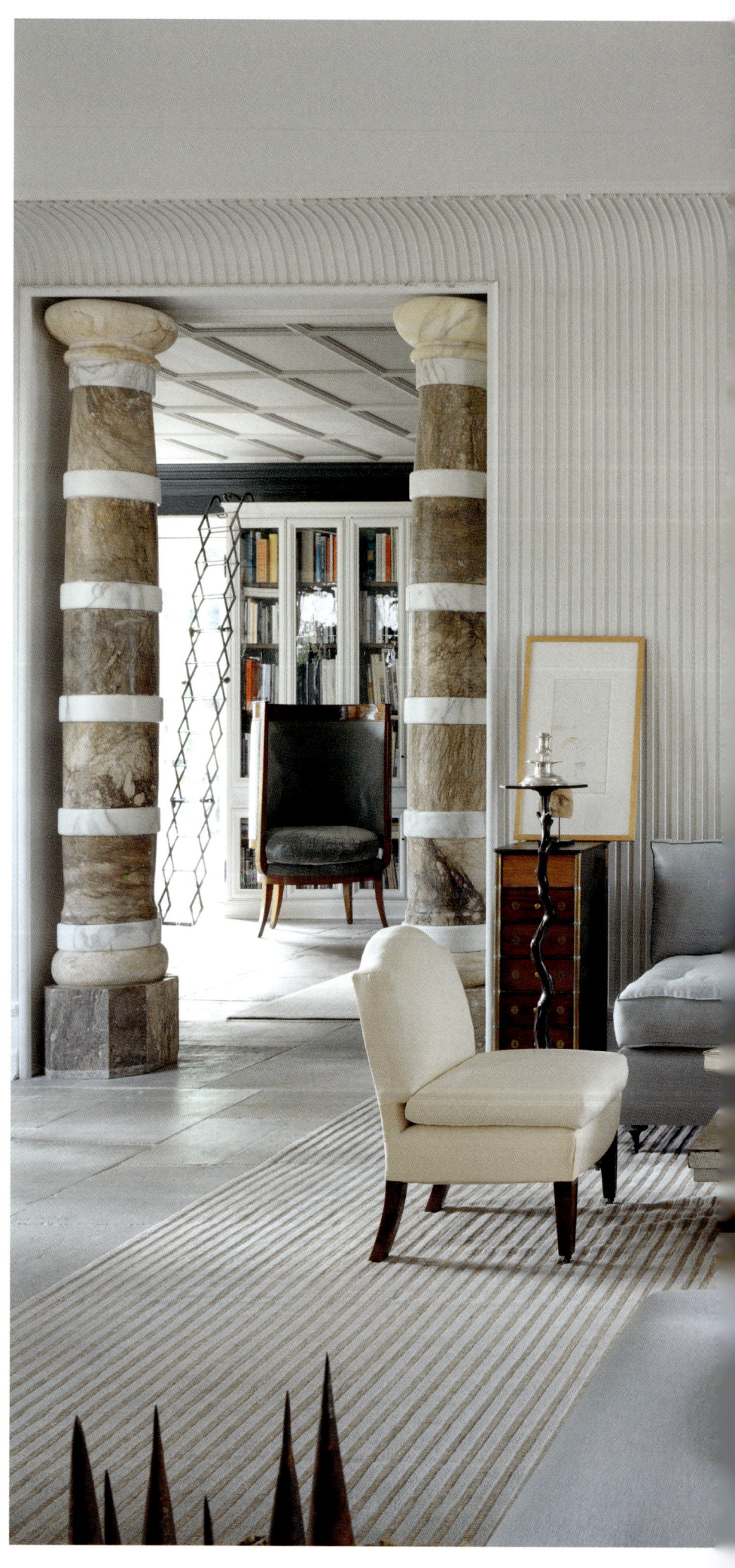

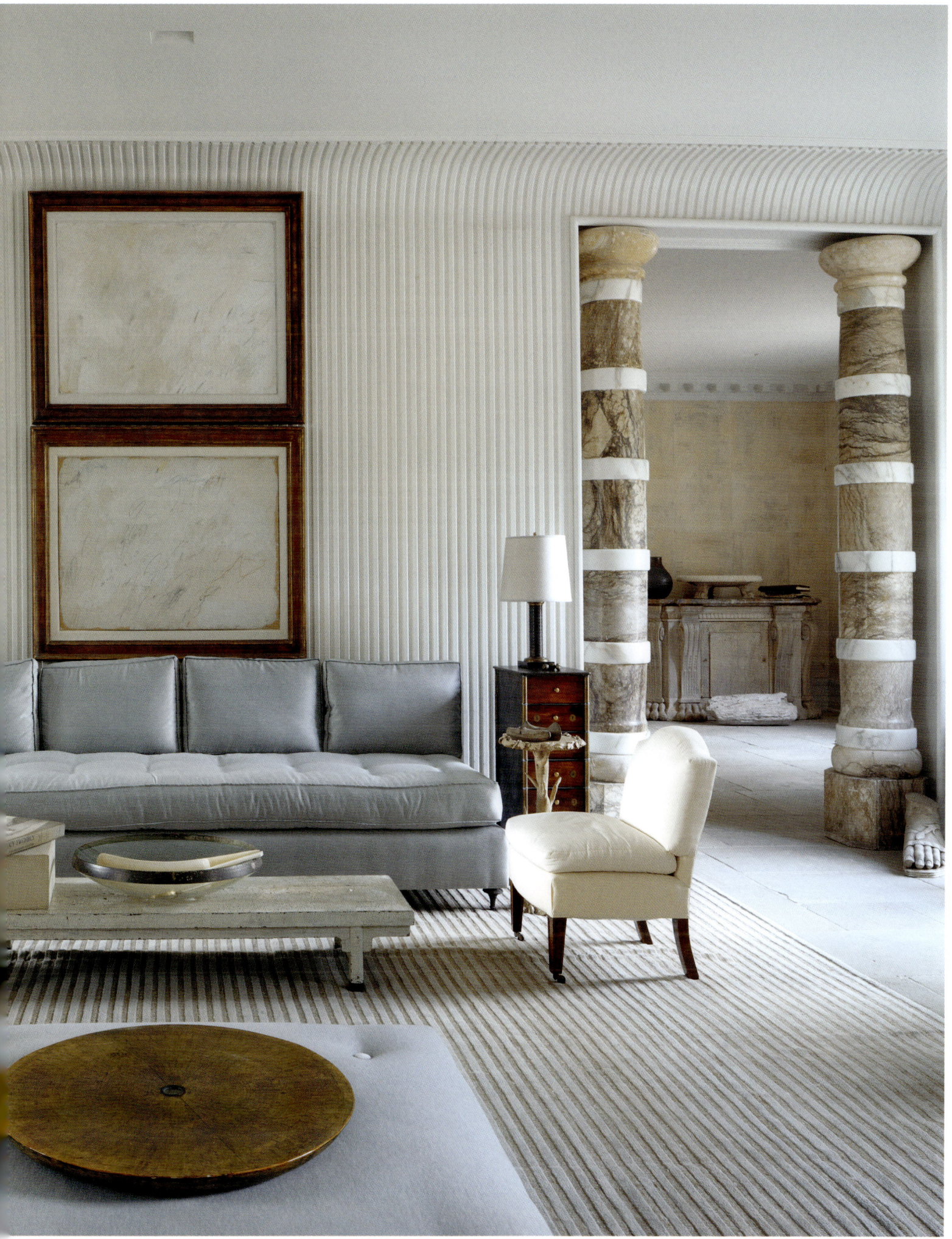

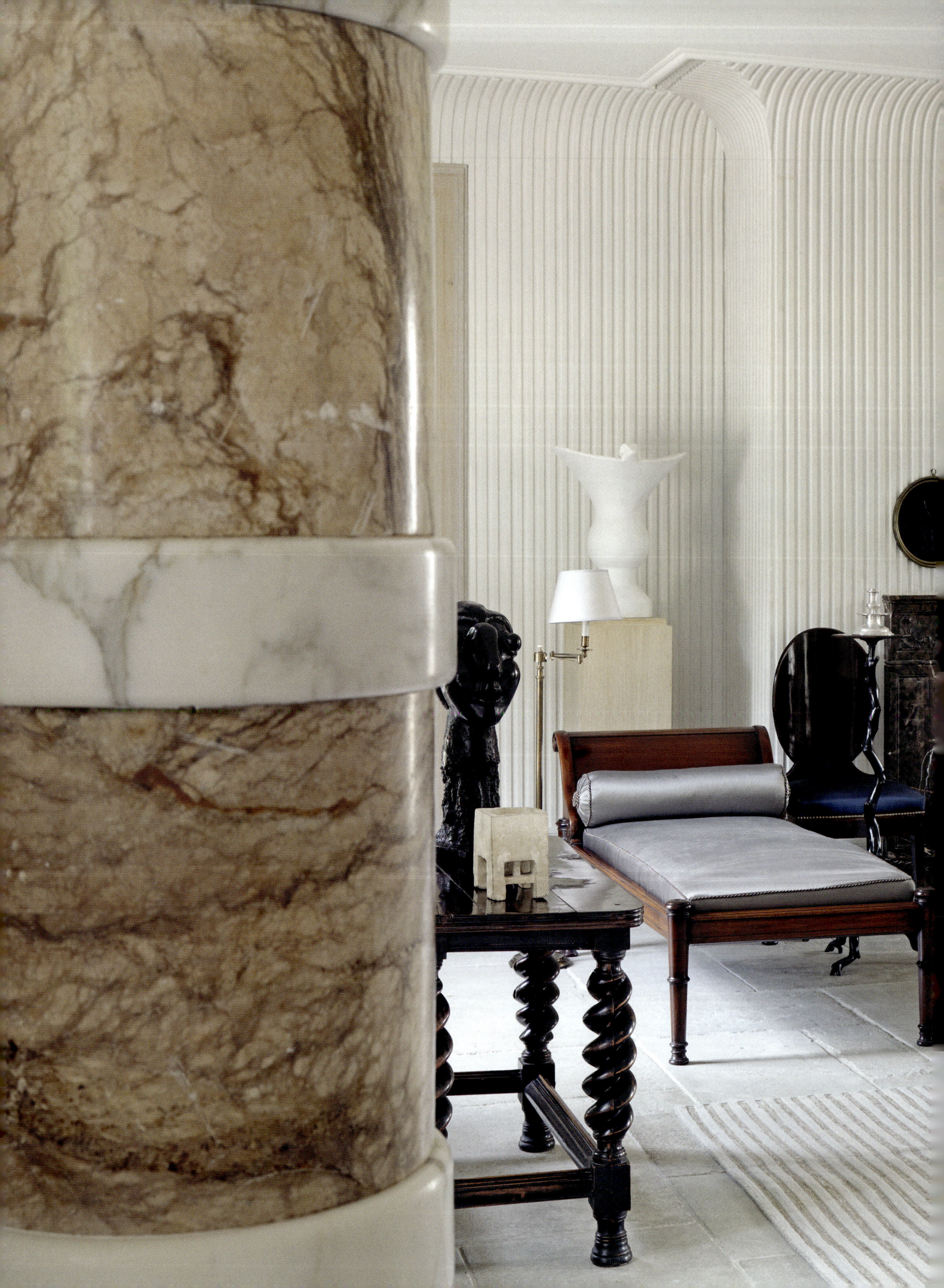

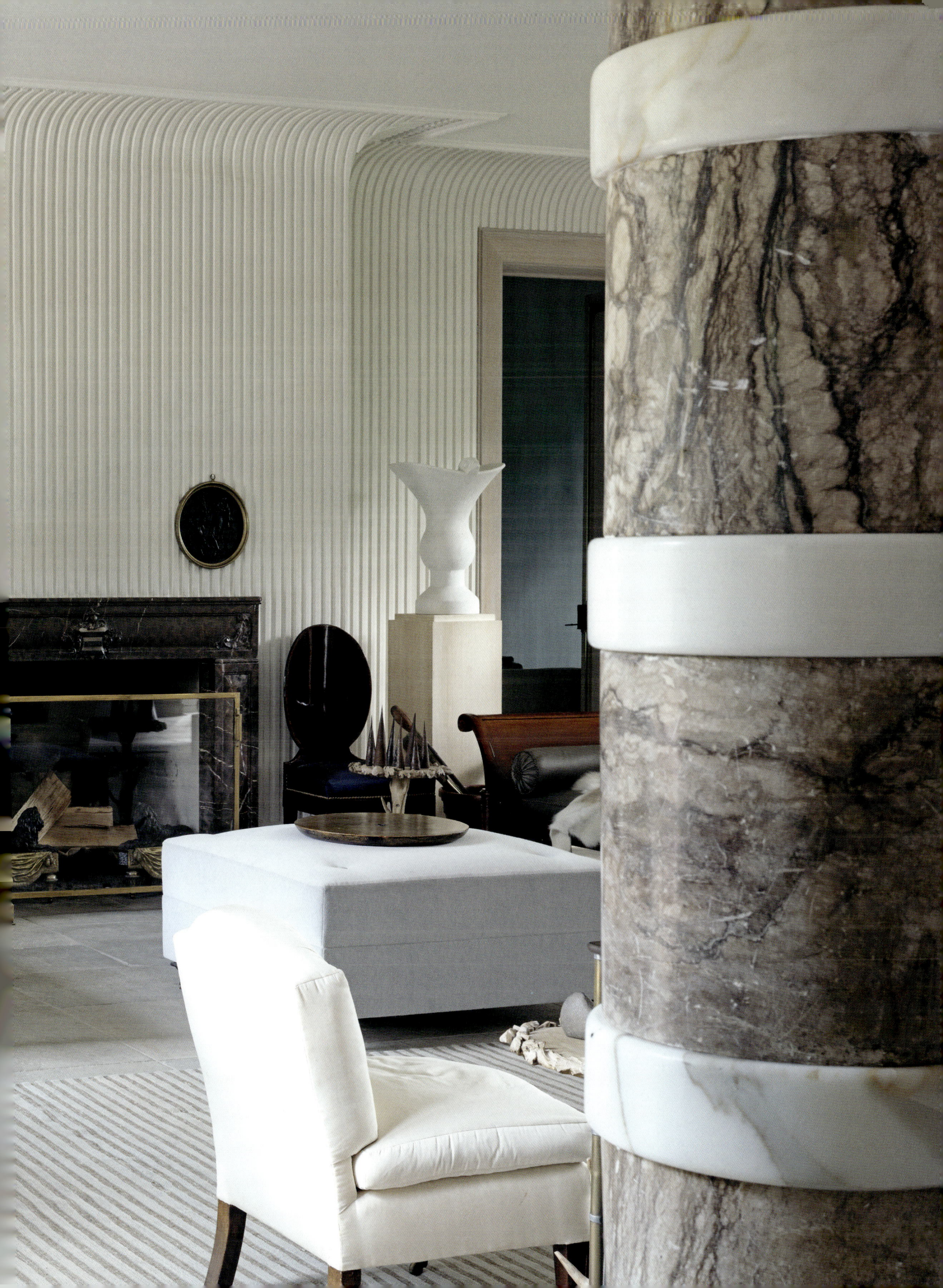

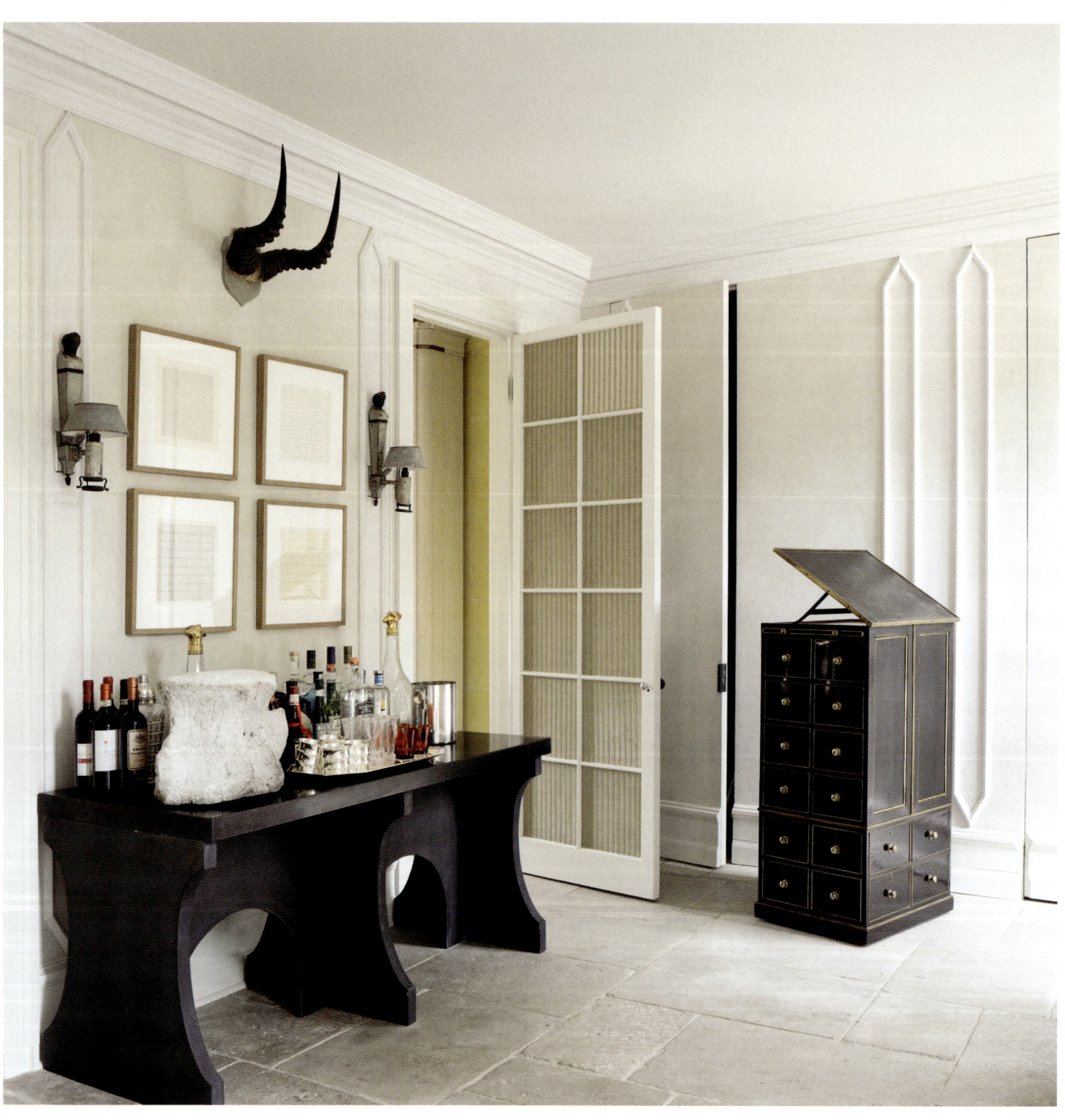

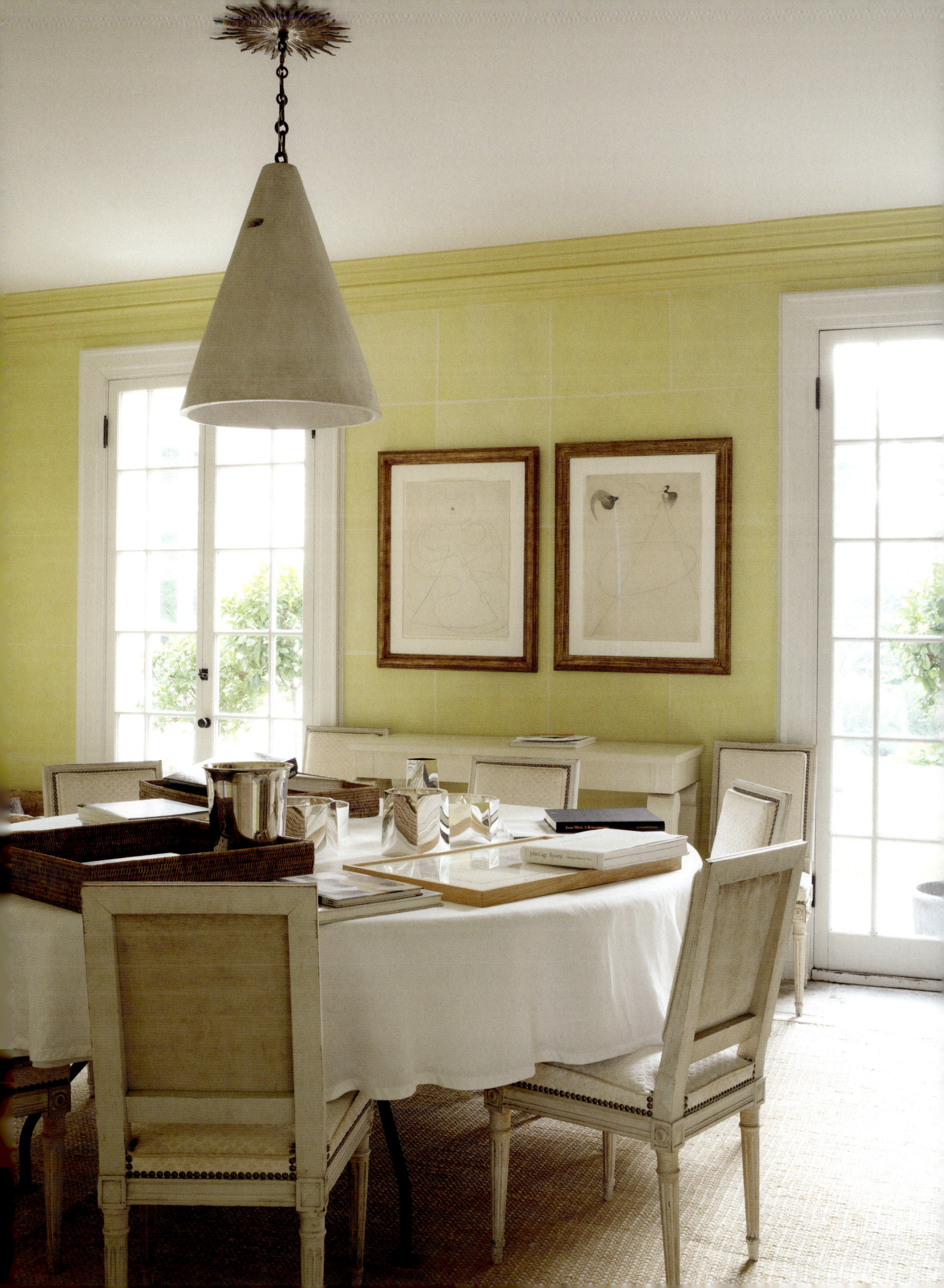

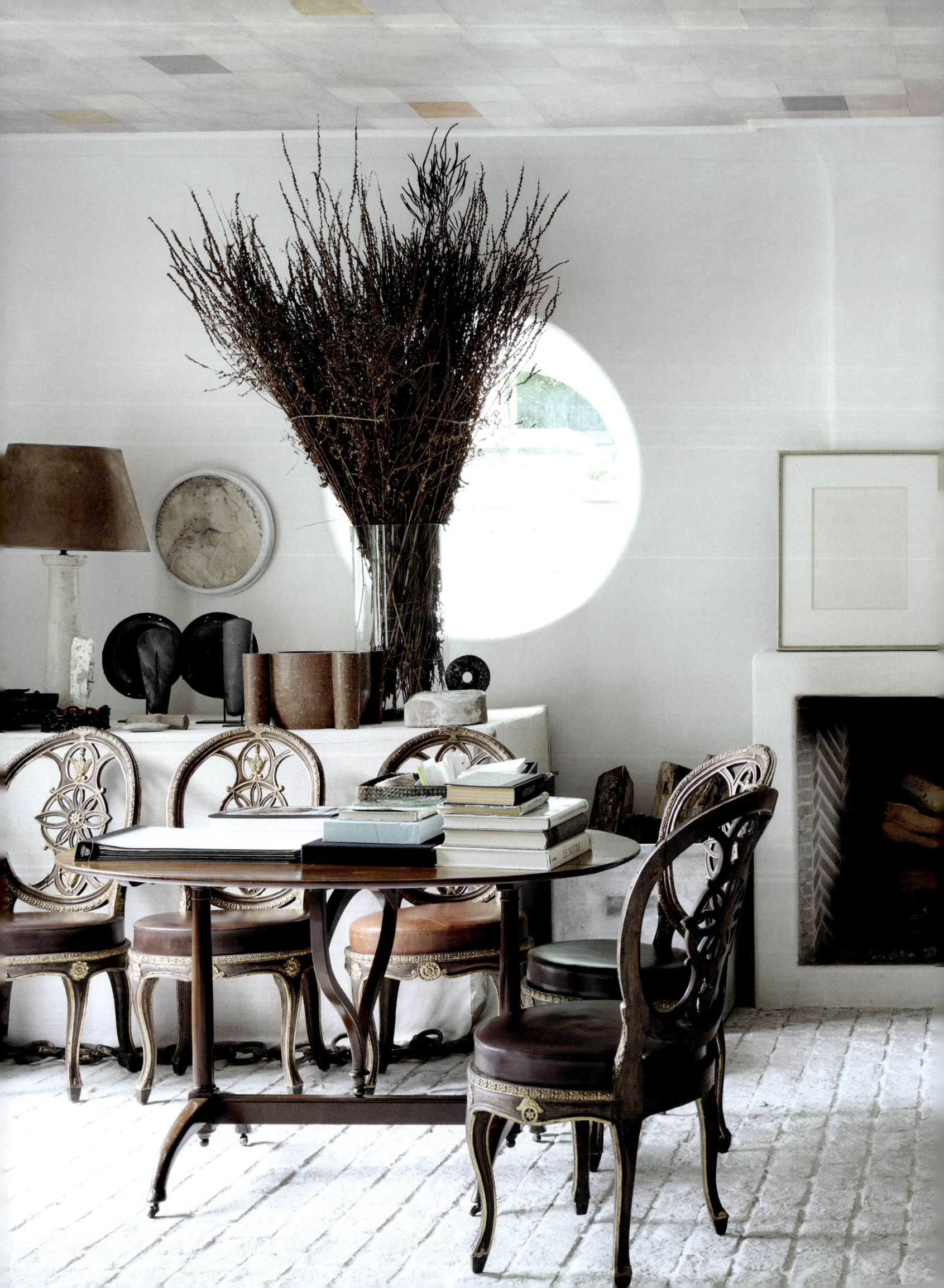

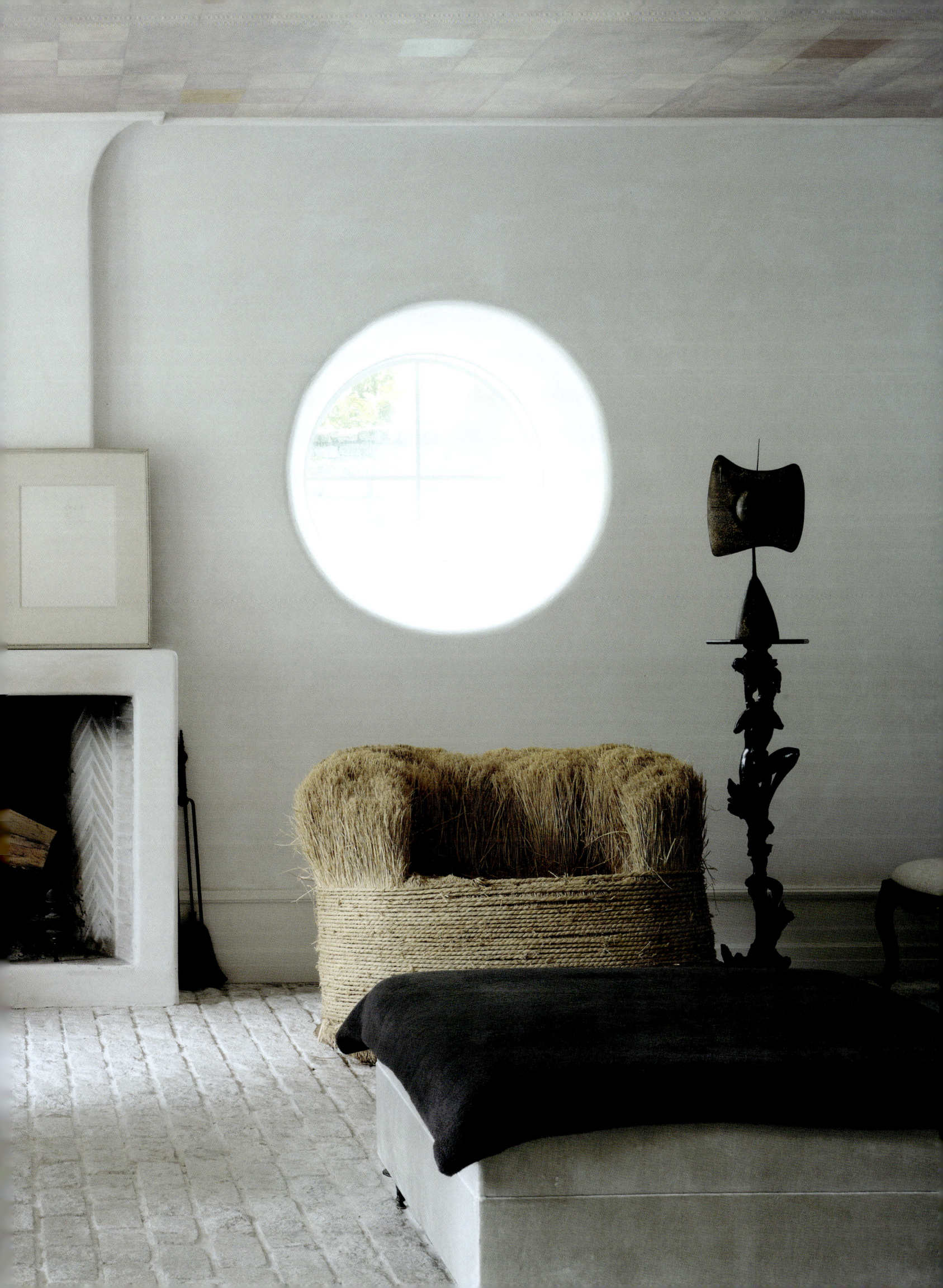

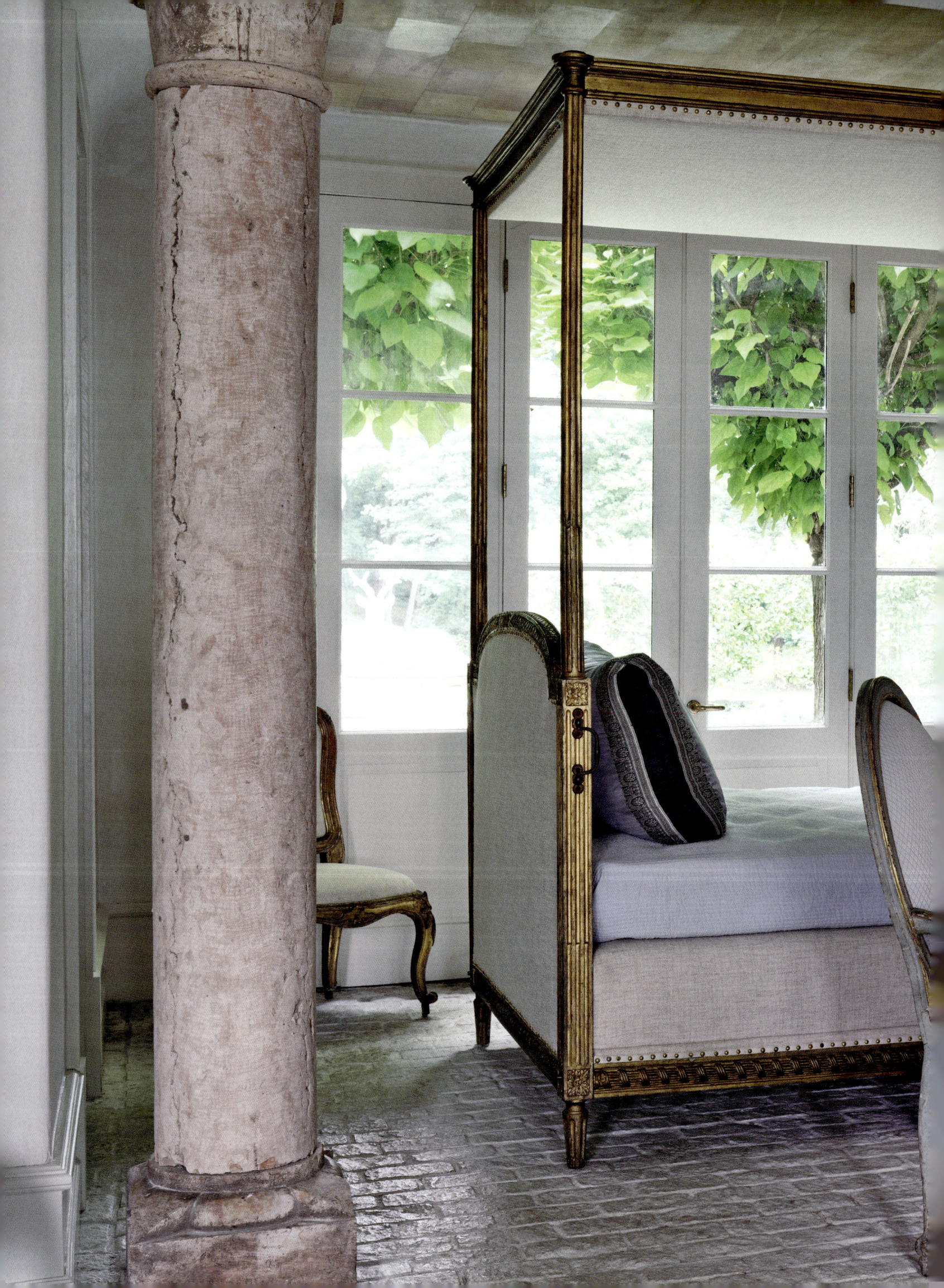

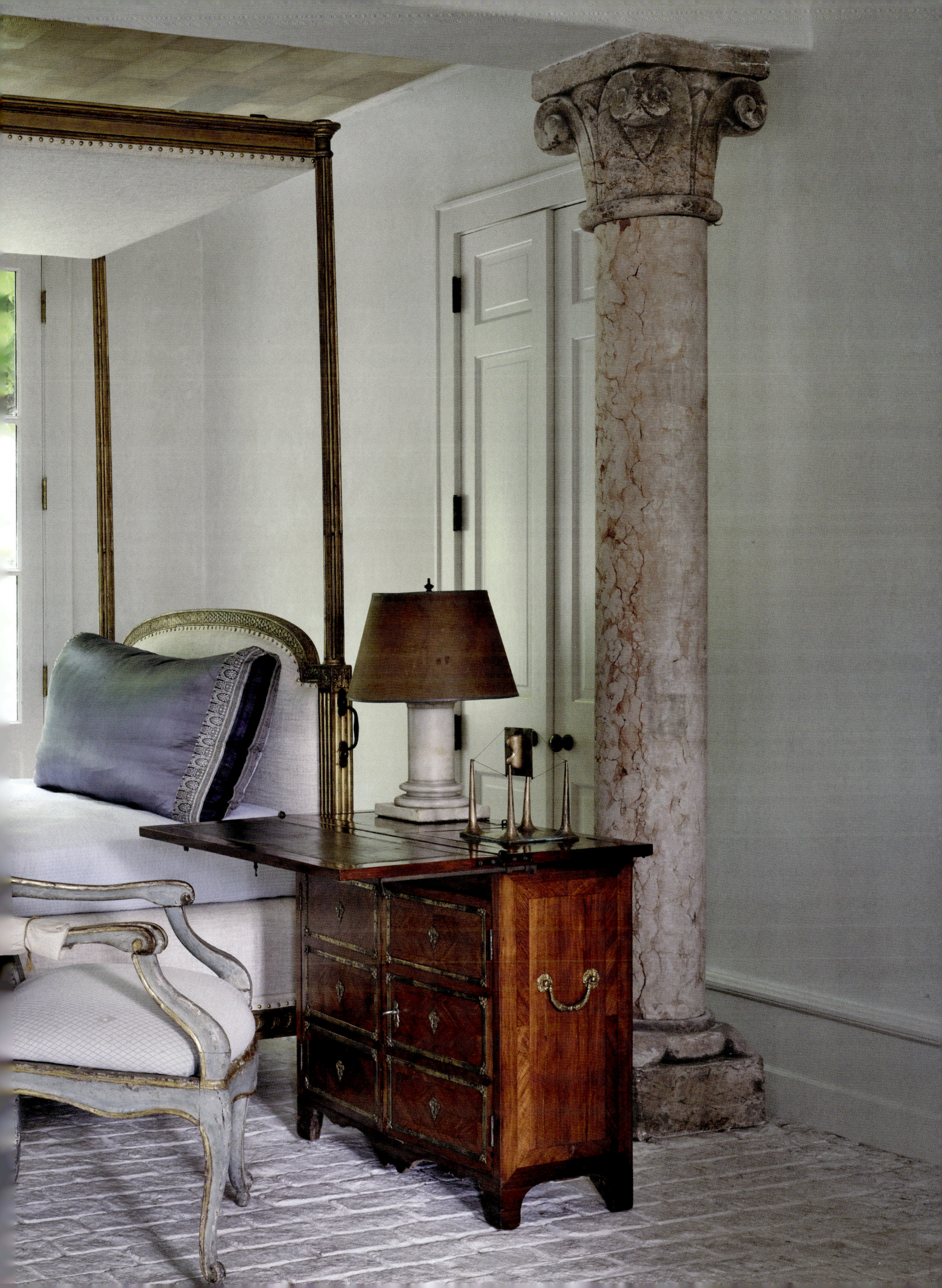

THEATER RURAL

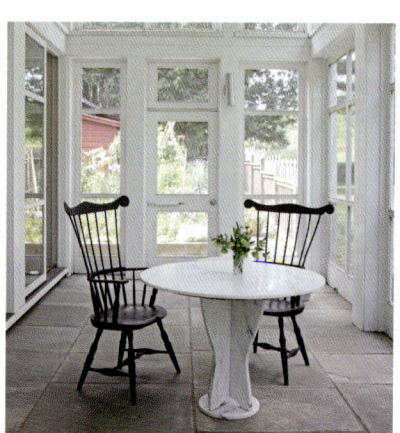

CARY LEIBOWITZ & SIMON LINCE

"Getaway" is not a word Cary and I have ever used. It sounds like an urgent escape destination! While it might not be where we have spent most of our days, this is very much our home and has become our primary residence, where we get to enjoy time with friends and family. No matter the season, we head to the country every weekend, although I am starting to spend more time up here, while Cary has no choice but to return to New York for work.

We had been looking for over a year, at a time when property was selling very quickly (those that weren't were either too derelict or already renovated to the max), and had primed friend and architect Robert Venturi well in advance of finding anything suitable. He tried to persuade us to buy an old property and not worry about him, but after a couple of false starts, we found this place. Owned by a couple who had moved here in the 1950s, it was almost too nice to do up as a project and originally too expensive. All its eighteenth-century details had been preserved and it had such a rich patina of history. Venturi loved it. We commissioned him to build an extension, which would include a Chinese facade made of metal, like a highway sign, and drew up an impressive list of rooms within rooms. As a Modernist, Venturi naturally suggested the new room should be entirely of glass—an irreverent nod to the classical architecture of the original house—yet neither of us felt that glass was really our thing. Nevertheless, we ended up with a glass extension, with the exception of the north- and south-facing walls, which, to comply with energy regulations, had to be insulated.

The simple utility garden—also designed by Venturi— has evolved over the years, and is protected from deer and wild animals with a custom-designed, larger-than-life picket fence. I have always admired English allotment-style gardens, and began our own equivalent venture by planting only vegetables. Today, it's a free-form mix of vegetables, roses, native perennials, and wildflowers. I love the unexpected combinations and I think the eclectic mix of plants has confused even the insects! While I garden, Cary cooks and tries to do things he doesn't have time for in the city. He always brings the laundry with him to do in the country, and returns to Manhattan laden with fresh food and vegetables.

Our favorite room is the bedroom, which is located on the second floor of the old house, with windows overlooking the garden and the woods, although we also love "The Room"—our big new extension—which we use nearly all the time. Our most treasured piece of art is actually a letter from our niece, Katie, who lives in England with her family. She sent us the note when she was learning to write, and it is such a sweet, unabashed expression of love—the perfect emblem for our country home. **SL**

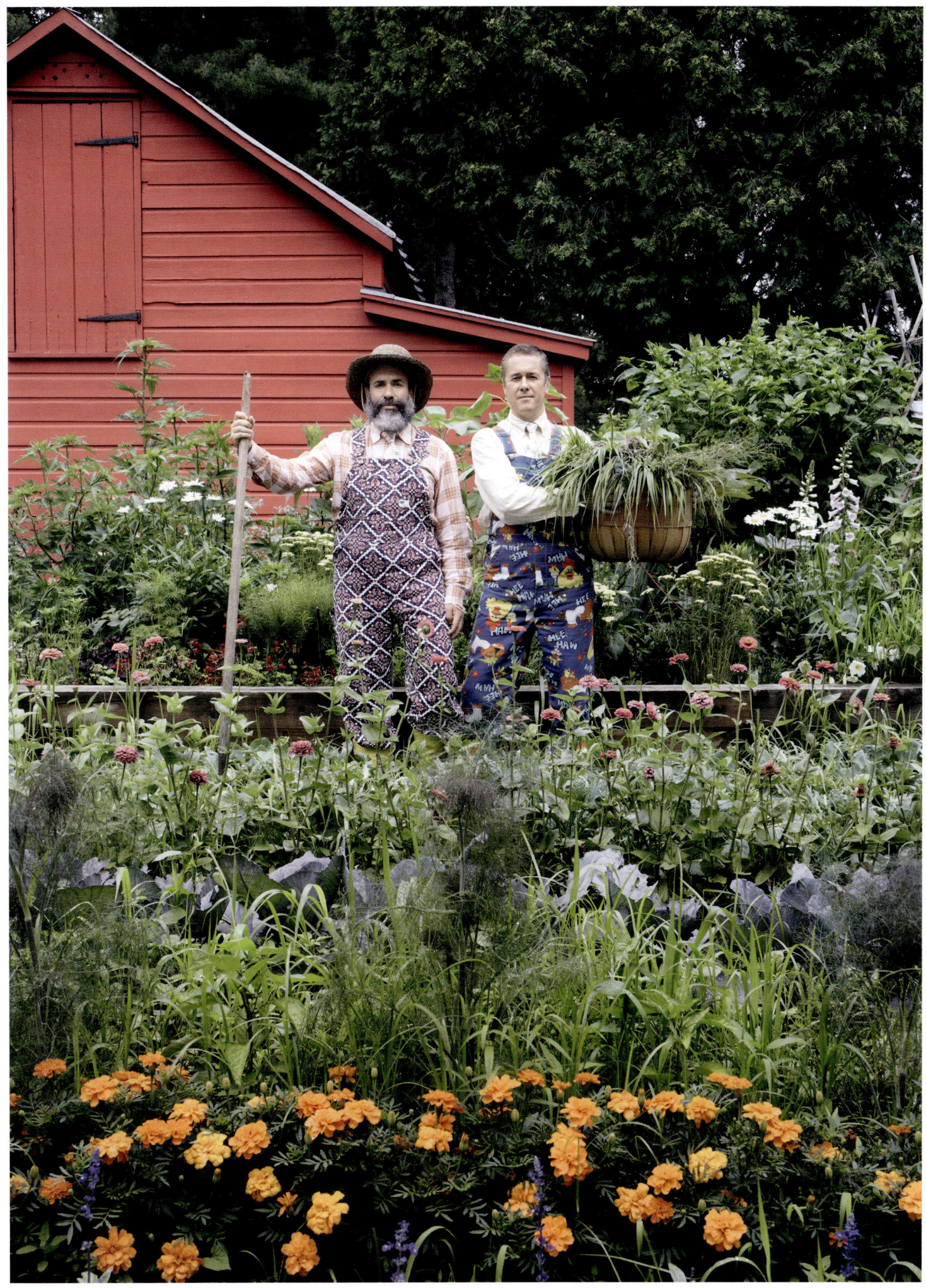

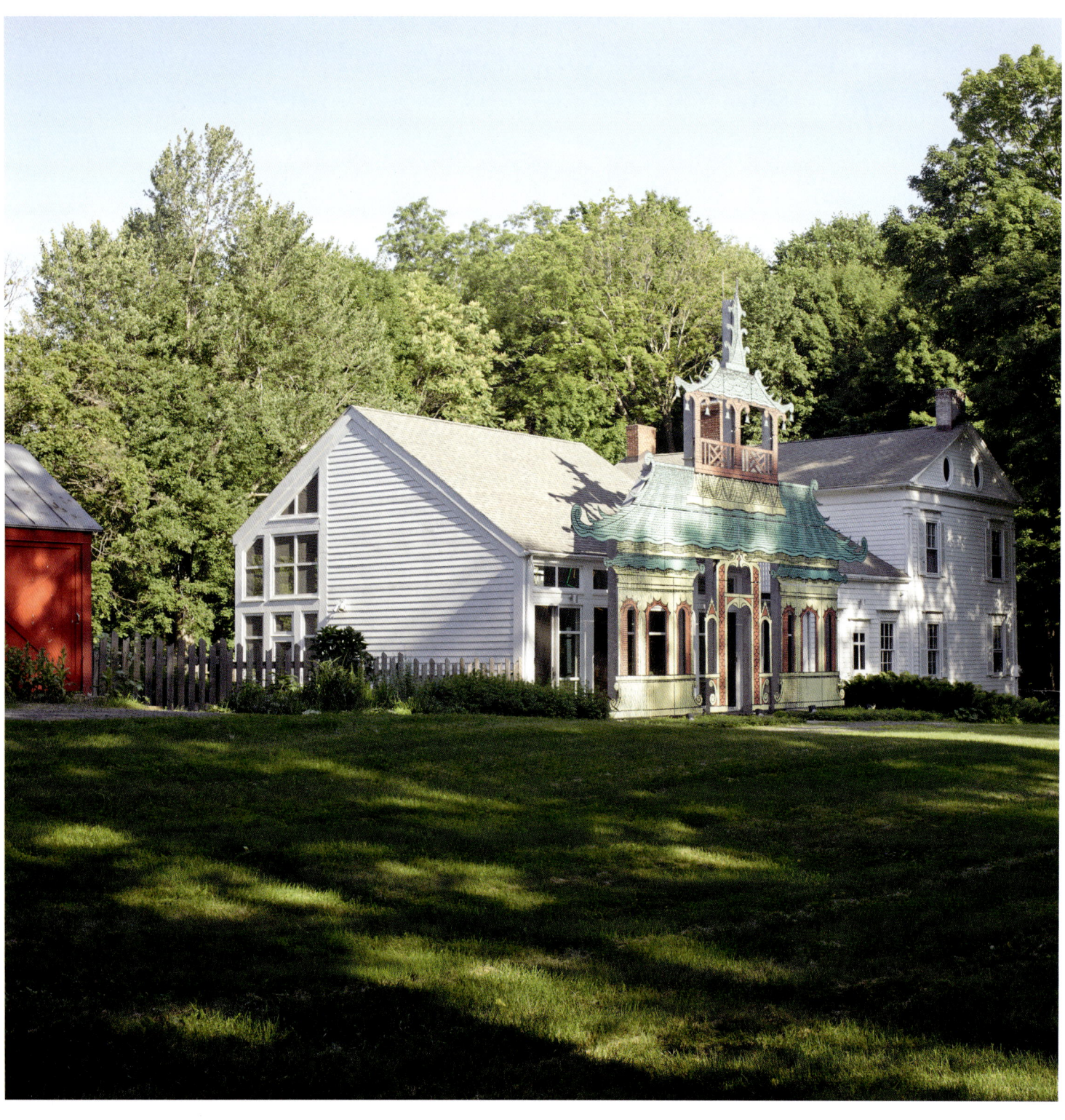

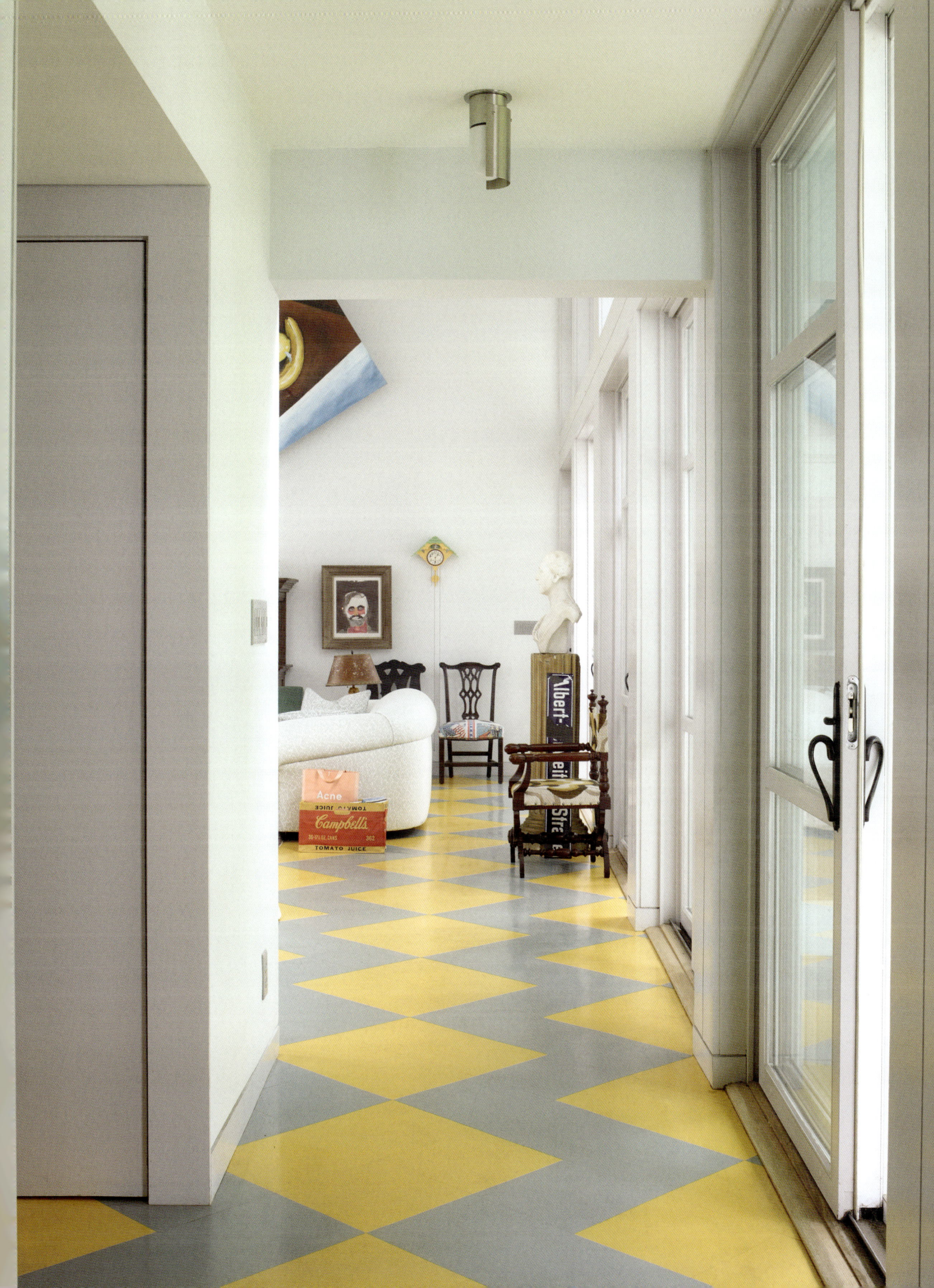

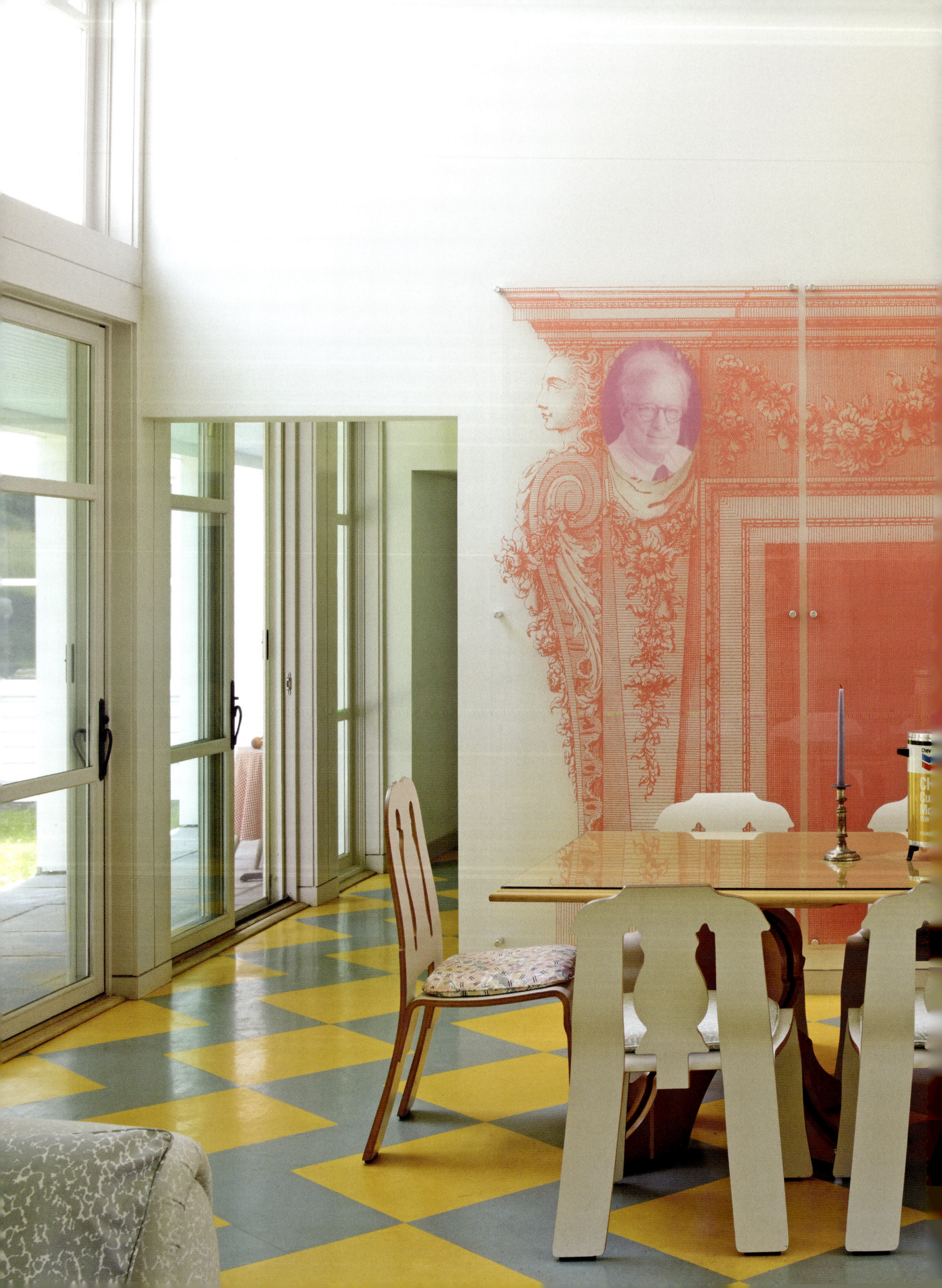

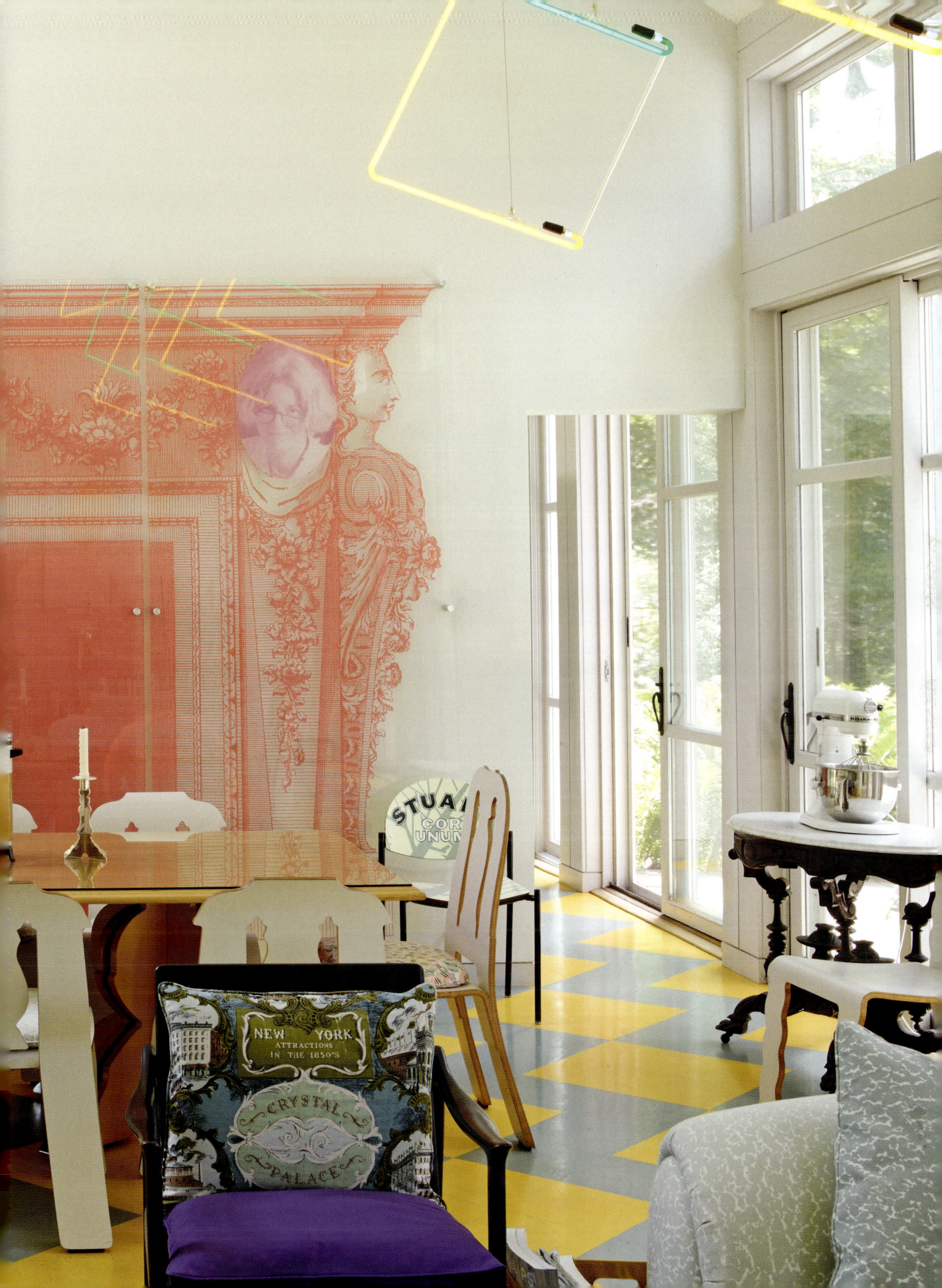

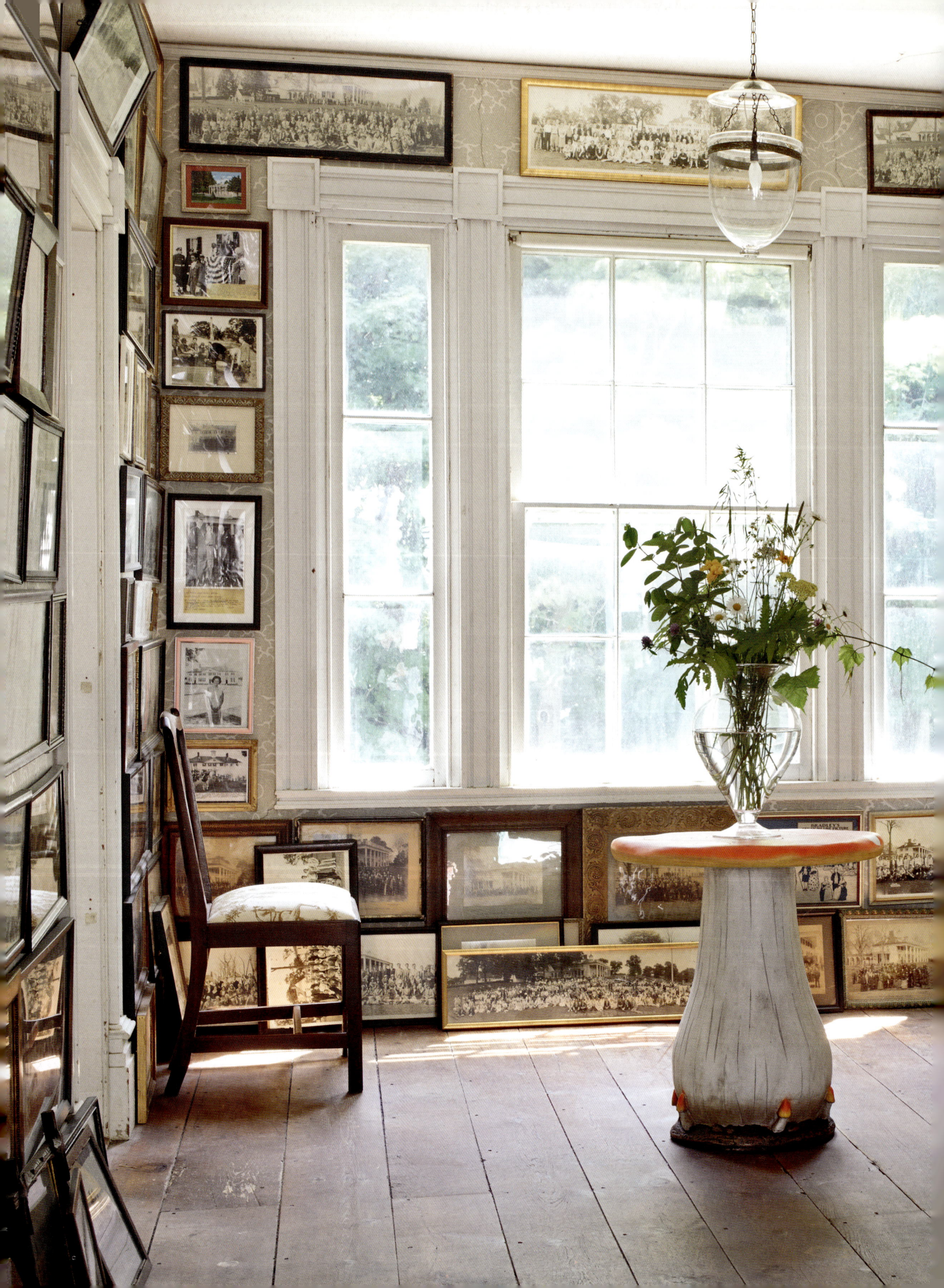

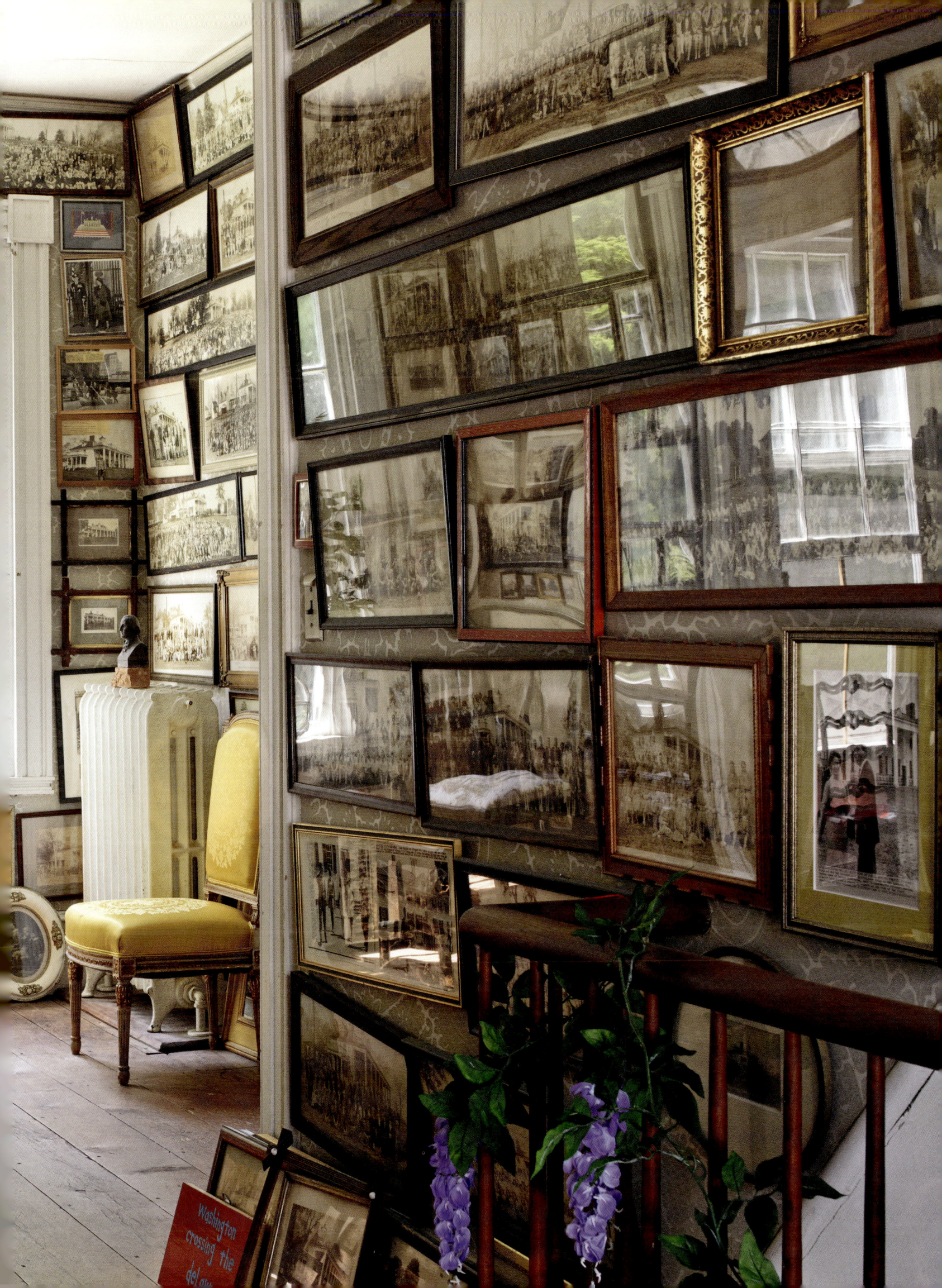

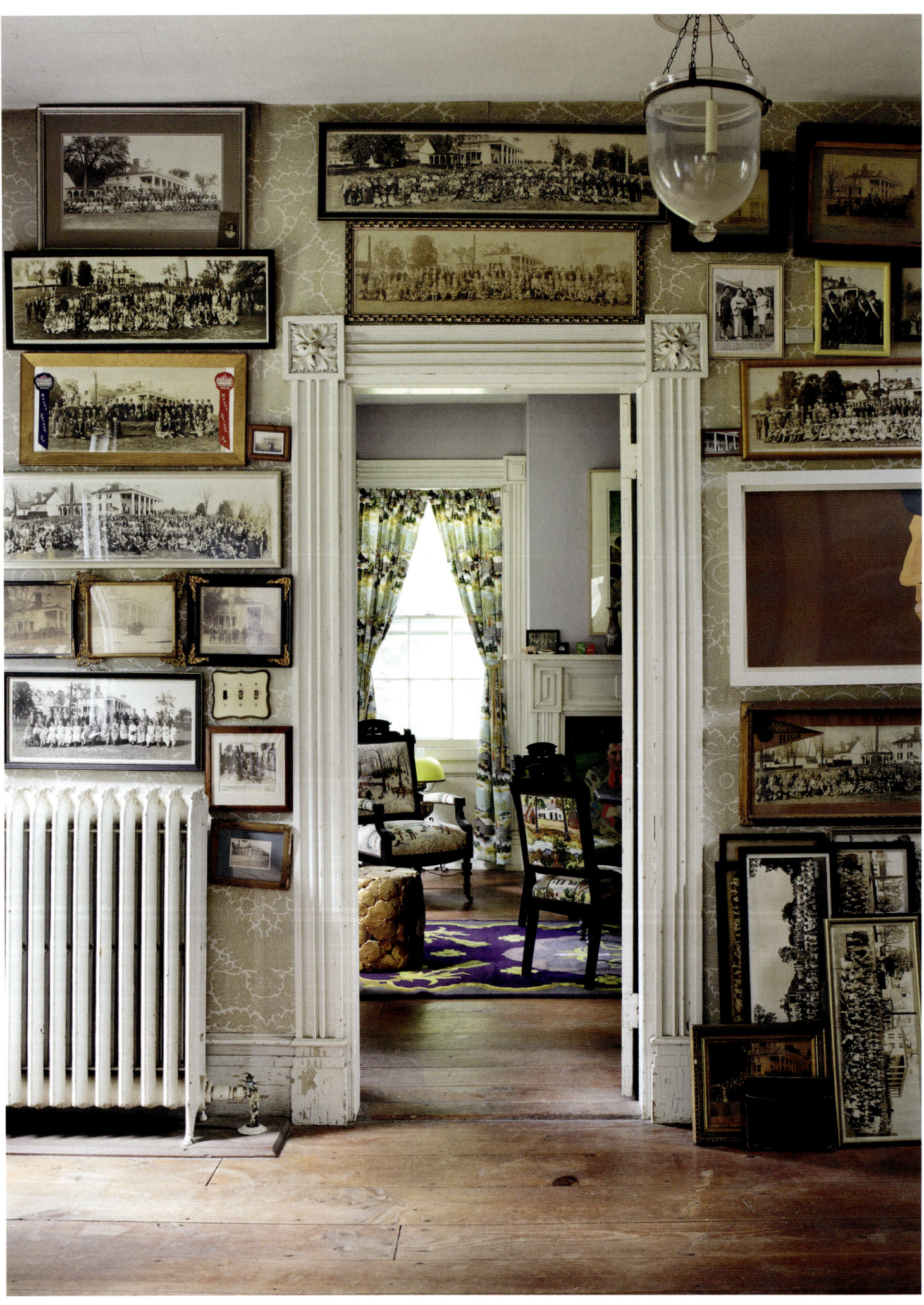

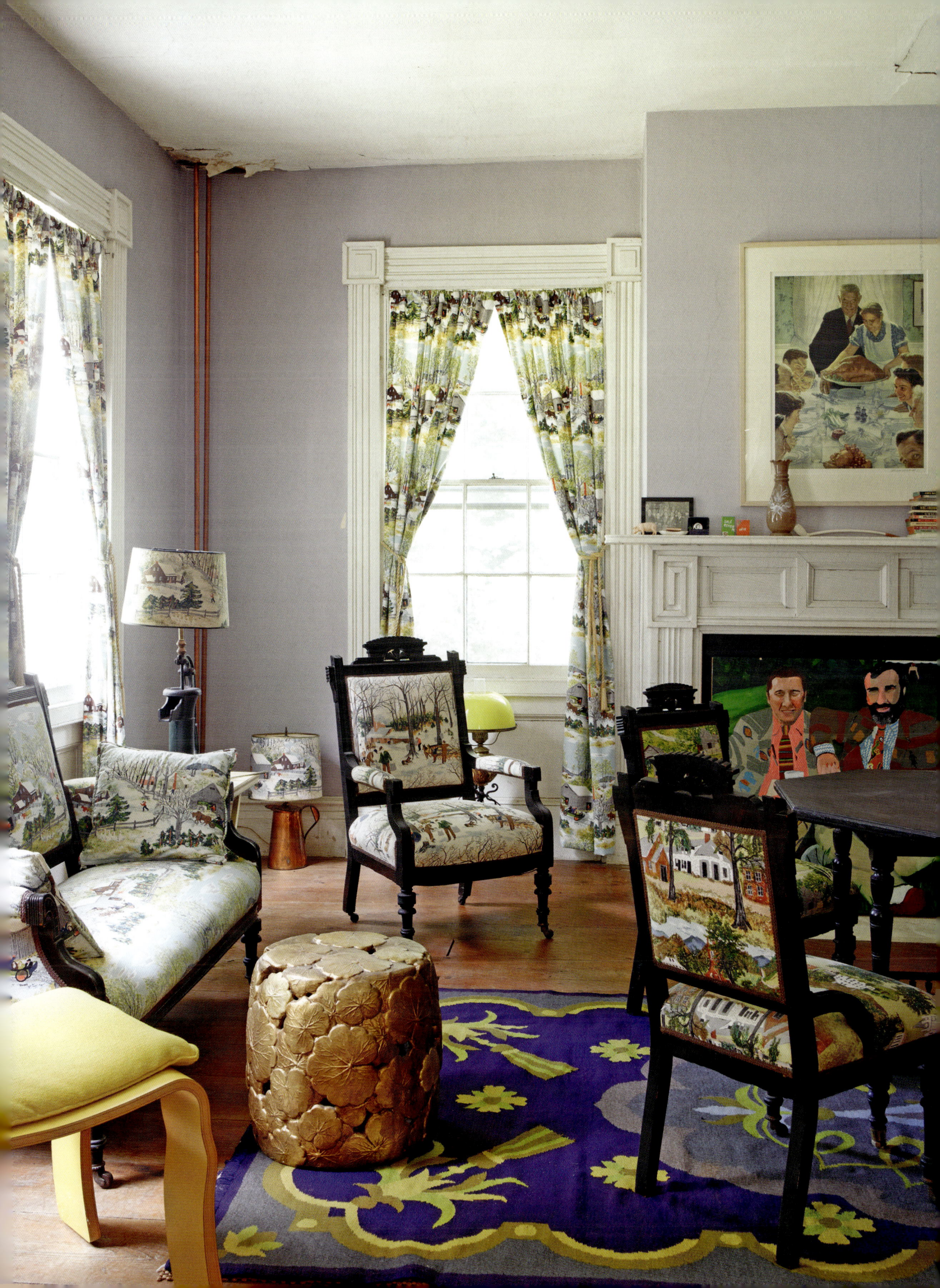

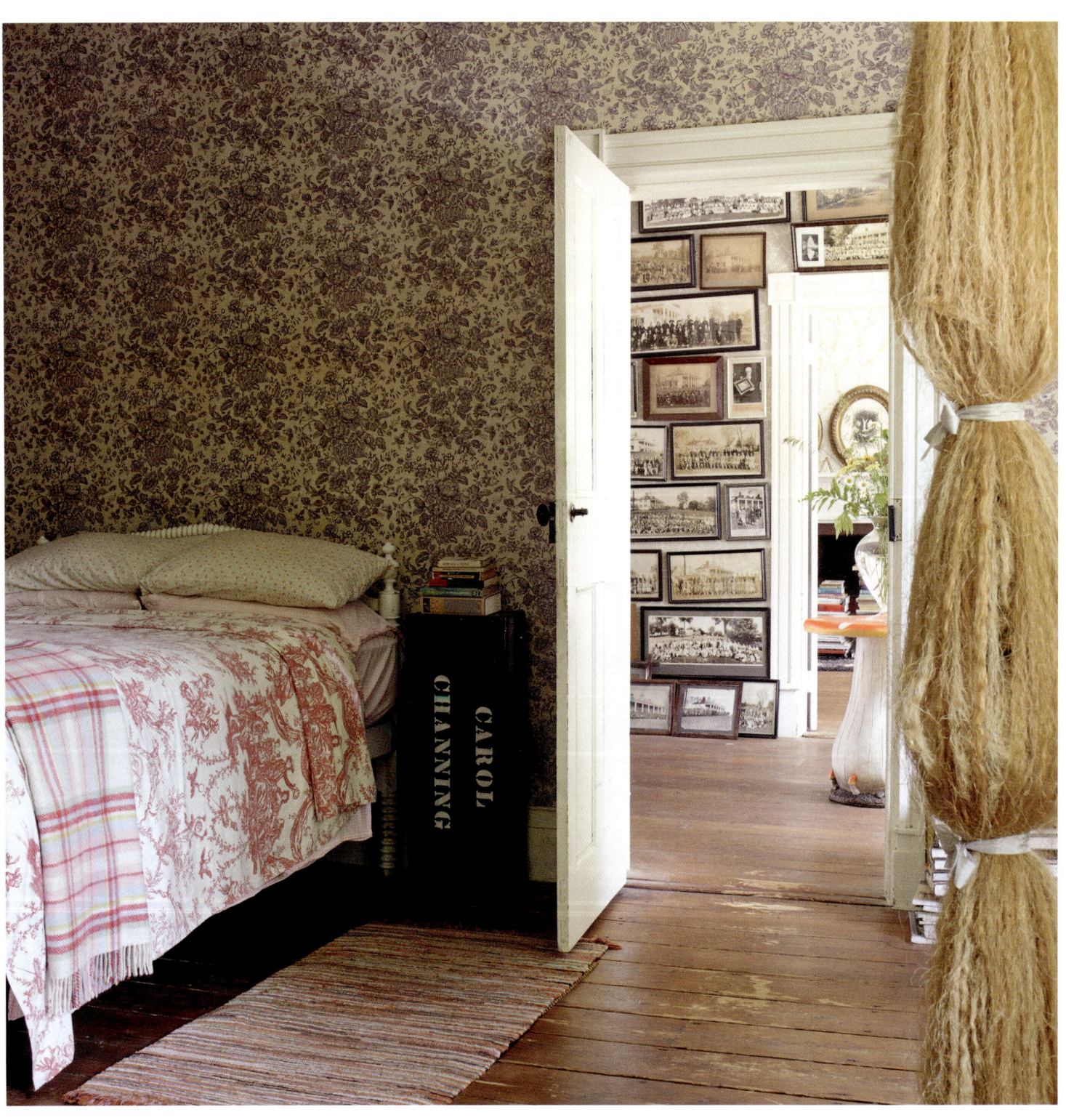

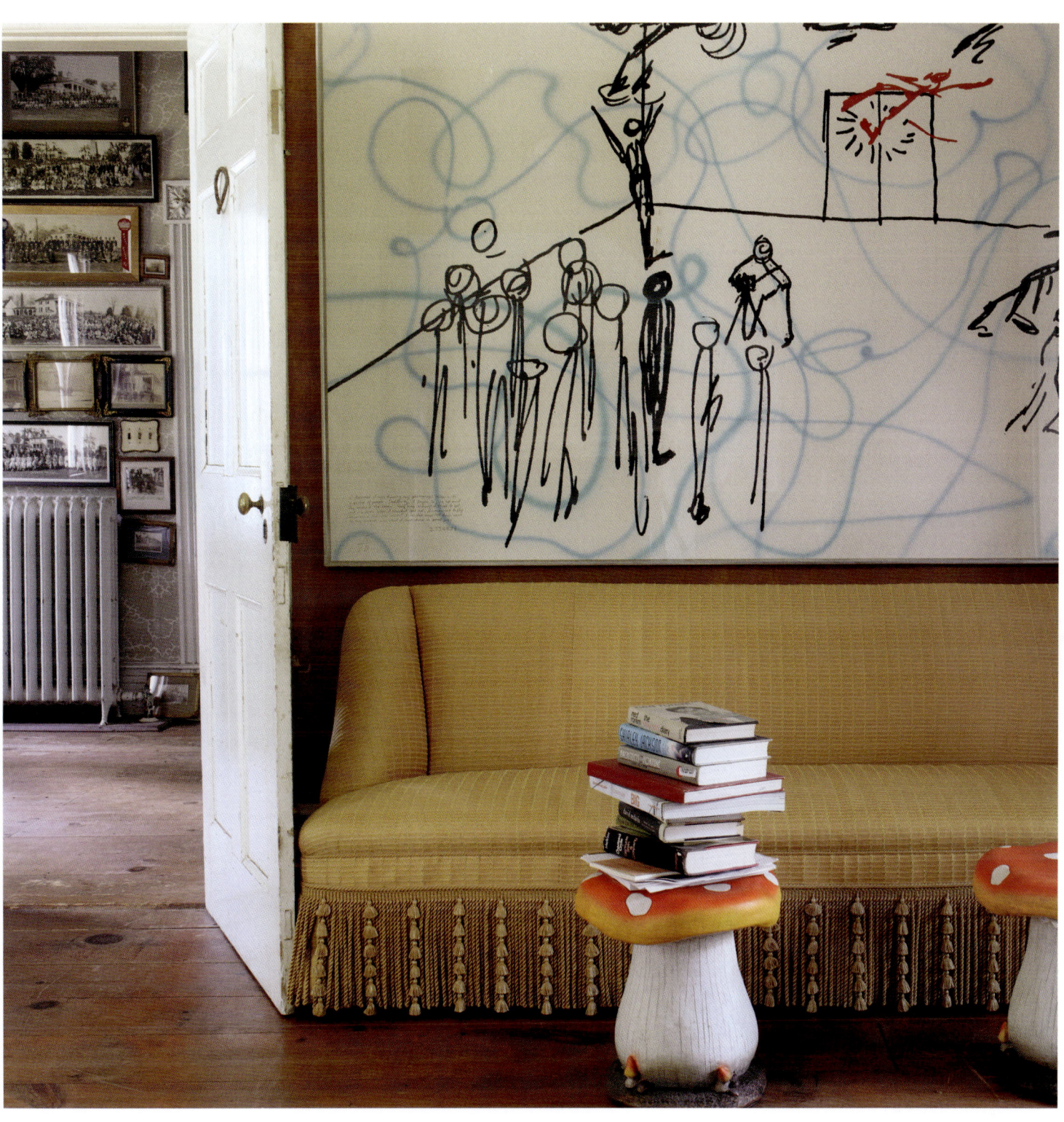

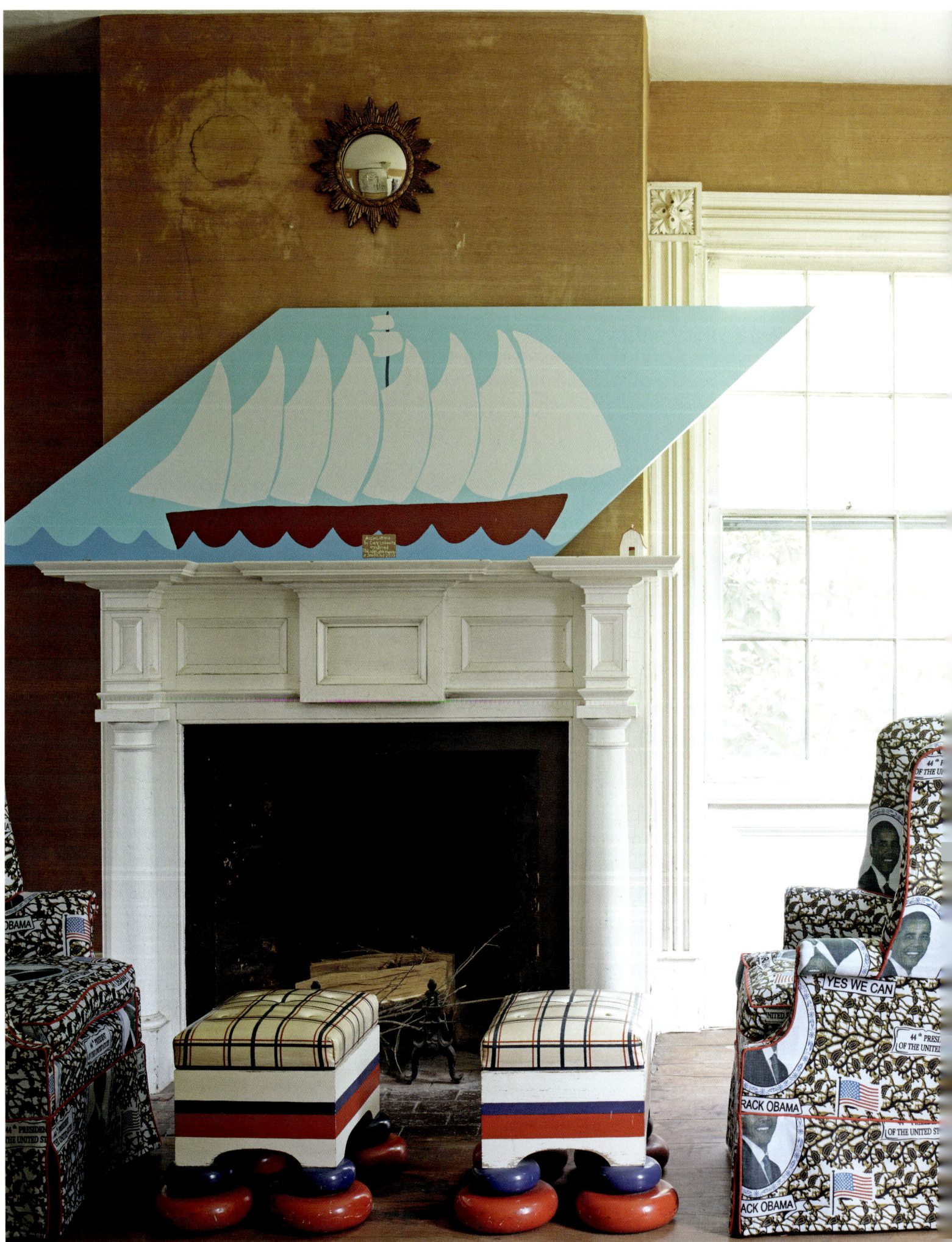

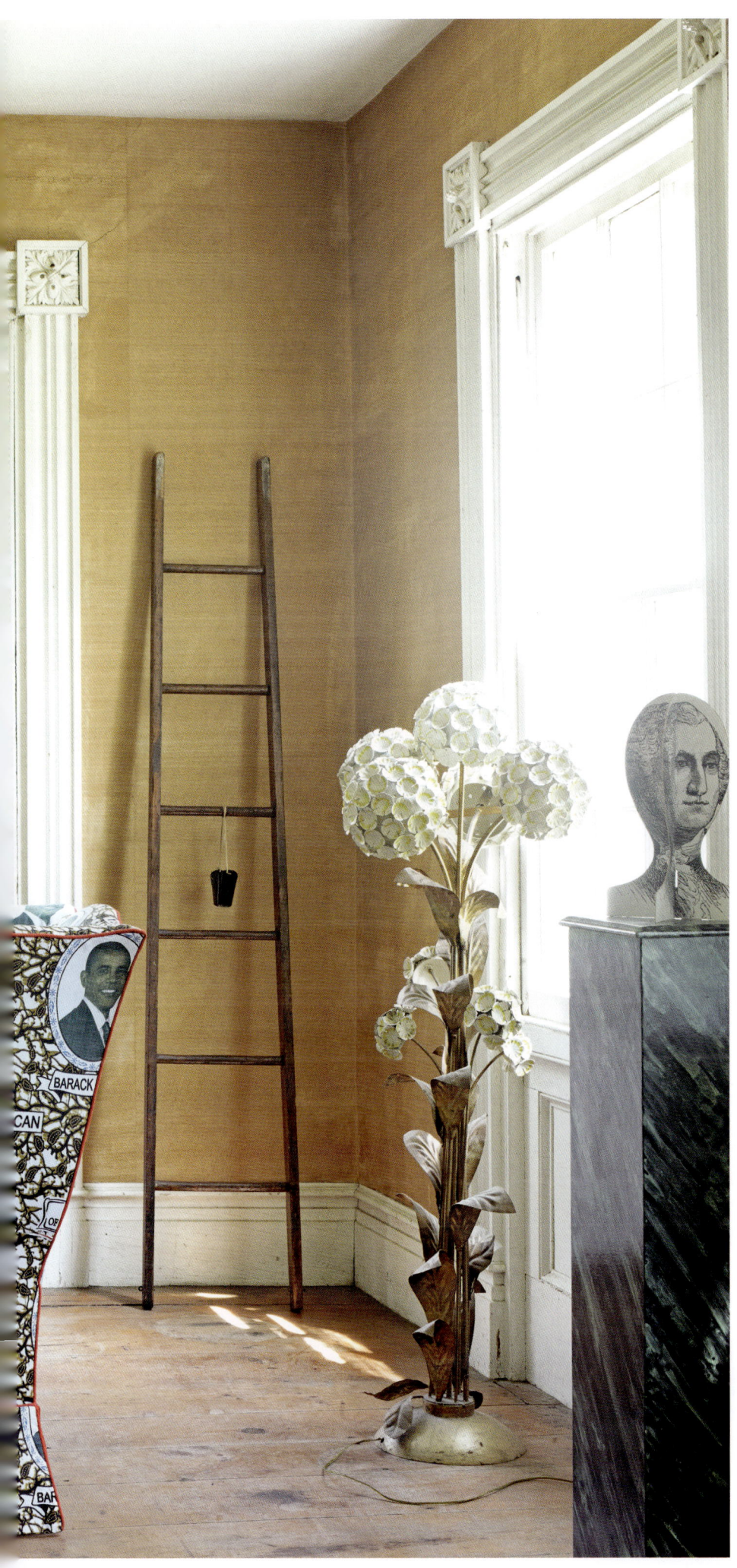

FEDERAL REVIVAL

STEVEN GAMBREL

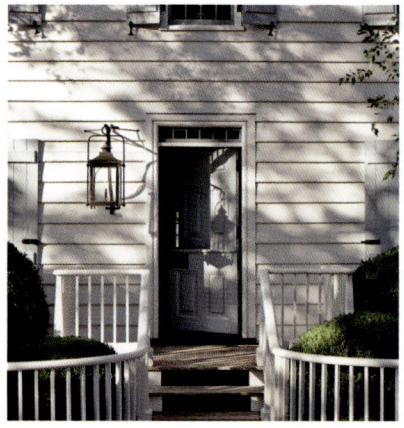

Although Sag Harbor was declared the first official port of entry into the United States in 1789, it rose to prominence in the heyday of the whaling industry. It became a prosperous town, with a diversity of people arriving off the whaling ships. When sea captains and sailors returned to the harbor at the end of a long trip abroad, they often brought back with them exotic furniture, lacquerware, and unusual paint pigments. In celebration of a successful mission, a shipbuilder was often engaged to embellish the facade or doorframe of a captain's simple house as an expression of the triumphant voyage.

The main street in the village is lined with elaborate and beautiful captains' houses, mostly dating from the mid-nineteenth century. Houses down the side streets are simpler and would have been occupied by shipbuilders and local business owners. Houses like mine on the waterfront would have been considered undesirable, because of the noise and stench from the whale blubber industry on the edges of the port. As whaling declined toward the latter part of the nineteenth century, Sag Harbor became a colony of artists and writers, seduced by its architecture and seafaring spirit. Since it is the deepest port on this stretch of Long Island coastline, during the summer months many private ships drop anchor here to enjoy the Hamptons.

Sag Harbor was a charming if sleepy town when I first discovered it as a student. I returned some years later and rented a simple shack—somebody's converted shed—and started renovating houses in the vicinity. In 2002, I had purchased a large, historic house and was working on it across the street from my current house. I had a puppy Labradoodle named Dash,

who would—unbeknownst to me—cross the street to get into the bay for a swim. Because of this, I got to know the owner at the time very well! One day she decided to sell the house and offered me first refusal. The house has been in my life for so long now that I can barely recall a time without it.

I rebuilt the entire house, basing the detailing on local vernacular that I had referenced during the restoration of previous projects. Because the building had been added onto for nearly a century, it needed clarity. I reimagined the house as one that had been owned by a successful nineteenth-century sea captain. The interior flooring came from a property in Maine and was reinstalled here. The paneling in the purple room was salvaged from a nineteenth-century house, and any extra needed made in simple pine, just as it would have been made in that period. In those days, purple pigment would have been too expensive and difficult to procure. However, as a front room it would have been seen by passers-by and acknowledged as a sign of wealth. I used this "aspirational" pigment as a reference of a society eager to display the prosperity of their voyages.

Sag Harbor and my house have been a "getaway" for me for nearly two decades. It is a place for creative reflection, a learning capsule of history, and a region full of coves to explore. We have a boat—the Dashaway—docked off the guest house, ready for hours of unplanned, unchartered exploration. The term "getaway" conjures a sense of freedom from obligations and a change in routine. In the ebb and flow of my full life, this house and Sag Harbor provide me with a link to the past, along with a sense of permanence in an ever-changing world.

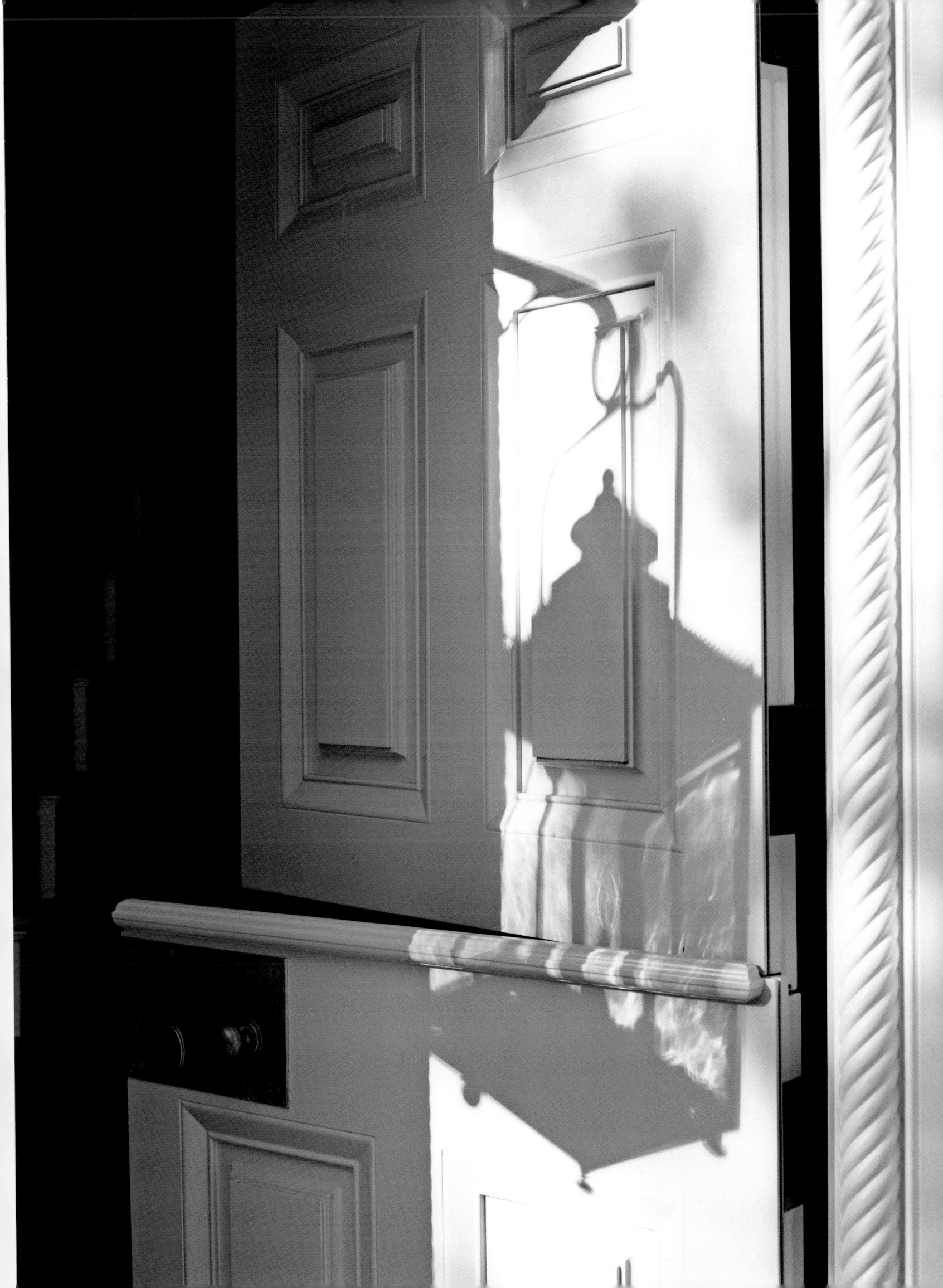

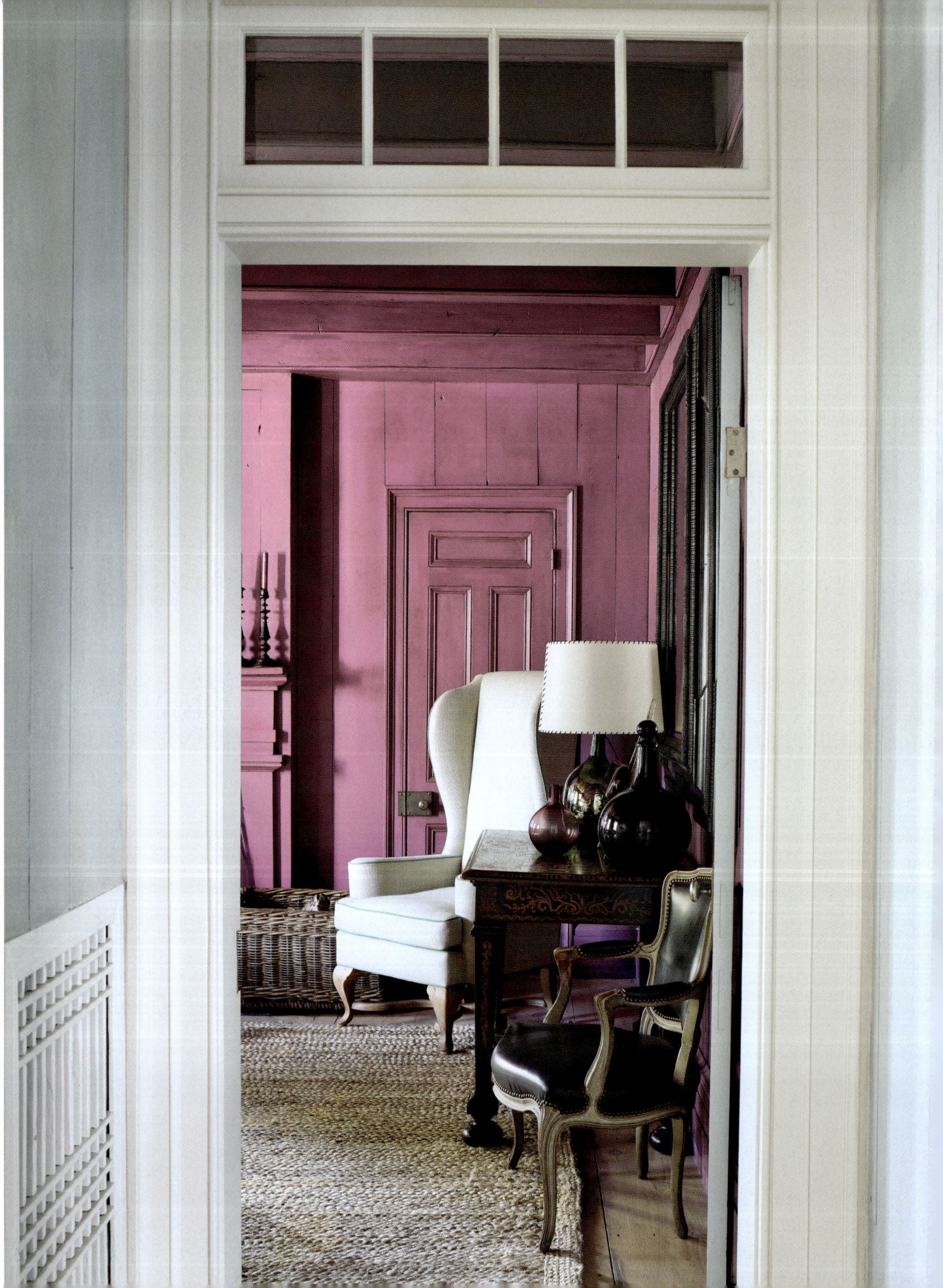

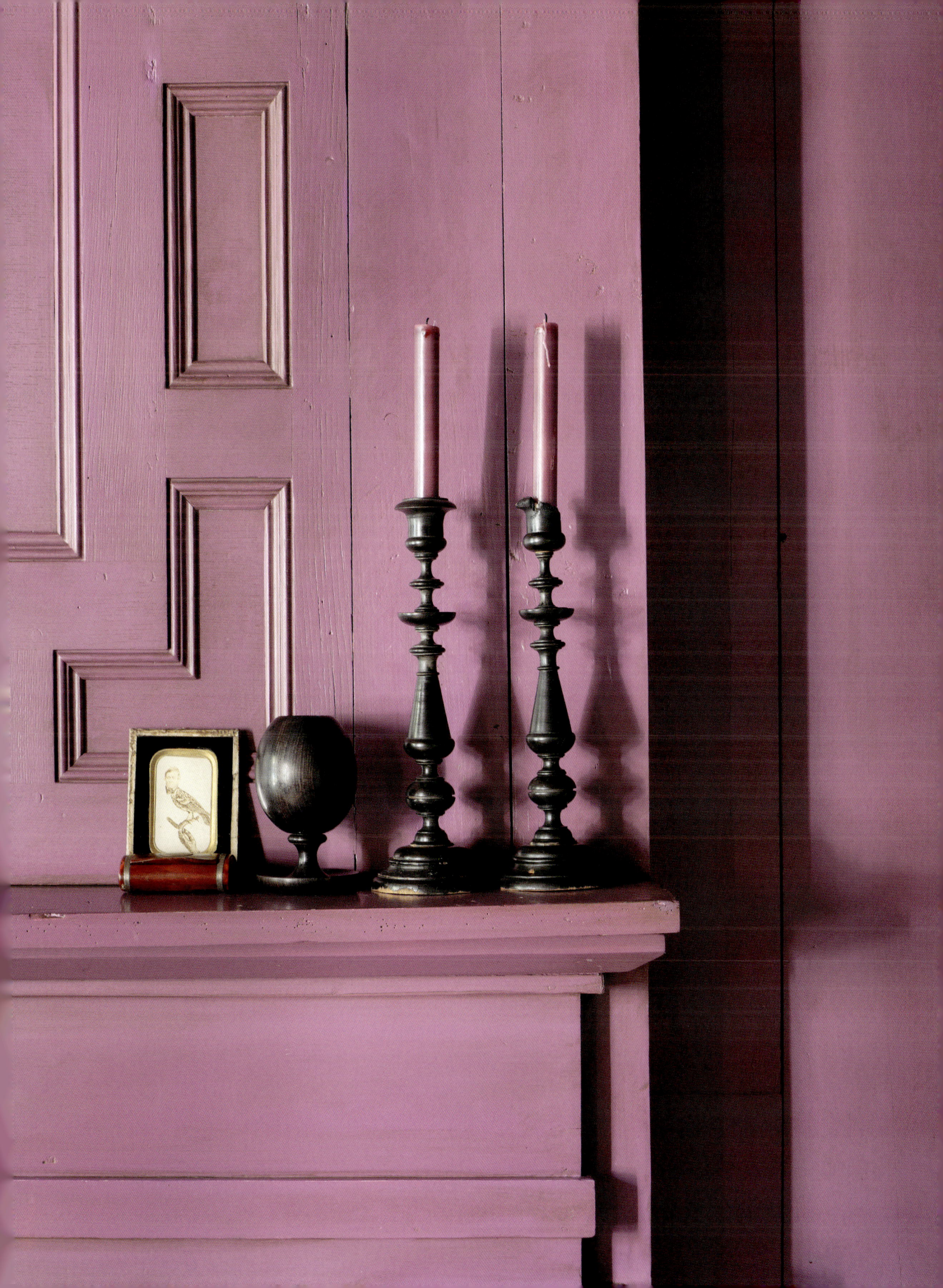

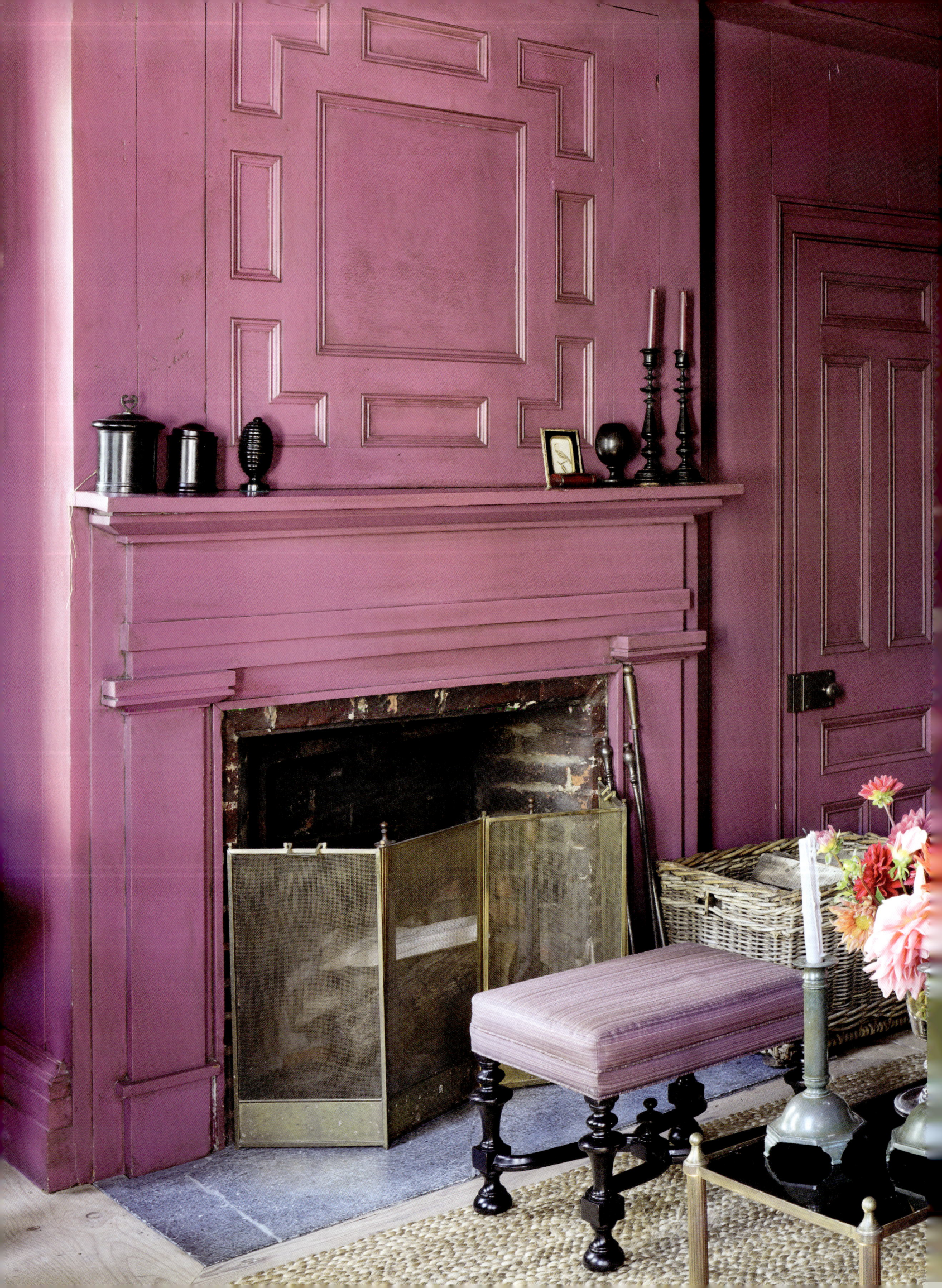

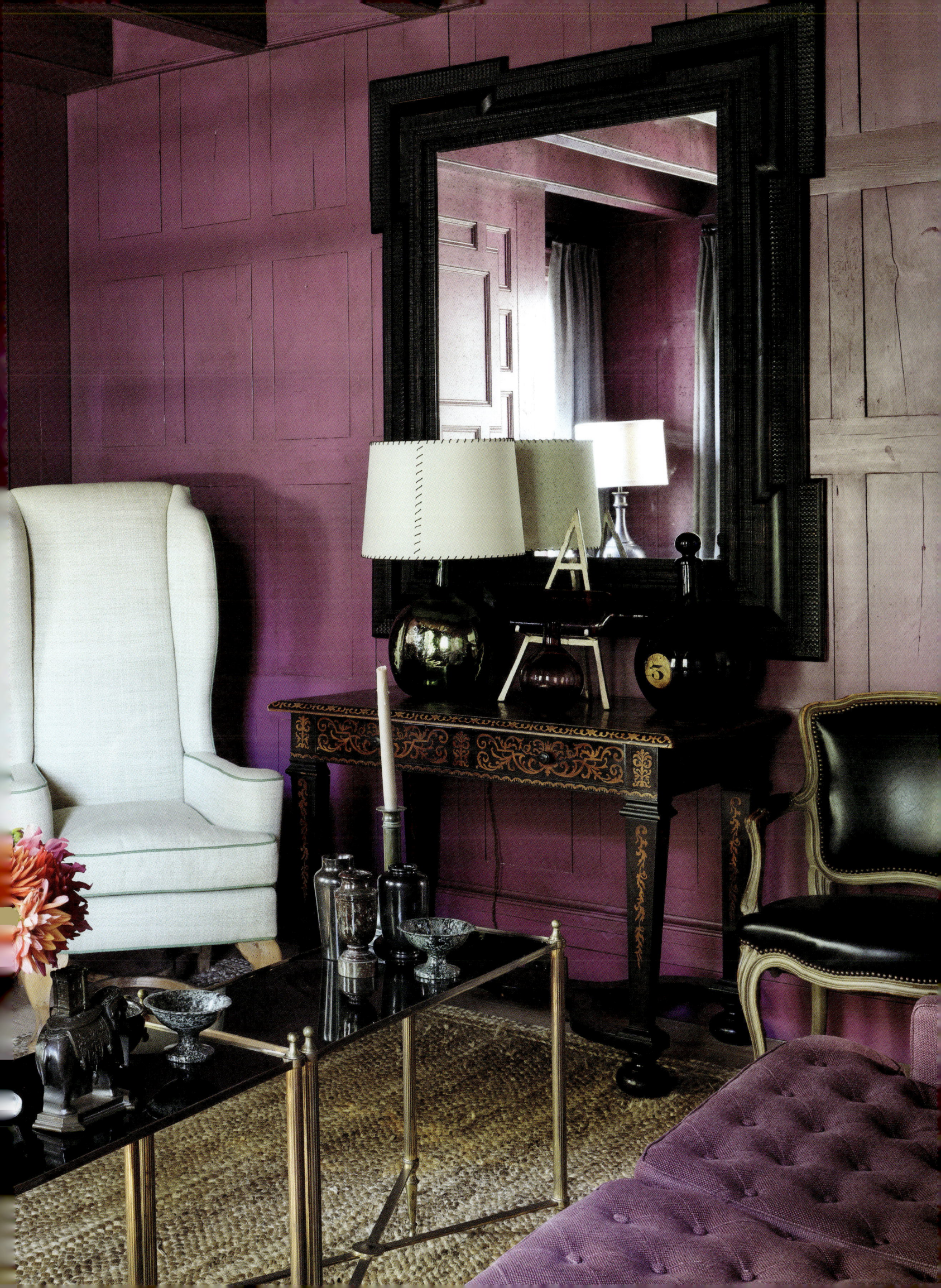

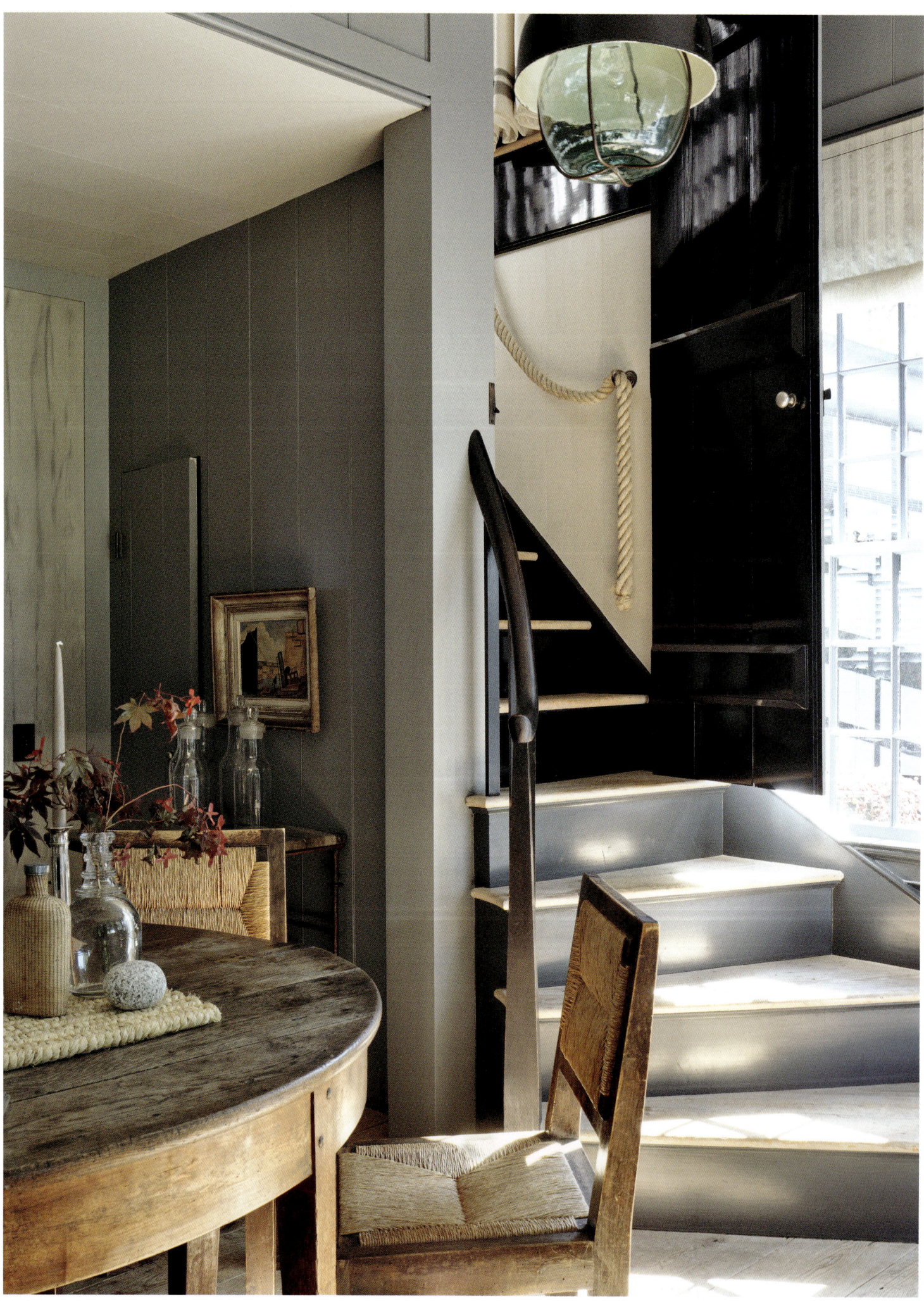

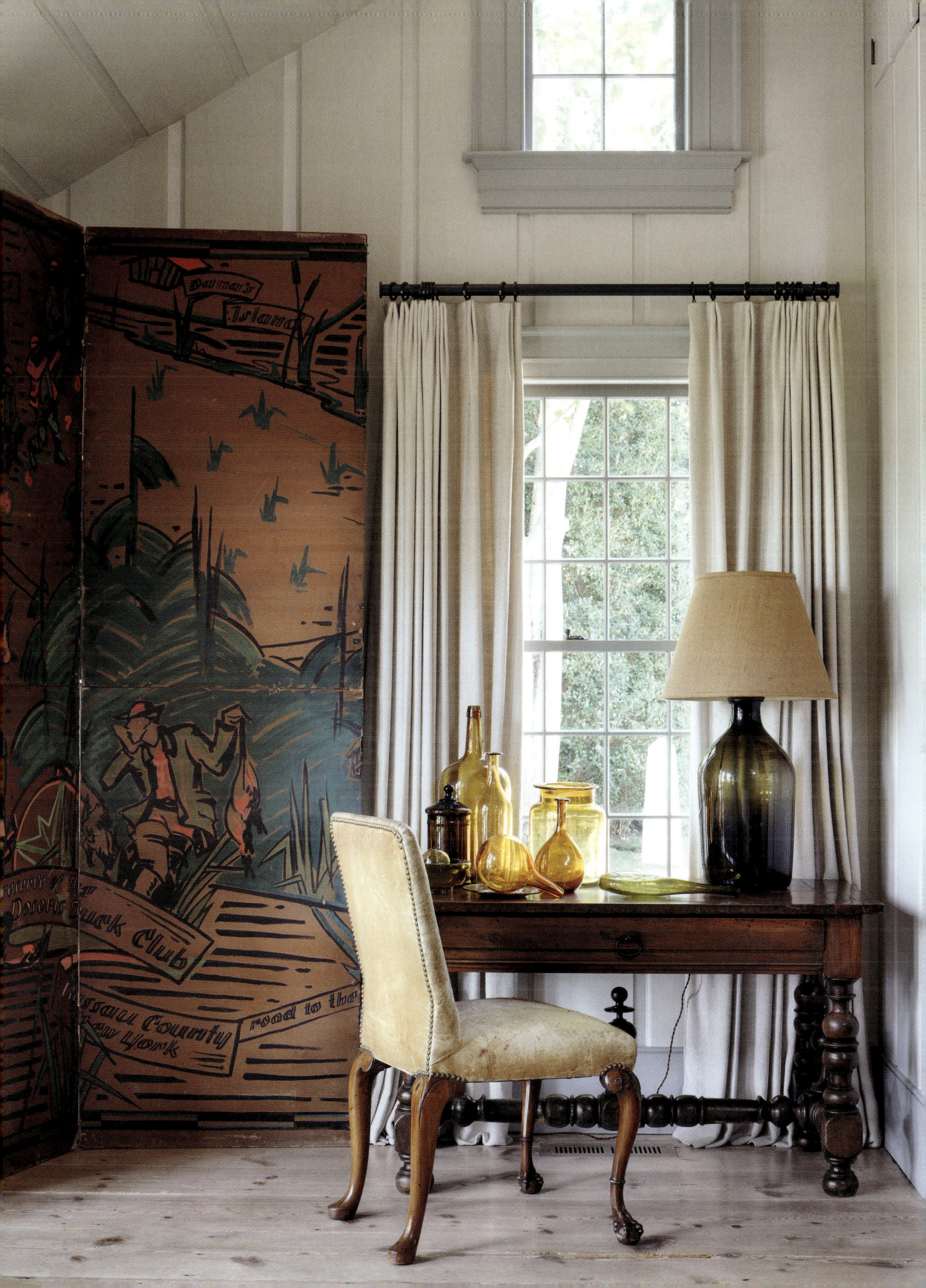

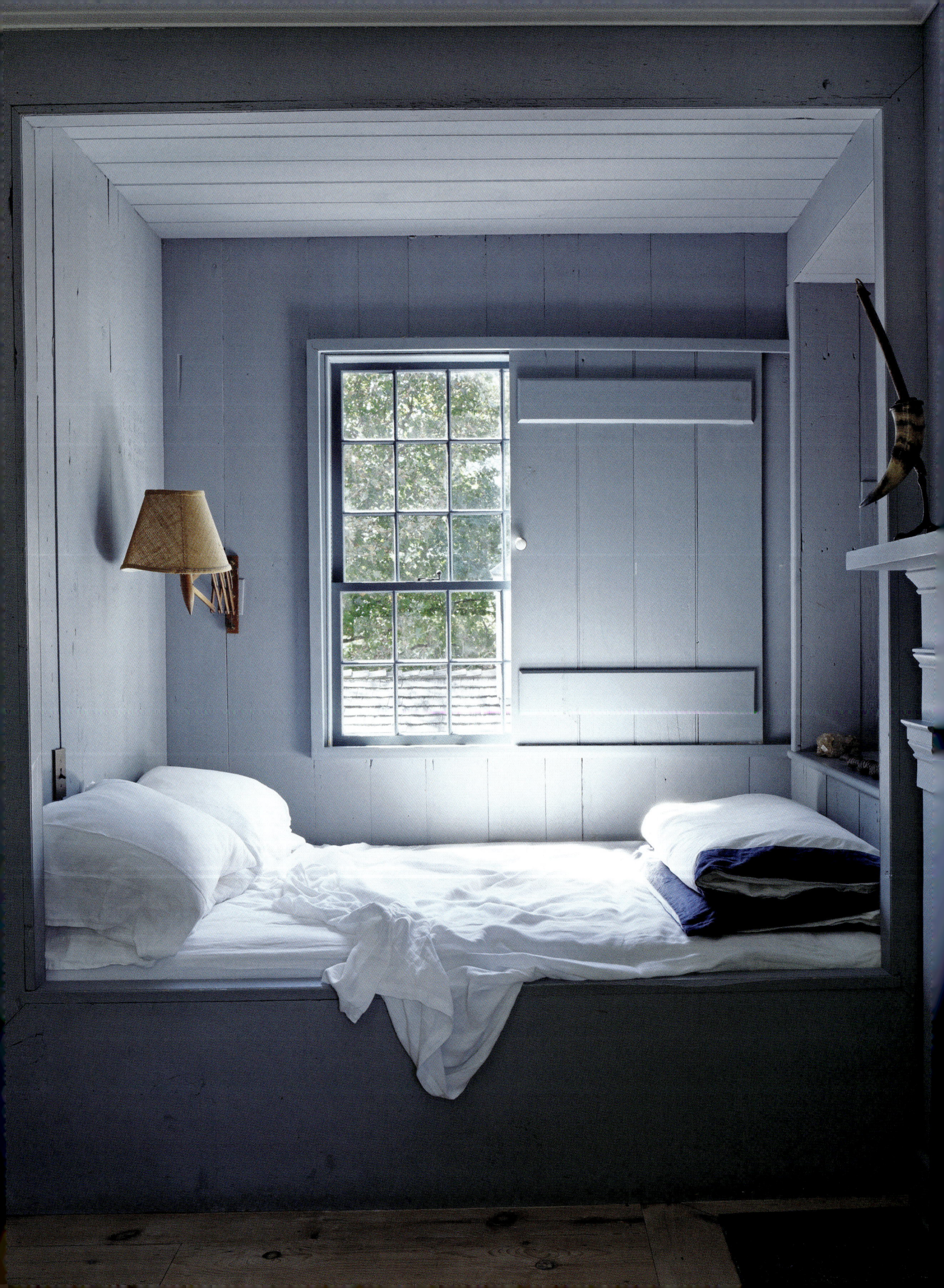

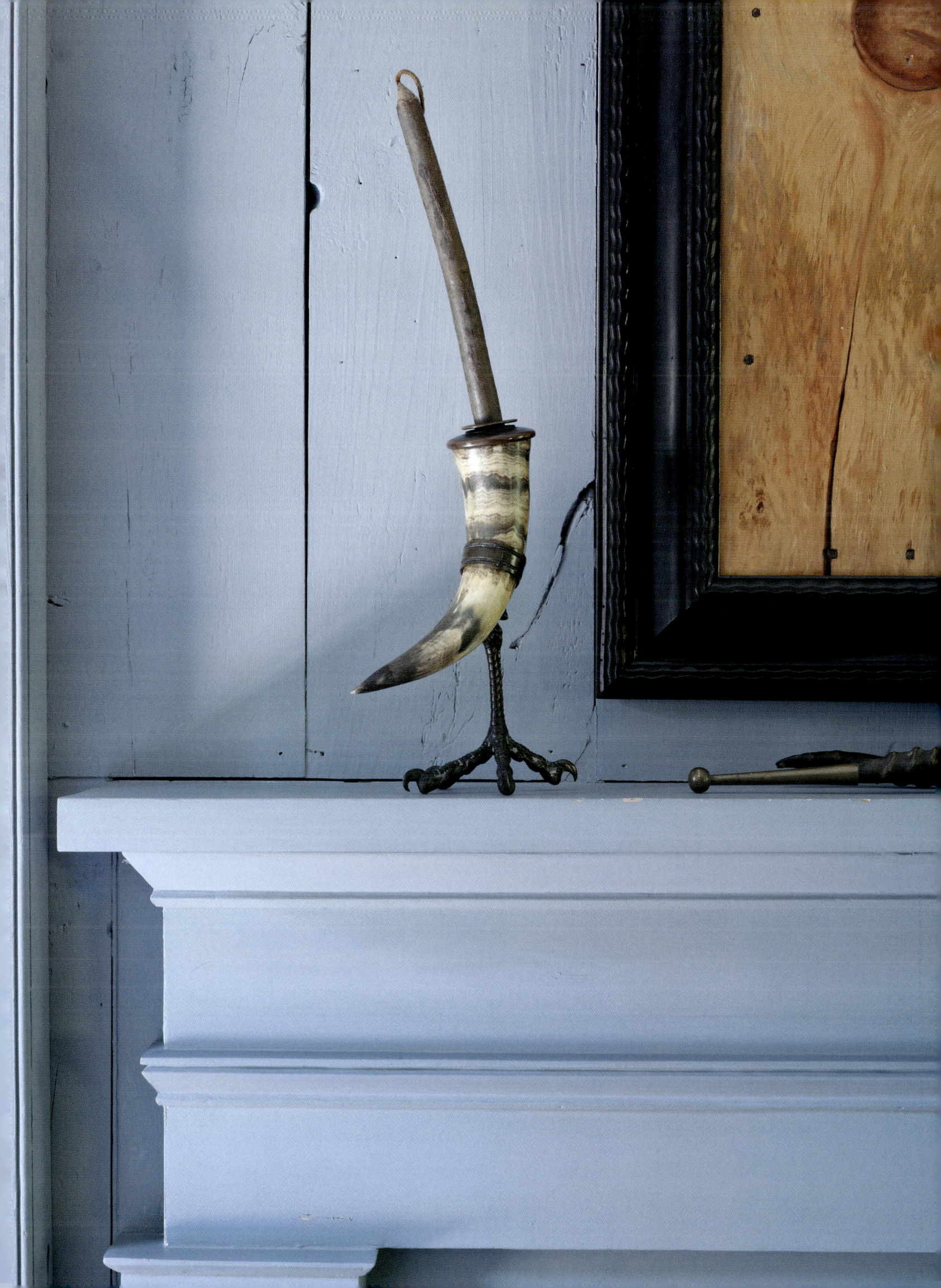

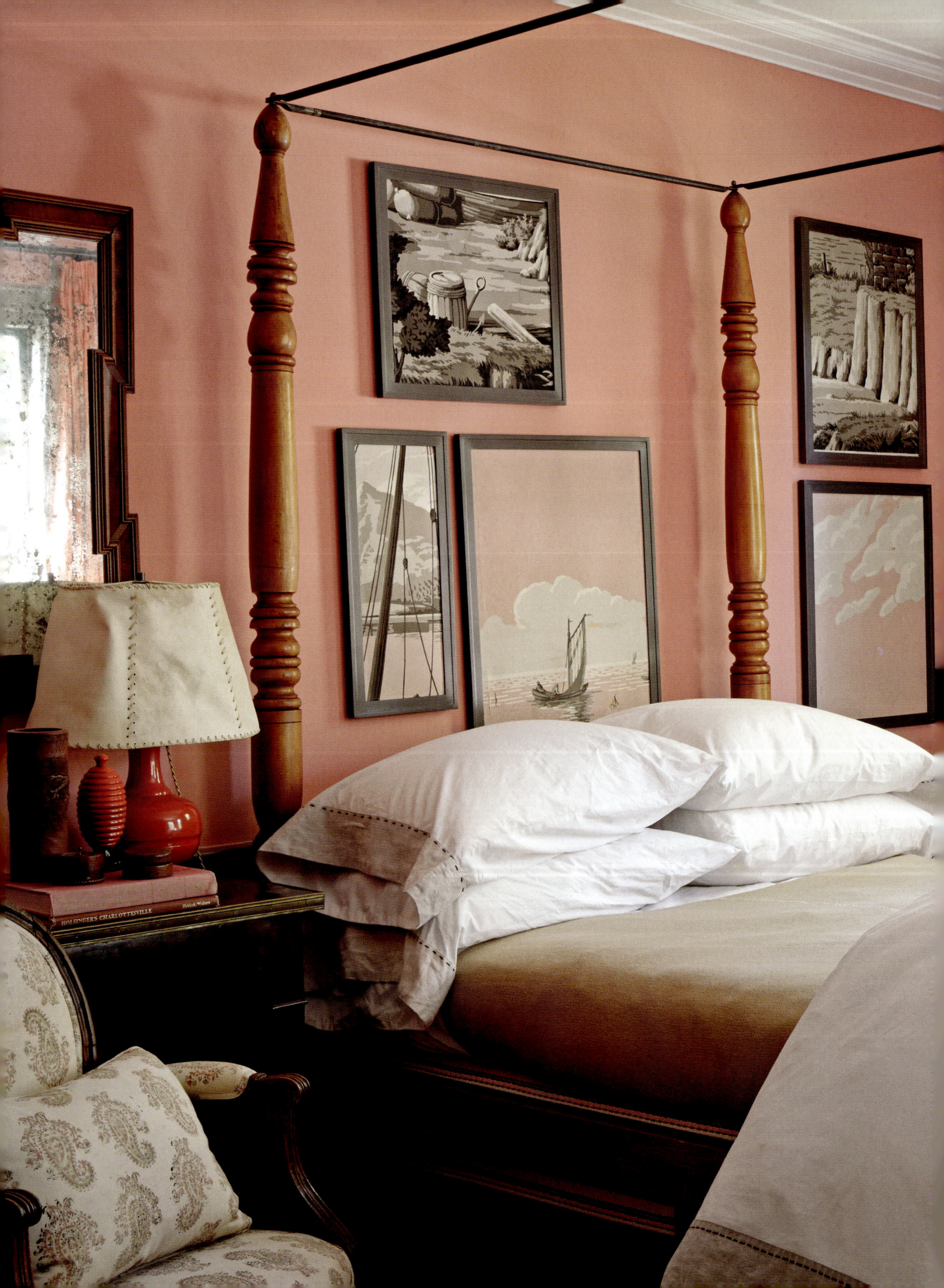

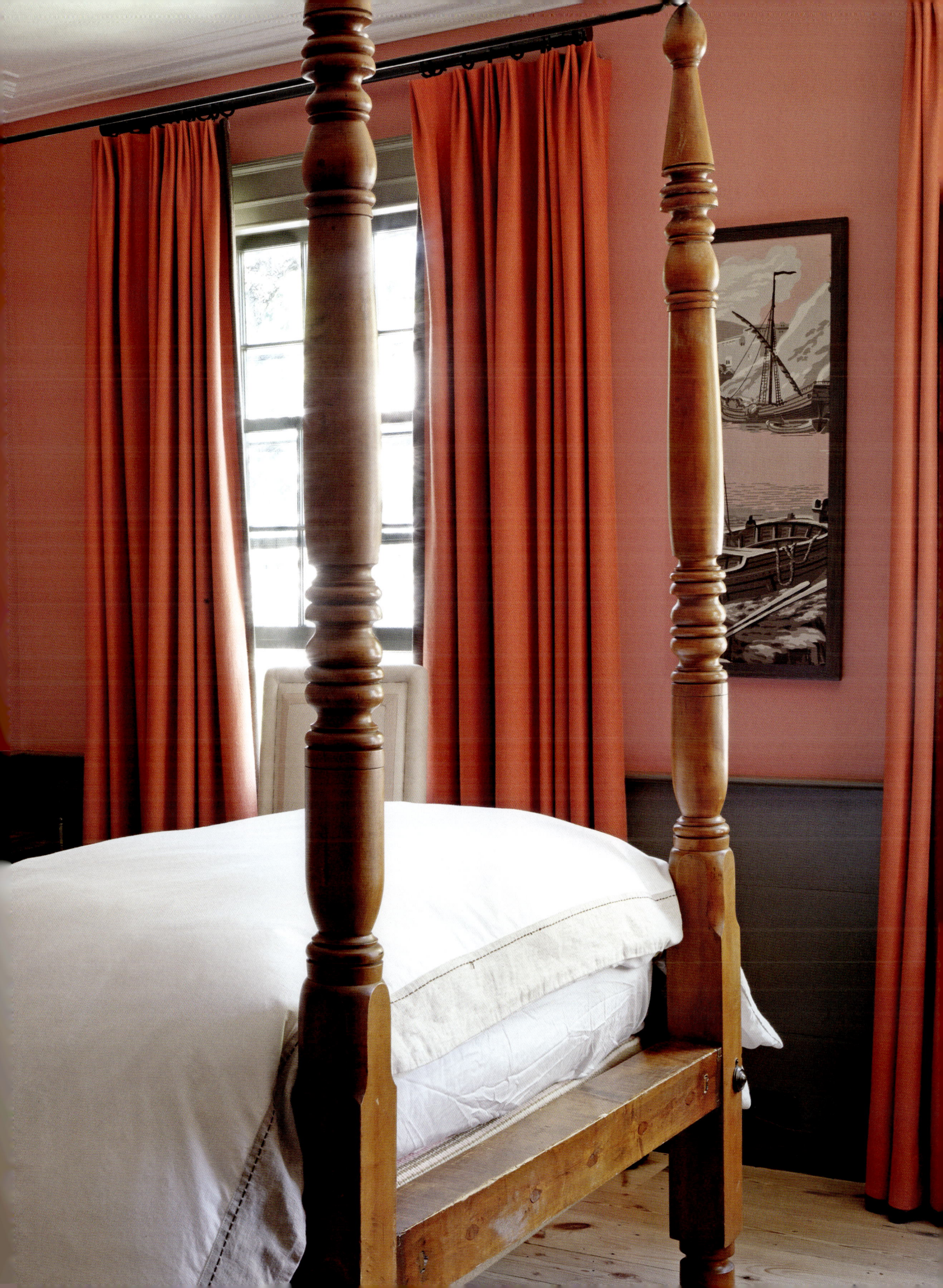

FOLLY DE GRANDEUR

MARIO BUATTA

"I am the original hoarder," the late interior decorator Mario Buatta would confess—an undisputed fact that earned him the sobriquet "King of Clutter." "I like to think of decorating a house the way an artist paints a picture: a dab at a time on the canvas, until the composition comes together. There is no such thing as decorating a room in six weeks or six months and saying it is finished, because no room is ever finished."

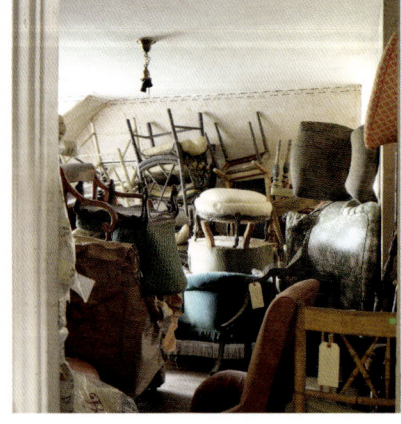

This approach to the undecorated-decorated look, which became an integral part of Buatta's signature style and imbued his projects with a sense of timelessness, would have been considered entirely appropriate when, in 1992, he purchased this eccentric and exuberant example of Gothic Revival architecture in Thompson Hill, Connecticut, over three hours' drive from his Manhattan apartment. Built in 1845 by William H. Mason, the prosperous owner of a local mill, the property had fallen on hard times and was in need of rescuing.

Buatta had great plans for the house. As he worked on ideas for mantelpieces and new moldings against a backdrop of peeling paint and wallpaper, true to form he was also buying furniture and objects at an extraordinary rate, and the house rapidly filled with antiques. "His collection was very important and emotional to Mario," affirms long-time friend, design historian Emily Evans Eerdmans. "He almost considered his collection to be his family."

Buatta's renovations—which included finials, pinnacles, and the addition of English-style chimney pots, adapting an exterior porch, and plans for a glass conservatory and a formal garden—stalled abruptly only four years into the work, after an apparently promising start. Disappointed by the slow progress, and struggling with illness and the harsh New England winters, Buatta visited Thompson Hill less and less frequently, and the property fell further into decline. The great English interior designer John Fowler, whom Buatta visited when in his early twenties and who had a great influence on his career, might well have summed up the scenario as "an undecorated look of romantic despair."

Mario Buatta died in October 2018. In January 2020 his collection of antiques went under the hammer at Sotheby's in New York and this eccentric house was put on the market once again. Local residents await the next chapter in its extraordinary history.

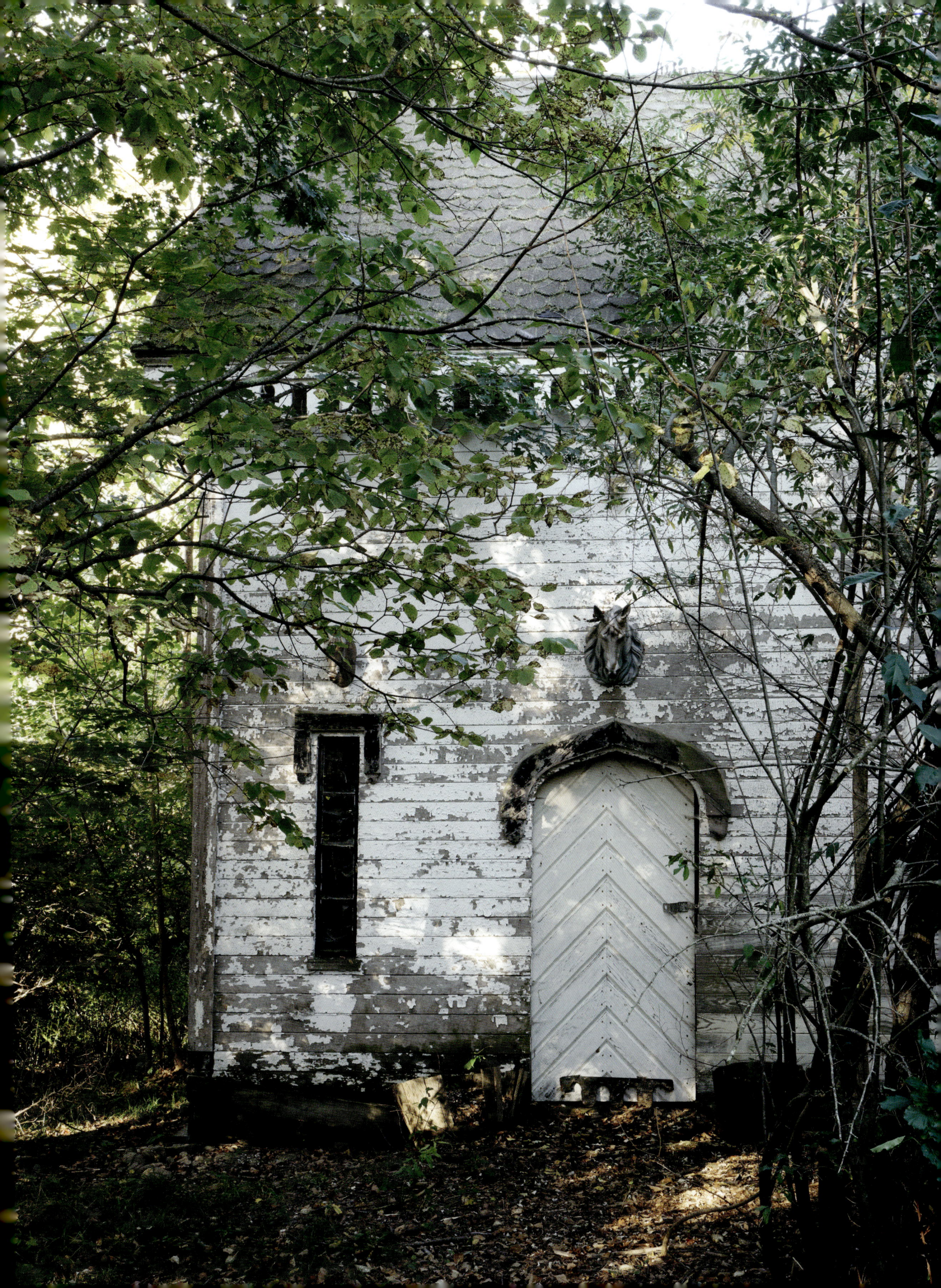

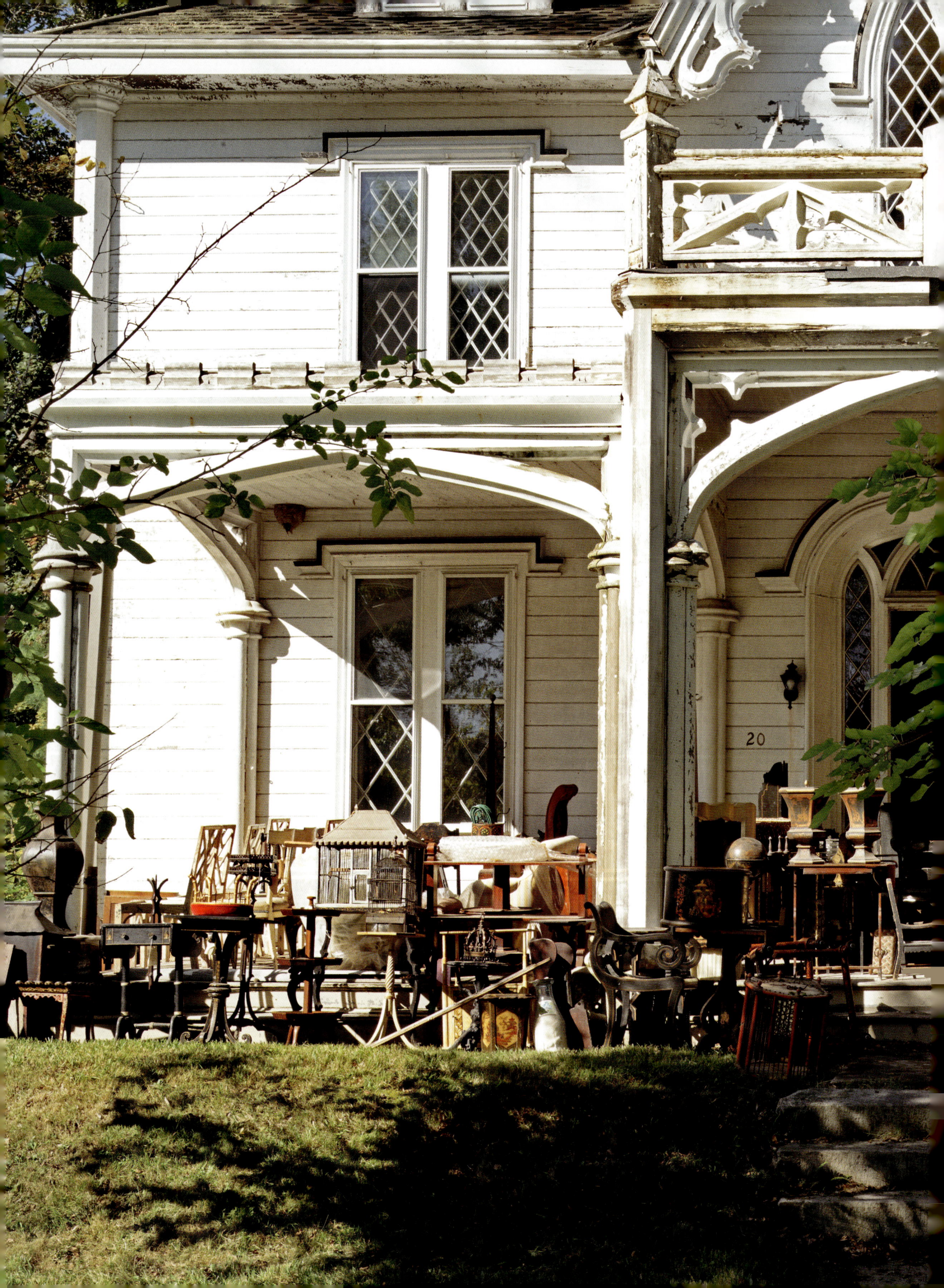

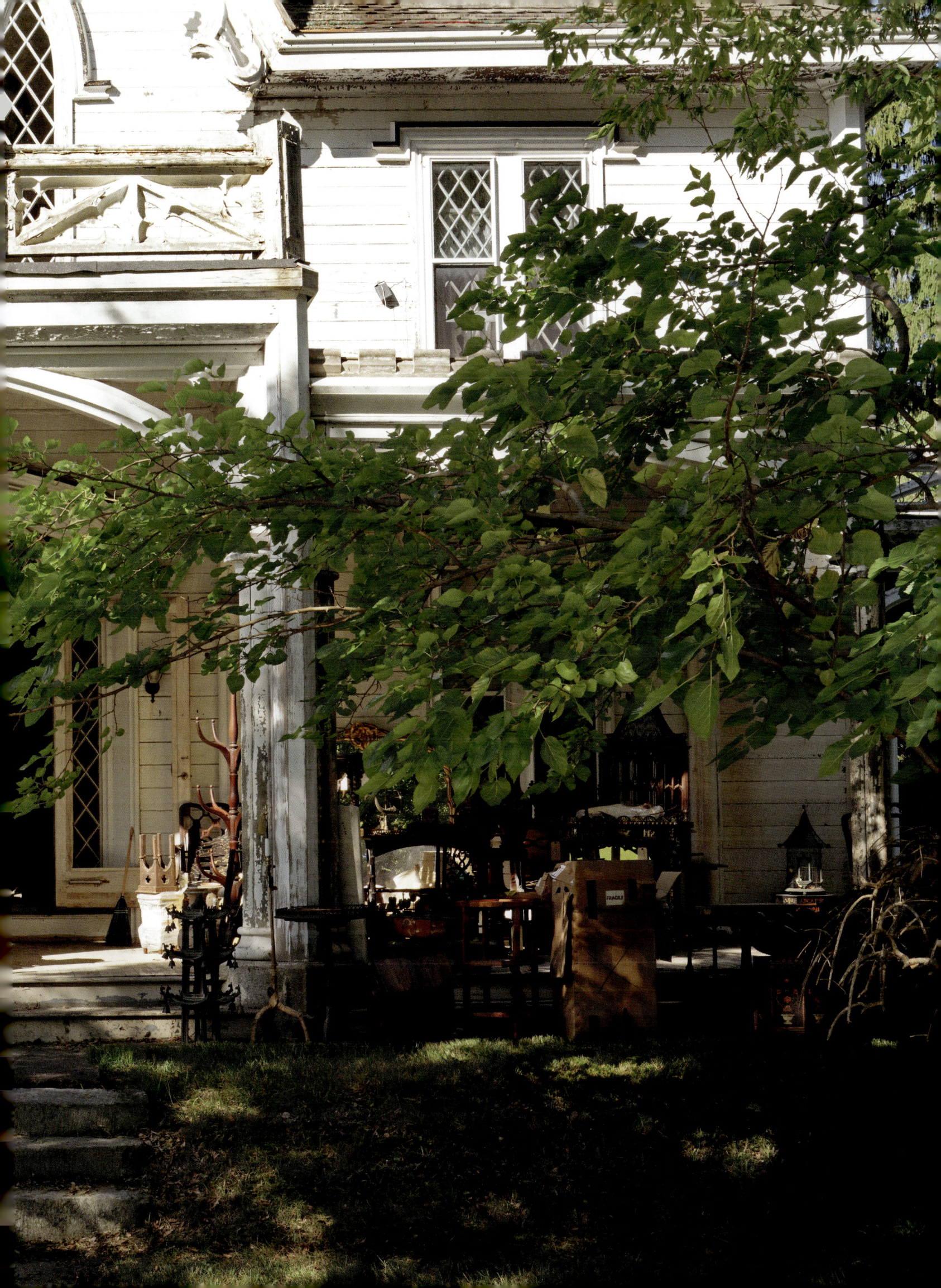

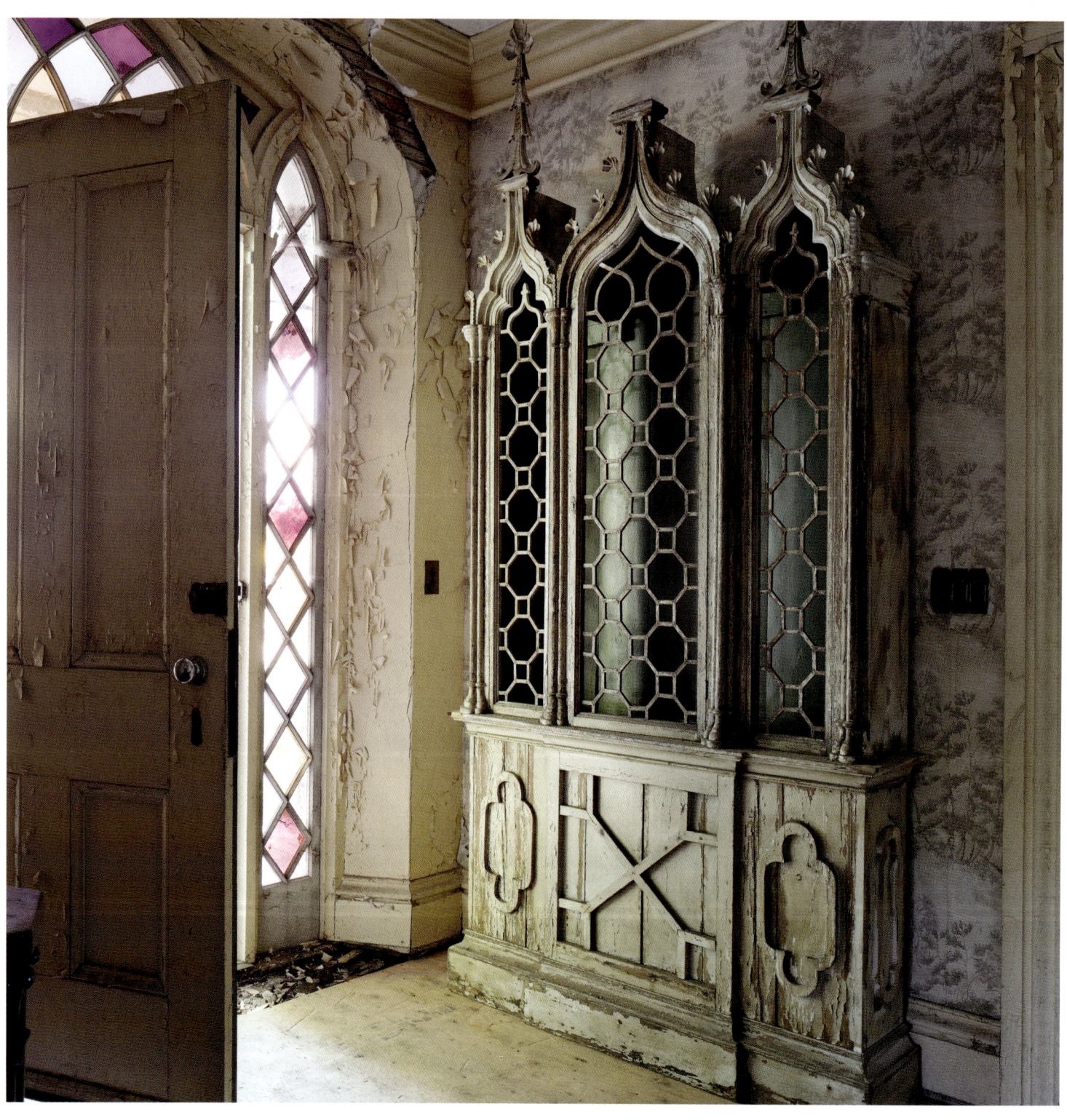

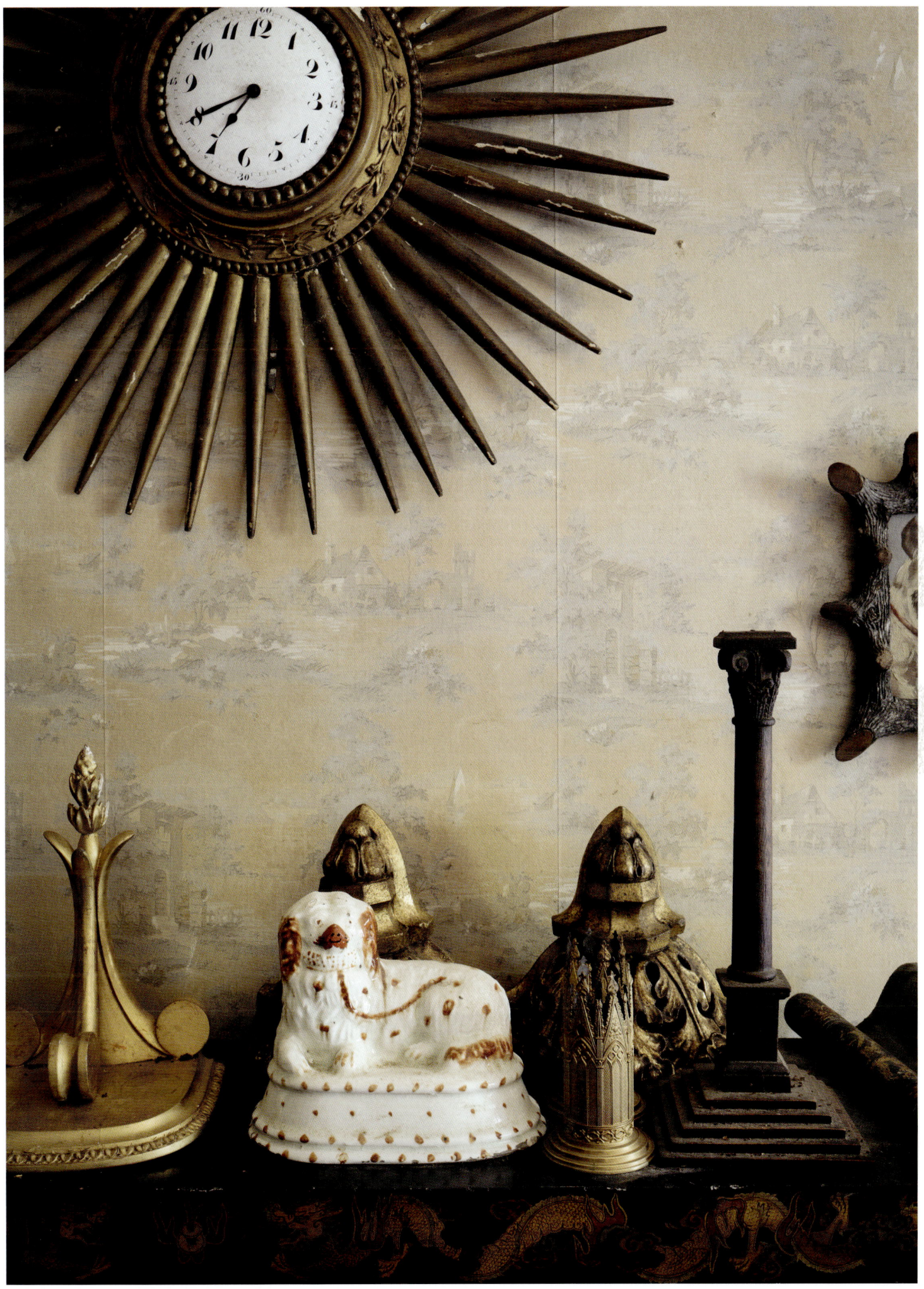

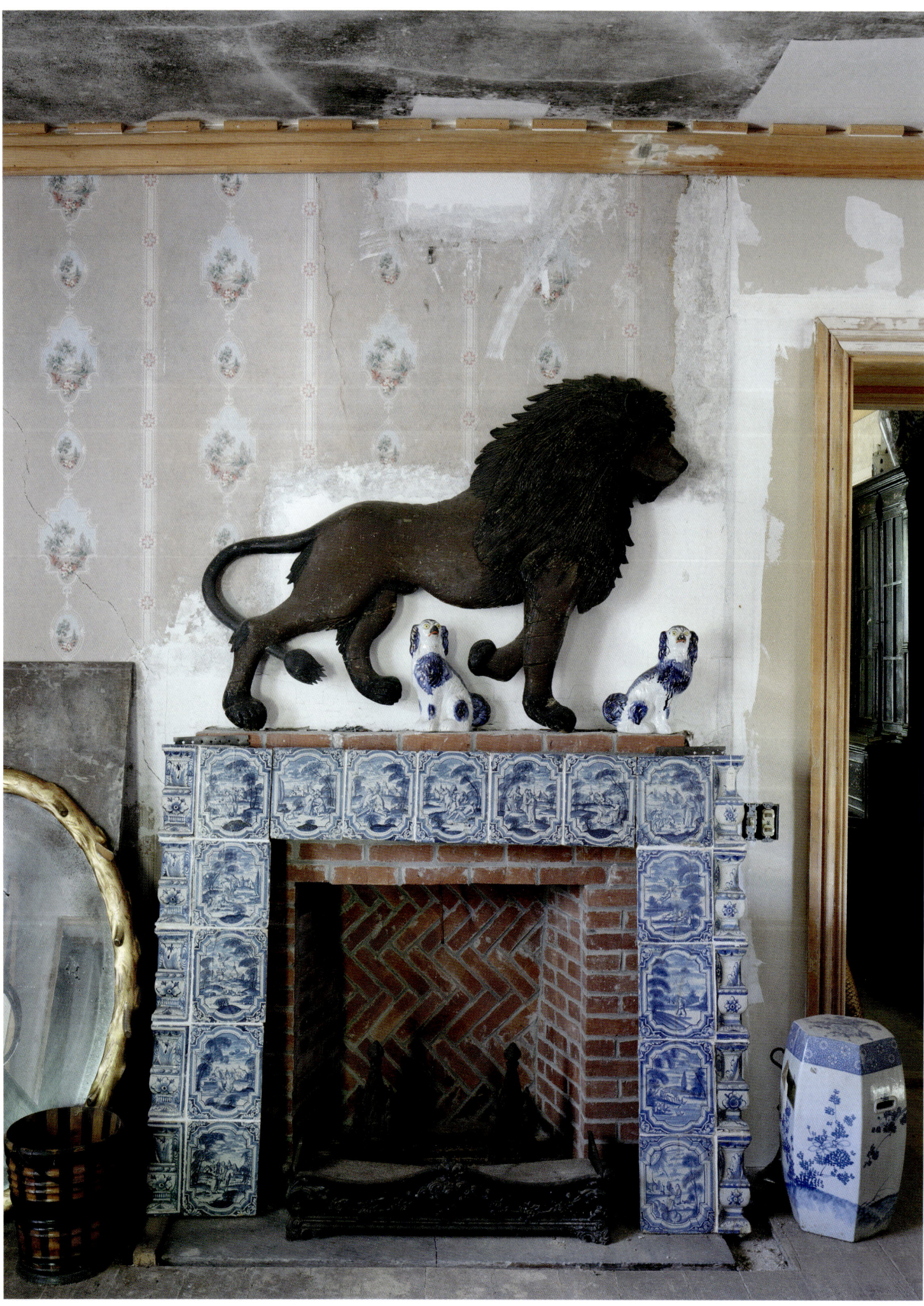

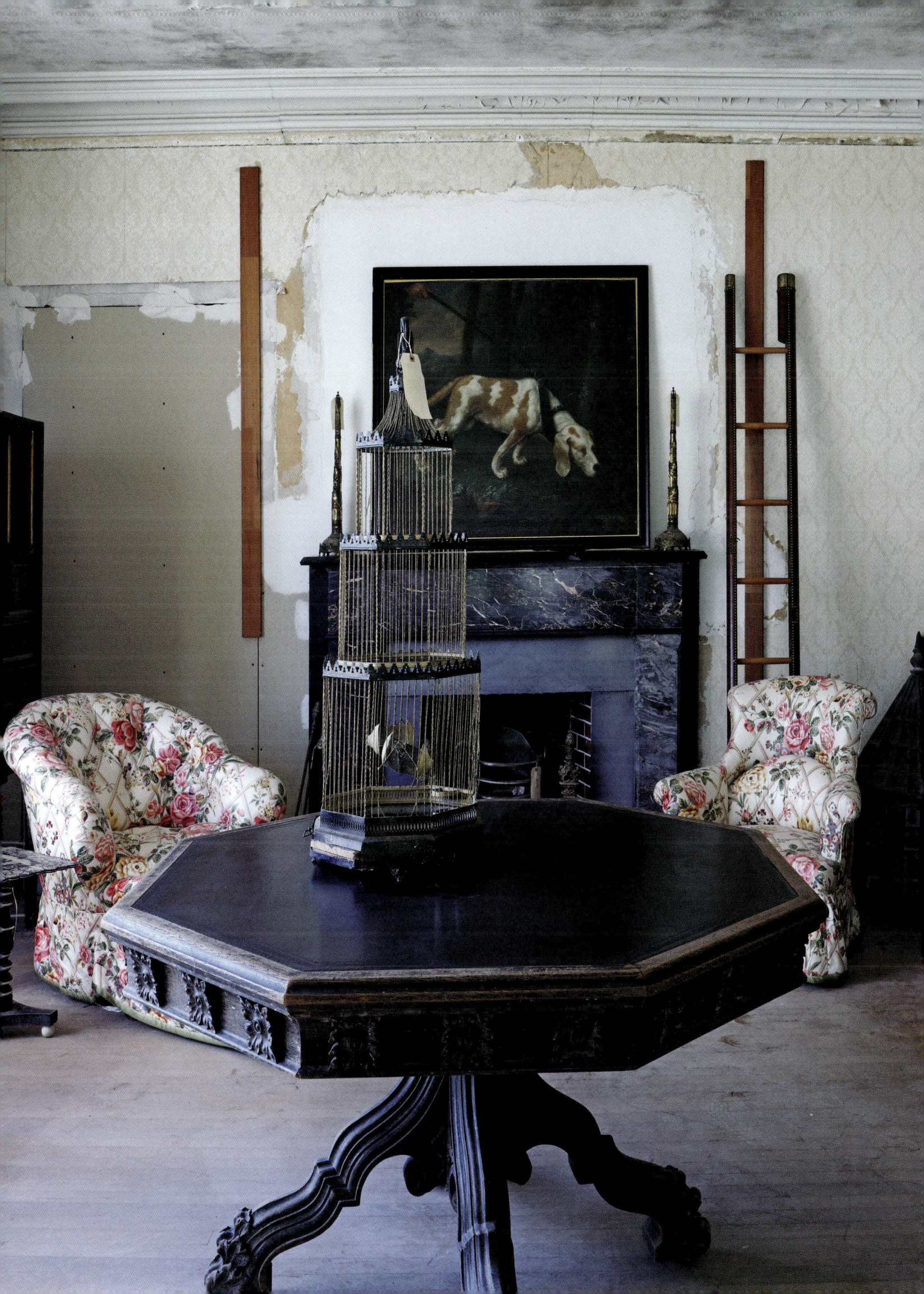

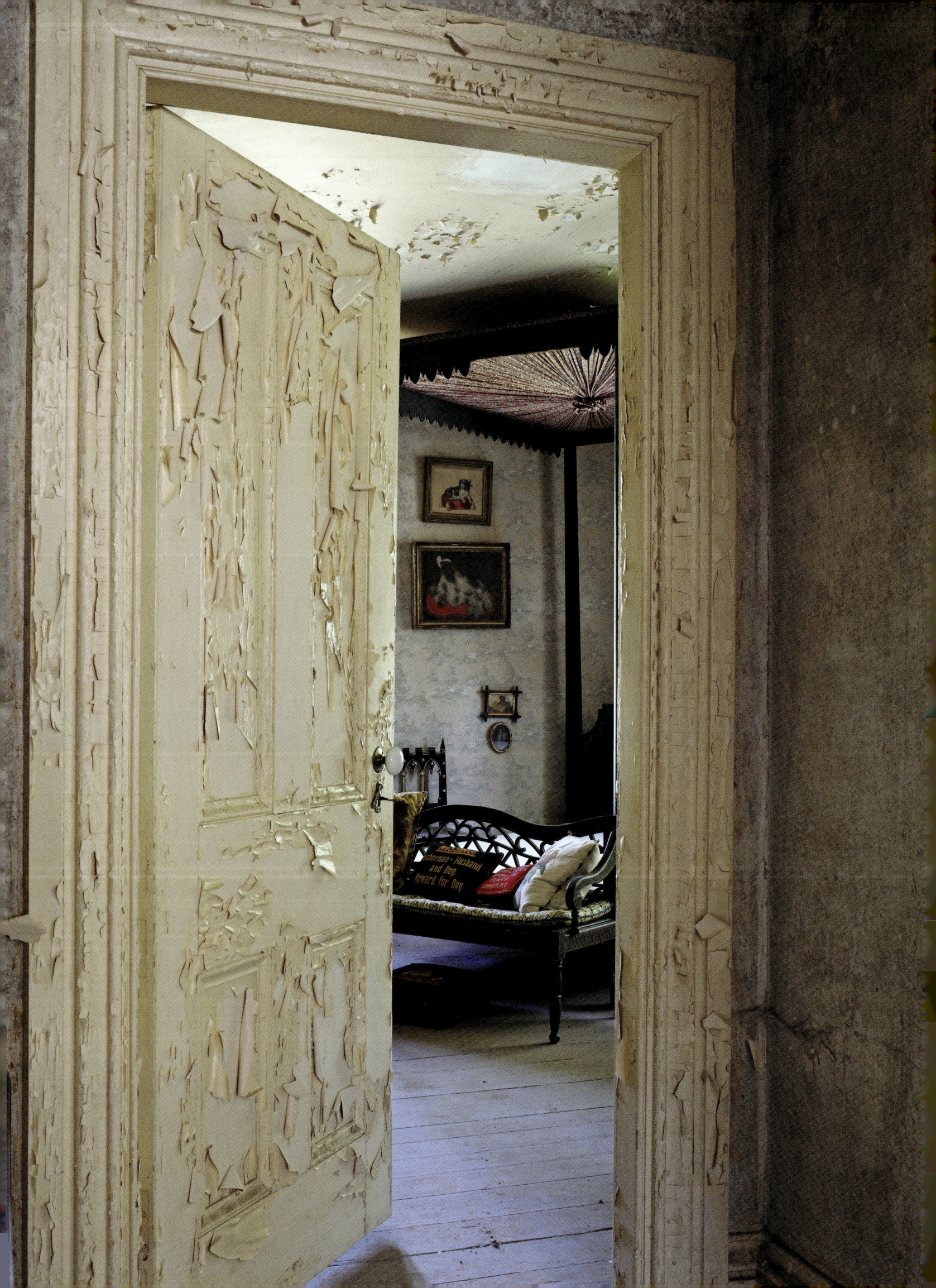

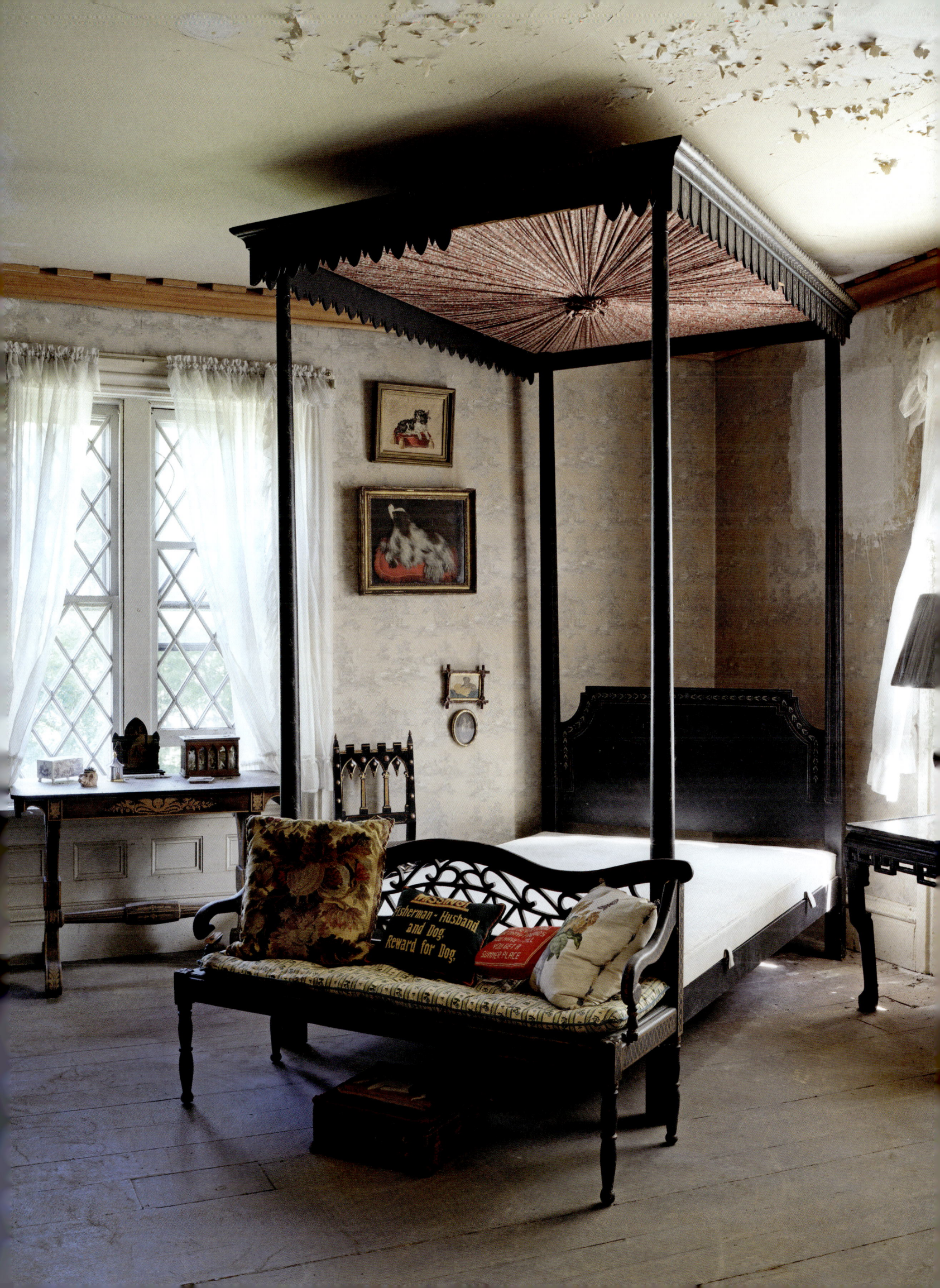

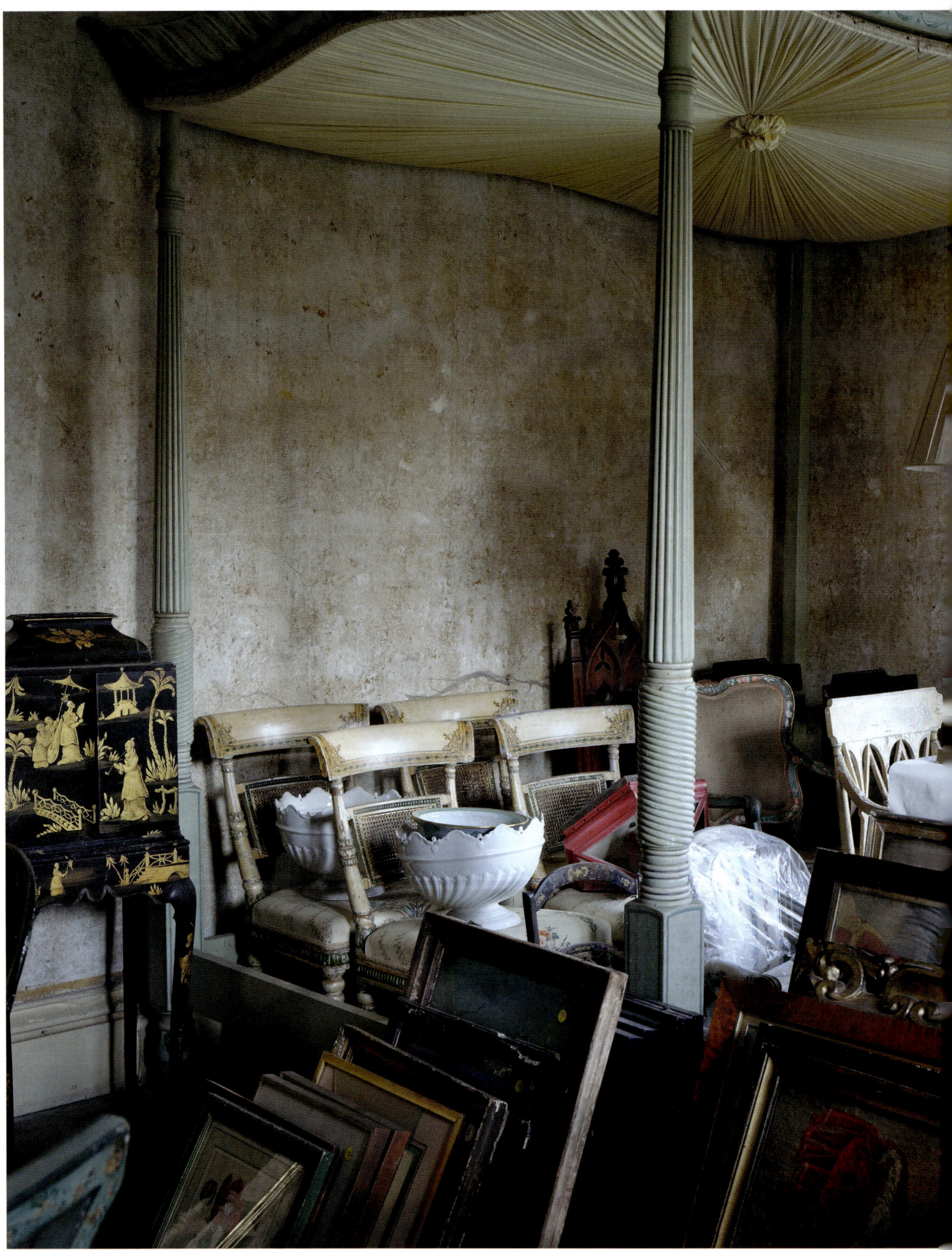

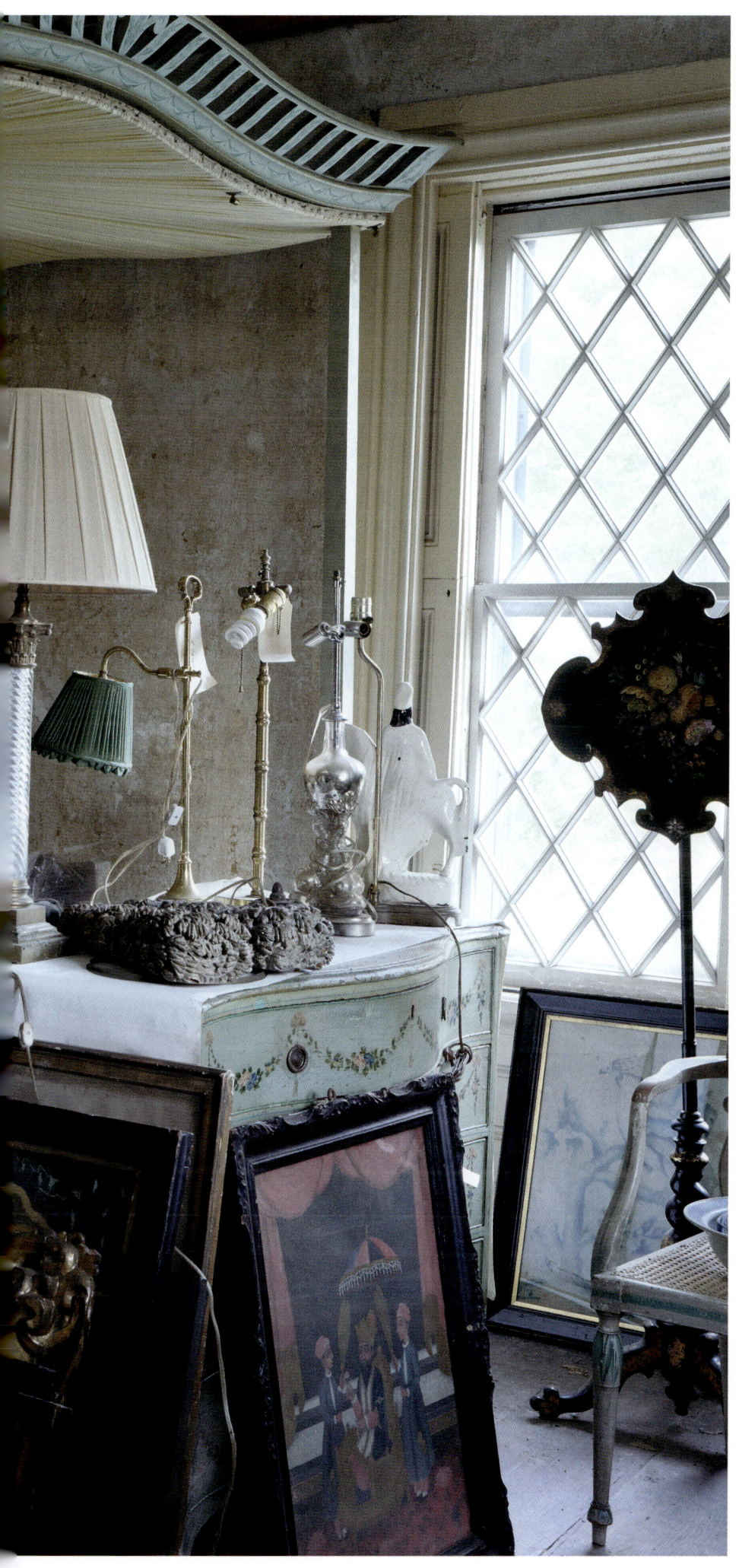

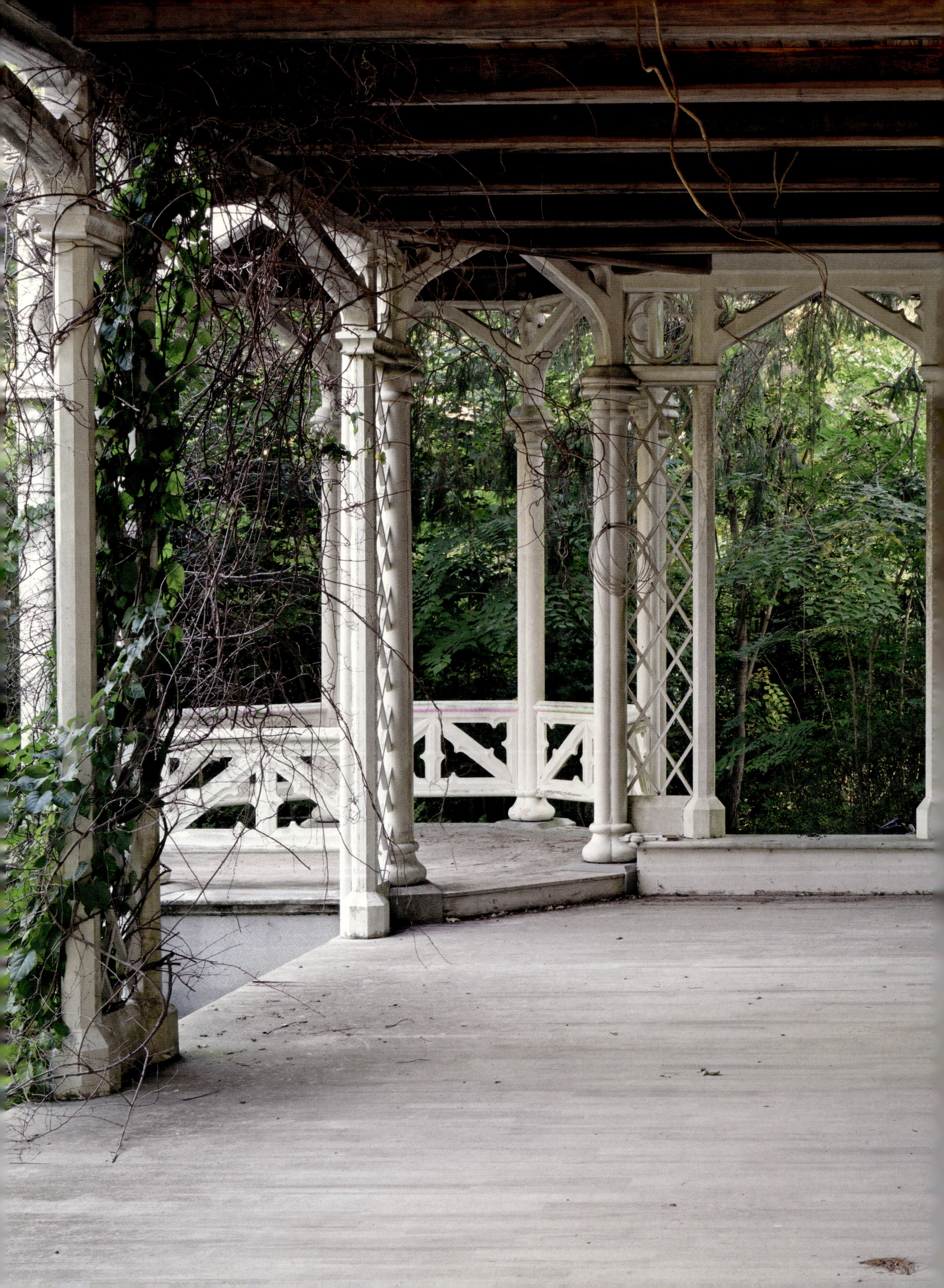

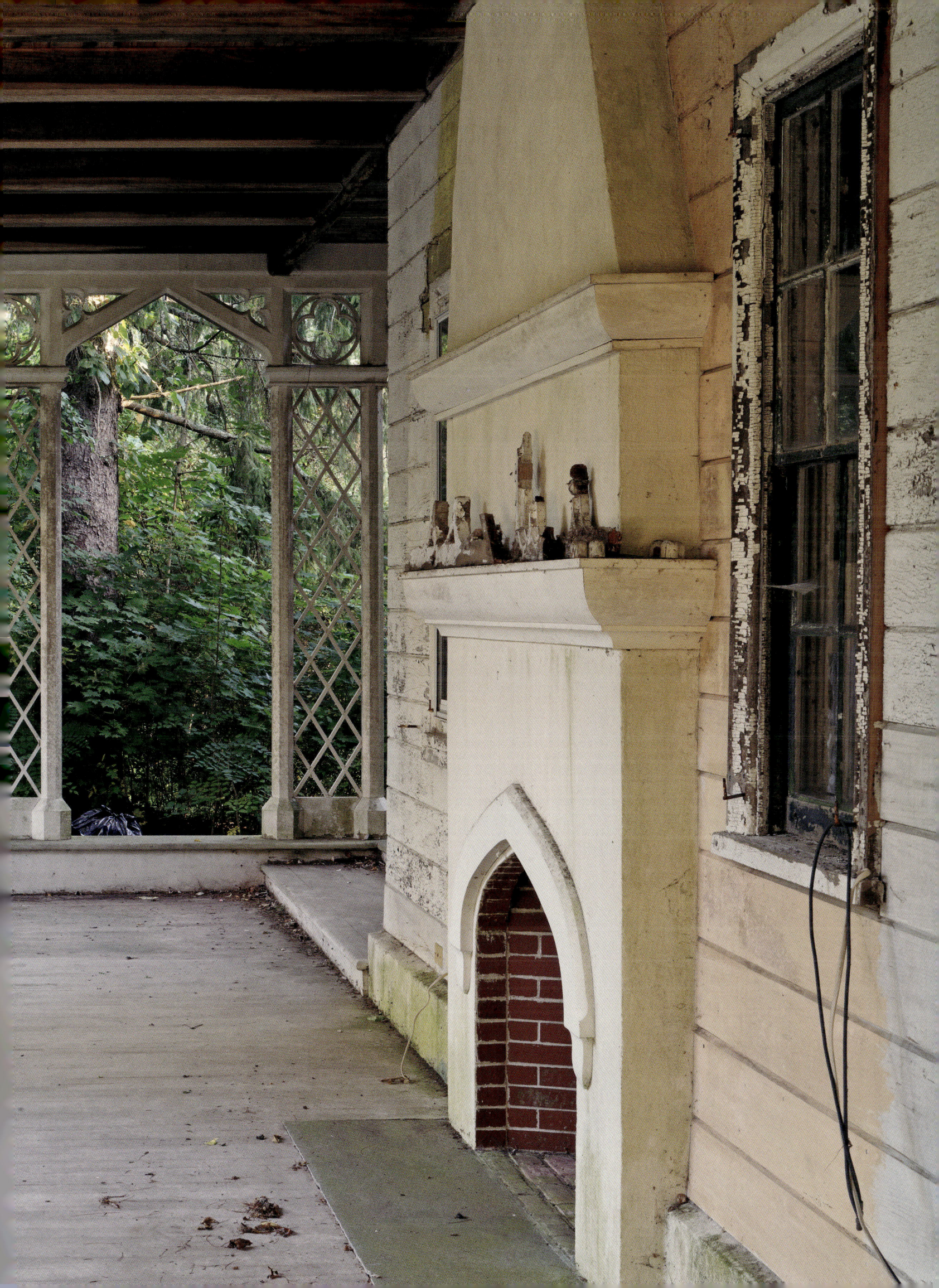

COASTAL RETREAT

DIANA PICASSO

Perched on the dunes overlooking Napeague Bay on the edge of Montauk in Long Island, this building was originally a 1950s kit house, which would have arrived on a flatbed and been assembled on site. Essentially a surfer's shack, it was designed to be used during the summer months and not "wintered." So when I took it on some 10 years ago, it was in a sad state of disrepair, a victim of the weather and general neglect.

At that time, I was in search of the peace of mind that only living by the ocean could bring, and, as an art historian, I knew it would be the perfect place to write. I had been looking for a cozy beach house—a place where wet, sandy feet did not impact; somewhere to relax. A mere stone's throw from the beach, I enjoyed long walks, paddleboarding, kayaking, and cycling, but especially beachcombing. The shells of The Hamptons vary incredibly in shape and color, and I was a passionate collector, those of a heart shape in particular.

This stretch of the beach overlooking the bay is private. My beach house was so peaceful, and the immersion with nature there quite overwhelming. Its location was the ideal orientation for a salutation to the sun. I loved being close to the fish farm and the Devon Yacht Club, and had many friends—artists, art collectors, art dealers.

Original properties here are few and far between, so the location of the beach house was relatively isolated. The nearby seaside village of Amagansett imposes strict building regulations for properties on the beach, and I would never have been granted planning permission to build something new on this site. There was nothing left of the old shack except its original footprint. Rebuilt from the inside out, it is entirely new. I kept the structure and modernized it: a perfect marriage between a Scandinavian home and a Japanese teahouse.

The wood on the walls of the living area is cedar rubbed with whitewash. The original brick fireplace against one wall was replaced with a suspended cast-iron wood burner, positioned in a corner of the room so as not to obstruct the view of the shoreline. Upstairs, the new shack was transformed into an open plan—yet intimate—space, while sliding doors opened onto a raised deck with a sheltered seating area, where I would sit and contemplate the sunrise or the sunset, according to my mood.

For me, this place was all about the beach—now a fond memory of a past chapter in my life.

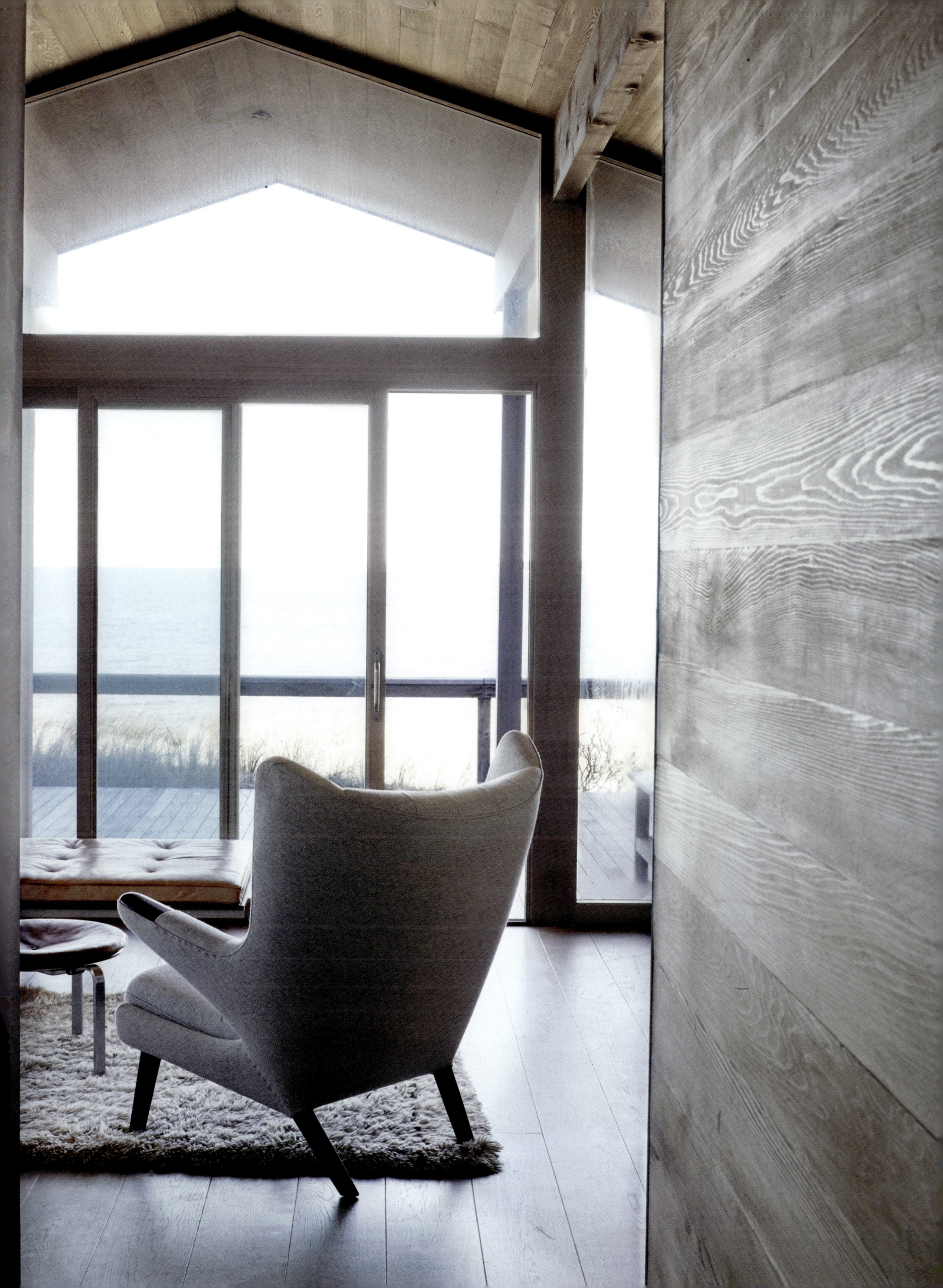

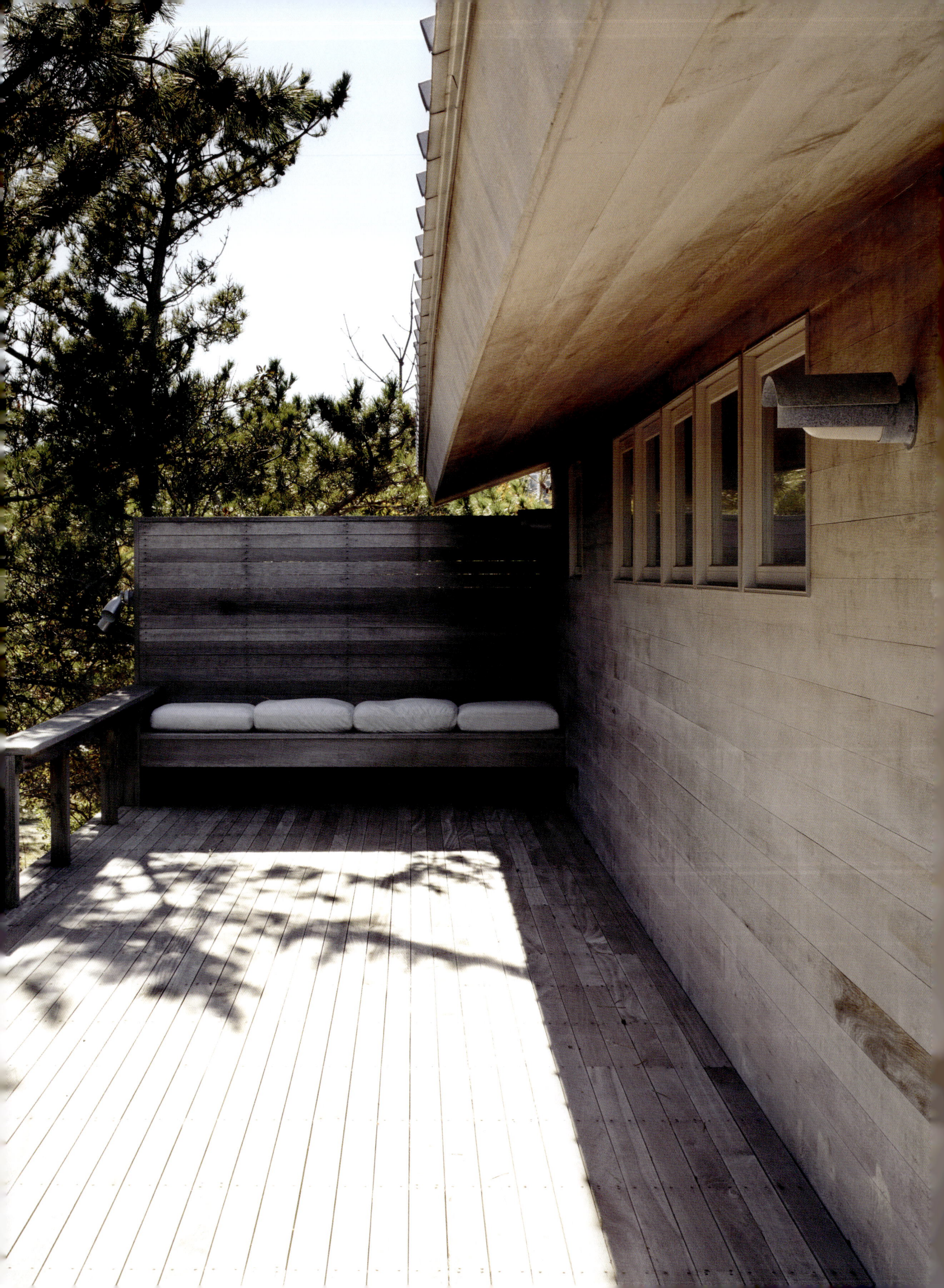

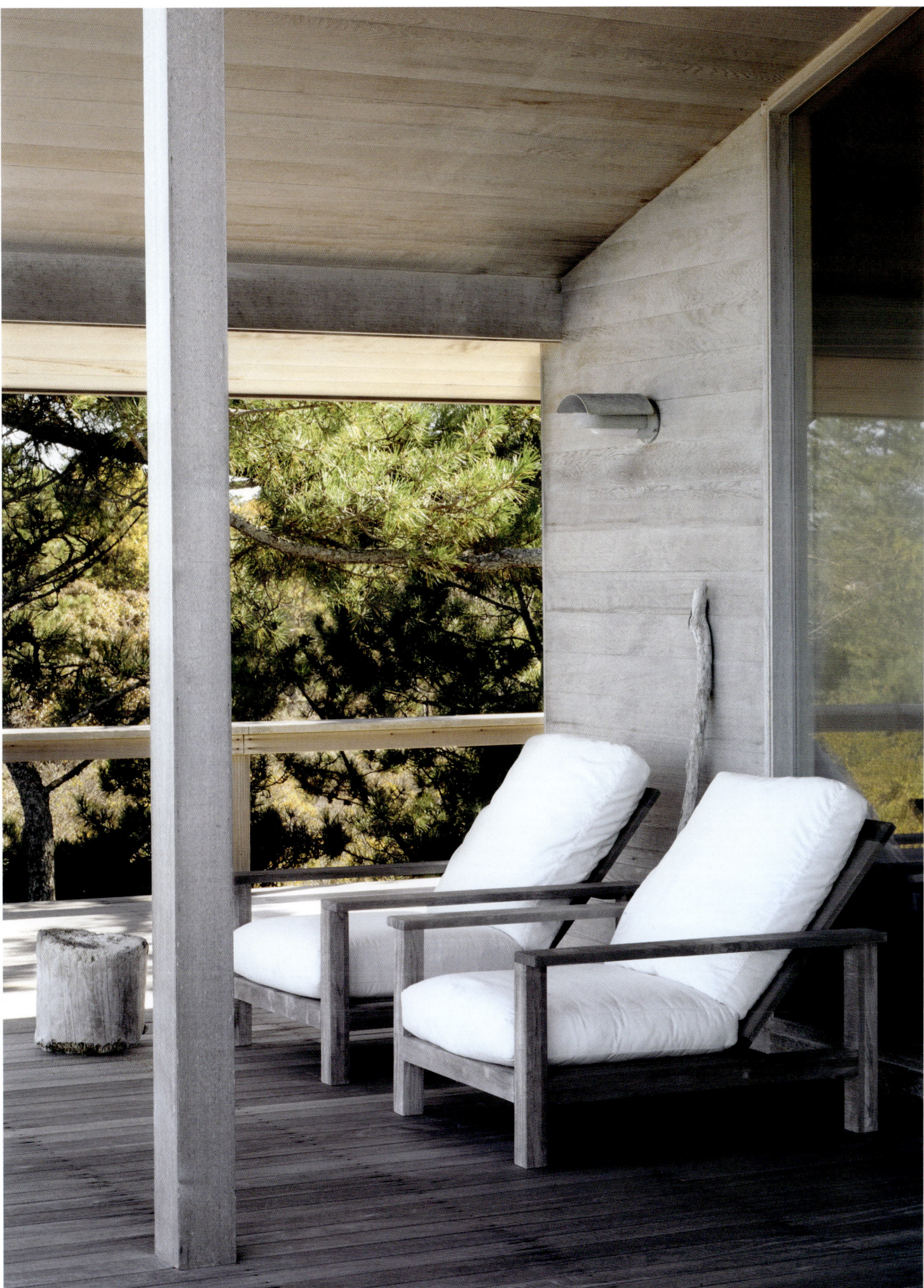

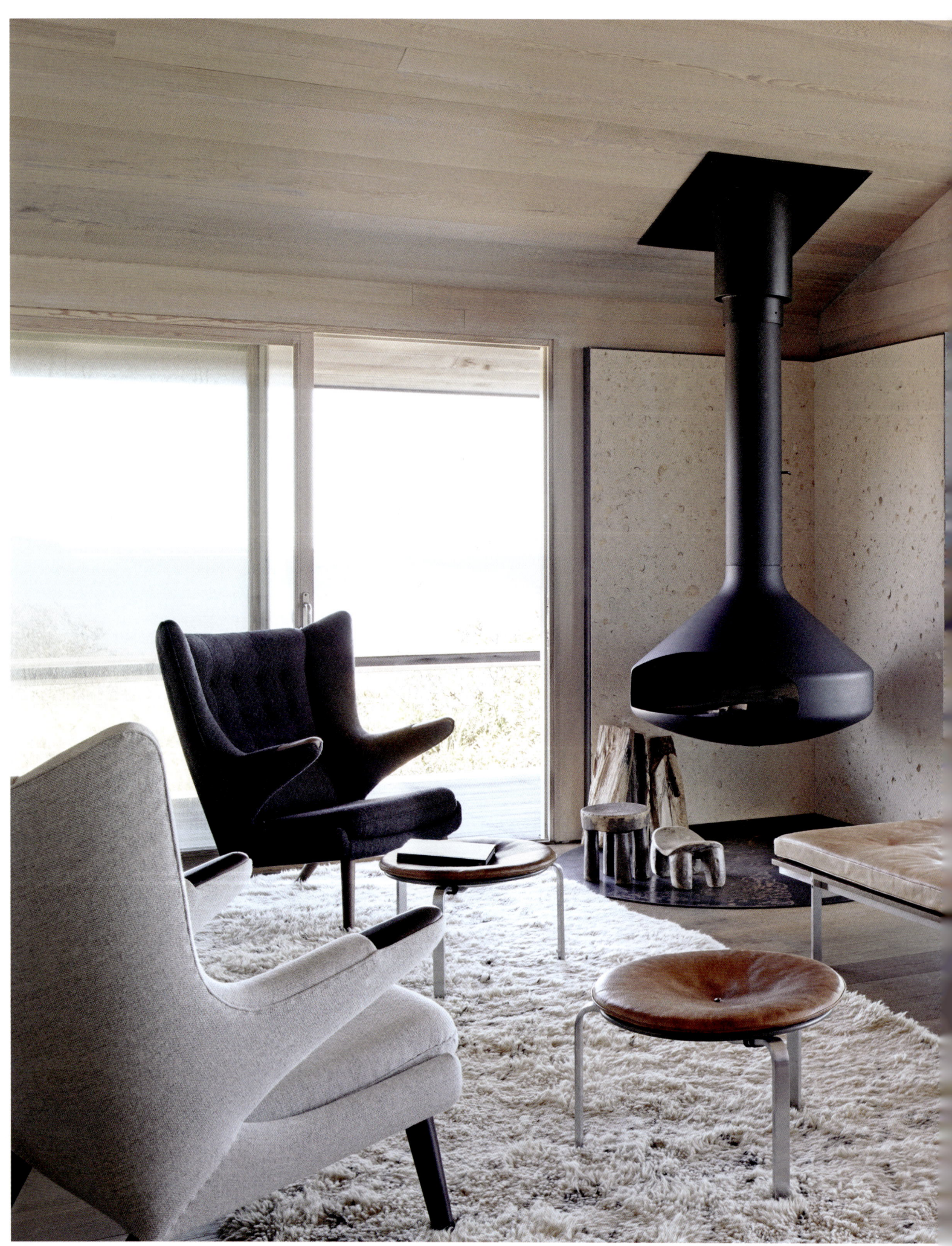

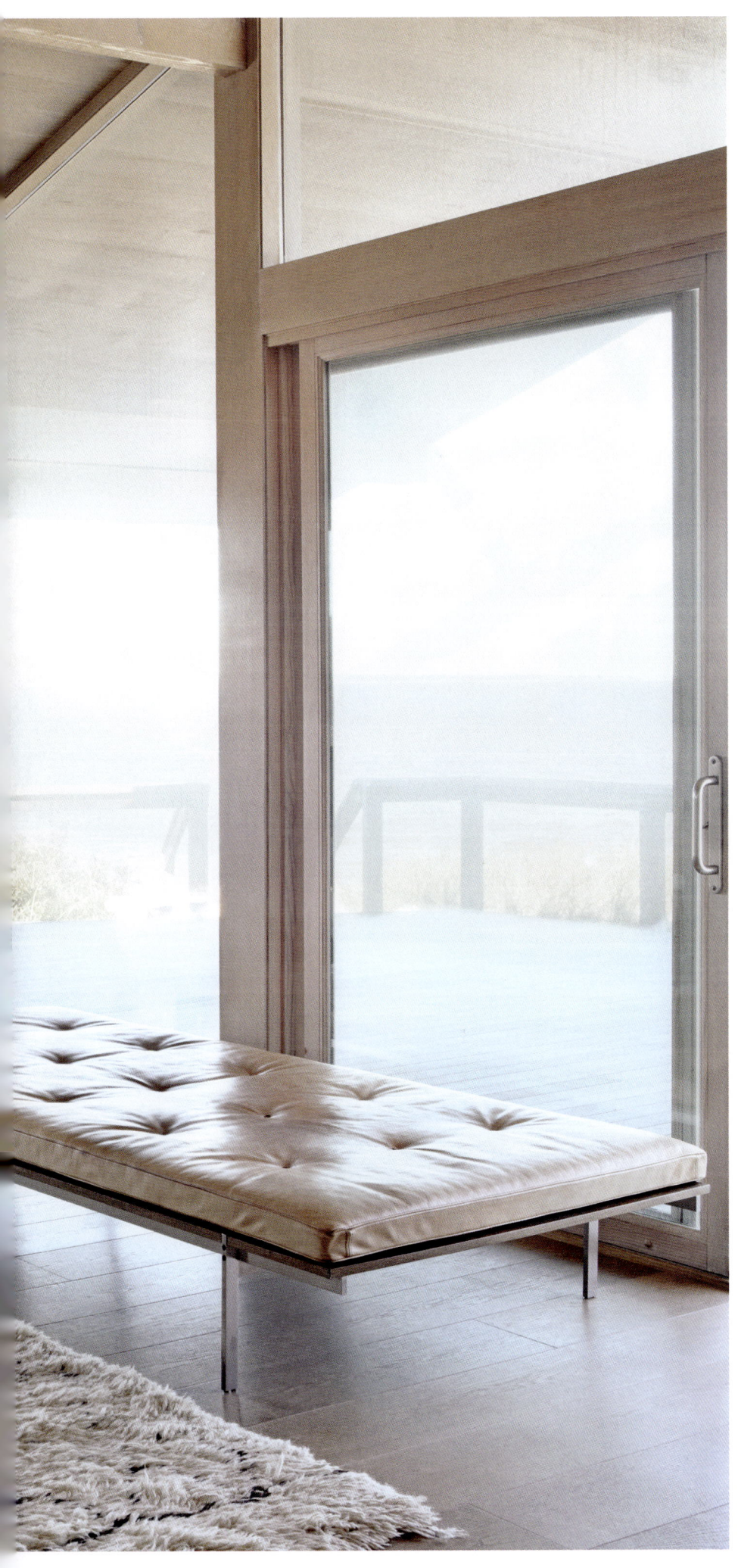

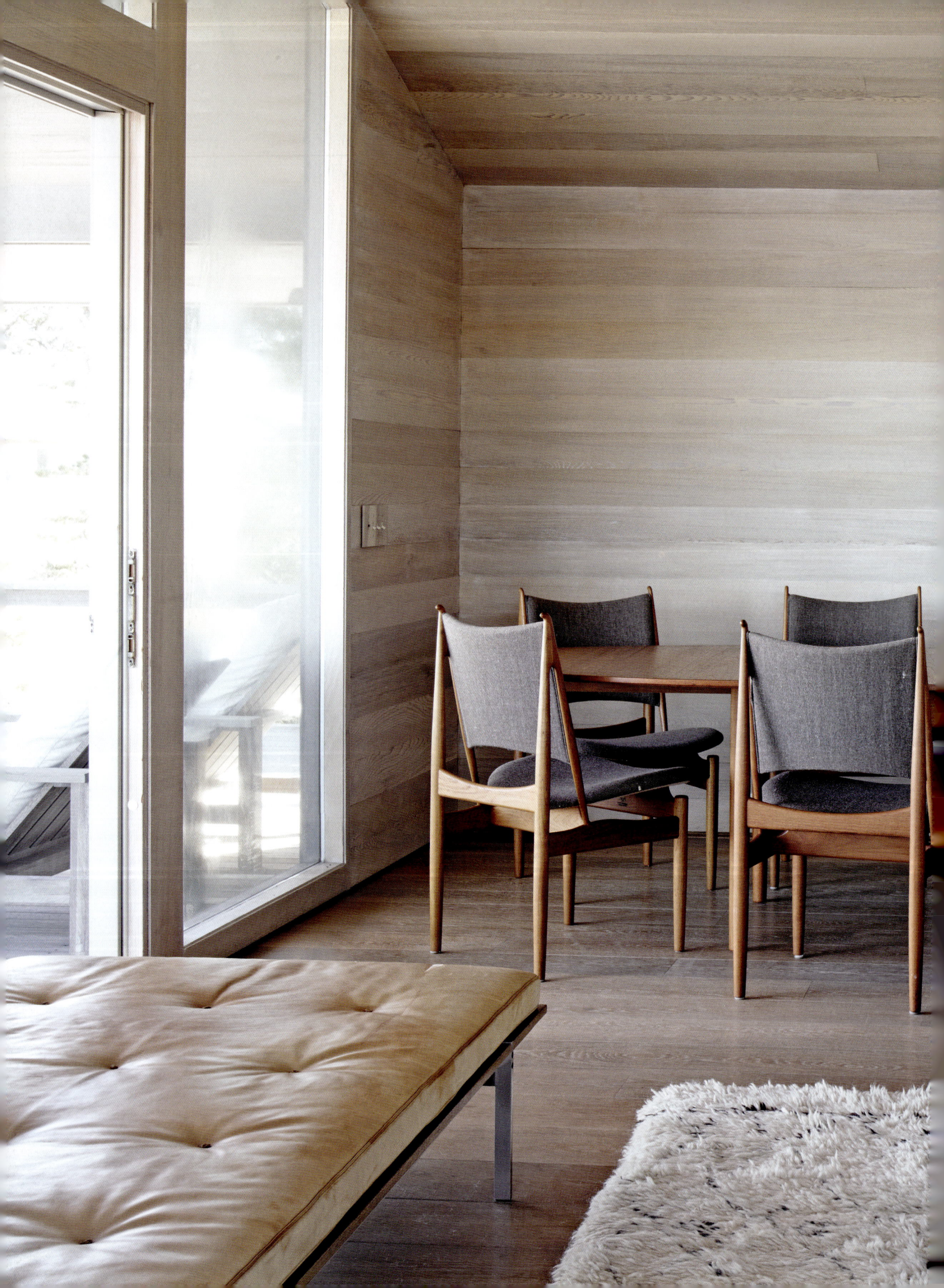

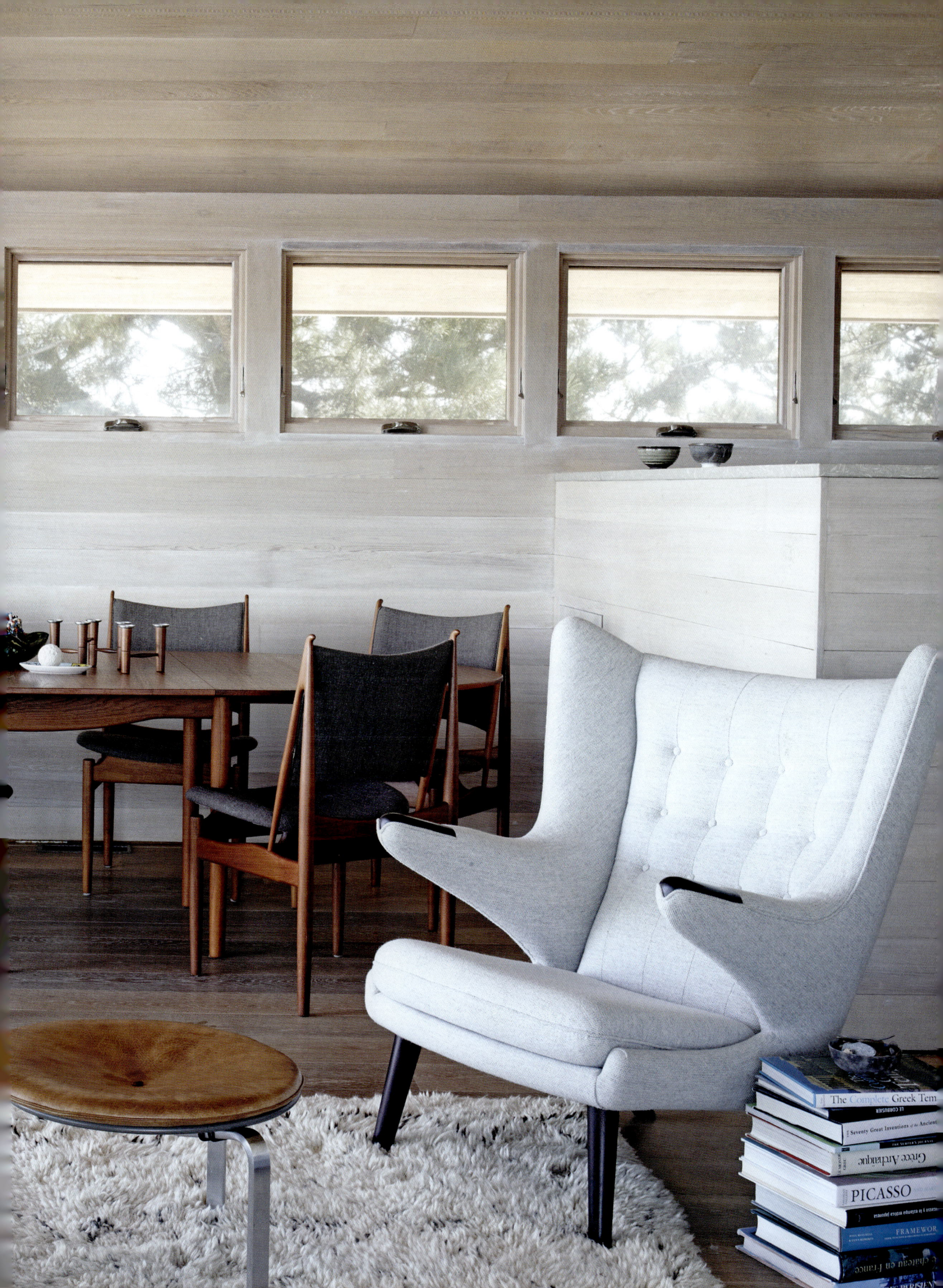

RESTRAINED RESTORATION

DAVID MANN

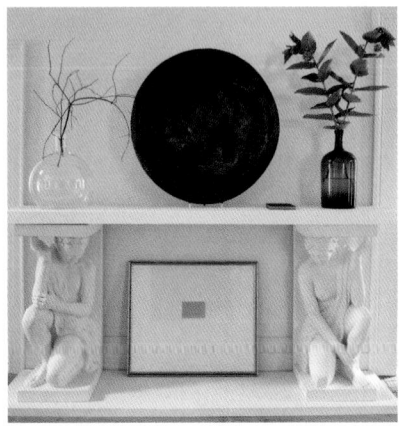

The Hudson Valley is gorgeous! The countryside is predominantly farmland, forest, and pine-dotted mountains. It has a relatively sparse population and there is no pressure. My partner Fritz and I like to explore, and seek out not just the beautiful old homes that exist out here but also the culture, as well as the friends that we have made over the years. It is a far quieter and simpler life to that of New York. I used to own a weekend house out West, but it proved to be too far away and would often take me a day to get there. This house is much closer and more convenient, but it still took me nearly three years to find. Wonderfully, Fritz had worked in the house as a stylist with Martha Stewart, and remembered that it had beautiful floors!

I used to work seven days a week. Owning a house in the country became the best reason to change my lifestyle and to escape into my own world at weekends, to do up my own home. The fact that I am a modern architect doesn't mean that I don't appreciate old buildings. This house has been a voyage of discovery and I have come to understand and appreciate how it has been changed over the years in order to cater to the different requirements of its various owners. It reflects centuries of lifestyle. It is essentially a Federal building that underwent a Greek Revival in the 1830s. The result is a layering of history, each period wishing to give the property a modern facelift!

We bought the house over 10 years ago. As an architect, I love and appreciate the space that exists around furniture and objects. In this house, I wanted to create an abstract feeling, so the first thing I did was to paint every room white. I used my favorite color—black—as punctuation marks and placed the furniture as if it were sculpture. In the old days, if people could afford it, they would paint the exterior of their houses white, to reflect the endlessly changing light throughout the day; the quality and variety of light in the Hudson Valley is extraordinary. With my white interior, furniture and objects become a play of shadows as the light moves around the house and artwork and furniture are spotlit in turn … The self-portrait by Benjamin Cottam in my bedroom and the wonderful 1940s French mantelpiece in the entrance hall are particular highlights.

Our favorite room is the dining room, not so much for its physicality but because it's where we spend most of our time and is the room we share with friends, talking, eating, and relaxing—the essential richness of life.

This house is our refuge.

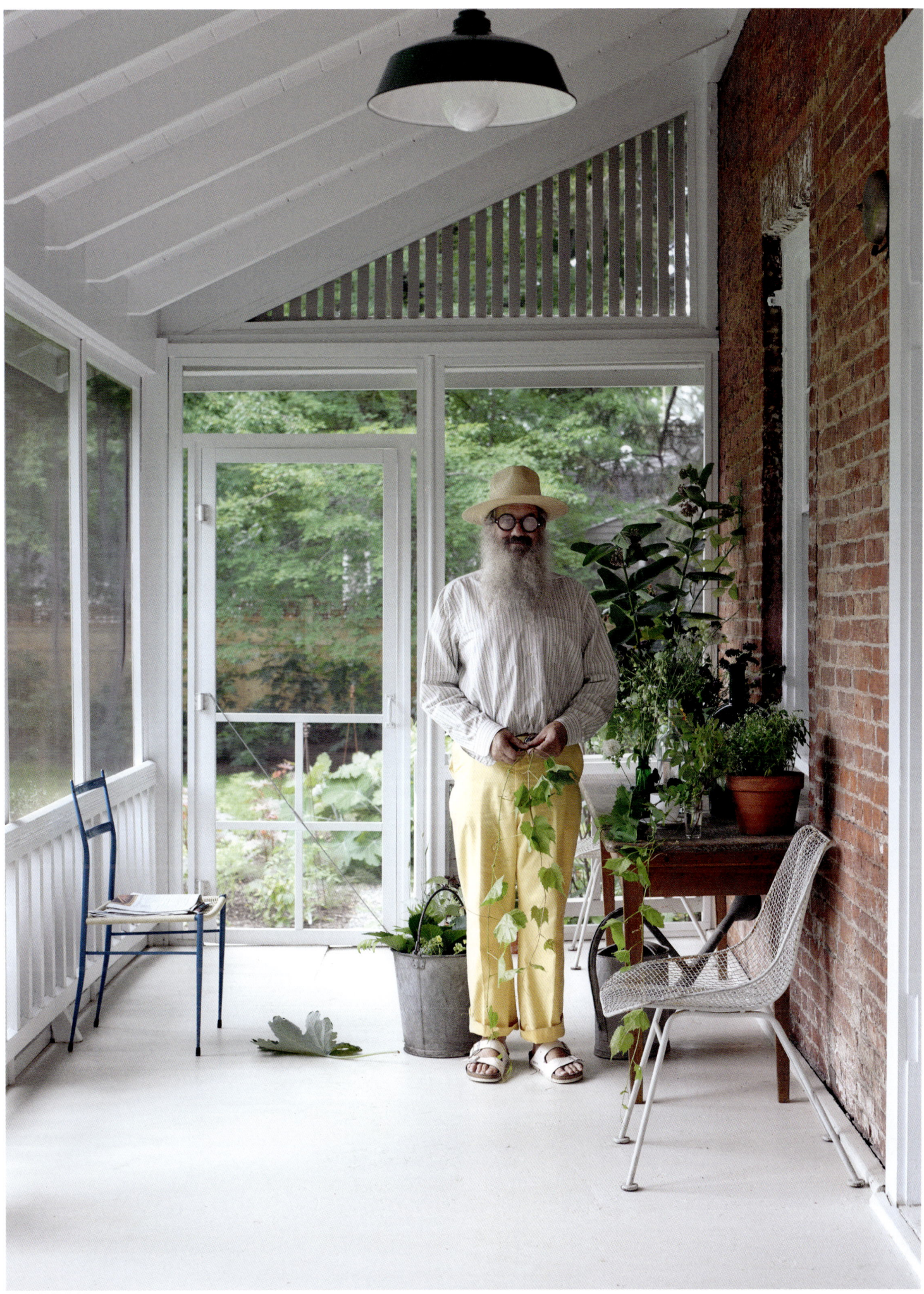

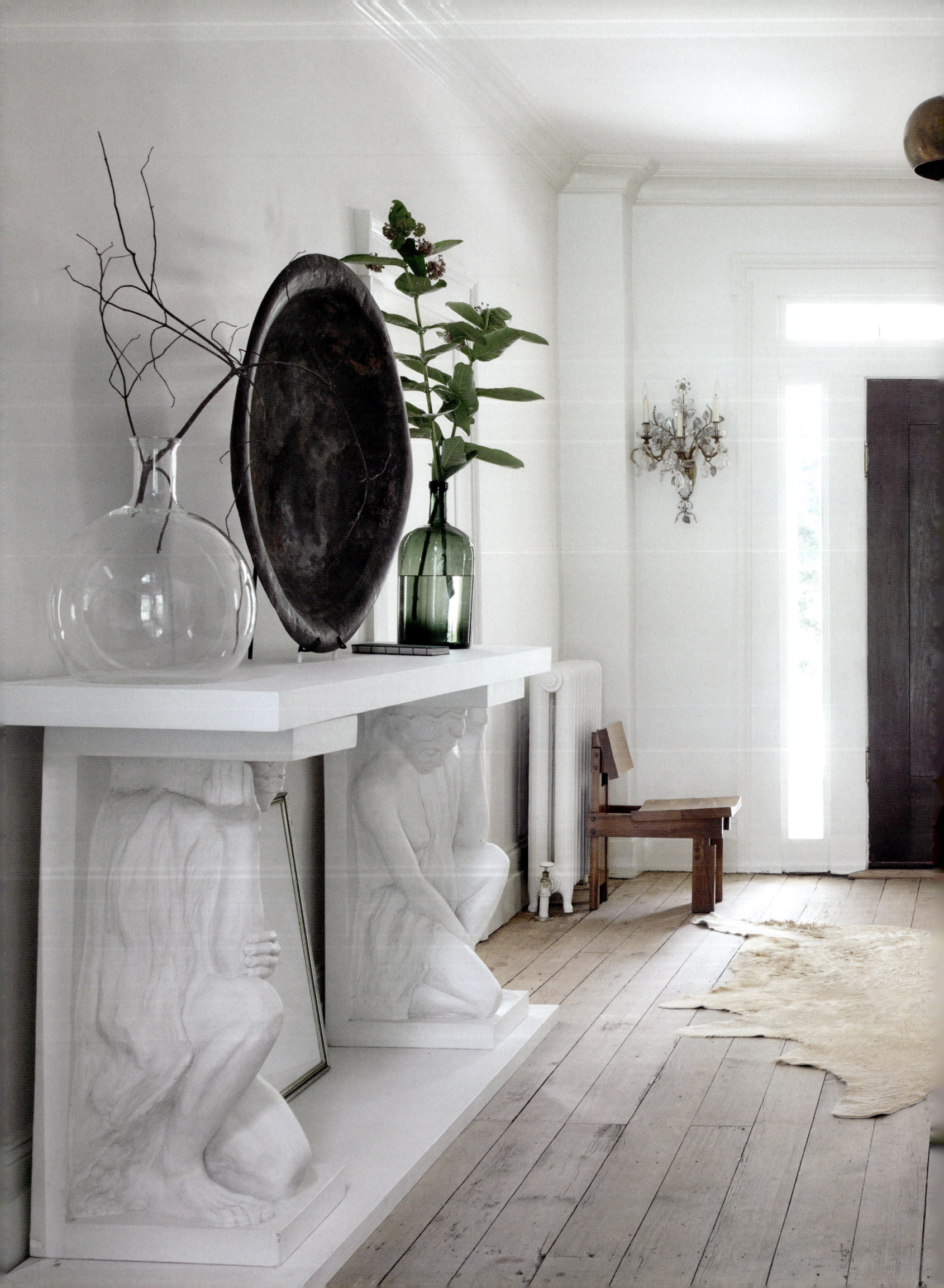

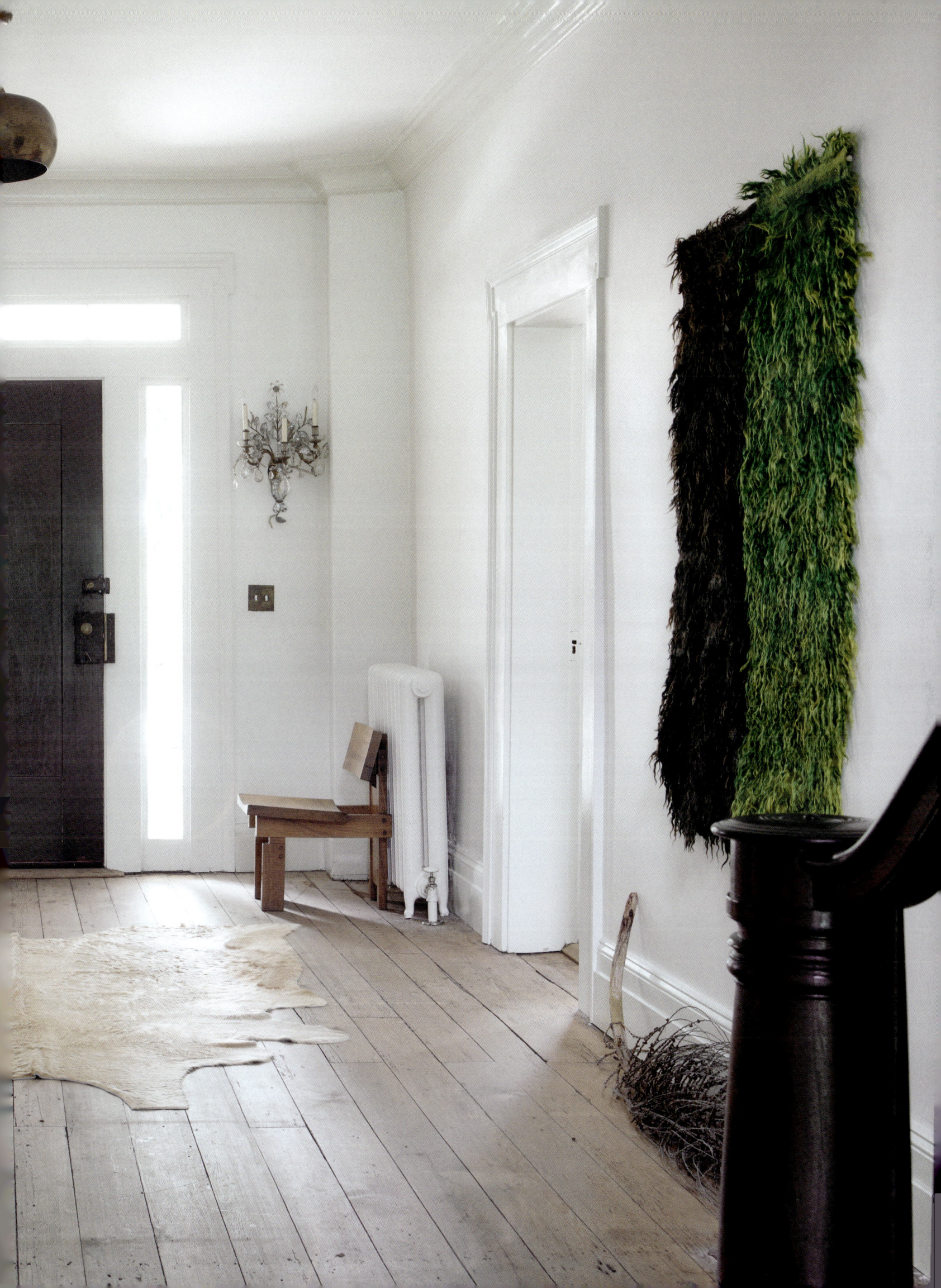

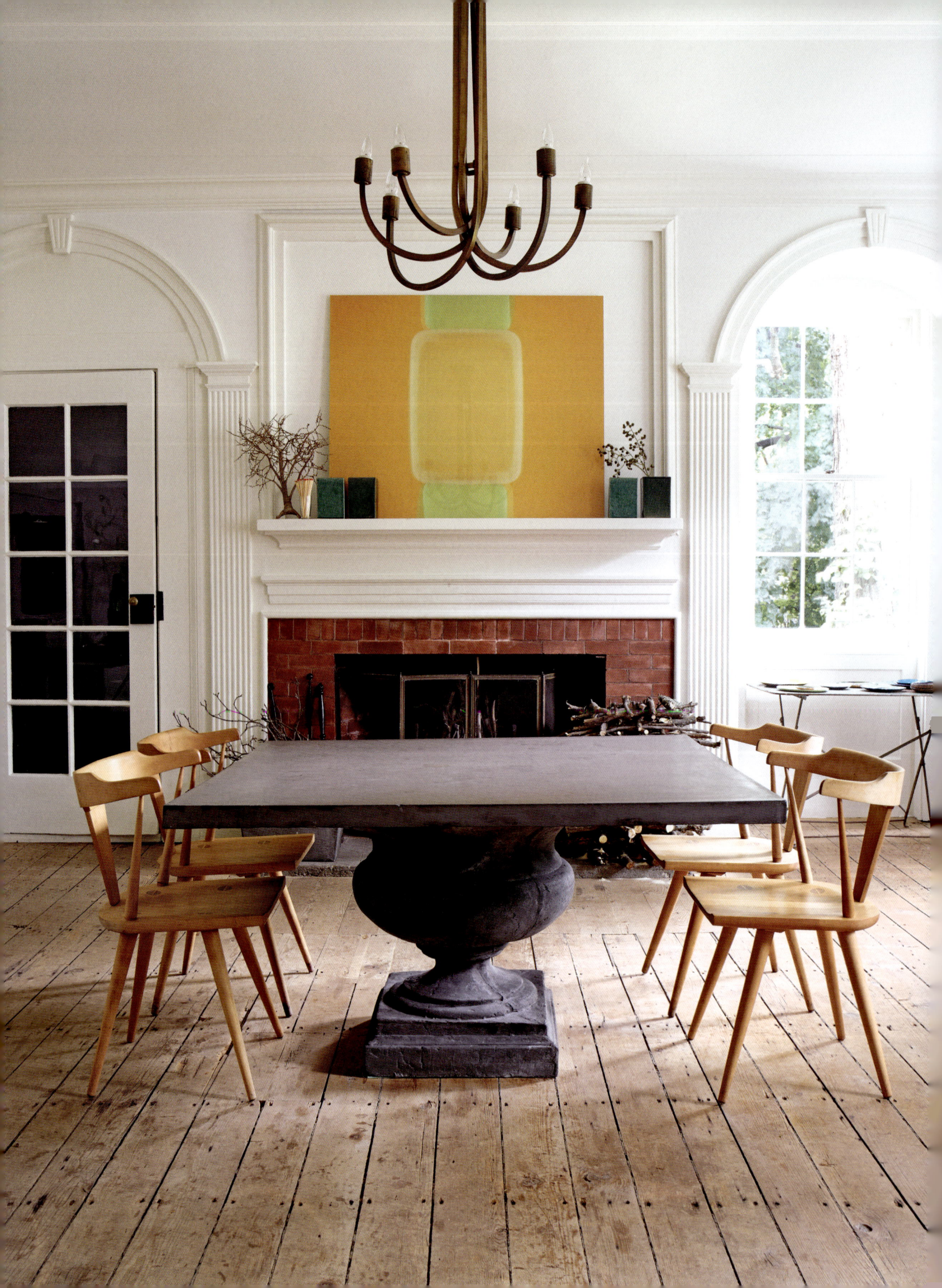

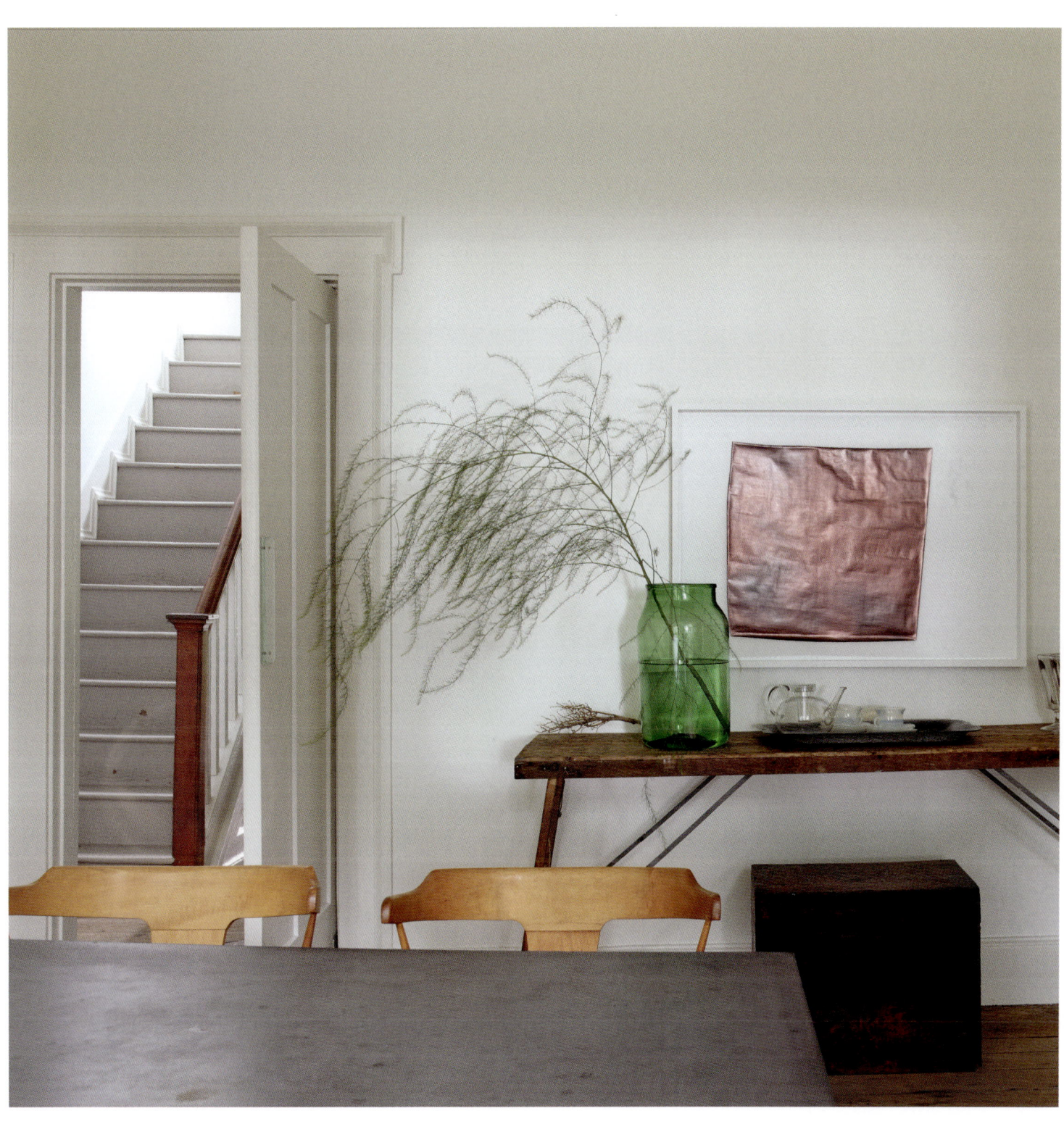

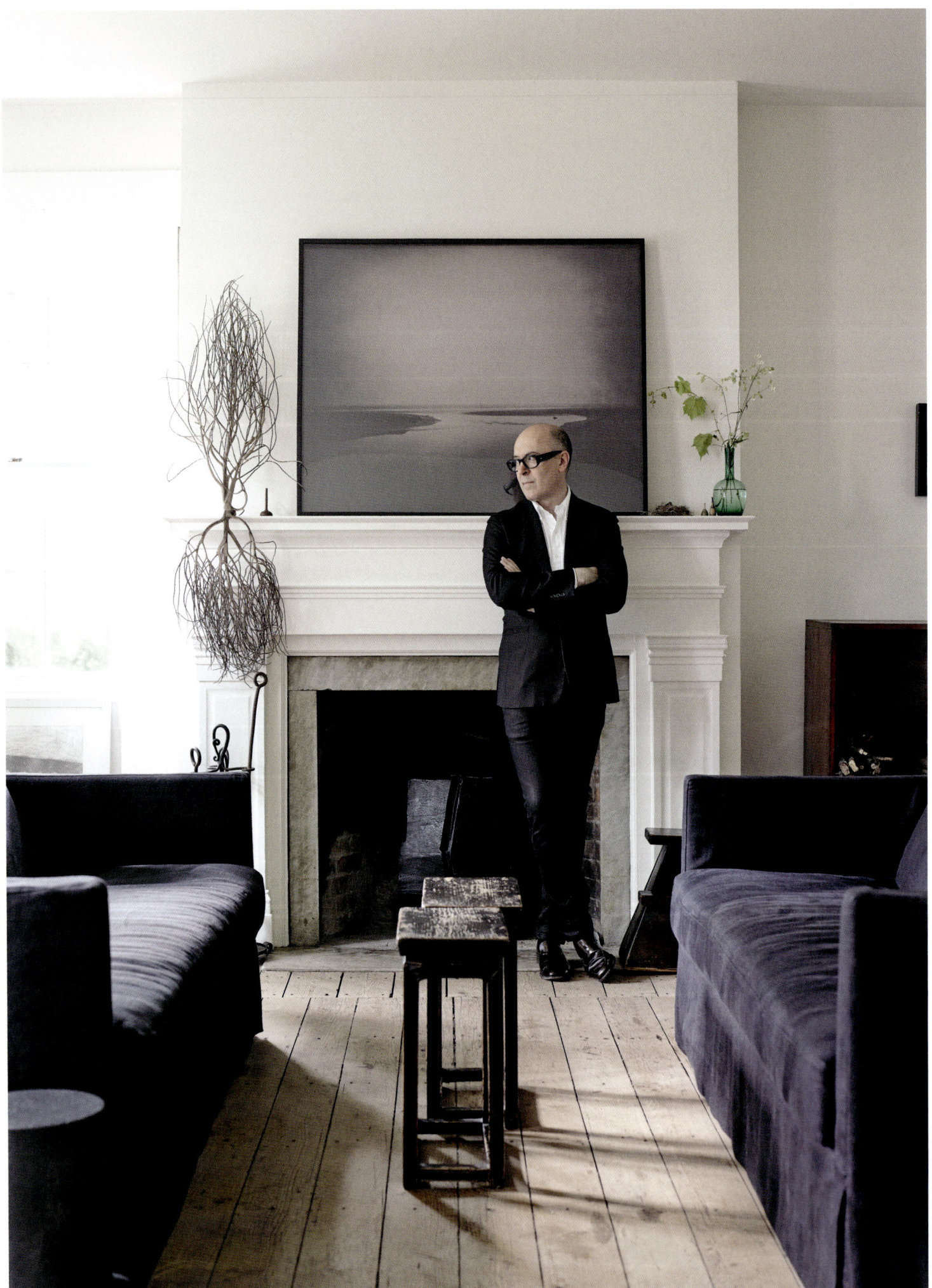

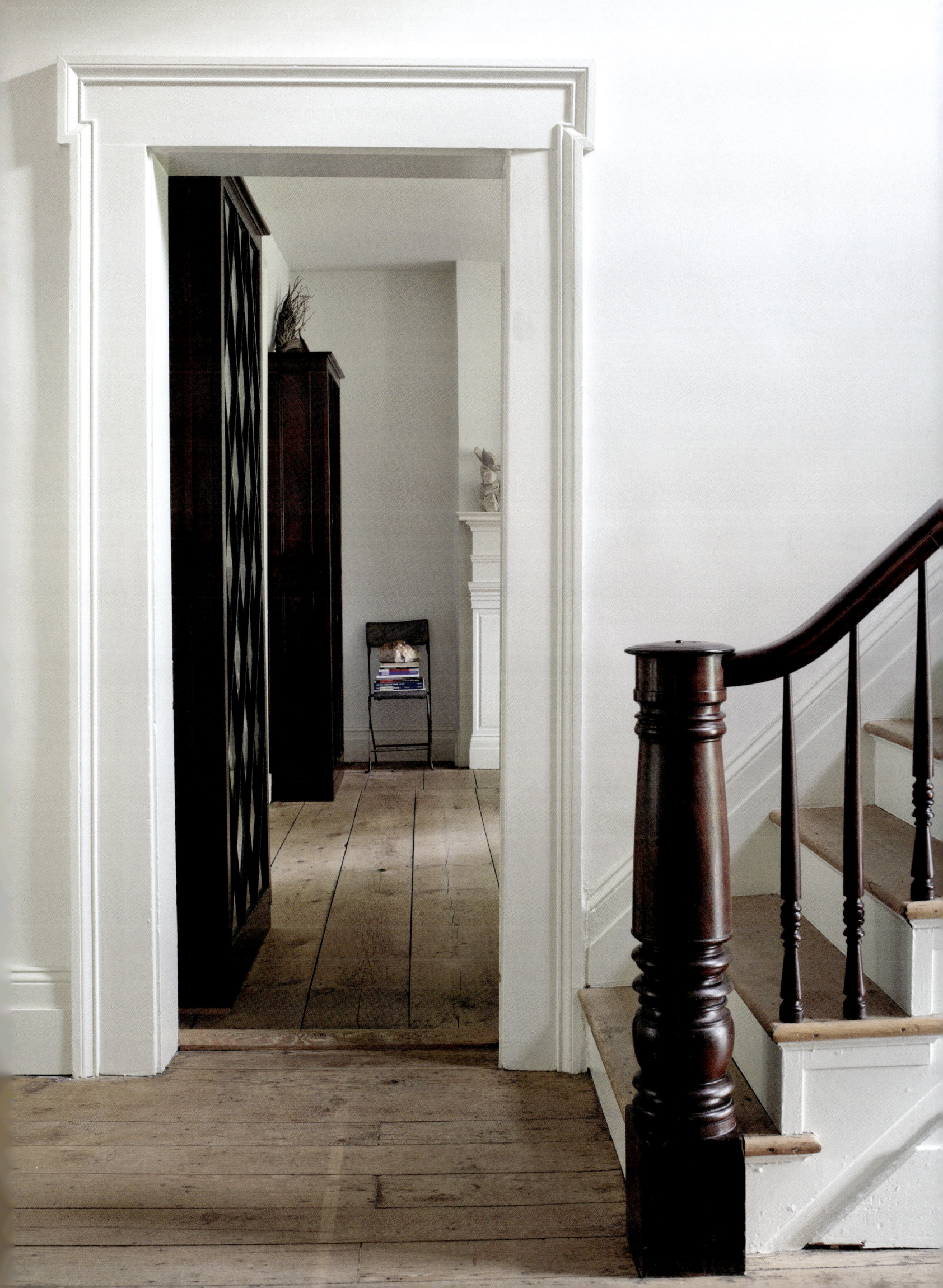

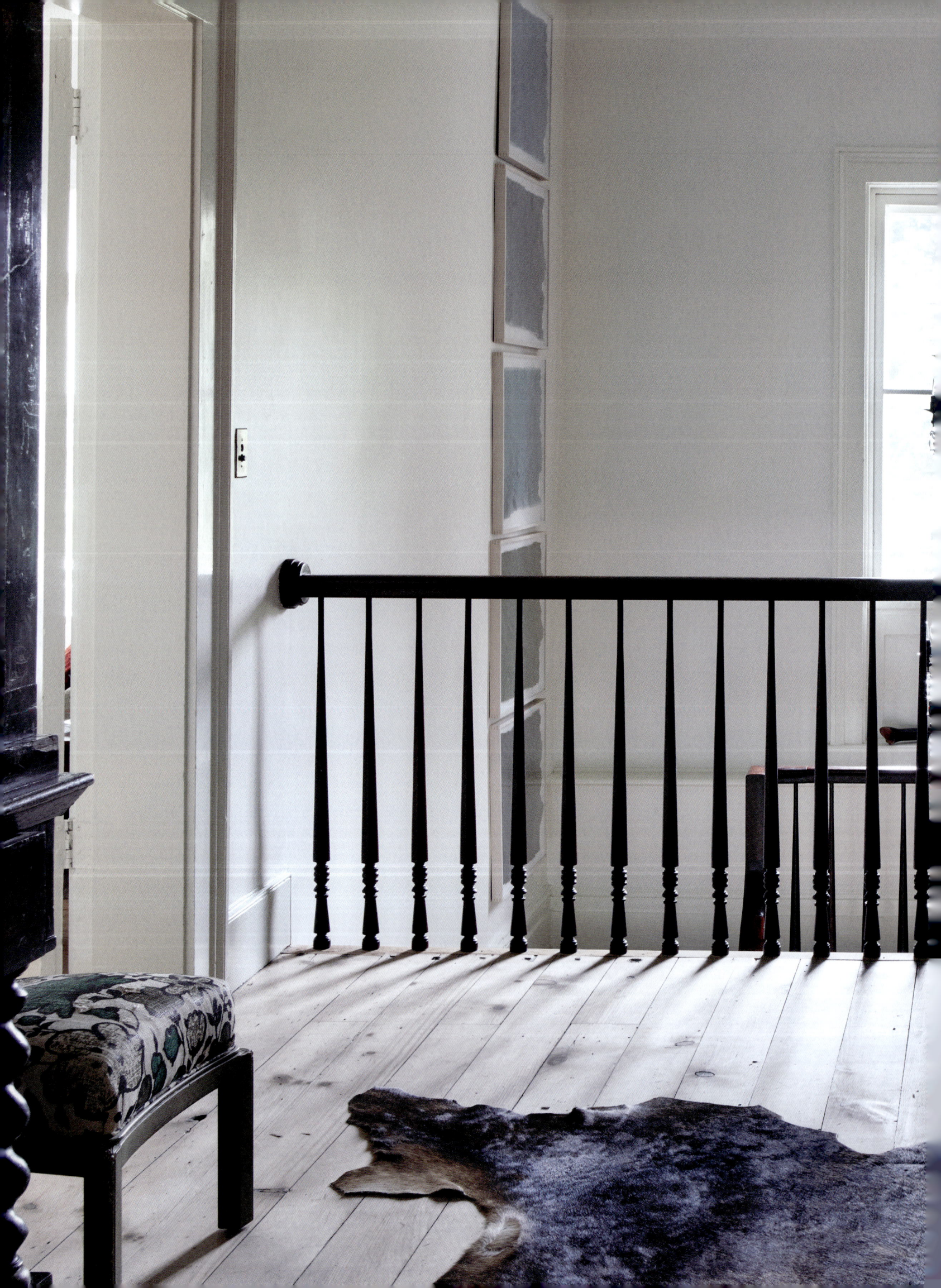

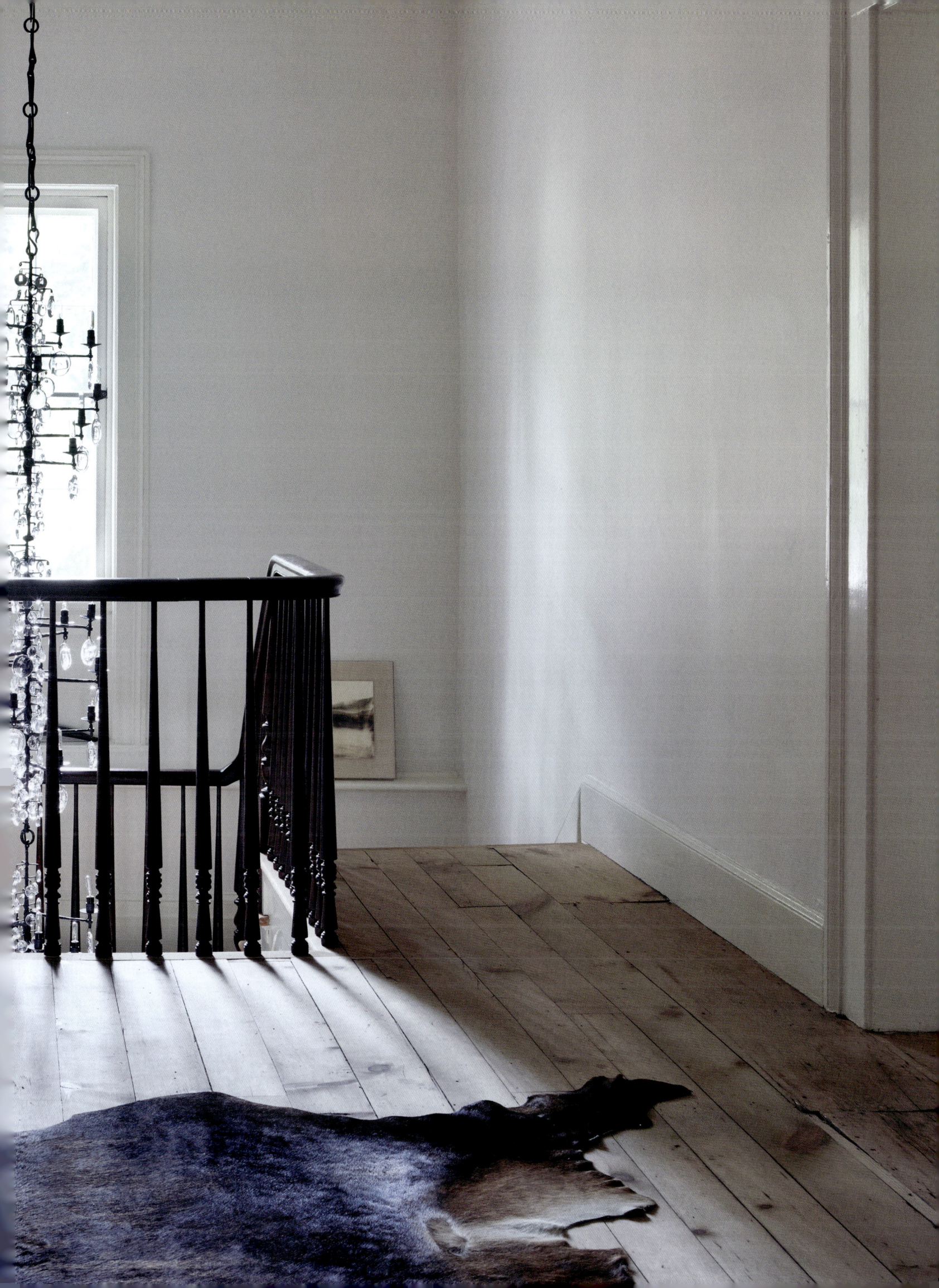

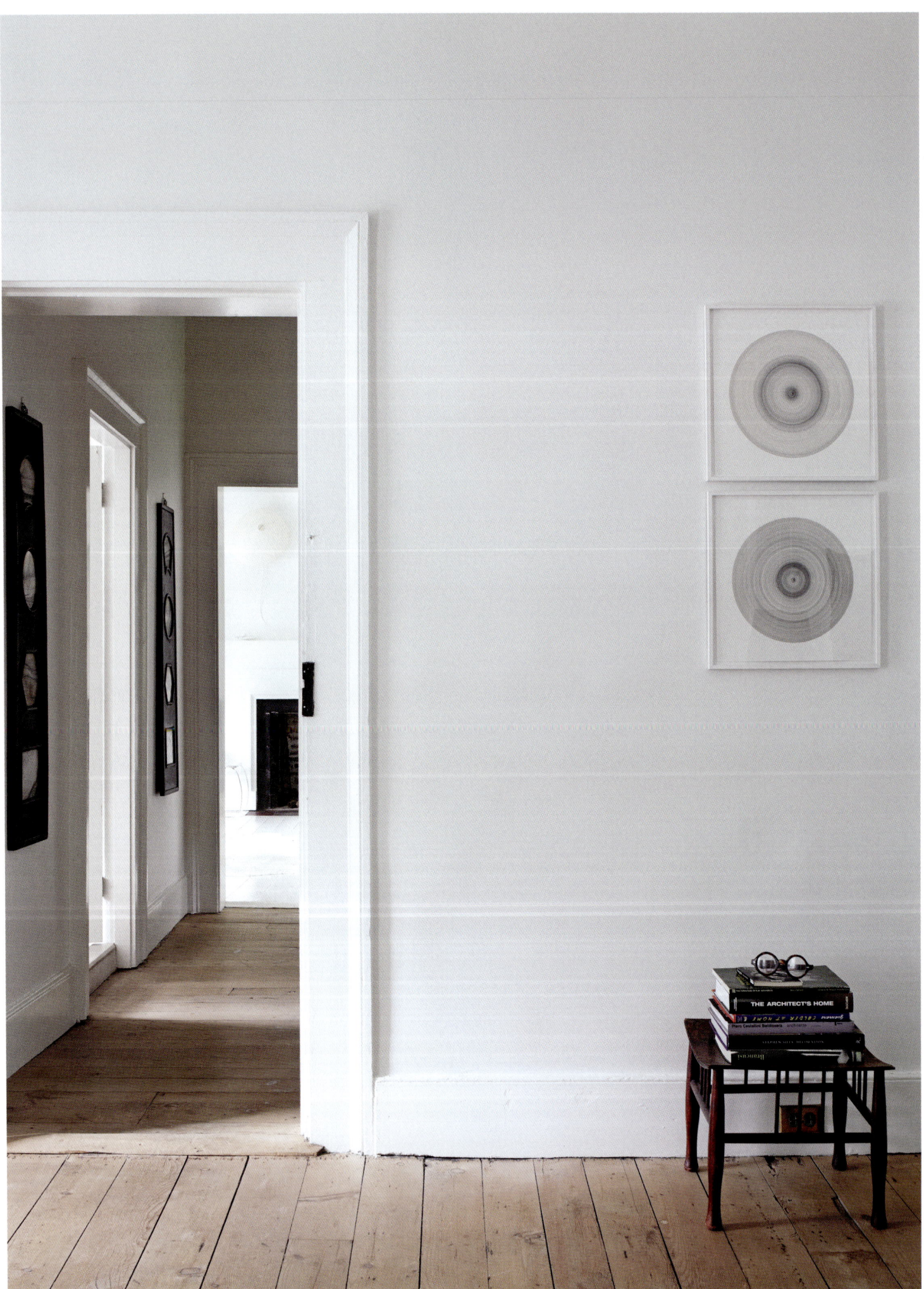

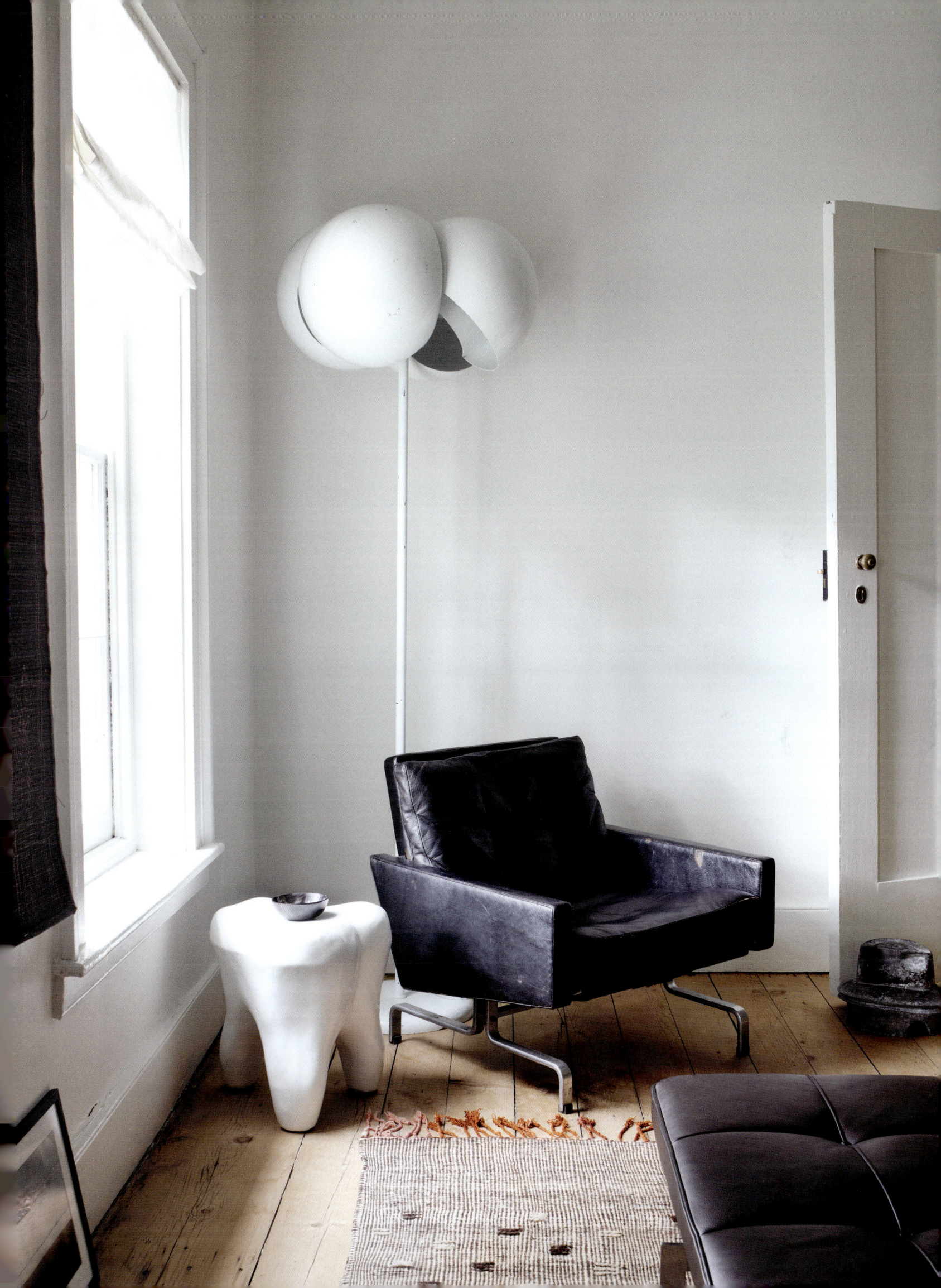

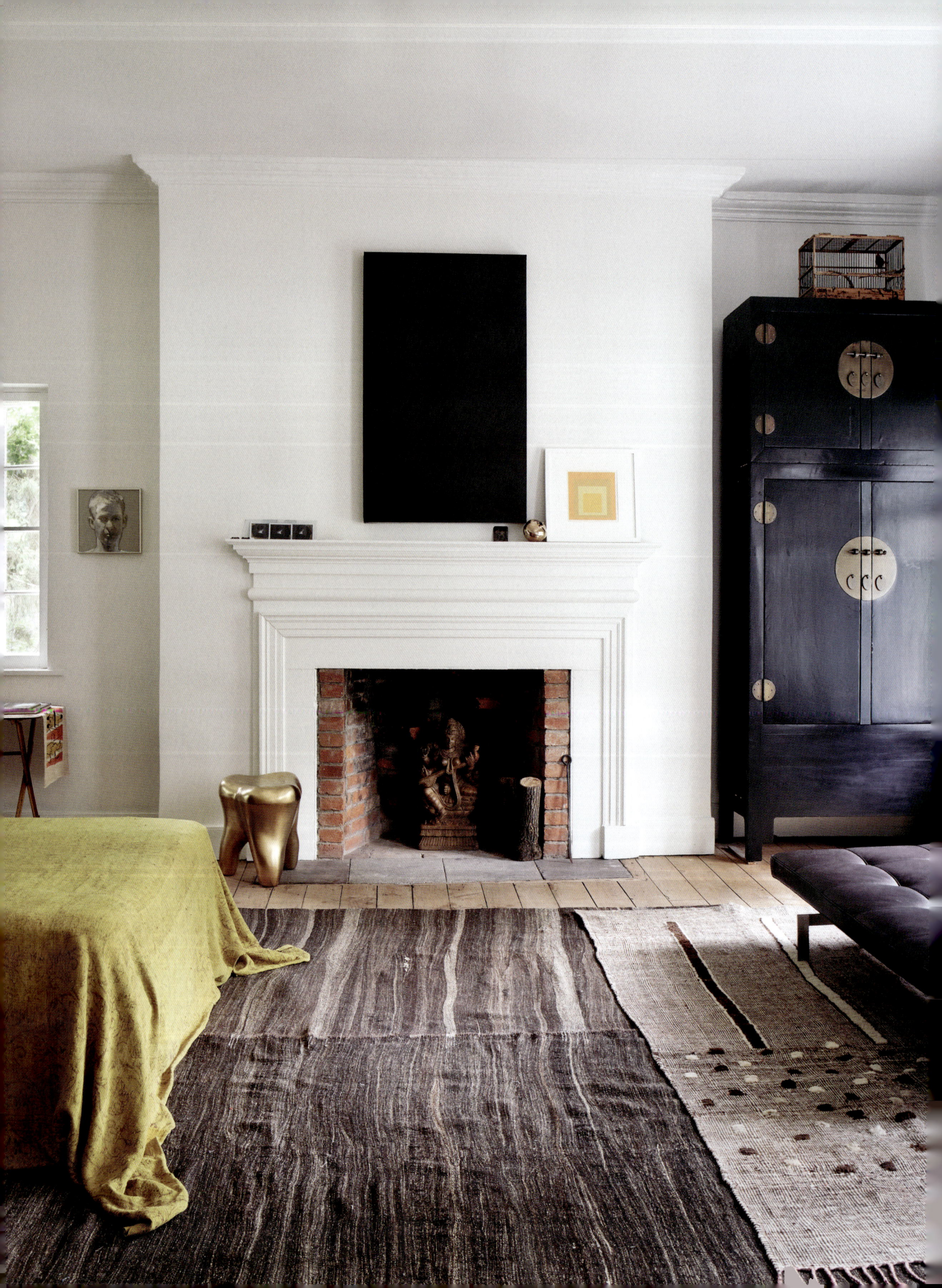

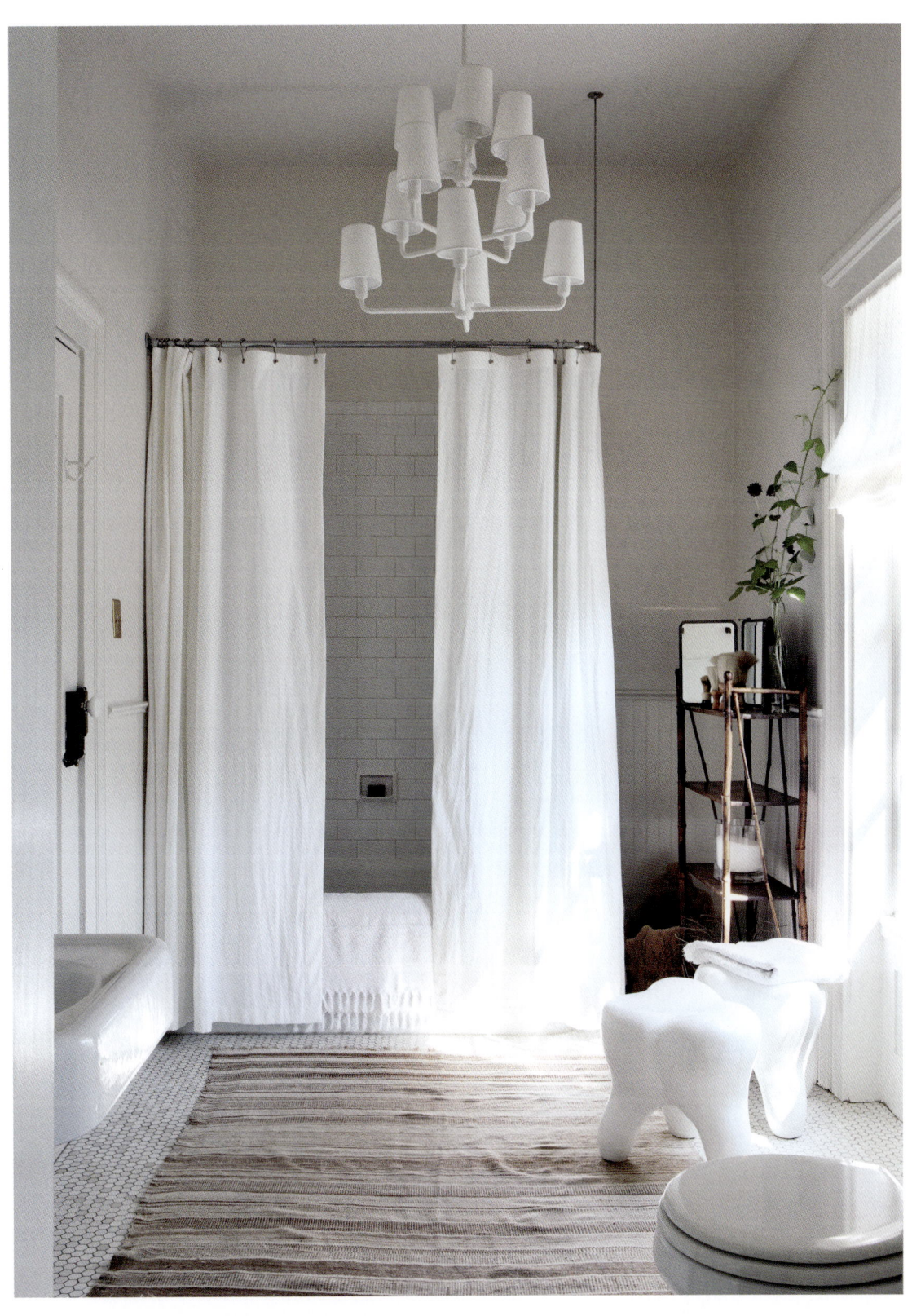

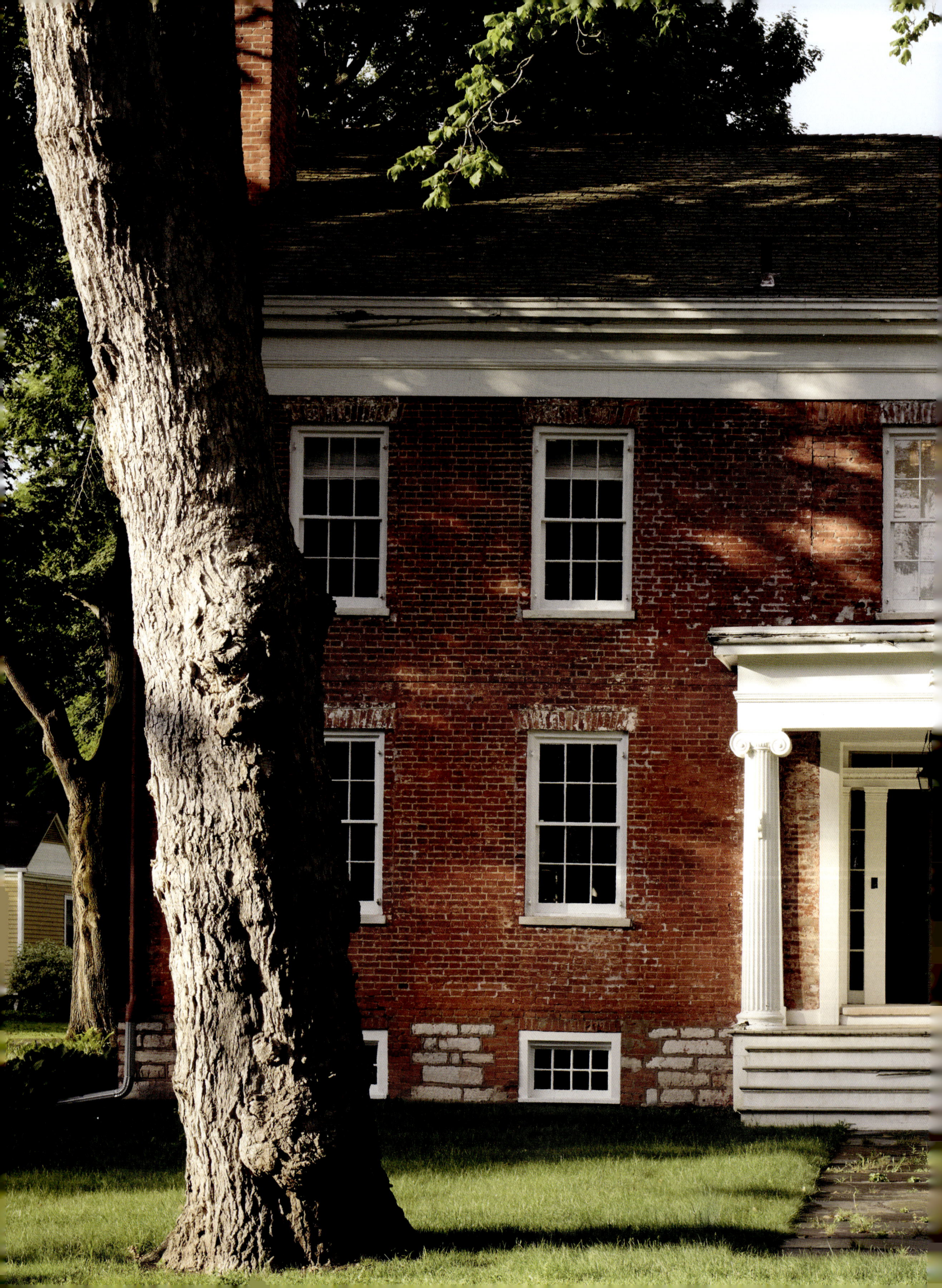

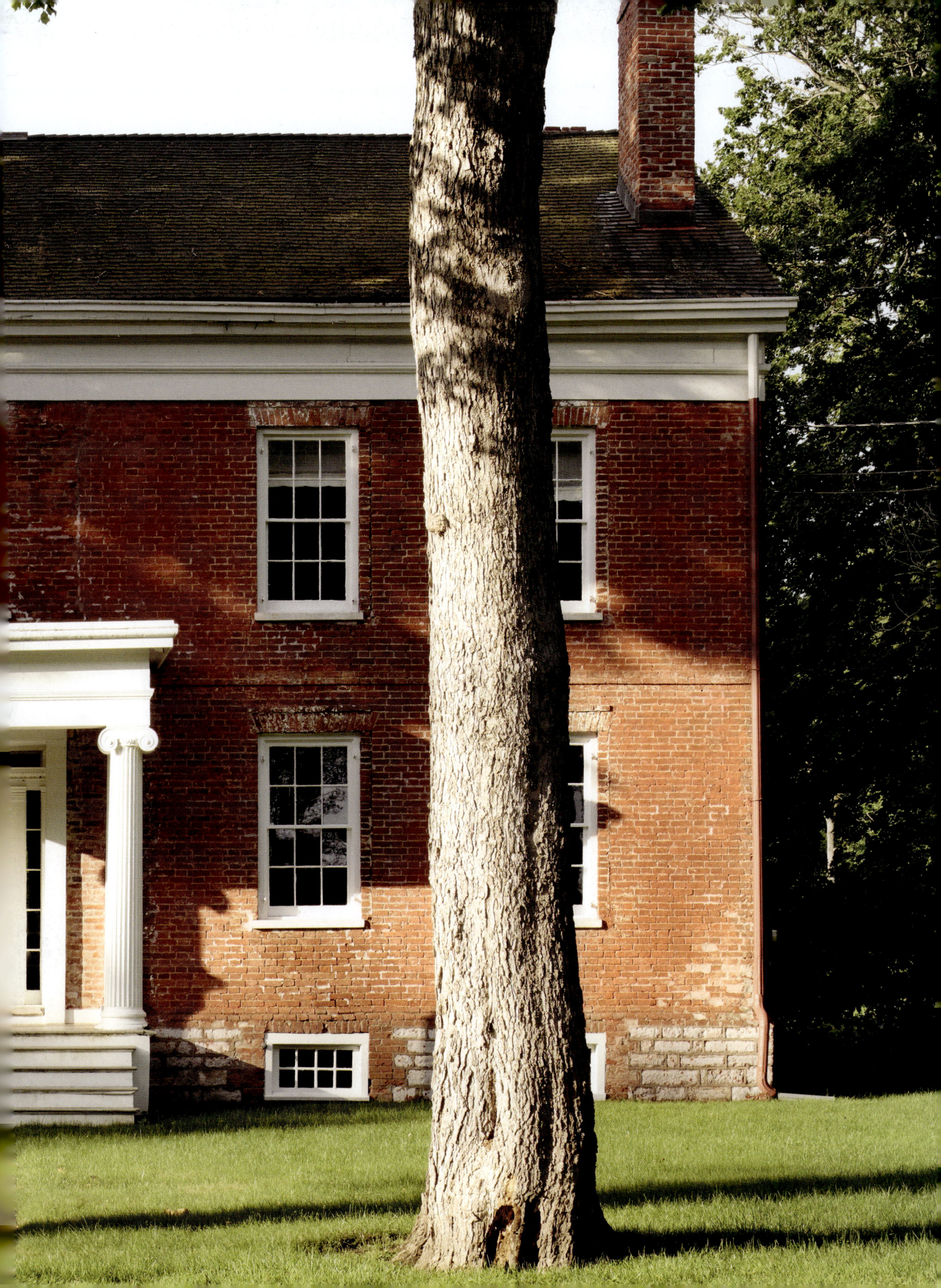

RURAL IDYLL

JACK McCOLLOUGH & LAZARO HERNANDEZ

Two years ago, I was commissioned by American *Vogue* to photograph the country retreat of Jack McCollough and Lazaro Hernandez, the creative duo behind Proenza Schouler. Accompanied by *Vogue* Contributing Editor Miranda Brooks, we set out from New York City for the wilds of the Massachusetts countryside and a relatively forgotten corner of the state, and arrived at a late-eighteenth-century clapboard farmhouse situated on its own 110 acres of land.

The sense of heightened anticipation I always feel at the start of every shoot was, in this particular case, surpassed by the sheer romantic beauty of the setting. Yet, as I was soon to gather from Miranda, who is not only a landscape architect but also a good friend of the couple, a great deal has been done over slow time to keep the surroundings as wild as possible. Over the course of the shoot, Miranda described the changes she made: planting enclosures of tall beech hedges for privacy from the road; preserving an eighteenth-century fieldstone patio discovered beneath an overgrown lawn; and clearing five acres of tangled woodland at the back of the house to re-create the original meadows and vistas. To one side of the property, she terraced the land for vegetable and bramble gardens. A mid-century concrete swimming pool—added by previous owners—was replaced with a low-key, dark basin, which she then surrounded with wildflower meadows and fruit trees, interlaced with a series of mown paths.

The interior of the house itself belies the state of disrepair it was discovered to be in. I was charmed by the authenticity and the spare, almost minimal fashion in which each room has been decorated. Stripped back, with historic detailing intact, the wide-plank floorboards and original plaster walls were carefully restored, along with the hand-stenciled designs in the dining room. The result: a photographer's dream shoot, and one that has stayed forever with me. **SIMON UPTON**

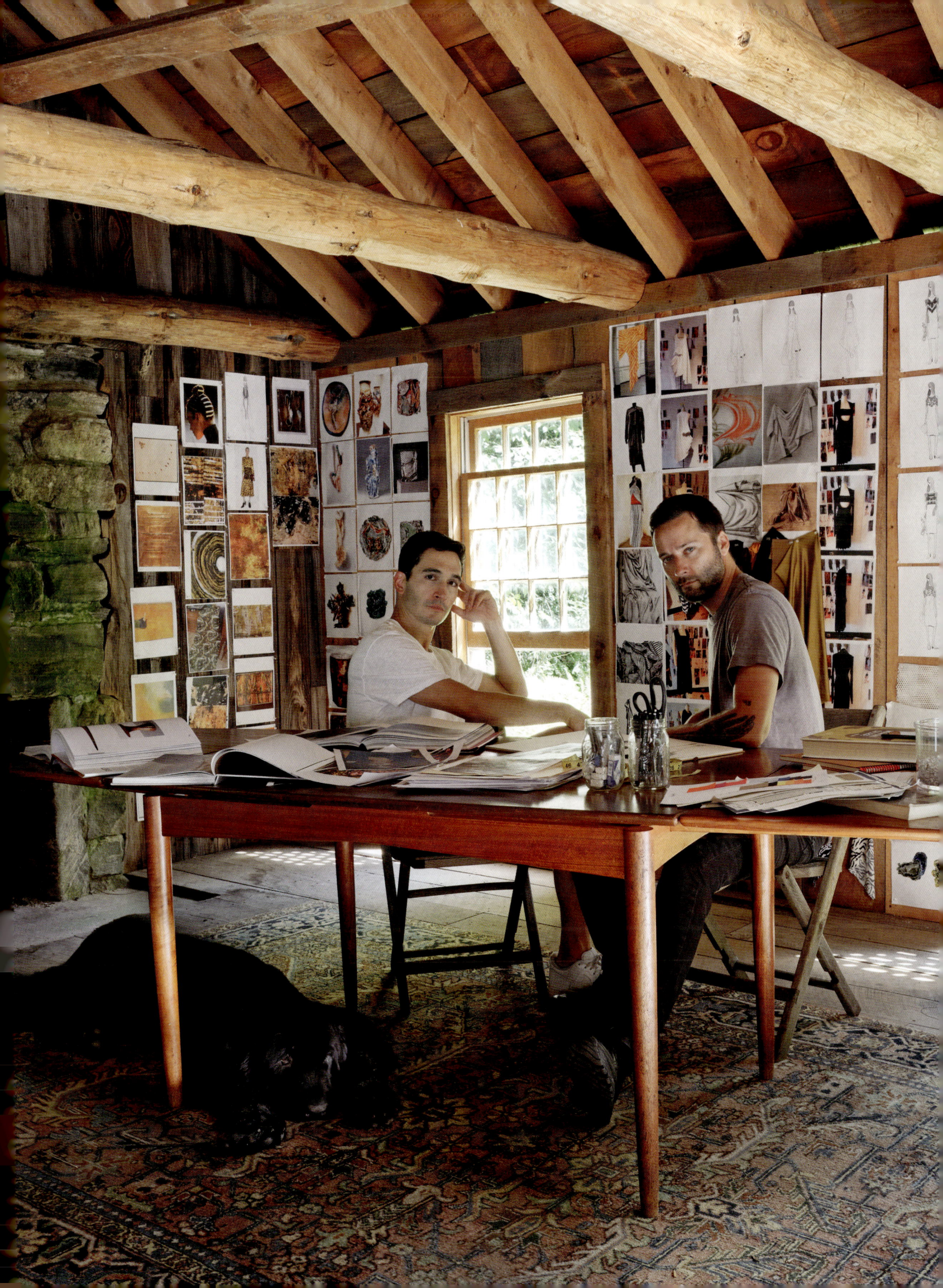

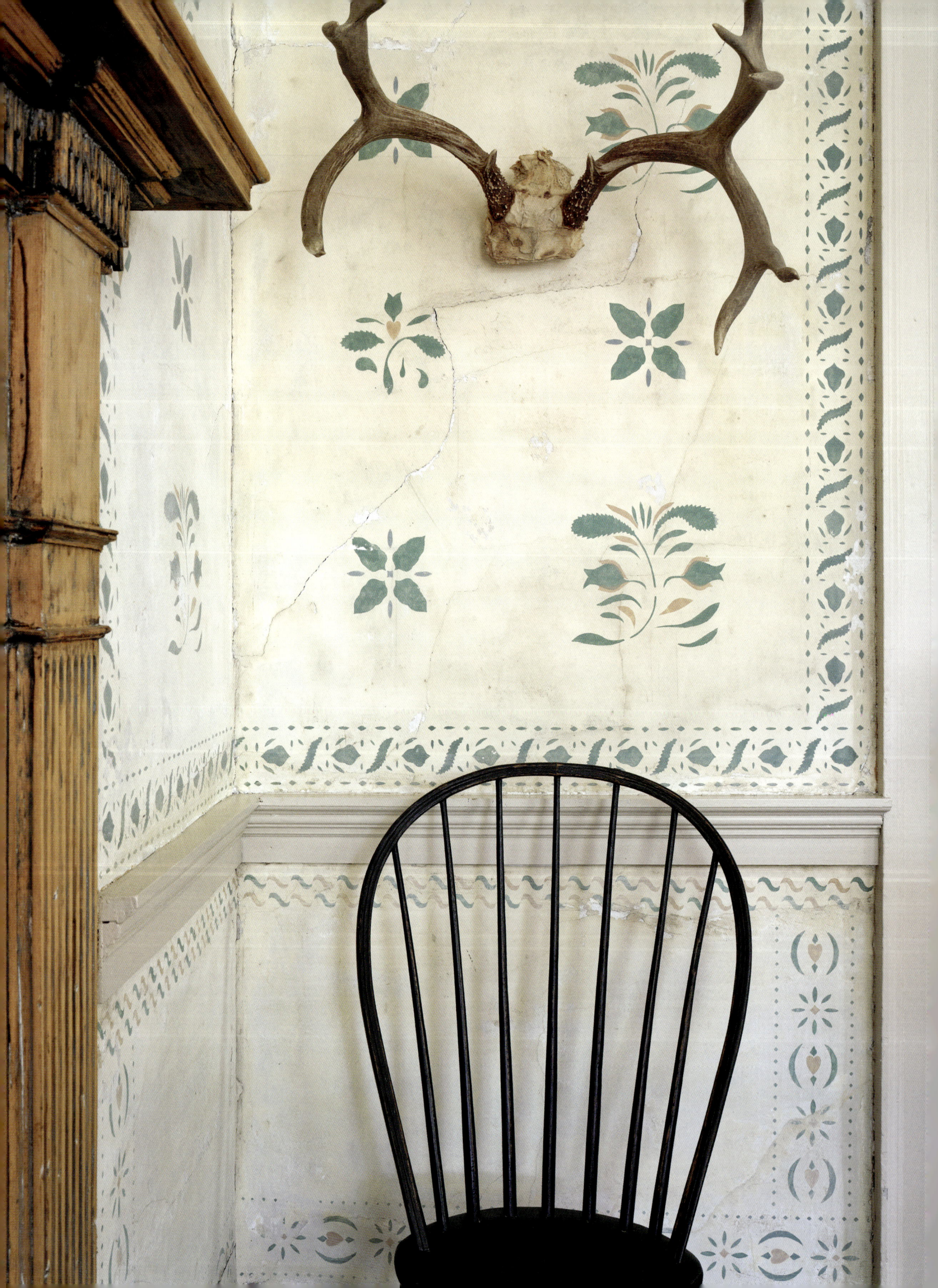

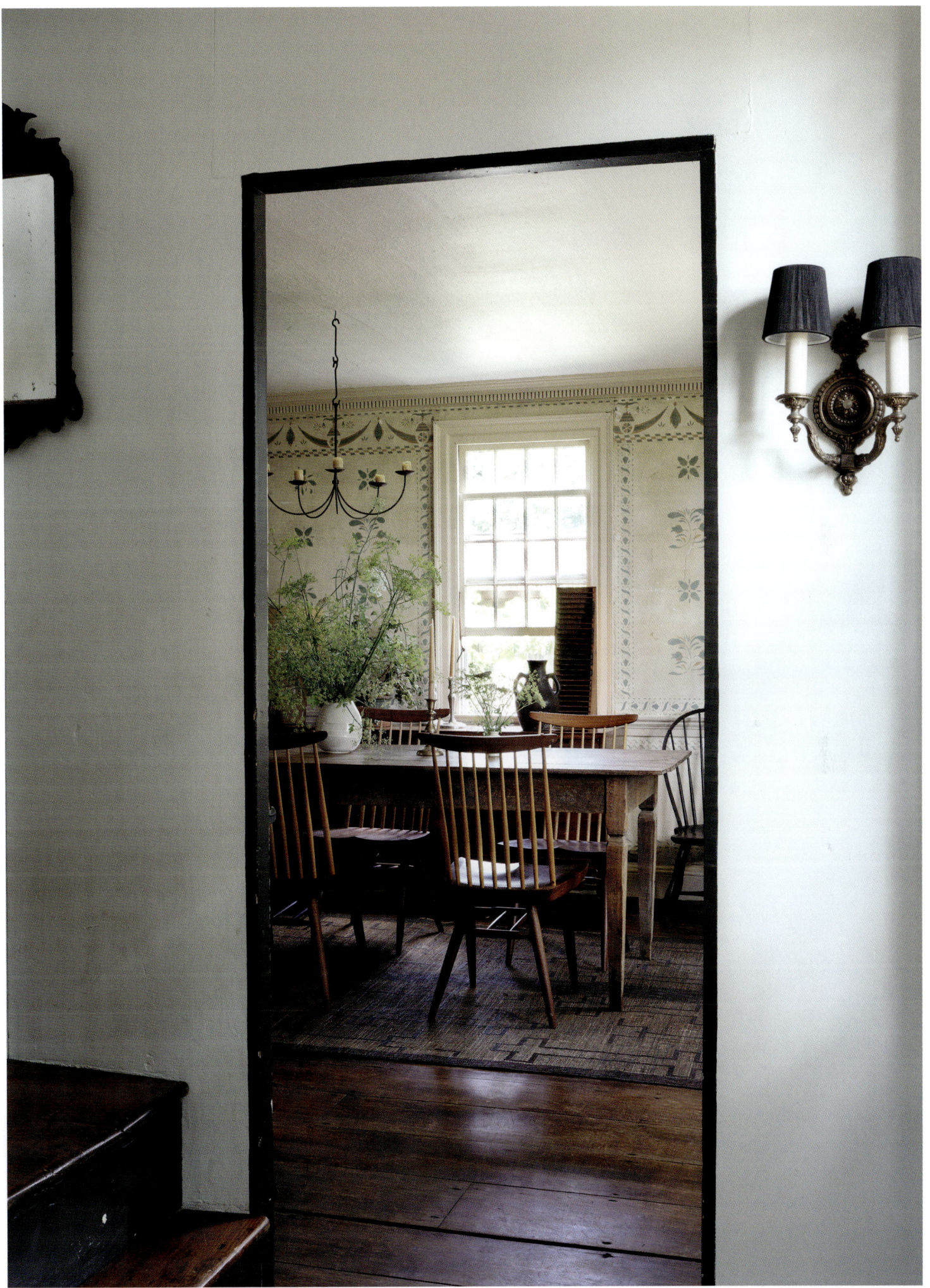

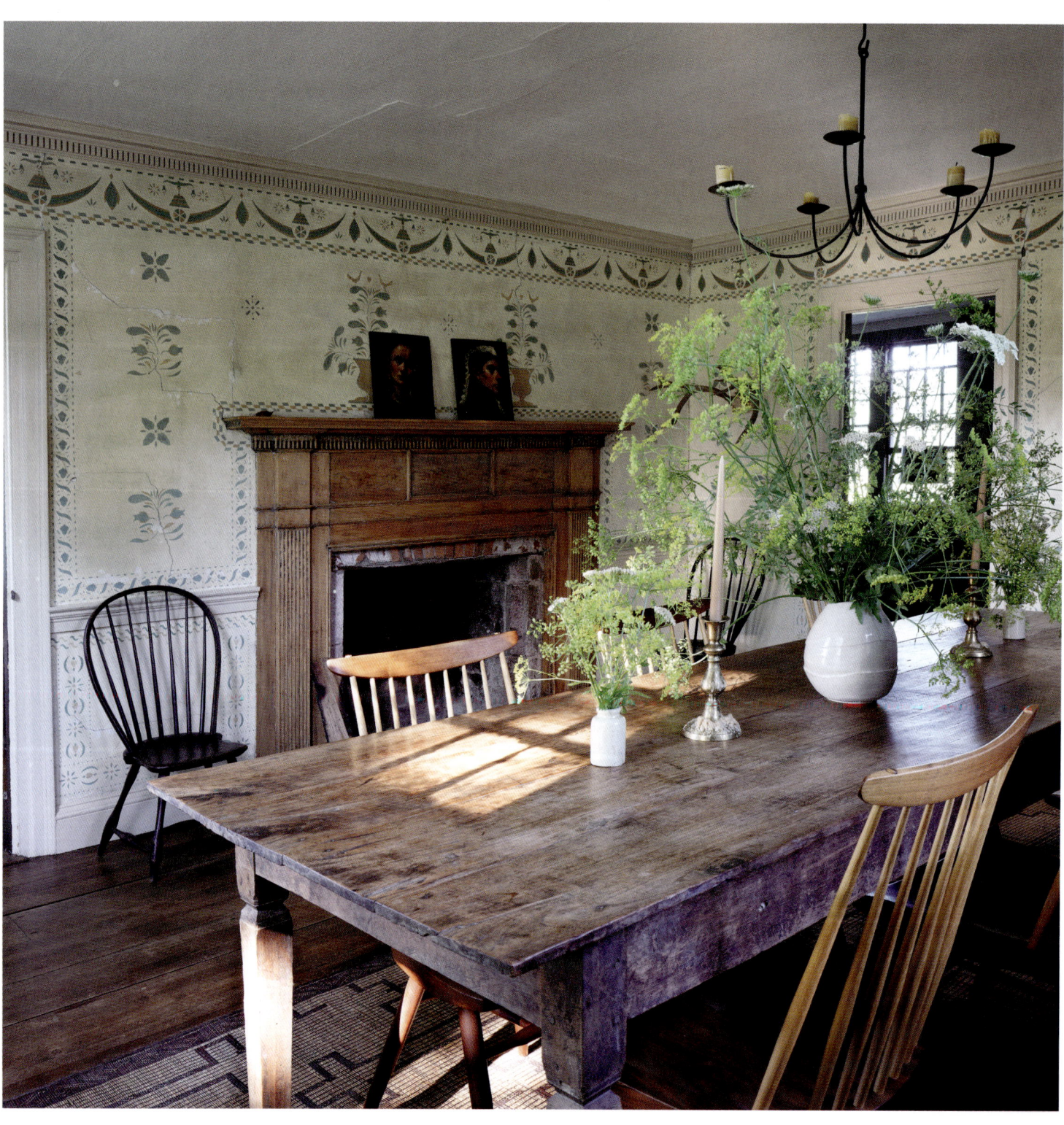

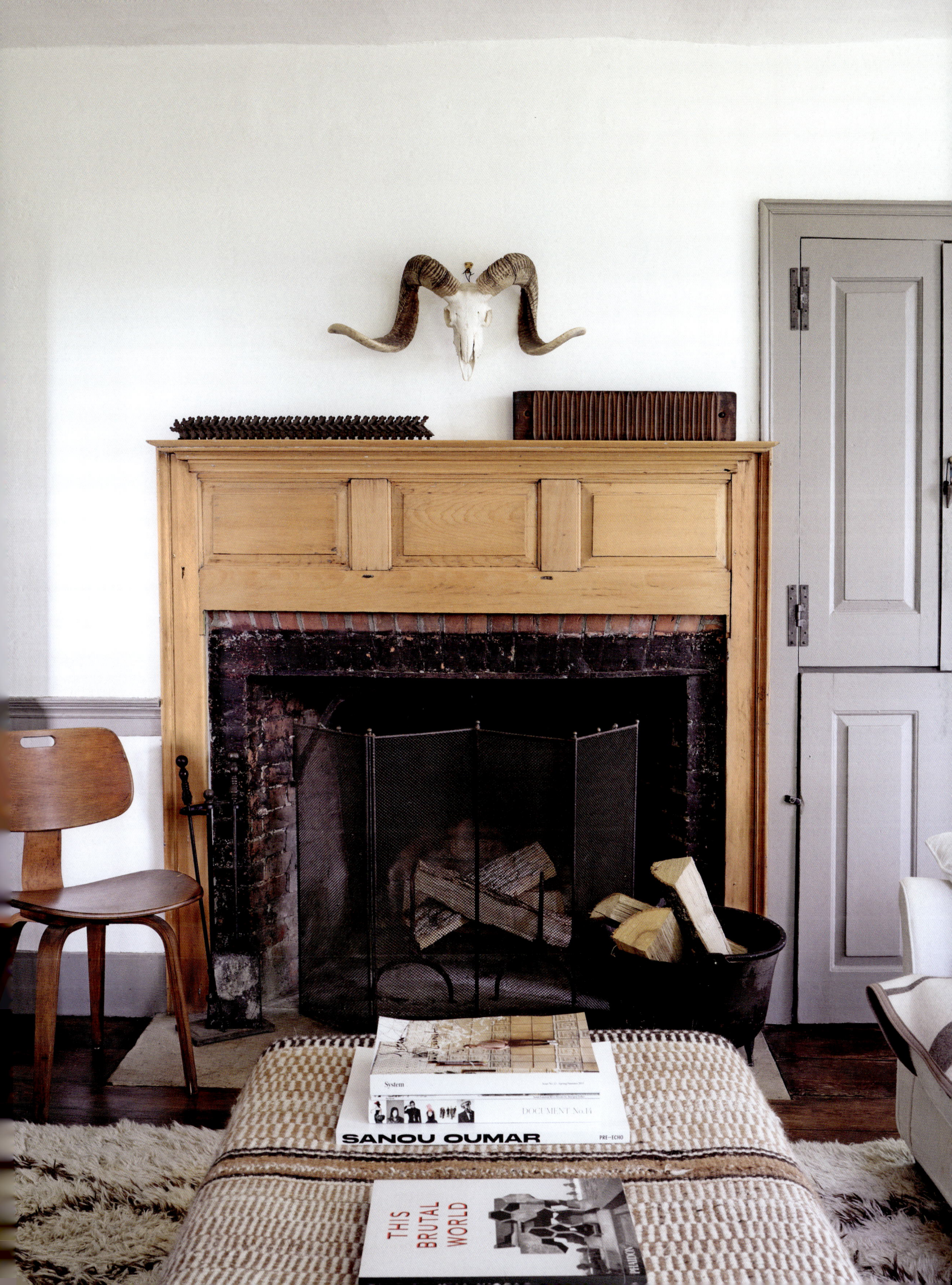

SANOU OUMAR

THIS BRUTAL WORLD

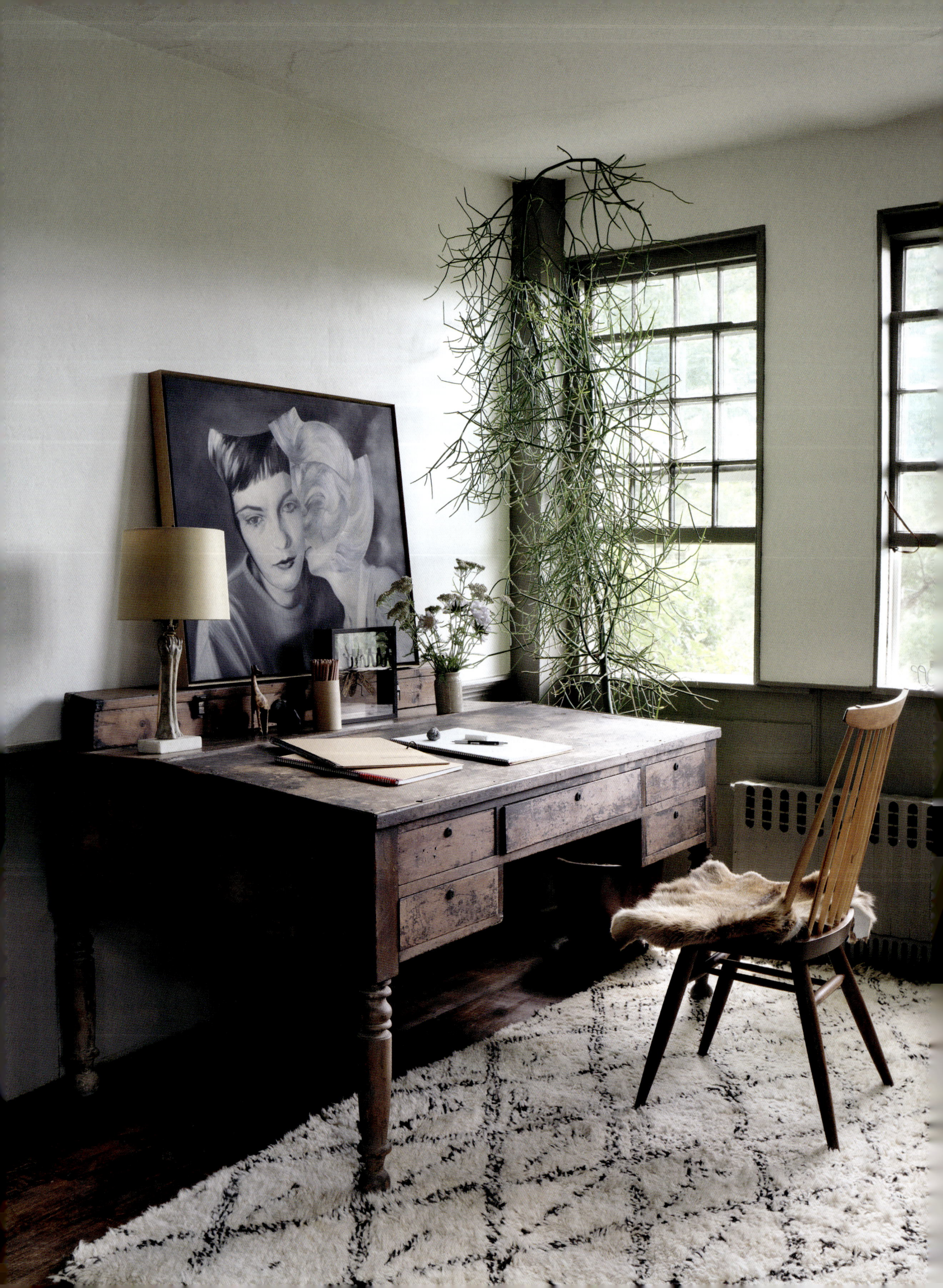

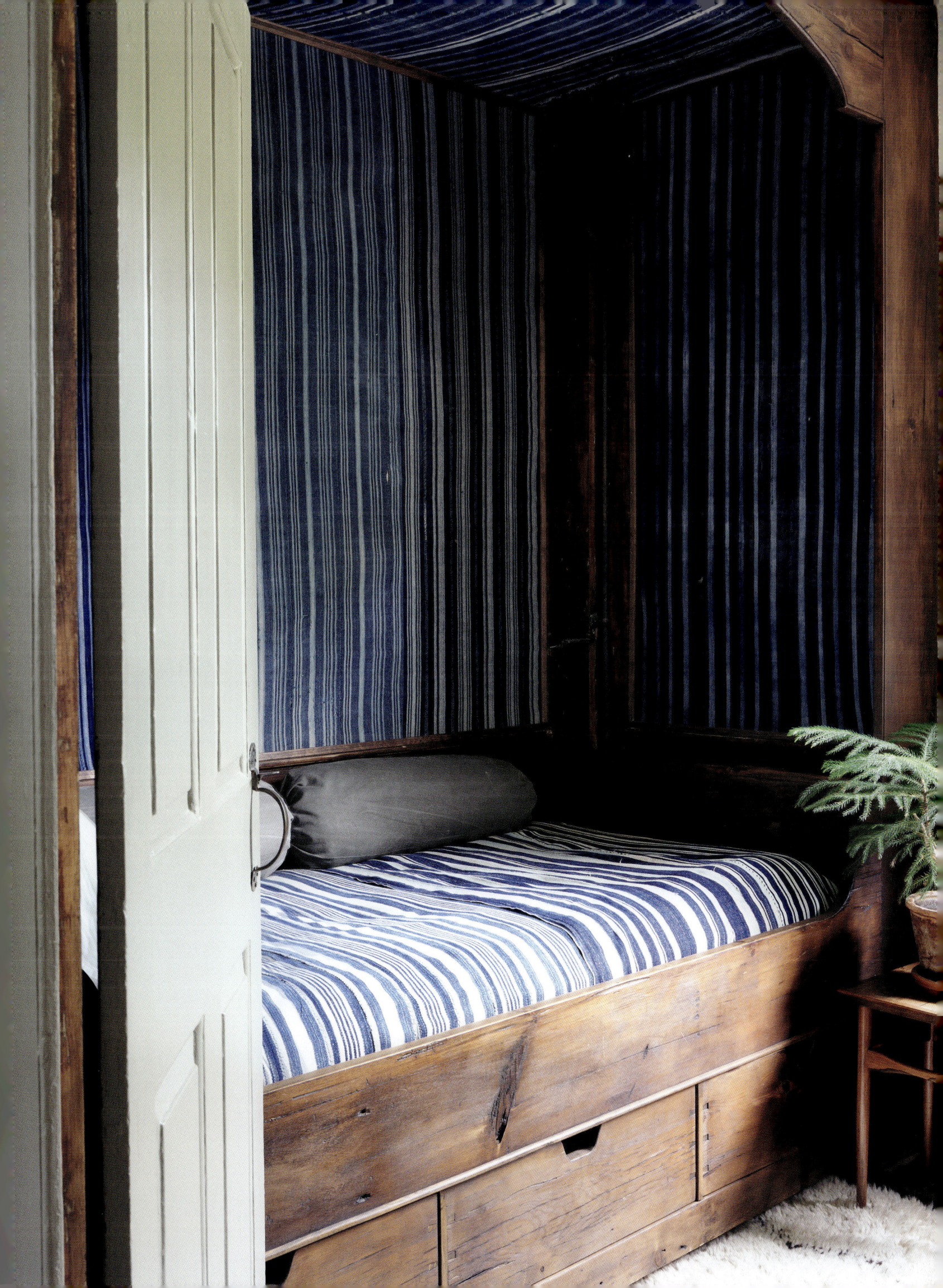

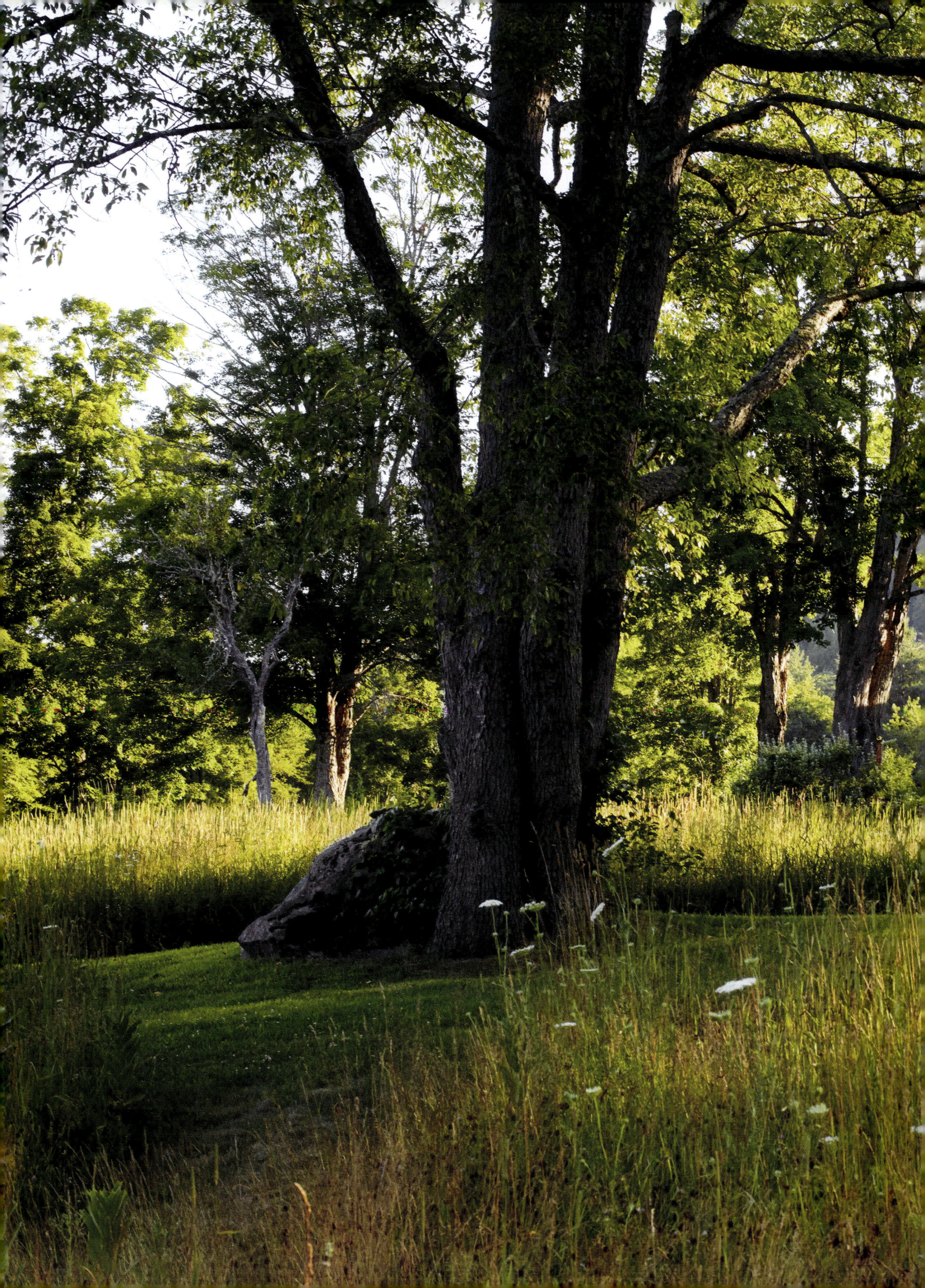

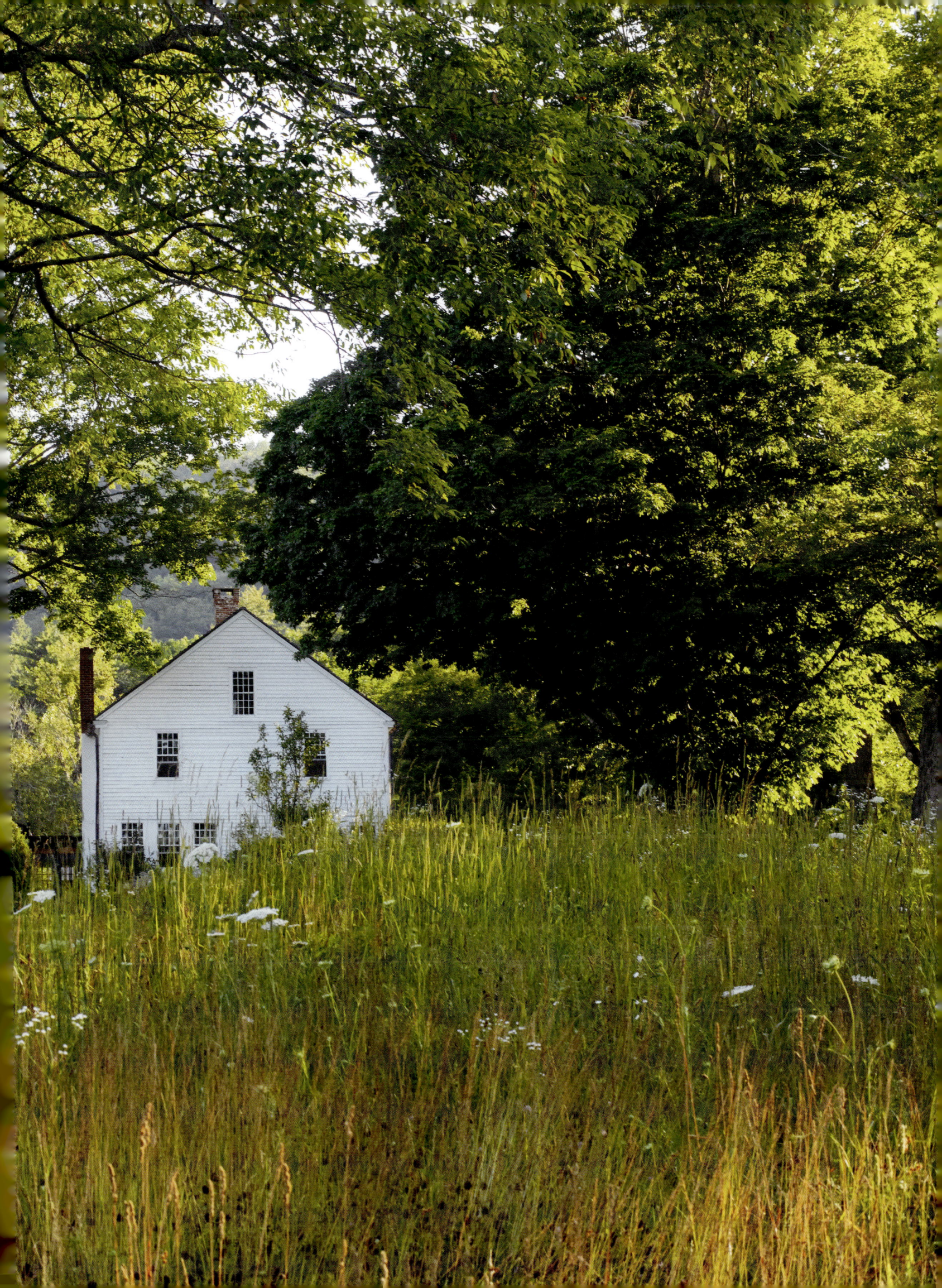

CREDITS

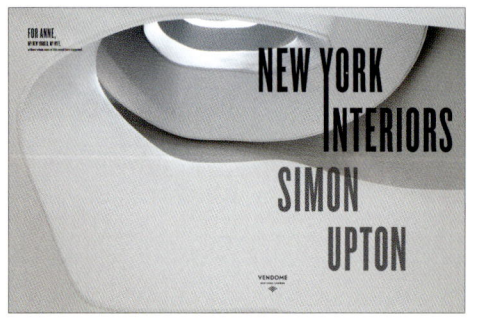

INTERIOR DESIGNERS: Haynes Roberts

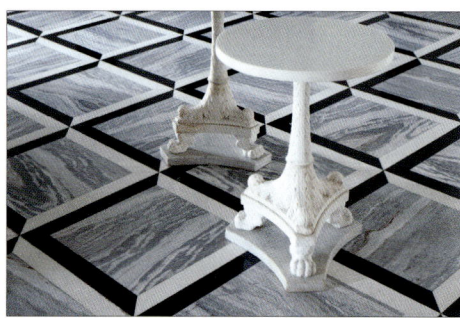

INTERIOR DESIGNER: Stephen Sills

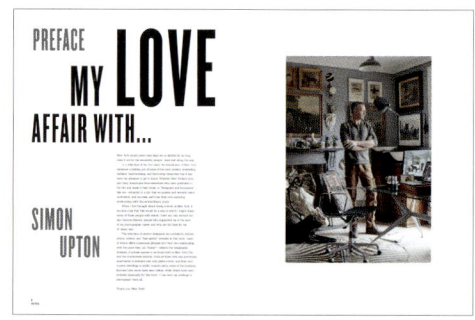

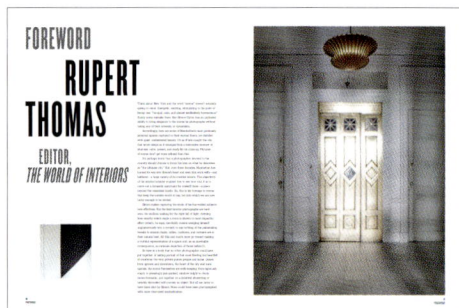

INTERIOR DESIGNERS: Haynes Roberts
ARTWORK: Ellsworth Kelly

CITY

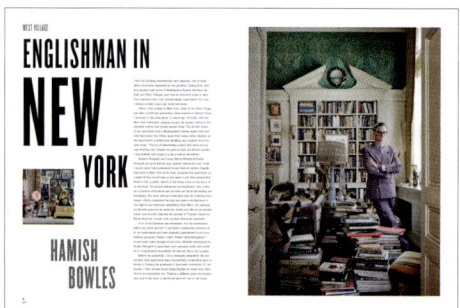

INTERIOR DESIGNERS: Roberto Peregalli and Laura Sartori Rimini of Studio Peregalli
FURNITURE: Casa Pupo
ARTWORK: Alfred Kingsley Lawrence, Lila de Nobili, Wolfgang Tillmans,
Tony Duquette, Elliott Puckette, Michael Landy

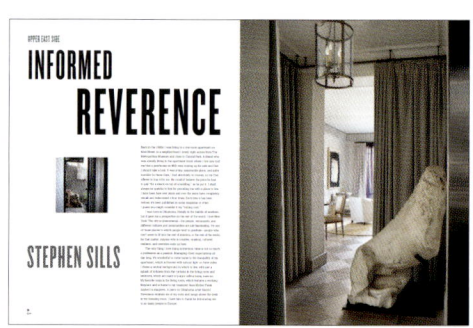

INTERIOR DESIGNER: Stephen Sills
FURNITURE: François Jordan, Georges Jacob, Jean-Michel Frank, Josef Hoffmann
ARTWORK: Man Ray, Richard Serra, Harold Stevenson

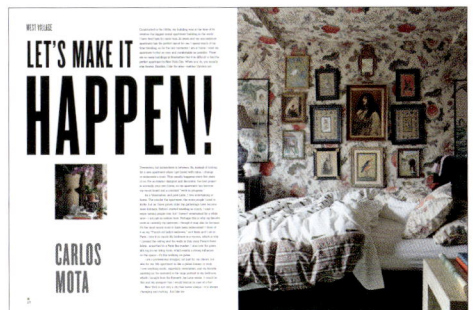

LET'S MAKE IT HAPPEN!

CARLOS MOTA

INTERIOR DESIGNER: Carlos Mota
FURNITURE & FITTINGS: Karl Springer, Rotin, Tangier, Carini Lang
ARTWORK: Lynn Davis

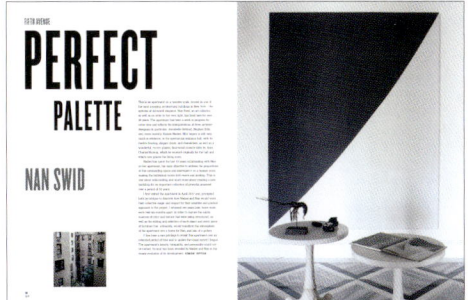

PERFECT PALETTE

NAN SWID

INTERIOR DESIGNERS: Stephen Sills, Annabelle Selldorf, Kazem Naderi
FURNITURE: Josef Hoffmann, Émile-Jacques Ruhlmann, André Sornay,
Jean-Charles Moreux, Jules Leleu, Maison Jansen, Le Corbusier, Jacques Adnet,
Ugo Zaccagnini, Fratelli Levaggi, Max Lamb
ARTWORK: Fernand Léger, Alfred Janniot, Jean Dunand, Nan Swid, Joan Miró,
Franz Kline, Ellsworth Kelly, Andrew Lord, David Smith, Roy Lichtenstein,
Brian Hunt, Alberto Giacometti, Richard Serra, Clyfford Still

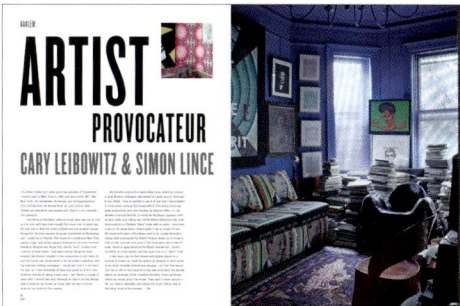

ARTIST PROVOCATEUR

CARY LEIBOWITZ & SIMON LINCE

FURNITURE & SOFT FURNISHINGS: Robert Venturi, Memphis, Frank Stella
ARTWORK: Peter Saul, McDermott & McGough, Ben Shahn, Angela Davis, Richard
Prince, Timothy Greenfield Sanders, Roy Lichtenstein, Richard Hamilton, Nicole
Eisenman, Vik Muniz, Andy Warhol, Steve Gianakos, Nolan Hendrickson, Frank Stella,
John Kacere, John Wesley, Chen Chen & Kai Williams, Jonathan Borofsky

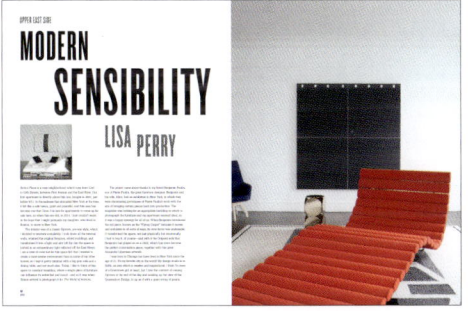

MODERN SENSIBILITY

LISA PERRY

FURNITURE: Pierre Paulin, Atelier de Troupe, Michael Anastassiades, Cappellini Fronzoni,
Hans J. Wegner
ARTWORK: Dylan Lynch, Alexander Liberman, Nick Darmstaedter, Grear Patterson, Joel Shapiro,
Max Bill, Ralph Mayer, Ed Garman, Philippe Decrauzat, Ernst Haas

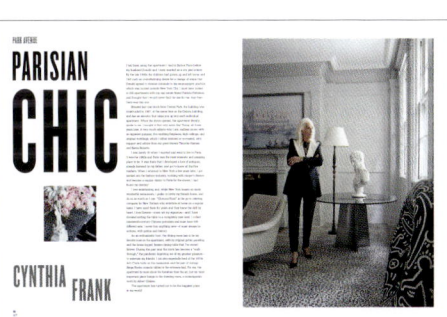

PARISIAN CHIC

CYNTHIA FRANK

INTERIOR DESIGNERS: Haynes Roberts
FURNITURE: Serge Roche, David Hicks, Maison Jansen
ARTWORK: Alberto Giacometti, Albert Gleizes, Alexander Liberman

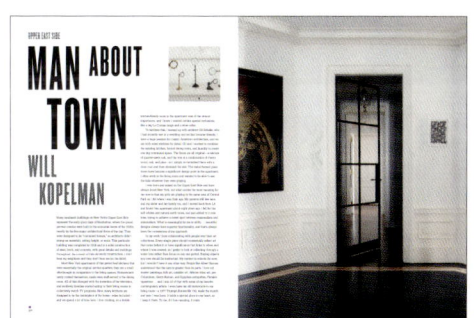

MAN ABOUT TOWN

WILL KOPELMAN

ARCHITECT: Gil Schafer
ARTWORK: Glenn Ligon, Frans Pourbus the Younger, Robert Perless, Mark Ryden,
Marc Quinn

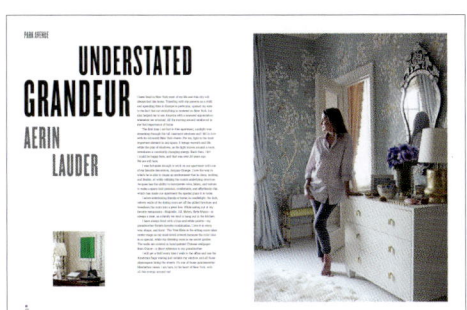

UNDERSTATED GRANDEUR

AERIN LAUDER

INTERIOR DESIGNER: Jacques Grange
ARTWORK: Sol LeWitt, Alexander Calder, Yves Klein, Marcel Broodthaers,
Piero Manzoni, Ed Ruscha, Mark Rothko, Jean Arp, Hiroshi Sugimoto, Franz Kline

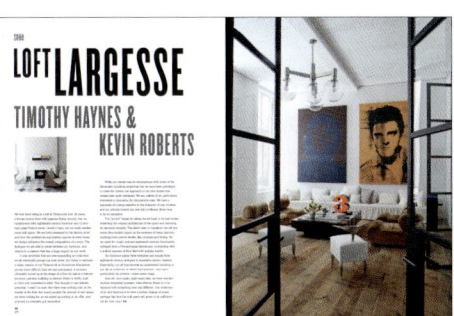

LOFT LARGESSE

TIMOTHY HAYNES & KEVIN ROBERTS

INTERIOR DESIGNERS: Haynes Roberts
FURNITURE: Axel Vervoordt, Klaus Uredat, Joseph-André Motte, Tommi Parzinger,
Gabriella Crespi, Milo Baughman, Tony Duquette, Verner Panton, Angelo Mangiarotti,
Garouste & Bonetti, Jean Royère, Gunnar Asplund, Gio Ponti, Charlotte Perriand
ARTWORK: Gavin Turk, Robert Indiana, Donald Judd, Rashid Johnson, Thomas Houseago,
Joyce Pensato, Frank Stella, Glenn Ligon, A.R. Penck, On Kawara

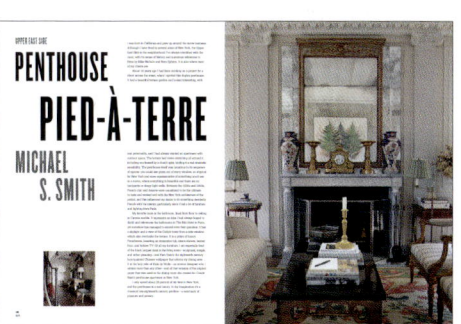

PENTHOUSE PIED-À-TERRE

MICHAEL S. SMITH

INTERIOR DESIGNER: Michael S. Smith
ARCHITECT: Oscar Shamamian, Ferguson & Shamamian
FURNITURE: Maison Jansen
ARTWORK: Philip Taaffe, Ellsworth Kelly, Elsie de Wolfe, Gracie Studio

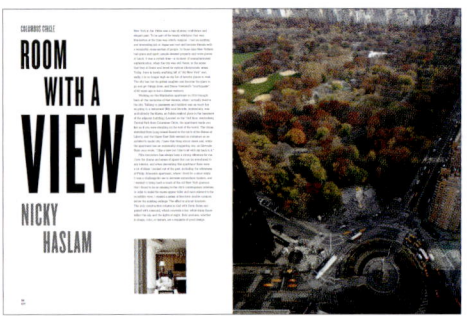

COLUMBUS CIRCLE
ROOM
WITH A
VIEW
NICKY
HASLAM

INTERIOR DESIGNER: Nicky Haslam

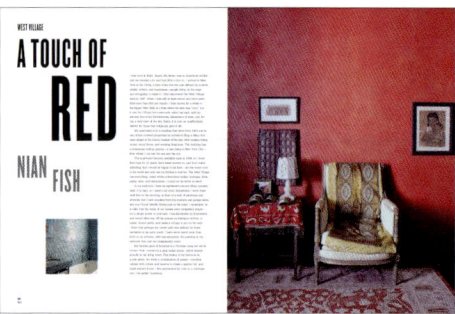

WEST VILLAGE
A TOUCH OF
RED
NIAN FISH

INTERIOR DESIGNER: Gregory Bissonnette

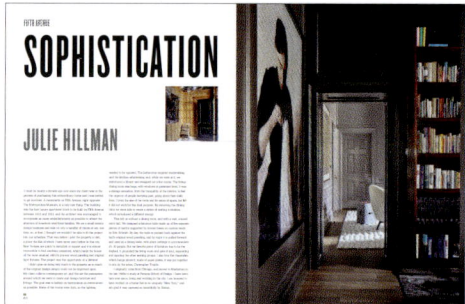

FIFTH AVENUE
SOPHISTICATION
JULIE HILLMAN

INTERIOR DESIGNER: Julie Hillman Design
ARCHITECT: Joe Vance, Joseph Vance Architects
BUILDING ARCHITECT: McKim, Mead & White
FURNITURE & FITTINGS: Grappolo, Eric Schmitt, Pierre Jeanneret, Le Corbusier,
Taher Chemirik, ALT for Living, Pierre Chapo, Charles Trevelyan, Serge Mouille,
Carl Malmsten, Fernando & Humberto Campana, Mauro Mori, Hubert le Gall,
Bruno Moinard Éditions, Gio Ponti, Stanford White (original paneling designer)
ARTWORK: Vik Muniz, Brigitte Tansini, Edward Burtynsky, Long-Bin Chen,
Elger Esser, Christopher Trujillo

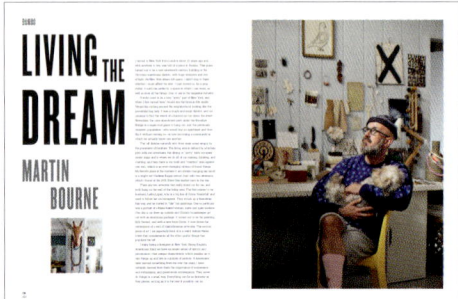

DUMBO
LIVING THE
DREAM
MARTIN
BOURNE

FURNITURE: Vladimir Kagan
ARTWORK: Gloria Vanderbilt, Ashley Hicks

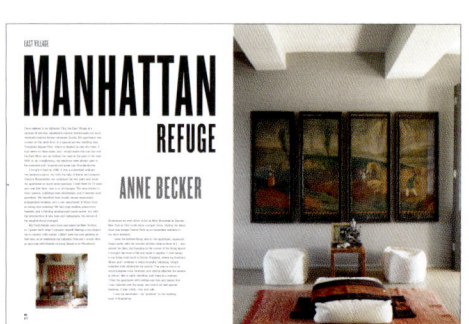

EAST VILLAGE
MANHATTAN
REFUGE
ANNE BECKER

INTERIOR DESIGNER: Gregory Bissonnette
ARTWORK: Anne Becker

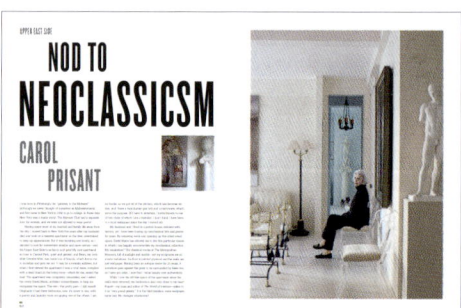

UPPER EAST SIDE
NOD TO
NEOCLASSICSM
CAROL
PRISANT

ARCHITECT: David Mann
FURNITURE & FITTINGS: Kismos, Émile-Jacques Ruhlmann
ARTWORK: Ostia Antica, Jean-Antoine Houdon

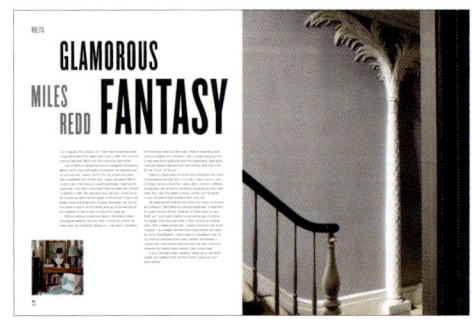

MALTA
GLAMOROUS
MILES REDD # FANTASY

INTERIOR DESIGNER: Miles Redd
FURNITURE: David Adler, Serge Roche, John Rosselli
ARTWORK: Tim Kent, Agustin Hurtado, Iksel, Carmen Almon, Kees van Dongen,
René Gruau

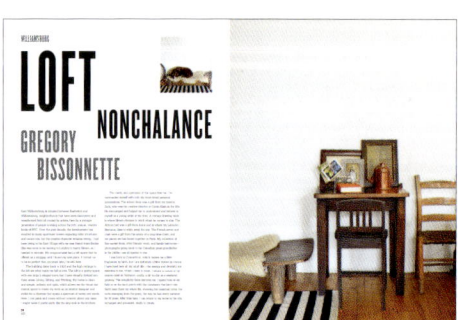

WILLIAMSBURG
LOFT
NONCHALANCE
GREGORY
BISSONNETTE

INTERIOR DESIGNER: Gregory Bissonnette

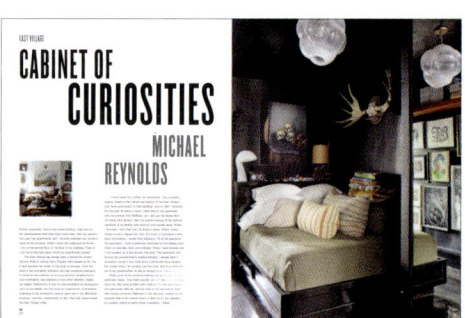

EAST VILLAGE
CABINET OF
CURIOSITIES
MICHAEL
REYNOLDS

INTERIOR DESIGNER: Michael Reynolds
FURNITURE & FITTINGS: Jeff Zimmerman, Wendel Castle, John Derian, Poul Kjaerholm,
Roger Capron
ARTWORK: François Halard, Lauren Drescher, Ain Cocke, Kehinde Wiley, Wilhelm von Gloeden,
Victoria Sambunaris, Robert Polidori, Mel Odom, Claudio Bravo, Tom of Finland,
Hellen van Meene, Johnny Smith, Robert Mapplethorpe, Louise Bonnet,
Inez van Lamsweerde & Vinoodh Matadin

GETAWAY

EAST VILLAGE
PERSONAL GALLERY
ALFREDO PAREDES

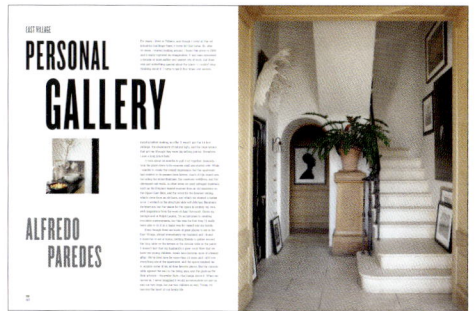

INTERIOR DESIGNER: Alfredo Paredes
ARCHITECT: Michael Neumann Architecture
FURNITURE & FITTINGS: Kevin Newling, BIBA, George Sherlock
ARTWORK: Richard Phibbs, Sheila Metzner, Victor Skrebneski, Max Dupain, Pat Steir, Richard Serra, Man Ray, Patrick Demarchelier, Jim French

PENNSYLVANIA
MILDRED'S LANE
J. MORGAN PUETT

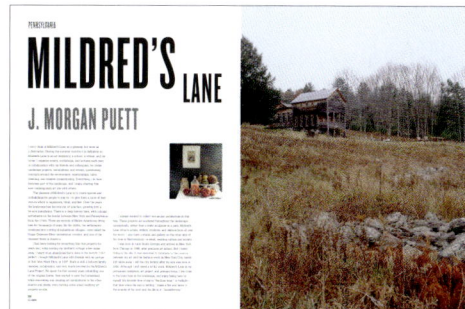

DESIGNER: J. Morgan Puett

BEDFORD
COUNTRY MANNERS
STEPHEN SILLS

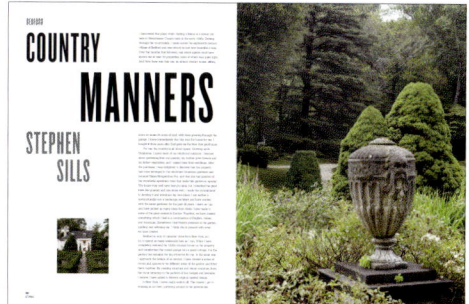

INTERIOR DESIGNER: Stephen Sills
FURNITURE: Georges Jacob, Jean-Michel Frank,
ARTWORK: Picasso, Jean Arp, Cy Twombly, Alberto Giacometti, Philippe Hiquily

HUDSON VALLEY
THEATER RURAL
CARY LEIBOWITZ & SIMON LINCE

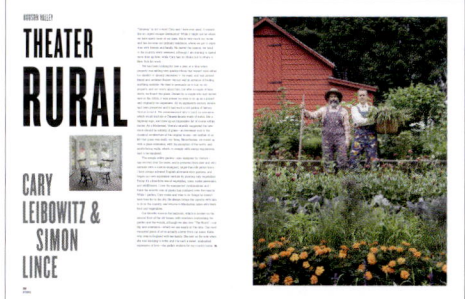

ARCHITECT: Robert Venturi
FURNITURE & FITTINGS: Robert Venturi
ARTWORK: Alex Katz, Norman Rockwell, Sara VanDerBeek, Katharine Umsted, Jonathan Borofsky, Cary Leibowitz

SAG HARBOR
FEDERAL REVIVAL
STEVEN GAMBREL

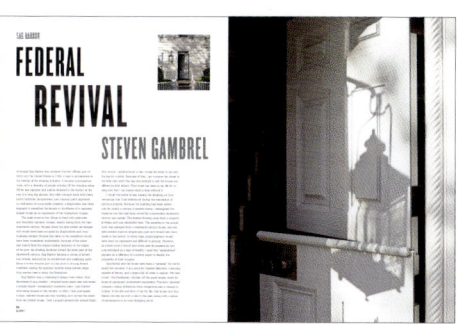

INTERIOR DESIGNER: Steven Gambrel

THOMPSON
FOLLY DE GRANDEUR
MARIO BUATTA

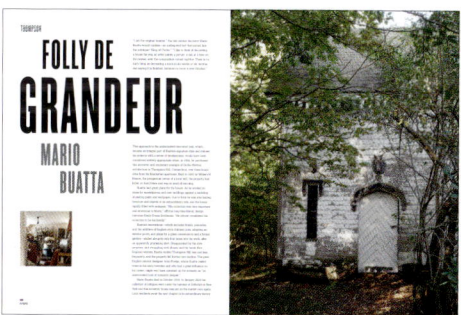

INTERIOR DESIGNER: Mario Buatta

AMAGANSETT
COASTAL RETREAT
DIANA PICASSO

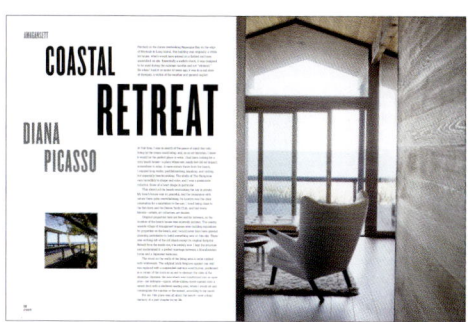

INTERIOR DESIGNER: Gregory Bissonnette

HUDSON VALLEY
RESTRAINED RESTORATION
DAVID MANN

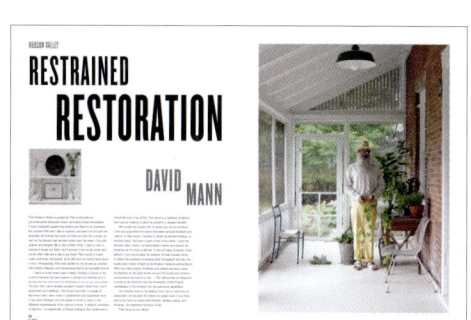

ARCHITECT: David Mann
FURNITURE & FITTINGS: Gio Ponti, Russell Woodard, Pierre Chareau, Paul McCobb, Stéphane Parmentier from Maison Gerard, Poul Kjaerholm, Erik Höglund
ARTWORK: Richard Caldicott, Lucia Bru, Benjamin Cottam, Björn Abelin, Spencer Finch, Jill Baroff

MASSACHUSETTS
RURAL IDYLL
JACK McCOLLOUGH & LAZARO HERNANDEZ

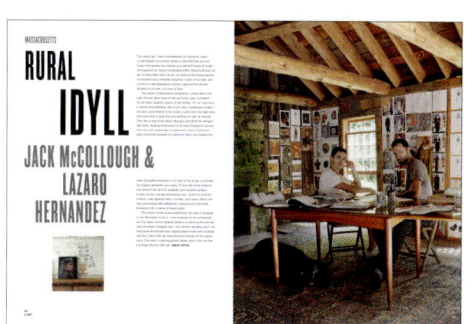

LANDSCAPE DESIGNER: Miranda Brooks

ACKNOWLEDGMENTS

In Memoriam **Carol Prisant**

Rupert Thomas, Editor, *The World of Interiors*

Karen Howes, my agent, editor and confidante

Isabel Parra, Socrates Mitsios, photo team and digital technician

Contributors
Anne Becker, Gregory Bissonnette, Martin Bourne, Hamish Bowles, Emily Eerdmans, Nian Fish, Cynthia Frank, Steven Gambrel, Nicky Haslam, Timothy Haynes, Lazaro Hernandez, Julie Hillman, Will Kopelman, Aerin Lauder, Cary Leibowitz, Simon Lince, David Mann, Jack McCollough, Carlos Mota, Kazem Naderi, Alfredo Paredes, Lisa Perry, Diana Picasso, J. Morgan Puett, Miles Redd, Kevin Roberts, Stephen Sills, Michael S. Smith, Nan Swid

Where would I be without the wonderful editors I have worked with?
Amy Astley, Ron Beinner, Michael Boodro, Miranda Brooks, Hatta Byng, Dara Caponigro, Graydon Carter, Howard Christian, Tom Delavan, Wendy Goodman, Mieke ten Have, Marian McEvoy, David Murphy, Deborah Needleman, Jim Reginato, Michael Reynolds, Robert Rufino, Mayer Rus, Margaret Russell, Anita Sarsidi, Michael Shome, Jacqui Small, Susan White, Anna Wintour

Magazines—thank you for my introduction to New York
The World of Interiors, Architectural Digest, American Vogue, Elle Décor, Veranda, NY Times

My Publisher, Producer, and Designer/Typographer
Vendome Press, David Shannon, Peter Dawson (Grade Design)

New York—and New Yorkers, for their wit and grit

New York Interiors
First published in 2021 by The Vendome Press
Vendome is a registered trademark of The Vendome Press, LLC
www.vendomepress.com

NEW YORK
Suite 2043
244 Fifth Avenue
New York, NY 10001
www.vendomepress.com

LONDON
63 Edith Grove
London,
UK, SW10 0LB
www.vendomepress.co.uk

Publishers: Beatrice Vincenzini, Mark Magowan, and Francesco Venturi

Distributed in North America by Abrams Books
Distributed in the United Kingdom, and the rest of the world, by Thames & Hudson

ISBN 978-0-86565-388-7

Editor: Tessa Monina
Production Director: Jim Spivey
Designer: Peter Dawson, Grade Design, London

Library of Congress Cataloging-in-Publication Data
[available upon request]

Printed and bound in China by
1010 Printing International Limited

First Printing